Strategic Management

4

Strategic Management
From theory to implementation
Fourth edition

David Hussey

*Visiting Professor in Strategic Management,
Nottingham Business School, Nottingham Trent University*

OXFORD   BOSTON   JOHANNESBURG   MELBOURNE   NEW DELHI   SINGAPORE

Butterworth-Heinemann
Linacre House, Jordan Hill, Oxford OX2 8DP
225 Wildwood Avenue, Woburn, MA 01801-2041
A division of Reed Educational and Professional Publishing Ltd

A member of the Reed Elsevier plc group

First published by Pergamon Press 1974
Second edition 1982
Reprinted 1984
Third edition 1994
Fourth edition 1998

British Library Cataloguing in Publication Data
Hussey, David, 1934–
    Strategic management: from theory to implementation. – 4th ed.
    1.   Strategic planning
    I.   Title
    658.4'012

ISBN 0 7506 3849 4

Composition by Genesis Typesetting, Laser Quay, Rochester, Kent
Printed and bound in Great Britain

FOR EVERY TITLE THAT WE PUBLISH, BUTTERWORTH-HEINEMANN
WILL PAY FOR BTCV TO PLANT AND CARE FOR A TREE.

Contents

The structure of the book

To write about any subject, however complex, it is necessary to follow a linear path. This has its limitations, in describing strategic management, as the connections between the subtopics are not linear, and resemble a plate of spaghetti where most strands are connected to many others. Perhaps a can of worms might be a better analogy, as the subject is continually moving and developing. One result of this is that many different choices could be made for the structure of the book, and for the cross-referencing inside the chapters. For this reason it is worth exploring how the parts fit together, to help readers who might come to the book with a different mindset.

The first three chapters set the scene for a study of the subject. Chapter 1 traces its evolution from the mid-1960s to date, showing the different schools of thought that have developed, and trying to help the reader put them in context. This is important because too many writers who develop a new slant to the subject overemphasise their own views at the expense of the existing body of knowledge. In reality, much that is new should supplement, instead of attempting to replace, that which already exists. Other chapters discuss the issues in achieving strategic success, and examine the concept of strategic management.

Part 2 of the book consists of five chapters which deal specifically with one aspect of strategy, the relation of the business with the external environment. Chapter 4 presents a way of thinking about the external environment which is more complete and integrated than the PEST approach (Political, Economic, Social and Technology) recommended in many books. This model lies behind some of the detailed techniques which are discussed later. It is also used again when industry analysis is considered later in the book.

Chapter 5 is about the need for setting common assumptions about the external environment by all those contributing to the development of a strategy. Chapter 6 has a broader scope than the business environment, and is about forecasting. It is positioned here because it is a key element of the discussion about external issues and trends, but the concepts it covers are applicable to other analytical aspects of strategic decision making. Chapter 7 provides some techniques and methods for ensuring that issues from the external environment are considered when strategies are being made. It includes discussion of scenario planning as a method of doing this.

In Chapter 8 the subject of ethics and morality is introduced. This is one of those chapters that could have been placed elsewhere in the book. It is in its present position because there is a close connection with what is considered to be ethical behaviour and the legal and social environment in which an organisation operates. A discussion on pressure groups shows how the business environment can be changed. The chapter also includes a discussion of the stakeholder concept, which if followed would link the internal elements of the organisation to the external in all its decision making. Because the stakeholder concept is not universally accepted an alternative approach is discussed, and this too requires a consideration of various elements in the business environment.

In Part 3 the emphasis is on a number of other aspects of the formulation of strategy. It has sixteen chapters which cover all the main concepts behind the making of strategy, and many of the techniques that can be used in analysis. In all cases the explanations are in depth, and emphasis is given to applying what is discussed to real situations. There is a research-based chapter on the use of a shareholder value approach in decision making. . . We look at concepts of vision and objectives, and start an exploration of the nature of strategy and the broad options that are available (for example, the virtual organisation, acquisition and alliances). There are specific chapters dealing with global strategies, technology, manufacturing, financial and human resource strategy. Finally in this part there are some chapters covering plan preparation and evaluation.

By this point in the book we have covered three of the five elements of the model presented in Chapter 1. There has been a lot on analysis, some emphasis on creative decision making and leadership, and we have started a consideration of strategic management as a process. In Part 4 full attention is given to the fifth element of this model, implementation, although one can argue that it has already received some attention in the emphasis I have given throughout to the application of concepts. The three chapters in this part cover both the system/administrative aspects of implementation and the behavioural issues, and include a way of thinking about transformational leadership.

In the final part of the book we return to complete the discussion of strategic management as a process, looking at the particular issues which arise when introducing such a process into an organisation, and examining the research evidence on the pitfalls of planning.

The final chapter offers some brief thoughts on the future direction of strategic management. A chapter analysis is provided below to help the reader see where particular concepts are covered.

Chapter	Main concepts covered	Some key authorities discussed
1 From planning to strategic management and beyond	Evolution of the subject and main modern schools of thought, against an increasingly turbulent and global environment. Comparison of many of the views. The chapter includes a five-point model showing the critical factors for strategic success, and ends by suggesting that a contingency approach may be more valuable than searching for the one right answer	Ansoff (1965), foundation of the subject, and later (1972), the concept of strategic management
The Boston Consulting Group contribution to analytical thinking. The PIMS database
Global strategy thinking of Prahalad and Doz (1987), Yip (1992) and Ohmae (1990). Ohmae (1982) (strategic thinking)
McKinsey 7S model

Chapter	Main concepts covered	Some key authorities discussed
		Porter industry analysis, competitor analysis, the value chain The incremental/emergent strategy views of Lindblom, Quinn, and Mintzberg Core competency approach of Hamel and Prahalad, Ansoff's modern views of a contingency approach, and related concepts from others
2 Strategic management: success or failure?	An analysis of the research evidence of the success of strategic management, contrasted with some obvious failings by some who claim to practise it. Failure of many acquisitions, and most BPR initiatives	The research quoted is from a wide range of studies. Part of this chapter is based on the experience of the author. The warnings about the things that can cause strategy to fail. Reference is made to the contingency/situational factors emphasised by Ansoff in his recent thinking, and Goold and Campbell's work on strategies and styles. Both authorities are treated more thoroughly in the next chapter
3 A look at the total process	The elements that must be covered when a strategy is considered (e.g. the effect of a marketing strategy on structure and processes, etc.). The importance of vision and leadership, and the brief discussion of an approach to transformational leadership. Styles of strategic management, a contingency approach to strategic management, research on the evolution of strategic management from long-range planning, description of strategic management, with illustrations of a planning process. Scenario planning as a process. Elements of a business plan	Much of this chapter is original to the author, although debts are acknowledged to various authorities in the thinking behind some of the conceptual models. Ansoff's scales of turbulence are discussed, and his recommendations are used to examine the findings of Gluck et al. on the evolution of planning. Strategy and styles relationships found by Goold and Campbell are explored. The main scenario planning authority referred to is van der Heijden
4 The challenge of the future	This chapter argues that organisations must heed the trends and forces in the environment, and discusses the need for creative thinking, and some of the things that block it. Most of	The issue of relating to the business environment is a commonplace in the literature of strategic management. The model presented here was developed by the author, and offers a

Chapter	Main concepts covered	Some key authorities discussed
	the chapter discusses a nine-step approach to considering the environment, with examples	more comprehensive and integrated approach than the familiar PEST method.
5 The environment: assumptions in planning	The examination of the business environment continues with a chapter dealing with the practical issue of determining the assumptions on which a strategy may be based. There is a discussion on certain aspects of risk	Much of this chapter comes from the experience of the author. The other authorities are some of the earlier researchers such as Ringbakk and Scott, whose focus was more on how organisations related to the external environment in practice. The emphasis of the chapter is more practical than theoretical
6 Forecasting	Various forecasting tools. These have value beyond forecasts of the business environment. The chapter is illustrated with an assessment of the environmental trigger factors which have been affecting organisations in recent years, and the sort of strategic reactions that have resulted. This has use beyond forecasting methods	References are given to further sources of information. There is no association with any method with a particular view of strategic management
7 Techniques for assessing the environment	The chapter begins with a discussion of the role of a strategic information unit, and moves to the exploration of a number of ways of making a strategic assessment of the factors in the business environment. The chapter concludes with a discussion of the strategic responses which can be made to environmental forces	Approaches developed by Harbridge Consulting Group, and Neubauer and Solomon are explored. Scenario planning is discussed as a technique (as opposed to the strategic management process view of Chapter 3), with references to van der Heijden, 1996, and to some examples.
8 Business philosophy (ethics and morality) and strategic management	The chapter discusses the relationship of an individual organisation's philosophy with the law, and with the views of society. The impact of pressure groups is explored. The issue of whether certain behaviours are obligations (stakeholder concept) or actions which are accepted as constraints is debated. Social audits are explored	Many references are given in this chapter, which includes numerous examples. The arguments for the stakeholder concept draw from the work of the Centre for Tomorrow's Company, and from Wheeler and Sillanpää (1997). The alternative view references Argenti (1997)

Chapter	Main concepts covered	Some key authorities discussed
9 The corporate appraisal– assessing strengths and weaknesses	It is much harder to define strengths and weaknesses than much of the literature implies. Five methods of assessment are discussed: polling managers, equilibrium analysis, independent analysis, critical success factors and core competencies. They are not intended to be mutually exclusive, and there is merit in using them all	Basic strengths and weakness analysis is a feature of most of the books on strategy. The chapter draws on the experience of the author. Equilibrium analysis is a simple technique developed by the author using force field analysis concepts. The independent analysis section includes some of the ideas of Drucker (1964). Hamel and Prahalad's views on core competencies are covered, and their practical application uses an approach based on that of Hinterhuber *et al.*
10 Analysing the industry and competitors	An integrated approach to competitor analysis is presented, moving from industry analysis through competitor profiling to building competitive advantage. In one sense this chapter can be seen as taking a different way of looking at the organisation in relation to the external forces of the market and competition, but this is to oversimplify the ground covered.	The chapter includes Porter's five forces, his view of mapping competitive groupings, and the value chain. It also includes various approaches which facilitate the application of industry and competitor analysis, which draw from the author's own experience.
11 Analysing the UK management development and training industry: a case history	In practice industry and competitor analysis is rarely easy. This chapter describes a real example, including the collection of information, its analysis, and the strategic conclusions that resulted. It is particularly useful in demonstrating ways of getting information when published sources are inadequate	Illustrates the use of some of the concepts of Porter and others
12 The search for shareholder value	There are two related elements to this chapter. The first deals with factors that create shareholder value and the second describes a method which measures value, and which is used as the basis of the strategic management process by certain organisations	In the first part Porter's views of moving from competitive advantage to corporate strategy are considered, supplemented by the findings from the PIMS database by Buzzell and Gale. The views of Goold and Campbell on the role that head offices play in creating or destroying value are included. The second part draws heavily on research by Handler, for Harbridge Consulting Group, and

Chapter	Main concepts covered	Some key authorities discussed
		shows the way certain UK organisations are applying the approach
13 Vision and objectives	A credible vision comes from the organisation's knowledge of itself and its potential. Vision, strategic intent, objectives, mission, goals and performance standards are related concepts which overlap, and are often used with different meanings. This chapter offers a view of the importance of vision, and an integrated approach that draws the various concepts together	Various authorities are discussed. The strategic intent of Hamel and Prahalad is also linked to the vision that occurs in the writings on transformational leadership
14 Strategy	A first step in thinking about strategic options and choices	Uses some of Ansoff's early thinking (e.g. a variant of the Ansoff matrix, and the idea of synergy). Some coverage of the satisficing, optimising and adaptivising views expounded by Ackoff
15 Strategic portfolio analysis	Portfolio analysis as one step to a more complex view of strategic choice. The evolution of portfolio analysis, and questions about the perception of the strategic arena in which an organisation operates. The factors considered are those of industry analysis	The Boston Consulting Group/Mckinsey, Shell Directional Policy Matrix (modified, with detailed method for plotting developed by the author). Porter's five forces concepts related to portfolio analysis. Risk analysis, a method developed by the author to add business environmental risk to the portfolio analysis
16 Portfolio analysis in practice	A worked example showing how to plot activities onto a portfolio chart, and to add information from the risk analysis method. Interpreting the results, and challenging some of the basic assumptions made in the example about the competitive arena. Using portfolio analysis as a dynamic tool	All based on the author's work in modifying the Shell directional policy matrix, and applying it in various situations
17 Strategic planning – a second look at the basic options	The main strategic options are examined and discussed (e.g. divestment, alliances, etc), including what should be considered in the	Information and concepts come from a number of sources and authorities

Chapter	Main concepts covered	Some key authorities discussed
	choice. The chapter includes modern views of close collaboration between suppliers and customers, and the outsourcing of activities. It stresses the high failure rates of some options, and suggests ways in which the prospects for success might be increased	
18 Multinational and global strategy	Globalisation occurs as a theme throughout the book. This chapter covers some of the underlying concepts. It explores the drivers which lead to an industry becoming global, and to the fact that an industry only becomes global when one or more of the competitors decide to do so. A diagnostic tool is provided to aid a consideration of the forces on a spectrum of local to global, and to see where the organisation now operates compared to what might be a better response. Strategic issues in multinational operations are discussed, as well as some of the risks	The chapter covers concepts from Yip, Cvar and Prahalad and Doz, as well as some developed by the author
19 Technology and manufacturing	Ways of thinking about technology strategies are discussed, including a technology audit, and the application of portfolio approaches to technology. The importance of technology in the overall strategy is emphasised. Manufacturing strategy covers modern views of manufacturing, in terms of method (e.g. CAD-CAM, flexible manufacturing), concepts (focused factory) and overall aims (world-class performance). The learning curve is discussed	Technology concepts come more from practitioners than academics (e.g. Henry). The academic contribution draws from Abell, Neubauer and Hamel and Prahalad. Manufacturing includes concepts by Skinner, Hayes et al., and The Boston Consulting Group
20 Financial planning	An examination of the strategic options to either ensure the financial resources needed by the organisation or to modify the strategy if resources are not available	

Chapter	Main concepts covered	Some key authorities discussed
21 Strategic planning for human resources	The whole area of strategic HRM is underdeveloped, with little movement beyond a measure of agreement that it is a good thing. This chapter draws heavily on original work by the author and colleagues, and provides a framework for strategic HRM, and some ways of applying this to different HR activities. Many practical tools are included	Mainly based on original research and the experience of the author in developing and applying workable concepts. Hofstede's concepts of intercultural management are discussed briefly, and the reader is referred to other methods
22 Preparing the strategic plan	This is a practical chapter which gives a demonstration of what a strategic plan might look like	
23 Evaluating a business plan	This is an important chapter because it is rarely discussed, the assumption being that knowing the concepts is enough to be able to judge a written plan. The chapter shows what to look for, and gives some ideas for testing a plan	
24 Operating plans	This chapter deals with plans at the operating level of the organisation. They may still be strategic, but deal with strategy in a different way than the corporate level. The level illustrated is of functions (e.g. marketing, production). Such plans form part of the process requirements of many, but not all, organisations. It is a practical chapter	
25 Project planning and appraisal	The chapter looks at the development of detailed project plans, their appraisal, and the process of monitoring and control	
26 From plans to actions	Covers some of the research which shows that strategies are not always implemented effectively, and discusses ways of ensuring that strategy is implemented. This chapter is biased towards the systems and processes issues, and most of the behavioural matters are discussed in the following chapter	Includes recent research findings from Kaplan and Alexander

Chapter	Main concepts covered	Some key authorities discussed
27 Management of change	This chapter looks at the degree of participation that is desirable in different circumstances (on a scale of collaborative to coercive), and shows the application of the transformational leadership model of Chapter 3. Resistance to change is discussed, as is the use of a management training initiative to aid implementation, and the issue of empowerment	Concepts of matching the degree of participation to the situation are derived from Stace and Dunphy. Some tools are developed from the research findings of Alexander
28 Introducing strategic management	This chapter covers issues arising from the introduction of strategic management as a process within organisations. It considers the role of the strategic planner, and the issues that should be considered for successful implementation of the process. It does not imply that all organisations should apply the same approach to strategic management	
29 Why planning sometimes fails	Based on a synthesis of research findings, this chapter looks at the factors that can cause a planning process to fail	
30 Strategic management to strategic change?	Looks at the way strategic management appears to be developing	

Introduction

My aim in this book, as in the previous editions, has been to cover the concepts and principles of strategic management, but not to stop there. Concepts and principles are of limited value unless people know how to apply them, and much of the book is devoted to application. In fact I would argue that those who never get deeper than the overall concepts are unlikely to know very much about their subject. But I would maintain also that those who believe they are expert in methods and techniques are only likely to have a true depth of expertise when it is built on a sound conceptual platform. Theory and practice are two sides of a coin, and the true expert will have both.

There are many ideas about strategic management, and the subject itself has evolved through several stages from its origins as *long-range planning.* Unfortunately some of those who promote new approaches feel that they also have to demonstrate the fallibility of everything that has gone before. This is a pity, because it confuses, and acts as an obstacle to a professional approach to the subject. True knowledge is built through the contributions of many people, and to try to deny parts of the past is to emerge with only a partial understanding of the subject, and to create the danger that the wheel will be reinvented, although disguised in different colours, time and time again. I hold to the belief that the 'right' approach to strategic management is more situational than many have believed, and that almost every idea or concept is right in some, but rarely in all, circumstances. The skill is to learn to know when. One aim of the book is to put the various concepts in context, and to help the reader to what should be a main objective of strategic management, the ability to undertake strategic thinking. This means that the reader will not find one dogmatic approach to every aspect of strategic management, but an attempt to show the richness and variety of what is available, so that the best choices can be made.

I have been fortunate in my own experience, which has enabled me to use almost everything covered by the book in real situations. From 1964 to 1975 I was a planner in various organisations, and before that I was in related but very different work in industrial development in a developing country. In 1976 I was invited to join the European arm of Harbridge House Inc, and a few years later I took over as managing director of the London company and the European operations. So I had the double task of developing and implementing a strategy for my own organisation, and consulting in strategic management and the implementation of strategy to various major clients. I became increasingly interested in issues of change and the implementation of strategy, and many of the assignments I was involved in were focused on this problem. The Harbridge Consulting Group had some very powerful ways of helping organisations to implement through the development of highly tailored management training programmes, which combined a measure of consultancy with skills which put company problems and issues into the heart of a specially developed programme. All this meant that even when I had not used a particular way of analysing a strategic situation, I was often exposed to the people who had used it in client organisations, and had access to the results.

In 1993 the Harbridge House organisation was sold to Coopers & Lybrand, and in November 1994 I left the organisation to follow my own interests. It was then that I received another benefit to my personal development through the invitation to become a visiting professor in strategic management at Nottingham Trent University.

Although there are some of my original methods of application in this book, by definition it has to be built mainly on the work of others. So I am grateful to all who have made a contribution to the subject. The reader will find references to, and explorations of, the work of all the big names in strategic management. But there are also contributions which have come from discussions and the exchange of ideas with people throughout the world. It is not possible to keep up to date on new concepts just by being a practitioner or consultant. Over the years I have gained much from the experience and knowledge of others. It was Professor Bernard Taylor of Henley who encouraged me to write my first book, *Introducing Corporate Planning*, and with whom I have had many opportunities to discuss strategic thinking. I should also mention Professor George Steiner, whose research at UCLA and books in the 1960s and 1970s were mines of information. George was always friendly and helpful in his letters, and I still regret that we have never had the chance to meet.

The father of strategic management is Igor Ansoff, who gave the first seminar I ever attended on corporate strategy, and he has always been helpful whenever I wanted to quote his work. In more recent years he has become a personal friend as well as a source of stimulation in his current ideas on environmental turbulence. I learnt from Professor Mike Porter, before his first book was published, when I attended the Advanced Management Programme at Harvard in 1978/9. At Harvard, too, I gained much from Professor Roland Christensen, who Porter acknowledges as one of the contributors to his own development.

I owe a debt to numerous former or present colleagues from the Harbridge House organisation, CIMID (the Center for International Management and Industrial Development), Nottingham Trent University, and the Japan Strategic Management Society (in particular, Professor Gen-Ichi Nakamura), my collaborators on the journal *Strategic Change*, and many past clients, both those who applied strategic management well and those who made something of a mess of it.

This edition owes a particular debt to Graham Beaver, of Nottingham Trent University, and Paul Joyce of North London, who as directors of their respective MBA programmes and professors of strategic management gave much help in shaping this new edition to the needs of modern MBA programmes.

Case studies are a new feature for this edition, and particular thanks are due to the authors, who are listed in the appropriate places. In particular, I should mention Professor Bob Mockler, of St John's University, New York, who offered me the choice from a number of new case studies, and Professor Per Jenster, now with CIMID, who was very helpful in finding tested case studies for me.

The result of all this is, I hope, a book which will be of use to students both for their studies and in their careers as managers. It has much to offer the practitioner, as well as the student, and I hope that all who read it will both enjoy the book, and find it of particular value in their own situations.

David Hussey

Acknowledgements

Short quotations are not included in this list, although they are all fully acknowledged in the text, as are the ideas of others which I have put into my own words. Diagrams and long extracts are acknowledged in the text and listed here. My thanks go to the publishers and authors who have allowed me to use this material.

American Management Association, New York, NY

- Figure 17.1 from Dooley, J. I. and Ciapolla, J. A., 'Guides to Screening New Products', in Martin, E. (ed.) *Management for the Smaller Company*, 1959.

Harbridge House Inc/Harbridge Consulting Group Ltd (acquired by Coopers & Lybrand)

- Figure 7.2, page 128.
- Figure 10.11, page 209.
- Figure 10.12, page 212.
- The questionnaire on pages 227–36.
- Various figures in Chapter 11.
- Figure 12.1, page 255.
- The extracts on pages 258–76 from Handler, S., *Value-based Strategic Management: A Survey of UK Companies*, London 1991.
- A Harbridge Consulting Group case study, (Grand Imperial by D. E. Hussey), is modified for Chapter 16.
- Figure 21.10, page 448.
- Figure 21.11, page 449.
- Figure 21.13, page 452.
- Exhibit 29.1, on page 597.

Dr Fred Hewitt

- Material to update the case study of which Dr Hewitt was a joint author, and which is acknowledged under the name of the publisher, John Wiley. The additional material is entitled 'Creating the Holistic Process-Oriented Learning Organisation: Xerox 1992–1997', and starts on page 688. It was written especially for this book.

Industrial Market Research Association

- Figure 6.2, page 109, which comes from Saunders, A. and Smith, N. J., 'Hydraulic Cranes from Armstrong's Elswick Works, 1846–1936: A Product

Life Cycle in Capital Goods', *Journal and Proceedings of the Industrial Market Research Association*, May 1970.

McGraw-Hill, Maidenhead

- Figure 9.5, page 184, from Denning, B. W., 'Introduction' in Denning, B. W., (ed.) *Corporate Planning: Selected Concepts*, 1971.

Pergamon Press (now an imprint of Elsevier), Oxford

- The extract on pages 32–3, which comes from Champion, J. R., 'Corporate Planning in CPC Europe', *Long Range Planning*, December, 1970.
- The extract on pages 33–4 which comes from Taylor, B. and Irving P., 'Organised Planning in Major UK Companies', *Long Range Planning*, June, 1971.
- Figure 3.6, page 67, which comes from Young, R. and Hussey, D. E., 'Corporate Planning at Rolls Royce Motors', *Long Range Planning*, April, 1977.
- Figures 7.3–7.6, pages 131–3, which come from Neubauer, F.-F. and Solomon, N. B., 'A Managerial Approach to Environmental Assessment', *Long Range Planning*, April, 1977.
- Figure 14.2, page 299, from Kami, M. J., 'Gap Analysis – Key to Super Growth', *Long Range Planning*, June, 1969.
- Figure 14.5, page 305, from Hargreaves, D, 'Corporate Planning – A Chairman's Guide', *Long Range Planning*, June, 1969.
- Figure 17.2, page 365, from Pavitt, K., 'Technological Innovation in European Industry: The Need for a World Perspective', *Long Range Planning*, December, 1969.
- Table 19.1, page 409, from Ford, D., 'Develop Your Technology Strategy', *Long Range Planning*, October, 1988.
- The two quotation on pages 412–13, from Hussey, D. E., *Management Training and Corporate Strategy*, 1988.

Stanford Research Institute, Menlo Park, CA

- Figure 3.7.

Strategic Management Research Group/R. Mockler, New York, NY

- Chapter 32, 'Colgate Oral Care Division in the Italian Market', Mockler, R. and Faccini, A., from *Cases in Multinational Strategic Management*, Mockler, R. (ed.) 1997.
- Chapter 34 'AGIP Petroli entering the Indian Market', Mockler R., Cornetti, C. and Scordino, in *Case Studies in Multinational Management*, Mockler, R., (ed.) 1997.

SWK Zimbabwe Ltd

- The extracts from the company brochure which appear on pages 613–16.

Urwick Orr & Partners (acquired by Price Waterhouse)

- Figure 3.8, page 69.
- Figures 26.3–26.5, pages 543–5.

John Wiley & Sons Ltd, Chichester

- Figure 1.1, on page 22, which comes from Hussey, D. E., Strategic Management: Past Experience and Future Directions', *Strategic Change*, 6.5.
- Figure 3.2, page 50, which comes from Hussey, D. E., *Business Driven Human Resource Management*, 1996.
- Figure 7.1, page 126, which comes from Butcher, H. and Mainelli, M., 'Strategic Information Management', in Hussey, D. E. (ed.), *International Review of Strategic Management*, vol. 1., 1990.
- Figure 9.6, page 188, from Hinterhuber, H. H., Friedrich, S. A., Handibauer, G. and Stubec, U., 'The Company as a Cognitive System of Core Competencies and Strategic Business Units', *Strategic Change*, 5.4, 1996.
- Figure 10.10, page 207 is reproduced from Crawshaw, H. S., 'Strategic Analysis for the Information Industry', *Strategic Change*, 1.1, 1992.
- Chapter 11 is an updated version of an article I wrote which appeared in *Strategic Change*, 1.4, 1992, entitled 'Analysing the Management Development and Training Industry; a Case History'.
- Chapter 35 is a version of Bounds, G. and Hewitt, F., 'Xerox: Envisioning a Corporate Transformation', *Stratgic Change*, 4.1, 1995. It contains additional material written by F. Hewitt.

Thanks are also due to John Robertson and the Shell Chemical Co Ltd for their help and permission to use and further develop the Directional Policy Matrix, the feature of much of Chapters 15 and 16.

Part 1

The Concept and the Need

CHAPTER 1

From planning to strategic management and beyond

Strategic management has a long history, although the words used to describe it have changed several times as the concepts have modified and developed. The aim of this chapter is to review the development of the subject from an approximate starting point in the mid-1960s, and to show how the modern approaches have emerged. The chapter is more than a history lesson, in that it also puts the various theories and concepts into a context, trying to cut through the confusion that results from the claims of certain authors that they offer the only true path to salvation.

In any aspect of management theory the enthusiastic practitioner is both a source of strength and a cause of weakness. Strength, because no concept of management can grow and develop unless it has the backing of keen supporters: weakness, because enthusiasm too often leads to an overselling of its benefits. The act of overselling causes a lack of precision and definition about the subject and surrounds it in a hazy vagueness.

Strategic management is no exception. It undoubtedly has a strong body of supporters, many of whom have contributed to the development of the subject. Without the people who apply the concepts, and those who research and think about them, the subject could never have developed. But some of the enthusiasts have never really understood the overall concept, some happily write and talk about its methods and techniques without ever having used them in real situations, and there are others who have overemphasised the benefits without also pointing out the difficulties. As a result it suffers from conceptual misunderstandings concealed under a semantic smokescreen. Too often it has been seen as a universal miracle cure for all corporate ills. Misused, it can block real strategic thinking, and can give rise to complacency. Too often its application is superficial, where platitudes take the place of the original thought about the future that strategic management is supposed to engender.

The evolution of the subject over time has led to a semantic confusion. New terms are often coined, sometimes without justification, to explain new nuances of emphasis, old terms are applied in a slightly different way, and because there is no standard dictionary of management, various authors attach different meanings to each of the apparently standard words. It is possible for two people to have a conversation about strategic management, using words which they both understand but the meanings of which are not shared. Such conversations can reach an end without either party knowing that they were not discussing the same thing.

Part of the problem is that as the subject evolves and changes, not every organisation or authority changes at the same speed. So although it is possible to accept research findings such as those by Gluck, Kaufman and Walleck[1] that provide empirical evidence of a four-phase move from basic financial planning meet budget), to forecast-based planning (predict the future), to externally oriented planning (think strategically), to strategic management (create the future), it is important to remember that, in practice, all the phases, and any others which might be identified since, coexist. Ansoff and McDonnell[2] who take a contingency view of the subject would go a stage further, and argue that different approaches should so co-exist, as organisations who face different levels of turbulence should approach the task of creating strategy in ways that are appropriate to the situation.

It is also common for job titles to be changed to whatever is fashionable, without there necessarily being any change in the role. This may be a particularly British habit, and can be observed elsewhere: sales managers became marketing managers overnight, often without doing any marketing, and most personnel managers are now human resource managers, but not all have the strategic orientation that the modern term implies. Concepts are often corrupted by the way that organisations use them, and problems that arise in practice are sometimes because of the way an approach is applied, and not the fault of the approach itself. An example is that portfolio analysis and industry analysis are sometimes criticised as looking at the past instead of the future: however, this is because those using the methods are not using them a dynamic tool which can help to explore the future. There are limitations, as there are with all techniques, but often they are not those of which they stand accused.

It is also true to say that many of the 'new' ideas, some of which move into common currency, are not as novel as the authors and readers believe. Many of the new thoughts of today are remarkably similar to many of the new ideas of the 1950s and 1960s. However, it would be wrong to imply that when this happens there is not also some movement of the subject, as what happens is not a simple recycling of the old but a movement more like a spiralling, which means that the loop when completed ends up in a slightly different place. The basic idea may not be as novel as the author believes, but it is not plagiarism, and may take the subject forward.

The strategic management literature can both enlighten and confuse for all these reasons. Although many of the ideas appear to pull in different directions, there is often more agreement between authors than they themselves acknowledge. And if you take a contingency view, they are probably all appropriate some of the time. What this chapter tries to do is to sort out some of the strands which contribute to the role of modern thinking about strategy, and to try to do this in a way that does not discard the old every time something new appears. There is great value in some of the older writing as well as in the new, and it is all of it, together with the first-hand experience of practitioners, and the contributions of researchers which enables strategic management to make a real contribution to the development and performance of organisations.

A historical perspective

Some of the conflicting views of strategic management can be explained by taking a historical perspective. This will show how the subject has developed as organisations tried to find better ways of developing strategies for the future, and also how changes in the business environment have led to new problems, and new subconcepts of strategy making. The main difficulty is where to begin.

We could choose a date somewhere around 320 BC when the Chinese military strategist Sun Tzu wrote *The Art of War*[3], a work which is said to have influenced the thinking of many modern Japanese businesses, and has led to a number of thoughts about how the 'art' can be applied to modern business. Wee[4] and Ho[5]

Landmark contributions to the development of strategic management

1963–70	Stanford Research Institute	Structured thinking about planning systems
1965	Igor Ansoff	Analytical approach to corporate strategy
1972	Igor Ansoff	Strategic management concept
1980	James Quinn	Logical incrementalism
1982	Kenichi Ohmae	Strategic thinking
1982	Thomas Peters and Robert Waterman	In search of excellence
1985	Henry Mintzberg	Deliberate and emergent strategies
C 1985	Igor Ansoff	Contingency approach (environmental turbulence)
1986	Noel Tichy and Mary Devanna	Transformational leadership
1987	Michael Porter	From competitive advantage to corporate strategy
1994	Gary Hamel and C. K. Prahalad	Reshaping industries (competing for the future)

are two examples. Strategic management is a modern concept, but was not the beginning of all thinking about business strategy. In fact I will not go back that far, as I do not have the scholarship to fill in the gap from the time of Sun Tzu to what most of us regard as the start of strategic management as a serious subject, the publication of an overall framework and methodology for the formulation of strategy. Ansoff's *Corporate Strategy* is still on the compulsory reading lists of many MBA programmes.[6]

From long-range planning to corporate planning

There had been previous books which, without necessarily using the term, gave very useful ideas on the formulation of strategy, many of which are still valid. In particular, there are two works by Drucker[7, 8] which helped to shape much of my early thinking on strategic analysis.

Just before Ansoff's seminal book was published, there had been a rise in interest in long-range planning. The total literature on the subject consisted of a few articles, and the earliest approaches were intended to give more control over the future by thinking beyond the annual budget. Not surprisingly, the resultant plans resembled an annual budget with a few columns added to give either three or five years, depending on the planner's taste. It may seem surprising to a modern readership, but at that time many of the debates were about how many years the plan should cover.

It would be fair to argue that the first phase of formal planning was no more than an extrapolation of current views, with little or no provision to do anything differently, and an inbuilt belief that the future would follow an incremental pattern. At that time jobs began to be created with titles such as long-range planning manager, and there are still echoes today in the title of one of the earliest planning journals, *Long Range Planning*, which is still at the leading edge, despite being saddled with an obsolete name.

The idea of the extended budget soon gave way to an attempt to be a little more active in the strategic content of long-range plans, and there was a shift of emphasis, although initially no change of name. Several things happened at roughly the same time. The Stanford Research Institute, Menlo Park, California, began to operate a subscription service on a membership basis, issuing reports which carried the warning that they were for the sole and confidential usage of clients of the service. Over the period around 1963 to about 1970 this service was very useful to its members in suggesting ways of thinking about the different types of plan that should be prepared, discussing the process, and giving insight into some of the early methods of analysis. I was fortunate in working for a member of the service when I first became involved in strategic management in 1964. What is worth emphasising is that the reports, and much of the other literature that began to emerge, had a focus on strategy, which moved thinking further away from the extrapolative budget concept of the early approaches. By the late 1960s the term 'corporate planning' tended to be used more frequently than 'long-range planning'.

Ansoff's *Corporate Strategy*[6], was published at a time when many people had been attracted by the idea of planning, and for those who were not SRI clients may well have been the only guidance that was available to them. There was an underlying throb of excitement as those involved believed that for the first time their organisations were able to work on shaping their future

Ansoff, in one of the SRI reports[9], traced the evolution of planning through four phases which he identified as Implementation (action instructions), Control, Extrapolative Planning, and Entrepreneurial Planning. Whatever the criticisms that may be levied at the early approaches to corporate planning, the intentions were much the same as those which appear in the preamble to many of the new paradigms offered in the 1980s and 1990s. Hamel and Prahalad[10], in their opening preface state: 'We believe that every company really does have the opportunity to shape its own destiny; no company is destined to be a laggard.' This echoes the title of a seminar I attended in about 1966, called *Corporate Planning, The Control of Corporate Destiny*. The idea of working on the future occurs in Drucker[8] and the quotation from this appears in the penultimate paragraph of a chapter called 'Making the future today':

> Tomorrow always arrives. It is always different, and then even the mightiest company is in trouble if it has not worked on the future.

The tools for better planning had begun to arrive a little before the publication of Ansoff's classic 1965 book. Merritt and Sykes[11] did much to develop and make usable the discounted cash flow approach to the analysis of capital projects, and many organisations began to use this approach for the first time around this period. The technique had been around for some time (I have the internal manual of one multinational company which sets out its approach to DCF, including risk analysis, which is dated 1958), but it was put on the map in the UK at by publicity over its use in an acquisition situation, and publication of the book by Merritt and Sykes.

Gap analysis (see Chapter 14) was used as a technique to help organisations find strategies to plug the gap between where they would end up without planning and where they wanted to be. A number of operational research (OR) techniques were co-opted into the planning arena: in fact there was one school of thought which took an OR approach to planning (see, for example, Ackoff[12]), just as there was another that saw the whole basis of planning as being dependent on accurate forecasting. New techniques for technological forecasting were promoted, and given further stimulation with the publication of Jantch.[13] The OR and forecasting schools of thought as the nub of planning have largely passed away, defeated by the discontinuities which began in the 1970s and continue to this day.

The term 'corporate planning' had almost taken over by the end of the 1960s, partly because it sounded better and partly because it stressed that here was an approach to management which embraced the whole organisation, was linked to both long- and short-term plans, and which enabled management to set strategies that would take the organisation to a different and predetermined future.

With hindsight it is possible to see that the tacit assumption behind much of the thinking was that the future was likely to be an incremental growth from the present. The main driver of the approach was planning, and the aim in most organisations was to produce an annually revised rolling set of plans to cover the whole organisation. Emphasis was on the process of planning, which in most companies was in theory a blend of top-down and bottom-up, under the philosophy that if line managers were involved implementation would follow naturally. This often led to the major changes in strategy being decided outside the planning system, and often these were opportunistic rather than planned. In many cases the organisation planned on the basis of the organisational units it had, instead of those that it should have, with the result that more emphasis was sometimes placed on justifying the status quo and much less on shaping the future.

Some landmarks in the development of analytical method

Time	Originator	Concept
1963–70	Stanford Research Institute	Thinking about planning systems and methods of analysis
1963	Merritt and Sykes	Promotion of discounted cash flow
Late 1960s	The Boston Consulting Group and McKinsey	Development of portfolio analysis and application at General Electric
1965	Roland Christensen, Kenneth Andrews and Joseph Bower	Distinctive competence of the organisation
1967	Jantch	Emergence of technological forecasting
1969–75	Wyckham Skinner	Seminal work on manufacturing strategy
1970	Toffler	Future shock: discontinuities in trends
1972	PIMS	Collection of data in order to assess results of strategic moves
1980	Michael Porter	Seminal work on industry analysis and competitor analysis
1980	McKinsey	7S framework
1985	Michael Porter	The value chain
1986	Hayes, Wheelwright and Clark	World class manufacturing
1987	C. K. Prahalad and Y. Doz	Global strategy
1990	Gary Hamel and C. K. Prahalad	Core competencies
1992	George Yip	Global strategy

Strategic planning

Before the next decade was reached the more advanced thinkers and practitioners recognised that strategy should be at the heart of the process. Although operational planning and strategic planning are intertwined, it is the latter which should be the driver. The short-term plans and systems should be driven by the longer-term perspective. Because of this more emphasis should be placed on strategy, and the title 'strategic planning' began to take over from 'corporate planning', but the latter persisted as a description, although many might have applied the more strategic orientation. The change was largely a shift of emphasis, not necessarily initially of the overall approach to the process of planning which still tended to focus on formal plans achieved through a corporate-wide process. The links that were intended from this shift of emphasis were not always achieved, and even much later research[14] found that very few organisations were succeeding in driving the organisation through the strategy, and integrating that strategy into the annual budget and the objectives and actions of managers throughout the organisation.

The strategic planning phase correlates with what Gluck et al.[1] called 'externally oriented planning', with much more attention being given to the external environment and to customers and markets.

Changes like this never appear like a thunderclap out of a clear blue sky, and a number of developments contributed. In the 1960s General Electric commissioned two consulting firms, McKinsey and The Boston Consulting Group, to undertake a strategic study of its activities. This may not have been the first time the technique of portfolio analysis had been applied, but the outcome was a new and superior way to look at the relative strategic importance of the various activities that made up an organisation. The many variants of the approach were influential in shaping the strategies of many organisations from the early 1970s. (Chapters 15 and 16 describe these approaches in some depth.) From this work was created the idea of regrouping business activities into strategic business units, which more closely matched the needs of the markets, and which gave a sharper focus than was possible over the more fragmented groupings of the 1960s. Portfolio analysis was one of many examples of how thinking about strategy was moved forward by consultants and practitioners, a contribution often overlooked by those bewildered by the outpouring of publications from academics. What was a trickle in the mid-1960s, became a stream a few years later, and had developed into a river by the late 1970s. It now resembles one of the Great Lakes of North America.

Portfolio analysis was the beginning of the development of superior ways to aid thinking about strategy, although even this was foreshadowed in Drucker[8], with his suggestions that the business should sort out its products into eleven categories, including yesterday's breadwinners, today's breadwinners, tomorrow's breadwinners, failures and investments in management ego. One of the differences was in taking the thinking to strategic business units, with many products, rather than leaving it at the product level.

Another contribution to better strategic understanding also started by General Electric, with the creation of a database which recorded strategic actions and related them to the consequences. In 1972 this was transferred to the Harvard

Business School and became the PIMS (Profit Impact of Market Strategy) programme. Now run by the Strategic Planning Institute, the database contains information submitted by PIMS members from throughout the world, and conclusions from the programme are regularly published for a wider audience (for example, Buzzell and Gale[15]).

Despite its intentions, the corporate planning phase had not given equal strategic attention to every aspect of the organisation, and 90 per cent of all effort was spent on marketing, finance and merger/acquisition. As with any generalisation, this statement was not universally true. Union Carbide, for example, applied a process of planned operational improvement as an adjunct to its growth-oriented planning. This was described in early editions of this book, but has been omitted on grounds of age from this new edition[16]. Conceptual development on the relationship between strategy and structure began at Harvard in the 1960s, and had a significant impact on thinking by the 1970s. Others began to put more effort into understanding that manufacturing could make a dynamic contribution to corporate strategy, and was not just a function that should passively react to the marketing strategy (see Chapter 19 for more details). However, many organisations gave scant thought to manufacturing strategy until the 1980s, when more were faced with global competition and new technologies began to have a significant impact.

Two factors in particular forced the abandonment of some of the assumptions behind the corporate planning phase, and brought a realisation that processes which assumed incremental growth could no longer stand up to the reality of a world where the future was full of shocks and surprises. The first big shock was the great oil price rise in 1973, when OPEC members got together and reduced supplies and increased costs. This was followed by, and partly caused, a period of shortages of commodities on a global basis, and a period of high inflation. The oil crisis followed the report of the Club of Rome[17], which argued that the world's resources were finite, and were being consumed at a rate that could not be sustained. Not surprisingly, authors rose to the challenge. Procurement was seen suddenly to be a strategic matter[18] and inflation not only called for a strategic response from organisations, but would also affect how the planning process should be applied[19, 20].

The fact that the future was going to be both different and discontinuous was increased by various publications which examined where some of the trends could lead. One such study, which was very influential at the time, was Alvin Toffler's *Future Shock* (1970).

At the same time as the environment was becoming more turbulent, there was a growing awareness that the nature of competition was changing, was more global, and that some competitors were behaving in a way that was different from the historical pattern. Later this began to develop into more structured thinking about global competition, but by this time strategic planning had itself evolved into its next phase.

Perhaps the best way to visualise the switch of emphasis was to see the task as setting a strategic direction for the organisation, whereas many had seen the task previously as preparing a blueprint for the future. I used the direction argument in a book I was writing during 1969, using the term 'objectives' in much the same way as we would now say 'vision'. The terms are explained in later chapters.

Objectives are something to aim at, although they should be regarded as a map grid reference rather than as a target at a rifle range. The company will not always find that the shortest distance is a straight line, and may have to make detours to avoid obstacles. But having made the detour it is possible to come back to the grid reference from another direction. Without a defined objective it becomes very difficult to measure progress: having detoured the company is likely to remain pointed in the wrong direction.[21]

Although the strategic planning phase put more concentration into strategy in relation to the business environment, markets and competitors, the most common process was still based on the preparation of corporate-wide plans, with submissions from the various business units being discussed with top management of the organisation. Some processes became very bureaucratic, bringing the danger that completing the annual round of forms was a more pressing task than strategic thinking. Not all top managements undertook what in theory was their task in looking across the boundaries of the SBU, and giving clear guidance on the direction of the organisation and what this would mean to each SBU. Sometimes the result was that the official plan for the whole was no more than the addition of the parts, and what actions were taken about developing strategies which were outside the scope of current SBUs, or fell across the boundaries of more than one SBU were unplanned. Some organisations modified the planning process to enable a broader strategic review to take place, and some used the techniques to determine a strategy, without relating it to a formal process of planning.

What was often missing was an emphasis on implementation, and a close relation between the analytical and behavioural aspects of management. It was the growing awareness of the shortfalls of the strategic planning phase, the way in which many organisations tried to overcome them, and the work of researchers and theorists that moved many organisations gently into the next phase.

Strategic management

The existence of strategic management in a job title does not inevitably mean that an organisation has changed to the new approach, and the position is further complicated by the fact that there are many different strands of thought about how strategic management should be applied. Although many of these have emerged in more recent years, a difference of opinion over how to manage strategically is not a new phenomenon, and many of the new ideas have their roots in the past, sometimes to a greater extent than many people realise. But first let us look at at what strategic management is, and how the new phase became popularised. Once again we can attribute the codification of a new way of thinking to Igor Ansoff.

Professor Ansoff gives a 1972 reference[22] as the first publication of the new name, and he should know. Mass appeal came somewhat later as more came to be written, such as Ansoff, Declerk and Hayes,[23] and more organisations took to the approach. Although there is no clear date, it was probably around 1980 when almost everyone switched to the new term, although even into the next century the words will be used by organisations that do not apply the concepts.

What is different about strategic management? First, it is about managing strategically as well as planning, so although the planning part may still be important, it is only a component. Strategic planning tended to focus on the 'hard' aspects of the external environment, and was concerned with markets and the products to supply them. It was about the formulation of strategy rather than its implementation. Strategic management includes the internal elements of organisation, such as style, structure and climate, it includes implementation and control, and consideration of the 'soft' elements of the environment. It is about the management of the total organisation, in order to create the future. Those who read this description will recall that these were the intentions of some of the earlier phases.

Ansoff[24] described strategic management as a new role for general managers, which was very different from the historic approach of management by exception. Discontinuous events rarely bring a response from functional managers, unless guided by general managers who tend to stick too long to the strategic knitting, often in the face of evidence that the market no longer wants it.

> The new general management role required managers to assume a creative and directive role in planning and guiding the firm's adaptation to a discontinuous and turbulent future. It required entrepreneurial creation of new strategies for the firm, design of new organisational capabilities and guidance of the firm's transformation to its new strategic posture. It is this combination of these three firm-changing activities that became known as strategic management (p. 7).

In the same paper, Ansoff suggests that an alternative name for strategic management might be 'disciplined entrepreneurship'.

Johnson and Scholes[25] argued that

> Strategic management is concerned with deciding on strategy and planning how that strategy is to be put into effect. It can be thought of as having three main elements within it . . . There is *strategic analysis*, in which the strategist seeks to understand the strategic position of the organisation. There is a *strategic choice* stage which is to do with formulation of possible courses of action, their evaluation, and the choice between them. Finally, there is a *strategic implementation* stage which is to do with planning how the choice of strategy can be put into effect (p. 10).

Although all this is true, this definition is almost identical to some of the descriptions used in the 1960s to describe corporate planning. What makes strategic management really different is the emphasis on managing the organisation through and by the strategic vision and the strategy, with the realisation that the soft issues in management may be more important in achieving this aim than the analytical processes.

This emphasis on both aspects means that strategic management can relate to and accommodate ideas such as those which emerged from the *in search of excellence* research,[26] which would have fallen outside the original planning orientation of the earlier years. Similarly the concept of the learning organisation (see, for example, Senge[27]) can fit well into the strategic management framework.

Ohmae[28] sums up the relationship of analysis (hard) and creativity (soft) in what is part of the essence of strategic management:

> ... Successful business strategies result not from rigorous analysis but from a particular state of mind. In what I call the mind of the strategist, insight and a consequent drive for achievement, often amounting to a sense of mission, fuel a thought process which is basically creative and intuitive rather than rational. Strategists do not reject analysis. Indeed they can hardly do without it. But they use it only to stimulate the creative process, to test the ideas that emerge, to work out their strategic implications, or to ensure successful implementation of high potential 'wild' ideas that might otherwise never be implemented properly. Great strategies, like great works of art or scientific discoveries, call for technical mastery in the working out but originate in insights that are beyond the reach of conscious analysis (p. 4).

Hold on to this idea of strategic thinking, add to it great emphasis on the leadership of strategic change, and the implementation of strategy, and we have what for me is what strategic management is all about.

Developments in concepts of strategic management seemed to come thick and fast during the 1980s, some related to the mainstream of the thinking, and others, which will be discussed later, moving down divergent tracks. The key name to emerge following the tradition of decisions related to sound analysis was Michael Porter. He, more than anyone, put competitor analysis into prominence. His thinking began before the publication of his first landmark book, with a background note used at Harvard from 1975, but he became prominent with his first work on techniques for analysing industries and competitors,[29] and this was followed by a more complex approach to building competitive advantage.[30] Some subsequent criticism of Porter's analytical approach that it analyses the past and not the future seems to be misplaced, as there is no reason why the analysis should not be applied in a dynamic way. Porter argued that there were three generic strategies available to all organisations: cost leadership, differentiation, and focus. I personally feel less happy with this idea than I do with most of his approaches to analysis.

From the late 1960s there were warning signs that old patterns of competition were changing, and that the biggest challenge would come from beyond national borders. It was not until the 1980s that the serious books on the development of a global strategy began to appear. Whereas books such as Brooke and van Beusekom[31] and Channon[32] largely reflected the conventional wisdom of applying planning systems to subsidiaries set up to manufacture for and market to their national economies, only a few years later the emphasis was on the global organisation that thought of the world as a market, and adjusted its activities accordingly. Such books help organisations which are global, and also those which are not, but who compete with global companies. Three landmark books are Porter,[33] Prahalad and Doz[34] and Yip[35].

Strategic management had thus shifted emphasis, happily accommodating books such as Ohmae[36] which dealt with the new logic of the global marketplace, and put joint ventures and alliances much higher in the list of strategic options. There was a realisation that businesses had to be world class in their standards of performance, thinking initially applied to manufacturing (see, for example, Hayes, Wheelwright and Clark[37]), and later to all areas of the business. Benchmarking became a tool of strategic management, also claimed by marketeers, and the total quality management movement. Whether strategic management would want to claim business process re-engineering and resultant UK/US fashion which was a feature of the 1990s for smaller, flatter organisations is a matter of opinion.

One of the differences in the strategic management approach compared to its predecessors is a closer blending of the analytical with the behavioural. The seeds of this were sown long before the new term was coined. The consultancy McKinsey made a great contribution with their 7S model, which brought structure, style, people and shared values together with skills, systems and strategy. The model has been published widely, and one place where it can be found is Peters and Waterman (p. 10)[26]. Some of the concepts behind this model go back many years, and will be discussed in Chapter 3, together with related developments. The 7S model put culture into the frame, and can be related to much more thinking on transformational or strategic leadership and the management of change. This is not the place for a detailed review of this thinking. Tichy and Devanna[38] and Bate[39] are useful samples of a much wider literature (see Chapters 3 and 27 for further discussion).

Although transformational leadership and change management are part of the armoury for the implementation of strategy, surprisingly for an approach to management which includes implementation as a major platform, much less has been written about the broader aspects of implementation. The earliest example of a book which I have found is Stonich,[40] although there have been articles on the subject. Bonoma[41] and Alexander[42, 43] made valuable contributions, and Hussey[44] provides a comprehensive collection of articles and case histories.

With hindsight we can see how what Ansoff originally called 'strategic management' has moulded and adapted itself to the changing challenges which businesses face. It is not hard to see how the different challenges organisations perceive (I use the word deliberately) that they face, the biases of the leaders of organisations, and the varying types of business activity have meant that the interpretation of what is involved in strategic management should vary from firm to firm. This in turn has led to a number of divergent and different schools of thought about business strategy and how it is, and should be, determined.

Divergence and differences

There are two problems in looking at what the authors claim are totally new ways of thinking about strategy. First, many of the claims to novelty and uniqueness only exist because the authors want them to, and what they really describe is the other side of an popular coin, and their work can be linked to much that has gone before. The second is that some of the theories are based on the analysis of what a few successful companies actually do, which is not always what they should be doing. This is one of the problems that beset the famous in search of excellence study (see Peters and Waterman[26]) for although it contains much wisdom, within a short time of publication many of the successful companies had fallen off their pedestals. There were obviously some missing ingredients in the make-up of what companies have to do to be successful. We can see another example of this. Quinn,[45] who was hailed by some as having made a breakthrough in understanding how strategic decisions were really made, based his theory of logical incrementalism on a study of nine companies, seven American, one Swedish, and one British. One of his successful companies was Xerox Corporation, who contributed to his theory that the right way to make strategy was through a process of logical incrementalism, where the organisation felt its way forward rather than going through a lot of formalised analysis (more of this later).

Now let us move forward to the work of another pair of 'new' thinkers. Hamel and Prahalad[10] also used Xerox in the development of their ideas, but this time as an example of a company that had failed strategically. They state:

> During the 1970s and 1980s Xerox surrendered a substantial amount of market share to Japanese competitors such as Canon and Sharp. Recognising that it was on a slippery slide to oblivion, Xerox benchmarked its competitors and fundamentally reengineered its processes. By the early 1990s Xerox had become a textbook example of how to reduce costs, improve quality, and satisfy customers. But in all the talk of the new 'American Samurai', two issues were overlooked. First, although Xerox succeeded in halting the erosion of its market share, it failed to recapture much share from its Japanese competitors. Canon still produces more copiers than any company in the world. Second, despite a pioneering role in laser printing, networking, icon-based computing, and the laptop computer, Xerox has failed to create any substantial new business outside its copier core. Although Xerox may have invented the office as we know it, it has profited very little from its inventiveness. In fact Xerox has probably left more money on the table, in the form of underexploited innovation, than any company in history (p. 17).

Bearing in mind that Quinn's work predated the changes Xerox did make during the 1980s, the choice of Xerox in his sample certainly raises some doubts.

So let us take what has come to be called the emergent strategy school of thought as our first discussion of modern divergent thinking. But how modern is it? How does 1959 grab you? It may even be earlier. Lindblom[46] described two ways of thinking about strategy. The first was the rational–comprehensive, or root approach, which is based on rational analysis to find the appropriate strategy. The second was the successive limited comparisons or branch method '. . . continually building out from the current situation, step-by-step and by small degrees'. The argument was that some strategies are too complex to be prethought on some sort of big bang approach, and the only way forward in these cases is to move forwards in incremental steps, continually reassessing where the organisation has got to with the strategy, and the appropriate next step. Lindblom was writing about public sector strategy, but his observations were equally appropriate for complex decisions in business. In fact, in a footnote Lindblom gives an alternative name to the branch method: 'the incremental method'.

Quinn's[45] conclusion was that successful business strategies did not arise from the highly formalised approach to planning that he felt was the recommendation of many text books. His findings were that in large organisations:

> The processes used to arrive at the total strategy are typically fragmented, evolutionary, and largely intuitive. Although one can frequently find embedded in these fragments some very refined pieces of formal strategic analysis, the real strategy tends to *evolve* as internal decisions and external events flow together to create a new, widely shared consensus for action among key members of the top management team (p. 15).

Later he concludes:

> The most effective strategies of major enterprises tend to emerge step by step from an iterative process in which the organisation probes the future, experiments, and learns from a series of partial (incremental) commitments rather than through global formulations of total strategies . . . The process is both logical and incremental (p. 58).

The other main proponent of this line of thinking is Mintzberg. In Mintzberg and Waters[47] a distinction is made between intended, deliberate, emergent and realised strategy. Deliberate strategy is based on precise intentions from rational analysis and examination of the situation: it is the portion of intended strategy which is actually realised, that is, implemented. Emergent strategy comes from patterns and ideas which are realised 'despite, or in the absence of' intentions. A consensus arises naturally as many different people in the organisation converge on the same theme or pattern, so that it becomes pervasive in the organisation 'without the need for any central direction or control':

> In other words, the convergence is not driven by any intentions of a central management, nor even by prior intentions widely shared among the other actors. It just evolves as the result of a host of individual actions.

Porter[48] criticises the idea of emergent strategy as described by Quinn and Mintzberg:

> Related in some way to the idea that strategic choices are unnecessary is another school of thought that has grown in importance in recent years – the need to stay flexible. Proponents of this view suggest that a company should not commit to any strategy at all. Because the competitive environment is always changing, they argue, choosing a position is always risky since it may soon become obsolete. These theorists believe that instead, a firm should be nimble, adaptive, and willing and able to pursue new strategies as new opportunities arise.
>
> Like most ideas that gain some acceptance among practitioners, this one contains an element of truth. However, the stay flexible school of strategy

defies competitive and organisational reality. Companies must indeed
innovate and improve constantly in pursuing their strategies in order to
sustain competitive advantage. Successful companies are those that recognise and respond to continually changing market and technological
possibilities to drive down costs or find new ways to differentiate. Yet my
research makes it clear that successful companies rarely change their
fundamental strategic positions ... They simply get better and better at
implementing them, through ongoing innovation (p. 273).

He then goes on to argue why consistency is so important in the marketplace, and
suggests that frequent shifts in strategy 'will leave a company mediocre at
everything'.

Readers have to make up their own minds about the emergent strategy
concept. Like Porter, I see some elements of truth in it, but I also see it as
providing an opportunity for mediocrity and an excuse for doing no thinking
about the future at all. The Ohmae idea of strategic thinking is a better
summation of what I feel is important for success, and anything that allows top
management to argue that the best strategies will just happen by accident is
dangerous. Your view may well be different.

Hamel and Prahalad are unlikely to be followers of the emergent strategy
concept, and although they have much to offer, they are really part of the
mainstream of strategic management thinking. Their main deviance from the
established path is their emphasis on the internal capabilities of the firm, through
the choosing and development of core competences which enable the firm to gain
competitive success. This in fact is not a completely new concept. Christensen,
Andrews and Bower,[49] the first edition of which was published in 1965, used the
term *distinctive competence of the organisation*. This went deeper than the
traditional strengths and weaknesses analysis. 'The distinctive competence of an
organisation is more than what it can do, it is what it can do particularly well'
(p. 256). 'The effort to find or to create a competence that is truly distinctive may
hold the real key to a company's success or even its future development. For
example, the ability of a cement manufacturer to run a truck fleet more
effectively than its competitors may constitute one of its principal competitive
strengths in selling an undifferentiated product' (p. 257).

Hamel and Prahalad have two main building blocks in their approach: the idea
of strategic intent and core competencies. The ideas are accessible in their most
comprehensive form in Hamel and Prahalad (1994)[10] and in the original form in
Prahalad and Hamel (1989)[50] and (1990).[51] Strategic intent is the animating
dream which will propel the organisation, which provides a sense of destiny,
direction and discovery. I have tried very hard but can see no difference in this
concept from that of vision which has already been mentioned. However, the
authors do a useful service in pushing the idea into a position of greater
prominence in management practice.

In Hamel and Prahalad (1996)[10] they deplore the fact that generations of US
and British managers have been turned into cost cutters, downsizers, and
reengineers, and have lost the capability to think strategically.

Although process reengineering dominates the top management agenda in
many companies, we've argued that to create the future, a company must also

be capable of 'reengineering' its industry. The logic is simple: to extend leadership a company must eventually reinvent leadership, to reinvent leadership it must ultimately reinvent its industry, and to reinvent its industry it must ultimately regenerate its strategy. For us, top management's primary task is reinventing industries and regenerating strategy, not reengineering processes (p. 21).

Not much in common here with the emergent strategy school of thought!

The second building block is core competencies, which they define: 'A core competence is a bundle of skills and technologies that enables a company to provide a particular benefit to customers.' (p. 219). It all rests on the contention that: 'Core competencies are the gateways to future opportunities. Leadership in core competence represents a potentiality that is released when imaginative new ways of exploiting that core competence are envisioned' (p. 217).

This approach to core competencies seemed to catch the imagination in the 1990s in the way that Porter's concepts did in the 1980s, and they will be discussed at some length in Chapter 9. Hamel and Prahalad[10] criticise the concepts of Porter as providing a map of the past, rather than about shaping up tomorrow's industries (although, as mentioned earlier, it is only the user who restricts the extent to which Porter's concepts are applied in a dynamic way).

Porter[48] in turn is equally critical of the competence concept which he bundles with other authorities whose concept of strategy is driven by capability or resources, the CCR in the quotation which will follow. He recognises the importance of competencies when related to the external situation, but

> The focus on CCR *independent* of industry, competition and activities, however, is fraught with danger . . . what makes a capability, competence or resource competitively valuable? What makes it a source of advantage? . . . Industry structure and competitive positioning define the value of competences, capabilities and resources. Skills in optics technology, for example, are worthless unless they allow specific customer needs to be met in ways that competitors cannot match (pp. 279–83).

(The dotted lines represent omissions which do not distort the meaning of the extracts quoted.)

Kay[52] builds on the competency and value chain concepts. He sees strategic success as deriving from the distinctive capability that an organisation can use in selected markets to achieve a sustainable position, and give customers added value. Distinctive capabilities arise from four sources: strategic architecture, reputation, innovation, and strategic assets. The first three are seen as the primary sources. Strategic assets are based on 'dominance or market position', through a natural or artificial monopoly, or through dominating a market with high entry barriers. Although in one place (p. 16) he includes strategic assets as a distinctive competence, it is clear that he sees them as something that is quite different (p. 113). Not every organisation can benefit from strategic assets.

Architecture is the capacity of organisations to develop relationships with other firms in the value chain, including customers, employees, and through networks. This provides the organisation with the capacity to develop and use organisational knowledge and to respond flexibly to changing circumstances. So strategic architecture has something to do with the learning organisation.

Reputation is the second powerful source of competence, but its importance varies between markets. It can also be costly and difficult to create, but is very easy to lose.

Innovation does not always deliver sustainable advantage, in that many innovations are easily copied. Kay believes that firms that are successful in innovation are often able to do so because of the strengths they have developed in their architecture, which enable them to generate a continuous flow of innovations, or move more rapidly than others to get an innovation to market.

A contingency approach to strategic management

The earliest concepts of planning were predicated on the assumption that the principles and concept were right for all businesses, although there might be some need for minor adaptation to fit the style and circumstances of particular organisations. Thus it was not expected that every planning system would be applied in precisely the same way, but the concept would be recognisable, and any differences would be in detail rather than the main ideas. This in fact was never true, partly because the fit of the universal concept to particular circumstances was never that precise, partly because new slants to the old concepts were being promoted all the time, and partly because many companies neglected to include many of the key elements when they applied the concepts. This idea of the 'right' way to do things persists in much of the literature to the present day, although there is probably more understanding of the reasons why changes have to be made to fit company circumstances, and in any case many of the modern ideas are intended to bring out the differences between organisations. Nevertheless, the underlying message of many of the authorities presented in this chapter is 'here is the only thorough way to develop strategy, and every one else is wrong in at least part of what they recommend'.

Some twenty years ago Igor Ansoff began to work on a dilemma which bothered him. Why do each of the methods suggested by the experts work well in some organisations and badly in others? I have been fortunate in having had many conversations with Igor, and he has often said that everything is right in some situations. But what are those situations? Igor has also claimed that few, if any, of the 'new' theories that are presented are based on sound research.

We can demonstrate this point by referring back to Quinn's work mentioned earlier. He investigated nine successful companies and drew conclusions that the way they reached their decisions about strategy were right because they were successful. However, he did not do the same detailed research among unsuccessful organisations, who were probably following the same approach, in which case the conclusion might have been that success was not due to the process but to some other unidentified factors. Similarly, it was impossible to say that the companies might not have been more successful had the strategy process been different: as we have seen, Hamel and Prahalad clearly believe this at least in the case of Xerox.

Ansoff began to research whether the processes by which strategies were identified and determined were not in some way contingent on the circumstances in which the organisation operated. Obviously there are many variables that will affect the quality of strategy, not least being the competence and judgement of the people who make it. Ansoff focused on something different, the external circumstances in which the organisation operated. What resulted was the definition of five levels of turbulence, with each of which was associated an optimal way of strategic management. There is face validity to this proposition, that, for example, an organisation in a level 1 degree of turbulence needs control more than it needs strategic change, and the old extended budgeting system of the 1960s is probably the best way of stopping people from developing new strategies that are not needed. At level 3 there is uncertainty and change, but quite a lot can be estimated with reasonable accuracy: therefore the strategic planning process that is the cornerstone of much of the present theory is appropriate. At level 5, the business exists in a state of massive turbulence, planning systems are too cumbersome to cope, and the approach to strategy must incorporate ways of finding and using weak signals about change, rapid response, flexibility, and a top management state of constant awareness. Level 5 organisations have to work to create the environment in which they are to operate: for level 1 organisations maintaining the status quo is more important.

Companies may move backwards and forwards along the spectrum. The computer firm Apple was at level 5 when first formed, as the PC market did not exist to any great extent and the technology was new. As it became established as successful it required a different top management approach, and probably operated at level 3 for a while. More recent industry developments and changes in where power lies in the industry has moved it to a higher level of turbulence again.

Ansoff's conclusions are described in Ansoff and McDonnell (1990)[2] (the first edition of this book appeared in 1984), and in shorter form in Ansoff (1991)[53]. The concept codifies the general management capability, culture/climate, and organisational competence that are appropriate for each level of turbulence.

Both the above references include some of the results of some of the research that supports the theory, and more complete summaries of this may be found in Ansoff et al.[54] and Ansoff and Sullivan.[55] The findings from similar research undertaken in various countries in different industries showed that the highest-profitability firms were those that had a good match between the level of turbulence and the appropriate approach to strategic management for that level. A mismatch of approach and turbulence by one level would reduce profitability considerably: a mismatch of two levels had the firms operating at a loss. The research method, in simple terms, compared the approach in the whole sample of companies to the level of turbulence and compared the result against profitability. It thus avoided the research defects mentioned earlier.

Until recently the new Ansoff concept has not been as widely supported or applied as one might expect, partly I suspect because it positions many of the other theories as being 'right' for only one level of turbulence: the Ansoff and

Sullivan reference includes a diagram which does just this for many of the authorities discussed in this chapter, and a few who I have not mentioned. However, others are beginning to think on contingency lines.

D'Aveni[56] proposes a different strategic approach for firms which operate in conditions of hypercompetition, which is the condition of ever higher levels of uncertainty, turbulence, diversity of competitors and hostility. Competition is nearly always a sequence of discontinuities, with few stable periods, and consequently competitive advantage erodes quickly. Competing firms make many major, rapid and unexpected strategic moves. 'Hypercompetition may be viewed, therefore, as just a faster version of traditional competition. But that's like saying that a hurricane is a faster version of a strong wind' (p. 217). D'Aveni provides tools and methods, as well as a philosophy for managing under conditions of hypercompetition, arguing that strategic management is no longer about creating long-term competitive advantage, which is unsustainable, but is about continually changing the patterns of markets, seeking temporary advantages, and maintaining the momentum of change. Rühli[57] explores these ideas and tests them against the electrotechnical industry. I am grateful for this article, as until I read it I had not come across the D'Aveni work.

D'Aveni examines a particular set of conditions. Coyne and Subramaniam[58] discuss a concept which emerged from an internal forum set up within the McKinsey consultancy. Like the Ansoff concept, it suggests different approaches to strategic thinking which are contingent on the degree of uncertainty about the future. They distinguish four levels. At level 1 it is possible to develop a usable prediction of the future through analysis: at level 2 analysis enables different scenarios to be made, although there is uncertainty over which will happen. By level 3 there is a condition of continuous uncertainty, where the outcome is likely to lie upon a continuum rather than a couple of discrete scenarios. Level 4 is a condition of great ambiguity. Readers who would like to compare these levels with those of Ansoff will need to refer to Chapter 3 where Ansoff's concepts are discussed in a little more depth.

The new McKinsey approach relates the levels of uncertainty to a new industry model developed on the foundation of Porter's approach. It has three dimensions: the structure/conduct of the industry, the basis of competition, and the external forces which affect the industry. They believe that the new model gives a more appropriate insight into what is important in making strategy, and that the process by which strategy is made should change with the level of uncertainty. They argue:

> Traditionally, strategic management has meant little more than staying the course. Today, however, it means actively managing the way in which strategy unfolds, month after month, year after year. That might entail drawing up contingent road maps in which reaching specific milestones will clarify the right strategy: it might equally mean recognising that strategy will have to evolve as industry conditions alter (p. 23).

Like Ansoff, they argue that existing concepts are of value, but are not universally applicable at all levels of uncertainty.

Where does this review leave us?

The changes in thinking that have taken place since the 1960s are signs of a healthy subject. We now have many better ways of thinking about strategic management in the round. I believe that it is dangerous to believe all the hype that comes out with each successive theory, that it is the only valid path to salvation. In fact it is only when we get to the contingency theories that authors of the new approaches appear to be willing to acknowledge that many different approaches and ways of thinking have value, but that this value is not the same in every situation. I am with Coyne and Subramaniam in their statement 'Consequently, strategists should be familiar with all of these concepts, but not biased toward any of them. They should narrow their focus to a specific submodel only after they have determined which one is most appropriate to their situation' (p. 24).

Figure 1.1 suggests that there are five areas of critical importance in successful strategic management, none of which should be neglected. In the centre, and affecting each of the other factors, are the capabilities of the business leaders. It is possible to hit on a good strategy without any analysis, but there are dangers in the approach which could be avoided. However, analysis rarely produces a sound strategy. Creativity and vision is required, and then analysis is needed again to examine the likely outcome of the strategy. The way in which strategic decisions are taken and the process the organisation uses to arrive at strategies will also affect the success of those strategies. Finally, the best strategy in the world will be useless if it is not implemented.

Figure 1.1
Critical factors for strategic success. (From Hussey, D. E. 'Strategic Management: Past Experience and Future Directions', *Strategic Change*, **6**, No. 5, 1997)

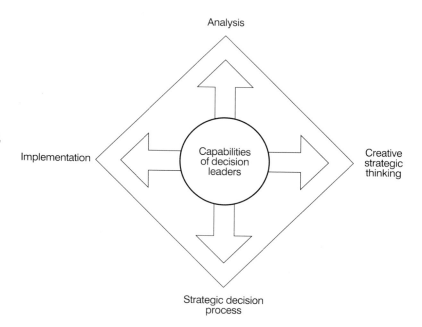

In the rest of the book it will usually be necessary to discuss one thing at a time, so please keep this model in mind so that there is a permanent reminder that all five factors have to be there.

I hope that this chapter has shown that an idea is not totally new just because an author claims it to be so, and that there has been a much greater continuity in the development of ideas over the whole history of the subject. I believe that many apparently disparate approaches link together rather well, and that the wise strategist will make use of all of them, some time, rather than using some of them always. There is no magic in any approach, and the right strategies for an organisation require much hard work and a willingness to continually work on improving strategic thinking.

References

1 Gluck, F. W., Kaufman, S. P. and Walleck, A. S. 'Strategic Management for Competitive Advantage', *Harvard Business Review*, July/August, 1980.

2 Ansoff, I. and McDonnell, E. *Implanting Strategic Management*, 2nd edn, Prentice Hall, Hemel Hempstead, 1990.

3 Sun Tzu, *The Art of War*, translation by Yuan Shibing, Sterling Publishing, New York, 1990.

4 Wee, C. H. 'Sun Tzu's Art of War: Selected applications to Strategic Thinking and Business Practices', in Hussey, D. E. (ed.), *International Review of Strategic Management*, Vol. 5, Wiley, Chichester, 1994.

5 Ho, S. K. 'Competitive Strategies Through Sun Tzu's Art of Warfare', *Strategic Change*, 6, No. 3, May, 1997.

6 Ansoff, H. I. *Corporate Strategy*, McGraw-Hill, New York, 1965.

7 Drucker, P. F. *The Practice of Management*, Heinemann, London, 1955.

8 Drucker, P. F. *Managing for Results*, Heinemann, London, 1964.

9 Ansoff, H. I. *The Evolution of Corporate Planning*, Stanford Research Institute, Menlo Park, CA, 1967.

10 Hamel, G. and Prahalad, C. K. *Competing for the Future*, Harvard Business School Press, Boston, 1996. (Note that the book was first published in 1994: the 1996 paperback version includes an additional preface.)

11 Merritt, A. J. and Sykes, A. *The Finance and Analysis of Capital Projects*, Longmans, London, 1963.

12 Ackoff, R. L. *A Concept of Corporate Planning*, Wiley Interscience, New York, 1970.

13 Jantch, E. *Technological Forecasting in Perspective*, OECD, 1967.

14 Kaplan, R. *Building a Management System to Implement Your Strategy: Strategic Management Survey: Summary of Findings and Conclusions*, Renaissance Solutions, London, 1995.

15 Buzzell, R. D. and Gale, B. T. *The PIMS Principles: Linking Strategy to Performance*, Free Press, New York, 1987.

16 Hussey, D. E. *Strategic Management: Theory & Practice*, 3rd edn, Chapter 25, Pergamon, Oxford, 1994.

17 Meadows D. H,, Meadows D. L., Randers, J. and Behrens, W. V. *The Limits to Growth*, Earth Island, London, 1972.

18 Farmer D. H. and Taylor, B. (eds). *Corporate Planning and Requirement*, Heinemann, London, 1975.

19 Hussey D. E. *Inflation and Business Policy*, Longman, London, 1975.

20 Hussey, D. E. *Corporate Planning: A Guide for Accountants*, Institute of Cost and Management Accountants, London, 1978.

21 Hussey, D. E. *Introducing Corporate Planning*, Pergamon, Oxford, 1971. (The 4th edition was published in 1991.)

22 Ansoff, H. I. 'The Concept of Strategic Management', *Journal of Business Policy*, 2, No. 4, Summer, 1972.

23 Ansoff, H. I., Declerk, R. P. and Hayes, R. L. (eds). *Strategic Planning to Strategic Management*, Wiley, Chichester, 1976.

24 Ansoff, H. I. 'Strategic Management in a Historical Perspective', in Hussey, D. E. (ed.), *International Review of Strategic Management, 1991*, Wiley, Chichester, 1991.

25 Johnson G. and Scholes, K. *Exploring Corporate Strategy*, Prentice Hall, London, 1984.

26 Peters, T. J. and Waterman, R. H. *In Search of Excellence*, Harper and Row, New York, 1982.

27 Senge, P. *The Fifth Discipline*, Doubleday, New York, 1990.

28 Ohmae, K. *The Mind of the Strategist*, McGraw-Hill, New York, 1982. (The page reference is taken from the 1983 edition by Penguin, London.)

29 Porter, M. E. *Competitive Strategy*, Free Press, New York, 1980.

30 Porter, M. E. *Competitive Advantage*, Free Press, New York, 1985.

31 Brook, M. Z. and van Beusekom, M. *International Corporate Planning*, Pitman, London, 1979.

32 Channon, D. F. with Jalland, M. *Multinational Strategic Planning*, Macmillan, London, 1979.

33 Porter, M. E. *Competition in Global Industries*, Harvard Business School Press, Boston, MA, 1986.

34 Prahalad, C. K. and Doz, Y. *The Multinational Mission*, Free Press, New York, 1987.

35 Yip, G. *Total Global Strategy*, Prentice Hall, Englewood Cliffs, NJ, 1992.

36 Ohmae, K. *The Borderless World*, HarperCollins, New York, 1990.

37 Hayes, R. H., Wheelwright, S. C. and Clark, K. B. *Dynamic Manufacturing*, Free Press, New York, 1988.

38 Tichy, M. and Devanna, M. A. *The Transformational Leader*, Wiley, New York, 1986 (reissued with a new preface in 1990).

39 Bate, P. *Strategies for Cultural Change*, Butterworth-Heinemann, Oxford, 1994.

40 Stonich, P. J. (ed.). *Implementing Strategy: Making Strategy Happen*, Ballinger, Cambridge, MA, 1982.

41 Bonoma, T. V. 'Making Your Marketing Strategy Work', *Harvard Business Review*, 62, No. 2, 69–76, 1984.

42 Alexander, L. D. 'Successfully Implementing Strategic Decisions', *Long Range Planning*, 18, No. 3, 91–97, 1985.

43 Alexander, L. D. 'Strategy Implementation: Nature of the Problem', in Hussey, D. E. (ed.), *International Review of Strategic Management*, pp. 73–96, Wiley, Chichester, 1991.

44 Hussey, D. E. (ed.). *The Implementation Challenge*, Wiley, Chichester, 1996.

45 Quinn, J. B. *Strategies for Change: Logical Incrementalism*, Irwin, Homewood, IL, 1980.

46 Lindblom, C. E. 'The Science of Muddling Through', *Public Administration Review*, 19, spring, 79–88, 1959. Also appears in Ansoff, H. I. (ed.) *Business Strategy*, pp. 41–60, Penguin, London, 1969.

47 Mintzberg, H. and Waters J. 'Of Strategies Deliberate and Emergent', *Strategic Management Journal*, July/September, 1985.

48 Porter, M. E. 'Competitive Strategy Revisited: a View from the 1990's', in Duffy, P. B. (ed.), *The Relevance of a Decade: Essays to mark the first ten years of the Harvard Business School Press*, Harvard Business School Press, Boston, MA, 1994.

49 Christensen, C. R., Andrews, K. R. and Bower, J. L. *Business Policy: Text and Cases*, 4th edn, Irwin, Homewood, IL, 1978.

50 Prahalad, C. K. and Hamel, G. 'Strategic Intent', *Harvard Business Review*, May/June, 1989.

51 Prahalad C. K. and Hamel, G. 'The Core Competence of the Corporation', *Harvard Business Review*, May/June, 79–91, 1990.

52 Kay, J. *Foundations of Corporate Success: How Business Strategies Add value*, Oxford University Press, Oxford, 1993.

53 Ansoff, H. I. 'Strategic Management in a Historical Perspective', in Hussey D. E. (ed.), *International Review of Strategic Management*, Vol. 2 pp. 3–69, Wiley, Chichester, 1991.

54 Ansoff, H. I. *et al.* 'Empirical Support for a Paradigmic Theory of Strategic Success Behaviors of Environment Serving Organisations', in Hussey, D. E. (ed.), *International Review of Strategic Management*, Vol. 4, pp. 173–203, 1993.

55 Ansoff H. I. and Sullivan, P. A. 'Optimizing Profitability in Turbulent Environments: A Formula for Strategic Success', *Long Range Planning*, **26**, No. 5, 11–23, October, 1993.

56 D'Aveni, R. *Hypercompetition: Managing the Dynamics of Strategic Manoeuvring*, Free Press, New York, 1994.

57 Rühli, E. 'The concept of hypercompetition – a new approach to strategic management in large multinational firms', *Strategic Change*, **6**, No. 7, November, 1997.

58 Coyne, K. P. and Subramaniam, S. 'Bringing Discipline to Strategy', *McKinsey Quarterly*, No. 4, 14–25, 1996.

CHAPTER 2

Strategic management: success or failure?

Is strategic management of benefit? In this chapter the research evidence will be examined, both into planning and into the success or failure of various company strategies. The chapter will provide a synthesis of the early research into planning success, and will also show that not all organisations that claim to apply strategic management are doing it well. Recent research into the success and failure of certain common strategic moves will be examined. The chapter will conclude with a list of common areas of weakness which are found in many organisations, and where careful attention would improve the quality of strategic decisions.

There can only be one justification for introducing strategic management into an organisation: a belief that it will lead to a successful future, and is more likely to do this than any other way of running the business. Indeed there is no sound reason why any chief executive should want to use this approach to management unless he or she had this belief.

It is a fact that many companies throughout the world practise some form of strategic management, and this provides circumstantial evidence that a body of chief executives hold this conviction. However, when we look more deeply into this, we find that what they all do under the name of strategic management is immensely variable. Some of the reasons for this have appeared in the previous chapter, and more will emerge later in this book. We should accept, too, that organisations may be dedicated to strategic management, and still take the wrong decisions.

The purpose of this chapter is to examine some of the available evidence about the benefits of strategic management, but not to take this at face value, and also to look at some of the things that strategic management should have avoided, but which have still happened.

Because the nature of strategic management has changed, as has been outlined, studies undertaken at different periods may be measuring different things. The evidence needs to be looked at in two sections. The first will cover the earlier studies of whether formal approaches to planning added value to organisations: essentially these examined whether the existence of a corporate planning process improved results. The following section will see what can be added to this evidence as the concept changes from corporate/strategic planning, to strategic management.

Planning does pay

Unfortunately, many of the benefits of a planning process are difficult to prove in absolute terms. This is because once planning is introduced, the company changes, and it is never possible to compare what has happened with what would have happened under different circumstances. It is rather like changes in the economic policy of a government. One can speculate – as the opposition parties usually do – that another and often totally opposite course of action would have led to better results. Such arguments can only rest on logic, economic theory and idealistic belief. It is never possible to turn the clock back, and neither is it conceivable that two economic solutions could be run in parallel on a test market basis to see which is best.

In addition, there is a major problem in identifying the costs of planning. Real benefit can only come if the additional profit earned exceeds the additional costs of planning. Quite apart from the conceptual problem of specifically separating the benefits of planning from those of other causes, it is almost impossible to identify costs. It may be easy to isolate the costs of any specialist planning staff, but this is only a part. It is very difficult to estimate the cost of the participation of other managers in the process – and an overwhelming task to try to see how the cost of their participation differs from what it would be under some other style of management. Under any circumstances managers will spend some time on planning: how much more (or less) they will spend where a company has a formal planning process can probably never be computed in meaningful terms.

Logical consideration leads to an expectation that planning procedures will bring more in profits than they cost. At one time it would have been necessary to close this chapter at that point – perhaps adding that the worthiness of many other aspects of management are also incapable of absolute proof – but a number of studies have changed this viewpoint. It is now possible to quote evidence which supports the contention that corporate planning leads to better results. These studies are not always perfect, frequently suffer from problems of sampling and usually can only try to measure one or two aspects of results. Those quoted in this chapter refer to a formal planning process, which may not necessarily be the same as strategic management under a modern interpretation.

Planning can be carried out well or it can be done badly. Again, there is an increasing body of knowledge on the degree of satisfaction felt by companies with their planning efforts and on the problems that arise in practice.

The findings of some of these serious attempts to measure the results of planning will be woven into the fabric of this chapter. Before this step is taken it is as well to return to the beginning and look critically at the evidence proving that companies actually do planning.

As might be expected, formal corporate planning as a contribution to the science of management arose in the USA and by the early 1960s had reached a high level of management acceptance. It arrived in the UK a year or two later and attained a high point of management interest by 1967 when the Society of Long Range Planning was formed. By 1970 this society had attracted about 1000 members all concerned in some ways with long-range planning. Numerous case histories have been presented at conferences or written up as articles in the journal of the society, *Long Range Planning*, mainly supplied by companies in the UK, the USA, or the continent of Europe. There are now companies which use this style of management in many countries throughout the world – one reason for this spread being through multinational companies applying a planning process throughout all their subsidiaries.

One of the first serious attempts to survey planning in the UK was undertaken by Denning and Lehr[1] in 1967. It was found that 25 per cent of companies from *The Times* top 300 (excluding financial concerns and nationalised companies) were practising some form of corporate planning. The survey showed, at that time, that it was only in seven industry groups that 25 per cent or more of the companies in those groups were definitely undertaking corporate planning. This led to some further analyses which will be referred to later.

Across the Atlantic, evidence that planning was acceptable was provided by the 1966 National Industrial Conference Board Survey of Business Opinions and Experience.[2] This revealed that over 90 per cent of manufacturers sampled practised some form of formal corporate planning. Similar studies in certain other countries have suggested that around 80 per cent of companies sampled have some kind of wide long-range plan. For example, Komo produced evidence of Japanese practice,[3] from 1965 to 1975, the Stanford Research Institute[4] surveyed the European situation in 1971, and Eppink, Keuning and de Jong[5] produced similar figures for Holland in 1976. The Dutch survey suggested that Holland lagged the USA and the UK by about five years.

Denning's and Lehr's and subsequent studies in both the UK and the USA proved that there were companies who had moved into corporate planning as early as the 1950s. Not all the evidence is straightforward. Another survey by Kempner[6] and Hewkins in 1968 found that few British companies had implemented corporate planning, while a number of executives rejected it completely. These results caused a certain amount of surprise because at that time many companies were known to undertake corporate planning: the fact that few of these emerged in the survey was probably partly due to sampling problems and partly to the fact that subsidiaries of external companies were not included. Thus the result did not purport to be typical of all companies operating in Britain. The Denning/Lehr survey also showed the skewed nature of the universe to certain industries, causing sampling problems on a small-scale survey.

A membership survey carried out by the Society for Long Range Planning in 1974[7] gave further confirmation of the differences of timing in the introduction of planning by type of industry. Table 2.1 illustrates some of the findings.

The median year of introduction would, of course, move if the survey were to be repeated today and if new firms had commenced planning. (Those not planning were organisations who had employees who belong to the Society, and the overall total not planning in the industry would be higher.) In the mid-1960s

Table 2.1 Introduction of planning by industry sectors

Industries	Replies	No. not planning	Median year of intro. planning
Food, drink, tobacco	30	1	1970
Chemicals, pharmaceuticals	35	4	1969
Oil and energy	10	–	1969
Metals and metal manufacture	17	1	1968
Mechanical engineering	22	2	1969
Electrical engineering, electronics	17	2	1968
Motor vehicles, aircraft, ships	13	3	1969
Textiles, fibres, footwear	8	1	1971
Other manufactures	51	5	1969
Construction	20	4	1969
Transport	16	–	1969
Retailing	13	5	1970
Banking, insurance, finance	39	4	1971

finding companies that planned in some industries (for example, banking) was rather like seeking needles in haystacks.

The fact that many companies were undertaking planning is one thing. Whether or not they were satisfied with what they were getting out of it was another. One of the first, and still one of the most useful studies on the implementation of planning, was that by Warren.[8] Much of his contribution will be left to Chapter 29, but it is worth mentioning that he found many misconceptions about what long-range planning really was. This is worth mentioning, because many of these early studies were made on the assumption that 'planning' meant the same in all the organisations studied.

Ringbakk[9] describes a survey of a sample of forty US companies identified in advance as having planning staffs. This confirmed that most companies had only begun corporate planning in the early 1960s, and established that many companies were disappointed by what they had achieved, and that not all the managements concerned practised planning as vigorously or accepted it as firmly as might have been assumed. A further general conclusion was that in most of the companies, planning was still in an evolutionary stage.

Perhaps one of the important points arising from this study is a reinforcement of a fairly obvious generalisation. Any new process of management can be applied well or badly, and the results achieved are affected by the skill with which the process is applied. To me this suggests that any company considering the introduction of a formal process of planning should take pains to learn how to do it well, and should be sure that it is the type of company that can benefit from such a system. More is made of these issues in Chapter 29 which examines a number of problems of implementation.

Irving[10] made a detailed study in 1969 of twenty-seven British companies (again excluding subsidiaries of overseas companies) which were identified as undertaking a planning process. (I personally feel some affection for this survey as I acted as the guinea-pig on whom his questionnaire was piloted.) He had little difficulty in identifying his sample, but, as in the Ringbakk survey, he found that many companies had only recently undertaken planning and that their systems were still in an evolutionary stage.

Taylor and Irving,[11] in an article based on this survey, stated:

> Corporate Planning in major UK companies is neither as well developed nor as fully accepted as one might expect. Less than half the sample companies were found to have complete corporate plans and a further 22 per cent had functional or divisional plans only, with little or no input from the corporate level. In a number of companies there was a heavy bias towards financial projections where objectives or action programmes had not been developed for the time period in question. In others, 'planning' consisted of little more than extended budgeting.
>
> Since an effort was made to select those companies who were thought to have made substantial progress in the development of corporate planning, one may conclude that industry in general is doing much less.
>
> These findings therefore support those of Ringbakk and Kempner–Hewkins concerning the present state of development of corporate planning in Britain and America.

In general, the conclusions of the survey evidence to this point was that an increasing number of companies were introducing this system of management, but many had a long way to go before they could be classified as effective planners. Since the mid-1970s, planning has become established in most organisations of any size, in most major countries. However, there has also been almost continuous research that has regularly thrown up the feeling that planning has not worked as well as it should have in many organisations. This theme will be returned to in later chapters.

The Society for Long Range Planning study[7] mentioned earlier provided fascinating evidence of what planning companies did and did not do. While most practised formal financial planning, forecast external events and reviewed performance against plan, only 25 per cent undertook contingency planning, 36 per cent diversification planning and 22 per cent divestment planning. Equally surprising, only 45 per cent undertook formal organisation planning and 53 per cent formal manpower planning.

Irving also provides some evidence of why companies decide to change to a system of corporate planning. In more than a third of his sample the introduction of planning was a direct result of major changes at board level. (My own personal experience has been that most of the planning appointments I have held have been the result of a change of chief executive. My consulting experience is similar.) In practically all cases, planning was initiated as the result of a perceived need to deliberately meet a factor of change which the company faced or expected to face. Less than a fifth of respondents stated that there was no specific event which caused planning to arrive in their companies.

Denning and Lehr[1] subjected their survey results to a detailed statistical evaluation in order to establish whether there were any particular characteristics of the planning companies when compared with the non-planners:

> If the introduction of formal long-range planning is, in fact, a managerial response to critical strategic or co-ordinative needs, one would expect evidence to that effect in the observed pattern of incidence. Vital strategic needs exist in situations of high financial risk or opportunity, whereas co-ordinative needs increase with the complexity of organizations. The following key parameters were selected for the analysis:
>
> Financial Risk/Opportunity – Rate of technological change
> – Growth and variability of turnover/profits
>
> Complexity – Size
> – Type of organization structure
> – Degree of vertical integration.

Each variable was analysed separately and the data were then subjected to a multivariate analysis. The main findings were that there was a strong positive correlation between the introduction of long-range planning and companies with a high rate of technological change and a clear positive relationship between planning and capital intensity. Growth and variability of turnover were found to affect the introduction of planning only marginally.

Only two of the 'complexity' factors could be measured, both size and organisational complexity having a strong relationship with the introduction of planning. Futher it was found that there was a tendency for the more complex companies to have introduced planning earlier than the less complex ones.

Two additional facts of interest emerging from the study were variation in the way that companies tackled the planning task and the higher proportion of subsidiaries of foreign companies who were doing corporate planning. While British companies included 23 per cent known 'planners', the foreign subsidiaries had 61 per cent of their number engaged in this activity.

It is possible to draw two alternative hypotheses from the Denning/Lehr survey:

- That the complex, high-capital, technological companies are the companies most likely to benefit from corporate planning; or
- That they are likely to perceive the need for planning before (as did the more complex companies in the sample) other types of company, and that where they lead other industries will follow. In my view the fact that over 40 per cent of companies had introduced planning for the first time in 1967, the year of the survey, lends some support to this hypothesis. This hypothesis seems to be supported by the other research quoted.

A number of case histories of planning activities are now available from companies in Europe and the USA, and many of these provide statements about the benefits of planning. Generally, such testimony tends to fall into three groups: those who judge the system by its efficiency as a system, those who point to short-term results, and those who attempt to describe the real long-term benefits being achieved.

The first type of argument is fallacious. (It is interesting to note that about one half of respondents in the Ringbakk[9] survey gave this sort of argument as demonstrating planning's contribution to corporate performance.) Certainly a planning process which does not produce clear objectives and logically evaluated plans will have little value, and the efficiency of the system is a very important factor in its success. In itself, it can never be an argument for corporate planning as a management activity. For example, there may be a fast and efficient train service between London and Manchester – poor consolation for the person who wants to travel to Cornwall. An efficient planning system must do more than simply be efficient: it must satisfy some economic need in a better way than would otherwise have been the case.

The next group of arguments are valid in an economic sense, but do not provide a long-term justification for planning. Certainly, the assessment of strengths and weaknesses may lead to immediate profit improvement opportunities, the coordinative ability of planning may bring an immediate improvement in communication, or planning may be the factor which leads to an organisational change. The results of all this activity can often be quantified and are frequently impressive. What should be realised is that in these cases planning is only one of a number of agencies which could have been used to secure the same results: for example, a firm of management consultants if properly briefed could have achieved the same benefit. I believe that these short-term results are the bonuses of planning, not the ultimate justification. Certainly they can pay for all the planning effort the company is likely to make in the future, so that, in effect, the other benefits are obtained free of charge.

In the third group of reasons there is a genuine effort to identify the real and tangible results of corporate planning. Such writers usually point to sustained growth and profitability, clarity of purpose, better communication, identification of additional opportunities, coordination, and better decision making. The following quotation from a case history by Champion[12] is representative of the type of general belief in the value of corporate planning which numerous writers have expressed:

> As regards the immediate results hoped for from the system, they were basically two. First, top management wanted to transform its European operations from a group of quasi-autonomous affiliates into a smoothly functioning integrated European unit. To do that it was necessary among other things, that the affiliates plan together within the framework of Europe-wide objectives. The planning system has unquestionably contributed to the achievement of this goal. CPC Europe is a solid unity today imbued by a team spirit which is nourished by effective dialogue up and down the management hierarchy and across functional and national boundary lines. Clearly, this major and very difficult achievement cannot be attributed exclusively to the planning system, but the system by establishing requirements and procedures for cooperation and coordination across all boundary lines and by stimulating the frank recognition and examination of common as well as particular business problems has aided importantly.
>
> Secondly, top management wanted to insure that all affiliates looked at their present and future business in a rational, analytic and systematic way. It is fair to say that CPC/E management has today a thorough and organized

understanding, at both the national and European levels of its present and future business potentials and that rational and organized planning has become a habit with the managers. Again, the planning system contributed significantly to the achievement by defining the parts into which a complex business and organization logically break down and by suggesting the means by which the functioning of these parts should be analyzed.

The second part of the question can be paraphrased into 'Has the planning system contributed indirectly to profits?' It is the most difficult question to answer. Profit-wise CPC Europe has done well since the planning system was installed. It would be ridiculous to assume that the company would not have done well without the planning system. The factors that make for success or failure in business are too numerous and too complex to make it possible to point to one as the determinant factor. But it is difficult to believe that an approach to planning which rationally structures the identification and evaluation of opportunities and the identification and measurement of risks does not in some small way at least contribute to sounder management decisions regarding which opportunities to pursue and which risks to take. This is not a completely satisfactory answer, but the truth is that planning systems, like management in general, must to a certain degree be accepted on the faith that their presence is beneficial.

This belief in the benefits of planning is echoed in Irving's[10] survey. Some of the responses are quoted in the Taylor/Irving[11] article:

Main Board Director of a large international group: 'I couldn't run the Company without a management planning system. The only way of controlling it is through management by exception. The old fashioned budgeting systems are absolutely worthless – the difference between management planning and budgeting is action. The biggest change is a change in attitude – the difference between saying that's what we expect to happen and that's what we are going to make happen.'

The General Manager of a Consumer Products Division of a large organisation commented: 'I feel planning is essential – without it, you don't know where you are going, it makes you look at a field in the widest possible sense, and consider alternatives. It makes you appreciate that there is change and the need to plan ahead to meet it. When you are in a fast moving environment, unless you can predict market trends, you will be continually behind.'

A main Board Director of a textile group said: 'If you have a long-range plan, you have to take a much closer look at the organization to highlight its strengths and weaknesses. It makes a managing director sit down and say "Where do I want to be in three or five years' time?" It's a thought provoking process – once you've been provoked into thought, benefits must inevitably follow.'

The Deputy Chairman of the same group said: 'We've been growing very rapidly as a group, therefore tidy setting down of objectives has been God's gift to us. We now realise how essential it is – we could have saved ourselves a lot of time and trouble had we had it before.'

The Chairman of the U. K. Division of a multi-national company said: 'I think it is impossible to operate without planning, principally because the size of investment means that you can't afford mistakes and also because of the lead time required to acquire, install and put into operation equipment. If we don't plan in advance, it takes at least two years to change direction, and we may miss opportunities – if you don't plan you cannot operate.'

A General Manager in the chemical industry said: 'The business and its component parts are all pointing in the same direction. Everyone knows what we are trying to achieve. Only by the process of planning can you really sort out what your objectives should be and apply analytical questioning to those objectives. It is inherently a control system – the chances of success are increased by the planning approach because you've done your homework. It's a way of living rather than a technique.'

A Senior Line Manager of a national building contractor observed: 'We couldn't exist without it – our resources would be over-stretched or under-utilized. You can't use your resources effectively without planning. It gives a target that must be worked to and indicates the implications of not meeting target. It motivates people all the way down the lines – one is always striving to improve on existing performance.'

These comments illustrate that planning is seen differently in different situations, but in each situation, if planning is to develop at all, it must satisfy a need.

What the testimony shows is that there are people who have strong personal beliefs in the efficacy of corporate planning. When taken in conjunction with the earlier evidence, the interpretations can only be that a large number of senior managers believe that planning works. This is an important factor, because, as stated earlier, no chief executive should introduce corporate planning unless he has this belief.

We do not have to rely on individual testimony, and there now are a growing number of studies which provide objective evidence in support of this belief.

Levitt[13] states:

> For many years the Stanford Research Institute has been studying the reasons why certain companies have outstanding growth records and others merely drift along at the national rate of economic growth. The major conclusions are as follows:
>
> (1) They systematically seek out, find, and reach for growth products and growth markets.
> (2) They characteristically have organized programmes to seek and promote new business opportunities.
> (3) They are consistently self-critical about the adequacy of their present operations and therefore consistently demonstrate superior competitive abilities in their present line of business.
> (4) Their top management slots are staffed by uniquely courageous, adventurous, high-spirited executives who bubble with dissatisfaction and are driven by an energetic zeal to lead rather than to follow.
> (5) The companies almost invariably have established formal systems of discovering opportunities and offsetting extreme risks by 'planning for the unseeable' with the context of clearly defined and growth-inspiring statements of 'company goals'.
> (6) The chief executives consciously and continuously, by word and by deed, establish an organizational environment of ruthless self-examination and effervescent high adventure.

Top management must see that the entire company becomes saturated with the idea of creativity and the merits of self-criticism. It must develop and transmit some guiding philosophy about the creative function – indeed, the creative necessity – of the really effective business enterprise.

A study by Thune and House[14] was carried out in the USA analysing the results of certain companies up to 1965. A sample of matched pairs of formal and informal 'planners' was selected from a larger sample drawn from six industry groups: drug, chemical, machinery, oil, food, and steel. Performance of the sample companies was then examined over periods of seven to fifteen years (depending on the date of the introduction of formal planning), in terms of five economic measures.

The significant results of the study were that the formal planning companies outperformed their counterparts on three of the five measures: earnings per share, earning on common equity, and earnings on total capital employed. In fact results for average sales and stock price appreciation were also better for the planners, but these measures were not statistically significant.

This is only a partial indication of results, and a comparison was also made of planning companies' performance before and after the introduction of planning. Again, the finding was that formal planning brought better results and planning companies improved their results on three of the economic measures: sales, earnings per share, and stock-price appreciation. (Data were not available for the other two measures.)

To confirm these findings, the performance of planning companies was compared against the informal planners for a period of time before the introduction of planning. There was no significant difference in results. The authors state:

> Thus the first major conclusion of the study is quite clear: formal planners from the time they initiated long-range planning through 1965 significantly outperformed informal planners with respect to earnings per share, earnings on common equity, and earnings on total capital employed. Furthermore, these companies outperformed their own records based on an equal period of time before they began formal planning. Finally, informal planners did not surpass formal planners on any of the measures of economic performance after long-range planning was introduced.

On an individual industry basis the findings held good for the drug, chemical, and machinery industries. Steel had to be omitted because of the length of time this industry had been planning. While food and oil showed generally better results among planners, there was no clear association of these results with the introduction of planning, since these companies also showed better results in the pre-planning era. These findings go some way to supporting the contention of Denning and Lehr[1] that some industries and company types are more likely to benefit than others from planning.

Herold[15] extended and validated part of the Thune and House study, although it was possible to do this for only five of the original eighteen matched pairs of companies used in the original study. All were in the drug and chemical industries. The conclusion was that those companies that engaged in corporate planning significantly outperformed those that did not.

Another study of considerable value, also performed in the United States, was carried out by Ansoff et al.[16] This examined the effect of planning on the success of acquisitions in American firms, and was limited to companies with a four-year acquisition free period, followed by an acquisition period during which no more than one year elapsed between successive acquisitions, followed by a post-acquisition period of at least two years. The universe for companies which met these criteria was 412 (from the sources used). All 412 companies were approached, resulting in 93 usable replies (22.6 per cent).

The study examined two types of acquisition behaviour: strategic planning (defining corporate objectives and acquisition strategies) and operational planning (identifying the means of acquisition, establishing search criteria, allocation of supporting budgets, and similar activities). Operational planning follows the strategic planning activities.

Corporate performance was measured against thirteen variables: sales, earnings, earnings/share, total assets, earnings/equity, dividends/share, stock price (adjusted), debt/equity, common equity, earnings/total equity, P/E ratio (adjusted), payout (dividends/earnings), and price/equity ratio. Three types of measurement were designed (average of annual percentage change, average percentage change over period, and the simple average value over period). The use, where relevant, of these three measures against the thirteen variables resulted in a total of twenty-one different measures of performance.

The questionnaire established eight characteristics of managerial behaviour during acquisition activity – four were concerned with strategic and four with operational planning. This enabled the sample to be divided into four subgroups: companies with little planning, companies with strategic planning only, those with operational planning only, and those with both types of planning. Overall, the 'planners' – that is companies exhibiting at least six of the eight characteristics – comprised 22.7 per cent of the sample.

A comparison of performance between what might be termed as the extensive planning firms and those with little or no planning revealed that on all the variables with the exception of total assets growth those firms which had extensively planned their acquisition programmes significantly outperformed those that did little or no formal planning. The variables which exhibited the most notable outperformance were sales growth, earnings growth, earnings/share growth, and earnings/common equity growth.

The investigators carried out a second analysis. The performance of twenty-two of the twenty-six 'planners' was compared with that of the forty firms which had no more than four of the eight characteristics. This study supported the findings of superior average performance by planning, and also revealed that the planners performed more consistently. The four most notable variables of outstanding performance were the same as those in the first analysis.

Further analysis supported the contention that planners did better mainly because they were able to avoid failure. A number of individual non-planners had performances which exceeded the best of the planners, but a much higher percentage of the non-planners had very poor performances.

The authors[16] conclude:

(1) Firms which engage in acquisition activity tend to take one of two distinctive approaches to acquisition planning. The first is an unplanned opportunistic approach and the other, a systematic planned approach. If a firm fails to plan any phase of the programme, it is likely to forgo planning altogether. If a firm does plan a phase, it is likely to make a complete strategic and operating plan.

(2) Firms which do plan tend to use these plans and to exhibit deliberate and systematic acquisition behaviour.

(3) Although subjective evaluation of results by management does not differ greatly between planners and non-planners, objective financial measurements show a substantial difference.

(4) On virtually all relevant financial criteria, the planners in our sample significantly outperformed the non-planners.

(5) Not only did the planners do better on the average, they performed more predictably than non-planners. Thus, planners appear to have narrowed the uncertainty in the outcomes of acquisition behaviour.

A further survey by Malik and Karger[17] in 1975 concluded:

So the answer to the question of whether long range planning is more promising than results seems clear: more results. Hard data suggests long range planning pays. And since studies by others have produced similar results, the weight of evidence is mounting rapidly. Companies engaged in long range planning are using a tool that has demonstrated its worth.

Yet another study, reported by Vancil,[18] is worthy of passing mention. This examined the accuracy of forecasts made by companies of the outcome of their plans and demonstrated that certain company characteristics and planning techniques were associated with more accurate forecasts. In particular the systems design features associated with the accurate forecasts were top-management involvement, association of subordinates in setting their own goals, discipline in linking the plan to the budget, and a philosophy that an important purpose of planning is to provide a frame of reference for the operational budget.

However, the author raised a stimulating question: the possibility that too much emphasis on accuracy could lead to self-fulfilling prophecies and below-optimum performance. If the contention of many planners that planning is a corporate mind stretching exercise is true, it may be that accuracy for its own sake is a less desirable trait than many believe.

Is strategic management of benefit?

The classic corporate planning process has postulated a blend of top-down and bottom-up thinking that in theory enables the final plan to be a rational amalgam of all viewpoints, argued out in a constructive manner. In fact we know that many different approaches to strategic planning and strategic management have evolved. In addition to the numerous approaches discussed in Chapter 1, research by Goold and Campbell[19] identified a number of different styles of planning in diversified organisations and argued that the most effective style depended on the business situation of the organisation. Goold, Campbell and Alexander[20] later extended this work to examine how different parenting styles could add value to an organisation.

Research into strategic management and its benefits has become more complex because of all the differences and nuances. The work by Ansoff and his colleagues, discussed in the previous chapter, demonstrated that the benefit comes when the organisation applies an approach to strategic management which matches the situation they are in, and that the wrong style may be harmful (see Ansoff *et al.*[21] and Ansoff and Sullivan[22]).

It seems that the totality of the research covered in this chapter proves beyond doubt that strategic management can be beneficial, but common sense tells us that it will not be beneficial in every situation. Even when the hurdle of fitting the approach to the situation has been overcome, strategic management is not likely to be successful if it is applied badly. There are also degrees of success, and not all organisations set a high enough level of expectation from their planning work, and are therefore too easily satisfied.

We can look at organisations on a case-by-case basis, and find some whose strategies have given them a clear edge. British Airways, for example, have a clear vision, the strategies to support it, and the courage to reshape the rules of the industry to build a position of competitive advantage. We can also put a date on when all this began to happen, which was when the organisation was privatised, and we can see that the benefits have come through consistently in the bottom-line results. By contrast, we can see other privatised British organisations, such as certain water companies, who earned very high levels of profits which their managements claimed was through management skill, but in fact was from a local monopoly situation. Examination of some of these companies' annual reports shows little sense of strategy and irrelevant diversification moves. More recent events have shown that many had not paid enough attention to their core businesses, with resultant water shortages, customer dissatisfaction, and in too many companies there were periods when the water supply was polluted. All this led to government interventions, such as the windfall tax, which were not in the interests of the firms.

So in arguing that the research points towards the success of strategic management, we should not ignore the fact that while many organisations would claim to be giving careful thought to the formulation and implementation of strategy, not all are as good at it as they could and should be.

Strategic management is in large part about setting corporate strategy in relation to the opportunities and threats of the marketplace and the business environment. What I have often found puzzling is the fact that so many large organisations in Europe and the USA, most if not all of which would claim to be practising strategic management, seem to produce similar strategic moves. Is it that all the analysts in an industry look at the same facts and reach the same conclusions? This might be true, but seems unlikely because many of the strategies have been reversed by the entire industry only a few years later. In the

Swatch – a successful strategy

Swatch is a name that will be familiar to all readers, yet it has, in industrial terms, had a short history. It came about through the drive and innovative approach of Dr Ernst Thomke, head of an organisation called ETA, which was a company within the SMH Group, Switzerland's largest watch producer. ETA made components and movements. Switzerland had lost its dominance in the world watch industry to Japan and South-east Asia, and ETA faced a declining demand for the integrated circuits it made for quartz watches. Its first strategy to work with its customers to standardise parts in order to increase volume and reduce costs was not a success.

Thomke therefore decided that ETA would produce an electronic watch to beat the Japanese at the low-cost end of the market. At that time ETA's production cost of a quartz movement was Sfr20, and this did not include the strap and case. Thomke wanted to design a watch which could be produced at a total cost of Sfr10.

The strategy was much more innovative than this implies, as in effect the opportunity he saw was to create a new segment at the lower end of the market, with the watch becoming a fun and fashion item, cheap enough to enable a consumer to own more than one, and for it to be replaced if it went wrong. The target market was the young and stylish, which was very different from the profile sought by other cheap watches. This creative thinking was also applied to a different design, made mainly of plastic, and using only part of the conventional quartz watch. To achieve this meant that ETA has to develop its own specialised machinery and computerised control and monitoring equipment.

Swatch has been a continuing success, and provided an example to the Swiss watch industry in demonstrating that decline could be reversed.

The key lessons from Swatch are:

- Good strategies are often very innovative
- The innovative thinking grew out of, and was supported by, analytical insight
- Marketing, development and manufacturing strategies were totally integrated
- The strategy was driven by a clear vision of what could be done.

mid-1970s it was fashionable for airlines to move into the hotel business: a decade later most had moved out of hotels to concentrate on the core airline business.

British retail banks began a rush in the 1970s to buy US banks, most of which could operate at the retail level in only one state. High prices were paid, and in some cases the loss over many years dragged down performance. The Midland Bank, for example sustained large losses, reputed to have reached £1 billion, made as a result of their acquisition of Crocker Bank in the USA in 1980: Crocker was sold to Wells Fargo in 1986. A second legacy of the acquisition was an overexposure in loans to Latin America[23].

Another strategic hare which the financial services industries followed like a pack of hounds was the acquisition of estate agents. The chase began in the mid-1980s, in the belief that the firms who acted as agents for the sale of houses would also be a vehicle for the sale of mortgages and house insurance. Banks, building societies and insurance companies paid vast premiums to acquire businesses, which for the most part plunged into loss, and by the early 1990s were being sold, sometimes back to the original owners, for a fraction of their purchase price. For example, Prudential Insurance is reported to have paid £230 million for its chain of estate agents. In 1989 alone it lost £49 million on them, and in 1991 sold the chain at a capital loss.

We see fashions in strategy: 'it's good to diversify' seemed to be the slogan of the 1960s and 1970s, yet by the 1980s the fashion was to revert to the core businesses. The 1990s seem to have been a period where de-layering, downsizing and cost cutting were the clever things to do, but these decisions were not always taken with forethought, nor was attention always given to how the organisation should operate afterwards.

There have been strategic failings by many British businesses over several decades. Whole industries have declined or disappeared and although in some cases this has been because of a 'natural' change in economic advantage, in others it has been because foreign competition has had a superior strategy to the British firms. There is no natural reason why Japan should have been able to destroy the British motorcycle industry, or become world leaders in the car industry: superior strategic thinking features highly as a reason. If a Japanese company could have done it, why could not a British company?

There is evidence over a long period that not all organisations have been willing to learn. Take the ever popular strategy of acquisition. Channon[24] noted the failure of many acquisitions in his landmark study of British companies' strategies through the 1960s. Few British companies attempted to rationalise their acquisitions. 'Frequently, acquired concerns were allowed to continue along much as before without real influence from the parent. The acquisition was in name only, but not in managerial action' (p. 240).

Buckner[25] found that, over the period 1960–70, over half of diversification moves were failures, and that the failure rate was higher when diversification was by acquisition rather than internal development. Similar findings on the failure of acquisitions have been found consistently in surveys in Europe, the UK and the USA right up to the present decade, suggesting that the issue is not unique to the UK, and that there is a constant failure of either the strategy, its implementation, or both. All but the first of the studies in references 26–32 found a failure rate of around 50 per cent.

The evidence on the results of some of the cost-cutting strategies is not of universal success. Kinnie, Hutchinson and Purcell[33] reviewed the published research studies:

> There is increasing evidence, however, to suggest that the majority of downsizings are unsuccessful – the anticipated economic and organisational benefits fail to materialise. In the USA between two thirds to three quarters of

Why does it take so long to get the message?

Since the late 1960s there have been numerous studies which demonstrate that only about a half of all acquisitions are successful, and that many destroy value. There have even been explorations of what can be done to improve the success rate. But organisations continue to repeat mistakes despite warnings that have been in the public domain for some thirty years.

Year	Country	Researcher
1974	UK	Buckner (over 1960-1970)
1967	USA	Kitching
1973	Europe	Kitching
1974	UK	Kitching
1986	UK	British Institute of Management
1987	USA	Porter
1988	UK	Hunt
1993	UK	Coopers and Lybrand

All this research except for Kitching (1967) found failure rates of 50 per cent or more. The failures appear to lie in :

● Failure to ensure a strategic fit of the acquired organisation
● Inadequate understanding of the acquired organisation
● Strategic thinking not carried through to the post-acquisition situation.

all downsizings are unsuccessful from the start[34]. A study in the USA by the Wyatt Co.[35] found that few downsizings meet their desired goals in terms of increased competitiveness and profitability. The majority of organisations meet their immediate cost reducing objectives but this improvement is not sustained in other areas, especially in the long range goals of improved service and increased competitive advantage. The findings of another study by Kenneth de Meuse *et al.*[36] show that for the three year period after the downsizing announcements firms making redundancies had ended up with lower profit margins and poorer returns on assets and equity than equivalent firms who do not downsize.

Business Process Re-engineering has also proved of dubious value in many organisations. Coulson-Thomas[37] found in his research across Europe (including the UK, of course) that most BPR exercises examined were really process simplification rather than re-engineering, and were being undertaken for medium-term cost and time savings and not for longer-term strategic benefits:

What is clear is that many of the BPR solutions being adopted are yielding cost benefits today at the price of inflexibility tomorrow. Thus paths and options are being limited and prescribed in order to 'speed things up' in ways that can reduce the scope for creative thinking and innovation.

This leaves us uncertain over whether the 59 per cent of UK organisations which reported BPR activity in 1995[38] were really applying BPR. Surveys in the USA show that a very high percentage of BPR initiatives are unsuccessful[39] (50–70 per cent failure). The success rate in the UK is unlikely to be any higher.

So although there is every reason for an organisation to commit to strategic management, there is also need for many more organisations to do a great deal more to achieve mastery over all aspects of the subject.

It would be unrealistic to believe that every organisation will achieve total success in everything it does. The realities of the global competitive arena mean that for every relative degree of success by one firm, another will experience a degree of relative failure. But my conclusion from the evidence discussed so far in this book is that, although many companies are good at strategic management, many more could dramatically improve their results by improving their strategic capabilities. There are four areas of weakness which I have observed in organisations, and which I think contribute to poor strategic performance, and these can be improved:

- Failure to analyse the situation before strategic decisions are made
- Failure to implement strategic decisions, including failure to think through the implications of a new strategy.
- Problems with the process of planning itself
- Incomplete understanding of many of the concepts by those claiming to apply them

Strategic management can make a difference.

References

1 Denning, B. W. and Lehr, M. E. 'The Extent and Nature of Corporate Long Range Planning in the United Kingdom, Parts 1 and 2', *Journal of Management Studies*, **8**, May 1971; **9**, February 1972.

2 Brown, J. K., Sands, S. S. and Thompson, G. C. 'Long Range Planning in the USA – NICB Survey', *Long Range Planning*, March 1969.

3 Komo, T. 'Long Range Planning – Japan – USA – A Comparative Study', *Long Range Planning*, October 1976.

4 Schuller-Gotzburg, V. V. and Dawson, R. W. *Organised Planning in 50 Western European Companies*, Stanford Research Institute, 1971 (Proprietary study.)

5 Eppink, D. J., Keuning, D. and de Jong, K. 'Corporate Planning in the Netherlands', *Long Range Planning*, October 1976.

6 Kempner, T. and Hewkins, J. W. M. 'Is Corporate Planning Necessary?' *British Institute of Management*, December 1968.

7 Knowlson, P. *Organisation and Membership Survey*, December 1974. Society for Long Range Planning.

8 Warren, E. K. *Long Range Planning: The Executive Viewpoint*, Prentice-Hall, Englewood Cliffs, NJ, 1966.

9 Ringbakk, K. A. 'Organised Planning in Major US Companies', *Long Range Planning*, December 1968.

10 Irving, P. *Corporate Planning in Practice: A Study of the Development of Organised Planning in Major United Kingdom Companies*, University of Bradford, MSc dissertation, 1970.

11 Taylor, B. and Irving, P. 'Organised Planning in Major UK Companies', *Long Range Planning*, June 1971.

12 Champion, J. R. 'Corporate Planning in CPC Europe', *Long Range Planning*, December 1970.

13 Levitt, T. *Innovation in Marketing*, McGraw-Hill, New York, 1962.

14 Thune, S. S. and House, R. J. 'Where Long Range Planning Pays Off', *Business Horizons*, August 1970.

15 Herold, D. M. 'Long Range Planning and Organisational Performance: A Cross Validation Study', *Academy of Management Journal*, March 1972.

16 Ansoff, H. I. Avner, J., Brandenburg, R. J., Portner, F. E. and Radosevitch, R. 'Does Planning Pay? The Effect of Planning of Success of Acquisition in American Firms', *Long Range Planning*, December 1970.

17 Malik, A. and Karger, D. W. 'Does Long Range Planning Improve Company Performance?' *Management Review*, September 1975.

18 Vancil, R. F. 'The Accuracy of Long Range Planning' *Harvard Business Review*, September/October 1970.

19 Goold, M. and Campbell, A. *Strategies and Styles*, Blackwell, Oxford, 1987.

20 Goold, M., Campbell, A. and Alexander, M. *Corporate Level Strategy*, Wiley, New York, 1994.

21 Ansoff, H. I. *et al.* 'Empirical Support for a Paradigmic Theory of Strategic Success Behaviors of Environment Serving Organisations', in Hussey, D. E. (ed.), *International Review of Strategic Management*, Vol. 4, pp. 173–203, Wiley, Chichester, 1993.

22 Ansoff, H. I. and Sullivan, P. A. 'Optimizing Profitability in Turbulent Environments: A Formula for Strategic Success', *Long Range Planning*, **26**, No. 5, 11–23, October, 1993.

23 Beaver G. and Jennings, P. L. 'Midland Bank Plc', *Strategic Change*, **5**, No. 4, 1996.

24 Channon, D. F. *The Strategy and Structure of British Enterprise*, Macmillan, London, 1973.

25 Buckner, H. 'Seeking New Sources of Earnings', in Hussey, D. E. (ed.), *The Corporate Planners' Yearbook, 1974–5*, Pergamon, Oxford, 1974.

26 Kitching, J. 'Why do Mergers Miscarry?', *Harvard Business Review*, November/December, 1967.

27 Kitching, J. *Acquisitions in Europe*, Business International, Geneva, 1973.

28 Kitching, J. 'Winning and Losing with European Acquisitions', *Harvard Business Review*, March/April, 1974,.

29 British Institute of Management. 'The Management of Acquisitions and Mergers', Discussion paper number 8, Economics Department, September, 1986.

30 Porter, M, E. 'From Competitive Advantage to Corporate Strategy', *Harvard Business Review*, May/June, 1987.

31 Hunt, J. 'Managing the Successful Acquisition: A People Question', *London Business School Journal*, **15** No. 2, Summer, 1988.

32 Coopers & Lybrand, 1993.

33 Kinnie, N., Hutchinson, S. and Purcell, J. Report by the University of Bath, *The People Management Implications of Leaner Ways of Working*, Issues in People Management No. 15, Institute of Personnel and Development, London, 1996

34 Howard, C. 'The Stress on Managers Caused by Downsizing', *The Globe and Mail*, 30 January, 1996.

35 Wyatt Company *Best Practices in Corporate Re-structuring*, Toronto, Ontario, 1994.

36 De Meuse, K., Vanderheiden, P. and Bergamann, T. 'Announcing Layoffs: their Effect on Corporate Financial Performance', *Human Resource Management*, **33**, No. 4, 1994.

37 Coulson-Thomas, C. J. 'Business Process Re-engineering and Strategic Change', *Strategic Change*, **5**, No. 3, 1994.

38 Grint , K. and Willcocks, L. 'Business Process Re-engineering in Theory and Practice: Business Paradise Regained?' *New Technology, Work and Employment*, **10**, No. 2, 1995.

39 Hammer, M. and Champney, J. *Re-engineering the Corporation: A Manifesto for Business Revolution*, Nicholas Brealey, London, 1993.

CHAPTER 3

A look at the total process

One aim of this chapter is to reach a deeper understanding of strategic management through a close examination of its components. Vision and leadership are put into the strategic management context. Important research into styles of strategic management and the contingency approach advocated by Igor Ansoff are summarised. The Ansoff scale of turbulence is related to the various planning stages found in a study of the evolution of strategic management. More depth is provided on process of strategic management, including strategic planning, including recent thinking about scenario planning. The final aim is to discuss in outline the elements that should appear in a business plan.

Components of strategic management

The previous chapter demonstrated that planning improves results, but raised concerns over whether even an apparently beneficial planning process always led to appropriate strategies. This chapter will begin to show how the two can go hand in hand, a theme that will be continued in later chapters. The emphasis will be on the management of strategy, although this chapter will also look at models for the completion of plans and of planning processes.

Strategy does not exist in a vacuum, and has both an influence on and is influenced by the culture of the organisation, its structure and the people it employs. How you want people to act is driven by strategy: how they actually act depends on reward systems, control mechanisms, and the climate of the organisation. Strategy management has to get all these things in harmony, and ensure that the strategy the organisation is following is appropriate.

Leavitt[1] drew attention in 1964 to the interlinking of task, structure, people and technology (tools) and showed how changes to one factor would cause changes to the others. Leavitt's 'diamond' was worked on by others, particularly Mckinsey and Company with their 7s model (see Peters and Waterman[2] and

Figure 3.1
Organisation and
the environment

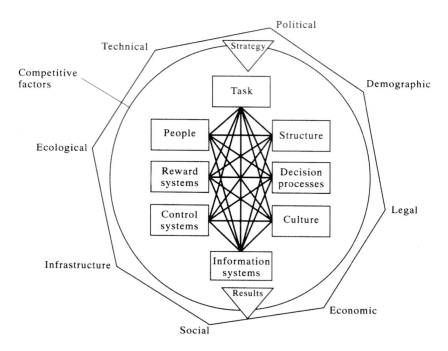

Galbraith and Nathanson[3]). These models began to add dimensions such as strategy, culture, and reward systems. Considerable research had been undertaken during the 1960s and 1970s into the relationship of strategy and structure (some details will be given when we deal with human resource planning in a later chapter).

Figure 3.1 draws on all this thinking to suggest one way of considering the elements that must be considered and put into some degree of equilibrium. Strategy is shown as the driver, interacting with the other organisational components to produce results. Even a poor interaction will lead to results, but to increase chances of getting the results we want. The 'organisation' is looked at in terms of eight boxes.

Tasks

A strategy leads to a need for certain things to be done by people. A change in strategy may change those tasks. For example, a strategy to be more customer responsive may require some tasks to be undertaken differently, and new ones to be added.

People

This means the nature, knowledge and skills of the various individuals already in the organisation, or who need to be recruited to the organisation to implement the strategy. The people required are influenced by the tasks, but also can influence the way the organisation looks at those tasks in the first place.

Reward systems

How people are rewarded will affect whether they perform the tasks in the way the strategy required. Frequently reward structures are out of step with the strategy. For example, the company may have an intention to sell the most profitable mix of products, but if the reward system pays sales bonuses in the total value of sales, the sales force are more likely to go for volume than for profit.

Control systems

How people are controlled will also affect what they actually do. Control mechanisms that emphasise individual effort, particularly if linked to reward, will affect behaviour far more than a management exhortation for teamwork. If teamwork is the important thing, then controls need to be designed accordingly. The nature of a control system can also influence, and is related to, the culture of the organisation. Delegated decision making, for example, will only happen if the control mechanisms allow it. In many organisations the exhortation is to take a long-term view, while the controls emphasise the short term. Action tends to relate to the control, and not the exhortation.

Information systems

Organisations are also affected by the way information is collected and disseminated. Empowerment of lower levels of management can only take place if they also receive the information needed to do the job. Information should also be related to the structure of the organisation. In many organisations it lags behind structural changes, making it harder for managers to manage. Strategy can become impossible to implement because of the failure of information systems to meet the needs of organisations. For example, there are still insurance companies that can only provide information by policy and not by customer. They cannot find out easily all the types of insurance held with them by a particular client. It is not hard to see how this could frustrate an excellent strategy for selling additional services to existing clients.

Decision-making systems

Where and how decisions are made, and who is allowed to make them will affect all parts of the model. The airline, SAS, caused a revolution in thinking in its organisation when it empowered the person in contact with the customer to make all reasonable decisions about matters that affected the customer. Previously these were all referred upwards in a bureaucratic process. This change had a fundamental impact on the culture of SAS.

Culture

The culture of an organisation is increasingly seen as one of the most important components to manage. Culture depends on all the other boxes in the model, and is also influenced by the nature of the company's business, its history, and where it operates. If culture does not fit with strategy, something will have to give, and it will probably be the strategy. Take a worldwide organisation, that operates individual businesses with full local autonomy, in various parts of the world. For good strategic reasons the company decides to integrate its businesses globally, standardising products, and rationalising many of its activities on a world basis. Will this all happen just because someone says it will? Unlikely! The existing culture will get in the way of the changes, so action would also be needed to bring about changes to this culture.

Structure

Finally there is the way the tasks are grouped into jobs, and jobs are grouped into organisational units. Structure like the other components of the model has a two-directional link with every other component, and can help a strategy to be implemented, or can make it totally impossible.

The circle outside the components of organisation represents the competitive arena in which the organisation operates. This has an obvious relationship with strategy, and much of this book will be about that relationship. It also impacts on the other components of the model, for example through the level of salaries paid to people in the industry, or the training provided by the educational system for people in that industry.

Outside is an eight-sided figure, which also will receive more attention later in the book. This represents the external business environment in which the organisation operates. One of the definitions of strategic management referred to earlier in this book stressed that it was about obtaining a good fit with the environment in which it operates. This is partly about strategy analysis and formulation, but it is also about managing the other elements in the model to achieve a harmony between them.

Vision and leadership

The description given above may strike the reader as little more than an assessment of the main tasks of top management in any organisation. That is exactly what strategic management is. All the interrelationships exist whether or not the organisation uses strategic management as the chosen means to bring about strategic change in the organisation. Under strategic management the driver is strategy, and the tasks of analysis and formulation are supported by a formal approach to planning.

One important element in the whole strategic management process is the development of a vision for the organisation by top management. This does not necessarily have to come out of the head of only one person, although sometimes it may. The vision is the view which goes beyond the life span of the corporate plans, which identifies the future nature and philosophy of the organisation. The quality of the vision is tied in directly with the quality of leadership, and, of course, a good system of planning cannot compensate for a lack of leadership. We will return to both vision and leadership later. The word 'vision' has many meanings. In this context it combines things like 'foresight', 'a vivid concept or mental picture', 'imaginative perception', 'a pleasing imaginative plan for, or anticipation of, future events' (all taken from *Chambers Twentieth Century Dictionary*).

The dictionary through some of the other meanings also reveals the pitfalls in the concept of vision, such as 'a revelation . . . in sleep', or a visionary 'given to reverie or fantasy', and 'out of touch with reality, impractical'. My own description of visions gone wrong comes through word association: 'vision . . . dream . . . nightmare'. Like so much else in strategic management, the chief executive has to get it right.

When thinking of vision in the context of strategic management we are really beginning to think of leadership, and it is an obvious fact that the success of an organisation is at least as much related to the quality of leadership as it is to the formation of a superior strategy. Much has been written about leadership, and it is a subject in its own right. However, it embraces many concepts, and people often mean different things when they think of leadership. John Nicholls[4] draws a useful distinction between micro leadership and macro leadership. Micro is related to the job or task, to the internal organisation, and to efficiency. It is about the here and now. Success comes from adapting one's leadership style to the various situations. The leading authorities on this aspect, which they term situational leadership, are Hersey and Blanchard.[5] Macro is related to the team or organisation, is concerned about how things could be, rather than as they are, is externally focused, and is concerned with long-term effectiveness. Leadership is performed through role in the organisation.

My own approach to transformational leadership draws from the above, supported by my experience, but does not claim great originality. I call it the EASIER approach, which stands for *E*nvision, *A*ctivate, *S*upport, *I*nstall, *E*nsure and *R*ecognise. The first three words deal mainly with the soft aspects of management: the last three cover the hard side, the systems and administrative tasks. Successful implementation depends on getting all six stages right.

- **Envisioning** This is the process of developing a coherent view of the future in order to form an overarching objective for the organisation. It blends the leader's view of external opportunities with the way internal competencies and resources relate to these opportunities.
- **Activating** Activating is the task of ensuring that others in the organisation understand, support, and eventually share the vision.

Figure 3.2
An approach to
managing change.
(From Hussey, D. E.
*Business Driven
Human Resource
Management*, Wiley,
Chichester, 1996)

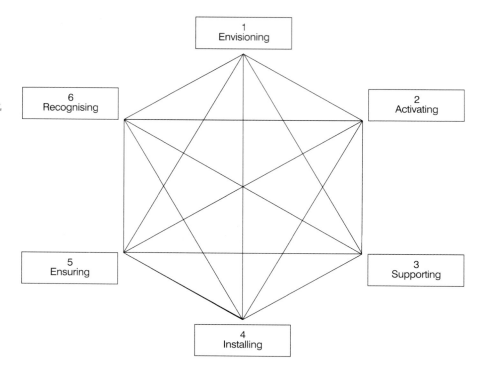

- **Supporting** Supporting is about motivating and inspiring people to achieve more than they otherwise might have believed possible, by providing the necessary moral and practical help to enable this to happen.
- **Installing** This is the process of developing detailed plans to enable the strategy to be implemented and controlled. There is nothing unique or special about the instruments such as plans, budgets, critical path analysis, Gantt charts or other tools which have to be developed to ensure that nothing is overlooked, and everything is coordinated. These are all the regular instruments of management.
- **Ensuring** Plans, structures for implementation, and policies may be formulated, and on paper the organisation may have covered everything. But this is not enough, and consideration must be given to the monitoring and controlling processes that will ensure that actions are correctly undertaken and results are as expected.
- **Recognising** This is giving recognition to those involved in the process. Recognition may be positive or negative, and should be used to reinforce the change, and to ensure that obstacles to progress are removed.

Dinkelspiel and Bailey[6] describe a model of organisational leadership which incorporates the concepts of both Figures 3.1 and 3.2, although in somewhat different form. This is the model developed by the consultancy Harbridge House Inc. of Boston, USA (now part of Coopers & Lybrand), and used in a variety of practical situations. The personal leadership element consists of vision, commitment and management (or execution), linked to an overriding require-ment of flexibility. Personal leadership drives the organisational context, which in the model is represented by the components of strategy, culture and structure/ systems.

Vision and the management of strategic change will be returned to in more detail in later chapters.

If leadership is important to strategic success, we might expect successful approaches to planning to vary with the beliefs and values of the leader. I believe that this is the right interpretation of another study into strategic management.

Styles of strategic management

Goold and Campbell[7] published an important research-based study of styles of strategic management. They saw the styles as arising from the attempt by top managers to determine the appropriate role for the corporate office *vis-à-vis* the business units, during which process trade-offs have to be made. The desire to give strong leadership from the centre conflicts with the desire to encourage entrepreneurial activity at the business unit level. Styles arise as a result of the way in which the group chief executive determines where the trade-offs have to be made.

A number of possible styles were identified on a matrix of planning influence from the corporate level (high, medium and low), and corporate control influence (flexible, tight strategic and tight financial). Of the nine possible positions on that matrix, three were found in the sample of companies studied. These were labelled *strategic planning*, with a high planning influence accompanied by flexible control, *strategic control*, which has medium level planning influence and tight financial control. Table 3.1 summarises the main differences between the styles.

There are strengths and weaknesses to each style, and the head office can both add and subtract value under each style. The authors conclude that the appropriate style is one that fits the situation of the business, and that appropriate matching is an important determinant of business success. In this way it is akin to situational leadership, where the right style is relevant to the situation in which the leader operates. Business factors fall under two headings, those related to the business situation, and those related to the resources in the organisation. Among the former are issues such as the ferocity of the competitive environment, size and length of payback of investments, and the shape of the corporate portfolio. Among the latter are the financial health of the company, the personality of the chief executive and the skills of senior management.

Although one might expect the situation faced by the companies to be the most important determinant of planning style, and indeed the next concept I will review provides a framework for such a consideration, my belief, fuelled by a close professional association with two of the companies in the Campbell and Goold sample, is that the individual differences between chief executives were a greater influence than the differences between business situations.

Table 3.1 Styles of strategic management (derived from Goold and Campbell[7])

	Strategic planning	*Strategic control*	*Financial control*
Strategy responsibility	Business level but multiple perspectives	Divisional and business unit	Unit and even profit centre
Review	Extensive to influence proposals and raise quality	Extensive – raise quality	Budget key planning process
Corporate support	For strategic themes	Avoidance of central strategies	Major use of acquisition (centre or unit)
Interdivisional coordination	Central coordination	Little strong division level coordination	Group-level MGRs flow into centre/units
Source of new ideas	Centre or unit	From units (divestment corporate)	Suggestions from centre
Source of goals	From plans	Objectives set	Short-term payback criteria
Reporting	Detailed to centre	Detailed	Frequent monitoring
Control	Flexible strategy key	Tight – incentives and sanctions	Budget as contract strong pressure on problem units-management change
Resource allocation	Centre allocates, sets priorities	Centre allocates and sets priorities	Centre funds all good projects

Environmental turbulence

The contribution of Igor Ansoff in developing a contingency approach to strategic management was outlined in Chapter 1. We now need to explore these ideas in a little more depth.

The Ansoff approach sought to identify the different environmental conditions under which different organisations were operating, and sought to match these with appropriate approaches to management and strategy. The starting concept was thus different from that of Goold and Campbell discussed above, where different concepts of strategic management were identified in organisations, but not related specifically to different sets of strategic conditions. The Ansoff approach suggests a scale of turbulence:

Level	State of turbulence	Strategic aggressiveness
1	Repetitive	Stable, based on precedents
2	Expanding	Reactive, incremental based on experience
3	Changing	Anticipatory, incremental, based on extrapolation
4	Discontinuous	Entrepreneurial, based on expected futures
5	Surpriseful	Creative, based on creativity

The approach to strategic decision making is different under each level, as the above description suggests. It follows that the optimum approach to strategic management should also vary with the turbulence level. Ansoff[8] suggests that for level 1 the appropriate system is management by procedures, since nothing is changing, and the best guide to the future is the past. However, it is doubtful whether this level of turbulence is currently experienced by many commercial organisations. For level 2, the right approach is what he terms financial control, where the emphasis is on control through budgets, rather than seeking new strategies. At level 3 the approach is extrapolative, and termed long-range planning: the emphasis is on sticking to the historical strategies of success, since the future is a logical extrapolation of the past.

At level 4 it is no longer safe to assume that tomorrow will be a continuation of the trends of yesterday, and the appropriate process is strategic planning. Ansoff[8] defines this as being '... focussed on selecting new strategies for the future and redirecting the firm's energies and resources to follow the logic of the new strategy development ... Thus strategic planning repositions the firm for success in the future environment.'

Ansoff argues that even before level 5 is reached forward-looking strategic planning is not adequate to ensure a speedy response to future events. This is particularly true when future changes are both violent and difficult to foresee. He suggests two 'real time' system responses: issue management, which can begin to supplement strategic planning from level 4, and surprise management. Issue management attempts to anticipate and respond to threats and opportunities. There is a link here with the scenario planning approaches which are used by some organisations.

By level 5 an increasing number of issues confront the organisation without prior warning. To cope with these the firm needs to add a further management system to deal with surprises. He suggests an emergency communication network, with a top-level strategic task force to cross organisational boundaries to deal with the issue. The key to success is to plan the surprise management organisation, and to train people in operating it. In other words, while issue management is a form of contingency planning for a predicted possibility, surprise management is a planned framework to deal with contingencies that cannot be foreseen.

The appropriate approach may vary in different parts of the same organisation. Thus it is quite possible for an organisation to have one strategic business unit operating under level 3 and another under level 5. The approach to strategic management should be varied by strategic business unit to take account of this.

In theory there are organisations operating under all levels of turbulence: there has also been an evolutionary movement from the lower to the higher levels.

Thus there are more organisations in levels 4 and 5 now than there were in the 1970s. It is reasonable to suggest that this increase in uncertainty will continue in the future.

Although not a specific part of the Ansoff model, from observation I would suggest that organisations make temporary changes to higher levels of turbulence from time to time, sometimes reverting back to their old position when the period of turbulence is over. It is reasonable to suggest that in severe economic recession even organisations that are normally at level 3 will for a period find themselves operating at level 5.

Evolution of planning approaches

Chapter 1 mentioned the study of the evolution of approaches to planning provided by Gluck *et al.*[9] who concluded in a 1980 study that there had been four phases in the evolution of formal strategic planning. The stages are shown in Figure 3.3. The dates are my own observations and do not appear in the study, but relate to empirical observations of my own and related observations on the evolution of planning approaches.[10] Approaches to planning tend to co-exist, which means that it is possible to find all forms in current use. Gluck and his co-authors noted that at the time of their work only a few companies were managing strategically, and that all of these were multinational and diversified companies.

Phase 1 could also be described as extended budgeting, and the approach is largely based on projecting the figures in the budget out for a few more years. This tends to emphasise the existing aspects of the business, and allows little room for major changes in strategy. In these companies any new strategic thinking occurs outside of the planning system.

In phase 2 the approach tries to match the company's strategies to the perversities of the real world. The feeling is that more accurate forecasting would lead to better planning, and the emphasis on this approach is on forecasting

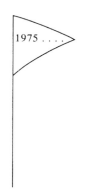

Figure 3.3
Phases in the evolution of strategic planning. (Derived from Gluck, Kaufman and Walleck, *Harvard Business Review*, July/August 1980)

1950 . . .   1965 . . . .   1970 . . . .   1975 . . . .

Basic financial (meet budget)   Forecast based (predict future)   Externally oriented (think strategically)   Strategic management (create future)

techniques and models. Operational research techniques were high on the list of the planner's tools when this approach was at its most popular. The Gluck study observes that one benefit of this approach was greater attention to resource allocation, and the growing use of portfolio analysis techniques to aid this.

Repeated frustration from the discontinuity of the events in the world in which we operate created a realisation that accurate forecasting was not possible. The figure suggests 1970 as the time when phase 3, externally based planning began to appear, but for the majority of companies the trigger was the 1973 oil crisis, which overnight put the world into a situation of unexpected turbulence. Externally based planning is characterised by more attention to markets, and the dynamic causes of market change, and much closer examination of competitors. Resource allocation takes a more dynamic role, and the approach was accompanied by the formal grouping of businesses with like strategic characteristics into SBUs, or strategic business units. Planners are expected to produce alternative strategies, an action which under the forecast-based approach would have been seen as indecisiveness. According to the Gluck study the weakness of externally based planning is that it imposes a burden of choice on top management which is too heavy, with the consequential result that many major decisions by default end up being taken by the planners rather than the managers.

Phase 4 melds strategic planning and management into one process. In their definition of strategic management, Gluck and his co-authors differ a little from the Ansoff and other definitions given in Chapter 1. They define it as 'a system of corporate values, planning responsibilities, or organisational responsibilities that couple strategic thinking with operational decision making at all levels and across all functional lines of authority in a corporation'. The main difference between phases 3 and 4 is of management philosophy rather than technique, and as the Ansoff view described earlier suggests, more emphasis is placed on the 'soft' internal aspects of management such as values and culture. Some of these themes will be picked up later when we look at the main behavioural advances in planning.

Without putting too much weight on the conclusion, I think we can roughly correlate the Gluck and Ansoff conclusions.

Ansoff turbulence level	Gluck planning stage
1	No equivalent
2	1
3	2
4	3 and 4
5	No equivalent

Strategic management

The stage has now been set for a deeper consideration of strategic management as a complete way of running a business. In the rest of this chapter an outline will be given of the total process of planning, the individual parts of which will be studied in greater detail as the book progresses. The aim is to introduce the components of planning and to relate them to each other. If the book so far has set the stage, the rest of this chapter offers a synopsis for the play, the individual scenes of which will be enacted as the book progresses.

It will have already become clear that there are several ways in which a planning process can be designed. It is important that each company which introduces planning should do so in a way that meets its own particular needs. The various examples examined here should be seen as starting points and should not be read too dogmatically. It will also already be apparent that part of the difference between planning systems in organisations is not the schematics showing what plans are prepared, or what should go into a plan, but where the analysis and decisions are undertaken. This is where all the ideas and research quoted so far in this chapter are particularly useful. A planning system will be examined in some depth, and this will be followed by illustrations of other approaches which although constructed differently arrive at approximately the same place. The chapter will conclude with a generalised model of what should be considered when a plan is prepared, although the detail of this will be considerably expanded in later chapters.

A strategic management process should aim to unleash for the company the benefits which have already been discussed in some detail – better results through better decisions, the identification of more opportunities, the consideration of more factors, improved coordination and communication, strong motivation, and the provision for the company of a means of coping with the pressures of change.

Any total planning process is concerned with plans of differing durations. It will incorporate plans for both the long and the short term. Immediately the words 'long term' are used they cause a flurry of concern among those who are newly come to planning. How long is a long-range plan? is a question which is frequently asked at introductory conferences, and it is a question which does not have a simple answer. Many planners believe that although the principles which guide the answer are important, the answer itself is nowhere near as vital as the questioners believe.

This is something of a paradox which deserves explanation. The first principle I would urge is that any plan which looks beyond the time horizons of the annual budget is taking a major step forward: even if the time span first chosen turns out to be wrong for the company, the benefits of moving out in time will more than outweigh the temporary disadvantage of having to adjust the period at the next planning cycle.

If plans were prepared on an absolutely rigid time horizon perhaps it would be more important to get the time right the first time around. In fact most companies work their plans on a 'rolling' basis. Every year the first year of the plan drops off and another is added at the end, so that the period provided for is always the three-, five-, ten-, or whatever years' span for which the company is trying to plan. This method gives the opportunity of regularly revising the plan, so that the company is not trying to follow a rigid path which has been outdated by events. The rolling system gives to planning that degree of flexibility which is essential in a fast-changing world and, as has already been seen, this degree of flexibility may still be inadequate when organisations are operating at the higher levels of environmental turbulence.

Exhibit 3.1 Some differences between the public and private sectors

Any generalisation is subject to many variations. There are as many differences between the various public sector non-trading organisations as there are between different businesses in the private sector. Yet there is some value in taking stock of some of the forces and drivers which cause differences in strategic management in many public sector organisations, compared to many private sector businesses.

- The private sector takes its stimulus from the market, and is often motivated by the need to grow. The public sector is driven by a need to respond to the pressures and demands of the public and politicians, who are not always in step with each other.
- Decision making in the public sector has to accommodate more stakeholders than in the private sector. A stakeholder approach is an option in the private sector. It is not in the public sector, where organisations have a much wider political interface within and without the organisation. A social services department of a local authority, for example, has to include other public sector organisations in its decision process, as well as agencies from the voluntary sector, pressure groups, its relationship with the local authority as a whole, the professional groups inside its own organisation, and external political influences.
- The legal framework often provides a greater influence on decision making in the public sector. Decision making is constrained both by what the organisation must do as a legal requirement, and what it must not do, because of legal limitations to its powers.
- The whole character of strategic decision making in the public sector is driven by a need to obtain consensus, and strategic plans have to be shared with many other organisations. Openness is thus an essential characteristic, whereas in the private sector it is an option.
- Resources are influenced more by external political decisions than by the needs of the public sector organisation, and what is available may be changed with little warning.
- The processes of strategic management are often driven by the requirements of an external agency, such as the Treasury, instead of the needs of the organisation. The format of the process, and its timetables, are not always conducive to the development of strategic thinking.
- Whereas innovation in the private sector usually derives in some way from the market, or at least has to pass the test of the market at some time, in the public sector the main emphasis for innovation may spring out of the strategic management process.

Not all companies use the rolling system. There are some who believe that an *x*-year plan should last *x* years and, upon expiry, be replaced by a further plan which will be followed with the same rigidity. A similar approach is often adopted by the national development plans of governments (e.g. the Indian five-year plan) and regional development authorities (the twenty-five-year general development plan of Rhodesia's Sabi-Limpopo Authority[11]). Those interested in the techniques of governmental economic planning will find Kidel's[12] description of the French fifth plan of value. There are valid reasons for the differences in approach, as the different types of plans are used for different purposes. A government development plan is not required as part of its process of management in quite the same way that corporate planning is used by business. The type of reactions that governments may make to adverse circumstances have little relation to those open to business.

However, even here the dangers of trying to plan too far in advance are very real, and are illustrated by one of the examples mentioned above. Rhodesia no longer exists as a country. Long before the twenty-five years of the plan had expired it became Zimbabwe, with a different style of government, operating under different market conditions. Droughts have dried up many of the dams which irrigated the area under the planning control of the authority, and the authority itself ceased to exist as a result of political changes before the ending of the civil war and the handing over of power to a government elected on a broader electoral franchise.

Each company should try to select a planning period which satisfies its particular and unique needs. There may be an identifiable cycle in a business which should be taken into account or some market or other factor which makes one length of time more appropriate than any other. A mining company might think in terms of the expected economic life of its mines: a company whose mines were expected to be depleted within ten years should be considering at least this time horizon in its strategies. It takes seven years to bring new plantings of apple trees to an economic orchard: forestry activities are on an even longer cycle. For a fashion business anything more than three years ahead may be groping in the dark because of the particular nature of the market. Other industries may find the question of lead time important: the number of years taken to introduce a new product, or to complete work in progress, or to effect some other change, may be important determinants of the planning period.

All this must be tempered with good sense. A business may have activities equivalent to growing mature oaks from acorns, but this does not necessarily dictate a hundred-year plan. A planning period that is too long will mean that none of the present managers will have much interest in it as they do not expect to be around that long. Warren[13] pointed out that division managers seldom stay at the same job for more than five years, and that the average tenure of office is under four years – which by implication means that many move jobs in an even shorter time period. When this is coupled to Pennington's[14] statement that a planner's 'life expectancy' in a US company is only three and a half years, the extent of the problem of choosing too long a horizon becomes very obvious.

There are thus human reasons why too long a period is not practicable for all parts of the organisation. Perhaps this is why many companies have settled for the five-year plan, which leads the field as the most popular time span. In fact for many companies five years is a good choice. It is far enough ahead to give the company perspective, yet not so far that it loses management interest or runs into severe forecasting problems (not that a forecast is any more than a building block for a plan). It is long enough for many actions to be implemented and for results to make themselves felt. A lesser period often gives rise to the problem that is

---

What some people say about strategy and strategic planning

Strategy is trying to understand where you sit in today's world. Not where you wish you were and where you hoped to be, but where you are. And it's trying to understand where you want to be. It's assessing the competitive and market changes that you can capitalise on or ward off to go from here to there. It's assessing the realistic chances of getting from here to there.

Attributed to Jack Welch, CEO, General Electric

The essence of strategic thinking is creating a sustainable competitive advantage.

M. Porter, The Economist, 23 May 1987

Know the enemy and know yourself, in a hundred battles you will never be defeated. When you are ignorant of the enemy, but know yourself, your chances of winning or losing are equal. If ignorant both of your enemy and yourself, you are sure to be defeated in every battle.

Sun Tzu, Art of War, c.400 BC, page 107 of the Wordsworth 1993 edition, translation by Yuan Shibing

Strategists do not reject analysis. Indeed they can hardly do without it. But they use it only to stimulate the creative process, to test the ideas that emerge, to work out strategic implications, or to ensure successful execution of high potential 'wild' ideas that otherwise never would be implemented properly. Great strategies, like great works of art or great scientific discoveries, call for technical mastery in the working out but originate from insights that are beyond the reach of conscious analysis.

Kenichi Ohmae, The Mind of the Strategist, p. 4, Penguin 1984 edition

It is a view of strategy that recognises that a firm must *unlearn* much of its past before it can find the future. It is a view of strategy that recognises it is not enough to optimally position a company within existing markets; the challenge is to pierce the fog of uncertainty and develop great *foresight* into the whereabouts of tomorrow's markets.

G. Hamel and C. K. Prahalad, Competing for the Future, p. 25, Harvard Business School Press, 1996 edition

shorter than the lead time of its most important projects, which means that their results cannot be included, and the business loses much of the potential benefit of thinking ahead. For this reason three years is generally far too short, and two years is nothing more than an extended budget.

Some companies may find that one time period meets all their planning needs. Most will almost certainly decide that some things should be treated differently from the period chosen for most of the plans. Thus the appraisal of specific projects might take a fifteen-year period into account, even though the normal planning time scale is five years. Equally necessary for many companies, although perceived less frequently, is the need to take strategic thinking further ahead than the formal five-year plan. This may be done through strategic scenarios which take into account longer-term influences, technological forecasts of the future, implications of research and development programmes, and other factors. Such scenarios help give perspective to the strategic plan.

The terms 'strategic' and 'project' plans have been used in this and previous chapters and, along with other types of plans, require definition. Although most writers are in broad agreement on the meanings of many of the terms, there are areas of semantic confusion. My purpose is not to make a comparative study of all the meanings assigned to the terms but to demonstrate how they are used in this book. The exception to this rule will be where alternative approaches to designing a system of plans are illustrated which use the words in a different way.

I see the strategic plan as something which defines the objectives of an organisation, and the means by which those objectives are to be attained: or more accurately this is a definition of strategy – the plan is its detailed specification. An alternative and more detailed definition, which helps to clarify the meaning of my shorter version, is quoted from Denning:[15]

> ...the determination of the future posture of the business with special reference to its product-market posture, its profitability, its size, its rate of innovation, its relationships with executives, its employees and certain external undertakings.

The strategic planning may be divided into subplans: ways of looking at this problem will be discussed later.

Operating plans are defined here as the plans of an existing area of the business. By virtue of the definition of strategic plans, they must be a spin-off from these, even though in practice the decision to continue in that particular area of business may be implicit rather than explicitly taken at the start of each planning cycle. Denning[15] states operating plans to be '... the forward planning of existing operations in existing markets with existing customers and facilities'.

In practical situations it may be more sensible to incorporate part of the strategic task in an operating plan since there are many activities, seen as purely strategic by the implications of Denning's definition of operating plans, which are very closely integrated with existing operations and which can only be isolated from them with difficulty – such as a decision to seek new customers. The fact that, for the more effective running of a system, management may delegate parts of its strategic task does not invalidate the definitions.

Project plans are plans covering particular capital investments, marketing or other operations. In the words of Denning[15]: '. . . the generation and appraisal of the commitment to and detailed working out of the detailed execution of an action *outside the scope of the present operations* which is capable of separate analysis and control.'

The italics are mine, for I do not agree entirely with this particular phrase and would argue that projects can emerge from both the strategic and operating areas. Techniques of appraisal and control are the same, regardless of the source of a project. This is a good illustration of how differences in viewpoint can lead to considerable semantic confusion unless they are clearly identified.

The term 'tactical plan' is sometimes used to suggest an essentially shorter-term action plan which leads to the implementation of the actions proposed in the strategic plan. Sometimes the term tactical is given a slightly wider meaning, as in the following quotation from Lander:[16]

> Strategic planning is carried out by the Chief Executive and his first line executives. It is concerned with the broad concept of the company in the future and the provision and allocation of total resources to product-market opportunities to realise the company's profit potential through selected strategies – tactical planning which embraces all the detailed plans and actions involved in implementing it can be undertaken by the first line executives and those who report to them.

In addition to its plans, every company practising corporate planning needs defined policies and procedures. Some will derive from specific plans, others will be attempts to bring order into the apparent chaos of the many areas of a modern business which are relatively unchanging and which do not justify any other form of planning. Future plans may alter established policy and procedure at any time.

An example of the derivation of policy and procedure from a plan may help to illustrate the relationships.

1 *Plan.* To reduce travelling expenditure of employees by 10 per cent in the following year by controlling class of travel, reducing frequency of travel, scrutinising expense claims more rigidly, and ensuring that all journeys are appropriately authorised.
2 *Policy.* All employees of the company are to travel second class on the railways unless the journey is of more than three hours (scheduled) duration.
3 *Procedure.* A defined system by which the policy is implemented and controlled – ticket-booking rules, expense claim forms and way of obtaining reimbursement, systems of authorisation of expense claims.

In any modern business there are hundreds of policies and procedures which must be applied if the organisation is to function at all. Definition provides a measure of uniformity, precision and control, and ensures that they are understood by all those who need to understand them. Where policies and procedures are of a 'permanent' nature they may beneficially be enshrined in books of regulations and standing orders. Every company has a host of these permanent areas: think for a moment of the areas of personnel, purchasing, office stationery, and general administration – although in many companies they are often implicitly rather than explicitly defined.

Careful attention to this area is a useful aid to better corporate planning. Often definition of a policy will lead to a recognition that it is incompatible with the plans and needs changing: if it is not defined it may be unknown to the people who would realise that it is inappropriate. The point should not be laboured, for there are no new principles involved, but it is nevertheless worth making.

An approach to corporate planning

Figure 3.4 shows a generalised approach to a process of corporate planning. This is conceived as a series of circles and segments of circles. In the centre are the three master plans which deal with the company's strategy: the strategic plan itself, and its interrelated and supporting plans for finance and personnel. These plans *together* fulfil the definitions of strategic plans given earlier in this chapter. Separately they show the main product marketing actions the company is to take in order to attain its defined profit targets and other objectives, the financial

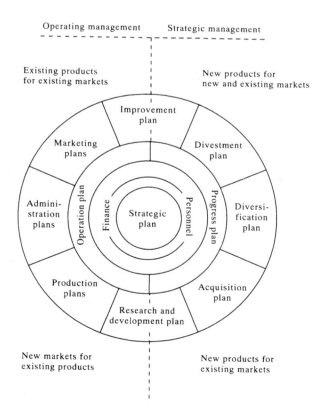

Figure 3.4
Generalised approach to corporate planning

resources which will be deployed (and the financial strategies employed) to enable the strategies to come about, and the human resources involved. The personnel plan embraces what is sometimes called manpower planning.

The diagram indicates the important difference between strategic and operating management tasks, both in relation to product markets and in relation to the types of plans. Operational plans cover marketing, production, and administration and deal with existing products. New markets for existing products are shown under this responsibility although it is also possible for this to be a major decision area.

Strategic management has divestment, diversification, and acquisition as three of its major components. Improvement, and research and development, are areas which may be either strategic or operating and are shown conceptually as coming under both (in reality it may be either) operating and strategic management.

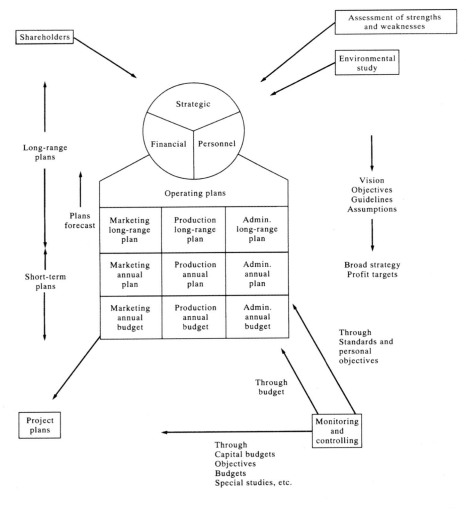

Figure 3.5
Generalised
planning system

The diagram sets out to illustrate the relationships between the various types of plans.

Figure 3.5 takes these concepts and turns them into a total planning system. Again this is on a generalised basis and is used to illustrate the principles. And, of course, each element of this system is examined in greater depth later in the book.

The circle and the box on which it stands illustrate a simplified view of all the plans in the system, while the other boxes and arrows show stages in the planning system and information flows. Once again, the heart of the system is seen as the strategic, personnel, and finance plans – all briefly described in earlier paragraphs and each the subject of considerable discussion in later chapters. It is fair to claim that a large part of this book is about this problem of planning the company's future strategy.

Strategy does not arise in a vacuum, and one of the first steps in planning is to perform an appraisal of strengths and weaknesses. This is likely to lead to a number of long- and short-term decisions, including many for profit improvement. An immediate spin-off from this stage in the planning process might therefore be projects – symbolised by the box in the bottom left-hand corner.

Most companies which practise strategic management try to achieve predetermined objectives which are related to the vision, and the process of setting these may be considered an integral part of strategic planning. Objectives are influenced by shareholders (although usually not explicitly) and, to some degree, by the assessment of strengths and weaknesses.

The third key stage is to relate the company to its business environment. This has an effect on strategies through the identification of opportunities, the anticipation of threats, and the improvement of forecasts. It may help the company to see where it has to take an avoidance action. Environmental study will cover a number of factors including the economy, political events, technology, market forces, legal implications, and social factors. The study of these factors may of itself be a complex operation, and involve the application of a number of management techniques.

The chief executive, the planner, and the top management team consider the various alternatives against the background of the objectives, strengths and weaknesses, and external factors. From this, more projects may spin off (bottom left-hand corner again) for detailed planning.

From the total corporate strategy may be derived objectives and guidelines for the operating plans, and from the environmental study and its consideration in the strategic planning process may come defined planning assumptions. For a simple company, such as that shown in the diagram, the setting of objectives and targets may be easy. Most companies are much more complex, and the multidivisional, multinational organisation may find it a very complex matter. These problems receive more treatment later in the book, and a deeper consideration is given to what is meant by objectives.

Long-range operating plans are properly the responsibility of those line managers in charge of the function or area concerned. The diagram shows three functional areas: in practice there may be more, or the company may be organised into subsidiaries or divisions. This additional complication does not change the principle, although it may make much harder the task of designing a planning system and introducing corporate planning. The detailed consideration of these points is also left until later in the book.

Operating planning gives rise to plans and forecasts which flow back to the strategic planning process, where they are considered in the light of the company's objectives and strategy, and may be either accepted or returned to operating managers for refinement. In turn, the considered plans of the operating units may lead to amendments to the thinking at strategic level and to changes in the strategic plans.

In this way there is a link between all the factors which go into the making of strategies and the thoughts of managers down the line. In many instances the managers who, as part of the top management team, work with the chief executive on strategic planning will be the same people who initiate work on the operating plans of their particular functional areas. This is particularly so in smaller companies. In the large multinationals the people who complete operating plans may play little or no part in the formation of corporate strategy except for the influence their plans have on the final plans. It is possible to devise methods so that these managers have more involvement in strategic thinking, and some companies have given a great deal of attention to making this possible.

Projects may be identified at operating level and give rise to further project plans.

The company now has a completely integrated and closely coordinated strategic plan covering all its areas of activity. It knows what it intends to achieve, how it intends to do it, and the expected effect on financial and personnel resources of these actions. Its next task is to move to implementation.

One way of doing this is through annual operating plans and the annual budget. The broad strategy and profit targets pass to the annual plans from the long-range operating plan. The annual operating plan shows the strategies and actions which have to be implemented over the forthcoming year if the plan is to be achieved. It takes these a stage further, and develops personal objectives for which named persons are responsible. If wished, this may be part of a complete system of management by objectives.

The annual budget becomes the expression in financial terms of the annual plan. Because this has strong links with the long-range plans, the budget is also closely linked with the long-range plans. It therefore becomes more than an instrument of management control in that it is a part of the implementation process of the total planning system.

Any implementation plan needs a monitoring and controlling mechanism, illustrated by the box in Figure 3.5 at the bottom right-hand corner. This mechanism ensures that the personal objectives are carried out; it checks the budget through normal methods of budgetary control and through various methods controls the performance of the projects. The outcome of measuring actual results against the plan might be a need to modify plans in some further cycle. Certainly the performance of the company is a factor which is related to its strengths and weaknesses and is then taken into account in the following year.

All this compresses and simplifies and makes little mention of the tools of the corporate planner. These tools include various techniques of management science, some of the more important of which will be discussed on later pages. The point to stress here is that the techniques are not the plan. There is sometimes a tendency for a planning system to be overshadowed by the techniques used in it. Although corporate models, forecasting models, decision trees, and networks may be invaluable tools, although a sophisticated management information system may be of great importance, the fact is that none of these are as important as the philosophy of planning itself.

One of the main difficulties in designing a planning process is to emphasise strategy. If strategic management is a key aim of the process, as it should be, the process should emphasise this. Although this can be done through the process illustrated in Figure 3.5 there is a danger of bottom-up operating plans swamping the strategy. All this would mean in the final event was that the 'plans' would bear little resemblance to what strategic decisions were taken at the top.

Vancil and Lorange[17] were among the first to suggest a three-stage planning process, consisting of a review of strategy: completion of plan; annual plan budget. This approach has been made into a workable process (see Young and Hussey[18]), following a few simple concepts.

The strategic review process is designed to provide a forum for agreeing the main strategic issues and decisions in discussion between head office and business unit. Its input is a number of working documents at both levels, and a summary of the main strategic points as seen from each viewpoint. Its output is a set of agreed strategic guidelines which are then used as the framework for the detailed planning stage. The main advantage of the extra step is that it allows a free discussion and careful focus on the appropriate strategic issues, with major inputs from corporate level, before business units have become locked into their plans, and before the main issues have been swamped by the volume of the plan. It is easier to change before the plan has been completed than after, if only because the volume of work in completing a detailed plan can prevent easy alteration. My experience is that this method facilitates strategic management. An example is given in Figure 3.6.

There are numerous other general systems which have been suggested from time to time, all of which have many similiarities with and some differences from the outline in the preceding pages. Two brief examples are given here, not because they are any more 'correct' than the others but because they may stimulate thought about different approaches. When systems are moved from the concept to a particular company situation they invariably need some modifications to fit that company. The aim should be to design a system that suits the unique needs of the particular business rather than to expect all companies to fit the textbook. Those interested may find numerous case histories, illustrating the way particular companies have solved this problem, in the pages of *Long Range Planning* and the *Journal of Strategic Change* or in Steiner[19] or Baynes.[20] Steiner deals with US experience, while Baynes's examples are from European companies.

Figure 3.7 shows the system of plans suggested by the Stanford Research Institute.[21] This, too, divides the planning task into two blocks (using the term corporate management where in Figure 3.5 I used 'strategic management').

It divides the strategic planning task into a number of subunits. Basically, in the sense of this figure, the strategic plan shows the potential of the company and

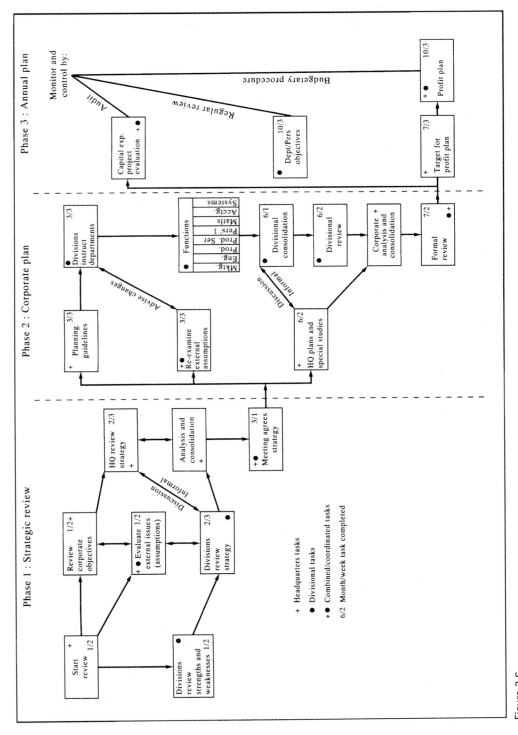

Figure 3.6
Three-stage 'strategic review' planning process. (From Young, R. and Hussey, D. E. 'Corporate Planning at Rolls-Royce Motors', *Long Range Planning*, April 1977)

Figure 3.7
System of plans
devised by the
Stanford Research
Institute (reprinted
with permission)

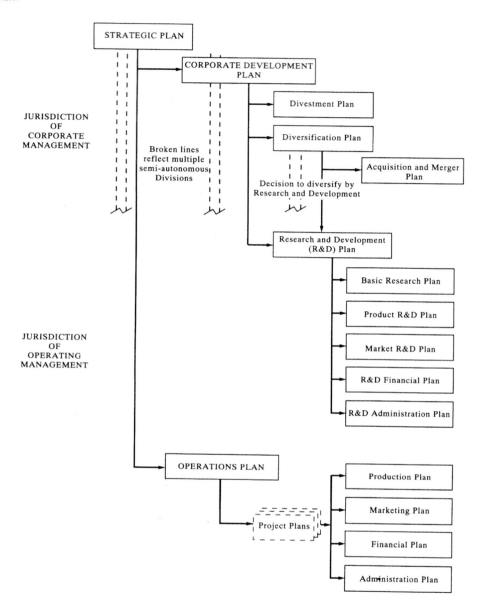

whether it can be attained from present operations. The development plan looks at the alternative ways in which the gap between potential and present operations may be filled, and moves through the two subplans for divestment and diversification. The second subplan again divides into acquisition and research and development. (In fact, although not illustrated in either Figure 3.4 or Figure 3.7 there are certain other methods of diversification which will be described in the chapters on strategy.)

Although not specifically mentioned, it is possible to make provision for top-level financial and manpower planning within the framework of this system.

CORPORATE PLANNING

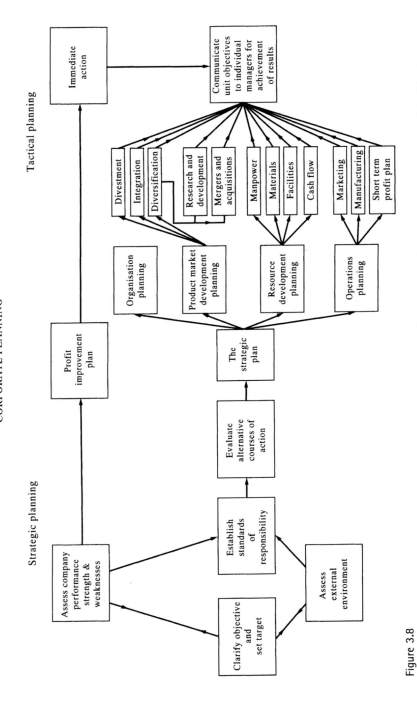

Figure 3.8
System of plans devised by Urwick Orr & Partners (reprinted with permission). *Note:* Urwick Orr are now absorbed into the Price Waterhouse organisation

The second approach is that developed by Urwick Orr & Partners Ltd., which is illustrated in Figure 3.8 with the steps which lead up to it. This diagram is thus directly comparable with that in Figure 3.5. (Urwick Orr was acquired by Price Waterhouse and no longer operates as a separate organisation.)

Here we have a system which, although it highlights certain factors that are different from those emphasised in the two earlier approaches, is still covering the same ground and, at the final analysis, is suggesting much the same thing. The Urwick Orr approach links closely with management by objectives, the process for which is described later. The meanings of 'strategic' and 'tactical' have been given earlier in the reference from Lander.[16]

The broad issues described in these pages are important because unless the delicate and interdependent relationship between the component parts of a planning system are understood, it becomes difficult to view planning in anything but a fragmented way. A strategic management system and its parts may be compared to a car engine. A few refinements may be added to give an improved performance: an occasional nut or bolt might drop off without making much difference to running. If the water tank bursts or the fan belt breaks, the engine will still operate in the short term although ultimately this will lead to severe damage. Most parts, although they may not look very important, will cause complete and immediate failure if removed. To understand any component it must be examined and studied individually – but it can only be used when related back to the total engine.

So it is with strategic management. Some modifications may improve the system; there is latitude in one or two minor areas. The system may appear to work in the short term even if certain key parts are neglected, but in the long term will destroy itself. Ignore most of the parts at your peril, for the system will never get started. Certainly each part of the process may be studied in depth as a separate entity – but its meaning will only emerge when it is considered as an integral part of the whole.

Scenario planning

Uncertainty and change are features that pervade much of the thinking about strategic management processes. In many of the approaches to planning discussed above uncertainty is taken account of through sensitivity and risk analysis. And as we have seen, there is some doubt that a highly formalised process of corporate planning can be flexible enough to cope with highly turbulent environments. It is also noticeable that many of the case histories and models of planning processes are not new. The newer thinking is mainly around the problem of rapid and violent change, improved analysis, and the behavioural aspects of strategic management. The outline models for preparing a plan seem to be fairly robust, although the process that lies behind them is situational.

There is a different approach to planning which has a long pedigree, although it has always been practised by only a minority of organisations. This is scenario planning, the development of which has been mainly by Shell, who have used the approach since the 1960s. A number of case histories of the Shell approach have been published (for example, Schoemaker and van der Heijden[22]). Chandler and Cockle[23] wrote one of the few books on the topic, based on their experience at Reed International. The most comprehensive text, likely to become the standard work on scenario planning is van der Heijden,[24] which takes the subject several steps further from the Shell experience. The author played a role in the Shell scenario planning process.

Van der Heijden argues that 'the less things are predicable the more attention you have to pay to the strategy **process**. Uncertainty has the effect of moving the key to success from the "optimal strategy" to "the most skilful strategy process"' (p. vii). He believes that the process is in effect one of strategic conversation, and that the best language for this conversation is scenarios.

Initial methods of scenario planning used a number of forecasts of possible futures, say three, of which one was designated as most likely. Plans were made for each, but inevitably the main concentration was on the most likely case. The modern approach is somewhat different. A number of scenarios of possible futures are developed, but none claim to be a forecast of what will happen. Major strategies are evaluated against each scenario, with the aim of ensuring that the chosen strategy will deliver value under any of the scenarios.

Van der Heijden claims that:

> Scenario planning distinguishes itself from other more traditional approaches to strategic planning through its explicit approach towards ambiguity and uncertainty in the strategic question. The most fundamental aspect of introducing uncertainty in the strategic equation is that it turns planning for the future from a once-off episodic activity into an ongoing learning proposition. In a situation of uncertainty, planning becomes learning, which never stops (p. 7).

Elements of a business plan

The descriptions of planning processes all require the preparation of plans. In addition, many managers may from time to time be required to write a business plan, even though their organisation may not operate a continuous process of strategic management. An all-purpose business plan framework is offered here in Figure 3.9. It is suitable for a strategic plan of a business unit, an operating plan, and as a general outline for a project plan. The concepts are appropriate for a complex, multidivisional organisation, but there will be differences at what is considered to be strategic compared to a simple single division business. These differences will become clearer from the later detailed chapters on strategy and strategic analysis.

There is a strong correlation between Figures 3.9 and 3.5, the main difference being that Figure 3.5 describes a process, while Figure 3.9 shows what topics should be covered in a plan. The only new concepts introduced in this model are assumptions, risk, and gap analysis. In addition, it separates strengths and

Figure 3.9

Outline components
of a business plan

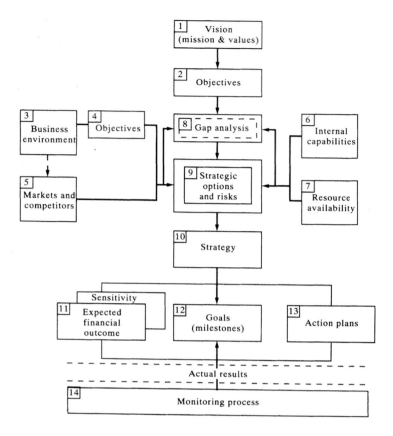

weaknesses into two parts, the internal capabilities (or lack of capability) and resource availability. The reason for this is that, although most successful organisations have access to resources of finance, skills and people beyond what is currently within the organisation, there is still a finite limit on resources which can affect what strategies are possible.

Assumptions are the subject of a separate chapter. For present purposes they may be defined as the statements about the environment on which the plan is based. The reason for making them explicit is partly to aid the interpretation of the plan and the risks to which it is subject, and partly to enable them to be monitored so that a fast reaction is facilitated should they prove to be erroneous.

Gap analysis is also described more fully later. It is a simple concept which looks at the expected future gap between objectives and forecasts of current activities, and how that gap might be closed.

Risk is an inherent part of the assessment of strategy. One does not take strategic decisions and then look at the risks involved, but assess the risks as part of the decision-making process.

The problem of business plan preparation will be returned to in Chapter 23 when we will look at how to evaluate a plan.

The exploration so far has given us a skeleton for strategic management. Bones by themselves have a useful but limited function. In the next chapters we will put flesh on these bones, to explore the process of strategy formulation in much greater detail. We will also explore how to put the breath of life into our process, so that it becomes a live, dynamic contributor to corporate success.

References

1 Leavitt, H. J. 'Applied Organisation Change in Industry: Structural, Technical and Human Approaches' (abridged version of a 1964 article) in Vroom, V. H. and Deci, E. L. (eds), *Management and Motivation*, Penguin, Harmondsworth, 1970.

2 Peters, T. J. and Waterman, R. H. *In Search of Excellence*, Harper & Row, New York, 1982.

3 Galbraith, J. R. and Nathanson, D. A. *Strategy Implementation: The Role of Strategy and Process*, West, St Paul, 1978.

4 Nicholls, J. 'Rescuing Leadership from Humpty Dumpty', *Journal of General Management*, **16**, No. 2, 1990.

5 Hersey, P. and Blanchard, K. *Management of Organisational Behaviour*, Prentice Hall, Englewood Cliffs, NJ, 1969.

6 Dinkelspiel, J. and Bailey, J. 'High performing Organisations: Aligning Culture and Organisation around Strategy', in Hussey, D. E. (ed.), *International Review of Strategic Management*, Vol. 2, No. 1, Wiley, Chichester, 1991.

7 Goold, M. and Campbell, A. *Strategies and Styles*, Blackwell, Oxford, 1987.

8 Ansoff, H. I. 'Strategic Management in a Historical Perspective', in Hussey, D. E. (ed.), *International Review of Strategic Management*, Vol. 2, No. 1, Wiley, Chichester, 1991.

9 Gluck, F. W., Kaufman, S. P. and Walleck, A. S. 'Strategic Management for Competitive Advantage', *Harvard Business Review*, July/August 1980.

10 Hussey, D. E. 'Evolution of Planning Approaches' *Professional Administration*, April 1979.

11 Stanbridge, P. J. 'Long Range Planning in Underdeveloped Countries – A Case History', *Long Range Planning*, December 1969.

12 Kidel, A. K. 'Techniques and Methodology of the French Fifth Plan', *Long Range Planning*, March 1969.

13 Warren, E. K. *Long Range Planning: The Executive Viewpoint*, Prentice Hall, Englewood Cliffs, NJ, 1966.

14 Pennington, M. W. 'Why has Planning Failed?' *Long Range Planning*, March 1972.

15 Denning, B. W. (ed.), Introduction in *Corporate Planning: Selected Concepts*, McGraw-Hill, New York, 1971.

16 Lander, K. E. 'Corporate Planning', *The Consulting Engineer*, December 1968.

17 Vancil, R. F. and Lorange, P. 'Strategic Planning in Diversified Companies', *Harvard Business Review*, January-February 1975.

18 Young, R. and Hussey, D. E. 'Corporate Planning at Rolls-Royce Motors Ltd', *Long Range Planning*, April 1977.

19 Steiner, G. A. (ed.), *Managerial Long Range Planning*, McGraw-Hill, New York, 1963.

20 Baynes, P. (ed.), *Case Studies in Corporate Planning*, Pitman, London, 1973.

21 Stewart, R. F., Allen, J. K. and Cavender, J. M., *The Strategic Plan*, Standford Research Institute, 1963.

22 Schoemaker, P. J. H. and van der Heijden, C. A. J. M. 'Strategic Planning at Royal Dutch Shell', *Journal of Strategic Change*, 2, No. 3, May/June, 157–71, 1993.

23 Chandler, J. and Cockle, P. *Techniques of Scenario Planning*, McGraw-Hill, Hemel Hempstead, 1982.

24 Van der Heijden, K. *Scenarios: The Art of Strategic Conversation*, Wiley, Chichester, 1996.

Part 2

The Changing Environment

CHAPTER 4

The challenge of the future

This chapter aims to show that strategic management is about coming to terms with a changing world. Strategic management is about both adapting to external changes and sometimes to cause the external environment to change. The chapter will provide a way of thinking about issues from the external environment and an understanding that there are interconnections between them.

One of the justifications given for subjecting a business to a process of strategic management is that it is the only satisfactory way of coming to terms with a changing world. Events in the environment in which the company operates have a direct effect on the success or failure of that company. Strategic management seeks, as one of its aims, to relate the company to its environment, and to identify in advance the threats and opportunities which environmental change brings. At the outset the unique character of each business should be stressed: the effect of change in factors outside the control of the company will vary not only between industries but also between companies in the same industry. What causes the effect to vary are not only the obvious things like the nature of business, countries of operation, and size of organisation: there are also the fundamental differences in the attitudes and abilities of various managements. What one manager views as a threat may be seized as an opportunity by another. Some accept the challenge of change as one of the factors which adds a stimulant to the task of management: others try ostrich-like to ignore it, or sit like Canute on the beach defying the inevitable movements of the tides of the times: still others see the change taking place and, like Nero, expend their energies on what – in the context of their problems – are frivolous activities. The Nero managers are the worst, because it is a management crime to see a threat and not to avoid it, to notice an opportunity yet not to understand it.

There can be few managers who are unaware that the world has changed. Even since the Second World War, revolutionary advances have been made through the impact of technology on day-to-day life. In many Western societies the car is now commonplace: just before the Second World War it was the richer person's prerogative (except, perhaps, in the USA where, even then, there was wider ownership). At the turn of the century, still within living memory, the car was a rarity, an innovation. From the horse-and-cart age of the first twenty years of this century to the motorised world of today is one vast turmoil of change.

Similar parallels can be drawn in other areas. The miracle of our first flight, the acceptance of flight as a normal method of transportation, the introduction of longer-range aeroplanes, and the invention of the jet engine, and – the ultimate master stroke – the development of the manned space ship. In medicine growing knowledge has pushed back the frontiers of disease in every country in the world; the identification of the real cause of many illnesses, the greater understanding of the human body (the science of biochemistry is a relatively new one), and the discovery of new drugs (of which perhaps penicillin is the shining example). Even the food eaten as a part of modern daily life is different. The great growth of the convenience food industry has occurred in the last twenty-five years.

The contrasts are not only in the fields of technology. In Europe and the USA there is a whole new structure of society. The underdeveloped countries may not have the same economic standards of prosperity as the industrial countries, but even here the comparison between everyday life today shows a vastly different quality from that of the primitive world of 1890. The British Empire is no more. Britain's pride of place in world affairs has been yielded to other countries.

This list could go on for ever, but the point has been made. What is of equal importance is not just that the world has changed but that the rate of change has increased. Change in all directions has occurred much more rapidly in the last twenty to thirty years than in the preceding forty to fifty. And the process continues to accelerate.

In addition, on many fronts (although not all) the expense of each technological development increases to the point where in industries such as aerospace it is almost impossible for private enterprise to operate without government support, and where one technological mistake can bring a giant like Rolls-Royce crashing to insolvency.

Throughout history inability to cope has led to extinction. In biological terms there is the example of the dinosaur, of whom the only traces are a few fossilised bones (although it is also relevant to point out that the dinosaur did survive for 140 million years). In business terms the company which makes no adjustments usually disappears with even fewer traces. Its only fossilised remains are its managers. Change in this context has many facets, some of which will be quoted later in this chapter.

Management books frequently refer to the failure of many businesses in the horse-and-cart age (horse-and-buggy in American writings) to come to terms with their changing environment. Many disappeared because of their inability to adapt. It is perhaps interesting to point to a business which did adapt.

In 1970 the London firm of Glover, Webb & Liversidge celebrated its 250th anniversary. The business was originally established as a carriage builder, and soon developed a respectable position in the market for phaetons, gigs, broughams, coaches, and farm and trade vehicles (this was in the pre-Nielson days of 1720). The company are still carriage builders and hold the Royal Warrant for the maintenance of the coaches and carriages of the Royal Mews.

The process of adaption began in the twentieth century when the company introduced motorised goods vehicles ('Gloverley'). In the 1930s it moved its attention to the refuse-vehicle business, building the first all-steel moving-floor dust-carts. Their main product areas are now dust-carts and security vans.

This company must owe much of its success over 250 years to its adaptability.

Not all companies are so adaptable. The inherent inflexibility of many of the larger companies often prevents them from seizing the opportunities that change can offer: lack of resources and sheer lack of ability frequently causes the smaller companies to resist any move which is different. Levitt[1] states:

> The inability or refusal of companies to see the opportunities produced by change often seems to be a peculiar affliction of big, well-organised companies. General Electric turned down the opportunity to get exclusive American rights to manufacture and distribute neon lights, saying there was no market for them. A new small company had to be organised by Europeans to pioneer this big profitable market. Frozen orange juice had to be started by a company not in the food business.
>
> The big hotel chains fought the motel idea for years, in spite of its greater customer satisfying benefits...
>
> Why do big companies so often seem to resist some of these changes so rigorously, acting only after the ideas are proved out, even when the companies pridefully promote their impressive slogans of progressiveness? Why is this complacency, this fat cat constipation, so often a big company problem?

Part of the duty of all managements is to make those strategic moves which ensure that the business grows, prospers, and therefore survives. Although all change is not caused by external events, frequently it is what is going on in the world outside which is its most forceful agency.

There is comfort and a feeling of false security in following the time-worn and well-known rut, often even to the extent that it goes deep enough for the sides to collapse and smother its occupant, killing all drive and initiative. One might also define a natural law of human inertia which can only be overcome by the restlessness and creative urge possessed by men of vision.

Most managers will be aware of the stock responses, the 'road-blocks' to new ideas which are produced automatically whenever the status quo is threatened (Figure 4.1). If all people observed these there would be no progress of any kind. In some cases the road-block may show the correct decision – but it is a result arrived at by emotional response rather than reason. In many more cases it is an unthinking reaction which kills initiative and preserves the false security of the known. At one time or another every manager will be guilty of road-blocking. Some do it all the time.

For the individual, change appears too frequently as a threat. A manager that sticks to the old tried and true course of action may be less often at loggerheads with colleagues, and may feel less at risk than if he or she 'sticks his or her neck out'. An error of omission is frequently less noticeable than one of commission: sometimes the missed opportunity is known only to the manager himself: everybody knows if he or she takes it and fails. Modern management calls for a

Figure 4.1

Examples of typical 'road-blocks' to new ideas

We're too small for that
Our competitors don't do it
We're too big
Shouldn't we do some market research?
The present system works all right
We've never done it before
Let's bring it up again in six months
What would our customers think?
It won't work
I've always done it this way
What about our sunk costs?
The Board would never approve
That's not the way we do things here
You're ahead of your time
The Union wouldn't like it
Why don't you go away and think it out again?
We could never market it
That's not our responsibility
Let them try it first
Too hard to sell
Not really practicable
We tried it before
Why not sleep on it?
Why should we be the first to change?

measure of courage, the willingness to take reasonable (but not reckless) decisions which change the current state of affairs. The company whose managers look always inwards to the 'safe' path will never be a leader: in many instances it will already have sown the seeds of its own failure. The challenge of the future with its gauntlet of change is faced by every company, large or small. Only those which square up to the situation and pick up the gauntlet can hope to succeed. Those that ignore it, or try to run away, will sooner or later come to grief.

It is by this unique ability to create change that humans have become the most successful of all the animals. Where the lesser animals are prisoners of their environment and can change only by the slow process of evolution (with the risk of extinction in the way), we have freedom to adapt and change the environment. This is part of our heritage.

At the same time it is understandable that change should be resisted since the psychological security of the individual may be threatened. Change may menace learned skills, a lifetime of experience, or a person's place in the community.

The fact that changes may be associated with risk has already been mentioned. Those who propose major changes may have to face the resentment – and sometimes ridicule – of their fellows. They may put at risk their prestige, their capital, and their livelihood.

In addition, the life pattern of each person is based on the present, and from this he or she may make assumptions about the future. Any change which threatens those assumptions may cause confusion. When the well-known landmarks are destroyed, even the most familiar path may become a journey to the unknown – a frightening experience. So we tend to resist.

Coping with a changing world calls for managers who have a measure of dissatisfaction. The restless person will always seek new methods and opportunities: the complacent rarely see a reason for doing things differently. Henry Ford is reported to have said 'I'm looking for a lot of men with an infinite capacity for not knowing what can't be done'. It is people who refuse to accept that things are impossible, who will not be baulked by difficulties, who strive to overcome obstacles, and see opportunities where others see threats: it is people such as these who possess what is perhaps the essence of real management.

This dissatisfaction, this refusal to bow down to the inevitable, requires another quality, creativity, and frequently both are found within the same person. The creative person is often restless. One of a chief executive's prime duties is to ensure that the company has a supply of creative managers. The organisational systems must encourage flair, initiative, and innovative skills. It is on these that the future success of the business lies. The planning manager has a particular duty to ensure that the planning system also encourages these qualities. All too often an ill-conceived and poorly designed process of formal planning does the opposite: it becomes an empty form-filling exercise which merely helps to maintain the existing situation. This is a state of affairs which no chief executive should tolerate and which no planner need allow to happen. Good planning methods, the principles of which are discussed in other chapters, will assist the company to develop those qualities which allow it to meet the challenge of the future.

'Creativity' is an important word. *Chamber's Twentieth Century Dictionary*[2] defines it as the 'state or quality of being creative: ability to create'. Both 'creative' and 'create' have meanings which include words like 'imagination' and 'originality'. Two meanings of 'create' are 'to bring into being or form out of nothing; to bring into being by force of imagination'. It is, I think, important to remember that creativity comes from people, although it may be the resources of the business or society which enables the original, imaginative solution to a problem to become something that can be implemented.

It is individual creativity, harnessed to achieve specific corporate objectives, which allows the company to innovate. Innovation is the function which enables a company to grow and profit from opportunities which arise from the changing world. In addition, another function which has already been mentioned is required – adaptability. This is the ability to adjust to new circumstances, particularly to avoid threats arising from the changing environment. Creativity must assist this function also, although more important are probably qualities of corporate self-criticism, flexibility, and the courage to change.

Change is an unavoidable factor in modern business life. As Drucker[3] has so aptly observed, tomorrow always arrives and is always different. What will happen in the future can never be certain, and the corporate planning process should take account of this. Change for the sake of change is not a good thing. The chief executive must retain a sense of balance. Just as in many companies it is next to impossible to get anyone to do anything differently, there are others – equally unhealthy – where nothing is constant, and changes are implemented with neither thought nor reason.

The rest of this chapter will examine in outline some of the main environmental factors which cause the challenge of the future. Succeeding chapters will show how these should be treated in the planning process, and some of the techniques of forecasting which the planner may need to use.

The external factors which affect performance and progress are, of course, legion. Not only are there many of them, but there are numerous interrelations: for example, technological change may bring about a different economic performance which in turn may change social attitudes. Although, for analysis purposes, it is necessary to group environmental factors under convenient headings, in practice the divisions are not absolute, other classifications are possible, and the real situation is a good deal more complicated. What this particular analysis tries to do is, through practical illustration, to draw attention to some of the factors which a chief executive should consider in the development of future strategies, and which for this reason should be systematically studied so that they may be adequately treated in the planning process. One of the tasks of the planner is to identify the relevant environmental factors to make the scope of the study manageable.

It is probably as well to try to dispel any illusions that taking account of environmental factors is easy. Although it is by no means difficult to consider factors in general terms, as we are doing here, it is very, very difficult to weave them into the fabric of plans. There are conceptual problems, disagreements, and uncertainties which ensure that the strategic planner's life is a very complicated affair.

The classification system chosen for this analysis is illustrated in Figure 4.2. Only a general overview is possible: every business must estimate for itself its own individual situation.

The diagram also makes the point that all the factors are to some degree interdependent. Changes in technology can, for example, have a profound effect on many or all of the other factors. Computers, and particularly the arrival of low cost but powerful computing, can be seen to have impacted many other factors:

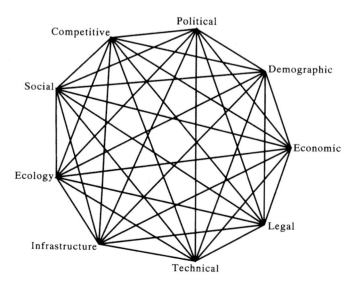

Figure 4.2
The environment

1 The economic situation has been altered by automatic trading in the stock market, with sales being triggered when prices fall to a predetermined level. This is blamed for stock market crashes and is accused of affecting business confidence and thereby impacting on economic output.

2 Social changes have been triggered. For example, more people are able to work at home, because information technology means that this is as effective as travelling to an office, although more lonely. The wall cash dispenser has changed social habits.

3 The competitive environment has changed, although there are few examples of permanent advantages being gained from IT. However there are numerous competitive *disadvantages* created for those organisations which do not keep up to date.

4 New legislation has come about through the need to protect data, prevent individual rights from being infringed, prevent copyright infringement, and many other areas.

5 Political events are changed because IT and opinion polls rapidly alter perceptions of what is important to the electorate.

At the same time, some of the lines of force are two-way. It is the backlash of social opinion against abuses, or expected abuses, of data by debt control and other firms that led to the legislation to control the use of databases (Data Protection Act) in the UK, and also in other countries.

The diagram includes the competitive environment, for completeness at this stage. In analysing this, as we shall see when we look at industry and competitor analysis later, my preference is to remove the factor from the outer perimeter of the diagram, and reposition it within the centre of the diagram, to study in more detail the impact of the other environmental factors on the industry, of which the particular company is a member.

It is also necessary to think of the speed of change, an issue discussed already when we looked at the concept of environmental turbulence.

Demographic factors

Populations change in many ways which are relevant to the business situation. It is not only the obvious generalisation that larger populations mean larger markets, assuming that economic prosperity continues: the altering structure of that population may be even more important.

A widespread trend in many parts of the world is for an ageing population, with fewer young people and more older ones. In addition, the older people are living longer. The trend holds true in the USA, much of Europe, Japan, and Singapore, and no doubt in many other countries that I have not studied. It is brought about by social changes which have led to falling birth rates, added to the longevity factor already mentioned. Such changes create strategic considerations for organisations, varying from the availability of people for employment to changes in markets because of different life styles. Politically, the retired are

The integrated environment

The external business environment is not a simple listing of factors. In assessing what is important, or how trends will develop, we need to consider how what happens to one factor may trigger changes in the others. The development of computer technology, and in particular the PC can be taken as an illustration.

This change in the technical factor of Figure 4.2 has had implications for every other factor. The following are examples and are not meant to be exhaustive.

- *Social* Among the social changes have been the growth in home ownership of computers, and the impact of computer games on the activities of children. Even more far reaching has been the fact that the computer has enabled an expansion of working from home, and has changed the nature of work in many industries.
- *Competitive* New business opportunities have developed, and old ones (e.g. mechanical typewriters) have declined. The technology has brought advantages to those who have seen opportunities, and changed the competitive positions of those that have not.
- *Political* New political views are formed, such as the British government's announced intention of linking every school to the Internet. To achieve this is leading to alliances with commercial organisations which would have been impossible for the Labour Party to contemplate a few years ago. There is also concern about the uncontrollable nature of the Internet.
- *Demographic* No changes are caused to the structure of the population, but it is possible to see how the technology could change the geographical location of the population.
- *Economic* The technology has contributed to the globalisation of the economy, and the volatility of share prices and foreign exchange rates.
- *Legal* New protections move from social concern, to political awareness, to legislation. An example of this is the Data Protection Act, which only applies to personal information stored electronically.
- *Infrastructure* In the developed countries an expansion of the infrastructure in the form of telephone lines has taken place, and new technologies have had to be introduced. In Third World countries an already inadequate infrastructure becomes even less able to meet the needs of business.
- *Ecology* A new mountain of non-biodegradable waste is created as faster cycles of obsolescence lead to more and more computers being scrapped. In turn this is causing pressure on manufacturers to produce products that can be recycled, and for legislation to control the wastage.

becoming a higher proportion of the electorate, and will therefore exercise a greater influence on government policies.

There is another, less obvious aspect of population change which has come to the fore in the USA, and is relevant for other countries. This is the diversity of the population, particularly those who are economically active, with increasing numbers from different ethnic and language groups in particular age bands, and occupations. This brings a need for greater intra-national cultural understanding, while convergence of countries, as in the European Union, makes international cultural understanding more important.

All these trends are potentially important in the planning of strategy. Fortunately, demographics are generally less turbulent than many of the other environmental factors. Most developed countries have a history of population censuses which means that the statistics are sound. Birth and death rates can be forecast with reasonable accuracy, and if the life expectancy at various ages is known, the movement of those of us who already exist into progressively higher age bands is close to a certainty. Immigration and emigration may be the greatest unknowns. Underdeveloped countries, and those developed countries such as what was once Yugoslavia, who have blundered into civil war are a forecaster's nightmare. Disease (particularly AIDS in Africa), famine and war mean that both life expectancy and live birth rates are unknown, and the death, and migrations of refugees mean that there is no statistical base from which to project.

Economic factors

Virtually all the demographic factors manifest themselves as an influence on another environmental function – the economy. As with all other factors, the effect on each country, each industry, and each business is not necessarily a constant, although every business is in some way under the influence of the economies in which it operates.

A study of all economic factors would be beyond the scope of this book, and would probably be an academic exercise unless carried out with the interests of a particular business in mind. Instead, a few examples are quoted to underline the importance of the economic factors, and it is hoped that these examples will illustrate the need for business to take them into account when preparing its corporate plans.

The problem is compounded by the increasing tendency for companies to become multinational in their scope. Although there are companies which still operate in one country only, many more will either be truly multinational or have at least an export trade. It follows that for many companies the economic factors to be studied are those applying in not just one but a number of countries.

Relation of company to the economy

Perhaps the first step is to try to relate company results to the general progress of the economy. Does the company mirror the ups and downs of the trade cycle or the general direction and rate of economic growth? Not all companies do – in fact some may thrive whatever seems to be going on in the wider economic front. Others may find themselves in a growth situation in times of prosperity, falling back very quickly in the event of a period of stagnation or decline (the situation with many consumer durables, machine tools, and construction).

Many companies straddle a number of industries, and it may be necessary to study each separately. Similarly, it may be desirable to study exports separately: certainly there is not an immediate major correlation to be expected between reflation in the UK and sales in Japan. These are commonsense qualifications, and others certainly will occur (such as correcting for abnormal patterns caused by a reorganisation). What should arise from a study such as this is a much greater understanding of the business and its economic environment, useful both for strategic planning and for analysing risk.

Inflation

A second economic factor is inflation. This, of course, is closely related to general economic performance. Inflation has its own implications for forward-looking management, and, indeed, is a problem which causes concern to most chief executives.

Inflation is a worldwide problem, but one which varies in intensity between countries. Lietner[4] quotes the example of Indonesia, which considered a national inflation rate in 1968 of 85 per cent, a great improvement over a previous figure of 360 per cent. Many South American countries have an inflation rate of between 20 and 50 per cent and the USA has tended to regard 5–6 per cent as a norm. Any increase over the norm can be traumatic and will move quickly to the political arena.

The immediate problem business faces is improving profits in a situation where rising costs are cutting into margins. Profits should increase at least as much as the inflation if the real return to shareholders is not to decrease and if the company is to provide its requirements of capital.

Inflation, like all other economic factors, will not affect all companies the same way. All other things being equal, a labour-intensive industry will feel the effect of inflation much more violently than a capital-intensive industry with modern plant and adequate capacity.

Some managers argue that the inflation element should be ignored in long-range planning since price rises will compensate for the inflation effect. There are a number of reasons why this argument is fallacious. Perhaps the most important is that the strategy for dealing with inflation is a matter of top management judgement, is a decision, not an automatic result, and in any case may be something other than a price adjustment. In addition, there are always time lags between cost and price increases, and even the cost increases do not incur all at once – labour rates may rise this week, raw materials next month, and transport costs next quarter; they may not have equal impact on all competitors. A third point, important for the implementation of plans, is that monitoring and controlling plans becomes next to impossible unless they are calculated at current prices.

So inflation, particularly the rates as applicable to the company, rather than the nation, is a key area of external influence. (A method of measuring internal company inflation is described in Hussey[5].)

Exchange rates

The multinational company has to take account not only of economic growth and inflation but also variations in exchange rates. Revaluation or devaluation can knock holes in any profit forecast. Some countries, for instance many of those in Africa, are subject to frequent and violent changes in exchange rates. Even those which are relatively stable are subject to change, as is demonstrated by the 1992 European exchange rate crisis.

Governmental economic policies

Government policies have a direct effect both on the economy at large and the individual company. Many of these are self-evident, and changes in fiscal policies have already been mentioned. These are by no means the only policies of concern to the company, as a few other examples will make clear.

In many countries, particularly the underdeveloped, government economic policies play a key part in the encouragement of new industry (e.g. protective customs duties). In the UK fiscal incentives were used for a long time as one part of a policy to entice industry to particular areas of the country.

At times of economic pressure policies are introduced which have an impact on business. Changes in hire-purchase legislation may be made for economic rather than legal reasons (raising minimum deposits and reducing repayment periods), credit may be restricted or expanded, and the liquidity of importers may be reduced through a system of import deposits.

Legal factors

Many of the economic policies will have the support of legislation. In addition, there are numerous aspects of the legal environment in which the company operates and which must be taken into account in the planning of strategy. Again, emphasis must be limited to a few specific examples.

The legal environment may be considered as having three parts: the existing pattern of laws under which every company operates, areas which change but where changes are advised in advance, and the unannounced introduction of new regulations or suspended clauses of existing laws.

In planning corporate strategy the pattern of existing laws is only of relevance for detailed consideration in so far as they are unusual, a particular constraint, or affect a type of business venture with which the company has no previous experience. It would be patently silly for a chief executive (or the planner) to list all laws which affect the business. However, the existing legal implications should not be forgotten, as it is possible for opportunities to be lost, or profits reduced, by failure in this area. An 'unusual' legal constraint might be one which affects one industry but not another. For example, in the UK the pharmaceuticals industry has to consider a number of special constraints which it cannot ignore when formulating strategy. It is not possible to market a new drug until clearance has been obtained from a government agency: to obtain clearance, various controlled trials must be performed and other data assembled to prove that the drug does its job and that all harmful side-effects have been identified, and that the problem of side-effects is not greater than the illness cured. To overlook this factor in long-term planning would be foolhardy since it has the effect of increasing the lead time before a new product can be introduced and can add to the risk of pre-launch failure.

On the other hand, I do not believe that better plans would be produced because *all* managers had expert personal knowledge about property laws, laws governing lighting in offices, or the host of day-to-day factors arising from commercial transactions. Each of these legal implications is important, and must be considered by someone in the organisation, but it is only infrequently a factor for strategic planning.

Areas of change in the legal environment are matters of greater concern in planning. Unlike many other environmental factors, changes in the legal situation are often known considerably in advance with a high degree of certainty. For example, British businesses had several years' warning of the date on which decimal currency would be introduced. To many this was just a cost-increasing factor, not particularly important to their overall plans. Others found in decimalisation an opportunity – not only the obvious increased market for cash register and calculating machine companies, but an opportunity for printers, publishers, educational, and training concerns. Less obvious, certain distributive concerns were able to offer an explanatory and training service to their customers, thus using decimalisation as an element of marketing strategy to increase sales of their normal products. No doubt many businesses ignored decimalisation, despite the warnings, until they were caught up in it.

This example shows that environmental factors may bring out a different reaction from different businesses. There are numerous other legal changes which fall into this 'advanced warning' area, and, indeed, in democratic countries most new legislation will fall under this category. Laws take time to be enacted and can rarely be introduced overnight. The warning may not always be as long as with decimalisation, although it is frequently a matter of years.

The third classification, factors which change without warning, presents business planners with a different sort of problem where plans have to be based on predictions and assessments rather than near-certainties.

Technological factors

The increasing magnitude and rapidity of technological change was discussed at the beginning of this chapter and was positioned as one of the key factors in the environment. It does not stand alone, and is interrelated with all the other factors (the Industrial Revolution, for example, was noted for economic, social, and legal change in addition to the rapid development of technology).

Bernal[6] maintains that we are currently passing through a new industrial revolution. Whereas the original was characterised by the harnessing of power to perform what were previously heavy manual tasks, the new revolution is the substitution of mechanical or electronic devices for individual skill. The new revolution introduces the speed, control, judgement, and precision of electronic instruments. It is a revolution '... in which planned scientific research is taking the place more and more of individual mechanical ingenuity'.

Certainly the company of today which ignores technology in its plans is very shortsighted. Technological change has, for most companies, at least two dimensions. The first is the change brought about for marketing reasons, often involving the creation of entirely new products or new uses for existing products. Thus metal guttering gives way to plastic, clay roofing tiles are replaced by cement, frozen vegetables replace the canned product, man-made fibres take a share of the textile market from natural fibres, and polythene bags cut into an area previously dominated by paper. These examples are all obvious because they have happened: many more problems arise from changes which might happen in the future.

The second dimension is change in processes, production methods, and other technology, which alters the way an established product is made. The basic product offered for sale may change only marginally: the way it is made may be totally new. Houses may be built by industrialised methods, far removed from traditional bricks and mortar with construction by on-site labour. Production lines may be automated and electronically controlled to give fine tolerances. An organic compound may be synthesised and produced from completely different raw materials by new processes. Machines may change in capacity and speed of production, in their efficiency rates, or in general reliability. Technological obsolescence is a factor not because of competition from new products in the market but because the company becomes increasingly uncompetitive in its costs. Extra-fast obsolescence can cause problems of under-recovered depreciation, increased capital requirements, and machinery sold for scrap long before its useful life is over.

Technological change may alter market structure without basically changing the product. Many of the requirements of office printing have been basically unchanged for many years. The availability of low-cost, efficient, and relatively simple office printing machines changed the place where printing takes place. It is both practicable and economic for office forms to be internally printed by even the smaller companies – business which has moved from the printing industry itself. Desktop publication has put high-quality book and report printing into the hands of the originator of the material.

It would be a mistake to assume that the only important technological changes are big ones. Relatively small changes in technology can have a disproportionate result.

For decades the world banana trade was based on a very simple system. Bananas were shipped in an unripe state on the stem on which nature grew them, usually loosely wrapped in straw (and later plastic). Each bundle was irregular in size and shape and was difficult to handle mechanically. Importing countries ripened the bananas in warehouses and, when this process was complete, the fruit was stripped off the stem in hands, packed into boxes, and delivered to retailers. Processes were generally labour intensive, there were problems over the disposal of quantities of vegetable matter in urban areas, and there was much double handling.

A relatively minor technological advance meant that green bananas could be picked in a standard carton in the exporting country and ripened in the same carton in the importers' warehouses, ultimately reaching the retail trade in the same container. Standard boxes enabled ships to use their cubic capacity to better advantage, and a greater weight could be carried on each voyage. Warehouses, for the same reason, could hold more produce. Mechanical handling became practicable. The amount of waste vegetable matter transported was reduced.

The results of this development have been so far-reaching that virtually all the world's leading banana companies have adapted to it. Many of the smaller wholesalers, which did not adapt, have vanished.

Like all environmental change, technological developments can bring both problems and opportunity. Part of management's challenge of the future is to come to grips with technology so that their businesses continue to prosper.

Another example of the balancing of opportunity from various technological development is provided by the British Oxygen Company, although their story is little different from that of other oxygen manufacturers elsewhere in the world.

The manufacture of oxygen is itself a response to technological development. With the expansion of demand, in particular from new processes in the steel industry, there came a greater increase in the volume requirements of individual customers. The company developed its techniques to meet these needs: had they not done so some of the new uses of oxygen would not have developed because transport costs would have made the gas too expensive.

The original type of small gas cylinder is still in use, and meets the needs of many small-volume users. For the larger-volume user there is a tanker delivery service which pumps gas into storage tanks on the customer's own premises.

Very large customers may have an atmospheric gas plant structured on their own premises, so that BOC can supply oxygen without any transport problems. A logical development from this was the installation of oxygen grids – pipelines which connected large users of oxygen with one or more oxygen plants. In this way a back-up service was provided against plant breakdown; customers whose usage did not justify a separate plant could be connected to the grid, and economies of scale could be obtained from the operation of large plants.

The British Oxygen story illustrates the snowballing effect of technological change. Each successive development took place to meet a demand created by the development which preceded it.

Factors relating to infrastructure

For most businesses which operate in the developed world the infrastructure is not a major planning problem. The situation is different in underdeveloped countries, where what is happening to the infrastructure may be the determinant factor in deciding what strategies are viable, or even possible. Many years ago I worked on development planning in what is now Zimbabwe. The importance of infrastructure became clear to me through my experiences: helping to bring rail communications to a remote area of the country; seeing the effect of the lack of a road bridge at a particular point on the River Sabi on the ability of farmers to get their produce quickly and cheaply to market; and of preventing a planned new airfield from being built in a position which would have had the runway leading to a new sugar mill of some height, the foundations of which were about to be laid. At a very personal level, the lack of telephone communications to a remote agricultural research station nearly brought my career to an end. An intricate itinerary was set up at short notice for a government committee of enquiry, which involved many visits, and careful transport planning. I had them arriving by small plane at an airstrip some few miles from the research station, but had still to arrange things with the station itself. My assumption that they were on the phone suddenly became critically wrong. There was no time to write. Fortunately I tracked down a government department that had a radio link with the station, and got the problem resolved. But it left me with a much greater awareness of the importance of the infrastructure, and of the value of not taking things for granted when planning.

Ecological factors

A few years ago ecology would hardly have been considered as an environmental factor worthy of inclusion in a serious book on corporate planning. Two things have happened in recent years that change this viewpoint. The first is a greater understanding of the balance of nature and of the effect of human activity on this balance. Science and the growth of human population have long been known to change ecological factors: what is now understood is that many of the changes bring penalties as well as benefits. The coin has two sides. The second factor is a change in social attitudes, at least in Europe and the USA, which has created a certain amount of public awareness and concern for ecological factors. There is now an ever-increasing weight of public opinion against things which threaten the ecological balance; much of this opinion manifesting itself in positive attitudes against pollution. The knowledge and attitudes have been reinforced by major disasters: nuclear power in Russia; oil tankers breaking up in the USA and Europe; poison gas escaping from a chemical plant in India.

There are a number of ecological factors which have implications for business. Part of the world growth in population is caused by upsetting the existing balance. Live birth rates have increased and the average span of life extended because of the benefits of modern medicine. In the Western world rising standards of living have led to social attitudes which have brought about a reduction in the overall birth rate and therefore in family size. In underdeveloped countries economic factors have not improved, the corresponding social attitudes have not developed, and family size continues to remain high. The result is that the poor countries tend to become poorer, while on a total basis the world population threatens to outstrip its resources.

Areas of land are swallowed up under urban developments, or different agricultural patterns which permanently change the natural animal and plant life. The availability of water supplies is a problem which is becoming increasingly acute in many areas; although technology and science can overcome some of the ecological problems (including the purification of sea water), the 'cure' often leads to further ills.

Most large organisations and some smaller ones increasingly have to consider ecological factors. Although not every aspect will affect every organisation directly, organisations are finding that problems they had not expected now arise to confront them. Toyota is reputed to have caused traffic pollution and congestion because of the way it operated its just-in-time system of production, which caused streams of lorries to converge on its Japanese plants at predetermined times throughout the day. This caused them to change their procedures.

Not so very long ago the major ecological concern organisations might consider was pollution, and the main consideration was prevention at the factory. Where once the main concern may have been controlling factory emissions, our greater level of knowledge means that there is a concern over the products of those factories. In addition to ensuring that the users suffer no long-term ill-effects from the products, many now see a need to build ecological considerations into products, so that the overall chain of environmental damage is reduced. Wheeler and Sillanpää[7] give some examples:

- Rank Xerox launched a strategy in 1990 for the recovery, re-use and recycling of copiers. By 1995 the greater proportion of copiers and about half of cartridges in Europe were recovered. The company is working to a long-term aim of developing waste-free products in waste-free facilities.
- In Japan a 1995 survey by the Japan Environmentally Conscious Products (ECP) Committee found that 89 per cent of the companies polled were marketing some ecoproducts, so called because their production minimised energy use, reduced waste, or enabled material recycling.

Most people will be familiar with the 'green' products, such as detergents, which have appeared on supermarket shelves over the past decade.

More than any other factors, ecological considerations illustrate the way changes have affected other factors in the model in Figure 4.2. Society becomes more aware of the interconnection of pollution and health, concerned over global warming, disturbed over oil spills, oil rig disasters and other major incidents, and worried by the increasing number of revelations that what was previously considered safe is in fact hazardous. Politicians react, often under the stimulus of pressure groups, and new laws are passed to control the excesses. There are economic pressures for organisations to take action, and new opportunities for those creative enough to see them.

Ecological factors should be considered from a strategic as well as an operational viewpoint. There is the issue of the attitude to social responsibility taken by the organisation (see Chapter 8), the need to ensure that the capital consequences of ecological issues are properly considered, and that the reputation of the organisation is upheld. Many organisations also need policies for dealing with pressure groups and for taking a long-term view of the impact that such organisations may have on their businesses.

But ecological factors are not just a threat. They can be a source of new opportunity and growth.

Sociological factors

Society is in a continuous process of change. Attitudes rarely alter overnight, but the time span during which they do alter is usually relevant to the corporate strategic plan. Two examples from the UK may help show the fundamental nature of some of the changes.

1 In the 1960s smoking was the norm, and any non-smoker who complained about the fumes in an office was seen as abnormal. By the 1980s, the non-smokers were in the majority, and non-smoking offices becoming common. By the 1990s it was the person who wished to smoke at a business meeting who was atypical, and smoking was increasingly becoming prohibited on public transport. The smoker is now seen as anti-social, whereas a decade or so previously the non-smoker bore this label.
2 Nudity is now common in films and television broadcasts, and causes no offence to the majority of people. What is normal now would have caused an outcry not all that long ago.

Some of the trends are related to different life styles. 'Portfolio careers', working from home, high levels of home ownership all result in different patterns of life, and different attitudes to what is acceptable and respectable. In the 1970s a manager who was made redundant carried a stigma. He – and at that time it would have been a he – 'could not be any good otherwise someone else would have been chosen'. Two major recessions and a decade of structural changes as companies try to reduce costs to be globally competitive have meant that now no one thinks the worse of someone who has been the victim of these changes.

There are at least three ways in which social trends are important for strategic planning.

1 Markets are directly affected by social changes, in the design of products, the trends in market size, and the way people make their buying decisions.
2 Social changes often lead to legal changes. Thus there is an increasing amount of social and employment legislation in most developed countries.
3 Expectations which people hold are important for human resource planning. It would be wrong to claim that in the UK women without exception have equal career opportunities with men. However, prospects are better than they were in the past, and are improving as we move into the future. Many men now have a deep belief that women are as equally competent as men in management

positions, and many more are willing to think about the issue. Other attitudes that are important for HR planning include work ethics, willingness to accept authority, and identification with the need for economic success. Future plans depend heavily on the view of how attitudes such as these will change over the years.

The results of changes do more than affect markets and our human resource policies. They have a massive impact on how organisations are managed, and how leaders have to behave if they want to have any followers. The impact is on strategic management, and not just on planning.

Political factors

Close to social changes come politics. In a democracy there is a two-way cause-and-effect relationship between social attitudes and the policies of the various political parties. Each may change the other. Leadership is required from a prime minister, but woe betide any who lead from the front and are too far ahead. In other societies politics may come from the barrel of a gun, and policies may be determined through other motivations.

For the strategic planner, particularly when involved in global strategy or multicountry operations, the key issue is political stability. The prognosis for this will not be the same everywhere, and is an important area for study.

In a domestic situation the concern is the changes in policy, and thereafter legislation and decisions, which would follow a change in political fortunes of the various parties.

The observant reader will have noticed that the competitive environment has not been discussed here. This is because the approach to thinking about and analysing this is somewhat different from the other factors, and is dealt with at some length later when we look at strategy and strategic analysis.

All the above thoughts sketch only briefly the challenge that environmental factors offer to business. The outlines can only faintly be drawn in any generalised description: only the individual company itself can turn the hesitant pencil marks into a drawing that has meaning and value.

This chapter has outlined the challenge of the environment, which still leaves the planner with the practical problem of how to actually use environmental factors in planning. This is an aspect which is taken up in the next chapter.

References

1 Levitt, T., *Innovation in Marketing*, McGraw-Hill, New York, 1962.
2 Macdonald, A. M. (ed.), *Chambers's Twentieth Century Dictionary*, W. & R. Chambers, Glasgow, 1972.
3 Drucker, P. F., *Managing for Results*, Heinemann, London, 1964.

4 Lietner, B. A. 'Prepare Your Company for Inflation', *Harvard Business Review*, September/October 1970.
5 Hussey, D. E., *Corporate Planning in Inflationary Conditions*, Institute of Cost and Management Accountants, London, 1979.
6 Bernal, J. D., *Science in History*, Pelican, London, 1969.
7 Wheeler D. and Sillanpää, M., *The Stakeholder Corporation*, Pitman, London, 1997.

CHAPTER 5

The environment: assumptions in planning

Strategy often has to be decided on the basis of assumptions about the future. The importance of clarifying assumptions and making them explicit is the basis of this chapter, which also demonstrates the need for decisions in different parts of the organisation to have a common base of assumptions, and shows their importance in considering risk.

The importance of the business environment to the company was stressed in some detail in the previous chapter. Strategic planning is about coping with change and uncertainty. As Scott[1] states:

> Planning is a process of groping forward. The future is enveloped in fog which grows denser the further we try to peer. Prediction of future events and circumstances means grappling with the uncertainties looming in this fog, and trying to make incomplete and indirect information as intelligible as possible.

Strategic management's problem is not only demonstrating to managers that they must accept the challenge of the future but also finding a way of dealing with those half-perceived and moving shadows in the fog. While the challenge has been analysed in depth in many excellent books on corporate planning, marketing, or general management, the way of handling that challenge in a practical and workable fashion has received less attention.

The purpose of this chapter is to try to provide a framework to help the company move from a perception of its future environment to a method whereby this perception can become the basis of all long-range plans. The premiss from which to start is that the future is always uncertain, and that the most talented of planners or managers will never be in a position to foretell all that will affect the company. Planning is not an exercise in clairvoyance, and planners do not have secret arts or psychic knowledge: nor does their portfolio of management techniques include those of the mystic.

Rational plans can only be made from a firm base. If a company's future success depends on the continuance of exports to a certain country, a plan can only be made if the company reaches some sort of conclusion about whether or not that country will continue to allow imports. A marketing manager who sits back and says 'I don't know so I won't say anything' and then still expects manufacturing to meet all requirements in any eventuality is not planning, but trying to opt out.

Refusal to face up to a problem is hardly likely to persuade that problem to go away, and no rational plans can be completed in these circumstances.

Although no manager can predict a future event with guaranteed accuracy, any manager can determine a logical outcome of events if the prediction is correct. It becomes possible to make a sound plan based on *assumptions* about the future which will be valid for as long as the assumptions are valid. If these prove to be wrong, it may be necessary to modify the plans or sometimes to completely restructure them.

Van Dam[2] reports how CP International Inc. looked at the problem of production for Central America. The area was studied in detail and the conclusion was reached that there would be a move towards a Central American Common Market. This conclusion became an assumption on which a strategic plan could be prepared for the area.

An assumption may be defined as a statement of opinion about the occurrence of an event which is outside the control of the planner. This statement is treated as fact during the preparation of plans, although the company must never delude itself into believing that the assumption is an expression of a certainty. Assumptions themselves do not remove any uncertainty although they should be used in subsequent analysis and actions to reduce risk: their task is to enable objective thought to take place about the nature, shape, and size of those shadows in the fog, so actions can take place which have a rational basis.

Assumptions, besides providing a foundation for plans, also have a coordinating effect. It is very important for all those involved in the company to base their plan on common assumptions. Failure to do this can only result in chaos. For example, a marketing manager might prepare forecasts of demand for a product based on one set of economic assumptions – those costing the product might be working on another set. Demand and supply calculations are thus on different bases and may be wildly incompatible.

In addition, unless all plans are based on similar assumptions, it becomes impossible for a company to identify the effect on the company if assumptions prove incorrect.

This, then, is one of the first rules in the use of assumptions. They must be common to all areas of the company, even if an individual manager disagrees violently with them. A measure of self-discipline is required, and this is frequently difficult to achieve in practice since managers tend to be individualistic and like to back their own hunches.

The second rule is that only assumptions which really affect the company should be included in the plans. There is always a danger that a company will fall into the elephant trap of corporate self-delusion. Because it lists a hundred and one assumptions on each and every factor in the environment it believes that it is taking account of these factors in its plans. Too often it is dealing in dreams, and too often the assumptions could be completely reversed without making the slightest difference to any of the plans and forecasts. This is a situation to be avoided.

In practical terms this means that not only must various forecasts and predictions be made of the environment but that some form of screening process must be set up to select those factors which really do have an impact on the company. There are a number of ways in which this can be done. One method is for the planner, or other person charged with preparing the forecasts, to complete an analysis of what is thought likely to be relevant. A second approach is for groups of managers to be drawn together in 'think-tank' type meetings, so that a number of minds are brought to bear on the problem. In other companies it may be more appropriate to use a combination of both methods. Whatever the solution chosen, the problem is one which deserves a considerable amount of corporate thought: there can, too, be side-benefits which arise from the process, and I have been present at sessions such as this which have led to the identification of new opportunities.

Assumptions are required at both the strategic and operational planning level. For the strategic plan the assumptions are assessments of those events outside the control of the company itself: many of these will be carried forward to the operating plans. In addition, at operating level, there may be certain assumptions about events which are under the control of the company – that is, as far as any future event can be said to be under the control of anybody – but which are not controlled by the manager of the department completing the plan. For example:

1 An assumption by individual operational departments that capital will be available to support their plans within the general framework of the guidelines provided. Ultimate analysis and the completion of the strategic plan may prove that this is an untrue assumption, and some modification may be necessary.
2 For production the sales forecast may be a basic assumption. The achievement of this is outside of the control of production: their job is to provide for the manufacture of the items specified in the forecast for delivery at the time required. Unless the forecast is taken as a basic assumption, no planning can be undertaken.
3 A marketing assumption that a new product will prove to be acceptable even though it is only in an early stage of development.

What is unacceptable is for operating managers to try to evade their responsibilities by defining assumptions about actions which *are* under their control. I have seen plans which included statements like:

● 'I assume my forecasts are correct.'
● 'I assume that I will cut labour costs by 10 per cent.'
● 'I assume that my new products will be test-marketed on the date stated.'

Assumptions have a very important part to play in the analysis of decisions and the avoidance of risk. They have no part to play in the avoidance of responsibility. And even with the basic environmental assumptions their purpose is not to provide an excuse for failure but rather to lead to a complex network of alternative decisions which enable the company to change its strategies quickly so that it remains on-course despite adverse circumstances.

So far the discussion on the setting of assumptions is of methods most appropriate for the smaller companies or those which have a relatively narrow span of diversity of operation. Some modification becomes necessary when assumptions are being set by multinational companies or companies with many subsidiaries in widely diverse operations. Here it is necessary to divide assumptions into those which are required to be set centrally, because of a need to apply a common approach to a number of subsidiaries, and those which should be decentralised, being more properly the concern of the management of the subsidiary. Part of the solution will depend on the degree of autonomy allowed subsidiaries, but even where this is wide there will still remain some planning assumptions which should be standardised internationally.

Exactly what should go into which group of assumptions is a matter for individual decision which will vary from company to company. The criteria should be that assumptions of major significance which are common to more than one subsidiary should be centralised, as should assumptions about the world economy (as opposed to those about a particular country) and assumptions derived from technological forecasts which lead to decisions about the future of research and development activity. Some examples of assumptions relevant to each of these three different sets of circumstances may make the explanation a little clearer:

1 If a multinational company has subsidiaries in two Asia-Pacific countries each should use the same assumptions about the future of the regional trade agreements. (Similarly, European subsidiaries should have a common assumption about new entrants to the European Union.)
2 The total group should operate to one set of assumptions about changes in the relative exchange rates of various international currencies. If this is not done international coordination is likely to be a matter of juggling 'apples and pears' rather than an examination of real corporate value.
3 Basic policy for the future direction of research and development should be a central corporate decision regardless of the location of the research and development unit, although this does not mean that projects which fit within the defined policy have all to be decided centrally. A fundamental assumption on, for example, world food supplies which leads to research into new sources of food – such as biotechnology – should therefore be decided centrally.

In each and every case, provided that the coordination of the inputs does not become an overwhelming task, there may be participation by the local subsidiary in setting the assumption. But the final decision should be a central one.

Every company will face another problem area – the varying 'quality' of the assumption. In the previous chapter mention was made of environmental factors for which advanced warning was available – as in, for example, changes to the legal environment. Assumptions that these events will come about have a high degree of 'quality': they are not certainties, but they are as close to being certain as it is possible to get when considering any future event.

At the other extreme there are assumptions which are necessary although the company may have little or no information on which to base its judgements. This should not prevent assumptions from being made, for every company would make an implicit assumption even if it did not state what this was (usually this is what is happening today will continue to happen tomorrow). There are many advantages in defining this type of assumption explicitly. Even if it is subsequently proved to be wrong, the company knows that it is wrong and that certain changes are overdue in its strategy.

In between there are varying degrees of 'quality' in assumptions, stretching from those derived from data that respond well to statistical analysis (e.g. medium-term population changes) to assumptions which can only be a matter of informed judgement. The next chapter will deal with certain techniques which can be used to improve forecasting (and therefore the quality of assumptions), but it must not be forgotten that there will always be many areas where an assumption has to be defined from very scanty data.

The sensible company will look very closely at the type of decisions made on low-quality assumptions. The less certain an event is, the more risk of failure there is likely to be in strategies which depend on it: some decisions might be rejected purely because the company does not have enough confidence on the assumption on which success depends. But there is much more to decision analysis than this, and we are anticipating later sections of this book.

Every company will also have to decide between what environmental studies are possible, and how much it can afford to spend. More and more effort can often be applied to enable more accurate assumptions to be developed, which in turn will lead to more effective decisions. Regular sources of data can be supplemented by special research studies, by complicated forecasting models, or by a massive investment in technological forecasting. For the multinational company the problem becomes more complex. It may be reasonable to make a comprehensive study of all factors for one or two countries. Is it necessarily reasonable to give the same attention to ten countries, or twenty countries, or to the whole world? Deciding where to sacrifice quality in making assumptions is just one of the many management tasks involved in a process of strategic management.

In effect, there is a corollary with what was stated earlier. Not only must factors be screened so that the irrelevant is rejected: the key areas must be identified and more attention given to making assumptions about these areas than any of the other possibilities. For example, a company engaged in food manufacture, processing large volumes of commodity raw materials, is likely to need to spend as much effort on making accurate assumptions about these as it does on factors influencing the market for its own products.

At this point it is worth mentioning that there are organisations which regularly publish environmental information, and others make forecasts of future trends. For example, in the UK the Registrar-General publishes population forecasts; there are a number of commercial organisations, such as the Economist Intelligence Unit Ltd. and Henley Centre for Forecasting; bodies such as the National Institute of Economic and Social Research; and a growing output of technological forecasts from a variety of sources. These may not make the task of setting planning assumptions easy, but they certainly make it easier.

Exhibit 5.1 Impact of the environment on an industry

Until 1986 the New Zealand footwear industry had protection through the customs tariff, and controls which limited imports to 18 per cent of the domestic market. Shoes were expensive, and the protection ensured that the industry was profitable. The protective regime began to be dismantled, with the aim of driving the local industry to become competitive against world standards.

By 1994 imports had penetrated to 72 per cent of the market. Now, the largest importer is a cut-price national retail chain which holds 30 per cent of the New Zealand market, and has ambitions to expand. Many manufacturers had operated their own retail outlets, and some have become importers.

International companies such as Bata and Clarks left the industry, as did a number of domestic firms. Although all businesses had access to the information about the impending change, not all reacted to it with any change in strategy. Some took a long time to perceive the implications of the situation. One manager said 'Something has to hit you before you realise ... when half the shoe factories are closing down over a year or so, when your own production drops from 3,000 pairs a week to about 800 pairs ...'

About thirty companies continue to make shoes, and are mainly those who assessed the situation and changed how they operated their businesses in order to succeed in the market. This new perception was partly due to the fact that many of the surviving companies had nowhere else to go. It was a question of finding a new way to operate, or lose the majority of their capital. Obviously, not all firms follow exactly the same strategy, but some of the features that seem to be common to the more successful of the survivors are:

- A switch from high-volume, low-priced products, where Asian producers had a great cost advantage.
- Stringent economic appraisal of all costs and all products. For many firms this included considerable retrenchment and improved efficiency, for example the introduction of CADCAM.
- The exodus of so many firms meant that it was possible to purchase modern shoemaking machinery at bargain prices, and many of the survivors benefited.
- In the short term it was possible to recruit the best people from the industry, although the reduction in size of the industry also means a long-run reduction in the skill base.
- More attention to the niches within a segmented industry.
- Diversifying into other leather products.
- Manufacturing for competitors to increase volumes.
- Increased attention to the design of footwear.

(*Source*: Harfield and Hamilton, 'Retreat from Volume:Strategies in a Declining Industry', *Strategic Change*, 6, No. 4, 1997)

Scott[1] suggests that the process of setting assumptions can be divided into three stages. First, there are the *initial assumptions*. At this stage in planning little may be known about the subject, and educated guesses may be used to form the bases of planning assumptions. These are really on trial, and are imposed so that corporate strategy may develop while further work examines the validity of the assumption.

Initial assumptions next move to the *working assumption* stage. Here further analysis and development take place, and those assumptions which are still valid and useful are used further in the planning process.

The last classification is *final assumptions*. These are those assumptions which find their way into the final written plan. Along the way their validity may be re-examined, so that what results is the most relevant and valid set of assumptions that the company can prepare. Scott makes the practical point that the written plan should only include those assumptions which are needed to use the plan or to understand the plan as a whole. The myriad minor assumptions which may have been used at various working stages in the planning process should be omitted from the final document.

So far only one use of assumptions in corporate planning has been discussed: clearly defined assumptions as a prerequisite for any form of logical and rational planning. By itself this use would justify the effort put into this aspect of planning, especially as it carries the side-benefit that environmental study also leads to the spotting of new opportunities. In addition to this, assumptions are very important tools which, used with skill and craftmanship, can help the company to weigh the chances of success in its favour. In effect they can be used to bias the corporate dice, so that some of the risk is removed from the throwing of it, that it may more often yield the high numbers.

It is probably fair to say that many companies do not get the maximum benefit out of their use of assumptions, and many still stop at the first and most obvious use. The majority produce 'one-point' plans: that is, plans which contain only one set of strategic forecasts leading to one estimated result. If a fundamental assumption fails, the plan fails. Plans such as this are likely to be somewhat inflexible. This need not be so.

Assumptions should instead be used in a number of positive ways as the basis for understanding the nature of the risks the company faces and for actions which eliminate or reduce those risks. This is not always easy, and in practical terms may be a planning refinement which comes only with the second or third planning cycle, but the methods will repay careful attention.

The subject of risk and sensitivity analysis will appear in more detail later in this book, for there are techniques which are worth using and these have a wider use than in conjunction with assumptions alone. Some things need to be said now because the sensitivity of various strategies based on key assumptions must be considered before it is possible to analyse ways of using assumptions to reduce risk.

Part of the key to risk analysis was given earlier in this chapter when the quality of assumptions was discussed, and in stressing the need to assess the importance of the assumption to the company. Good planning requires management to look closely at the effects a wrong assumption would have on the strategies selected: first, to quantify the effect of error, and, second, to assess the probability of error. It is always a good idea to look at the best and the worst which might happen. A large adverse effect is patently more worrying than a small one.

In making decisions based on assumptions it is often easy to forget that they are not firm facts. The importance of quantifying the effect of wrong assumptions cannot be overstressed. In general terms a situation where a wrong assumption would bankrupt the company is to be avoided, even when the probability of a wrong assumption is fairly low. At the other end of the scale, a company may tolerate an assumption with a fairly high risk of failure if the total effect of failure on profits is small. (It must not be overlooked that there are alternative strategic choices possible from one assumption, each with its own pattern of risks of success or failure: this point is made use of later.)

Assessing probabilities can be a complex task and is sometimes impossible in any scientific way. However, it is always possible for any manager to assess 'betting odds' on any assumption he or she uses, and for corporate management to reach some measure of agreement on the 'betting odds' of the chances of any proving to be true. Although this part of exercise may not be justifiable mathematically, it has the effect of helping managers to accept that part of their difficult task as managers is to make decisions in conditions of uncertainty.

For the time being the difficulties of sensitivity and risk analysis will be passed over and attention focused on other important uses of assumptions – the reduction of risk.

Risk may be positively reduced in three ways:

1 Choice of strategies with lower adverse effects if assumptions are wrong
2 Contingency plans
3 Hedging actions

The first of these is part of the process of strategic decision making, and is an extension of what has already been said. Where a strategy would bring the risk of the complete collapse of the company should its base assumptions prove incorrect, it is eminently sensible to choose an alternative. Although the alternative may have a lower earning potential, the effect in case of failure may be far less disastrous. It is, of course, this form of reasoning which leads to test marketing and other forms of experimental marketing research to try alternative strategies before making irreversible decisions to implement them.

Another example is provided in a backwards integration situation. On the basic assumptions sales forecasts may be developed, for the ultimate product, and it is possible to envisage a situation where it appears profitable to integrate backwards and to provide all the necessary raw materials. Closer consideration of risk might indicate that a better decision would be to produce, for example, only 60 per cent of each raw material, buying the rest from other sources. In this way demand can fall heavily before the plant producing the raw materials is in any way affected. The acknowledgement of the risk element inherent in any decision which affects the future may take the company down a completely different strategic path. This path may meander more than any other, but if it avoids the pitfalls and hazards of the direct route, the extra effort expended is well worth while.

This key use of assumptions in strategy has further relevance in another area – contingency planning. However much work a company has put into its assumptions, however much faith it has that the assumptions will prove to be correct, there is still an element of uncertainty. The man who turns up at his railway station to catch his morning train to work does so on the assumption that, even if his train does not run, there will be another train to catch. If he has caught a train at this time every working day for the past twenty-five years, he may reasonably assume that there will be a train today. Yet his assumption may be wrong: there may have been a strike, a train crash, the collapse of a bridge, a landslide, or many other such chance events. If he is a careful man he will have already made his contingency plan for just such an eventuality, and have worked out an alternative way of reaching his destination.

In ideal circumstances every strategy would have a portfolio of alternative or contingency plans which can be swung into action in the event of the failure of an assumption. These may vary from contingency plans which enable the continued pursuit of a basic strategy to complete alternative strategies into which the company may move without losing stride as it follows a new path to its objectives. Circumstances are seldom ideal. Companies can only very rarely afford the work to develop a comprehensive portfolio of alternatives which may never be used, and in practice it is usually necessary to concentrate on a few key areas, where failure would have a significant effect.

A leading British food wholesaler and importer distributed most of its products from the port of importation to its chain of depots by a rail-container system. This was the most economic form of transport for its particular situation. All its forward plans were based on the assumption that the rail service would not be upset by strikes, industrial unrest, or labour disputes. Indeed, the rational planning of marketing activities and depot requirements would have been impossible under any other assumption. At the same time the company was not blind to the fact that the assumption might be wrong, and that rail services might be disrupted on a short-term basis. For this reason it also had a contingency plan – a plan for a complete alternative distribution service which could be put into effect almost instantaneously. This plan was fully documented and attempted to foresee – and plan for – every adverse effect of rail disruption which might occur, including failures in the postal service.

Those British companies which had prepared contingency plans to cope with a failure of postal services generally fared better in the last major British postal strike than the many firms which gave the matter no thought at all until *after* the strike had begun.

It would, of course, be wrong to imply that contingency plans could be developed for all risks. There are many that have to be faced without any fallback position. It is nevertheless true that many organisations do not give enough attention to this aspect of planning.

The food wholesaler provided a short-term contingency plan to meet an operational difficulty. An example of contingency planning at the strategic level comes from a former government agency of what was then called Rhodesia.

The Sabi–Limpopo Authority is a statutory body which was set up to coordinate and expand a major irrigation development scheme which would ultimately irrigate 600 000 acres. Much of the development which had already been effected, and much of that planned, was based on sugar, on the assumption that 'moderate' prices would obtain. This assumption was made at the time of the 1963/4 situation of unusually high prices. At the same time, although sugar was the key strategy, both private developers and government had devoted some effort to examine other alternative crops. After UDI, the Rhodesia's export sugar market vanished under the onslaught of United Nations' sanctions. Thus the base assumption proved false. Without any major difficulty the Sabi-Limpopo Authority changed an entire estate, which was being set up for sugar, over to wheat. The alternative strategy was ready and was capable of speedy implementation.

A development of this train of thought has been the use of scenarios for strategic planning. These provide a number of complete views of possible future states combining networks of assumptions, and strategies are developed to meet each. This provides an opportunity to compare different possible strategic paths, to assess the degree of commonality of variance between strategies, and leads to conscious decisions to build in flexibility into the plans (see Chapter 3).

Hedging actions have been practised since business began, and may often be a legitimate way of avoiding risk when assumptions prove to be incorrect. For example, for many years UK corporate planners had to forecast whether – and if so when – the UK would enter the EC, when not even governments knew the answer. Even where a company planned on the assumption that the UK would not enter, it frequently made sense to 'hedge', to establish business with the EC countries that would stand the company in good stead even if it were wrong.

A similar problem is facing not only British organisations but also foreign companies considering investments in the UK in 1997. Will European Monetary Union go ahead on schedule, and will the UK join in with the first wave, or even at all? Although this would affect all businesses, it is of so great a concern to financial institutions that forethought, hedging actions and contingency plans must be on the agenda of such companies.

Perhaps the last thing that should be said on the subject of assumptions is that it is very, very easy for the expected results to be taken as truth and the underlying assumptions forgotten. An assumed happening very quickly takes on the character of a sacred oath: the fact that it *is* only assumed vanishes with a rapidity which would do credit to any stage magician's sleight of hand. This is something which every manager must beware of, and one of the most effective ways of doing this is to establish a system of monitoring, revision, and control which constantly keeps the company aware of the changing validity of its assumptions. This subject is taken up again in Chapter 12.

The whole process of setting planning assumptions calls for much creative corporate thought. It is a task which should not be skimped, for failure to put adequate effort into planning at this stage may bring all the subsequent plans tumbling down like a house of cards. The key to flexible plans often lies in the assumption stage: it is a key which helps the company open many of the barriers which lie between its present position and its future objectives. Yet it is a key which remains invisible to many of those engaged on the planning task.

References

1 Scott, B. W. *Long Range Planning in American Industry*, American Management Association, 1962.
2 Van Dam, A. 'Corporate Planning for Asia, Latin America and Africa', paper presented to the International Conference of Corporate Planners, Montreal, 9 December 1971.

CHAPTER 6

Forecasting

Managers make forecasts all the time, although many are implicit rather than explicit. The aim of this chapter is to review the main forecasting methods that are available, and to show what should be considered in choosing the best method for a particular situation. Examples of composite forecasts are provided, which have the added value of demonstrating some of the trends which face modern business.

Forecasting is not the same as planning, although a plan may be based on certain forecasts: for example, of some of the environmental factors discussed earlier. One of the byproducts of a plan may be a forecast of the results that will be attained if it is implemented. So forecasts may be both part of the raw material of planning and a manifestation of its outcome.

All forecasts deal with matters of uncertainty – a point which has already been discussed – and the more this uncertainty can be reduced, the better the chance a company has of planning the right decisions. Although we have already seen (Chapter 2) that too much stress on the accuracy of results may reduce the value of planning, the same cannot be said of environmental forecasts which cause the company to commit resources to achieve a particular plan.

Any person may make a forecast and, indeed, every person does from time to time. The method of forecasting may vary from a blind guess, through informed judgement, to the use of a more scientific approach. Some forecasting techniques are very complicated, and it is easy to fall into the trap of believing that complexity is beneficial for its own sake: simple methods may often be the most cost-effective.

Marshall,[1] the great English economist, had a word of sense to say about an approach to economics when in 1898 he wrote: 'It is doubtless true that much of this work has less need of elaborate scientific methods than of a shrewd mother wit, a sound sense of proportion and a large experience of life.' The same might be said about approaches to forecasting.

Some writers on the subject distinguish between a forecast, a prediction, a projection, and an anticipation, but as there is little common agreement on the use of these terms, no attempt is made here to assign particular meanings to the words.

The product life cycle

One concept which is of value in many forecasting situations is that of the product life cycle. This suggests that all products pass through a series of growth curves (the first part of which is S-shaped), until they reach a point when they either level out or begin to decline. The concept is illustrated in Figure 6.1.

Figure 6.1
Product life-cycle curve

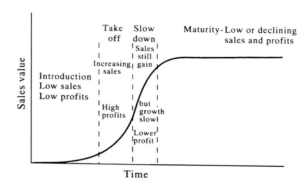

The curve begins with a period of low sales and low profits as the new product is introduced to the market. This is followed by a period of take-off associated with rapidly increasing sales and relatively high profits: the period during which the product is gaining acceptance and has little competition. At this stage any competitive activity tends to increase the total market. At the same time unit costs are lower because the benefits of increasing scale of production are achieved.

By the third stage the rate of growth has slowed considerably as more competitors enter the market and as, in any case, it becomes more difficult to increase sales penetration. The additional expenditure to increase sales and to meet competitive activity reduces the profit per unit (although it may still increase in total).

The product moves to maturity, where it has a situation of low or declining sales growth and a fall-off in profitability. Yet another final stage may result, where the product declines rapidly to obscurity.

One forecasting problem can be seen from a study of Figure 6.1. A statistical projection made at any one of the stages of the life-cycle curve would have resulted in a completely wrong forecast (this can be seen by imaging a trend line at each stage).

The second forecasting problem is that the time span of the life cycle might be months, years, or decades. This is further complicated by the fact that actions may be taken accidentally or deliberately to extend the product life cycle, and thus distort the expected pattern. Levitt[2] gives an example of various stages in the life cycle of oil:

(a) Crude oil as a medicine.
(b) Paraffin for lighting.

108

(c) Paraffin for space heating.
(d) Petrol for internal combustion engines.
(e) Oil for central heating.
(f) Petrochemical industry.

Such actions to alter the shape of the life cycle may be taken by a company: in fact one aspect of strategy might be to do just this. Shape may be altered by the introduction of actions to extend the cycle (e.g. the introduction of a successful ethical pharmaceutical product as an 'over-the-counter' product supported by promotion). Alternatively, action may be taken to lengthen each phase of the cycle by changing the rate at which things happen: for example by heavy advertising, or changes in price. Kotler[3] provides an extensive analysis of marketing strategies that are applicable at various stages of the life cycle.

Figure 6.2 shows a 'real' product life cycle from an analysis of the demand for hydraulic cranes over a ninety-year period carried out by Saunders and Smith.[4] This is a good illustration of the fact that the cycle may last many years and that it will show some deviations from the theoretical pattern.

Figure 6.2
Modified life cycle. Hydraulic cranes from Armstrong's Elswick Works. Reprinted by permission from an article by Saunders and Smith[4]

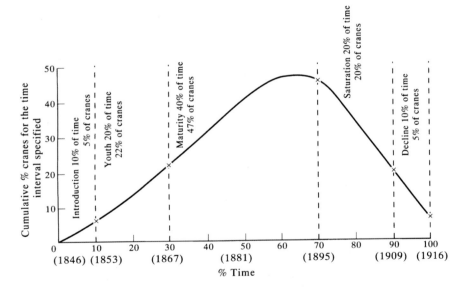

Statistical projections

There are a number of techniques which provide a projection of a statistical series into the future and which rely entirely on analysis of the series. They are based on the assumption that past performance will be a guide to the future.

Whether such an assumption is correct depends, of course, on many factors, including the age of the product, the point reached in its life cycle, and the length of time for which the forecast is made. There are many methods which are very valuable for short-term forecasts of a few months, but which are rarely accurate beyond this.

One use of these methods is to gain perspective: to see where a trend *might* lead. If this projected position is patently impossible the forecaster will have learnt something about the data.

(i) Simple growth pattern

A commonly used method of forecasting is based on the average annual growth rate calculated over a period, simply worked out by expressing the latest year as an index of the earliest and working out the growth rate from a book of compound interest tables. Variations on this theme include allowing for erratic movements in the data or in a typical year. It may also be postulated that the expected change is a particular percentage of the previous growth rate.

(ii) Moving averages

A moving average is a method of eliminating regular seasonal or cyclical patterns from the data to indicate the underlying smoothed trend. (Having calculated the trend, it then becomes possible to eliminate it statistically, to enable a study to be made of the seasonal factors.) Each point in the moving average is the mean of a number of consecutive points of the series: the number of data points is chosen by judgement to give the period which best eliminates the seasonal irregularities. The average used may be the arithmetic or geometric means, or the median.

Moving averages are rarely useful for long-term forecasts. One of their disadvantages is that they always fall short of the actual data available: any projection has to cover not only the future but also some of the past.

(iii) Exponential smoothing

Another technique for short-term forecasting, which has a particular value for inventory and production control systems, is exponential smoothing. The method is based on a moving average which is exponentially weighted so that the more recent data is given a greater weighting, and that the past forecasting error is taken into account in each successive forecast. A full description of the method is given by Coutie et al.[5] Statistical confidence limits may also be calculated.

A more sophisticated variant of exponential smoothing is the Box–Jenkins method which is even more accurate in short-term forecasting (up to three months).

(iv) Mathematical trends

A number of mathematical formulae are available for calculating a trend line in a time series and extending this line to some future point. The simplest, and often a valuable starting position, is to fit a line on a graph by eye, using a ruler so that the area on the graph under the trend line is approximately equal to the area above it.

By eye alone the line of 'best fit' is difficult to place exactly, but may be calculated mathematically by the method of least squares. An indication of the likely validity of a least squares trend line as a method for predicting the future trend of a series of data can be obtained using the Cartesian coordinate method. This will reveal whether the data has any correlation or if it is completely dissociated. A full description of these methods will be found in most books on elementary statistics, e.g. Moroney.[6]

There are many other methods, including logarithms, square roots, and ways of fitting a curvilinear trend. All these methods have value in medium- and long-term forecasting, but give little indication of turning points in the data. Thus in the product life-cycle diagram, it is probable that the methods would be useful during much of the time for each period in the curve, but would lose their validity each time there is a change in shape to a new period of the cycle.

Marketing and market research methods

When thinking about forecasting it is very easy to concentrate on mathematics and operational research and to forget some of the other time-tested methods which are used continuously by practising managers. Many of these methods may be grouped under the heading of marketing and marketing research and include experimental marketing, special surveys, comparative studies, and similar approaches. Even a relatively routine piece of market research is used as a minor forecasting tool: assuming that the information gathered when the fieldwork was carried out a few weeks ago is still valid when decisions are based on the report.

(i) Comparative studies

A useful forecasting method is to examine the performance of something similar to the item being forecast. For example, a company launching a new proprietary pharmaceutical, say a cough cure, might well study the price, promotion, and progress of other types of proprietary products introduced in the previous five years. An analogy might be derived from the performance of these similar products, which can be of value in predicting the likely results of the new item about to be launched.

Similar analogies may be drawn from studies of promotional expenditures and market performance of competitive or similar products. Methods such as these may be used to give a greater understanding of the forecasting situation, thus enabling forecasts by other methods to be interpreted intelligently. In some cases the analogy may be drawn against performance in another country.

Many forecasters find it valuable to use past performance in the USA as a guide to future performance in the UK. It is not only sales and market forecasts which may be compared in this way but similar events. For example, those forecasting the effects of decimalisation in the UK learnt from experiences in South Africa and Australia.

(ii) Leading indicators

The leading indicator should, more correctly, be classified as an economic research method, except that it seems to have some similarities with the comparative studies mentioned above. A leading indicator is an event which always precedes an event of another type, thus giving a prior warning of change. Thus an economic output figure for the building industry might be used as an indicator for other economic activity. Forward attendance bookings at management seminars, or figures of executive advertisements, may also give an advance indication of general movement in the economy. It is essentially a tool for forecasting the short term.

(iii) Experimental market research

Under this heading I include all marketing tests designed to yield information that can be used to assess the profitability of the proposed move and to give quantitative data that may be used for forecasting. If the experiments are well designed and properly controlled, so that they measure what they were intended to measure, valuable information can be yielded which can be extended from the test area to a wider universe. Examples of such experiments are test-market operations, advertising weighting experiments, price experiments, and marketing methods: an example of the last is a telephone-selling operation which could be tested in a small area before a decision was made to change.

The disadvantage of such tests is that a true experiment eliminates all variables except the one being measured: this is not always possible in practice. In addition, the experimental area is rarely a replica in miniature of the whole country. Nevertheless, much useful data may be collected: at worst this enables the company to be more accurate about the probability of success or failure (a product which fails in test market is most unlikely to succeed on a national basis); at best it provides a means of making simple forecasts and of providing data on causal relationships which can be used for more complex forecasting models.

(iv) Intention-to-buy surveys

These may be used for both consumer and industrial goods. There are two main uses: first, for gaining information about proposed new products, and, second, to calculate an index for existing products, on a regular basis, which can be related to actual performance, thus providing a predictive index for forecasting future sales. Occasionally, with industrial products where there are few customers, these data may be reliable enough to be used raw.

The use of such surveys in connection with new products is usually part of wider concept work, and leads to the design of market tests rather than firm forecasts.

(v) Marketing judgement

There are many occasions when few or no data exist on which to base a forecast of a product or environmental event, but where the knowledge and experience of the company's employees can be called upon, or when common sense can be used to forecast bands of possible results based on some other data.

New products are among the most difficult of forecasting problems. It is frequently possible to keep the forecasts within the bounds of possibility if various likely, reasonable, and impossible parameters are set up in connection with some other data. For example, the total number of households is known. A company planning to launch a new food snack may make initial working forecasts based on:

Likely: each household buys one packet per month.
Reasonable: each household buys one packet per fortnight.
Impossible: each household buys two packets per week.

This sort of exercise depends a great deal on assumptions, many draw heavily on desk research and in-house surveys, and although it suffers from many disadvantages is considerably better than just guessing.

McCarthy[7] provides a further example of quantifying 'judgement' in his procedure for building a subjective demand curve. This probes the judgement of key executives by asking what quantity they believe they could sell at various prices, and enables a theoretical demand curve to be derived. Kotler[3] gives further insight.

(vi) Other surveys

Marketing research can also provide much information which can be used in forecasting situations. A consumer usage and attitude survey might well be used to identify the dynamics of demand, which in turn may be used in forecasts or marketing models. Cause and effect are not always easy to identify. For example, in the UK cars are polished more frequently where the owners do not have garages. Is this because they have no garages and give extra protection this way – in which case it might be a predictive tool? Or is it that people without garages tend to belong to a grouping who for other reasons polish their cars more frequently?

Analytical forecasts and models

Some of the most exciting forecasting techniques require complicated econometric and mathematical skills before they can be applied. They may draw heavily on market surveys, economic research, and desk studies for valid explanations and assumptions which may be incorporated into the forecasting model. Although most of the earlier statistical forecasting techniques can be calculated manually, these more complex models rely heavily on the computer. One forecast may require many thousand calculations: possible in theory without using a computer, but hardly practicable.

(i) Regression analysis

The advantage of the regression analysis technique is that it explores the mathematical relationships of other variables with the one being studied and relates this data into a joint equation. Variables selected for this analysis must have a causal relationship – completely unrelated data, although it might well fit statistically, cannot yield meaningful results.

Parker and Seguara[8] argue that:

> Regression is more powerful than subjective estimation because it enables the forecaster to measure explicitly the apparent association between variables over time, thus eliminating a large portion of the guesswork. If the user finds a statistical association between the level of growth in sales and the movement of four or five other variables, then this relationship becomes the basis of the forecast itself.

Although variables are examined statistically, their initial identification as possible influence factors is a matter of judgement. Market surveys may help to identify related factors although such identification is of most value when it is possible to obtain a number of years of history for each variable.

The strength of the regression analysis method is that it provides a rational way of using management judgement. A marketing manager might believe that the market for a product is influenced by changes in, for example, the adult population, disposable income, the building of new houses, industry promotional expenditure, and the average daily temperature. Regression analysis provides the means of identifying and using for forecasting purposes those factors which are statistically significant. As with all forecasts that rely on past data, the implicit assumption is that past relationship will continue: as with all forecasts, this may not be true.

(ii) Economic models

An economic model is an attempt to represent, in mathematical terms, the interdependent relationships of a number of variables which affect a particular activity. Models may be built to forecast numerous fields of activity, e.g. sales, market performance, the economy, commodity prices.

Such models may be very complex, and may be built to take account of all known factors which have a causal relationship with the item being forecast. Thus a sales forecast would, in addition to the factors causing demand, take account of all the other factors in the distribution system, such as inventory levels.

Apart from the mathematical skills, an econometric model builder needs to be able to identify and understand the causal factors which have a bearing on his or her forecast. Gathering the necessary data is often of itself a complex task; information is seldom available exactly as the model builder would like it. A decision to build a model can bring a requirement for considerable economic and marketing research.

(iii) Input–output analysis

The first national input–output table was published by W. W. Leontieff in 1937. Originally developed on a national basis to show the inter-industry flow of goods and services in the total economy, these tables have now been developed as a means of studying a company or a market.

Every industry appears twice in the table – once as an input and once as an output. The table shows what flows of inputs must occur to produce a certain flow of outputs: thus causal relationships may be explored, provided sufficient care and attention has been given to constructing the table in the first place. A change in output of the motor-vehicle industry would, for example, require inputs from the iron and steel industry. This input is the output of this industry, and, in turn, causes a demand for inputs from other industries.

Most countries now produce input–output tables to reflect past economic performance. A number of agencies have also produced tables relating to the future, which incorporate forecasts from different industries and economic sectors. For the normal company an effective input–output table can be a very expensive tool to develop, and the additional benefit conferred by such a model would need careful study against its cost.

Combination forecasts

Many forecasts are arrived at by combining forecasts of numerous variables. This is a situation met in many common business situations: for example, a forecast of results to be expected from a capital expenditure project. Such a forecast would be a composite of forecasts of sales of various products, production and distribution costs, and capital expenditure. In addition, the analysis would call for a forecast of corporation tax rates.

A similar composite approach may be used in other situations, e.g. forecasting the economy.

Technological forecasting ('futures')

The term 'technological forecasting' has come to be applied to a group of techniques which have been developed in recent years. In fact this is something of a misnomer, for the techniques are used in many forecasting situations as well as the future state of technology: they may be as useful for forecasting social patterns and economic activity as for suggesting new products and approaches to their manufacture.

Unfortunately many of the practitioners of technological forecasting have thrown a semantic smokescreen around their subject, coining words that have no meaning to the manager who is expected to base decisions on the results of those forecasts. There is also an aura of mystique around methods which purport to give forecasts of what will happen twenty to thirty years hence. My view is that a technological forecast should be interpreted not so much as a prediction of what *will* happen, but as an indication of what is possible and which can therefore be made to happen. Used in this sense it can be seen as a major contributor to strategic decisions, helping the company to choose its commitments to the future from a more rational base. It has particular relevance in research and development strategies, particularly those with a long time span, and for major capital investment decisions such as the siting and nature of a new airport.

It is by no means new for an entrepreneur to have a sense of vision which shapes all his or her strategies, and many of the world's biggest companies started with little more than determination, a willingness to work, and a dream. Similarly, judgement forecasts about any event have always been (and probably always will be) a feature of the management scene: they have already been discussed in this chapter. Many of the techniques of technological forecasting systemise and improve some of the vision and judgement. They provide a framework for assessing the logical interrelationships of isolated forecasts: they provide a means of combining the judgement of many experts. Frequently they present the decision makers with a number of alternative futures to give a measure of choice and control over their own future.

There are now a number of techniques grouped under the broad heading of technological forecasting. The use of many of these is becoming more widespread, and there are now a number of institutes and commercial companies in both Europe and the USA which specialise in 'futurology'. Many of the studies, by bodies such as the Club of Rome, on the future availability of the world's sources have been given wide publicity and are publicly available.

(i) Delphi technique

Perhaps one of the best-known techniques is Delphi, which has the advantage that it can be organised fairly inexpensively and may be carried out by post. Essentially the technique is the use of a panel of experts to forecast future events or developments through a sequence of questionnaires. Results of one questionnaire are used to produce the next, and each expert is made aware of any additional information about actual developments which is contributed by any of the other experts. Successive questionnaires also show to each expert the extent to which his or her opinion differs from the others. They are given the opportunity of modifying or adding to their first statements, and to show how far they agree with aspects of opinion which are additional to their own.

Many Delphi studies are carried out entirely by postal questionnaire, and the experts never come into contact with each other; all contact is through a coordinator. The selection of the panel is a matter of some importance, for the identification of genuine experts is often a matter of difficulty. One approach used in a long-range study of medicine, is reported by Teeling-Smith[9] as an 'expanding nucleus' technique. As experts were identified they were invited to suggest other qualified people who could serve on the panel. From a small beginning with 'people from different fields of medicine and from the pharmaceutical industry – selected on a personal basis because they were known to have expert knowledge and to be generally forward looking', eighty experts were identified from which a panel of fifty from various parts of the world was constructed.

The advantage of the Delphi technique is that it stimulates creative thinking and corrects the bias of individual personal judgement without swinging to the other extreme of domination by majority opinion. The questionnaire usually is designed in such a way that it forces a quantified answer: for example, the percentage of households with two cars at a certain date or the probability of an event happening by a certain time.

Some Delphi studies invite the chosen expert to consult with other people he knows when formulating his opinions. Others ask the experts to leave blank questions which they feel they are not personally competent to answer. It is also possible to build in a weighting system into the answers, so the opinion of those most competent to judge is given more attention than that of those with less knowledge on that particular question.

The relative ease of conducting a Delphi study, and the current vogue for pronouncements about the future, have led to a large harvest of published Delphi studies about practically every topic under the sun. Unfortunately, it is not always easy to separate the tares from the grain, and many of the studies have little positive value.

(ii) Scenarios

A scenario is an attempt to describe a sequence of events which demonstrate how a particular goal might be reached. For example, a number of exercises have been carried out extrapolating various trends which would lead ultimately to the destruction of the world. The scenario technique might take this as background, postulate an alternative state of affairs which is to be preferred, and identify the various actions which have to be taken over time to reach this preferred goal. Scenario writing is a creative exercise which attempts to correlate various necessary actions and their effect on each other, and to assign a time scale to these. It is very much a forecast of the possible.

As scenario writing is creative, it benefits from the involvement of several people. It is possible to use the technique in a much narrower area than the future of the world discussed above: for example, a number of alternative developments of a particular technology might be postulated, and experts asked to write scenarios showing what implications the developments will have.

Scenarios may also be used in conjunction with other techniques: for example, to provide the questions which are to be incorporated into a Delphi study.

(iii) Impact analysis

In many ways only a branch of scenario writing, this technique concentrates on the impact which various forecast technological developments might have on particular industries. Where the scenario shows a route to a goal, impact analysis concentrates on analysing the effects of an expected development which may or may not be desired. The analysis provides the company with the opportunity of spotting opportunities or taking avoidance action where appropriate.

(iv) Extrapolative techniques

There are a number of extrapolative techniques of technological forecasting which have an obvious link with general economic forecasting. They are based on the study of technological trends and their extrapolation into the future.

For example, it is possible to plot the development of a particular end-use over a span of years, setting up a graph with an efficiency rating on the vertical axis and time on the horizontal. The end-use might result from a number of different technologies. It is possible to imagine such a graph plotting the development of military weapons: the efficiency index might be the weapon's destructive ability.

On this imaginary graph it is possible to plot our first weapon, stones, and one of our latest, H-bombs. In between are swords, spears, bows and arrows, guns, bombs, and many more. Each successive development showing a great increase in destructive ability, and occurring in an ever-decreasing time span. Thus the past is established in a series of points through which a trend line may be fitted. The next step is to extrapolate the trend to a likely new technological development and its position on the efficiency scale, although one hesitates to forecast anything more destructive than the H-bomb even as an imaginary exercise.

The technique has many faults, although its validity is improved when applied to a genuine problem. Perhaps the military weapon example is a little unreal, but it is not hard to move from this point to a real problem: for example, energy output, food processing developments or something similar.

It becomes a more real analysis when the forecaster applies a second technique in conjunction with the first. This studies the life-cycle curve of each individual technology, extrapolating the curves so that it becomes possible to see when one technology is reaching its turning point or is being overtaken by another. Some efficiency ceilings are predictable for a particular technology – the maximum energy output of, say, a windmill under the optimum theoretical circumstances is calculable – and if these ceilings are below the requirement of the users of the technology it indicates that a change of technology is imminent.

The life-cycle curve will normally take the typical S-shape discussed earlier in this chapter. Imagine a chart showing bow-and-arrow and gunpowder technologies. Bows and arrows would have a relatively short development time (the bottom of the S), a relatively short climb over a short period as maximum destructive efficiency increased and a long top to the S, lasting centuries, as the technology reached a peak beyond which it could not improve. Gunpowder technology would start with a destructive ability something below the top of the bow-and-arrow curve. For a period both technologies would overlap. For several hundred years destructive efficiency would increase until this technology, too, reached its peak of performance and turned round the top of its S-curve.

Although this technique may give an early warning of the expected onset of a new technology, it will not always enable management to predict exactly what will replace it. However, it may identify a problem which could then be analysed by one of the other techniques covered in this chapter.

There are several other extrapolative techniques of varying complexity, including the consideration of multiple trends and 'technology precursors'. A description of these will be found in most comprehensive works on technological forecasting.

(v) Morphological analysis

This technique possesses one of the tongue-twisting names that helps build that semantic barrier between 'expert' and manager. Essentially the method consists of an exhaustive analysis to identify all the technological requirements of a product and the relationships between them. The dimensions are plotted in a multidimensional matrix so that possible alternatives may be explored.

The technique is useful for considering a multiplicity of technological or environmental options. It is, however, a method which is very difficult to apply in practice, and which is both complex and involved.

Choosing the best technique

This wealth of available techniques brings an inevitable problem. How may a company choose the best method? The answer to this question is that selection is a matter of judgement supported by experience. However, there are some principles which can assist.

1 The purpose of the forecast should be clearly defined and, therefore, the degree of accuracy required. Is it an area where a close approximation is all that is

required for decision making (e.g. for setting salesmen's targets), or is it an issue of key importance on which a whole network of major decisions will be based?

2 The ability of the company to use the forecast is also important. Time and time again managers use environmental forecasts in an unsophisticated way, often only partially taking account of them in plans and decisions. A major change in environmental forecast is not always reflected in a change of action by the manager. Where a company is in this state it cannot justify the more complex forecasting methods that it may require at a later stage when it improves its planning ability.

3 Cost-effectiveness is one of the most important of criteria. Will the additional cost of a complex technique be recouped in better decisions? If it will not, a cheaper and simpler method should be prescribed. The cost is not simply that of producing the forecast, and includes the collection of any special data needed. A forecast that can be made from readily available data is likely to be cheaper, regardless of technique, than one which calls for special studies and research surveys.

4 The ability of the company to use sophisticated methods is a key factor. Although any company may buy out forecasting skills by using consultants and software packages available from computer manufacturers and bureaux, it is frequently inadvisable to use methods which the management of the company cannot understand and to which key individual managers may be hostile. Every company has at any point in time a threshold of sophistication beyond which it cannot immediately rise: this principle runs through the design of any aspect of a planning system.

5 The speed at which forecasts are needed is also very important. A forecast needed today cannot be met by the construction of an econometric model taking two months or more to build. In these circumstances the fact that an econometric model may be more accurate is an irrelevance.

6 The frequency with which a forecast has to be made will also have an impact, particularly on cost-effectiveness. An econometric model which may be used for successive forecasts at different times as the value of its parameters change is of potentially more value than a model designed to solve a particular isolated problem. Similarly, a forecasting routine which is part of a total company model, using a computer for the analysis of alternatives, will have different requirements again.

Examples of comprehensive forecasts

The final part of this chapter will provide examples of forecasts made by different methods. They are drawn from published works. In addition to illustrating an approach, the first provides valuable insight into the changing management trends, brought about by different patterns of competition, technology changes, social and demographic changes.

Management in the 1990s

The first study was undertaken in the UK, although the research base was European. Its conclusions were echoed by a less rigorous but similar study in the USA. Both were based on market research-style methods, with interviews conducted with key managers from organisations which had already started to experience the new trends. From these interviews it was possible to present a form of scenario about the main challenges. The UK study claims to provide insight rather than a prescriptive picture of the future.

What results from considering all this evidence is a coherent picture of at least a major element of difference between managing through the 1980s and managing in the 1990s and beyond.

Although comparable research may not be available for other countries, it is reasonable to suggest that results can be extrapolated outside of the research area, although with caution. This is because many of the triggers for change are of a global nature.

The landmark UK study was Barham et al.,[10] carried out in 1988. This was later expanded by Barham and Bassam in 1989,[11] and it is from this latter reference that this summary is drawn. The research identified a number of factors or pressures which the respondents saw as critical for the future:

- *Intensifying of competition* This was seen as a continuing trend, with pressure coming from two main sources. First there is the continuing trend for many industries to become more global, which not only brings new competitors into play, but also changes the critical success factors of the industries concerned. The second source is the continuing merging of competition, as companies in related industries changed their boundaries: for example building societies moving into retail banking. Both sources cause discontinuities, and neither is expected to abate.
- *Information technology* The effective management of IT is seen as an important factor for the 1990s. The authors also cite the problem of managers whose uncertainty is increased because they now have too much information, but insufficient time to enable them to use it.
- *'City' pressures* Tension between the short-term requirements of investors and the long-term needs of the business is seen as an unfortunate reality today and in the future.
- *Organisations to become more dynamic* As a response to competitive pressures, organisations will be more dynamic. Expectations include decentralised structures, managers at all levels to take more responsibility, more entrepreneurial organisations, and mechanisms such as task force management.
- *Market focus* Organisations will be more market focused, with segmentation becoming even more critical. In response to pressures, organisations will also become more customer driven. Relationship building is critical, and service will increasingly be seen as part of the product. There will be a greater need for innovation.
- *Quality* Total quality management becomes obligatory, and is driven as much by customer demands as by the will of the organisation itself.

121

- *Speed of product development* As product life cycles shorten, the need to speed up product development increases
- *Acquisitions* Acquisitions continue to be a key element in corporate strategies, now frequently triggered by the need to become more global.

These findings have many similarities with those of Sullivan[12] whose research was undertaken in 1989. The findings related to the USA, and were classified as business forces and the trends in organisational response. In Exhibit 6.1, the findings of the two studies have been combined. As well as illustrating the outcomes of studies of the future, this table offers information which is of interest to any one concerned with strategic management.

The next example is something which fits the image of a futures study. It used thematic, trend and impact analysis, and sequential logic, resulting in a number of scenarios showing the new order of nations in the year 2010. Assumptions are clearly stated.

The study is by C. W. Taylor[13] and was published in 1992, written on behalf of the Strategic Studies Institute, US Army War College. Some elements of the study deal with military issues. Of wider interest are the first chapters that deal with world international order, world population, world interdependence and socio-

Exhibit 6.1 Trends which affect management

Trigger factor	Organisational response trends
• Intensifying competition/global competition	• World-class manufacturing • More dynamic and flatter organisations • Market focus • More strategic alliances • Continuing acquisition activity • Effective harnessing of IT
• Customer demands for quality and service	• Service becomes part of the product • Customer-focused organisations • Total quality management
• Accelerating technological obsolescence	• Innovation given more priority • Reduction of time in product development
• City pressures on short term profits	• Short-term/long-term tension • Emphasis on shareholder value
• Demographic trends	• Culture/strategy issues • Smaller, flatter structures • Different work practices • People seen as more important • Managing cultural diversity

Table 6.1 Percentage of world population by stage of development

	1986	2025
Post-industrial	20.1	13.5
Advanced industrial	1.3	1.6
Transitioning industrial	5.5	5.3
Industrial	48.5	45.6
Pre-industrial	24.7	34.0

political change, and world technological issues. In fact some of the forecasts which support the scenarios go beyond 2010 to 2025. It contains worrying forecasts, such as the proportion of world population in developed countries falling from 23 per cent in 1991 to 16 per cent by 2025 (see Table 6.1).

Taylor provides a view of the world of the future which is of considerable interest, particularly to those following a global strategy. By 2025 he suggests the pattern of population outlined in Table 6.1.

The book provides a coherent scenario against which plans could be made, the above figures being a tiny extract in summary form. There is no guarantee that its predictions will come true, and certainly other scenarios could be developed.

Another example was published by the Royal Institute of International Affairs.[14] It offers three scenarios to 2015, which it terms 'postcards from the future', which dwell chiefly on the concerns of the industrialised world. The three scenarios deal with the social, political and economic consequences of different rates of change and turbulence. Although none would claim to be a forecast of what will happen, they show three ways in which the world could develop, and therefore are very useful as a basis for strategic thinking.

Forecasts, although an extremely valuable aid to strategic thinking, are only useful if the environmental factors they cover are given due consideration in the strategy process. Chapter 5 gave a model to facilitate systematic consideration of these factors. The next chapter will explore some of the ways of ensuring that issues from the business environment are identified and incorporated into strategic thinking.

References

1 Marshall, A. *Principles of Economics*, 8th edn, Macmillan, London, 1956.
2 Levitt, T. *Innovation in Marketing*, Pan, London, 1968.
3 Kotler, P. *Marketing Management: Analysis, Implementation and Control*, 8th edn, Prentice Hall, Englewood Cliffs, NJ, 1994.
4 Saunders, A. and Smith, N. J. 'Hydraulic Cranes from Armstrong's Elswick Works, 1846 1936: a Product Life Cycle in Capital Goods', *Journal and Proceedings of the Industrial Market Research Association*, 6, No. 2, May 1970.

5 Coutie, G. A., Davies, O. L., Horsell, C. H., Millar, D. W. G. P. and Morrell A. J. H. *Short-term Forecasting*, ICL Monograph No. 2, Oliver & Boyd, Edinburgh, 1964.
6 Moroney, M. J. *Facts from Figures*, Pelican, London, 1951.
7 McCarthy, E. J. *Basic Marketing: A Managerial Approach*, Irwin, Homewood, IL, 1964.
8 Parker, G. G. C. and Seguara, E. L. 'How to Get a Better Forecast', *Harvard Business Review*, March-April, 1971.
9 Teeling-Smith, G. 'Medicines in the 1990s: experiences with a Delphi forecast', *Long Range Planning*, June 1971.
10 Barham, K. A., Fraser, J. and Heath, L. *Management for the Future*, Ashridge Management College and the Fountain for Management Development, UK, 1988.
11 Barham, K. A. and Bassam, C. *Shaping the Corporate Future*, Unwin/Hyman, London, 1989.
12 Sullivan, P. Managing in the 1990s, unpublished research, Harbridge House Inc, Boston, USA, 1989.
13 Taylor, C. W. *A World 2010: A New Order of Nations*, Strategic Studies Institute, US Army War College, Carlisle Barracks, PA, 1992.
14 Royal Institute of International Affairs. *Unsettled Times*, The 1996 Chatham House Forum Report, Royal Institute of International Affairs, London.

CHAPTER 7

Techniques for assessing the environment

This chapter aims to move the discussion of concepts for looking at the external environment to methods of practical application. It explores the setting up of a strategic information unit, and describes several ways in which external issues may be systematically examined, leading to strategic decisions. The aim is to move from a simple listing of opportunities and threats to a more fundamental understanding of how an organisation can determine what is really important to it, and thereafter think deeply about the issues.

So far we have explored a model to help the strategist think of the various factors in the business environment, we have seen how the task of formulating strategy is assisted through the setting of assumptions, and we have looked at some of the approaches to forecasting. What we now need to do is to explore ways to help determine what the critical environmental issues are for a particular organisation, and some ways of dealing with uncertainty. En route to these issues we should also give some thought to the setting up of a strategic information unit within the organisation.

The model in Figure 4.2 has a particular strength in that it draws attention to the interrelated nature of the various factors that make up the business environment. It also illuminates a difficulty that we have as humans: it is very hard for us to consider a large number of variables simultaneously. The approaches in this chapter all try to help with this problem.

Setting up a strategic information unit

It is not impossible to make plans without accessing detailed information about the business environment, but the probability that sound plans will be prepared will increase if attention can be given to the collection and analysis of

Figure 7.1
Role of strategic planning unit. (From Butcher, H. and Mainelli, M. 'Strategic Information Management', in Hussey, D. E. (ed.), *International Review of Strategic Management*, Vol. 1, Wiley, Chichester, 1990)

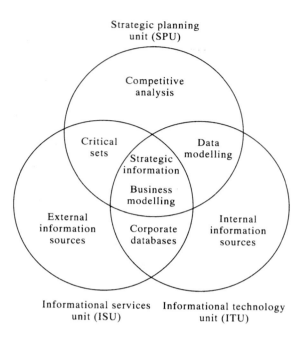

information on a regular basis. The effort that can be given to this will, of course, vary with the resources of the organisation, but in these days of databases that can be accessed at reasonable cost, there is little reason why even the smallest organisation should lack information. Ruth Stanat[1,2] suggests undertaking a strategic information audit, to evaluate what is being provided at present compared with the real needs of the organisation. The audit would also cover the effectiveness of current information sources, and of the means by which information is distributed within the organisation. Although the scheme I am following chooses to treat industry and competitor analysis as a separate subject to be discussed later, any strategic information system should cover these needs as well as those arising from the broader environment.

Figure 7.1, from work by Butcher and Mainelli,[3] relates the role of an external information unit, to information systems and strategic planning units. A key aspect is being aware of the interfaces where more than one of the units has both a need and a responsibility. Successful strategic information management involves managing these to avoid duplication, and making sure that the responsibilities of all three are considered.

Butcher and Mainelli divide information into three types:

Information for assumptions: tends to be trend information for stable assumptions, e.g. average customer size, and discrete events for unstable assumptions, e.g. an assumption of new entrants in a market would be contradicted by news of a major acquisition of a competitor.

Information for decisions: on a strategic level, the information tends to be voluminous and oriented to specific new projects or cancellations, e.g. should a new product be launched.

Information for success factors: measurement tends to be exact for internally supplied information, but base statistical information may be all that is available for external information, e.g. a success factor of press coverage could be measured by column inches multiplied by impact factor of publication.

We will look more closly at information requirements for competitor analysis, and ways of compressing information so that management can track the important issues, in later chapters, including a case history which deals with both the task of obtaining relevant information in a legal and moral way, and the tracking problem. Anyone who wants to follow a continuity of thought about information could jump to Chapters 10 and 11 now.

In this chapter we will next look at ways of determining what issues are relevant to the strategic management of a particular organisation. However it is worth stressing that none of the techniques illustrated does more than take a photograph, at a given point of time. Some information scanning mechanism is desirable as discussed above, with periodic repeat analysis using one or other of the techniques described here (or other similar approaches which are available) to ensure that there have been no changes in what is important.

Relating to the environment

There are similarities in a number of the methods available, and many of them seem to have been developed around the same time, in the mid-to late 1970s. I have chosen to illustrate two methods in some detail, one developed by my own consulting organisation and the other by Fred Neubauer, who is now a professor at IMD, Lausanne. For the record I should also like to refer the reader to some of the similar approaches, for example Hargreaves and Dauman,[4] Hofer and Schendel[5] and McNamee.[6]

Facing up to change

The approach developed by the Harbridge Consulting Group has not been published outside the firm, but has been used widely with clients over a long period. It is capable of use as an analytical check list, but is more often used in small group work to facilitate thinking about the environment among line and other managers who are involved in the strategy formulation process.

The heart of the approach is reproduced in Figure 7.2. The categories listed on the left-hand side are similar to those in Figure 4.2. Under each heading there are subheadings showing the type of factor that may be important. The aim here is to provide a starting prompt list. It is not the intention to suggest that all items are relevant to a particular organisation, nor that only items on the list should be considered. The analysis really begins with column 1, where respondents identify the issues that appear important. An effective method is to have the

Category	Check list of possible changes (Examples only)	1 Possible changes for your company	2 Impact	3 Probability	4 Overall importance	5 Preparation	6 Who is aware of the change?	7 Whose responsibility?	8 Is effective action likely?	9 Are the resources available?
Demographic	School leaver availability	Demographic								
	Ageing population									
	Minorities									
	Women									
	Graduate availability									
Social	Consumer attitudes	Social								
	Employee attitudes									
	Attitudes to training									
Economic	Inflation	Economic								
	Reflation/recession									
	EEC harmonisation									
	Employment levels									
	International trade									
	Balance of payments									
	Interest rates									
Political	Change of domestic government	Political								
	Changes of government in other countries									
	Privatisation									
Ecological	Pollution	Ecological								
	Waste									
	Climate									
Technological	New materials	Technological								
	Patents									
	Product life									
	Information technology									
	Production methods and processes									
	Machine replacement									
Legal	Equal opportunities legislation	Legal								
	Health/safety/welfare									
	Taxation									
	Competitive interference									
	EEC harmonisation									
	Information disclosure									
	Participation									
Infrastructure	Transport systems	Infrastructure								
	Communications systems									

Figure 7.2

Extract from *Facing up to Change*. (Copyright Harbridge Consulting Group Ltd, 1976, 1990)

questionnaires completed individually by a number of managers, preferably including line people who know the business well, and others who may have access to environmental information. The individuals come together in groups to agree what is important. If done well, one value of this approach is that it encourages a deep consideration of more factors, and forces thinking about their relative importance.

Columns 2 to 4 require respondents to reach a view on the importance of each identified factor to the organisation. This is achieved through a scoring method which converts opinions into numbers. The rules are:

Impact

What impact would it have?	Score
Extremely High Impact	6
	5
High Impact	4
	3
Relatively Low Impact	2
	1
Don't know	7

Probability of it happening

A Certainty	100%	6
Very Likely	84%	5
Quite Possible	67%	4
As Likely as Not	50%	3
Probably Not	33%	2
Highly Unlikely	16%	1
Don't Know		7

Overall importance is calculated by multiplying the impact score by the probability score. 'Don't know' scores high so that something important is not overlooked through ignorance. Attention is focused on those factors which have the highest overall scores.

Column 5, headed *Preparation*, is the response to another question. How ready are you for the important changes? The word 'you' refers to the unit for which the strategies are being considered, and could be a total company, a business unit, a department or a product. Again a numerical score is entered:

Completely prepared, including an implementation plan	6
Fairly well prepared, with tentative plans	5
Have decided a general approach	4
Not well prepared, with only a general idea of response	3
Vague awareness	2
Not at all prepared	1

This time attention is focused on the low scores for preparedness, concentrating on those items with a high score for impact.

129

Columns 6 and 7 begin to explore the possibilities for action. First, who is aware of the threats and opportunities represented by the change? This would be a superfluous question if all the decision makers were working on the questionnaire, but becomes important if the group is of planners or middle managers, or does not include all the appropriate top people. The next column pins down responsibility for dealing with the change. Complex issues may lead to multiple responsibilities, such as changes in the demographic mix affecting Human Resources and Marketing, for different reasons, or being a problem for one division but an opportunity for another.

Columns 8 and 9 both use numerical scales, varying from 6 (the best) to 1 (the worst). One column probes perception of whether effective action will in fact be taken. The other assesses whether the organisation can/will make the appropriate resources available to deal with it.

The rest of the approach consists of a number of other questions and headings which are designed to lead to action. These are not reproduced here.

One should not be trapped by the neat mathematics. The tool is an aid to thinking about the right things, and the numbers are a way of helping focus on the most important. In the end the value of the approach lies in the awareness it creates and the actions stimulated. By themselves the numbers have no value and are merely a means to an end.

An additional technique has been developed around columns 1–5 of Figure 7.2, and related to methods of portfolio analysis. This is called risk matrix, and will be described in a later chapter, as it is not possible to make sense of it independently of portfolio analysis, a topic in its own right.

The Neubauer/Solomon approach

This method was published by the authors in 1977,[7] having earlier been proved by them in various situations. It uses a briefer classification of environmental factors: natural/man-made, social/cultural, technological, political, and economic. However, the classification postulated in Figure 4.2 could be substituted if desired. Two types of environmental conditions are considered, Trends and Constituents. Trends are self-descriptive. Constituents refer to those individuals and institutions in the environment who may impact the business, such as trade unions and governments.

The method identifies the critical factors and their impact, as will be explained, and studies the threats and opportunities that they create. In turn these are related to the mission and strategies of the organisation. The final part of the exercise examines organisational responsiveness, including constraints and capabilities. Figure 7.3 illustrates the steps that the approach takes to reach a new strategy, if required: shown as a modified strategy in the figure.

For the purpose of this analysis the authors define strategy as the 'major decisions and/or action programmes employed by the company to fulfil its mission'. Mission in their terms is the answer to the three questions: whose and what needs are the company satisfying, and what value does it provide to those whose needs it is satisfying? The authors suggest restricting the strategies listed to no more than eight, which should all satisfy the criteria of having long-term

Figure 7.3
Neubauer/Solomon
Method Parts A and
B

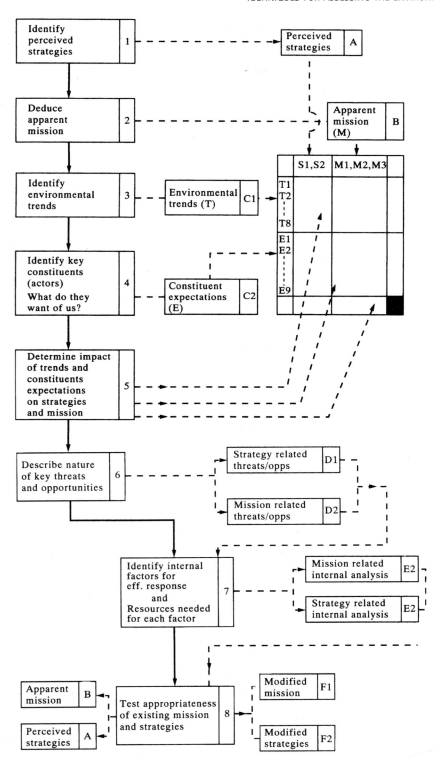

Figure 7.4

Neubauer/Solomon
Scoring Matrix

			Selection Criteria												
			Strategies								Mission			Impact	
			S1	S2	S3	S4	S5	S6	S7	S8	M1	M2	M3	+	-
External forces for change	Trends	T1													
		T2													
		T3													
		T4													
		T5													
		T6													
		T7													
		T8													
	Const expectations	E1													
		E2													
		E3													
		E4													
		E5													
		E6													
		E7													
		E8													
		E9													
Impact		+													
		-													

M1 = Whose needs   M3 = What value

M2 = What needs

impact, being crucial to the survival and development of the organisation, having breadth of scope, being hard to reverse, and involving the commitment of resources. Similarly they suggest reducing mission to the three answers to the questions posed above.

With this background we can begin to look at Figure 7.4, which is an enlargement of the matrix within Figure 7.3, and into which the analyst will enter scores which relate the impact of the environmental factors on the strategies and mission of the organisation. This figure is shown uncompleted, and it will be noted that in addition to restricting the number of strategies considered, the authors also suggest limiting the external factors to eight trends and nine expectations of constituents. A larger number may be examined in the initial stages of analysis, but only the most important will be carried through for this detailed study.

The rating scale is shown in Figure 7.5. Zero is neutral: a negative score represents a threat and a positive score an opportunity. The larger the number scored, the greater is the impact on the organisation.

Scores are entered into the matrix, as in the example in Figure 7.6. This gives a great deal of information. Reading across the matrix we can see from the final two columns which trends and constituent expectations impact the organisation most, in either a beneficial or harmful way. Reading down the matrix we can see which strategies and which elements of the mission should be reconsidered,

Figure 7.5
Neubauer/Solomon
Rating Score

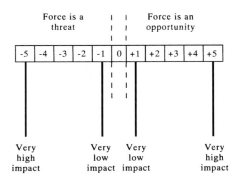

Test each external force for change against
each strategy/mission. Enter number in
appropriate box in matrix.

Figure 7.6
Neubauer/Solomon
Completed Matrix

			Selection Criteria												
			Strategies								Mission			Impact	
			S1	S2	S3	S4	S5	S6	S7	S8	M1	M2	M3	+	−
External forces for change	Trends	T1	0	0	0	+5	−3	−5	+3	0	+1	0	0	+9	−8
		T2	0	−5	−4	−4	+1	0	0	0	0	+5	0	+6	−13
		T3	+1	−2	−1	+3	0	−2	+2	0	0	+5	−5	+11	−10
		T4	+1	−1	+3	0	0	−1	+4	0	0	0	−5	+8	−7
		T5	0	0	+2	0	+3	0	+1	0	+2	0	−4	+8	−4
		T6	0	0	0	+3	0	+1	0	0	0	+5	0	+12	−1
		T7	+4	0	0	+2	+2	−3	0	0	0	0	0	+8	−3
		T8	0	0	0	0	+2	0	0	+5	−1	+5	0	+12	−1
	Const expectations	E1	−5	+1	−1	0	0	−5	−2	−2	0	0	−5	+1	−20
		E2	−1	0	0	0	+1	−5	−1	−3	0	0	−5	+1	−14
		E3	−1	0	+1	0	0	0	−2	0	−1	0	0	+1	−4
		E4	0	+2	−2	+2	−3	0	0	0	0	0	+1	+5	−5
		E5	0	0	0	+5	−2	+1	+1	0	+2	−5	+5	+14	−7
		E6	+1	0	+2	−1	−3	−3	+1	0	0	0	+5	+9	−7
		E7	0	0	0	0	0	0	0	0	−1	0	0	0	−1
		E8	−3	−1	0	+2	+1	−4	0	+1	−2	+1	0	+5	−10
		E9	+2	−3	0	0	0	0	−1	0	−1	+5	−3	+7	−8
Impact		+	+9	+3	+8	+22	+10	+2	+12	+6	+5	+26	+11		
		−	−10	−12	−8	−5	−11	−28	−6	−5	−6	−5	−26		

M1 = Whose needs   M3 = What value
M2 = What needs

either because of threats or opportunities. An alternative action might be to
continue a strategy, but with a better understanding of its risks, which in turn
might indicate some hedging strategies, or a modification so that a risky strategy
is still followed, but the organisation's involvement reduced: for example,
through an alliance to share risk, rather than doing everything itself.

Scenario planning

One way in which an organisation can take account of an uncertain world is through scenario planning. We encountered this in Chapter 3, and scenarios appeared again in Chapter 6, but it is worth considering again in the present context. In a nutshell, scenario planning consists of preparing a number of scenarios of different possible futures the organisation might face. It would be possible to develop a different strategy for each, although this still leaves the problem of choosing a strategic path from what could be divergent directions. A more effective way is to follow the advice of Van der Heijden,[8] and choose a strategy which is robust under all the scenarios, although this is not necessarily an easy task.

Scenarios can also be used to build understanding, and to help reveal a possible course of action. Industry analysis is the subject of a later chapter, but it is worth mentioning that I have used a very simple form of scenario analysis to create a dynamic view of possible directions. By looking at changes that could be made to the whole industry by actors at various positions in the industry, it is possible to see ways in which the industry can be made to change the way you want, and also to see actions that can be taken to anticipate and prevent changes which you do not want to happen. This may not be scenario analysis in the way the exponents of scenario planning describe it, but it is a very useful way of stimulating strategic thinking.

Scenarios can raise awareness in managers and help avoid surprise. Different scenarios of the future can broaden the outlook of managers to the external forces that shape the future of the organisation, and sensitise them to the vulnerabilities and to the opportunities.

Longley and Warner[9] provide a case history of the use of a scenario to identify future issues in the British National Health Service. The exercise was undertaken to help bring about an understanding of how the forces for change impacted not only on the health service, but also to agencies outside whose activities contributed to the overall state of health of the population. The exercise led to a greater understanding of the key strategic issues for the health service, and to a reappraisal of what was currently being done. The article describes the development of one scenario to help bring together all the numerous forces acting on the future of human health

British Airways used a scenario planning approach for the first time in 1994/5. The initial experiment involved the development of two comprehensive scenarios, which were used in a series of workshops to generate possible strategies. Strategies were developed for each scenario, and mapped on a matrix to show the fit with the alternative scenario. Present strategies were also mapped for fit with both scenarios. In addition to gaining a better understanding by managers of the trends in the external environment, workshops were also held with groups such as the trades unions and alliance partners, so that they could understand the factors that were affecting the thinking of British Airways. (Moyer[10] provides a detailed description of this exercise.)

Proponents of scenario planning argue that the examination of the strategies developed for all the scenarios leads to the selection of a best-fit strategy for all scenarios. In other words the 'best' strategy for one scenario may not be chosen, because of the possible impact on it of the others. My view is that any approach that helps an organisation to consider the outside world in a coherent manner is worth following. Of all the plans which come to me for comment as a consultant, very few address the impact of the external world in an adequate way, because of the sheer difficulty of handling numerous variables. In organisations subject to considerable uncertainty, it is worth considering scenario planning as an addition to the techniques already discussed. In fact research into scenario planning, such as that by Malasca et al.,[11] suggests that it is indeed these types of companies which lead the way in scenario planning. Some of the conclusions from the Malasca study are of interest:

> Companies operating in the most turbulent environments and companies with long term experience of strategic planning have been pioneers in adopting MSA (*multiple scenario analysis*).
> MSA is able to remove some of the drawbacks of strategic planning and especially to improve control of the uncertainty and unpredictability of the corporate environment....
> There is no uniform method of procedure with MSA, nor is there likely to be in the future....

Before we leave scenario planning to look at responding to the environment in another way, we should also remember Ansoff's views about environmental turbulence described in Chapter 3. Where turbulence is extreme, perhaps even scenario planning will be too lengthy a process to enable fast response to new circumstances.

Ways of responding

The implication so far has been that things go on in the outside world, and the organisation can only react. This is only partly true, in that in some circumstances the organisation can change the trend. Figure 7.7 provides four quadrants for thinking about the environment.

One axis deals with the organisation's willingness and ability to influence the direction of the trend. The other is its willingness or ability to change its strategies. The top left-hand quadrant has the organisation in the position of being able to exert some influence on the trend, but not altering its strategy. How successful this will be will depend on how far the trend can be influenced. A minor change may still affect the organisation adversely: a major change may be very favourable. The common methods of influencing the trend consist of lobbying, and the effective use of information to provide a reason why something should be done or not done. Frequently the best approach is through pressure groups, such as industry associations, and through representation,

Figure 7.7
Responses to
environmental
change

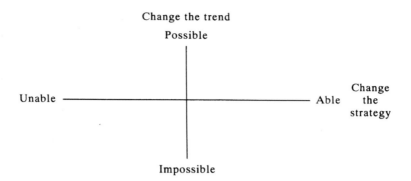

usually through such groups, on advisory bodies, such as those setting standards. For some issues this may be no more than a measure aimed at the civil servants to ensure that regulations are drawn up in a beneficial way, for example standards or labelling. For others it may involve influencing ministers and members of parliament, convincing them that a proposed or expected policy would be bad for the economy, and therefore for votes. Really big issues may involve ways of influencing public opinion through mass public relations and even advertising.

Pressure groups are not restricted to business and one approach to changing the trends might be to provide a counter to the activities of other pressure groups. Of course there are many pressure groups that are not important to the organisation, but those that are should not be ignored. Nestlé experienced massive loss of sales because of the activities of INFACT, an organisation set up in the USA in 1977 to force Nestlé to change its marketing and promotional activities for baby milk in the Third World, where there were many deaths because the product was used inappropriately by many mothers. Among the weapons was an attempt to boycott all Nestlé products until it conformed to INFACT's demands. Hartley,[12] who provides a case study of this event, maintains that the impact on Nestlé was wider than loss of sales and profits, as it also caused action by governments and world bodies.

The top right-hand side of the diagram states the situation where action is taken both to affect the trend and to change strategy. In the Nestlé example the company did much through its own public relations activity to combat the power of the pressure group. An alternative, suggested by Hartley, might have been to be seen to cooperate with them, and to ensure that there were no grounds on which accusations could be levelled. What the strategic change might be is very dependent on the circumstances, but might include measures to reduce risk, or to deal with the partial modification of a trend which still left the organisation needing to adjust its actions.

In the bottom half of the matrix we have a situation where either on grounds of practicability or cost, the organisation intends to take no actions to influence trends. This may be a general view that applies to every aspect of the environment, or may be applied only to specific trends: for example no companies are in a position to change the world's demographic trends!

Where the underlying strategy is also not to be changed, the bottom left side of the figure, it may be sensible to take actions that enable the organisation to reduce risk. This may include careful monitoring of trends, and actions inside to reduce lead times for reacting. Lead times before changes can be made to different conditions may involve setting up different decision processes, taking steps to reduce the time needed for new product development, or installing flexible manufacturing methods which make it easier to change what is produced.

The bottom right-hand corner can cover an enormous variety of possible changes to strategy. There are also types of strategic decisions which may reduce risk. Among these are shifting risks to others in the chain from first supplier to ultimate buyer, perhaps by changing contract terms so that inflation risks were taken by someone else, or by franchising so that certain risks were avoided. It may be preferable to work through alliances and joint ventures rather than taking on the whole risk oneself (often at the same time increasing the chance of success by neutralising a potential source of competition). There may be major investments to build a different strategic position. For example one of the reasons behind Sony's purchase of film studios in the USA is believed to be to avoid losing a future video configuration battle, if producers do not use it for their products: a reaction to its failure with an earlier video system, which had technical superiority and no cost disadvantage, but failed because there were few videos for rental in that configuration.

There is still another aspect to relating the organisation to the business environment that we have not yet covered. This is the issue of business ethics and social responsibility, and the concept of the social audit which achieved some popularity in the late 1970s and early 1980s. A dimension of the social audit which remains topical is concerned with the physical environment, and the requirement to be 'green'. These are issues for the next chapter.

References

1 Stanat, R. *The Intelligent Corporation*, Amacom, New York, 1990.

2 Stanat, R. 'Trends in Data Collection and Analysis: a New Approach to the Collection of Global Information', in Hussey, D. E. (ed.), *International Review of Strategic Management*, Vol. 3, Wiley, Chichester, 1992.

3 Butcher, H. and Mainelli, M. 'Strategic Information Management', in Hussey, D. E. (ed.), *International Review of Strategic Management*, Vol. 1, Wiley, Chichester, 1990.

4 Hargreaves, J. and Dauman, J. *Business Survival and Social Change*, Associated Business Programmes, London, 1975.

5 Hofer, C. W. and Schendel, D. *Strategy Formulation: Analytical Concepts*, West, St Paul, USA, 1978.

6 McNamee, P. *Management Accounting: Strategic Planning and Marketing*, Heinemann in association with CIMA, London, 1988.

7 Neubauer, F-F. and Solomon, N. B. 'A Managerial Approach to Environmental Assessment', *Long Range Planning*, **10**, No. 2, 1977.

8 Van der Heijden, K. *Scenarios: The Art of Strategic Conversation*, Wiley, Chichester, 1996.

9 Longley, M. and Warner, M. 'Future Health Scenarios – Strategic Issues for the British Health Service', *Long Range Planning*, 28, No. 4, August, 22–32, 1995.

10 Moyer, K. 'Scenario Planning at British Airways – A Case Study', *Long Range Planning*, 29, No. 2, April, 172–181, 1996.

11 Malasca, P. *et al.* 'Scenarios in Europe – Who Uses Them And Why?' *Long Range Planning*, 17, No. 5, 1984.

12 Hartley, R. F. *Marketing Mistakes*, 3rd edn, Chapter 4, Wiley, New York, 1986.

CHAPTER 8

Business philosophy (ethics and morality) and strategic management

There are three aims of this chapter. The first is to examine the issue of ethics and morality in modern business. The second is to present two different ways of thinking about such matters, either as constraints or as obligations under the stakeholder concept. A final aim is to describe the social audit, a process through which an organisation can measure and monitor its standards of behaviour.

Most managers would accept the statement that every business has to observe certain obligations which modify the way it operates. There would be widespread disagreement over the extent and nature of these obligations and the way in which they should be allowed to influence or interfere with business decisions and actions. In general terms it might be said that every business has obligations towards its shareholders, employees, customers, suppliers, and to the community. Yet the way in which it observes these obligations will vary from staying just on the right side of those which are enforced by law to having so violent a conviction about a particular principle that application of it becomes almost a crusade. There is as much variation in the business philosophies of corporations as there is in the standards of ethics of individual people.

It is no part of the study of strategic management to moralise on what is the 'correct' business philosophy. Much more relevant is the appreciation of the need to define the most significant aspects of a company's particular philosophy as one of the stages in the planning process, the understanding of how the philosophy affects the plans of the company, and knowing something of the dynamics of change which mould and alter society's approach to standards of business ethics and behaviour. Perhaps this last point is among the most important because, by definition, strategic management is concerned with the long term, and the norms of society are under constant and continual pressure from the forces of change. What is sacred to one generation may become profane to the next.

The pattern of development frequently involves government legislation. A pressure group builds up in the society and challenges a particular norm often in the teeth of ferocious opposition from business: certain business executives react faster than others (or may, indeed, themselves be members of the pressure group) and adjust their business philosophies accordingly: government may submit to the pressure by introducing a law which forces all to adhere to the new standards. There are variations to the process, which range from the failure of the pressure group to make any significant impact, to a spontaneous change without the need for government interference. It would be nonsense to suggest that every minority viewpoint eventually becomes the norm, or that no change can take place without government assistance, and, of course, in a democratic community government actions tend to be linked with the wishes of society.

During the medieval period the Church had great influence on business. It had definite views on the charging of interest which, to say the least, were different from those accepted by modern society. The doctrine of the 'just price' was a constraint accepted by many Christians. Heaton[1] states:

> In selling, as in lending, greed was anathema. Some church writers inherited the ancient aristocratic contempt for the trader: others condemned some of his methods. To St Thomas Aquinas (about 1250) trade was an undesirable calling, a badge of man's fall from grace; but since it was a necessary (or inevitable) evil, it might be tolerated if the seller was content with a *just* price. Let him be satisfied with a return which covered his material costs and paid him for his labour; let him meet the needs of a modest living standard and give any surplus to the poor; then his activities would be lawful and Christian. . . . But all writers agreed that justice was violated when any man monopolised the supply of a commodity and sought to extract exorbitant prices from the consumer.

The Swiss hotel business in the Geneva of Calvin conformed to a different business philosophy from that of today.

> In 1546 the inns of Geneva were re-organised as 'abbeys' and placed under strict government supervision: and a precise code of behaviour for guests and hosts was laid down. Among other items it included the following:
>
> If any one blasphemes the name of God or says, 'By the body, 'sblood, zounds' or anything like, or who gives himself to the devil or uses similar execrable imprecations, he shall be punished. . . .
>
> *Item*: The host shall not allow any person of whatever quality he be to drink or eat anything in his house without first having asked a blessing and afterward said grace.
>
> *Item*: The host shall be obliged to keep in a public place a French Bible, in which anyone who wishes may read. . . .
>
> *Item*: The host shall not allow any dissoluteness like dancing, dice, or cards, nor shall he receive anyone suspected of being a debauchee or ruffian.
>
> *Item*: He shall only allow people to play honest games without swearing or blasphemy, and without wasting more time than that allowed for a meal. . . .
>
> *Item*: Nobody shall be allowed to sit up after nine o'clock at night except spies. . . .[2]

Not all business executives have followed the ethics and standards of the day. In the height of the bad period of the Industrial Revolution, with all the well-known abuses of child labour, long hours, and inhuman working conditions, some employers stood alone. For example, Robert Owen (1771–1858):

> For twenty-three years he experimented in making a model mill and a model village. He gave up using pauper apprentices, forbade children under ten to work and sent them to school instead. He limited hours to twelve a day, less 1¾ hours for meals. He established a store to sell food at cost, improved houses, provided medical care, set up a sick fund, and founded a savings bank. Though his plans frightened his partners, he made profits, and New Lanark became one of the seven wonders of Britain.[1]

Many of Robert Owen's actions, advanced though they were for the times, would be considered to demonstrate an antiquated philosophy by the standards of today. So the pattern continually changes and reforms: the *avant-garde* philosophy of today becomes the traditionalist view of tomorrow. Whatever top managements' views on its obligations, business is part of the fabric of the society of the present, and its long-range plans will be implemented in the society of the future. (We have already considered in Chapter 4 some of the sociological trends which should be considered in planning.)

Hargreaves and Dauman[3] suggest that there are three levels of distinct but interrelated areas of social responsibility:

- *Basic responsibilities* generated by the existence of the organisation. This, they define, includes the need to keep within the letter of the law, to observe formal codes of conduct, to safeguard basic shareholder and employee interests, and to deal honourably with customers, suppliers and creditors.
- *Organisational responsibilities* which meet the changing needs of stakeholders (we will come back to this term), respond to changing attitudes, observes the spirit of the law rather than just the letter, and anticipates changes in legislation.
- *Societal responsibilities*, which help create a healthy environment in which the organisation can prosper, and help to solve key social problems which if not dealt with could affect the long-term prospects of the organisation.

While most people would argue strongly that every organisation should behave in an ethical and moral way, it is possible to see from the above classification that it is possible to be ethical and moral at each of the three levels. So because an organisation chooses to restrain itself to the basic level, it does not mean that it lacks integrity. Of course, the cynics have argued that the term *business ethics* is an oxymoron, and certainly some businesses fall far short of what is generally accepted moral and ethical behaviour.

As an organisation moves from the level of basic responsibility to embrace all three levels, it moves into situations of conflict. Jackall[4] observes:

> Even more difficult is fashioning some working consensus about the meaning of 'corporate social responsibility', a consensus that includes top management, external publics that top management is trying to appease, and middle

A matrix for considering social responsibility

Groupings	Level		
	Basic	Organisational	Societal
Shareholders			
Employees			
Customers			
Suppliers			
Community			

Note: Basic means keeping within the law and dealing honourably. *Organisational* means responding to changing attitudes, anticipating changes in the law, and meeting the spirit of the law and not just the letter. *Societal* means taking actions to help create a healthy environment and aiding the solution of long-term social problems which might otherwise affect prospects for the organisation.

The degree to which the organisation moves beyond the basic level is a management decision. What is your organisation doing under each cell in the matrix? Do you think it should do less or more, or is it about right?

> management that must implement a policy. Here the precariousness of ideological bridges between the interests of a corporation, individual managers, and the public are most apparent (p. 199).

Of the five groups to whom the company has obligations the one which would cause least surprise is the duty owed to shareholders. In general terms we may describe this as a duty to earn the shareholder an adequate return on investment and to preserve assets for the future. Chapter 12, dealing in detail with corporate objectives, defines this generalisation in more detail and in a way which can be meaningly quantified for planning purposes. For the present purpose the general concept of profit is sufficient. Other duties to shareholders may be harder to define and cause more differences of opinion – consider, for instance, the paucity of information given to shareholders by many companies: despite improvements by some, many annual company reports are designed to conceal more than they reveal.

What perhaps is of more significance to a study of business philosophy and ethics is the lack of influence that shareholders have on the day-to-day management of the companies they own. The *Financial Times*[5] reports Galbraith as arguing that:

> Some 40 per cent of the Gross National Product of the U.S. is controlled by 2000 giant corporations in manufacturing, merchandising, transport and the

utilities. If the great state corporations are included in the 'technostructure', a similar proportion of the national product in Italy, France and Britain is controlled by an equally small number of concerns.

Their ambitions may not coincide with those of society as a whole. Shareholders, Galbraith maintains, no longer have much influence on the day-to-day management of corporations. As a result managers have become more concerned with growth than with earnings. So long as a corporation makes a reasonable rate of return its managers have virtually complete power and their brief concern is to enlarge the scope of their operations and increase the size of their company.

The enormous size of some of the modern multinational corporations means that they have the ability, e.g. the sheer power of their investment, to transcend the policies of the governments of their host countries.

In one way the freedom of action of managers is subject to a constraint: at least the reasonable rate of return referred to by Galbraith must be earned if shareholders are to be contented and managers keep their jobs. This definitely has an effect on the development and application of actions resulting from matters of conscience. Carr[6] points out:

> Perhaps there are some executives who are so strongly positioned that they can afford to urge their management to accept a reduced rate of return on investments for the sake of society of which they are a part. But for the large majority of corporate employees who want to keep their jobs and win their superiors' approbation, to propose such a thing would be inviting oneself to the corporate guillotine.

In recent years there has been more attention given to the concept of shareholder value, both in terms of the strategies that create this, and ways of looking at it. The modern concepts apply discounted cash flow approaches to the measurement and selection of strategies. Chapter 12 will explore these concepts in some detail.

To move into this area of business moral and ethical behaviour is to move into an area of double-talk and public relations puffing. It is an area of platitudes, of noble-sounding statements which frequently have no bearing on the real way in which the business operates.

The matter is complicated further by the fact that in addition to these doubtful areas of public relations opportunism and inept platitudes there is a further confusion between genuine moral restraint and corporate strategy. This difference is not always very easy to identify, and is often known only by the top management of the business concerned – and even here, in the process of time, there may be a merging so that the two are inseparable. This mixture of moral actions caused by personal beliefs, and strategic actions which achieve the same results, is part of the process of development and change which is continually taking place. And, indeed, it may be a tactical move for a manager to position a genuinely held moral conviction to shareholders. In fact Carr[6] suggests that executives with a conscience should position this sort of problem as a longer-term profit improvement exercise if they are to have an impact on profit-motivated top management.

The confused world of morals and ethics is bemused even further by the incompatibilities of the modern business situation. It is not even necessary for a chief executive to compromise his or her own moral standards to run into circumstances where he or she cannot win. For example, it is a genuine intention of many companies that they be 'good citizens' of the countries in which they operate. This is the task which immediately brings a conflict of interest. How can an American parent company be a good citizen of both the USA and the UK when both countries are facing balance of payment problems (e.g. when the UK government would like dividends of the UK subsidiary reduced and the US government urges that they be increased)? Similarly, actions to direct exports to the cheapest source of supply can result in production switches away from overseas subsidiaries, a strategy which runs contrary to the national interests of the countries concerned. When governments themselves are in conflict, the ability of the chief executive to live up to a 'good citizen' motive becomes even more difficult.

It is important for these problems to be faced seriously and for the chief executive to determine in advance what really is intended and how the organisation will react in the sort of circumstance described above. Honesty of thought is much more important than high-sounding words, for employees in any company react very quickly to double standards. The sort of statement which some chief executives frequently hand out to all employees is often disbelieved on sight: if credibility is wanted the meaning behind the words must be demonstrated. And if a chief executive wishes anyone to act upon his or her words, for the statements to have an impact on the way business activities are performed in the company, for the moral constraints which he or she considers important to be built into the fabric of the corporate plans, he or she must, above all, obtain this necessary measure of credibility.

Setting difficult and sometimes costly standards for operating a business is rarely easy. For most chief executives the avoidance situations like not cheating the customers, not offering bribes, and not breaking their word, may be found relatively easy in a world where honesty in business has gained some acceptance as a welcome ideal. Those philosophies which require a positive action – like investing capital to reduce pollution beyond the requirements of the law – may not be so easy to face. Not every chief executive is a Robert Owen, willing to move ahead of his time. Yet, as we shall see, in addition to the moral issues it is often in industry's own interest that it keeps to the fore of the field because this renders government interference unnecessary.

Many business executives would claim that there are two standards: the one they use for their private lives, and the one used for business. The stereotype of the regular churchgoer and supporter of charities who habitually exploits the employees, gives short measure to the customers, and sends the suppliers into bankruptcy will probably always be with us. If chief executives can live with standards such as these, this is their privilege. A business normally reflects the philosophies, ethics, and morals of the person at the top, and it must be for these qualities as well as the ability to earn profits that a person is selected by the owners to run that business. I believe that it is both right and proper that a chief executive should have definite views on the way in which the corporation should behave.

Wates[7] states:

> . . . that the proposition that there are values which I endeavour to uphold as a private citizen which I must abjure as an industrialist, is totally untenable . . . In academic and in churchy circles one frequently meets the 'two worlds' view of business and the rest of life, which seems to be based on the idea that business consisting as it does of exploiting and manipulating markets in the interests of higher profits, is itself basically immoral and therefore anything goes in that jungle. Indeed in this respect business is its own worst enemy since the shorthand way some business men have of talking about maximising profit as an end in itself, lends colour to this view. Such people stand capitalism on its head and make it indefensible. They certainly provide no answer to those compelling arguments based on 'social justice' with which alternative economic systems appeal with such great effect to the young and to the underdeveloped countries. These arguments have to be faced; I simply cannot accept that business is by definition immoral; in fact I believe that capitalism both needs and has a moral base.

Personal standards in business are not restricted to chief executives. One of the larger firms in the UK fruit and vegetable trade operates a 'travelling wholesaler' section – the business of selling to the retail greengrocer off a lorry. A driver/ salesman employed by the company consistently refused to call on a particular customer on his round because the retailer habitually swore at him and treated him in a degrading way. 'I may be only a lorry driver, but I am entitled to be treated as a human being.' For this driver his self-respect was more important than the risk of losing his job.

The point that should be emphasised is that chief executives must be true to themselves. This is not always easy, and it must be accepted that it is a simpler task for the chief executive of a family business, or a company in which he or she happens to have a very high shareholding, or the small private company (where the shareholders are known personally) to reconcile a private moral position with a duty to the shareholders.

The remaining obligations listed earlier each bring their own particular moral and ethical problems to the chief executive of a modern company. An attempt is made to examine some of the possible implications, although again it should be stressed that there is no intention to moralise. There is little doubt that philosophies will vary between companies, since not all chief executives share the same beliefs, attitudes, and opinions; and, indeed, it is desirable that there should be differences.

The community

Obligations to the community (or to society, to put it another way) probably include the most complex, the most contentious, and the most thought-provoking aspects in any chief executive's business philosophy. Perception of the company's obligations will vary from a feeling that as long as the company is growing and making profits the community is well served, to a fundamental belief that business is a sociological process which has numerous obligations to others. Unfortunately, some of the issues faced by modern business make it more and more difficult for any chief executive to take the extreme viewpoints: they are no longer as simple as deciding whether factory premises play a part in local community relations.

Perhaps the most serious issues can be clustered under one word – green. Carr[6] argues that:

> The public shrugs at the company president who conspires with his peers to fix prices. It grins at the vice president in charge of sales who provides call girls for a customer. After we have heard a few such stories they become monotonous.
>
> We cannot shrug or grin, however, at the refusal of powerful corporations to take vigorous action against great dangers threatening the society, and to which they contribute. Compared with such a corporation or with the executive who is willing to jeopardise the health and well-being of an entire people in order to add something to current earnings, the man who merely embezzles company funds is as insignificant in the annals of morality as Jesse James is compared with Nero.

Pollution of the environment has only recently been recognised as an international problem, threatening the entire ecology of the world and the survival of the human race itself. Business is not the only cause of pollution; government and local authorities are themselves deeply involved. In the USA and Europe there is some evidence of government concern: on the other hand, other countries appear quite willing to accept a higher degree of atmospheric pollution as part of the price of economic growth. Pollution takes many forms – the poisoning of the air with smoke and gas emission, the discharge of industrial wastes, the pumping of sewage into rivers, canals, and the sea, the uncontrolled use of insecticides and herbicides, the mountains of unrottable rubbish which cities create daily, and the pollution of the countryside with litter, old furniture, and abandoned cars. Ironically some of the companies which purport to exist to improve public health are among the worst offenders: many of the companies engaged in pharmaceuticals also have interests in chemicals and dyestuffs, and historically have discharged noxious wastes into rivers or the sea.

The chief executive's dilemma if the organisation operates in one of the many industries which cause pollution is to decide whether to take a moral attitude on an acute and life-threatening problem or to pretend the problem does not exist and wait until government forces action. The trends make it harder not to notice the problem. Twenty-five years ago it would rarely have been a subject that called for top management action. Today the better understanding of the real issues has led to public protest and pressure groups, as well as attention by the government and industrial and academic scientists. If, in the 1970s, Ralph Nader's protest movement can shake a giant like General Motors, and if in the 1980s the world can be shocked into action by a nuclear accident in Russia, chemical plant explosions in India, and oil tanker disasters in the USA, it is highly likely that issues of responsibility to the community will loom even larger through the 1990s and beyond.

It is easy to simplify the problem. Let us look at the dynamics of a current situation: fluoride in the water supply. Some water companies have added fluoride because of the undoubtedly beneficial impact it has on dental health, and following extensive lobbying. However, the anti-fluoride lobby claims that it has evidence that this practice causes fluoride poisoning and shortens the lives of a small number of those that drink the water over a long period. Should the manufacturers of fluoride refuse to sell it to water companies for this purpose, and should water companies cease to add fluoride? Further, should water companies take steps to remove fluoride from the water supply in those areas which it occurs naturally? Is it their job to assess an issue that is not completely certain, or should they say that it is up to government?

A similar problem faces any business that sells nuts or incorporates nuts into its products. A very small proportion of the population will die if they put even a small quantity of a product containing nuts in their mouths, and some are said to be so allergic that they can be affected by someone else eating food containing nuts nearby. Should businesses, in the light of this knowledge, cease to deal in nuts, when for most of the population they are a healthy product? And if this does happen, what about the effect on the communities that grow the nuts?

Many major organisations see the value of maintaining positive relationships with government, local government and the community, and the growth in government and public affairs departments. More than 80 per cent of the *Fortune 500* companies are reputed to have public affairs offices in Washington. Organisations of varying sizes will also work through trade associations on an industry basis. Such offices are usually established to influence and lobby, and to put over the company/industry viewpoint, rather than with the prime aim of benefiting the community.

Chief executives may, for moral reasons, feel that part of their obligation to the community lies in determining types of business in which they will not participate. The activities prescribed in this way may be within the law but outside of their own code of ethics (in fact we need not concern ourselves with firms which intend to act outside the law since they are unlikely to be involved in the sort of management approach described in this book). Thus for these reasons a company may decide not to enter fields such as gambling, night clubs, alcohol production, or the tobacco industry. The decision is personal to the company: others may quite happily enter these areas without any feeling that they are behaving immorally.

Ethical problems appear in other directions. Another subject of increasing concern is the use of industrial espionage and the differences between this and legitimate marketing research. In considering industrial espionage we are moving away from the more contentious motives into an area related to simple standards of honesty and basic integrity. Yet not all companies are averse to gaining advantage over competitors by means such as these.

Related in some ways with the attitude to industrial espionage is a chief executive's philosophy towards competitors. This may be based on fair dealing and high standards of integrity, or it may be completely the opposite. Keen competition can still exist under conditions of amicable relations, although not all managers believe this.

The manager of one of the divisions of one company operating in the UK was annoyed when his chief executive agreed to show a major competitor how a system of profit improvement was designed and implemented. 'You may help the enemy, but you don't clean their rifles for them,' he grumbled.

Some years ago in South Africa one cigarette manufacturer took another to court. Salesmen of the rival company had been spreading the rumour among African consumers that the claimant's cigarettes caused sterility, causing a large decline in sales.

It would be tedious to attempt to analyse all aspects of a company's possible obligations to society. Such topics as race relations, equal opportunity for women, the use of sex and nudity in advertising, and the support of political parties are among the many issues on which a chief executive might be expected to take an attitude which may make the task of fulfilling duties to shareholders that much harder.

Employees

Obligations to employees may seem, at first glance, to be an area of little difficulty. Of course, most modern companies, in whatever country they operate, recognise that Victorian attitudes are no longer acceptable and that they have a certain responsibility for the health and wellbeing of those they employ. On the other hand, few chief executives would be wise to give every employee a life-long guarantee of continuity of employment.

Many companies which practise strategic management build some form of policy statement about their attitude to people into their vision statement and policies.

We are all familiar with the statement that many companies make in their annual reports – 'our employees are our greatest asset', or words to this effect. The vision statement of the chief executive of a British group with widespread interests included the following statement:

> I sincerely accept the statement that human beings are always more important than machines, systems or organisation, and that all decisions should therefore adequately reflect this understanding.
> . . . I believe it to be imperative that due regard be given to the motivation of individuals and that consistent with the basic purpose of the Group we must seek to meet these needs.

The 'basic purpose' of this company refers to profit objectives.

Another British company with a number of overseas subsidiaries and operating mainly in the grocery field, defined its broad obligations to employees.

> The Company exists for the benefit of all its owners and will operate in such a way that it holds the net profit returned to its owners as the prime consideration in all decisions: subject to the constraints that the Company

will endeavour to be a 'good citizen' of each country in which it operates, that it will always conduct its business in an ethical manner, and that it will have the regard of a 'good employer' for the health and well-being of its employees.

In its own long-term interests the Company will act in such a way that it is regarded internally and externally as a progressive and dynamic concern, giving fair treatment to customers and to employees.

These are typical examples of what companies say. How they live up to the statements is another matter, and only those inside the company know whether what it says bears any relationship to what it does. Indeed many organisations that had even more dedication to employees enshrined in its policy statements were among those who simply ignored them when they followed the fashion and joined the large number of organisations which de-layered, downsized, and reorganised their processes.

It is not that organisations should never make people redundant: it is the care and caring with which such an action is taken. Woodward[8] gives an example from his experience as leader of a job club, which shows that the treatment of employees sometimes leaves something to be desired:

> Robert, a cost accountant, was tidying his desk at the end of just another Friday afternoon, when the finance director paused on his way through the office. 'Don't come back on Monday, Robert', he said, 'You've been made redundant. details are in the post – they should reach you tomorrow'. Robert was 56 and had worked for this company for 35 years.

However, for many companies the responsibility to employees is taken more seriously and has an effect on the strategies the firm pursues. The example given here is rather old, but still of interest, and dates from 1971 when the company was considering expansion into South Africa, during the apartheid period. A British firm of builders and contractors, Wates Ltd, have definite objectives for their relations with employees which they express as 'to grow people'. This is further stated as a policy of 'optimising individual and the company goals'. Implementation of this objective was a little unusual in that it led Wates to a decision that 'the idea of doing business in South Africa is totally unacceptable' on the grounds that conditions in that country would prevent the company from fulfilling this objective. It was against all the moral and moralistic idealistic beliefs of the board that they should voluntarily begin business in a country where they were prevented by law from offering equal opportunity to all employees, regardless of race.

This example is important in that it demonstrates how a particular philosophy can shape a company's attitude to its opportunities for profit. Not everyone would agree with Wates' decisions: the significant factor is not *what* was decided, but *why*.

Failure to think through all the implications of responsibility to employees, can be expensive, as the basic responsibility level is not always quite as basic as it seems. The first successful legal claim in the UK for work-related stress, *Walker v. Northumberland County Council* (1995), was won by the employee. Initially the employer intended to appeal, but settlement was reached out of court for around

149

£175 000. There is health and safety legislation, but there is no specific law that the employer should take action to help an employee in a stress situation.

Wheeler and Sillanpää[9] quote the example of Texaco who faced a law suit in 1994 by 1500 present and past employees for racial discrimination for half a billion dollars. They settled in late 1996 when conversations which had been secretly taped showed that Texaco executives referred to black employees in offensive terms. At about the same time Texaco (UK) was chosen by the Industrial Society as one of six companies to illustrate best practice on diversity.

Many more issues in the future will be covered by legislation, and whether the business intends to act at the basic responsibility level, or accepts that there is more that should be done, it is important that what is said in the vision statement and board room utterances reflects the real values of the organisation. Platitudes plucked out of the air can be damaging, as insincerity is swiftly revealed.

Customers

Obligations to customers appear at first sight to present few philosophical problems: how a business treats its customers is on the surface a matter of commercial self-interest, bound up with its marketing strategy and the desire to retain and expand its customer lists. Few companies adopt the 'selling refrigerators to Eskimos approach' (at least without an after-sales service!), and, for most, cheating or misleading the customer would be a matter of economic suicide.

Moral issues can, in this area too, run deep below the surface, and the company may accept obligations which are more far-reaching than those dictated by commercial prudence or enforced by legislation. On the other hand, it may not.

Some years ago the American government banned as harmful the use of cyclamates (a sugar substitute) in the manufacture of food. Following this ban products containing these chemicals disappeared from the US market. Despite the evidence and government action, many American companies continued to export these products to countries where no legal ban had been imposed. In these companies the obligation felt towards overseas customers was obviously minimal.

The world's pharmaceuticals companies have generally had a high standard of moral behaviour to consumers long before governments began to legislate for the control of new drugs. This was undoubtedly partly through self-interest (claims for damages – such as in the thalidomide cases – can be expensive in terms of both compensation and adverse publicity) and partly through association with the medical profession, which itself is renowned for its high ethical standards: in addition, many managers in the pharmaceuticals industry have a pride in their moral obligations to their consumers which transcend the bare minimum.

Safety of the health and wellbeing of customers is not just a moral issue which faces the food and pharmaceuticals industries. Many other businesses have to decide on the extent to which they accept similar obligations which avoid harming the customer: examples are toy manufacturers (and many potentially harmful toys are made, particularly in South-east Asia), the car industry, clothing (many deaths have been caused through the use of inflammable acrylic fibres in children's nightdresses), toiletries, and electrical appliances. Printing a warning on their plastic bags about danger to young children probably did not gain the British retail giants Marks & Spencer a single extra sale, and certainly would have involved them in thought, if not cost.

Chief executives might well have differing views over pricing policies. Is it immoral to make abnormally high profits on a transaction if an opportunity arises? Attitudes to price policies and competition vary between individuals, between groups in the society, between government and industry, and often the government attitude to different industries. Government may take a very lofty attitude if it discovers two competing consumer goods companies have had 'discussions' on price rises: yet it will consider a rate-fixing cartel like IATA, or one of the shipping conferences, as something which is completely justified. Is there really any difference? While many chief executives would agree that forming a ring to frustrate normal tendering procedures would be immoral, I suspect that many would not be quite so concerned about 'suggesting' to a competitor that rising costs justified price increases. As society and government have different standards, it must be equally difficult for a chief executive to decide what is ethically right or wrong. This ambivalence carried through public attitudes to business. Much of society will congratulate a company for its efficiency in gaining profit growth, and at the same time pillory it for increasing its margins. The borderline between profit and profiteering is a fine one.

Suppliers

Various philosophies are possible in relation to a chief executive's obligations to suppliers. On the one hand, there is the chain store which sets out to ensnare small suppliers in such a tight web that eventually they face the choice of bankruptcy or selling their businesses, to what has become their only customer, at only a fraction of their real value. At the other extreme there is the company which goes out of its way to assist its suppliers, and gives its creditors better treatment than it receives from its debtors. Somewhere in the middle there is the company who elects that its only obligation is to pursue a path of commercial probity, giving neither more nor less to suppliers than they are legally entitled to have.

Again, the choice falls on the chief executive: it is philosophy and outlook from the top which will condition a company's behaviour to its suppliers.

An interesting example of how a business may go out of its way to help its suppliers is provided by Marks & Spencer, who have already been mentioned in another connection in this chapter. This company operates a production engineering unit at its London headquarters which provides a service to its smaller suppliers to help them become more efficient. In addition, with the help of Urwick Orr (management consultants), it arranged a series of training courses for the production staffs of its food and garment suppliers. No doubt there is a commercial benefit, as well as a feeling of ethical satisfaction, from these moves – yet the position of the company in relation to its suppliers could not be further from the type of chain store which is prepared to trample its suppliers underfoot in its search for additional profit.

There is also room for ethical considerations in considering price attitudes. Obtaining supplies at the lowest possible cost is, of course, an essential aspect of efficient management. Many chief executives would consider it unethical to band together with competitors in order to create a monopsonistic situation. However, it is not unknown for 'rings' of antique dealers to be exposed from time to time in the UK, and no doubt other countries. The ring rigs auctions in such a way that they are able to buy at low prices and share the profits among ring members. A ring such as this has featured in the BBC's longest-running soap, *The Archers*, so no one can have any doubts that they really exist!

Modern concepts of continuous improvement, or total quality management, stress that suppliers should be treated more as alliance partners than adversaries. Those that follow this concept are moving into a different pattern of supplier relationships, where there may be preferred suppliers with whom there is a long-term relationship, with both contributing to the continuous improvement of quality. This changes what might previously have been an ethical choice into enlightened self-interest.

Business ethics and planning

Earlier in this chapter it was mentioned that much of the pattern of changing ethical standards is conditioned by society, and frequently government plays a part by legislating to change standards to conform to the norms of the age. In all countries there are laws governing certain aspects of conduct towards employees, and in most there are complex legal safeguards of fostering the interest of customers and the community.

Often it is in the interests of business to keep ahead of legislation, since governments frequently tend to over-react. Governments, of course, will always err on the side of the event which is most visible and of most public concern. It will legislate to prevent a recurrence of a thalidomide type of disaster rather than consider the virtually unidentifiable lives which might be saved from a less time-consuming system of control.

Similarly, governments throughout the world will begin to react more stringently – and frequently overreact – to the pollution menace. In these circumstances industry could be penalised to a greater degree than if it had acted independently. The fact that an industry can exercise a self-control which obviates the need for legal enforcement has frequently been demonstrated. For example, in the UK, advertising ethics are controlled by the industries concerned.

The advent of government interference is one of the factors which changes social values and is, therefore, important. It departs a little from the main theme of the chapter, which is concerned more with the constraints chief executives voluntarily observe, rather than the ones to which they are compelled to surrender.

The difference between the two is not always easy to define, and is of minor significance in planning treatment.

Some attention should now be given to relating moral and ethical philosophies to a concept of modern management and strategic planning. The point has been made, and must be stressed, that the decisions made in this area are personal to the chief executive. In planning terms there is no difference in treatment between the company whose chief executive has low standards of integrity and is happy for the entire company to cheat, lie, and defraud without the slightest twinge of conscience and the company whose affairs are conducted on a higher plane. The chief executive of the former company will have less to consider or define than that of his or her counterpart. The freedom of each executive to decide these things for himself is a very important point of principle. Drucker[10] states: 'No one but the management of each particular business can decide what the objectives in the area of *public responsibility* should be.'

There are two schools of thought about how issues such as social responsibility should be treated in strategic management. Both accept the need for organisations to behave in a responsible way, and the difference is largely in whether this is an obligation where opportunities to do better should be actively sought out, or something which is a voluntary constraint on the organisation's freedom of action.

The stakeholder concept

The first of these has become known as the stakeholder concept. It is not new, and certainly dates from the 1960s and may well have existed long before this. Its

Figure 8.1
Stakeholders in an organisation. (Classification used by Wheeler and Sillanpää[9])

	Primary	Secondary
Social	Shareholders & investors Employees & Managers Customers Local communities Suppliers Other business partners	Government & regulators Civic institutions Social pressure groups Media Academic commentators Trade bodies Competitors
Non-social	The natural environment Future generations Non-human species	Environment pressure groups Animal welfare organisations

fundamental argument is that the organisation should be run for the benefit of the stakeholders in it.

Wheeler and Sillanpää[9] define stakeholders under four headings, which I have put into the matrix (Figure 8.1). They do not, of course, mean that organisations all have these stakeholders, and many writers on the stakeholder concept use the classifications I have used in this chapter.

The stakeholder proposition is that

> ...the long-term value of a company rests primarily on: the knowledge, abilities and commitment of its employees; and its relationships with investors, customers and other stakeholders. Loyal relationships are increasingly dependent upon how a company is perceived to create 'added value' beyond the commercial transaction. Added value embraces issues like quality, service, care for people and the natural environment and integrity. It is our belief that in the future the development of loyal, inclusive stakeholder relationships will become one of the most important determinants of commercial viability and business success.[9]

Features of the stakeholder corporation include:

- Efforts to understand the requirements of stakeholders, and to develop a vision and strategies that reflect and balance these needs
- Ways of measuring that the benefits are being delivered
- Communication, including surveys, that enables the organisation to understand the needs of stakeholders.
- Openness and transparency
- The belief that business can deliver commercial success and social value.

One reason why the concept has come back into prominence in the UK is the publication of the Royal Society for the encouragement of Arts, Manufactures, and Commerce's (RSA) report on 'Tomorrow's Company'.[11] This was followed by the establishment of the RSA company, The Centre For Tomorrow's Company, to promote the approach developed by the inquiry. What emerged from this inquiry by a team of twenty-five heavyweight business leaders was what the RSA call 'the inclusive approach', which builds successful relationships with stakeholders: employees, customers, suppliers, and the community. The belief of the inquiry was that a focus only on shareholders leads to short-termism, and that organisations with the balanced approach are more successful over the long term. Goyder[12] illuminates the cycle of failure by examining what happened to Britain's top company from the journal *Management Today*, over the period 1979 to 1989. Of the eleven top companies, four collapsed, two were acquired, and only five were still profitable.

Proponents of the inclusive approach include Willett International, Unipart, the John Lewis Partnership and the Co-operative Bank. The Body Shop is an enthusiastic supporter of the stakeholder concept, and much of the content of Wheeler and Sillanpää[9] draws from experience in that organisation. In November 1996 Kleinwort Benson launched the first Tomorrow's Company investment fund. The bank claims that a back test of companies chosen for the portfolio showed that they had superior performance on share price.

The constraints approach

There are opponents of the stakeholder approach as well as supporters. Argenti[13] argues:

> If 'the stakeholder approach' merely asserted that 'companies perform better the more closely they engage everyone affected by their operations' there would be little dissent: even the most rabid capitalist could accept that. But the theory goes far beyond that; it declares that the company should be run for all those who may be deemed to have a stake in it.

His criticisms are based on owner's rights, the lack of homogeneity between the various stakeholders, and practical problems. He concludes:

> The stakeholder theory is an idea whose time has long run out. It claims that companies should be run for the benefit of all, an impossible dream which, significantly, inspired such well-meaning disasters as nationalisation. In reality human organisations involve two distinct relationships: they are designed to confer advantage on one specific set of people – their intended beneficiaries. But, in order to operate effectively, they must engage the enthusiasm of all those other people who are affected by their activities and so must offer them some inducement. The stakeholder theory is not just philosophically misconceived, it has practical consequences to society that are profoundly damaging and deeply unethical.

The approach of many writers on strategic management is to suggest that ethical and moral obligations are constraints which the organisation sets according to it perception of how it should behave. Constraints may be defined as things which for moral or ethical reasons the company will not do, despite the fact that to do them would put the company a long way towards the achievement of its profit objectives. Ansoff[14] uses a simpler definition: 'constraints are decision rules, which exclude certain options from the firm's freedom actions.' Argenti[15] provides a basically similar approach.

Ansoff[14] makes a distinction between constraints and responsibilities. Under his classification a responsibility is something which a company accepts and which adds to its expense without in any way reducing its freedom of strategic action. Thus a company may, as many companies do, accept a liability to support a particular charitable foundation, or an employee's pension fund, but these actions in no way exclude any options from its strategy. The difference between a responsibility and a constraint is that a constraint does inhibit a company's freedom of action.

An important principle is that constraints must be defined and written down as part of the planning process (and, of course, this also includes certain of the major constraints imposed by law). Only when they are clearly defined can the chief executive be sure that they are clearly communicated through the organisation. The fact that this sort of policy action is called a constraint does not mean that it is in any way negative. The negative 'Thou shalt not steal' can be interpreted as the very positive 'be honest'.

It must be stressed that it is as important to define the constraints as to define any other element in a corporate plan. Only after this act is it possible for the organisation to be sure that its plans and day-to-day actions truly reflect the philosophies of the chief executive.

The defined constraints become an integral part of the company's corporate plans, and should be one of the criteria against which the plans and strategies are measured. The reason for clearly stating the constraints is practical, not academic. It is so that they can be used in the running of the business. In their application in planning constraints stand next to objectives, which means that most of the discussion on this subject (Chapter 12) also has a bearing on the subject.

In an ideal world more attention would perhaps be given to defining the constraints caused by ethical and moral considerations than is usually customary in modern business. Argenti[16] is perhaps a little idealistic in his views:

> Unfortunately, however, it was found to be only too easy to run a company so that it satisfied the shareholders – but failed to satisfy – indeed bitterly dissatisfied – other groups. Gradually, therefore, over the past few decades the shareholder has dropped from first beneficiary to the last – or so it would appear at first sight. In fact, he has always been last, he had always been the residual beneficiary after all other expenses of running the company have been met; the difference is only that most companies now recognise what some did not before, that it is not morally acceptable to take advantage of one's employees, suppliers, or customers even if it were possible (and in modern conditions, with full employment and vigorous competition, it seldom is). Thus the shareholder received, and still receives, whatever profit was left over from the company's operations; the distinction being that nowadays there is less left over because companies in general meet their social obligations instead of neglecting them.

Drucker's[10] view of what should happen is perhaps a useful note on which to summarise the debate so far.

> But what is most important is that management realise it must consider the impact of every business policy and business action upon society. It has to consider whether the action is likely to promote the public good, to advance the basic beliefs of our society, to contribute to its stability, strength and harmony.

How pleasant life would be if all chief executives of all businesses approached their problems in this way!

Cadbury[17] should have the last words on ethical issues, from his article that won the *Harvard Business Review* 1986 Annual Ethics in Business Prize. Among his many practical and thoughtful comments are two statements. One is that 'shelving hard decisions is the least ethical course' of action for a chief executive, and of course, many ethical decisions are neither easy to take, nor pleasant to implement. My own interpretation of this is that the golden glow of righteousness over a no-bribes policy in the Third World is easier to maintain when it does not mean making a large number of people redundant in the home country through lack of work. Moral decisions with no consequences are not the ones that cause sleepless nights!

The second is that 'actions are unethical if they won't stand scrutiny'. He argues that openness and ethics go together.

> Openness is also, I believe, the best way to disarm outside suspicion of companies' motives and actions. Disclosure is not a panacea for improving the relations between business and society, but the willingness to operate an open system is the foundation of those relations. Business needs to be open to the views of society and open in return about its own activities; this is essential for the establishment of trust.

Social audit

Hargreaves and Dauman,[18] whose book (published in 1975) unfortunately is now out of print, state:

> The idea of a social audit for organisations, particularly in business, is new. Indeed the term 'social audit' itself is still interpreted differently by different people. To some it means the public disclosure of a company's social performance. To others it means the internal (confidential) evaluation of a company's social responsibility performance. Others go further and define the social audit as a comprehensive evaluation of the way a company discharges all its responsibilities, to shareholders, customers, employees and suppliers, to the wider community, indeed to all its stakeholders.

They suggest a number of reasons why organisations should conduct a social audit. First, social responsibility is becoming an issue which is important to the growth and survival of the organisation. Second, like it or not, many organisations, without giving consent, are subject to social audits by external organisations. Many of these have a particular political axe to grind. Reports have been published on a number of companies by the Public Interest Research Centre, and Social Audits Ltd of the UK and by the Project on Corporate Responsibility in the USA. Companies such as General Motors, Tube Investments and Avon Rubber have been the targets. A third reason advanced by the authors is the ever-increasing requirement for disclosure in various countries, and their belief that industry is better off moving in advance of legislation, and thereby setting the pace and the rules that follow. They see as a fourth reason the pressure by shareholders for more information. Since they wrote their book there have been developments on all fronts, including the setting up of a number of ethical unit trusts which will only invest in companies that make acceptable products and behave in an ethical way, as defined by the unit trust.

There is no one universally acceptable way of conducting a social audit. Wheeler and Sillanpää[9] provide a detailed description of the method used by The Body Shop which is of value to anyone who may wish to explore the subject in detail.

One school of thought moves into social accounting, the idea that all social actions, negative and positive can be quantified and presented either as a broad numerical statement, or even more precisely as a form of balance sheet. This concept is very difficult to make workable. There are enough problems over the judgement areas in normal accounting, to show the problems that could arise when almost every statement was a judgement.

If the intention is to use the social audit as one element in the formulation of strategy within a company, and the purpose is totally internal, the resultant report should become another way of helping to relate the internal elements of the organisation to the external environment. Such an audit might be approached by listing the critical issues, some of which may also be partially covered by legislation, and the constituents who have a concern with the firm. Against these lists it is then possible to evaluate every strategy, policy and operating practice of the organisation. It would probably be necessary to repeat this exercise at various organisational levels: by business unit, by functional area, by geographical location, and by department. Immediately one can see that this is not a small task, while those that have been involved in quality audits for BS 5750 (ISO 9000) accreditation will be aware of the work involved in a much narrower aspect of policy and performance audit.

The types of issue that might be considered will vary over time, as what is considered socially important changes over time, as we have seen. However, they might include consumer responsiveness, health and safety, environmental pollution, use of scarce raw materials, Third World actions, employment of women or of ethnic minorities, energy utilisation and many more. Constituents have been defined in the preceding chapter when we looked at the Neubauer/ Solomon method of analysing the environment. Indeed, one can visualise the construction of matrices with scoring systems to help identify the success and problem areas.

In periods of recession, pressure on organisations to conduct social audits tends to alleviate, as organisations grapple with the more immediate task of staying solvent. *Green* issues have now become the most pressing, and some authorities now urge organisations to undertake audits of green issues. Vandermerwe and Oliff[19,20] argue that consumers are willing to buy *green*. They argue the need for a green audit, and the development of strategies across all functions. Most organisations have given some thought to green issues, and my experience is that they are even more complicated than other social issues. An organisation may clean up its own act, and be convinced that it creates no pollution, but unless it looks right across the chain of supply through to the ultimate consumer, it may simply be shifting the problem elsewhere. Perhaps it uses a raw material which is in itself safe and non polluting, but the supplier who makes it has to create a toxic waste. Maybe the packaging used is beautifully clean and hygienic, but will not biodegrade after use. Any audit needs to be very broad, and conducted with action in mind.

Vandermerwe and Oliff argue that organisations should set green goals. They list:

- Identifying benchmarks for green performance
- Determining the opportunities and risks from the 'green wave'

- Extend strategic planning to cover a broad range of green scenarios
- Undertake a careful assessment of the costs and benefits of being a green company.

References

1 Heaton, H. *Economic History of Europe*, Harper & Bros, New York, 1948.
2 Smith, L. N. *The Horizon Book of the Elizabethan World*, Paul Hamlyn, London, 1967.
3 Hargreaves, J. and Dauman, J. *Business Survival and Social Change*, Associated Business Programmes, London, 1975.
4 Jackall, R. *Moral Mazes*, Oxford University Press, New York, 1988.
5 *Financial Times*, 7 April 1971.
6 Carr, A. C. 'Can an Executive Afford a Conscience?' *Harvard Business Review*, July–August, 1970.
7 Wates, N. Social Responsibilities in Industry, Lecture to the Runnymede Trust, 15 October 1971.
8 Woodward, W. J., 'The Human Price of Change', *Journal of Professional HRM*, No 2, January, 1996.
9 Wheeler, D. and Sillanpää, M. *The Stakeholder Corporation*, Pitman, London, 1997.
10 Drucker, P. *The Practice of Management*, Heinemann, London, 1955.
11 RSA Inquiry. *Tomorrow's Company*, Gower, Aldershot, 1996.
12 Goyder, M. 'Tomorrow's Company', *Journal of Professional HRM*, No. 7, July, 1977.
13 Argenti, J. 'Stakeholders: the Case Against', *Long Range Planning*, 30, No. 3, June, 442–445, 1997.
14 Ansoff, H. I. *Corporate Strategy*, McGraw-Hill, New York, 1965.
15 Argenti, A. J. A. *Corporate Planning: A Practical Guide*, Allen & Unwin, London, 1968.
16 Argenti, A. J. A. 'Defining Corporate Objectives', *Long Range Planning*, March 1969.
17 Cadbury, Sir Adrian, 'Ethical Managers Make Their Own Rules', *Harvard Business Review*, September/October, 1987.
18 Hargreaves, J. and Dauman, J. *Business Survival and Social Change*, Associated Business Programmes, London, 1975.
19 Vandermerwe, S. and Oliff, M. D. 'Customers Drive Corporations Green', *Long Range Planning*, 23, No. 6, December, 1990.
20 Vandermerwe, S. and Oliff, M. D. 'Strategies For The '90s Mean Full Green Ahead Say Top Executives', *Strategic Management Review* (Tokyo), 16, No. 2, 1991.

Part 3

The Making of Strategy

CHAPTER 9

The corporate appraisal – assessing strengths and weaknesses

The assessment of strengths and weaknesses is an early stage in strategic thinking, and one where it is very easy to end up with meaningless lists of so-called strengths and weaknesses. The chapter will explore five ways of looking at strengths and weaknesses: assessment by managers, often resulting in what many books call SWOT analysis; equilibrium analysis, which is one way of forcing managers to make a more careful consideration of strengths and weaknesses; a process to 'audit' the facts, drawing conclusions from a detailed analysis of the organisation; the critical success factor approach; and the core competency approach. For each method, the chapter deals both with the concept and ways of operationalising it in a real situation.

So far this book has examined the broader aspects of strategic management and has looked at the process of planning in relation to a changing environment. It is now time to concentrate on a very specific step in the process – the assessment of corporate strengths and weaknesses. Planning literature refers to this important stage under various headings: the corporate appraisal, the position audit, and assessing the present position[1,2]. The particular terminology used is not important: the action itself is vital.

The corporate appraisal should be one of the first steps in the process of preparing strategic plans, and should provide both the platform from which the corporate objectives are established and the baseline of the strategic plan. Attempting to plan without carrying out this fundamental step is rather like trying to reach the top floor of a building without using the stairs or lift: the ascent is possible, but is highly dangerous and calls for much more effort. Omission of the basic step may lead the company to adopt the wrong strategy, to take decisions which at best restrict its achievement of its highest potential, and at worst lead it on the road to ruin.

In many ways the corporate appraisal may be one of the most difficult stages top management has to face. It sometimes means striking at the established practices and business areas of the company. It means facing up to unpleasant facts, an action which tends to destroy the wall of false security behind which it is so easy for even good managers to take complacent shelter. It can easily be considered as criticism by managers and accordingly resented. This is the area in which emotional responses may easily be roused. It is probably for these reasons that most companies which have a process of strategic planning – except when they have installed it with the aid of an outside management consultant – will confess to have either omitted this step entirely or glossed over it so brusquely that they pay only lip service to the concepts.

It is by no means unknown for a company to take stock of itself without practising any form of formal planning. Cost reduction areas and productivity increases are frequently sought by companies which are pointed much more to the present than to the future. General consultancy assignments are carried out in many companies by management consultants. It is perhaps because so many of the elements of the corporate appraisal are long-established management procedures that many books on planning do not dwell very much on the process of the corporate appraisal. Nearly all stress the need to assess strengths and weaknesses, but few give any indication how to set about it. The word 'strategy' conjures up visions of daring action on the corporate battlefield: the driving off of competitors; the subjugation of another company through acquisition – perhaps it even becomes the prize for winning a duel with other competing bidders; the conquest of new markets; and the deployment of massive resources of men and finance in gigantic projects. These emotive phrases may describe where strategy will eventually evolve. They are certainly not the starting point. And it is perfectly possible for a company to produce a sound strategy that is based almost entirely on opportunities uncovered during the corporate appraisal.

I like to think of the corporate appraisal as a process of establishing the corporate identity. There is a direct comparison between the guidance offered by a career counsellor to an individual person, and the use of the corporate appraisal by a forward-thinking management. No good career counsellor would consider the job well done if he or she simply provided the applicant with a list of situations vacant. What the counsellor tries to do is find out a great deal about the aspirations, ambitions, education, general intelligence, abilities, experience, and personality of the person being helped. Instead of a name he or she begins to deal with an identity; a real person who can be matched to a career which will complement his or her own individual and personal characteristics. So it is with the company. A superficial list of 'opportunities' can be produced in five minutes for any company. And it will probably be worth less than the time spent thinking about it. Instead the corporate identity should be established, and this unique combination of skills and experience, faults and abilities, matched to opportunities which exploit the strong points and correct the weak ones.

An appraisal should be conducted with the future in mind. Much of it will, of necessity, be equivalent to a photograph of the current position, but there will be many areas where it is possible to extend this static picture into the future. The appraisal should be designed to help solve the problems of tomorrow and, wherever possible, should be made dynamic rather than static. The fact that a particular product *today* contributes 80 per cent of profit is interesting: it becomes much more interesting when linked to information about competitive activity, and whether it is in a declining or growth market. Although at this stage in planning it may not be possible to be too specific about the future, the general indications should be given wherever the appraisal can identify them. Drucker[3] stresses that it is as important to identify 'tomorrow's breadwinners' as it is to identify today's. It is because of this future-oriented outlook that I believe the term 'appraising the company's present position' to be a poor description of what should happen.

No company in the world, however profitable, can afford to neglect opportunities for cost reduction and profit improvement. (It may deliberately opt not to implement them, but this is decision, not neglect.) Although the main purpose of the appraisal has to do with the future, the immediate profit potential which arises is a strong additional reason for not ignoring this step in the planning process. It is possible to argue that taking any cost-reduction opportunity is a positive way of removing a weakness and avoiding the perpetuation of an unsatisfactory situation, and any additional contribution to cash flow reinforces the company's ability to exploit new opportunities.

There are several ways in which an organisation can set out to undertake a corporate appraisal, although none of them are mutually exclusive. Although the aim of this chapter is to focus on the internal elements of the analysis, in reality the strengths and weaknesses should not be completely separated from the opportunities available to and the threats facing the organisation. It is also true to say that strengths and weaknesses require to be matched against the needs of customers and the capabilities of competitors, so the next two chapters on industry and competitor analysis are also relevant to the final conclusions that should be drawn from a corporate appraisal. In this chapter it will be necessary to stray a little from a total focus on strengths and weaknesses, but as far as possible we will keep to the internal elements. But remember that in the end it is the market which is important.

The five ways of looking at strengths and weaknesses are:

- Assessment by managers
- Equilibrium analysis
- An analytical method which assesses the key facts, from which strengths and weaknesses can be determined
- The critical success factor concept
- The core competency approach

Assessment by managers

The method which appears in almost every book on strategic management goes under a variety of names. It has been called SOFT (strength, fault, opportunity, threat), SWOT (strength, weakness, opportunity, threat), TWOS, TOWS, and WOTS

UP (the final letters standing for underlying planning). The end product is a list, frequently presented on one sheet of paper, under the headings in the order suggested by the acronym. The S and W are the internal elements, and the O and T come from the external environment, including the competitors and the market. Such a list usually leads into either action plans or projects to put things right.

Of course, a list of this nature may well be generated by the analytical approach which is discussed in some depth later in this chapter. The self-assessment method does not work this way. Instead it asks managers, either alone, or in groups, to complete the list under the chosen headings. As these are really the same, and only the order changes to make the various acronyms, we can shorten this to SWOT analysis. They may be asked to assess the whole organisation, or just the part that they work within.

There is some validity in the underlying belief that managers at various levels have knowledge of what the organisation is good or bad at, and that they can add a great deal to the understanding of the corporate situation. Unfortunately, the self-assessment method often fails to release this knowledge, and can reinforce existing perceptions of the strategic situation at a time when they should be challenged. Typically managers find it hard to identify the real strengths of an organisation, and many SWOT charts produced at workshops of managers leave the observer wondering why the organisation has any business at all.

Weaknesses are often a mixture of minor operational issues with a few strategic matters. What appears to be a weakness may in some circumstances be a strength. For example, the fact that order-handling costs are higher than those of competitors may be a weakness: on the other hand, it could be a strength if the extra effort put in meant that customers received their orders much faster than they would from competitors, *and that they valued this*. If managers have no perception that the industry is changing, or that they should take action to change it, their perception of weaknesses will inevitably be related to the past rather than the future.

There is also the problem that SWOT analysis tempts people to be superficial, and that sometimes what is said, and believed, has little relationship to reality. An example is work that I did with an organisation that made scaffold poles and cement-forming equipment. Managers genuinely believed that they sold or hired their product to the major contractors, and that these were their key customers. They further believed that the company was the market leader in scaffold poles: in fact the name of the company was used on construction sites in place of the somewhat longer 'scaffold pole'. So among their strengths was their relationships with these customers, and their dominant position in the market for scaffold poles (but not for cement-forming equipment). Among the threats was that recession had devastated the market.

Sales analysis, which they had never undertaken before, revealed a different story. Although they had major contractors as their customers for the forming equipment, in the past year they had had business with only one contractor for scaffold poles. The customer base for scaffolding was now almost completely small local builders (they had a chain of branches across the UK), and most transactions were of much smaller value than the managers believed. Further work showed that they no longer held the leadership in market share, and that recession was a cause, but not the major cause, of their sales decline. Market research among contractors revealed that they had asked my client some years ago to provide a hire-and-erect service for scaffolding, and had been rejected as the client did not wish to get into the business of erecting and dismantling scaffolding. As a result, the contractors had encouraged the formation of specialist companies, and in most cases had sold their own stocks of scaffolding to these companies. Now they no longer needed to deal with my client.

The introduction of some hard facts not only showed that the managers' perception was faulty, but also made it clear that they needed a complete reappraisal of their strategy. .

Although the self-assessment route can be of value, the message is, approach it with care, and ideally combine it with an analytical approach.

Under the SWOT approach an attempt is made to establish what has to be done to maintain the satisfactory things and correct the faults, to ensure that opportunities are exploited, and threats avoided or reduced in impact. This is what all the methods of conducting a corporate appraisal aim to do. Where this approach does differ is that it is basically a self-appraisal scheme. Managers are asked to comment under this classification on aspects of their own operations: to record their own opinions, which may often not be the same as current company policy. As analyses may be obtained from various levels in the organisation, a variety of opinions and ideas may be forthcoming. These are analysed and discussed, and eventually refined to working lists.

Equilibrium analysis

One problem I have found in practice is stimulating managers to take a balanced view of strengths and weaknesses. Often all that results from a self-appraisal is a shopping list which is often painfully inadequate. To help managers be more objective I often use what I call the equilibrium approach in group discussions. This is illustrated in Figure 9.1 and is probably the simplest technique ever designed. It consists of a scale and a line.

The line represents the current state of something – anything – that is to be considered. Examples are current market share, state of labour turnover, present profitability. Above the line the group are asked to identify the factors which keep it as *low* as it is. Below the line they are asked to say what keeps it as *high* as it is. In practice it helps to switch to and from with remarks like 'You've identified so much that holds it down that I'm surprised you have any business at all! Why is it that you are doing as well as you are?'

Arrows can be drawn from each key item identified, using the scale to provide a judgemental view of the importance of the factor. Longer lines are more important than short ones. The final stage is to identify what issues (a) can and (b) should be addressed, to remove negative factors or strengthen positive ones. This simple approach is very effective in achieving balance and consensus.

It is perfectly feasible to use this approach as well as one of the other methods.

167

Figure 9.1
Equilibrium Analysis
(example)

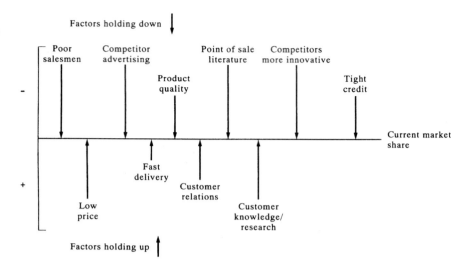

One of the most difficult things to encourage is a *continual* inward-looking approach. It is very easy to regard a corporate appraisal as a once-and-for-all exercise, which, of course, it should never be. While the process of studying environmental opportunities, which are readily perceived to be always changing, is a planning tool which becomes sharpened with use, the internal self-criticism of the company's affairs, which do not always appear to be altering, can easily become a very blunt probe.

The analytical approach

The analytical approach seeks to analyse the business using data rather than opinion. Any organisation that decides to undertake a corporate appraisal in this way must first decide how to set about it. One method might be to put the whole thing into the hands of consultants: but this is really begging the question, as the consultants themselves would apply a certain methodology, so even if this route is chosen, the organisation should give some thought to the sorts of things that should be investigated.

A second approach might be for one person in the organisation to undertake the study – the chief executive personally, or the planner, or some other appropriate person. On an individual basis, the ability of any one person to probe deeply is limited by the size and complexity of the group: a vast multinational giant would have to decentralise its approach if it were ever to finish.

The third approach uses a series of teams on a part-time basis, led by – depending on size – a number of people who had been allocated full-time to the appraisal, with all the work being coordinated and controlled by one person. This method has the merit that it really works and, provided the coordinator gets the teams working in the right areas and seeking answers to the right questions, it goes a long way to ensuring that the results are objective and emotionally detached.

The corporate appraisal should not be seen as being completely isolated from the studies of the environment. There are interrelationships, and although the two stages are conceptually separate, each impinges on the other. Thus the first appreciation of the appraisal may be modified by what is learned about environmental trends and expectations. Turning the microscope inwards also involves a measure of peering outwards. Market share and the performance of competitors are but two examples of external factors which properly form part of the corporate appraisal. There is no hard-and-fast line where it is possible to say that the corporate appraisal ends and environmental trends begin, just as on a hazy day it is not possible to be precise about the exact spot on the horizon where the sky disappears and the sea is seen. This does not mean that the appraisal is not different from the environmental study – and no one would argue that sea and sky are the same, even though their extremes are confused.

What factors should be considered in the appraisal? The answer will vary between organisations, and although a generalised view can be given, a real situation would call for some critical selection. So the items which follow should only be treated as indicative.

There is another problem. The written word gives the impression that events follow in logical sequence, like loops in a chain. Life is not like this because there are few events in real situations which are completely divorced from every other event. In a real situation the factors studied hang together like a spider's web. Strands are linked to other strands directly and indirectly.

A number of basic concepts should be carried in mind as the appraisal progresses, and performance rated against these.

1 It should always be assumed that there might be a better way of doing anything until the contrary is proved.
2 It is usually a relatively small amount of effort which produces most of the return. Actual figures will vary, but will generally prove that a large amount of profit, say 80 per cent, comes from, say, 20 per cent of effort. The remaining 20 per cent of profit comes from 80 per cent of effort. Unfortunately, it is rarely possible to be specific about the *exact* point when effort could profitably be curtailed, although any action which reduces the amount of less profitable action should lead to corporate improvement.
3 Often knowledge of what is being done is not as perfect as managers within a company believe. One of the tasks of the corporate appraisal should be to ascertain the facts. This can often be a very difficult exercise. Incorrect answers are often supplied to the investigators' questions out of ignorance, and in good faith.
4 When *what* is being done has been established, the question Why? should be asked.
5 The future is more important than the present, where the trends and effects on the aspects studied can be foreseen.
6 The appraisal should cover all aspects of the company.

Trends of results

An obvious starting point is the company's historical pattern of performance: trends in profit, sales, capital employed, and then all the various ratios which may be derived from these to measure efficiency. To make sense the analysis should be broken down by subsidiary companies, departments, or areas of performance (such as home and export sales). Practical difficulties may arise in the detailed analysis because of lack of information: for example, capital employed may be difficult to calculate for divisions using common facilities for even the current year, quite apart from any past data. The whole basis of accounting may have changed over the period, so that definitions are not strictly comparable. Accounting systems may even vary between subsidiaries – even more probable with companies operating in several countries. All this means that there may be gaps and imperfections in the data collected.

The examination of these historical figures will show whether the company is improving or worsening its position; it becomes possible to see the broad activity areas contributing to the results and – even at this early stage – to isolate poor performances for further thought. At this point it may be possible to add a few question marks to the data which take account of some of the future aspects – perhaps indicating a market area which is likely to change radically, or a major change that might be expected in a subsidiary because of economic trends in a particular country.

Sources of profits

Analysis by broad department or subsidiary can only be regarded as a starting point. The next stage should be a detailed examination of profitability and prospects on a product basis, in terms of geographical sales, where relevant (e.g. by export market), and by distribution method.

This is one of the many stages when the accounting methods of the firm should be queried. Although most companies have detailed costs by product, the exercise should question the bases on which these are calculated. This usually means looking at the way in which certain costs are allocated.

Queries of this nature do not necessarily mean that the cost accounting system is 'wrong'. In fact workable alternatives to the allocations used by the cost accountants may be difficult to establish for *regular* reporting purposes, although they may be ascertainable for an *ad hoc* exercise such as the corporate appraisal. The cost accountant's job is to ensure that all costs are apportioned somewhere, so that at the end of the day the company does not find items it has not recovered. The planner is more interested in the dynamics of change: he or she wishes to see what would be left if a particular product or activity were carried out in a different way.

Many costs which are allocated to products or activities are apportioned on some form of percentage basis, spread evenly across the activity. Thus it is quite common to find transportation costs charged at a flat percentage of sales value: order-processing costs, sales force costs, and various other variable overheads may be allocated in the same way. The assumption is that all these costs fall on products in a normal distribution.

In fact this is an erroneous assumption because these costs fall unevenly in a highly skewed distribution. Transport costs will vary with order size and distance from depot. Order processing costs will vary with the number of lines on the invoice: it costs no more to process an order for £1000 than for an order of £1 of the same product.

Drucker[3] indicates the value of allocating costs like this on a 'transaction' basis – making an attempt to re-examine product and activity profitability when costs are allocated in a way which is much closer to the way in which they really fall. This part of the exercise may require the support of work study or O&M specialists, but can repay the effort handsomely, often bringing a completely new perception of the business.

A food manufacturer found that after reallocating its transport and order-processing costs by number of orders instead of by percentage of sales value, a whole class of distributive outlet was shown to be unprofitable. These outlets accounted for some 55 per cent of orders but under 7 per cent of sales. Within the class of outlet there was some profitable business, and it was possible to lay down broad parameters showing activities that should either be eliminated or changed to improve margins. This was a completely new perspective for the company.

In another part of the same exercise it was noted that an identical product with different labels (government contract and normal trade) was sold at a lower price to one type of distribution outlet than to another. The product costings showed that the cheaper-priced label cost less to produce than the more expensive one. Common sense indicated an error somewhere and investigation showed that certain overheads had been allocated *pro rata* to selling price. On the same assumption, if the product had been given away, it would have incurred no overheads.

Fyffes Group Ltd have documented[5] how by applying a 'transaction' view to physical distribution problems they were able to reduce their lorry fleet of over 300 vehicles by 20 per cent during an eighteen-month period of increasing turnover.

It is studies such as these which enable the appraisal to identify the real 'breadwinners' in the organisation. At the same time they also indicate changes which should be made to various levels of strategy within the company. One of the most frequent strategic decisions which emerges is the reduction of variety, the elimination of certain products, or a pricing or order size change which effectively eliminates certain classes of customer. Many firms take pride in the length of their product list: many would make much more profit if they eliminated those which did not adequately contribute to profits.

Even where products do make a positive contribution, this may sometimes be increased if the number of varieties can be reduced, or greater standardisation introduced, of raw materials, packaging, or product.

Wander Ltd,[4] food and pharmaceuticals manufacturers, found that they had fifty-three varieties of their main product, Ovaltine. Immediate action reduced this to below fifty, and by careful thought, leading to the combination of various exports labels, within two years the number of label and size variations had been further reduced to about two dozen. As many of the export tins were of lithographed metal, these moves brought inventory savings all the way through the production line.

Risk

The investigators now have a clear indication of the company's main sources of profits. The next stage is to examine some of the risks attached to these products.

First, there is the obvious situation where a company is very dependent on one product for its profit. There have been many companies in this position, and they can carry on for decades making good returns and seemingly giving little cause for concern. Yet there is a problem, and overdependence on one product – or indeed, to a lesser degree one market – carries a high probability of future problems.

Second, a similar type of risk is where the bulk of a company's business is tied up with a few customers. This is often the case with certain industrial products, and is an increasing tendency in certain types of retailing. Again the business may be quite safe, although there is a strong indication for strategic development elsewhere. In some cases the strategic implication may mean a new approach in the same market, widening the pattern of distribution: in others it may indicate different products or completely new types of business.

Third, there is raw material risk which may vary from a world difficulty of supply to overdependence on one supplier.

Market risk should also be examined. The market position of each main product should be established. It is equally important for the firm to understand the areas in which it has leadership. What is it that makes its products unique so that people are willing to purchase them? A product does not have to be a brand leader to have uniqueness or particular attributes in which it has a leadership position. This is the point in the study when market research reports should be linked with the internally derived data and supplemented with informed judgement from people inside the company. Market risks are an important consideration in the study of which of the products will develop as future breadwinners and which are likely to decline or die.

Finally, technological risk should be considered, not only the possibility of product obsolescence but also the likely changes in production processes which are likely to cause the company problems in the area of plant and machinery. Anything which affects the company's future competitive position is a risk which should be carefully considered.

Manufacturing activity

With this developing profile of its products in mind, the company should turn its attention to the processes by which these are made, looking for areas of potential cost reduction, alternative production methods, alternative formulae or composition of products, and technological developments which could improve costs. To aid this study, it may be useful to use work-study techniques or value analysis.

There is frequently a general assumption in companies that its production processes are efficient. This they may be. The question to be answered is whether they can be more efficient, or is it possible to achieve the same end product by cheaper alternatives. This is the point in time when the company should examine make-or-buy situations for its components, and should look at the prices of outside services in comparison with its own costs.

The graph in Figure 9.2 provides an answer to those who argue that production is a sacrosanct area. This shows efficiency ratings on a theoretical yield basis for the processing of a basic commodity in a food plant. For years the plant had had an average efficiency of about 94–95 per cent. Suddenly it slumped dangerously. Corrective action brought a modest improvement. At this stage a process engineering team was brought in – not as part of a corporate appraisal but as an operational necessity. Successive actions gradually increased the yield, which soon passed the old average of 94–95 per cent. Improvement continued, and at one point a yield greater than the theoretical

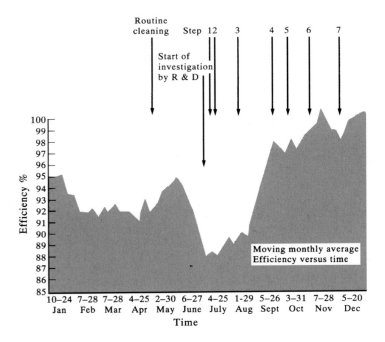

Figure 9.2
Improvement in the efficiency of a food process

maximum was obtained. The point of the story is that after the study the plant was operated more efficiently than it had ever been, although earlier in the year management would have argued that it was already efficient. In this case it took what proved to be a happy accident to bring about improvements.

Consideration of the process should include the raw materials, the standards set for their purchase, and the efficiency of the company as buyers.

Rationalisation of resources

Another aspect of the study, particularly in companies with many sites, is whether facilities of plant or buildings can be rationalised or relocated. Where two plants or two office buildings can be amalgamated into one, considerable cost savings may frequently be obtained. A similar approach should be applied to distribution depots: many companies have made a substantial impact on their profit position by drastically reducing the number of depots operated.

A company with plants located in different countries should re-examine its supply and demand patterns. Perhaps a particular plant should be closed or the source of supply to a particular importing country changed. International studies such as this are invariably complex and involve more than factory cost comparisons. Marginal costs should be considered, the effect of change on fixed overheads, investment requirements, and differing tax liabilities. There may also be legal problems to be considered where profits are, in effect, transferred from one legal entity to another.

Organisation and management structure

Facilities are important, but they are not the only resources a company has to deploy. Even more important are people. The corporate appraisal should look at the people resource from a number of viewpoints.

A good place to start is the basic organisational structure. What is the company's organisational structure? A simple question that a surprisingly large number of companies are unable to answer because no one has ever set down the structure on paper.

Once the structure has been identified it becomes possible to look at impending management problems such as succession and the strengths and weaknesses of the key managers and their teams. In many family businesses succession to the top management slots is often a problem, recognition of which does not always come until the death, illness, or retirement of a key manager. The assessment of managerial capability is a very delicate task, yet it is one which is most important. There is very little point in deciding to launch a range of new products if it is known that the marketing manager is incapable of making a success of the venture. Assessments such as this can only be made at the highest level in the organisation, which is one reason why the chief executive must be very closely involved in the appraisal.

In a very large company, organisational and managerial capability assessment may be a complex problem – and particularly complex where the company is also multinational and the appraisal is complicated by the need to make examinations across a very wide front.

Organisational problems may exist at every level in the company, as may the question of the quality of individual performance, and it is sensible to also examine other aspects of the people resource. What are the company's labour relations like – are these a strength or a weakness? How does productivity compare with that in other industries?

In one study of a small warehouse depot of a large organisation, I found that the company was paying a very high overtime bill, with employees working very late on certain days of the week. However, on other days they were finishing their work by lunchtime and either carrying out unnecessary tasks (like sweeping a floor twice) or were actually going home before closing time. Overall, they were working less than the normal weekly number of hours, yet at the same time were drawing considerable sums in overtime payments. Simple rescheduling of the workload removed all the overtime. (However, it should be noted that in most circumstances other problems will arise if take-home pay is reduced.)

The appraisal should also consider the company's relation with its trade unions, and whether anything should be done to improve or maintain these. What, indeed, is the company's policy to trade unions?

Perhaps most important of all is the general morale of employees (which may vary by sector) and their attitudes to the company. There is also often a sort of 'corporate motivation' which may be important: thus sometimes whole companies think only in terms of their major product. In other companies there may be absolutely no feeling for profit. Still others may think only of profit and never of people. If 'judgement' assessments backed by overt evidence, such as a number of labour disputes, are distrusted, it is possible to use a more scientific approach to establish these factors using opinion research techniques.

Financial resources

At this stage an assessment should be made of the company's liquid resources and probable future cash-flow position. A company with a very high debt must take a different view of its future strategic options from one with a surplus of cash. This aspect of the appraisal should also consider the effects on cash flow that could result from internal changes, such as a reduction of inventories or debtors, or the disposal of certain fixed assets. Even at this early stage thought should be given to the future, and the company's financial potential identified in some detail.

Corporate capability

In addition to the corporate motivation discussed earlier, every company has – often for no easily discernible reason – a number of things it is good at and a number at which it is mediocre or poor. On paper the individual people frequently appear no different from or no better than those in other companies: yet collectively they often obtain a level of synergy which is difficult to explain. So one company may be particularly effective in its customer service, another may be excellent at physical distribution. It may be possible for one company to utilise design skills more skilfully than its competitors. Another may have a particular and unique marketing flair.

These strong and weak points should be identified where possible – again using marketing research, internal opinion, and company results as the sources of data.

Systems

The corporate appraisal should also look at the systems used within the company, attempting to identify areas of strength and areas of weakness. Again a future-oriented examination is called for: it is not only a question of current effectiveness but also how the system could stand up to expected changes. Can the order-processing department cope with a dramatic increase in the number of new products? How efficient is the costing system – and will it creak under the strain of new requirements? Does the budgetary control process really work – is it dynamic enough for modern business? Are there any written policies in existence in the form of 'standing orders', or is everything always decided on an *ad hoc* basis? What are the systems of decision taking? How effective is the inventory control procedure? Have the warehouse routines ever been subjected to work study? What methods are used for the evaluation of capital expenditure projects?

The inquiry should probe into every corner of the company, seeking information which will help to provide colour, form, and shape to some of the blank pieces which contribute to the total jigsaw which is the corporate identity.

Use of resources

One of the objects of the study is to produce a pattern from the jumble of facts that has been collected – to put some of the pieces of the puzzle together so that tentative conclusions may be made about the form the whole picture will take.

An important step is to examine the allocation of resources between products and to compare this with their real profit contribution. 'Resources' means not only money, buildings, and plant but also what are probably the scarcer resources of management talent, capability, and technical skills.

Analysis of this nature usually is imperfect because it has to attempt to divide what is often the indivisible, and may bring particular problems of management when dealing with the less-specific data. Nevertheless, sensible conclusions can be drawn. What so often happens is that the study shows where emphasis is misplaced. Too frequently a declining product area is given to the best managers to 'put on its feet'. Corporate pride will not allow the company to let the product die – or to deliberately kill it – and resources of time, money, and effort are squandered when they could be spent wisely if used on a successful product area that can be made more successful.

Divisions that can boast of past glories frequently obtain the lion's share of all the available resources, even though other business areas offer more potential. Research & Development effort may be misdirected; perhaps trying to breathe new life into a dying product when the company should be practising euthanasia.

Out of this aspect of the appraisal should come an understanding of which products are what Drucker[3] calls an investment in management ego – projects carried on through feelings of personal or corporate pride, which greedily swallow resources and contribute neither to present nor future profits.

If nothing more than a change of emphasis emerges, this aspect of the appraisal will have contributed much, and occasionally it may result in a complete reorientation of the company.

The next two chapters will deal in detail with industry and competitor analysis, both of which contribute to the corporate appraisal, the formulation of strategy, and the monitoring of the outcome of that strategy. There is one extension to industry analysis which should be mentioned here. It is related to the modern trend for many organisations to find that the competitive arena has moved from a multicountry operation, where each country could be seen as an almost independent strategic decision unit, to a global market. When an organisation has a global strategy it has to think of all country markets at once, and develop an approach that takes the maximum advantage from size without losing all its ability to respond to local needs. Global strategy will feature in a later chapter. It is an area where most of the writing is new, and much is still evolving. The point for the appraisal is to check that the organisation is managing in the best way for the situation it is in. Head-on competition with a global marketer by an organisation that manages on a multicountry basis (that is, all decisions taken locally and independently) will in almost all cases lead to ultimate failure. Therefore, if the company is running its business in a way which is a mismatch with the competitive arena in which it operates, this should be a point of debate from the appraisal. The words 'competitive benchmarking' might be mentioned here, as a further trailer to matters germane to the appraisal, but which will be expanded in the next chapter.

Reporting on the appraisal

By this stage in the investigation those engaged in the appraisal will be ready to complete the final report. What they should have is a mass of data, some already partly assembled, some in the form of detailed reports which have to be summarised and integrated, and the rest in the form of brief notes. The final report will draw on data generated in the study as well as information and reports which are already existing.

In theory the report will cover all areas of the company with equal efficiency, and will contain all relevant data to enable immediate profit improvements to be made and to provide a foundation stone for every future strategic decision. In practice things will be somewhat different. The report should bring improvements; it should help in the formation of strategy, but it will be neither complete nor perfect. Some of the data will be more reliable than the rest; there may be complete gaps where it has been impossible to make any analysis. In other areas tentative estimates may be all that is possible, yet – despite these imperfections – the final report can be a document of great value to the company.

In practice, too, there may have been an implementation of some of the recommendations as the subreports are completed, and some action may have been taken before the formal unveiling of the final report. This is, indeed, what should happen, and it is a mistake to see the report as something which has no part in the management of the company until the final dramatic moment when it is dropped on the chief executive's desk. Yet although the appraisal will have unearthed many things on which immediate action can be taken, it should – if it has done its job well – draw many conclusions which are a surprise to the company. It may make recommendations which bring out a strong emotional reaction from individual members in the company.

Such a reaction should not take the investigators unawares. Frequently, appraisals of this nature challenge the established order of things and bring the company face to face with the impact of change. Often, the factual information can lead to a number of different actions, and there may be strong differences of opinion over what these may be. The report may shake the existing power structure within the company, and aspects of it may be resented by those whose positions are challenged. And often, what appears to be the firm rocky ground on which the company's past and therefore its future is based is revealed as about to turn to a quivering quicksand: this can be hard to accept.

It is possible to argue that, unless some differences of opinion occur within the company, either the appraisal has not got to the root of the situation or the company is one of the lucky few that is doing everything well. In order that they may be sure that they will obtain really effective corporate appraisals the chief executives must choose the investigators wisely. It must be possible to rely on their objectivity and professional integrity, and they must be mature and senior enough not to bend their conclusions to suit personalities in the company.

At the same time the team must be given a measure of protection and the chief executive must ensure that effective use is made of the report and that it is not shelved merely because it is unpleasant. There must be a willingness to accept that certain conclusions might even be construed as criticisms of his or her own present or past actions. Indeed, the chief executive should try to get the management team to view the document not as criticism of the past but rather as an objective analysis of what the company must now do. This is often more difficult in practice than in theory, since it is very hard for most managers to forget their personal involvement and view the recommendations and conclusions with objectivity.

Normally, a corporate appraisal such as this should be available to the whole of the senior management team, while some of the subreports and extracts may be shown to managers of lower levels. There may be some aspects of the report which the chief executive wishes to keep confidential – e.g. the appraisal of individual management abilities: the chief executive may well have carried out these parts of the exercise personally, and even the investigators may be unaware of the chief executive's conclusions in these areas.

Because the corporate appraisal is so important, a great deal of thought should go into the writing of the final report – not only in the quality of the content but also in the format and presentation of the report. There are many 'right' ways of writing this, and it is an area about which it is dangerous to be dogmatic.

My own approach has been to prepare a brief summary report showing the main strengths and weaknesses of the company and the strategic implications of these. Each statement is backed up by a more detailed report and analysis, examining the subject in considerable depth. Significant figures and charts may be attached as appendices. The method is not perfect but it enables the conclusions and recommendations to be presented in a way that has considerable dramatic impact and which forces the main issues to the attention. The volume and variety of the appendices will depend very much on the individual circumstances. A simplified, abbreviated example of this style of presentation is given in Figure 9.3.

The example is not meant to illustrate a real company; and certainly an organisation in as bad a way as this might well have to consider closing down. In this particular appraisal the reader is asked to assume that the aspects not shown provide the management with grounds for believing that improvement is possible. But no wonder morale in marketing is reported to be low.

Before leaving the analytical method, I should mention one summary approach which I have found useful. This is the ROI Chart shown in Figure 9.4 (sometimes called a Dupont chart). This is a way of looking at the economic structure of the business, by putting the balance sheet and income statement onto one sheet of paper. The figure is adaptable. In the example columns A, B and C could be taken as SBUs, subsidiaries, or products, and charts could be completed at various levels of resolution. Thus the summary chart might be by SBU, and for each SBU there might be a regional analysis, and for each region, a product analysis. It then becomes very easy to see where the profit is coming from, and also whether the use of capital is related to the size of profit contribution. Unfortunately there is always some work to do to fill in the columns, as the final accounts rarely use figures in precisely this way. The insight such a chart can bring can repay this effort.

PART 1: Weaknesses/Limiting Factors

Factor	Strategic Implications
1. Management	1. Management
(a) Chief executive age 65, no obvious successor.	(a) Recruitment, merger, or sale of business. Main priority for action.

(b) Middle management can be graded as:
 	
         % of Managers
Weak   50
Mediocre 10
Good   40
	(b) (i) Recruitment in weak areas.
	    (ii) Management development and training.
	   (iii) Reorganisation.

(c) The company undertakes no management development or training of any kind.	(c) Investigate feasibility of systematic approach to management development.
(d) Organisational lines and relationships are undefined. No organisation chart exists.	(d) Implementation of the reorganisation proposals (recommended in separate report).
(e) Marketing manager 60, has been seriously ill and is unlikely to be able to cope with change or expansion.	(e) See reorganisational proposals. Problem must be solved if company to develop.
2. Marketing	2. Marketing

(a) 75% of profits emanate from product A. Market declining at 10% per year. Market share under attack from competitors with superior product.	(a) (i) Reduce dependence on this one product – see separate report.
	    (ii) Examine market strategy to seek improvement (see also 2b).
	   (iii) Improve product.
	   (iv) Cost reduction – value analysis, process development.

(b) Advertising and promotional expenditure is haphazard, dispersed over various types of media and methods, and is without any form of follow up to measure impact or effect.	(b) (i) Relate to new marketing strategy.
	    (ii) Cease promotion through sponsorship – saving £50,000 per year.
	   (iii) Market research to measure impact of current advertising.

(c) Fifty-six variations of pack or label of product A.	(c) Reduce variety to ten, saving £30,000 per year in packaging, warehousing, finance, and production costs.
(d) Fifteen products (one hundred variations) account for 12% of sales and contribute no profit. Ten of these are in a loss situation (two make a loss on variable costs).	(d) (i) Cease production, re-deploy resources on twelve products. (ii) Develop marketing plan to exploit three products in growth markets.
(e) 45% of order transactions account for $2\frac{1}{2}$% of sales. There is a loss on these transactions.	(e) Review minimum order sizes, price structures, and physical distribution methods.

PART 2: Strengths

Factor	Strategic Implications
1. Management	
(a) Skilful and competent production management.	(a) Exploit in managing new product production and costs reduction on existing products.
2. People	
(a) Strong sense of loyalty to company, and morale high in factories (although not high in marketing).	(a) (i) Make best use of this in reorganising for change. (ii) Ensure that managerial style encourages these feelings.
3. Marketing	
(a) Strong image among consumers for service. Quality image remains although suffering from impact of competitors' better product.	(a) Transfer to other products.

Figure 9.3

Example of one method of summarising strengths and weaknesses

Product	Current annual sales (£000)	% of total sales	Sales growth past 5 years	Market prospects	Competitors	Brand share	True profit contr. (£000)	% Total profit contr.	Utilisation of resources					Remarks
									% fixed assets	% working capital	% R%D time	% Prod. capacity	% sales force time	
A (56 variations)	3000	50	2% p.a.	-10% p.a.	Strong and strengthening	40%	300	75	60	45	5	40	95	Present bread-winner, doubtful future
B (3 variations)	600	10	15% p.a.	+25% p.a.	Weak–new competition probable	75%	4	1	5	10	25	12	1	Future bread-winner. Profit can be improved by new process just developed
C (1 variation)	300	5	New product	+10% p.a.	Nil–will change within two years	100%	60	15	2	4	30	10	3	High profitability will not continue once product under competitive attack
D (30 variations)	30	1	Nil	+25% p.a.	Many competitors	10%	-4	-1	10	1	12	10	Nil	No future for this product
E (10 variations)	30	1	+2½% p.a.	Not known	No information	Not known	4	1	1	1	Nil	1	Nil	

Figure 9.3 Appendix A
Product Contribution and Resources

Figure 9.4
ROI chart to show
the economic
structure of the
business

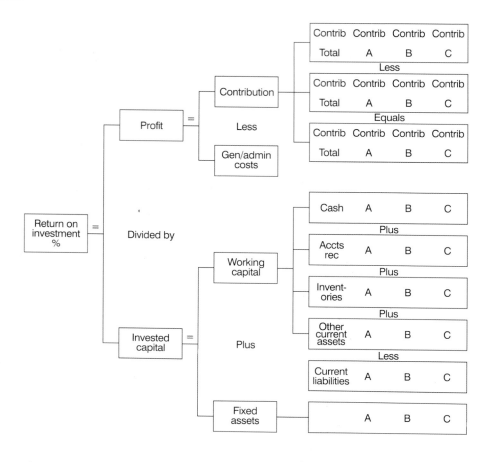

The critical success factor concept

Critical success factors are also known as critical skills, or sometimes the word 'critical' is replaced by 'key'. One way to make SWOT analysis more meaningful is to assess the half dozen or so critical skills that the organisation must possess in order to be successful in its marketplace. Once these have been identified as a standard, it becomes possible to compare the level to which the organisation has these skills. Denning[2] suggested a variety of skills that may be important, and these are shown in Figure 9.5. In this figure he has identified what he believed to be the critical skills required of an international oil company and a car manufacturer. The important thing is not whether this analysis is still correct but that the skills needed for the two businesses are different.

The critical success factor concept provides a link back from the market place to the organisation's strengths and weaknesses. If we want to succeed in this market, we have to be very good at these critical success factors. If we are weak in one of these factors we have a strategic weakness. It may well have been a weakness that we might have overlooked without a critical success factor analysis. It also follows that once we know where we have to do well, we also have a standard against which we can assess competitors, and the concept will appear again when we consider competitor analysis.

The analysis can take place at various levels in the organisation. For example, if the concept were applied to Hanson Trust, different critical success factors would be expected at the corporate level from those that would be found at the business unit level. In addition, the brick-making activities would have different critical success factors from the battery business.

The core competency approach

The core competencies concept became well known in 1990, with the publication of an article in the *Harvard Business Review*.[4] The concept actually appears in earlier work (see, for example, Prahalad and Doz[5]), and no doubt the dedicated researcher could turn up other references. The argument is that organisations should base their strategies around their core competencies, as it is these that enable organisations to reshape industries and to gain lasting competitive advantage.

> Core competence does not diminish with use. Unlike physical assets, which do deteriorate over time, competencies are enhanced as they are applied and shared. But competencies still need to be nurtured and protected; knowledge fades if it is not used. Competencies are the glue that binds existing businesses. They are also the engine for new business development. Patterns of diversification and market entry may be guided by them, not just by the attractiveness of markets.[4]

What are core competencies?

If the idea is to have any value in the corporate appraisal and beyond into corporate strategy, we must first define what is meant by the term, think about how core competencies may be used, and try to solve the problem of how an organisation can discover what its core competencies really are. The value of the concept is dependent on the ability of organisations to make practical use of it. Hamel and Prahalad[6] state:

> A core competence is a bundle of skills and technologies that enables a company to provide a particular benefit to customers. At Sony that benefit is 'pocketability', and the core competence is miniaturization. At Federal Express the benefit is on-time delivery, and the core competence, at a very high level, is logistics management. Logistics are also central to Wal-Mart's ability to provide customers with the benefits of choice, availability, and value. At EDS the customer benefit is seamless information flows, and one of the contributing core competencies is systems integration. Motorola provides customers with the benefits of 'untethered communications', which are based on Motorola's mastery of competencies in wireless communication (p. 219).

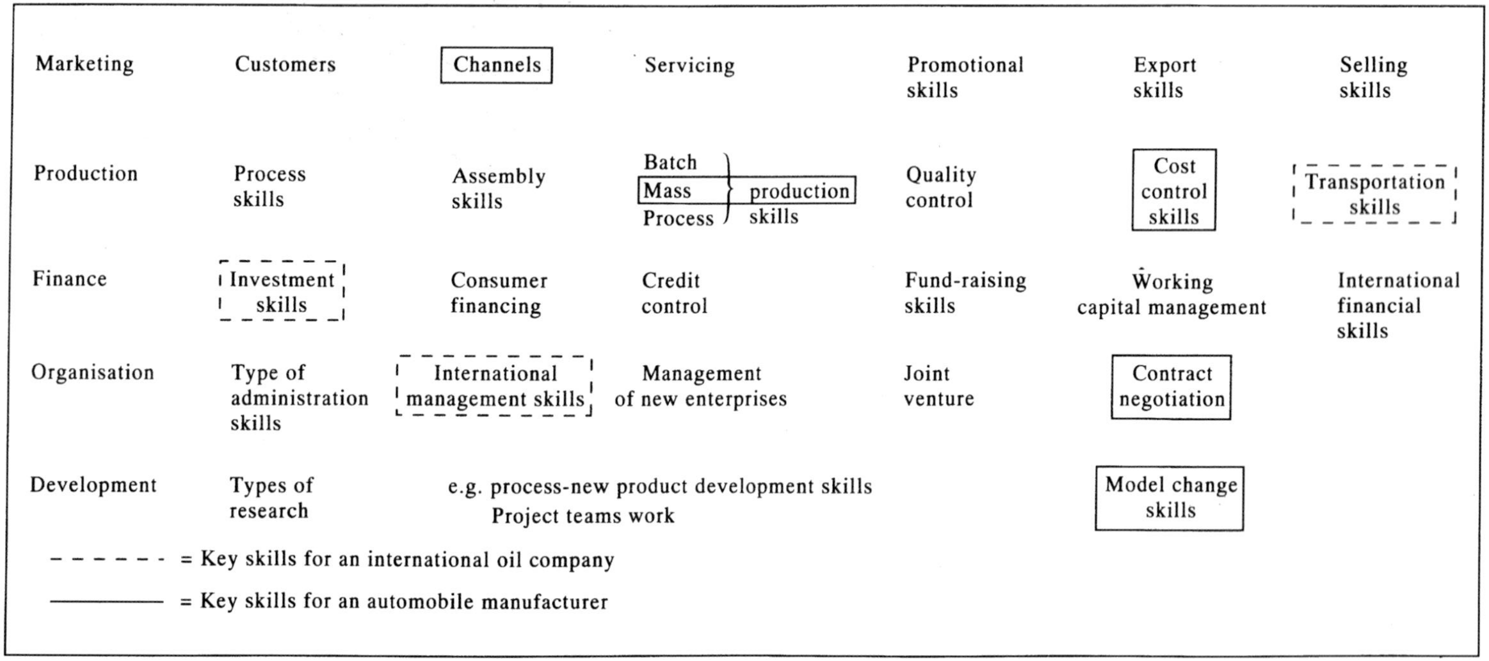

Marketing	Customers	Channels	Servicing	Promotional skills	Export skills	Selling skills
Production	Process skills	Assembly skills	Batch / Mass / Process } production skills	Quality control	Cost control skills	Transportation skills
Finance	Investment skills	Consumer financing	Credit control	Fund-raising skills	Working capital management	International financial skills
Organisation	Type of administration skills	International management skills	Management of new enterprises	Joint venture	Contract negotiation	
Development	Types of research	e.g. process-new product development skills Project teams work			Model change skills	

- - - - - = Key skills for an international oil company

———— = Key skills for an automobile manufacturer

Figure 9.5
Capability profile and key skills. (From Denning, B. W. Corporate Planning: Selected Concepts, McGraw-Hill, Maidenhead, 1971)

This takes us a little way forward, and we need to backtrack to see what Hamel and Prahalad consider a competence to be, before examining how we can tell whether or not it is core. Hamel[7] says: '. . . a competence is a bundle of constituent skills and technologies, rather than a single, discrete skill or technology' (p. 11). A core competence must:

- Give access (or potential access) to a wide variety of markets
- Deliver a clear benefit to the customer (or more accurately, a benefit that the customer perceives)
- Be hard for competitors to copy, so that it provides a clear basis for differentiation

A core competence is not, therefore:

- A single skill
- A competence that all competitors have
- A product
- Something possessed by only one small area of the organisation.

It is worth stressing that a core competence does not have to be something done entirely in-house. It can be achieved through strategic alliances (although this will require an additional competence in the successful management of alliances), or close relationships with suppliers, distributors or customers.

The use of core competencies is to provide the engine which enables the organisation to invent the future, and to continually stay ahead of the competition. To do this the organisation must ensure that it has an appropriate 'strategic architecture', to use the term described by Hamel and Prahalad.[6] They see the strategic architecture as 'a high-level blueprint for the deployment of new functionalities, the acquisition of new competencies or the migration of existing competencies, and the reconfiguring of the interface with customers' (p. 118). The organisation should be seen as a portfolio of core competencies, rather than a portfolio of businesses. A corporate appraisal of core competencies also needs to give attention to all the components of organisation which were discussed in Chapter 3. It is not enough to decide on the core competencies: the organisation must also create the capability to exploit them.

Determining the core competencies of an organisation

One of the problems of trying to determine the core competencies is that the works referenced spend much more effort on persuading that the approach is the right one to use than they give practical guidance on how to get over the first hurdle. All the good advice on how to use and manage core competencies is only of value if you know what they are. My personal view is that many of the organisations that are mentioned as good examples in these works arrived at their core competencies by entrepreneurial flair and happy accident, rather than careful analysis. Using them as an example of how organisations benefit from the approach is a form of rationalisation after the event, whereas the rest of us have to first find our own rocket launching sites, if we want to use the concept to fly to the stars.

Fortunately others have worked on the practicalities of assessing core competencies. The detailed approach described here draws heavily on Hinterhuber et al.[8] supplemented by some methods suggested by Klein and Hiscocks.[9] What is described below is thus a synthesis of the views of both authorities.

A five-stage approach is suggested:

- Determining current competencies
- Assessing the relative strengths of the competencies
- Identifying those which deliver value to current customers
- Establishing which are needed for the longer term
- Examining the portfolio of competencies.

Determining current competencies

Four sources are suggested:

1 What can be gleaned from the organisation's structure (for example, if the organisation has a telephone sales operation, it is likely to have some competencies in this area).
2 Discussions with key people inside the organisation. Just who is key will vary with the organisation, but a good rule is to cast the net wide. Some very important competencies may be buried inside departments in the organisation, and may not be visible to top management.
3 Competencies which are obvious from an examination of the activities, products and services of the organisation. Often the intangible elements are taken for granted within the organisation, although the competencies required to achieve them may be among the most important for the organisation.
4 What can be learned from customers and suppliers, both from market research reports and from discussions and focus group interviews.

At this stage the organisation will have a long laundry list, which will probably contain individual skills which need to be grouped into competencies, and will certainly include many competencies which are neither strategic nor core.

Assessing the relative strengths of the competencies

The internal perception of the extent to which a competence is possessed may not be the reality. Sometimes a closer correlation between truth and beliefs can be achieved through further internal assessment, performed by a panel of managers from within the organisation who have knowledge of customers and competitors. Scoring the organisation against each main competitor can sometimes help to assess the strength relative to competitors. External expert knowledge may be used to perform a similar function. The most objective method is benchmarking, against direct competitors, other firms which are high-performers in one or more areas of competence, and internally across the organisation to assess the extent to which the competence is truly shared.

By definition, any competence which is common to all in an industry, and which every competitor is good at, cannot be a core competence (although it may still be important).

Identifying those competencies that deliver value to the customers

A competence should deliver value to at least a significant segment of the market. The identified competencies may be compared to the value chain (see Chapter 10), which is a method for determining which of the various activities of the organisation deliver added value to customers, and thus become sources of competitive advantage.

Hinterhuber et al.[8] recommend identifying '... the articulated, and if possible non-articulated customer wishes concerning product characteristics and product-related services'. With this information, and the critical success factors discussed earlier in the chapter, they suggest that it is possible to move onto a two-phase evaluation chain to identify what is important, and to show visually the relative strength of each element analysed. The first matrix they propose enables each critical success factor to be compared with the performance characteristics the customers are seeking. Symbols are used to indicate the organisation's strength (or otherwise) in each of the cells in the matrix. The second matrix compares the same performance characteristics with the competencies needed to support them, using a similar system of symbols. Both matrices include weighting and scoring, one use of which is to aid the positioning of each competence in a portfolio of core competencies.

Establishing which competencies are needed for the longer term

If an aim is to use core competencies to change the industries in which an organisation operates, it follows that some attempt should be made to think beyond the current range of products and services, and to explore what may be core in a more future-oriented manner. Klein and Hiscocks[9] offer one method for doing this, although this is built on an analysis of skills rather than competencies. They call it the opportunity matrix, a method which requires the use of an appropriate computer database. Skills are listed and scored, and entered as one axis in the database. Possible diversifications and potential future products are then listed, and scored for the level of skill needed. A five-point scale is used, varying from 'skill not required' to 'world-class capability essential'. The database may be programmed to identify opportunities which match skills, and which could represent opportunities for the organisation.

Skills still need to be clustered into competencies. However, the approach could also be used to analyse current products and services, and the resultant matrix used as a basis on which they may be grouped into competencies. The assessment of all this evidence can help to determine which competencies are indeed core.

Figure 9.6
The portfolio of
core competencies.
(From Hinterhuber
et al.[8])

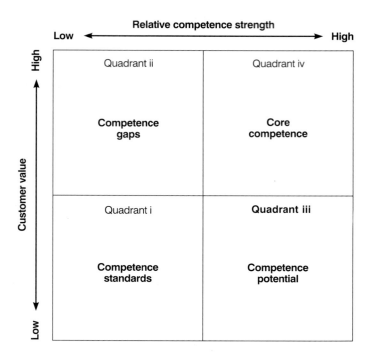

Examining the portfolio of competencies

Hinterhuber *et al.*[8] use the scores from their correlation chain to position the organisation's competencies. The matrix is reproduced in Figure 9.6, and positions could be plotted judgementally, provided there is some evidence to support the contentions.

The three most interesting positions are quadrants ii, iv and iii. Quadrant ii may indicate areas of weakness which the organisation should either correct or render unimportant by changing its activities. Quadrant iv contains the core competencies which require management if the organisation is to be able to sustain and develop its competence. Quadrant iii may provide opportunities to use some of these competencies to develop products which the customer would value. The danger of this quadrant is that these competencies may include those needed for the future rather than the present, and that a more dynamic assessment might decide that some of them are really core.

Although the portfolio examination of competencies has a lot of appeal, and indeed is following suggestions made by Hamel and Prahalad, there is one weakness. The fact that a competence has high customer value, and is an area of high corporate ability, misses out one key dimension: uniqueness. This could be solved when competencies are listed on the chart, by showing with a symbol against each the degree to which the organisation shares the competence with competitors. The quadrant would be renamed 'critical and core competencies'.

Validity of the core competence methods

A good deal has been claimed for the core competence approach, although I do not believe that the methodology for applying it has yet been proved, through repeated application, to be robust. Hamel and Prahalad, in their various works, claim that other foundations for the development of strategy, such as industry analysis, are pictures of the past rather than the future. This is a criticism with which I do not agree, as it is possible to use many methods dynamically. However, although the logic of core competencies has much of value behind it, there is a danger that when organisations assess their core competencies they too will look at the present and past, rather than the future. The methods for identifying competencies and skills look reasonable and robust, although very complex in large multibusiness, multinational organisations, but the chance of error is high, and it is much harder to determine which are core for the future.

My belief is that core competencies are a useful tool in the corporate appraisal, and will help strategic decision making, but they do not prevent an organisation from being wrongfooted by turbulent change, nor are they enough by themselves to provide a total basis for making strategic decisions. They are a method for seeing the strengths, weaknesses, opportunities and threats in a different way, and they help move towards a solution, but do not do more than this.

However the corporate appraisal is tackled, whether by any of the methods outlined in this chapter or by a different approach altogether, there is no doubt that it is an essential first step in the process of strategic planning. It is the springboard from which the great leap may be made into the mists of the future.

References

1 Ansoff, H.I. *Corporate Strategy*, McGraw-Hill, New York, 1965.

2 Denning, B. W. *Corporate Planning: Selected Concepts*, McGraw-Hill, New York, 1971.

3 Drucker, P.F. *Managing for Results*, Heinemann, London, 1964.

4 Prahalad C. K. and Hamel, G. 'The Core Competence of the Corporation', *Harvard Business Review*, May/June, 1990.

5 Prahalad C. K. and Doz, Y. L. *The Multinational Mission*, Free Press, New York, 1987.

6 Hamel, G. and Prahalad, C. K. *Competing for the Future*, Harvard Business School Press, Boston, MA, 1994. (My page references are to the 1996 paperback edition, which has an additional preface.)

7 Hamel, G. 'The Concept of Core Competence', in Hamel, G. and Heene, A. (eds), *Competence Based Competition*, Wiley, Chichester, 1994.

8 Hinterhuber, H. H., Friedrich, S. A., Handlbauer, G. and Stubec, U. 'The Company as a Cognitive System of Core Competencies and Strategic Business Units', *Strategic Change*, 5, No. 4, July–August, 1996.

9 Klein, J. A. and Hiscocks, P. G. 'Competence -based Competition: A Toolkit', in Hamel, G. and Heene, A. (eds), *Competence Based Competition*, Wiley, Chichester, 1994.

CHAPTER 10

Analysing the industry and competitors

The aim is to provide an integrated way of thinking about industry and competitor analysis. Much of the conceptual inspiration is from the work of Professor Porter, and the concepts are described. The chapter shows how to operationalise these concepts, and suggests eight major stages in assessing the position of the industry and competitors. The steps include practical application tools developed to take the concepts into real situations. The chapter includes an outline questionnaire, which can be used as an aid to collecting information for industry and portfolio analysis.

An approach to competitor analysis

In the next two chapters we will explore some ideas about industry and competitor analysis. The concepts are discussed in this chapter, to be followed in Chapter 11 with a case history showing some of the applications. Industry analysis is a sort of half-way house between strengths and weakness analysis and strategy formulation. It provides another way of measuring the internal elements of the organisation against what is going on in the wider world, but it is also' an essential to the formulation of sound future-oriented strategies. As we will see, there can also be a connection between industry analysis and portfolio analysis. The questionnaire in this chapter can be used both for industry analysis and to collect information for the directional policy matrix, which is described in more detail in a later chapter.

It is useful to think of the various components of industry and competitor analysis as a linked series of steps leading to the building of competitive advantage. Figure 10.1 shows this approach as one overall process, as a series of eight steps built around sources of strategic information. It may not be essential for every organisation to go through every step each time, but it makes sense to make what to do or what not to do a matter of rational decision.

Figure 10.1
Approach to
competitor analysis

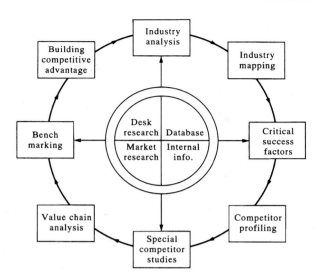

The heart of the diagram is the strategic information system, which has been shown broken down into four very different sources of information. Information was discussed in an earlier chapter, so what will be covered here will be only those aspects which are peculiar to competitor analysis.

The outer ring follows a logical sequence. It is recommended that the sequence is maintained, even if some steps are omitted, because each step provides information which is useful to the steps that follow.

Industry analysis is a way of looking at the relative power of all the players in the chain of supply through to consumer. The purpose is not just diagnosis, but should lead to strategies to improve the position of the company. A large part of this chapter will be spent on the principles of industry analysis.

Industry mapping is a way of presenting the results of industry analysis, so that the information is accessible, and conflicts between different pieces of information are forced into the limelight.

We have already met critical success factors. Here we will look more closely at how they might be derived from industry analysis, and used as one element of competitor analysis.

Competitor profiling is a way of compressing the strategic information about a competitor so that it can be used more effectively. The method can be extended to customers and suppliers, where the strategies that they are following are important for your own organisation's success. It is a small jump to use these profiles to generate a series of different scenarios about where strategic change might be triggered, and by whom.

Special competitor studies are needed sometimes to look at particular aspects of strategy. They may be narrowly focused into, say, one product, activities in specific countries, or particular issues, such as production methods.

Value chain analysis is an approach to help the organisation identify its sources of competitive advantages. It is thus as much about identifying differentiation compared to competitors, although not restricted to market differentiation, as about the company in relation to its markets.

Benchmarking is one of those activities that need not be restricted to competitors. It may be desirable for a bank, for example, to compare its counter service with that of competitors. More frequently benchmarking may be used to lift a level of activity to the best it can be compared with, inside and outside the industry. Thus a study of customer service by one type of retailer might cover many non-competing retailers. Total quality management might be benchmarked against the leaders in the field regardless of industry. An aim of benchmarking is usually to seek excellence in performance by reaching world-class performance in any area of activity which is relevant.

The final box in the diagram is about bringing all the components together to develop strategies that create sustainable competitive advantage. Unfortunately sustainable advantage needs continual improvement, as others seek to emulate. Part of the strategic task is therefore to find ways of keeping ahead.

Industry analysis

The person most associated with competitor analysis is Michael Porter,[1] who did an excellent job in drawing together the threads of analytical thought about industry analysis, and then went on to develop the value chain concept. The basic ideas of industry analysis have been around for many years. Entry barriers have been described in economic textbooks almost since economics became a subject. The idea of studying suppliers as well as competitors can be found in many books which pre-dated those of Porter, for example Farmer and Taylor,[2] while the earliest of marketing books talked about studying customers. Porter's contribution to industry analysis was first, to take these random threads and turn them into a rope, and second, to write about his concept in such a way as to make it the main thrust of strategic thinking during the 1980s. This was no mean achievement.

The basic model appears in Figure 10.2. This version is a little different from Porter's original in that it is set within the environmental diagram, which was described in full in earlier chapters. In addition, his original five forces have been expanded to show that substitutes are a force between the industry and its suppliers, and between the industry and its buyers. A third difference is that exit barriers have been separated from entry barriers. To be strictly correct, another force should be shown on the figure, although this is based on my own experience and is not mentioned in the original Porter concept. This is the role of influencers, who also may operate between the industry and its suppliers or buyers. By influencers I mean individuals or firms who may determine the purchase, but are not themselves buyers. A doctor, for example, prescribes drugs, which the customer buys from the chemist. However, even this is a simplification in a welfare state, where all or part of the purchase may also be influenced by the national equivalent to the UK's Department of Health. An architect may specify the lift that is installed in a new building. It may be a consulting engineer that determines the specifications of a new sewage-treatment plant, and by so doing may change the number of competitors who are able to bid. No study of the industry can afford to ignore any influencers who might operate within the industry.

A second problem with industry analysis which Porter does deal with is the need to determine the appropriate competitive arena. This has two dimensions, one of geography and the other of product. Anyone who analyses an industry has to decide whether the right basis of analysis is the world, a region such as the European Union, a country, or a local area within a country. If the picture is too broad, it becomes impossible to undertake a meaningful analysis. If it is too narrow, it is likely that the wrong signals will be read, and that what appears to be a powerful position is in fact very weak. A later chapter will deal at length with global strategy and the forces which drive organisations to take a global view. However, for present purposes the guidance that can be offered is to decide what is relevant by studying the customers and the competitors. An individual company may be the driver that turns an industry global, but the company that refuses to acknowledge that an industry is global is hardly likely to change it back. To analyse a global industry there is a need to cascade down from a global overview, through regions, to key countries.

At the product level it is an easy trap to take a market segment as the industry. In my time with the food company that markets Ovaltine, I remember the claims that we were the market leaders. In beverages including tea and coffee? In food type drinks like Horlicks and drinking chocolate? In malted milk beverages, of which our product was one? No, in brown malted milk products. This might be a useful classification for marketing purposes, and might indeed have been the product that served particular segments of the market. It would have been useless as a basis for industry analysis.

It is important to remember that industry definitions change over time, and that there may be strong overlaps with other industries so that the industry becomes different, although all sectors are not necessarily in competition. Not so long ago there was a typewriter industry, a telephone industry, a computer industry, and a video industry. What we have seen over the last decade or so is a merging of these so that it becomes possible to argue that they are now all parts of the same industry, or if they are not they soon will be. It would clearly be a nonsense for anyone to analyse the typewriter industry without also including computers. Would it make sense to look at telex in isolation from computers, electronic mail, and fax? In this particular set of product categories the boundaries are still changing.

There are a number of general principles that can be determined for each box in Figure 10.2, and it is possible to say that if a certain condition occurs, it is likely to lead to more or less aggressive behaviour between competitors, or to move the balance of advantage from the industry to a buyer or a supplier. The check list approach is useful, but the skill in interpretation comes from looking at the interaction of all the factors. What gives the buyer an advantage may be offset by another factor that favours the industry firm. An example is management consultancy, where the product is perishable (yesterday's unused time has no value) and entry barriers are low. These factors put bargaining power in the hands of the buyer. However, the better firms in the industry do not suffer

Figure 10.2
Basic elements
affecting industry
profitability

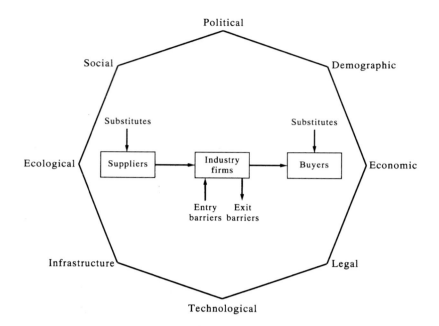

continual erosion of margins, because they may offer scarce skills, large potential benefits, proprietary approaches, and have reputations that allay fears present among buyers of intangibles. There are thus offsetting factors which neutralise or reduce some of the adverse factors. However, competitive positions in what is a highly fragmented industry are variable, there are many segments to the market, with competition strong in some and weak in others. Some firms offer a clearly differentiated service: others are at the commodity end. Setting a competitive strategy in this industry is not a simple matter of plucking a couple of issues from a check list and devising actions in response. It is a matter of applying human ingenuity to the composite impact of all the factors taken in conjunction with each other. And so it would be if we were to use another industry as an example.

With this caution in mind, it is possible to make more sense from a study of the individual elements of industry analysis.

Industry firms

It is traditional for analysts to examine such factors as market shares and to pay some attention to the different positioning of each firm in the marketplace. Industry analysis tries to identify all the factors which affect the intensity of competitive behaviour. The competitiveness of the industry is not revealed by brand shares alone, although these are important. Competitive behaviour is also influenced by many other factors, including the following.

Growth rates of the industry

Competitive behaviour tends to be less aggressive if industry growth rates are relatively high, because each firm can increase its sales without necessarily increasing its market share. This statement is considerably modified by the firm's position on the life-cycle curve. In a new industry high growth rates may bring in new competitors, which will tend to lead to aggressive behaviour. In almost all industries, a fall in the growth rate will tend to intensify competition. Often it is the change that causes new patterns, rather than the growth rate itself. Other things being equal, one would expect to find more aggressive behaviour in an industry whose annual growth rate has fallen suddenly from 10 per cent to 3 per cent than in an industry whose growth has stabilised at 3 per cent.

General level of profits

Lack of profits among the industry (or significant firms in the industry) will tend to make competitive behaviour less predictable. Where profits are high for all, there may be a measure of tolerance of competitors. A change to lower profits may trigger a more aggressive attitude.

Level of fixed costs

Where investment is large, highly specialised and fixed costs are a relatively high proportion of total costs; competitors tend to 'hang on', selling at less than full costs, when the market slumps or there is overcapacity for some other reason. Shipping, oil refinery and petrochemicals all provide examples where competitive behaviour may lead to low profits or losses over a very long period of time, because the alternative is plant closure at a time when assets cannot be realised.

Economies of scale—experience curve

Competitive behaviour is likely to be more aggressive when there are clear advantages in being big. This may happen when cost levels are dependent on high volumes, or when the experience curve effect means that progressively higher volumes will lead to progressively lower costs. Lower costs mean prices can be reduced, which in turn means that even higher volumes can be gained. In a growth market, where demand is elastic and the product subject to mass production (e.g. motorcycles, calculating machines, electronic components) the experience curve effect can bring dominance to the firm that gets far enough ahead. Competitive behaviour is likely to be very aggressive during this period.

Degree of differentiation

Market imperfections give a degree of protection to individual firms and reduce the impact of competition. Thus it is reasonable to expect the fiercest competition when all firms are offering products of commodity status, and the most peaceful behaviour when each firm offers such a highly differentiated product that it is almost unique.

Number of firms and market shares

A fragmented industry, with no one firm having a significant market share, tends to be more competitive than one which has a clear market leader who is in a dominant position. To some degree, these tendencies may be modified by the position on the product life cycle. It is unwise to assume that mature markets will all have gone through the shakeout period. Some are highly fragmented because the economic circumstances do not favour large firms (e.g. many service industries).

New entrant

In long-established industries, firms often reach unspoken forms of accommodation with each other, softening aggressiveness of competition. This will often change with the entry of a new firm who either does not know or chooses to ignore these implicit 'rules' (e.g. the impact of Laker on the Atlantic air routes). A similar effect may occur if one of the companies appoints a new chief executive from outside the industry.

Nature of product

A perishable product (e.g. airline tickets, fresh produce) is likely to be more susceptible to random price cutting than one which can be stored easily and cheaply.

Buyers

There are two reasons for studying the structure of the industry along the channel to the ultimate consumer. The first is to ensure that the whole of the present structure is known, as this may reveal new strategic options, including the all-important one of changing the 'rules of the game' by finding another way to get the product to the consumer.

A second reason is to determine the relative influence on profits exercised by the various stages in the chain, and the way power is likely to shift in the future.

It is not necessarily the industry itself which determines its own margins and profitability; sometimes the greater power is in the hands of the buyers. Factors which influence the relative location of this power and influence include the following.

Relative size

If the industry includes firms which are considerably larger than their customers, sheer weight of resources may put them in the dominant position. The opposite may apply when the buying organisations are the larger. This is not a universal truth, as other factors may outweigh size in importance. For example, UK grocery products are largely controlled by supermarket chains, who not only have most of the retail outlets but have also developed their own-label products that they can adjust in volume and price if the brand manufacturers do not toe the line. In this way they may determine the profitability of manufacturers whose organisations may be considerably larger than those of the supermarkets.

Dependencies

Bargaining strength may lie with the least dependent of the two parties. This is a composite of the number of industry firms contrasted with the number of buying firms (what flexibility does each have?), and the importance of the product to the profits of each party.

Profitability of the buying industry

The industry firms are likely to be in a healthier position when they are selling to a profitable industry. Where buyers are unprofitable or have low profits there is likely to be stronger resistance against price increases. This resistance will increase when the buyer is facing an elastic demand curve, and cannot easily pass on his or her extra costs.

Experience of buyers

Buyers purchasing from a mature industry are likely to have more experience than those dealing with a new one. Thus, the more mature the industry, the weaker its bargaining position may become (subject, of course, to other factors). Where the buying industry is also mature, there may be a tendency for the degree of product differentiation to fall, making it more difficult for the industry to sustain high margins.

Threat of integration

The industry firm that patently has the capability and strength to integrate into its buying industry possesses a key bargaining point. If the buying industry thwarts its profit aims, it has the potential to remove the blockage. The opposite applies when the buying industry can offer a credible threat of backwards integration. In either case the credibility of the threat is enhanced when both parties are aware that such a move would be economically viable. Do not forget that the actions of *your* customer may be affected by the power of *their* customer.

The key factor in successfully analysing the customers in a particular industry is segmenting them into groups and distinguishing them either by the reason they buy or how they buy. Criteria for segmenting customer groups include:

● Industry or market segment
● Geographic location
● Size of purchase
● Frequency of purchase.

Suppliers

It is traditional for an industry to believe that it holds the edge over both its buyers and suppliers, a statement that patently cannot always be true since the industry itself is a buyer to its supplier. Relations with the supplying industry are rarely studied as a matter of strategic importance. In reality the analysis of suppliers is the converse of the analysis of buyers. The factors to consider are therefore the same: industry or market segment, product application, geographic location, size of purchase, and frequency of purchase.

Suppliers exercise power in an industry in a number of ways: by lowering the quality of goods for a given purchase price, by tightening payment and service terms, and so on, to the extent that suppliers in general, or particular supplier groups, exercise significant power; as a result, industry costs increase and profitability diminishes.

Substitutes

The availability of substitutes may have a dramatic effect on the prospects for an industry, and will unleash a further set of competitive relationships. Emergence of a new substitute may bring new firms with different cost structures into the competitive arena. A substitute will often increase the power of the buyer and reduce the power of the seller. The emergence of potential new substitutes is therefore a possibility that should be studied for each industry.

Where the number of existing substitutes is large, the possibility that the industry has been ill-defined should be considered. It may be that a production view has been taken rather than a marketing view. In any event, the substitute industry should be studied as rigorously as the firm's own industry.

Entry and exit barriers

The entry and exit barriers will affect the profitability of an industry and the way in which competitors behave. Entry barriers can only be interpreted in relation to the attractiveness of the industry. Relatively low barriers will deter firms from entering low-profit/low-growth industries. The barriers may have to be very high to keep a new entrant out of a highly attractive industry.

Examples of entry barriers which *raise the costs* of a new entrant are:

1 Economies of scale/the experience curve factor may raise the capital costs of entry to a very high level (e.g. electronic calculators).
2 *Highly differentiated products* may require extensive advertising support before a newcomer can break in (e.g. household detergents). This may raise costs to prohibitive levels.
3 *The nature of distribution* may require entry at a high level of output (e.g. supermarkets will not stock brands which are slow-moving and have low market shares).

Other entry barriers may create a legal restriction to entry, or in some way deny access to a critical part of the market:

● Patents
● Legal controls (e.g. auditors, television broadcasting companies)
● Control of distribution outlets (e.g. the British film industry until recently)
● Contracts with key customers or suppliers.

Where entry barriers are very low the industry may become fragmented and competition fierce, with new competitors regularly coming into the market. Industry profitability is to a large extent dependent on market imperfections, and one element of corporate strategy might be to find ways of raising the entry barriers.

Exit barriers are the factors which tie a firm to the industry and make it difficult or impossible for it to leave. Where they occur, the firm will hang on, trading as best it can, and depressing profits in the industry.

Exit barriers may be around the need to write off specialised assets for which there is no buyer, particular contracts, or legal requirements which make it costly to meet severance payments to employees. There may also be government pressure on the firm to stay in the business.

Exhibit 10.1 Changing the balance of power in an industry

A US subsidiary of a British engineering firm, let's call them XYZ Environmental, made a machine for use in sewage works, the function of which was to separate solids from liquids. Although the company had a product that was superior to those of competitors, this delivered no advantage because the customers were mainly from the public sector, who had to take the lowest-priced competitive tender which met specifications. Consulting engineers set the specifications, which set the conditions for the tender. They were conservative in their thinking and rarely moved from the safe performance specifications of the past. Entry barriers to the industry were low, increasing the intensity of competition.

The solution was to persuade the buyer that part of the bidding process should include side-by-side tests of the competitive machines to confirm that they could meet requirements. The idea was for each bidder to mount a machine on a trailer, and connect it to the sewage-treatment plant, demonstrating what performance could be delivered in operating conditions. The processing speed, quality, and reliability of the XYZ machine was proved. Buyers then began to put the higher performance specifications in their requirements to the consulting engineers. Higher specifications began to eliminate some of the competition, and cause problems to others that had to upgrade.

XYZ succeeded in making side-by-side tests a regular part of the bidding process, giving a continuous opportunity to demonstrate superiority. The staff that operated the test rig were highly trained, as XYZ knew that technical superiority required effective operation of the rig. Entry barriers were increased, because new entrants had to incur the increased capital costs of one or two rigs and trailers. To demonstrate confidence, XYZ began to persuade buyers to ask for performance bonds from successful tenderers. These were easy to obtain from XYZ's banks, because of the overall financial strength of the group, and no money had to be deposited to cover them. This was not the case for competitors with weak balance sheets, who sometimes found it hard to obtain the necessary bank backing. In this way more entry barriers were created.

The result of this and actions to ensure first-class aftersales support were that better prices were obtained, and market share rose.

(*Source*: Case study written by D. E. Hussey for a client's private use in the annual managing directors' conference)

Industry mapping

So far the discussion of industry analysis has been to illustrate the principles. It is possible to move straight from concept to practical application. However, this is rarely easy, so I should like to suggest an approach which I have developed over numerous studies of different industries, and which I know to be helpful. I call this industry mapping.

One of the considerations in a real-life study is that the headings used so far are too broad. Buyers, for example, are of many types and may perform many different functions. Some of the products of a components company, for example, may go to original equipment manufacturers. The sale of spares and replacements may take quite different channels. Really we are interested in all stages to the final consumer. A related issue is that the components company cited above would be classed as a supplier if we had been looking through the eyes of an OEM company. However, it was the 'industry' in my study. If the industry studied was one stage back I could have looked at the electronic components that my component factory buys to put into their product. If I had done this my stream of analysis would have covered only one of the buying channels for these electronic supplies.

In industry mapping an attempt is made to plot the whole chain from first supplier through to final consumer, examining the relationships of each link in the chain. We still have to define what we are doing. If we took the view of my components company we should probably not want to study in detail all that happened to the rest of the output of the electronics supplier, but we would want to consider any other industries we supplied to, apart from the one mentioned. The OEM company might take an even narrower focus than us. But even they may have different ways of reaching their customers: direct sale, distributors and agents. They may feel a need to study the second-hand and retrofit markets, since these may have a direct bearing on their prospects.

All these examples add up to a need to think very clearly about the industry. The industry mapping approach starts by drawing an outline diagram showing all the links in the chain. Figures 10.3–10.6 give some examples of outline maps for a number of industries. It should be stressed that at this stage the need is to look at the industry and not just the firm. This may not seem a profound statement, but I have seen many businesses which can draw such a map for what they themselves do, but have no knowledge of channels which they do not use.

One way of developing the outline is to define the industry in diagram form by thinking of the logical ways in which business might flow through the channels. This provides a hypothesis for discussion with those inside the company who have appropriate knowledge. The next step is to relate the draft diagram to company market research and any external published information.

When drawing the boxes, keep in mind the next part of the analysis, when all the key information about the industry will be recorded on the diagram.

In the next stage of analysis the key information that enables the industry to be interpreted is recorded on the block diagram. Figure 10.7 provides a summary

Notes on Figures 10.3–10.6

Figure 10.3:   Note that the two main product areas are shown, which in reality may have different sets of competitors. Also included are consulting engineers who influence the buying decisions but are not themselves buyers. Note that, as with the other examples, it might be desirable to group buyers by their characteristics, and in some industries it may be worth looking beyond the buyers to their customers. Similarly, it is sometimes useful to explore the chain of supply into those links that support the suppliers.

Figure 10.4:   In this sort of industry there are often two different supply channels for the OEM and aftermarket. There may even be different competitors in each. OEM companies may influence the replacement market to a greater degree than the diagram suggests.

Figure 10.5:   We may want to break down retailers into several boxes, particularly if there are wholesalers that specialise in different outlets (e.g. chemists). If we were looking at household detergents we might want to break down the competitors into product headings, and take the supply chain back several stages. The example makes it clear that competitors have several main routes to the end-consumer.

Figure 10.6:   This is an initial model for a complex industry which handles many unrelated products. Every stage illustrated is capable of being analysed further.

Figure 10.3
Example industry
map outline. Plant
such as water
purification, power
generation, etc.

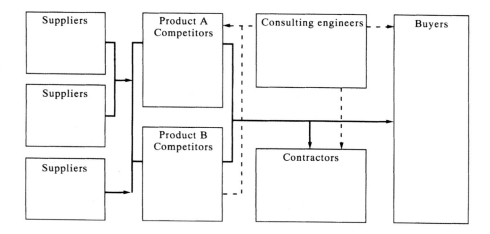

Figure 10.4
Components for
original equipment

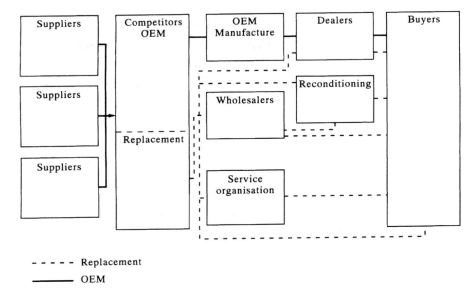

- - - - - Replacement
———— OEM

Figure 10.5
Products such as
toiletries (e.g. hair
care)

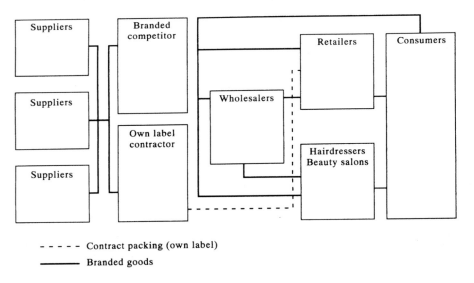

- - - - - Contract packing (own label)
———— Branded goods

of the nature of the information that we will want to record. The points are all directly related to the concepts of industry analysis discussed earlier, except that we will want to change the data requirements slightly to fit the nature of each box we have identified on the block diagram. Thus the buyers' headings would be different if we were looking at a manufacturer, retailer or end-consumer.

The industry map becomes complex once the information is added. For this reason, the examples shown are incomplete – they are given to show how the map is built up.

Figure 10.8 is a very rudimentary outline of what must have been (c. 1969), and probably still is, one of the most convoluted industry structures imaginable. On

Figure 10.6
Generalised outline
model – general
insurance

	Competitors	End customers
	National/International brokers	International
Reinsurance	Regional and 'one office brokers	Large corporate
		Other corporate
Suppliers(e.g. computers)	Other Intermediaries	Personal
	Influences	

Figure 10.7
Summary of factors
in industry analysis

Entry barriers/Exit barriers
Economies of scale
Product differentiation
Capital
Access to distribution channels
Government policies
Dedicated plant
Market growth
Experience
Fixed/variable costs

Threat of new entrants

Suppliers
Few or many companies supplying customer firms

Profitability of supplying firms

Do they fight with substitutes to customer firms

Capacity and utilisation

Are customer firms significant for suppliers

Can suppliers integrate forwards

Bargaining power of suppliers

Ratio

Firms
Number
Relative size
Actual size
Market share
Profitability
Margins
Added value
Significance of key suppliers
Credibility to integrate forward/backwards
Capacity increases large in scale
'Personality' of competitors
High strategic stakes
Exit barriers

Bargaining power of customers

Ratio

Buyers
Demands for quality
Playing off competitors
Are they concentrated or large buyers
Are products a significant element in buyer costs
Are bought-in products standard
Are they low profit earners
Potential for backward integration
Quality of purchase e.g. safety equipment, medical
Can retail buyers influence ultimate customer
Number
Growth
Profitability
Margins
Power of supplying firms relative to buyers

Threat of substitute products or services

Substitutes
Products
which offer better price/ performance than firms offering above
which come from high profit industries

the map we have started to record information about the number of firms in each box. How we complete the rest of the map would depend on our business interest. If, for example, we were an importer, we would probably be interested in the whole structure, and the really critical information would be who controlled the retail outlets, and the percentage of our type of product that passed through the various channels. We would probably want to plot some of the integrated players like Fyffes and Geest on the map, and some of the main importers like Jaffa. We would probably group many of the other players, rather than trying to study them individually.

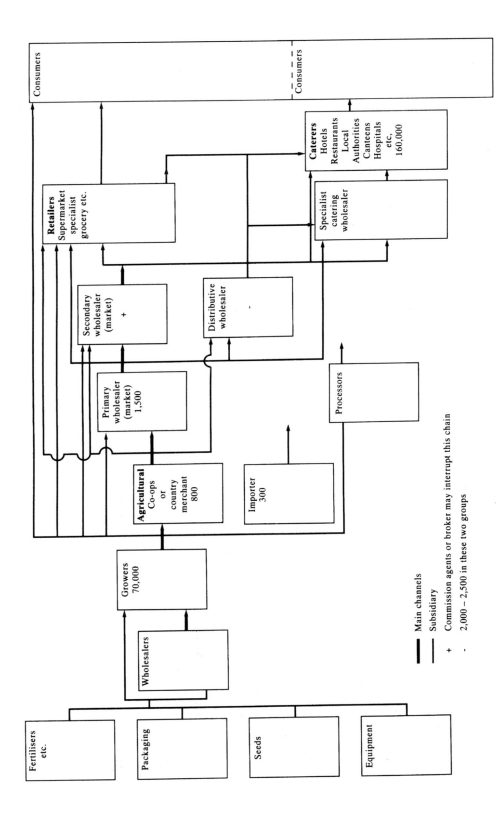

Figure 10.8

Fruit and vegetable distribution. (From Hussey, D. E. *Introducing Corporate Planning*, Pergamon, Oxford, 1991)

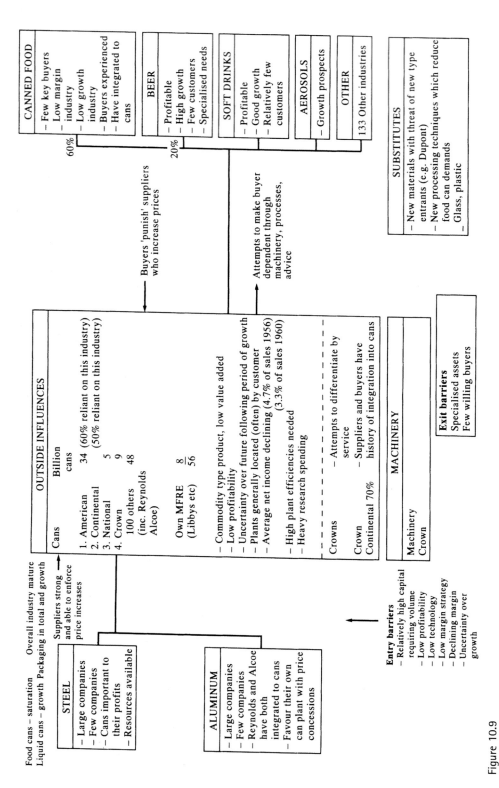

Figure 10.9

Metal container industry (1962) – USA (From Hussey, *Introducing Corporate Planning*)

Figure 10.9 shows a more complex map. Again it is simplified and represents the metal container industry in the USA as it was in 1962. Before looking at the data, note that the map ends at the buying industries. In a real situation we might have a need to examine the customers of these industries – in most cases the consumer, but sometimes another manufacturer. If the product had been chicken-killing equipment, for example, we would have an incomplete analysis if we stopped at poultry processors, since the main forces in this industry are the supermarkets on the one hand and the fast food firms on the other.

On the map in Figure 10.9 you will notice that, although there are obvious gaps in information that could have been plotted, we have a very clear summary picture emerging from the forces which will affect competitive behaviour among can manufacturers. There are two dominant competitors in an industry squeezed by suppliers and customers and subject to both backwards and forwards integration. Further inspection shows markets such as brewing, soft drinks and aerosols where the needs are more specialised, the buyers more profitable, and markets growing. Had we taken this analysis to the competitor profiling, we should have found that one competitor, Crown Cork, had spotted this and had a strategy aimed particularly at these segments, lifting it a step above the commodity nature of the industry.

Just by reading the information on the map, we can gain a picture that would have taken about 20 pages of narrative description. And we can also see the obvious important gaps in the information that we would need to plug.

Figure 10.10 comes from an article by Crawshaw[3] which describes a case history of an industry mapping exercise. In all these examples, information has been recorded in note form. A practical point is that a dossier of information in a more detailed format should be built up by those preparing the map. This

Figure 10.10
Outline map of the information industry. (From Crawshaw[3]: used with permission)

PRODUCERS/PUBLISHERS   'RETAILERS'   MARKETS/SECTORS

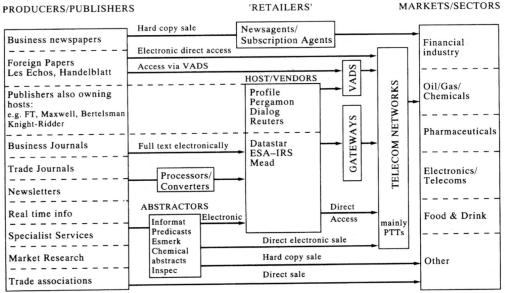

© INFORMAT 1989

becomes a reference book of source material, which of course should include the sources of all information.

Typical problems observed in building up these maps offer a very good reason why for most companies this is a useful approach:

1 Perceptions of the competitive arena often differ from the reality, resulting in suppression of options when competitive strategies are formulated.
2 Often only one part of the problem has been perceived. Acrow, a once-great scaffolding pole company with a hire or sale strategy, ignored the growing hire-and-erect competitors who eventually took over most of the market. This contributed to the demise of the company.
3 Market segmentation is often confused with strategic segmentation. The former may be achieved by product positioning and promotion but has few entry barriers. The latter offers a longer-term position because it is defensible. The ultra-luxury car is a strategic segment of the car market: the upmarket versions of, say, the Ford Escort represent a market segmentation.
4 Data used by the company are often incorrect, mainly because they have been used functionally and go unchecked against other sources (e.g. manufacturing people using capacity information about the industry, and not relating this to the market-share data used by marketing).
5. Information is often missing, leading to the need to decide its potential importance and whether action should be taken. This is a straight cost–benefit decision. Few of us need perfection.

Critical success factors

In the previous chapter we touched briefly on the idea of critical success factors. Industry analysis provides one way through which these can be derived, and the analyst has a rich vein of information to mine from the industry map and the data that lies behind it.

Critical success factors may be defined as the things that have to be done well if the companies in the industry are to be successful. There may be additional factors to add which are unique to the competitive positioning for which the organisation is striving, but the core factors will apply to all competitors operating in the same sector of the industry. They therefore provide a useful standard for measuring both one's own performance against them and that of key competitors.

In doing this analysis, it is important not to overlook the fact that the same industry may contain sectors with widely differing critical success factors. A good example is the own-label contractor and the branded competitor classifications of Figure 10.5. Both produce virtually identical products, but the critical success factors of the two sectors have little in common.

Thus we might expect those for the contractor to include:

- Flexible manufacture, with the ability to change lines quickly
- Low-cost manufacture

● Ability to formulate quickly copies of branded products
● Negotiation ability, since there are relatively few buyers and these are supplied on contract.

The branded competitors' critical success factors might not include any of the above, but would cover:

● Segmentation and promotional skills; the ability to create markets
● Marketing research skills to identify new marketing needs
● R&D skills to invent new products
● Distribution skills
● Pricing skills to ensure the right margins.

Strategic implications

Tentative strategic conclusions can begin to be drawn as the industry mapping analysis progresses. I have found it helpful to present maps on A3 paper, organised so that when opened out there is a map on one side and a narrative sheet on the other. The narrative highlights all the strategic issues arising. Some of the headings I have used in the past include:

● Key points observed in the analysis
● Concerns over the availability or accuracy of some of the information
● Trends which may change the map
● Problems in competitive positioning
● Critical success factors
● Strategic issues and points for consideration.

This should not be undertaken in isolation from other elements of strategic analysis, particularly the impact of trends from the business environment, as these can change the shape and structure of an industry.

One of the exciting things about this type of analysis is that we are taking a photograph of what exists today. Often strategies can be derived which when

Figure 10.11
Strategy matrix.
(Copyright
Harbridge
Consulting Group
Ltd: used with
permission)

		Activity	
		Same	Novel
Structure of Industry	Same	• Niches/segmentation • Improvement strategies	Niches/segmentation
	Changed	• Acquire competitors • Create new channels	Create new opportunity

implemented will change the shape and structure of the industry. Figure 10.11 shows in matrix form some of the strategic options which may emerge from an industry mapping exercise.

Cell 1: same activity, same structure

Here the strategic options are about improving position. This may be gaining advantage through a changed cost structure (for example, the complete relocation of the Vickers Armoured Fighting Vehicle plant in the early 1980s from multiple Victorian buildings to a one-building, greenfield site). It may include careful segmentation or other marketing strategies which beat the competition.

Cell 2: new activity, same structure

This is the group of strategies which deals with the introduction of an alternative, better product (not merely an improved copy of an old one). For example, the lightweight, self-propelled booms to give access on construction sites both found a new market and removed a major share from the previous heavy, cumbersome telescopic booms that were previously used. The firm that introduced the self-propelled booms gained a considerable advantage over the companies that had been market leaders in this area.

Cell 3: same activity, changed structure

This is the strategy followed by companies that have tried to achieve leadership in a fragmented industry through acquisition of competitors.

Cell 4: new activity, changed structure

An old example is the supermarkets who began by offering a different approach to grocery retailing, and went on to change the structure of the industry through increasing buyer power as they gained control of the channels. A more recent example is Sears Roebuck in the USA, which brought together its insurance company, Allstate, and several new financial service company acquisitions, a new general credit card (launched on the back of the store card), and its retail network to offer a new way of marketing consumer financial services.

Competitor profiling

Industry mapping helps us to understand the forces which determine competitive behaviour in general, and also to identify which competitors should be studied at an individual level. The next stages of competitor analysis are designed to achieve a number of aims, which include:

1 Formulation of an appropriate strategy in the reality of the competition. An appropriate strategy might be one which chooses those areas for the industry analysis that avoid ferocious competition. Or, for a dominant competitor, it may mean ensuring that it retains this position.
2 Finding a superior strategy that gives competitive advantage.
3 Being prepared for competitor actions and expected reactions to your strategies.
4 Influencing competitor reactions, by trying to get the competitor to do what you want.
5 Developing an alliance strategy with competitors. Relations with competitors do not always have to be hostile, and in some industries there are opportunities which can best be exploited as a joint venture or alliance.
6 Identifying the true competitors. Not all the players in an industry are necessarily all competing against each other. The case study in the next chapter gives an example of an industry where there are so many segments and so much fragmentation that many players in the industry are neither offering similar products, nor selling them to the same buyers.

Competitor profiling provides a way of looking at competitors, and presenting the results in an easy-to-read form, again on one A3 sheet of paper. Sometimes more pages are needed, particularly when a competitor has to be studied at different levels (product or geographic), but the principle of reducing the analysis to summary statements can be preserved. This process increases understanding of the competitor, focuses attention on the appropriate issues, and provides a format which eases internal communication and can be stored in a database.

A pro-forma competitor profile is provided in Figure 10.12. In practice this will require modification to suit the types of competitor in the industry. Each block of information is discussed below.

Financial results

Choose the key figures that mean the most to you. Typically these would include sales, profits, and key ratios such as earnings per share, return on assets, return on sales and growth rates. The example shows that there may be a need to repeat this information at various levels, such as the total group, the division and the business unit. These headings will change with the objectives of the analysis and the structure of the competitor. What can be recorded is, of course, limited by the information that can be legitimately obtained, and the special knowledge of the analyst which may allow certain estimates to be made. At the broadest levels, the information will probably come from annual reports: at the lowest levels it may be necessary to estimate sales and profit figures from market research and other sources.

Financial Results

	Group					Division					Unit				
	YR	YR	YR	YR	YR	YR	YR	YR	YR	YR	YR	YR	YR	YR	YR
Sales															
PBT															
PAT															
ROA															
ROS															
Sales Growth															
EPS															

Product Analysis

Product	Sales			Direct Costs			Contribution			Market Share		
	YR	YR	YR	YR	YR	YR	YR	YR	YR	YR	YR	YR
1												
2												
3												
4												
5												
6												
7												
8												

Marketing and Sales Activity

Sources of Competitive Advantage

SOURCE	NOTES
Infrastructure	
R & D	
Logistics In	
Operations	
Logistics Out	
Marketing	
Sales	
Services	

Importance of Activity to Group

Scope of International Operations

Key Factors

Apparent Strategy

Strengths **Weaknesses**

Implications **Implications**

Organisation Philosophy

CSF Ratings

Factor	Competitor	Own	Index

Personnel Policies

Notes
Assess each factor 0–10 index is

$$\text{COMPETITOR SCORE} \over \text{OWN SCORE}$$

Figure 10.12
Outline competitor profile. (Copyright Harbridge Consulting Group Ltd: used with permission)

Product analysis

This is another breakdown of the information into products or product categories. Data may come from annual reports, but will invariably have to be supplemented by market research information and possibly analysis of the competitive product so that cost structures can be estimated. The ability to complete every cell will vary with the information that can be obtained, and the justification of the effort that should be put on this will vary with the importance of the competitor. Very often the analyst will have to be satisfied with a less than complete answer. This section incorporates market shares. It could also be extended if appropriate to show segment shares: again a judgement has to be made on the value of this information and whether it can be obtained.

Marketing and sales activity

This is a notepad to record key information about how the competitor influences the market. It may include information on advertising spends, the size of the sales force, direct mail activity, or whatever else is strategically important.

Importance of activity to group

This part of the form assesses the significance of the industry being analysed to the total operations of the competitor. The reason for this is to establish whether the activity is core to the competitor, in which case more resources might be made available to fight off a competitive threat. Something which is peripheral may not receive the same management time, nor have additional resources made available. One complex way of showing this is to draw a portfolio chart of all the competitor's activities.

This is always difficult, and particularly so if the competitor operates in a number of industries on which the analyst has little real knowledge. Just how difficult will become clearer in a later chapter which deals with portfolio analysis. An alternative method is illustrated in Figure 10.13, which immediately shows the importance of an activity to a competitor as a source of turnover, profits and growth.

Figure 10.13
Importance of corporate activities

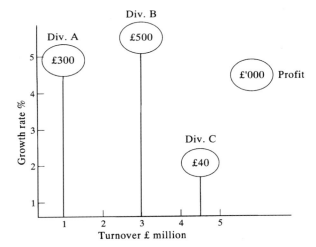

Sources of competitive advantage

This box begins to tie into value chain analysis, and is an attempt to identify just what it is which is giving a competitor an edge. Are they a particularly efficient manufacturer? Is the edge in their ability to develop continuous product innovations? Is it a superior aftersales service? An extension or alternative to this box could be to try to identify the core competence of the competitor. Prahalad and Doz[4] stress the importance of studying the core technologies and competencies of organisations as well as their particular product market attributes. They quote, as one example, Honda and argue that its competitive strength comes from engines, a core technology, as well as brand recognition.

Scope of international operations

This box provides a notepad to record information about the operations of a competitor outside of any particular country which may be being studied. The two main aspects which should not be ignored are any marketing advantage given by international operations and the way in which the competitor runs its international operations. The competitive reactions to your strategy will be very different if the competitor operates on an individual country basis, what has been termed 'multilocal', than if it manages globally through an integrated strategy. One European-wide grocery products company I studied operated at a competitive disadvantage because each country operation was treated as a separate business, and had to achieve its return on investment targets as its main priority. Its major competitor, who was winning all the battles in every country, treated Europe as one strategic area and would put resources into any country to beat off a competitive threat, regardless of the short-term impact on that subsidiary's bottom line. The virtually uncoordinated country strategies of my client meant that it could rarely win against the superior strategy of the competitor. Knowing how your competitor views global operations is a critical first step to understanding and predicting how it will behave in different circumstances.

Key factors

This is another notepad to record any major points about the competitor which do not fit under the other headings.

Apparent strategy

This box records what the competitor's strategy appears to be. I use the word 'apparent', because it can only be a deduction, based on the analysis of all the information (the factual situation drawn from the market research and hard data, and the assessments made from statements in annual reports, press announcements, interviews, and company literature). This is one of the most important pieces of information on the profile and should be discussed at some length within the company that is doing the analysis.

Strengths and weaknesses

The purpose of this box is self-evident. It will be easier to complete if hard data and specific market research into the view from the customer are used, as well as the impressions of your own managers. It is very easy to attribute to competitors strengths and weaknesses that they do not possess, or which are of trivial importance in the marketplace.

Critical success factor ratings

The critical success factors discussed earlier can be used as one way of comparing competitors against one's own operations. I have found it useful to score the competitor and the company on whose behalf the analysis is undertaken against each critical factor. If possible, I have this exercise undertaken by a number of informed managers individually, argue out the extreme views, and average the final answers. What usually becomes apparent is a series of strengths that may not have emerged from the first exercise.

Organisation philosophy

This matters because how a company organises itself will affect how it behaves in the marketplace. One dimension of philosophy was discussed when we looked at the international operations box. There are many others, including the degree of centralisation/decentralisation, where strategic decisions are taken, and whether organised into strategic business units or subsidiaries. Is the main owning organisation a holding company, perhaps operating like a Hanson, or an integrated part of the overall business, like British Petroleum? Goold and Campbell[5] provide useful insight into the various philosophies for the organisation of strategic decision making.

Personnel policies

The final box records those personnel policies which impact on strategy. For example, the type of people recruited, how they are developed, the reward policies applied, and the importance placed on people are all aspects which have potential strategic importance.

The next chapter provides a case history of the application of competitor analysis, using the methods described in this chapter. It includes an example of a completed profile.

The process of profiling is beneficial in itself, as it forces systematic consideration of competitors. It also offers a way in which masses of information can be sifted and reduced to something that the human mind can handle. I have used such profiles as the foundation of a database enabling electronic storage and retrieval.

The compression of lots of data into a one-page information sheet is very helpful when a number of managers are working together to formulate strategy. It is at least possible to get everyone reading the same information at the same time!

Such profiles can also be completed on any key players on the industry map, and it may be of equal value to study the strategies of key industry customers in a similar way.

Competitor groupings (strategic groups)

Unfortunately, competitor profiling cannot deal with all the competitive situations we may meet. In a fragmented market, for example, there may be hundreds of relatively small competitors, many of whom may never be met in a competitive situation. Studying each individually may add little insight. This is one reason why we have to find another way of looking at competitors. Porter[1] argues that competitors can be studied on the basis of strategic groups. His definition is:

> A strategic group is the group of firms in an industry following the same or a similar strategy. . . An industry could have only one strategy group if all the firms followed essentially the same strategy. At the other extreme, each firm could be a different strategic group.

One solution to the fragmented industry would be to identify strategic groups and study these. Some authorities, including Porter, would recommend this for all industries. The identification of criteria for strategic groups has exercised many minds. McGee and Thomas[6] provide an excellent review of many of the research studies into strategic group identification. McNamee and McHugh[7] give a case study of defining strategic groups in the Northern Ireland clothing industry. A number of matrix classifications have been used to identify groups. Porter[1] suggests specialisation and vertical integration as the two axes of a matrix for plotting the strategic groups. In his example of the US chain saw industry, he uses quality branded image as one axis and the mix of channels used as another. The McNamee and McHugh[7] argument is that such diagrams need also to display the intensity of competition in each group plotted.

McGee and Thomas should be left with the last word on the usefulness of the strategic group concept in competitor analysis:

> By occupying an intermediate level of analysis between firms and industry, strategic groups are helpful for identifying issues about an organisation's competitive position (e.g. Who are the direct competitors? What are the competitive forces? What are the distinct competitive assets?) Indeed the key to understanding industry evolution lies in the way in which firms change their asset structures, in other words, the ways in which mobility barriers change and redefine the strategic groups thus enabling predictions about future industry evolution to be advanced. . .
>
> (1) Groups can be used to preserve information characterising individual firms which is typically lost in industry studies using averaged and aggregated data.

(2) Because groups allow us to investigate multiple firms concurrently, they allow us to assess the effectiveness of their strategic actions over a wider range of variations than a single firm's experience affords.

(3) Group analysis can be used to summarise information to bring key dimensions into high relief, for example to facilitate an assessment of the consequences of a collective movement by many firms into similar competitive postures, or to verify similarities of strategic direction across an industry.

Special competitor studies

The profiling approach will cover most competitor analysis needs most of the time. However, sometimes there may be a requirement to undertake a special study of one competitor or of several competitors in a comparative study. The latter comes close to benchmarking, which will be discussed later.

There is little difference in concept between undertaking a special study of a competitor to build competitive advantage or of a competitor or other organisation as an acquisition candidate. The sources of information are the same, although the purposes may be different.

A special study of a competitor may be more focused. It may be restricted to a functional area, such as their use of information systems, or a country (are they doing anything in Poland?), or to an attempt to predict the direction of their Research and Development. Such reports have to be designed to fit the purpose, so very little guidance can be given on their shape. Perhaps more interesting is an idea of some of the legitimate sources of information that can be tapped. This will be left until the end of the chapter, as it applies to every aspect of competitor analysis.

Value chain analysis

The concept of value chain analysis was another innovation from Michael Porter.[8] Hussey[9] defined value chains as:

> A method for separating the activities the firm performs in order to identify the underlying areas of competitive advantage. All broad stages of the process from *in-bound logistics* to after sales service are identified. They are then broken down into more detailed chains of activity, so that areas where the firm has advantages can be studied. Similar analysis is undertaken on competitors, leading to more effective competitive strategies and a fuller understanding of how each competitor is achieving differentiation.

Before probing more deeply into what this all means, it is as well to give some thought about what Johansson *et al.*[10], call 'the new value metrics', which are the ways in which the value to customers can be increased, and competitive advantage gained. They give the following details:

Quality
- Meeting customer requirements
- Fitness for use
- Process integrity, minimum variance
- Elimination of waste
- Continuous improvement

Service
- Customer support
- Product service
- Product support
- Flexibility to meet customer demands
- Flexibility to meet market changes

Cost
- Design and engineering
- Conversion
- Quality assurance
- Distribution
- Administration
- Inventory
- Materials

Cycle time
- Time to market
  - Concept to delivery
  - Order entry to delivery
- Response to market forces
- Lead time
  - Design
  - Conversion
  - Engineering
  - Delivery
- Materials
- Inventory

Porter[8] argues that: 'Value is created when a firm creates competitive advantage for its buyer – lowers its buyer's cost or raises its buyer's performance' (p. 53). The value metrics mentioned above are all ways of doing one or both of these things. In Porter's view,

> Competitive advantage cannot be understood by looking at the firm as a whole. It stems from the many discrete activities a firm performs in designing, producing, marketing, delivering and supporting its products. Each of these activities can contribute to a firm's relative cost position and create a basis for differentiation (p. 33).

The analysis of the firm's value chain requires an examination of these activities, their costs, and what they contribute to buyer value. In fact the position is a little more complicated than this, as the ultimate buyer's value chain is affected by every organisation along the way, which would include not only the firm but also its suppliers and distributors. In some situations the best way to look at improving customer value can be through a collaborative examination with others in the overall chain to see what overall changes could be made.

Porter defines two overall elements in the value chain: value activities and margin. Margin is the difference between total value and the overall costs of performing the value activities, and, of course, becomes part of the costs of the next organisation's value chain. Value activities are those which are technologically and strategically distinct. They are rarely the same as accounting definitions, which makes the tasks of looking at the costs of each value activity much more difficult. The firm has primary activities, which are directly related to the products and services the firm offers, support activities, which aid the value activities in specific ways, and an infrastructure which contributes in a more general sense.

Porter[8] provides a diagram in the form of a rectangle with one pointed end, divided horizontally into two equal halves: that at the top contains 'firm's infrastructure' and 'support activities' and that at the bottom the 'primary activities'. The reason I am not including this often-quoted diagram is that I have seen it misused too often in spurious analysis, where a firm's organisation chart is regrouped under the headings on the chart without any analysis of the actual activities performed, and every other page in Porter's 557-page book is ignored. So rather than contribute to the further misuse of the Porter concepts I will describe the approach in a different way.

Support activities

Three activities are suggested: human resource management, technology development, and procurement (purchasing). Each of these is capable of being analysed for the contribution made to each value activity.

Primary activities

The five primary activity areas are:

1 *Physical distribution, in-bound (in-bound logistics)* All the activities concerned with the receipt, storage, handling and recording of the raw materials and supplies obtained by the organisation
2 *Operations* The activities performed by the organisation to transform the inputs into final finished form
3 *Physical distribution, out-bound (out-bound logistics)* Activities from warehousing the finished product to getting it to the customer
4 *Marketing and sales* The provision of a means by which the customer knows about the product and can purchase it

219

5 *Service* The activities which enhance the value of the product, such as aftersales service, spare-parts availability, installation and training.

These headings are generic, and may be modified to suit a particular organisation. They are also only a starting point, and have little value unless each primary heading is broken down into the activities the organisation actually performs. Thus the marketing and sales activity for a replacement window company might break down to:

Marketing management
Promotional materials
Sales administration
Telephone sales
Shop operations
Sales people
Direct mail
Media advertising

The word 'might' is used deliberately, as my personal knowledge of this industry is as a customer of one large firm and a victim of the regular telephone sales operations of all the others. However, the headings give the flavour of what has to be done.

Each of the primary activities has to be taken to this sort of more detailed level, and the only warning that needs to be given at this stage is that the grouping may not be precisely that in the organisation chart. For all I know, the replacement-window company I was thinking of might not have the shops reporting to the marketing and sales operation. However, we are concerned with a way of analysing the activities, and should follow this line of thinking rather than that of the formal structure.

All this is the easy part. The first, more difficult, step is to analyse each of the support activities, so that we can see what they do to enable the primary activities to deliver value. Although broad descriptions, like recruitment or training under the HRM support activity may be a starting point, the analysis should be more specific: what has really been done, and what did it contribute?

An even harder step is to re-analyse the cost structure of the organisation so that it is possible to see what each activity costs. An easy statement to make, but very complex in practice.

And the hardest step of all is to put a measurement to the value that each activity gives to the buyer. One way of doing this is to rate each activity on a 1 to 10 scale (recording the evidence for the conclusion), and this is likely to be more accurate when it incorporates information from the buyer. It is possible that some activities have a negative value.

The analysis undertaken on the firm gives a picture, and may reveal ways to change the situation. However, it is more meaningful if also carried out on major competitors, even if less detailed on costs, because in this way it is possible to make a comparative assessment of where competitive advantage can be gained. Preece, Fleisher and Toccacelli[11] describe the use of value chain analysis at Levi Strauss and suggest a way of making this comparison, and some of its strategic and tactical uses in the area of corporate reputation.

Value chain analysis may lead to ways of building competitive advantage by relating the analysis to the value metrics. The real value is not in static analysis but in seeing where changes can be made, such as through the application of improved technologies to various links in the value chain. It may well lead to businesses process re-engineering, to develop an organisation which has a closer fit with what would add most value for customers.

However, the health warning is that the old maxim rubbish in, rubbish out applies to this analysis as to any other. Perhaps because it is complex I seem to have seen more rubbish around this method of analysis than any other (although the garbage content of many other examples of strategic analysis which I have examined has often been too high for comfort).

One aspect that requires particular attention is to be sure that something you see as beneficial, is also seen this way by customers. Not all activities add value.

Benchmarking

Benchmarking is a process through which the organisation seeks to identify the best practices that are relevant to the industry. It is thus different from a study that merely seeks to identify what a competitor does, because first, our interest is only with the best, and second, good practice is not necessarily restricted to those in the industry.

I am grateful to Bengt Karlöf[12] for giving me sight of the manuscript of the English translation of one of his Swedish books, and thus drawing my attention to the two concepts of best internal practice and best external practice.

Best internal practice is a benchmarking concept that can be applied by any organisation that has replicated activity within a country or across the world. This may be duplicated factories, branch operations, or service operations. Karlöff recommends breaking down the operations into comparable value chain activities. If this sort of analysis is to be meaningful it has to cluster activities by relevant differences. If we take as an example the service operations of a European elevator company, there may not be much to be gained from comparing one country with another. There may be a great deal to be learned by sorting service centres into groups with similar characteristics, and seeking best practice within each group, regardless of within which country it falls. The advantages of the best internal practice approach is that data can be obtained on whatever parameters are determined to be appropriate for the study, and it is possible to find out the reasons for variances, thus enabling action to be taken. The disadvantages are that the organisation's best may only equate to competitor's worst, that such comparisons often become bogged down by company politics, leading to defensive behaviour and manipulation of the figures.

Best external practice is easier for support activities across industries than it is for detailed cost analysis between competitors. Occasionally it is possible to get support from all competitors for an honest broker to collect and analyse the figures, and to present them in a meaningful but non-confidential way. The non-confidential data are helpful in putting a particular organisation on a league table, but does not necessarily help in identifying what it is that contributes to the best performer's figures.

Some things can be benchmarked relatively easily. Service levels can usually be measured through market research studies. Productivity levels or manufacturing processes are a much tougher proposition. As always in this book, I am only referring to information that can be obtained by legitimate means. My own standard is that if I would feel uncomfortable telling a competitor how I obtained my information, I should not use that source.

Interindustry benchmarking studies can yield valuable information. My own organisation has found little difficulty in undertaking some of these studies for clients, for example in particular aspects of human resource management (in one case the policies and approaches used by organisations in the USA and the UK to manage cultural diversity in the workforce), and in policies for customer service. These sorts of studies really fall outside of the analysis of competitors, but may lead to ways of building competitive advantage.

Building competitive advantage

Competitor analysis can be used in an avoidance sort of way. By being aware of what competitors are doing it becomes possible to avoid activities which would lead to a head-on battle on ground which was not of your own choosing.

Building competitive advantage is a high-sounding aim. In reality, much of the competitor analysis is about removing competitive disadvantage rather than creating a permanent gap between your activities and those of competitors. There are comparatively few actions that cannot be copied by competitors. However, it is usually much harder for a competitor to regain ground that has been lost, so even a temporary advantage may be beneficial, particularly if accompanied by an intention to take the next set of actions that enables the organisation to stay ahead.

Porter[1] argues that there are only three generic strategies that can be followed. He provides a matrix with 'industry-wide' and 'particular segment only' as the two positions on one axis and 'uniqueness perceived by the customer' and 'low-cost position' as the two positions on the other. This results in either an industry-wide differentiation strategy, or an overall cost leadership strategy, or a focus strategy. In a later work[8] he modified these conclusions to accept that a focus strategy, could be differentiated or cost based. He used the phrase 'stuck in the middle' to describe firms which failed to make a clear choice between one of the three strategies. I find it hard to agree with such a simple view of the choices, and believe that they are too stark and uncompromising. Within a cost-leadership strategy there is room for differentiation. It is possible to argue that all supermarket chains follow a cost-leadership strategy, but there are also key elements of differentiation. Few people would see Tesco, Sainsbury, Waitrose and Asda in the UK as being identical companies. Differentiation is created by image, by the range of products stocked, originality in own-label brands, location and layout of stores, and no doubt many other factors.

What I do believe is important is clarity over what it is that the organisation is trying to do and the implications of the various options, compared to the offerings and approaches of competitors. However, the strategies themselves must emerge from a study of the market opportunities, tempered by the sort of analysis suggested in this chapter. It would be naive to suggest that competitor analysis is all that matters. It is the mechanism which helps to fine-tune a strategic idea, a way of avoiding expensive errors, a method for ensuring that customers are provided with reasons to buy your product rather than that of someone else. However, if there is no market, or the advantages you offer are not valued by the market, there will be no success. Industry and competitor analysis are important, they help in understanding markets, and in strategic positioning, but they are only one of the elements needed to create a sound strategy.

Information for competitor analysis

The need for strategic information was discussed in an earlier chapter, and competitor information is only a subset of this. In addition, as already mentioned, there may be little difference between information for competitor analysis and for acquisition or alliance purposes.

The lengths that should be gone to are a matter for cost–benefit analysis. How important is that missing piece of information that may be very costly to obtain? Is it worth commissioning a special piece of market research only to assess the strengths and weaknesses of competitors as seen through the eyes of customers? These sorts of decisions require careful judgement on a case by case basis. Will the information be likely to lead to different decisions? How critical are these decisions? Will the costs of getting the information exceed the benefits?

An example of what can be involved is provided by Gulliver,[13] the former chief executive of the Argyll Group, writing about the impact on Argyll of the Guinness affair and the battle to acquire Distillers.

> My team went back 15 years with the Distillers accounts and up to ten years with the principal trading subsidiaries. With a total of about 80 trading subsidiaries we were able to prepare a group consolidation which gave us a good feel for the contribution of individual profit centres. In addition, we scrutinised analysts' reports and trade and financial press cuttings back to the 1960s. Drink industry reports were obtained, and independent market research on Distillers' products were commissioned on the pretext of Argyll examining new market opportunities. We also looked at its industrial relations.
>
> Finally we made a pavement inspection of Distillers' properties. After checking trade directories and *Yellow Pages*, a small team photographed and produced a report on every Distillers' property we could find.

Legitimate sources of information are summarised in Figure 10.14. Many of these are self-evident, but there are one or two less obvious sources which are worth special mention.

Figure 10.14
Sources of
information.
(Reproduced from
Hussey, *Introducing
Corporate Planning*)

Types of Initiative	Examples
1. Library research	Annual reports Press/journal material Investment analysts' reports Government reports Published market intelligence Company literature Company history Academic case studies Computer-based information services Competitor advertising
2. Interviews–secondary sources	Investment analysis Journalists Academics Others with special knowledge
3. Direct contact	Visits to plants Trade associations
4. Conferences, etc.	Industry associations Industry conferences and seminars
5. Primary market research	Consumer surveys Trade(retail/wholesale) surveys Industrial market research Retail audits Diary panels
6. Sales analysis	Bids loss/gain analysis
7. Engineering/R & D	Product comparison
8. Soft information	Own managers Own sales staff

The thing to remember is that every organisation has to communicate: to shareholders, customers, employees and prospective employees, to certain officials, and in some cases to special interest groups that can affect its business. I find it worth-while to think through the various ways in which a particular company may be doing this. If we take prospective employees the immediate and obvious source is recruitment advertisements. These may give information on new activities, through different skills being sort, new locations, expansion strategies, and in a few instances hard facts like 'join our team of 25 applied psychologists', 'all the main UK banks use our systems', or 'we manufacture in five locations round the world'. Small snippets often help the jigsaw of miscellaneous information to fall into a pattern. Many companies also produce recruitment brochures, particularly if they recruit graduates. These brochures often provide information and insights that may not be published elsewhere, as do speeches to professional bodies or business schools.

The company newspaper or journal is often a very good source of information, and there are libraries which keep collections of this type of material. Of course, it depends on the publication, and if it serves a purely social purpose, little will be gained. Often it provides explanations of policies, details of new ventures, and many other insights.

Shareholders receive information directly through annual reports, which can be a mine of good information. There is also indirect communication through press statements, speeches, and statements to investment analysts and journalists. To obtain the support of shareholders it is often necessary for organisations to explain their strategies, and library searches or database services are a good source of such information. The databases may be particularly useful because they may include world-wide reports. A company chairman may be called upon to give explanations in one country which are not reported in his or her home base.

Customers receive communication through sales literature, trade press announcements, advertisements and sales calls. The hard aspects of communication are usually easy to obtain: few companies will refuse to give a copy of their brochures when requested by a competitor, because they could easily be obtained by other means. Often original research is the only way to identify what the image is among customers of key competitors. In a bid situation much can be learned from failures as well as successes. I know of one organisation who bid for about 80 per cent of contracts in their market segments. By constructing a database, which included information about who won the contract and in most cases the price in which it was let, they had a source of hard information, capable of being analysed

Information for competitor analysis and acquisition studies

One way of thinking about where competitor information might be obtained is to think logically about how and why information becomes available in relation to the specific competitor. The methods apply equally to any organisation you may wish to study, including potential acquisition candidates, alliance partners or even customers and suppliers.

1 *The evidence left by its activities* This is the forensics, the traces it leaves for others to find because it trades, builds factories, or runs fleets of lorries. The evidence can be found through marketing research, the analysis of products, and observation of promotional displays, shop layouts and prices, factory buildings, etc.
2 *The organisation's own need to communicate* Every organisation has to communicate with customers, current and potential shareholders, present and potential employees, and sometimes the politicians. So annual reports often give more information than the bare minimum, brochures describe products, internal newspapers reveal facts about new building, structure, and vision, and recruitment advertisements sometimes reveal useful facts about plant location, capacities, structure, and new products. Articles may be written, or encouraged, which reveal facts about the organisation.
3 *Legal obligations* Things the organisation is obliged to reveal by law, or because it wishes to take advantage of the law. Annual reports, patent applications, monopolies enquiries, and similar requirements will put information into the public domain.
4 *Unwelcome activities of outsiders* Sometimes other organisations obtain and publish information about an organisation and against its wishes. This may include investigative journalism, court cases and tribunals.

by geographical region, competitor, customer, influencers, and type and size of installation. The value of this in competitor analysis is self-evident.

Patents have to be filed and may be a rich source of information, although they need to be scanned by appropriately qualified people. Information moves into the public domain as a result of special government enquiries.

Reverse engineering of products is often valuable to determine technical or other advantages, and also to calculate the costs of production.

Fuld[14] provides a number of examples of such sources of competitor analysis and how to make use of them.

There is always more information available than might at first be expected. Often the missing elements can be deduced from the parts of the picture that can be seen. One of my clients analysed their competitors. They then had somebody analyse their own organisation from published sources, and were amazed how much of what was thought of as a confidential strategy could be deduced by an intelligent analyst. But remember that strategy is not just what people say: it is what they do. For the most part, actions such as a new product, concentration on a particular segment, or a geographical expansion produce evidence that can be observed, and measured in a way that is independent of any statements by competitors.

In the next chapter there is a case history of the application of industry and competitor analysis. This should help show the practical advantages of this type of analysis, and also the limitations that occur in any real-life situation.

References

1 Porter, M. E. *Competitive Strategy*, Free Press, New York, 1980.

2 Farmer, D. H. and Taylor, B. *Corporate Planning and Procurement*, Heinemann, London, 1975.

3 Crawshaw, H. S. 'Strategic Analysis for the Information Industry', *Journal of Strategic Change*, 1, No. 1, 1992.

4 Prahalad, C. K. and Doz, Y. *The Multinational Mission*, Free Press, New York, 1987.

5 Goold, M. and Campbell, A. *Strategies and Styles*, Blackwell, Oxford, 1987.

6 McGee, J. and Thomas, H. 'Strategic Groups and Intra-Industry Competition', in Hussey, D. E. (ed.), *International Review of Strategic Management*, Vol. 3, Wiley, Chichester, 1992.

7 McNamee, P. and McHugh, M. 'The Group Competitive Intensity Map', in *Hussey, D. E. (ed.), International Review of Strategic Management*, Vol. 1, Wiley, Chichester, 1990.

8 Porter, M. E. *Competitive Advantage*, Free Press, New York, 1985.

9 Hussey, D. E. 'A Glossary of Management Techniques' in Hussey, D. E. (ed.), *International Review of Strategic Management*, Vol. 3, Wiley, Chichester, 1992.

10 Johansson, H. J., McHugh, P., Pendlebury, A. J. and Wheeler, W. A. *Business Process Reengineering*, Wiley, Chichester, 1993.

11 Preece, S., Fleisher, C. and Toccacelli, J. 'Building a Reputation along the Value Chain at Levi Strauss', *Long Range Planning*, 28, No. 6, December, 1995.

12 Karlöf, B. Strategisk Precision, Affärsvärlden Förlag AB, Stockholm, 1991. (Note an English edition was published by Wiley in 1993 under the title *Strategic Precision*.)

13 Gulliver, J. 'How Scotland Lost Out to Back-street Hammersmith', *The Times*, 31 August 1990.

14 Fuld, L. M. *Competitor Intelligence*, Wiley, New York, 1987.

Further reading

Day, G. S. and Reibstein, D. J. (eds), *Wharton on Dynamic Competitive Strategy*, Wiley, New York, 1997.

Karlöf, B. and Östblom, S. *Benchmarking: A Signpost to Excellence in Quality and Productivity*, Wiley, Chichester, 1993.

McGonagle, J. and Vella, C. M. *Outsmarting the Competition*, McGraw-Hill, Maidenhead, 1993.

Pitts, A. and Lei, D. *Strategic Management: Building and Sustaining Competitive Advantage*, West, Minneapolis/St Paul, MN, 1996.

Watson, G. H., *Strategic Benchmarking*, Wiley, New York, 1993.

Appendix: outline questionnaire

1. Definition of Industry

1.1. How would you define the industry in which you operate (by product and services)?

1.2. What is your definition of the relevant geographical scope of your industry? (You may find it important to analyse more than one geographical area, grouping regions with similar product life cycles, competitors or Government policies.)

1.3. Is your activity directed at a definable market segment or segments? What are these?

1.4. What is the approximate size of the market(s)?

1.5. What is the range of profits for your industry (in terms of ROCE)? Are they

above average for all British* industry	☐
average	☐
below average for all British* industry	☐

1.6. How stable are the profits in your industry?

	Year to Year	Within a Year
Very stable	☐	☐
Stable	☐	☐
Unstable	☐	☐

This questionnaire was designed to facilitate analysis of an industry. It should be modified for the characteristics of the industry being studied, and is particularly useful for a company which operates in several industries. The design of the questionnaire means that it collects the information in a way that enables both industry and portfolio analysis to be undertaken. © Harbridge Consulting Group Ltd. Used with permission.

*Amend according to relevant geographical area.

2. Competition

2.1.   *As the number of competitors increases, or as they become more equal in size and power there is a tendency for growing contention in the industry.*

2.1.1. List the competitors in the industry by major segment (as defined) (including your firm) with approximate market shares and position description (defined below):

Competitor   Market Share   Position Description

Position Description – use the description which best fits each firm:

Leader   a company which by virtue of its market position is likely to be followed by others in pricing.

Major   the position where no one firm is a leader, but where a number of approximately equal dominance.

Minor
Negligible

(Note: these definitions are based on those used in the Directional Policy Matrix, a portfolio analysis tool originally developed by Shell Chemicals).

2.1.2. Which word best describes the type of competition in your industry?

friendly ☐   gentlemanly ☐   polite ☐
bitter ☐   warlike ☐   fierce ☐
cut-throat ☐

2.2.   *Contention increases as growth rates slow*

2.2.1. Which phase of the life cycle characterises your industry and your products?*

	Industry	Your Products
Introduction	☐	☐
Take-Off	☐	☐
Slow Down	☐	☐
Maturity	☐	☐
Decline	☐	☐

*Refer to Figure 10.3.

2.2.2. What rate of market growth (in volume terms) occurs in your industry?

	% p.a.
Last five years	_____
Forecast next five years	_____

2.3.   *Rivalry increases where fixed costs are high, efficient increments to capacity are large, or external factors lead to recurring or chronic excess capacity.*

2.3.1. What is the approximate percentage of fixed costs to total costs in your industry?   _____

2.3.2. What is the lead time required to increase capacity?   _____

2.3.3. What is your estimate of current utilisation of capacity? (Normal shifts)

	%
Your industry as a whole	_____
Your firm	_____

2.3.4. Are periods of chronic excess capacity a characteristic of your industry?   _____

2.3.5. Are margins maintained when capacity exceeds demand?   _____

2.4.   *Competition increases when the product is perishable or difficult or costly to store.*
(Note: an air-line ticket, a consultancy service, and a banana are examples of very different perishable products).

2.4.1. Does your industry fall under these categories?

Perishable ☐
Difficult to store ☐
Costly to store ☐

2.5   *Contention increases the more standardised the product and the less differentiated it is in the eyes of the buyer, reaching a peak as it nears commodity status.*

2.5.1. How do the buyers view the products in the industry?

Standardised/Interchangeable ☐
Substitutes ☐
Differentiated ☐
Requiring a major change (e.g. engineering, formulation, or manufacturing process) if products changed ☐

---

*Note: A similar change may occur when a chief executive changes.

2.5.2. Does pricing behaviour in the industry suggest that the industry regards its products as standardised?

_____

_____

(Note: these questions may need to be considered separately for different market segments).

2.6.   Competition becomes more unpredictable as firms in the industry develop different 'personalities' or when recent entrants have different historical origins and ignore the 'norms' of industry behaviour.*

2.6.1. How would you describe the firms in your industry?

Club or fraternity (homogeneous interests)	☐
Tend to act according to the unwritten 'rules'	☐
Little common interest	☐
Irrational in behaviour	☐

2.6.2. Are the firms in the industry long established, or have there been recent entrants to the industry whose values and objectives appear to be different?

_____

_____

_____

_____

_____

_____

2.6.3. Are there one or more 'mavericks' in the industry who regularly upset the industry?   _____

3. Suppliers

3.1.   (a) Industry profits may be reduced when the bargaining power of the suppliers of the major items increases. This will happen as a supplier industry becomes less competitive.
(b) The bargaining power of suppliers tends to reduce if the purchasing industry is highly concentrated.

3.1.1. What is the ratio of suppliers to industry forms for each of the most important supplies?

3.1.2. To what extent are the most important supplies:

Standardised/Interchangeable ☐
Substitutes ☐
Differentiated ☐
Tied to the industry through particular processes, plant, etc.
(e.g. if the firm changed, its supplier would have to modify
its product, manufacturing process, etc.) ☐

3.2. *(a) Suppliers will tend to try to influence the growth of the purchasing
industry when it accounts for a large proportion of the total output of the
supplying industry.*
*(b) The availability of competing substitute products will tend to reduce the
power of suppliers and increase purchasing industry profitability.*

3.2.1. To what extent are the supplier industries dependent on the sales of your
industries?

_____

_____

_____

_____

3.3. *Suppliers may increase their bargaining power if they can demonstrate a
credible threat to integrate forward.*

3.3.1. List any suppliers which have integrated forwards in the industry:

_____

_____

_____

(Note: backwards integration is covered in Question 3.4)

3.3.2. How does profitability in your industry compare with those in your
suppliers' industries? (If higher, the threat of integration is increased, since
the supplier will tend to judge the investment opportunity against his
present returns).
(Note: this is not the only factor they will consider – opportunity cost of
capital is also important.)

Rates of return:
Very much higher ☐
Higher ☐
The same ☐
A little lower ☐
Considerably lower ☐

3.3.3. Is the volume of business in the hands of any one supplier sufficient to justify their operation in your industry? (That is, sales volume in relation to efficient scale of operations). _____

3.3.4. Could the supplier obtain any economies by integrating? _____

3.3.5. Consider the barriers to integration.

3.3.6. Does the industry act as a barrier to thwart suppliers' technical innovations and new products? _____

3.4. *On the other hand the purchasing industry can reduce the power of the suppliers if it can offer a credible threat to integrate backwards.*

3.4.1. List any firms in the industry which have integrated backwards.

_____

_____

_____

_____

_____

3.4.2. Are the entry barriers to backward integration high or low? _____

4. Buyers

4.1. *The availability to increase prices is reduced when the buying industry has a low value added.*

4.1.1. How significant is the value added at each stage in the industry, e.g.

	Very High	High	Medium	Low	Very Low
Supplier					
Industry					
Buyer					

4.2. *(a) The power of the buyer is higher the more it is dominated by powerful customers, the fewer the number of buying firms, and the greater their percentage purchases from the industry*
(b) The power of the buyer decreases as the industry becomes more concentrated.

4.2.1. What is the percentage of industry firms to buying firms? _____

4.2.2. Is the market dominated by a small group of powerful customers? _____

4.2.3. What percentage of sales goes to each of the various categories of buyer:

Category   Industry   Your Firm

4.3. *The power of buyers is reduced by a credible threat of forward integration by the industry: it is increased by a credible threat of backwards integration by the buyers.*

4.3.1. List any firms in the industry who have integrated forward.

_____

_____

_____

4.3.2. List any buyers who have integrated backwards.

_____

_____

_____

4.3.3. Are there any significant economic advantages in integration?

_____

_____

_____

4.3.4. Does the volume of business justify the buyer considering operation in the industry (i.e. sales volume in relation to efficient scale of operations)? Or vice versa?

Backwards by buyer   _____

Forwards by industry   _____

4.3.5. How does profitability of the buyer firms compare with that of the industry?

Higher   ☐
Same   ☐
Lower   ☐

4.4. *As buyers become more experienced, normally as a market matures, they may exercise more influence over the profitability of suppliers.*

4.4.1. What proportion of business (by each main category of buyers), is by competitive tender?

_____

_____

_____

4.4.2. How effective are the buyers in imposing their standards on you and your competitors?

_____

_____

_____

4.4.3. What is the nature of the buying decision process in the main categories of buyers?

_____

_____

_____

4.4.4. Please describe the nature and importance of firms which may influence the buying decision, but who are not themselves buyers.

_____

_____

_____

5. New Entries: Exits

Some of the factors which make an industry attractive to new entrants have already been covered: profitability, growth, degree of competition etc. In addition there might be added a lack of entry and exit barriers.

5.1. *Entry barriers make it more difficult for an outsider to get into the industry.*

5.1.1. Are economies of scale important in your industry, sufficient to ensure that new entrants have to make/set up a significant capacity at high capital cost in order to compensate?   _____

5.1.2. Would vertical integration provide significant additional economies? _____

5.1.3. List any absolute cost advantages possessed by your firm and each of the major competitors.

Advantage	Competitor (Name)
Patents on products or processes	
Control of proprietary technology	
Control of raw materials	
Availability of low cost capital	
Experience	
Ownership of effective depreciated assets	

5.1.4. To what degree does each of the major competitors (including your firm) have a barrier of brand loyalty (product differentiation)?

5.1.5. Does success in the industry require access to tied distribution networks (e.g. dealers in the motor car industry)?

Yes ☐   No ☐

Could a new entrant secure these?

Yes ☐   No ☐

5.1.6. How would firms in the industry react to a new entrant?

5.1.7. Do any of the following exit barriers exist in the industry?

Specialised, durable assets which have little resale value ☐
High fixed costs associated with exit ☐
Inter-relatedness with other businesses ☐

6. Substitutes

6.1. *The extent to which substitutes have been included in the analysis will depend on the definition of the industry. If current substitutes have been excluded, their industry should be subjected to an analysis similar to the foregoing.*

6.2. What threats, if any, do you see from new substitutes?

235

7. Strategic Issues

What issues arise from the analysis?

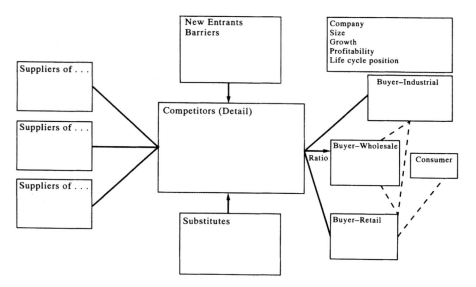

Note: This diagram should be drawn on A3 paper and used to summarise the findings from the questionnaire.

CHAPTER 11

Analysing the UK management development and training industry: a case history

Industry and competitor analysis, and the steps covered in the previous chapter, are important to strategy formulation. The objective of this chapter is to show how the practical tools were used in a real situation, both to demonstrate how the approach has to be modified to fit a different situation and to illustrate that with the right amount of effort much can be discovered even in an industry which has no reliable statistics, and has numerous competitors whose legal format means that they do not register annual returns that are available to the public. A further aim is to show that such an analysis gets better over time, but also requires a commitment of considerable effort.

Scope

Case histories of industry and competitor analysis are difficult to obtain, because of their confidential nature and because it is not always ethical to make public one's value judgements of competitors. In this chapter I have tried to demonstrate the results of a practical application of competitor analysis techniques using

This chapter is a modification of an article of the same name which was published in *Journal of Strategic Change*, 1, No. 4.

mainly real information. However, I have used simplified examples in some of the analytical displays, and where necessary for ethical reasons I have used fictitious exhibits, rather than disclosing my opinions of real competitors. Such exhibits have been reduced to a minimum and are included only where necessary to ensure understanding of the methods actually applied.

One of the difficulties of competitor analysis is knowing what information to obtain. The problem often varies between the extremes of having too few data for meaningful analysis and having so many that it becomes difficult to make sense of it. Once a decision has been taken on the information that is needed, the problem shifts to one of how to obtain it using legitimate and ethical methods. Finally, we reach the crunch issue of what to do with the information that we have collected.

The industry that I have chosen is one of two overlapping industries in which Harbridge Consulting Group operate. It is typical of many industries in that definition is difficult and there are hazy borders with related industries. It is also subject to certain international forces for change, although it is by no means a global industry. It is fragmented, and is unusual in having a mix of private- and public-sector competitors. Within the private sector, there are organisations that gain tax advantages from being registered as charities, although this means that they have to operate under certain rules. Among the other private-sector businesses is a mix of one-person businesses, partnerships and limited companies. Like so many other industries, many competitors also have operations in other industries, making it difficult to interpret their results. Many aspects of our situation have echoes in other industries. It is a professional services business, although there is some competition from 'products' such as videos. Many of its characteristics would be recognised by other professional services businesses, such as solicitors, accountants and surveyors.

All the methodologies illustrated have relevance in other industries, and I have used them with clients from the whole spectrum of business activity.

The outline approach

Figure 11.1 shows the outline approach (this is a simplified version of Figure 10.1), which we have been using continuously on this and other industries since the early 1980s, although some elements of our approach are even older. The analysis of information goes through four linked stages, which also helps to identify what information is required to enable meaningful analysis to take place.

All the information sources shown on the diagram have been used to a greater or lesser extent in applying these methods to various situations. In our own industry, databases are less helpful than other sources of information, which is a reflection of the structure of the industry, the few quoted companies in the industry, the lack of published statistics and the relatively small size of most of the players.

Figure 11.1
Approach to
competitor analysis.
(Copyright
Harbridge
Consulting Group
Ltd: reprinted with
permission)

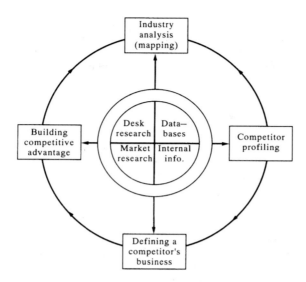

Before going deeper into the methods that were used, I should like to explain the reasons for starting what became an increasingly detailed competitor analysis system.

In early 1980 we had virtually no information about our market in the UK or that of our competitors, which made strategic planning a hit-or-miss affair. The UK side of the firm had shown little or no growth for many years. It also followed the classic consultant's situation of basing a business on the skills of its professional staff and changing emphasis with the departure or engagement of every key employee. What we wanted to do was to position the firm in areas where we would build and sustain competitive advantage, to understand properly the pressures on the industry and to identify our real competitors from the 600 or so businesses that operate in the UK management training market. We wanted to improve our ability to plan, so that we could do at least as well as the best in growth years, and better than most in lean years. We wanted information that would enable us to speak authoritatively about all aspects of management development.

We had one additional reason, which is probably the only one that is not similar to that of any firm in any other industry contemplating competitor analysis. We needed a 'laboratory' in which we could try some of the concepts that we were developing for use with clients. What better laboratory was there than our own business, where we could be free from the restrictions of client confidentiality and develop examples that could be shared with others?

My advice to anyone starting competitor analysis is to think through the aims of the exercise first. Competitor analysis may be undertaken for many reasons and that for purely tactical purposes may take a different form from that for strategic reasons. Our intentions were mainly strategic, although as I shall show later, we did gain some tactical benefit. In addition, some types of analysis are best done as benchmark studies, rather than using the method shown here. If, for example, the need is to identify the best human resource management practice in

239

the industry, how the best competitors are using information technology or what is being done about customer responsiveness, then a benchmark study would be a more appropriate approach.

Industry mapping

A journey around the outer circle of Figure 11.1 begins with what I see as the essential first step in competitor analysis: obtaining a detailed understanding of the competitive arena. To do this, we used the principles of Porter.[1] For our total strategic analysis, we set industry analysis within the context of the outside environment, as in Figure 10.2, although for the purpose of this chapter I will not discuss environmental issues.

Our method explodes the supplier/competitor/buyer boxes of the 'five forces' model to mirror the total channel from the first link in the supply chain to the final consumer. The first task is to develop this in block diagram form, using knowledge of managers, logic and available market information. We tend to incorporate substitutes into this diagram if they are already significant or appear likely to become so. In addition, we analyse influencers of a buying action. In some industries, the influencers may do more to shape the competitive forces than the competitors themselves.

In theory, the development of such a block diagram should be easy. In practice, we find that many of our clients face difficulty, tending to draw diagrams that reflect their preconceived ideas or the elements of a channel that they use. When we began our journey towards useful competitor analysis, we found similar problems. We knew what we did and who some of our competitors were, but knew surprisingly little about buying decisions, substitute products or the overall structure of the industry. How we began to collect this information is discussed later, but the example that appears in Figure 11.2 is the result of several analyses and is not the original.

As we began to develop our understanding, we were able to use the block diagram to record key information about the industry. Figure 11.2 gives a simplified view of our industry map. The main difference between this map and the real one is that the real map contains more competitor assessments, uses a personal system of abbreviations and includes more analysis of the buying decision. Figures 11.3 and 11.4 show our assessment of the evolution of the market for the type of service that we provide.

These three diagrams, supported by the additional information that I have omitted for simplification or sensitivity reasons, provide the basis for a detailed strategic evaluation using Porter's[1] principles. Before I discuss a few of these findings I should like to mention two decisions that we had to make about the arena that we were charting.

There were good reasons for studying the UK as the geographical area, and much of the market is still local to the UK. However, like most industries there is an international dimension. Recently we have explored this in more detail, in particular researching other countries in Europe and, of course, having access to

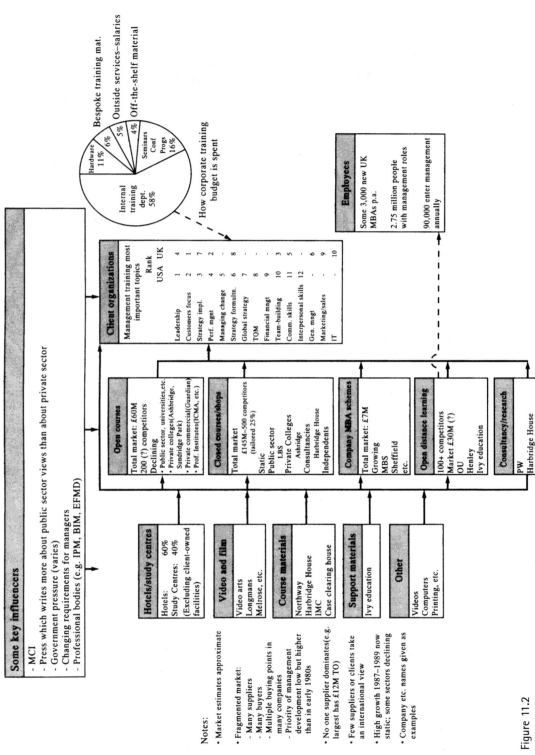

Figure 11.2

Industry map – Management training and development

Figure 11.3
UK market for management development and training. (Copyright Harbridge Consulting Group Ltd: reprinted with permission)

	1985	1989	1990	£M 1991
Open public subscription	45	60	55	40
Closed in-company	75	145	150	123
Company MBA scheme	-	4	7	7
Open/distance	10	30	33	30
Consultancy/research	26	50	55	50
	156	289	300	250

Figure 11.4
Management training market: professional fees, etc. (Copyright Harbridge Consulting Group Ltd: reprinted with permission)

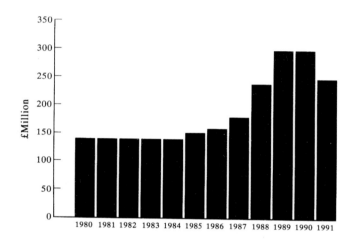

information about the United States of America through our parent company. These findings have had a profound influence on our strategy, although including the detail of the analysis would expand this chapter to book length.

The second decision centred on the problem of industry definition. Figure 11.5 highlights some of the issues. The provision and delivery of management training and development services sounds a neat industry.

However, the suppliers to it, of which a few are illustrated in the figure, are frequently engaged in related businesses. This has at least two implications: how statistical information is collated; and the gradual merging of some of the activities outside the circle with those inside it. For example, the Management Consultancies Association publishes statistics on the consultancy industry. In their figures is included a sector that covers management training. Users of these statistics might be tempted to think that this covers the output of the management training industry. But this is not so; such data exclude the activities of the other providers as not only are they not members of the association but most of them are not eligible to be members. Similarly, government frequently looks at the industry as if it was supplied only by academic institutions (which in

Figure 11.5
How industries overlap in the management training and development industry. (Copyright Harbridge Consulting Group Ltd: reprinted with permission)

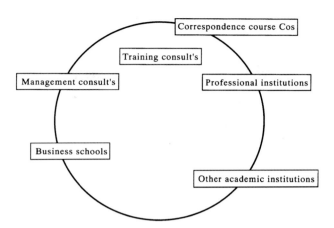

the UK are mainly in the public sector), and often speaks of total UK training when it actually means non-managerial training. The private sector holds a larger market share of the management training market than does the public sector, even before we count the in-house training activities of the 'buyers'.

The related activities of providers change the dimensions of the circle. Three examples clarify this statement:

1 As management consultants, we frequently combine consultancy and training skills to produce a solution for clients that broadens the traditional use

Figure 11.6
Strategic groupings: a hypothetical example from the training industry. The terms 'low' and 'high' are relative to each other and do not imply that one is 'better' than another. (Copyright Harbridge Consulting Group Ltd: reprinted with permission)

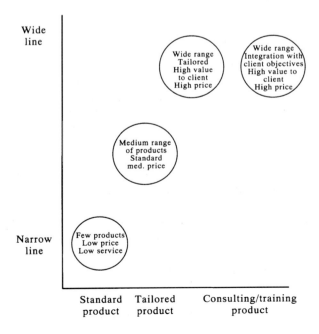

243

of training and lies both inside and outside the circle. It is indeed one of the areas of differentiation that we seek.

2 Academic qualifications moved into the industry when business schools began to offer tailored MBA degrees to individual companies and consortia of companies. An additional twist is that we run courses for two clients that are accredited by two different business schools towards their MBA degrees.

3 Distance learning has been a growth sector of the industry. Not surprisingly, some of the traditional correspondence schools have developed products that compete in the industry, and organisations such as the Open University offer their products to corporate customers, as well as to private individuals.

From what I have said, it is apparent that the boundary of the industry, even as defined, is constantly changing. It is also apparent that different views could be based quite logically on the actual boundaries of the industry. This suggests a need for careful study of some of the key competitors, including some with whom we do not compete directly, to identify the directions in which they could move and which would change the shape of the market in which we compete.

Interpreting the industry analysis

It would be boring to most readers if I offered a full interpretation of the industry map. What I should like to give is enough of a description of some of the findings to carry the case study along, to help later when we look at how the information was obtained and to make the value of such industry maps a little clearer. All the points that I mention are strategically important to us and have been used in formulating our own strategies.

1 The industry is fragmented. There are numerous competitors, no one organisation has more than a 10 per cent market share (although shares are higher in specific segments), and there are numerous buyers.

2 There are no universal patterns by which the buyers organise their management training activity. It is not possible to look at an organisation from the outside and predict whether management training is centralised, decentralised or a mix of both; or to identify the level at which management development decisions are taken, how much training is performed or what proportion is undertaken by the organisation's own staff.

3 Entry barriers to the industry in general are low, but few new entrants are able to grow into significant competitors, although an exception is when the new entrant is a spin-off from an existing competitor. Barriers are much higher in some segments than in others.

4 Not only do most buyers undertake a proportion of their management training with their own resources, but a number effectively become competitors by offering their services to other organisations.

5 In addition to the sectors shown on the map, there are numerous segments. Competitors can be grouped roughly into those who offer a 'commodity' product, and those who are highly differentiated and who support their activities with proprietary approaches. For example, we do not compete with most of the 600 organisations in the UK management training market, and the number of competitors in our chosen segments usually varies between one and twenty. The story would be very different if we were at the commodity end of the spectrum, and I suspect that we would be a much smaller firm.

6 There are 'switching' costs, although they are not large enough to hold a dissatisfied buyer. The nature of these costs is that only differentiated competitors are likely to benefit from them.

7 The product is perishable in that much of what is offered is time based. Yesterday's unused consultancy time has no resale value.

8 Interesting issues surround the way that most buyers make their buying decisions. Management development/training departments are controlled through budgets that measure the costs of training rather than the benefits. Not surprisingly actions follow what the system appears to demand, and most buyers would rather save £500 in the costs of an initiative (on which they are measured), than spend an extra £500 in order to gain an additional £10,000 of benefit from training (on which they are not measured).

9 Many relationships between competitor and client exist at the personal level, with the advantages and disadvantages that this suggests. The key for an organisation that wishes to grow is to add a parallel relationship between the consultancy and client organisations, while not destroying personal relationships.

10 As the range of subjects and methods within management training is so great, there is always an opportunity to innovate. The cost of concept development is a growth barrier to the independent one-person business.

All this can be summed up in the statement that 600 competitors are not frightening if you can take strategic actions that result in your competing with a manageable number. The opportunities to add value are very great, and the more that this is done, the greater the distance the differentiated firm can gain over the bulk of the competitors.

The purists might query whether all these conclusions could have been read from the example of the industry map presented here. As it is abridged, some could not have been read off this map, although more can be seen from the originals that we use ourselves. However, all conclusions could have been reached through the exercise of completing the map, while the mapping process itself throws up areas where the 'facts' do not make sense, shows clearly where there is a lack of knowledge and often helps missing information to be arrived at by logical deduction.

Profiling competitors

From what has been said so far, it is clear that we do not have to study 600 competitors in detail. Many can be grouped, as they behave in roughly the same way. Figure 11.6 shows some of our thinking on competitor groupings in this industry. This diagram could be expanded by adding the dimension of type of ownership, as public-sector organisations, for example, have very different ways of operating from those of private-sector firms.

More ideas on competitor groupings are given in McGee and Thomas,[2] McNamee[3] and Porter.[1]

Currently, we keep tabs on about 120 competitors. This includes the twenty or so that are most significant to us, a number of which have the capability of becoming more significant, and enough of the others so that we have a feel for the total situation. We do not keep information on any sole practitioner.

When we started the exercise, we had very little idea of who our competitors were. This may sound surprising to someone who is used to a typical industry structure where there are clear market leaders, but less so I suspect to someone from a similar fragmented professional services market. The steps that we took to find out will be discussed later.

It took 2–3 years from our first researches to develop profiles in the form illustrated in Figure 11.7. The profile shown is a fictitious example, but I have tried to make it realistic by not completing every information cell. Complete information on any competitor is very rare. What the profile shows is where the competitor gains its revenue and a series of notepads for recording strategic information, focusing on what really matters when we formulate our own strategies. Notepad items were explained in Chapter 10.

What this profiling has done for us is to provide more discipline to our collection of information. It has given us the opportunity to deduce missing parts of the jigsaw puzzle, provided a means of storing information in an easily retrievable way and given us a series of documents that, with the industry map, allow us to survey a vast array of information painlessly when making our own plans. It has become easier for us to identify firms in the industry where collaboration is possible and to pinpoint appropriate competitors who we would recommend to clients (strange as it might seem, this happens, and if we are making a recommendation we like to be sure that we are pointing the client to the right people).

While we have by no means reached perfection in our profiling, and still tend to update our records in blitzes, rather than as a continuous process, we have been able to develop a much better understanding of our industry map through this additional work.

We have also been able to draw up some very useful generic comparisons of strengths and weaknesses between ourselves and different competitor groups (for example, business schools), while understanding the individual differences within each competitor group. In a fragmented market, it is more useful to find a strategy that builds advantages over the majority of competitors, rather than trying to beat each one singly. Products, image and philosophies that result from this exercise have to stand the test of the market.

Figure 11.7

Competitor profile:
Super Consult Ltd
(subsidiary of World
Consulting Services).
(Copyright Harbridge
Consulting Group Ltd)

Financial Results

	Group Super Consult Ltd								Division Training								Unit				
	19XIV	19XX	19XI	19XD	19XII	19XIII	19XIV	19XI	19XD	19XII	19XI	19XD	YR	YR	YR	YR	YR	YR	YR	YR	YR
Sales £M	100	91	87	80	75	65	61	50	40	15											
PDT £M	100	8	8	7	5																
PAT																					
RDA																						
ROS																						
Prof Impl No	85	80	75																		
Fees per Prof	118	114	109	107																		

Product Analysis

	Sales			Direct Costs				Contribution				Market Share			
Product	19V	19XIV	19XII	YR	YR	YR	YR	YR	YR	YR	YR	YR	19XIV	YR	YR
1. Tailored £M	5	2											1%		
2. Other In Co £M	30	25	20										1%		
3. Public Courses £M	30	34	30										5%		
4.															
5.															
6.															
7.															
8.															

Marketing and Sales Activity

1. Quarterly newsletter
2. Regular exhibits
3. Regular promotional seminars
4. Monthly direct mail campaign

Sources of Competitive Advantage

SOURCES	NOTES
Infrastructure	
R & D	
Logistics In	
Operations	Own printing facility
Logistics Out	Mainly use own staff for delivery
Marketing	
Sales	Specialist sales force
Services	Strong customer service orientation

Importance of Activity to Group

Super Consult is:

10% of WCS Revenue
7% of WCS Profit

Growing twice as fast as the whole group

Scope of International Operations

Total group is strong in North America, UK, Singapore. Weak in the rest of Europe and other S. East Asian countries

Key Factors

1. Own training college
2. Offers training (Management) in all European languages
3. Ties into world network
4. New CEO's in parent and SuperConsult. Watch for changes
5. Clients from bottom half of Times 1000 and similar European companies
6. Prices at high end of their sectors

Strengths

1. Reputation in standardised training and open courses
2. Strong financial backing but parent Co wants dividend growth

Weaknesses

1. Not well known among larger Co's who buy tailored
2. Employs the wrong people for tailored work
3. High staff turnover

Implications

Could solve all problems but corporate cash box only available for quick return prospects

Implications

Strategy may be defeated by HR issues

CSF Ratings

Factor	Com-petitor	Own	Index
Quality Image	6	9	67
Quality of Staff	8	6	133
	6	9	67
	5	5	100
Financial Resources	6	4	200

Notes

Assess each factor 0-10 Index is

COMPETITOR SCORE / OWN SCORE

Apparent Strategy

1. Targeting tailored training market
2. Developing new products (recent advert for development personnel)
3. Will not expand UK college
4. Expected to open French college 19XV
5. Major expansion of continental client base

Organization Philosophy

Historically country companies have all reported to US parent

Recent announcements suggest a change to a more global approach

Do not use external associates employees only

Personnel Policies

Professional staff have degrees or professional qualifications. Recent adverts seek post graduate degrees.

Salaries at academic scales plus profit sharing. Some difficulty recruiting.

No equity participation. A quoted US company.

Defining a competitor's business

Some of the original thinking about business definition comes from Abell,[4] who suggested plotting businesses on a three-dimensional chart showing customer functions, customer groups and alternative technologies. Many variations on these themes are possible, and indeed one could delve much deeper into the literature on segmentation to develop the ideas further.

We used simpler matrix displays, which helped to show the difference between ourselves and other organisations in a diagrammatic way. Figure 11.8 shows some of the actual charts that we made, although I have taken off the names. These made us realise the considerable difference in focus of business that we had seen as roughly comparable to ourselves. Some, although of high standing and quality, do not really compete with us at all, although we still monitor them because they may change!

In a less fragmented industry, I would have spent further time on this more detailed type of analysis; however, the number of competitors, and their low market shares, means that the value of going deeper than we have is questionable.

Obtaining the information

None of this analysis would have been possible if we had been unable to obtain any information. In the beginning, the task was daunting and it would have been easy to decide that nothing could be done as the information was too sparse. In the early years, desk research yielded negligible information, because little was published at that time. This meant that we had to consider primary research if we were to obtain any information at all. Our first major competitor study was undertaken in 1985, and this set a foundation that helped us to make sense of information from other sources. After that time, there was an increase in the number of published research studies, which meant that our information became more complete.

Our first piece of research into the market was completed in 1983. This was not, at that time, intended to help us follow the competitor analysis approach described in this chapter, but was the first of a series of reports that we have carried out into management development and training to increase our knowledge of the 'state of the art' and to gain marketing information. Most of these reports are published so that they can be shared with other interested parties, and although they have contributed greatly to our understanding of buyer behaviour and awareness of changing needs and responses, they are not primarily market research reports.

In 1985, we undertook two interrelated pieces of research. We wanted to find out whether the market for our type of training was expanding. Were we getting our fair share of the growth? What were the factors that the buyers considered when choosing a supplier?

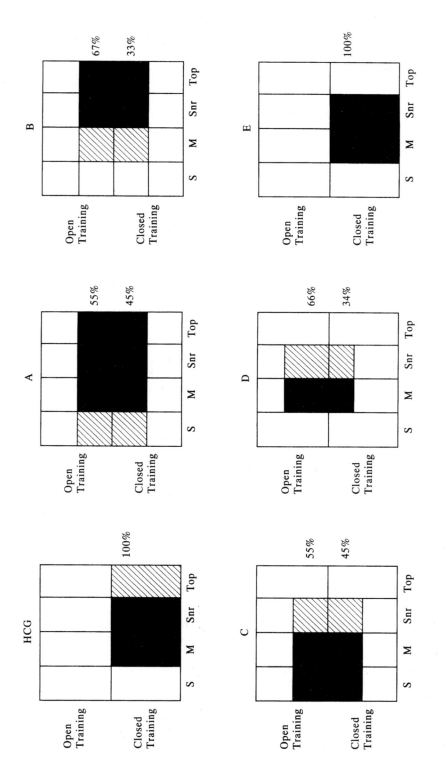

S = Supervisory

M = Middle

Snr = Senior

Top = Top Management

Figure 11.8

Management training activities: sample of competitors. White = normal activity, black = heavy activity, shaded = some activity. (Copyright Harbridge Consulting Group Ltd: reprinted with permission)

Figure 11.9
Primary research
undertaken by us
for the analysis.
'Published' means
published by us

Date	Published information	Unpublished information
1983	Management training in UK companies	
1984	MBA and UK industry	
1985		Competitor study
1986	Tailored management education	
1986	Distance learning	
1987		Competitor information project
1988		Innovation training
1988		Management skills
1989	Consortium/Co MBAs	Management training Europe part 1
1989		Management training Europe part 2
1989		Hotel/study centres
1990		Competitor update
1991	Management training in large UK companies	
1993	Management training in medium sized UK companies	
1993	Management development in Germany	

We knew many of our competitors, but did we know them all? There was a great gap between the ones that we could list and the columns of names shown in directories. Who were the competitors who might be considered to be most critical to our future? Who did the buyers think were our competitors, and who did our competitors think were their most serious rivals? We wanted to know if we were competitive in price, quality, speed of response to the client and in our overall philosophies. And we wanted to answer the same questions for each major competitor. From this, our first intention was to prepare a market-related assessment of our strengths and weaknesses, compared with those of competitors.

A sample survey was conducted by telephone of forty-three buyers of our type of training service, exploring aspects of all the research objectives. We interviewed on a personal visit nine major competitors, building up our list of real competitors from information supplied by buyers and competitors. We were able to check most of the information provided by competitors from the interviews with buyers. All this research was done honestly and openly by one of our consultants.

The information from this survey provided the base from which we could build and develop on the lines already discussed, and led to immediate tactical and strategic decisions. Meanwhile, we continued to add more valuable data from our research for publication and focused some of this on areas of the industry map, which were hitherto blank. We published a report on distance learning, for example, in 1986, and another in late 1989 on consortium and company MBAs.

Although not part of the published report, this survey enabled us to quantify the size of this sector of the market.

In 1987, we used an MBA student to build up the files of competitor information, which we had started to compile. This involved collecting brochures from competitors, annual reports (where available) and press cuttings. In addition, we established our first database, using an earlier format of competitor profile. We did the usual searches at Companies' House, and probably bored the Charity Commissioners with our complaints about competitors who were registered as charities and who had not lodged their returns for several years.

Most of this activity is typical of competitor analysis generally. Three activities that yielded useful information were:

1 Continued direct contact with competitors, including the exchange of information that would be in the annual report if we were all public limited companies. The competitor analysis system that we have built up means that there is somewhere to put the results of all these formal and informal comments, as well as information that comes to us about a competitor from elsewhere in the industry.
2 Obtaining feedback from clients when there is a pre-qualifying exercise or a competitive bid (whether we win or lose). This has been an invaluable source of information. On occasion, buyers have prepared an analysis of all the bidders that they have been willing to share.
3 Helping journalists to write about the industry and suggesting who they should approach for the collection of data for league tables. In this way, we filled several gaps in our own information, especially as a few firms who had refused to exchange information with us on the grounds of confidentiality did not have the same inhibitions when it was a question of gaining publicity.

Published information and market intelligence have become more important since 1987. Several studies have been completed, which when supplemented by our own studies have enabled us to quantify the sectors on our industry map. There is still no sound statistical base for the industry, but the combination of all of our sources means that we believe that our estimates are as accurate as they need to be for the type of decisions that have to be made.

In 1989, we reworked our competitor database, and now store information in a form similar to that of the profiles in this article. We had hopes of creating a dynamic database that would enable us to update the industry map automatically every time a competitor profile was updated. This is not economic at present. We have also done some concept work with an information house to develop something similar for more general use, but commercial prospects are not right.

The main conclusion that can be reached from our work is that a competitor analysis system will improve over time if continuous effort is applied, that even small pieces of information can be coordinated and used if there is a mechanism to handle them and that lack of published information about an industry and competitors may make analysis harder, but need not prevent it.

We have begun to extend the scope of our study to other countries in Europe and have spent more effort on identifying organisations that we can build alliances with, rather than undertaking a complete competitor analysis.

251

Building competitive advantage

None of this analysis is worth while unless it leads to actions. The sort of strategic and tactical actions that we took may give an indication of the benefits that readers might obtain from competitor analysis.

1 We identified much more clearly where we could gain differentiation, and where there were market segments where we could gain clear advantage.
2 As a result, one of the things that we did was to build our geographical and language capability, so that through our own resources or alliances with other organisations, we are able to run the same course for a multinational company in every West European language. This is especially important when the course is intended to support a Europe-wide strategy by the client.
3 We started many new initiatives to build image and awareness, including our regular publication *Management Training Update* (ten issues per year and free to management development and human resources personnel). We redesigned all our stationery and literature to achieve a common image.
4 A strategy was developed for operations in other countries in Europe.
5 Several different products and concepts were developed.
6 The growth of in-company MBA schemes made us seek to become better informed about what was happening, and to find ways in which our work could gain academic accreditation in certain circumstances, without in any way losing our commercial image for that of a pseudo-business school.

At the tactical level, we are now able to identify more accurately those competitors who are significant for different types of assignments, and their respective strengths and weaknesses. Even when we do not know who else has been asked to bid, this helps us to plan our own proposals and presentations in a way that emphasises our advantages.

We redesigned our basic approach to proposal writing, so that our strengths, in so far as they were appropriate to the assignment, were presented in such a way as to invite the client to probe to see whether other bidders also possessed them. Our research had shown significant areas where we knew that many of the competitors likely to be asked to bid did not possess similar strengths. Almost immediately after completing our 1985 competitor study, we had opportunities to apply these tactical concepts and won two major assignments on competitive bids in quick succession. We have been fortunate in developing strong relationships with both clients, and continue to run major management training programmes for them.

Our strategy has helped us to grow faster than the market since the mid-1980s, and our concepts of industry and competitor analysis have helped us to develop these strategies. Add this to the benefits that our clients gain from similar approaches, and the value of competitor analysis becomes clear. However, it is not without cost and anyone thinking of undertaking it needs to decide whether they are looking for a one-off injection of competitor data into their strategy formulation or they wish to set up a continuing system. Both need dedication of effort, and the continuing system needs some attention to organisation and resources.

In either case, and whether the aim of competitor analysis is tactical or strategic, the only justification for the costs and effort is the action that results from the new knowledge. I hope that this case history has given some indication of the benefits, as well as a methodology, of competitor analysis and that it shows that an initial lack of competitor information can sometimes be overcome.

References

1 Porter, M. *Competitive Strategy*, Free Press, New York, 1980.

2 McGee, J. and Thomas, H. 'Strategic Groups and Intra-industry Competition', Hussey, D. E. (ed.), *International Review of Strategic Management*, Vol. 3. Wiley, Chichester, 1992.

3 McNamee P. 'The Group Competitive Intensity Map: A Means of Displaying Competitive Position', in Hussey, D. E. (ed.), *International Review of Strategic Management*, Vol. 1, Wiley, Chichester, 1990.

4 Abell, D. *Defining and Business*, Prentice Hall, Englewood Cliffs, NJ, 1980.

CHAPTER 12

The search for shareholder value

The aim of this chapter is to explore the concepts of shareholder value, and the various methods that are available for its measurement. Examples are given of how the value approach is applied in two British companies. The information is drawn from an original research report. The chapter shows both the advantages and the practical difficulties of applying the value approach.

In the next chapter we will explore some concepts of objectives, which may be important both in the formulation and implementation of strategy. In order to do this topic justice we need first to explore some of the modern ideas about creating shareholder value. This is an important concept and the treatment given here will be partly about strategic concepts, and partly about ways of measurement which can be incorporated into objectives. The second part will be illustrated with some examples of how certain British companies are applying concepts of value-based strategy, drawing on research conducted by my colleague Sylvia Handler[1] and published by Harbridge Consulting Group Ltd. I am grateful for permission to use this material, and indeed for the existence of the research which means that I can support a description of the theory with some examples of practice.

Some concepts of strategy

Supporters of value-based strategy believe that the creation of value is measurable, using discounted cash flow concepts. This will be the second part of the chapter. It is a truism to say that some strategic decisions made by organisations add to the value of the shareholders' investment, while others reduce it. When Hanson bought Imperial Foods it paid £2.1 billion. Within a few months it had sold the brewing interests for £1.4 billion. Other disposals and cost reductions left Hanson with a very profitable cash-generating tobacco company, after it had regained most of the purchase price from the disposals. There is no doubt that Hanson added to the value of its shareholders. There is also no doubt that on the stock market the perception was that Imperial as a whole was worth less than the sum of its parts, an example of the so-called 'conglomerate discount' on share prices. Decisions taken in the past by Imperial did not add as much to shareholder value as decisions taken by the acquirer. More recently another organisation with mixed interests became the subject of a hostile bid. In this case an organisation was established by various interests to mount a bid for BAT, which at that time was involved in insurance, tobacco, retailing, and various manufacturing interests. BAT split off many of its interests, effectively creating separate entities in which its shareholders could choose whether they wished to retain their investment or sell it. BAT became a two-industry business, with more focus and less suspicion that good businesses might be propping up bad ones. The bid failed.

These examples led to the conclusion that although shareholder value is created when returns on old assets and new investments exceed the cost of capital, in a diversified organisation there has to be something that increases the overall value, so that there is synergy. In the examples given there was a reduction of value of businesses through being bound together in a group. This raises the question: how do diversified companies create value?

Figure 12.1 shows five ways in which diversified companies can affect shareholder value. The chart is derived from ideas from three sources: Goold and Campbell,[2] Porter,[3] and Buzzell and Gale.[4]

Shared resources or activities between components of a company offer one way to increase shareholder value. An example might be a distribution system which is used by all the SBUs, which because of overall size offers real economies of scale. In addition, because total costs are shared among all users, the cost for each may be lower than if they all had to provide such a facility. Purchasing, research and development and sometimes management development are other examples where value may be added by sharing. Such sharing sometimes offers increased potential for differentiation. However, there are also dangers of

Figure 12.1
How diversified organisations create value. (Copyright Harbridge Consulting Group Ltd: reprinted with permission)

diseconomies from sharing activities, particularly from loss of flexibility and the advantage of time through increased bureaucracy. Central purchasing and supplies gone mad has, for example, resulted in situations where a replacement light bulb could only be obtained from a central warehouse some miles away. An organisation has to sift the evidence very carefully in order to ensure that the value gained is real.

Related to shared resources are the spillover benefits that may be gained between SBUs from activities undertaken by any one of them. This may create windfall gains for the other divisions. For example, Buzzell and Gale[4] state that GE's research in turbine engines helped its aircraft engine business. GE, under Jack Welch, have periodically combined SBUs under a common sector management when it appears that there should be spillover benefits which are not being realised.

The third area on Figure 12.1 is shared knowledge and skills. Buzzell and Gale[4] found from the analysis of the PIMS database that clusters of businesses in similar environments have been found to outperform clusters of dissimilar businesses. Knowledge and skills, whether technical, managerial or commercial, can be passed from one business to another, thus improving performance in a way that might otherwise not have happened. Porter[3] set three criteria:

1 The shared matter must be meaningful.
2 It must be in activities which are key to success.
3 It must give a real advantage to the receiving unit.

Buzzell and Gale found that SBUs could benefit from a shared image. A good reputation of one SBU could spill over into sister businesses. In particular, bad businesses gain from association with good ones. However, this is not without penalty, because the bad business can drag down the performance of good ones.

The final area of investigation has been touched on in Chapter 3 when we looked at the styles of planning identified by Goold and Campbell. Part of the reason for this research was to establish how the corporate centre could add value. The modern trend has been to reduce the size of the centre, and to return tasks to the businesses, eliminating duplication and delays. Some of the frustration caused by some head offices in the past is reflected in the name given by all subsidiaries of one of my clients to the person charged at head office with the tasks of evaluating capital projects. Everyone outside called him the project preventer.

Trends to closeness to the customer, an appreciation of the strategic value of speed, and a need to reduce costs have led to the elimination of layers of management in businesses, and to the removal of many head-office functions. The question of how each remaining function adds value to the organisation is one that should be regularly studied.

Value is too important to be left as an accidental occurrence. All the areas mentioned above have to be managed. Prahalad and Doz[5] emphasise the need to examine dependencies across different units of a global business to determine which are critical. The analysis may be very complex, with many cross-dependencies. They suggest areas of cost and areas of benefit.

Costs include loss of top management focus on particular businesses, and an accompanying loss of visibility of the true results of a business. Flexibility may be reduced and so may innovation. The very need for coordination costs money at business unit and head office levels. These costs are the downside of the positive aspects of value creation suggested in our earlier analysis.

Although many of the benefits they see from managing an interdependent global system are similar to those already discussed, their main points are listed for completeness. Shared resources bring opportunities for cost reduction and an increase in added value, technological integrity can be assured, a global infrastructure may be essential to meet global competition, there may be core technologies which stretch across businesses, and size gives bargaining power with host governments.

It is easy to miscalculate the value of one activity to another. In the 1980s many British building societies and insurance companies followed each other like lemmings into the purchase of estate agents, in the belief that this would provide a good source of insurance and mortgage business. The reality was that few knew how to manage such businesses, and that the theoretical market connections did not exist to the degree expected. Consequently many divested these expensively acquired businesses, some selling back to the people they had bought from, but at a lower price. Prudential Assurance is reported to have paid £230 million for its chain of estate agents. It lost £49 million on them in 1989 alone, and in 1991 sold them for a fraction of the purchase price. Instead of adding value, the strategy reduced it.

Measuring shareholder value

There is some evidence that, contrary to popular opinion, the stock market is not oriented to the short term and that capital gains are usually preferred to dividends. One element of evidence is that new product investments and major capital expenditures, when announced, frequently increase share price, although the short-term effect may be to reduce earnings. Investors are concerned with the increase in value of their investments over a reasonable time period. We have seen some of the ways in which multiactivity companies can increase or decrease value. The problem for managements is how to develop a way of measuring value, which will enable the organisation to be run in a way that consistently increases value. The answer is a process called Value-based Strategic Management (VSM), although, as we will see, there are several ways of applying it.

Much of the world's experience in applying VSM comes from the USA. The Harbridge Consulting Group's research in 1991 (Handler[1]) found that there was little awareness of the approach in most UK companies, although interest was growing, and there were a number of companies who were staunch advocates. The remainder of this chapter consists of extracts from this report, including case histories which show how two companies are applying the approach. To make the extract easier to read, I have not used inverted commas. The report contains much more information, including case histories of a further five companies.

257

The extracts used here are not in the same order as they appear in the report, and I have omitted many sections. This suits my purpose, and I do not think I have created any distortions through this treatment. Anyone who is concerned can obtain the report.[1]

Extracts from S. Handler – *Value-based strategic management: a survey of UK companies*

1. Economic value

There are a number of variations on the theme of value assessment, but all are based on an analysis of the future cash flows which will be generated. This analysis involves the discounting of future cash flow values by an appropriate cost of capital. Economic value appraises future expectations rather than current and past performance.

The limitations seen by the companies in the survey relate mainly to its practical application, for its usefulness relies heavily on making the correct assumptions and preparing the cash projections.

The advantages, it is argued, outweigh the limitations, making it the clearly favoured approach, because:

(i) It measures cash, not accounting profit, which can be distorted by accounting conventions such as those for depreciation, stock valuation and provisions.

(ii) Accounting measures concentrate on the past and the present profits, not on the future. Investors focus on future cash generation, looking for dividends and capital gains.

(iii) It considers the time value of money, unlike the other methods. It is concerned with the timing of all cash flows.

(iv) Empirical studies show that future cash flow is a better indicator for potential value creation.

2. Accounting model

The traditional accounting model involves various standards of performance based upon reported profits:

Earnings per Share (EPS) Growth in EPS (after-tax profit attributable to ordinary shareholders divided by the number of ordinary shares) is used to measure performance and the return to shareholders. If EPS is growing, shareholder value is assumed to be enhanced.

The limitations include:

(i) The calculation of EPS is based on accounting conventions.
(ii) The time value of money is ignored.
(iii) The element of risk is ignored.

P/E Ratio The P/E ratio relates the market price per share to the earnings per share. As it is based on EPS, it suffers from the same limitations. One fallacy of this model is that it assumes that P/E multiples never change. But in fact, P/E ratios are constantly adjusting to account for changes in the 'quality' of a company's earnings in the wake of acquisitions, divestments, future investment opportunities, and changes in financial structure and accounting policies. And that adjustment makes EPS an unreliable measure of value.

Return on Capital Employed (ROCE) ROCE is calculated by relating some measure of profit to the book value of the assets as, for example:

$$\frac{\text{Operating Profit}}{\text{Capital Employed}} \times 100\%$$

The return is then compared to the company's cost of capital. If the ROCE is consistently greater, then shareholder value is considered to be created.

The limitations include:

(i) It is based on accounting profit, which may have little to do with economic value.
(ii) It ignores the future potential of the investment.
(iii) The timing of cash inflows and outflows (not the least of which is tax) is ignored, as is the residual value of the assets.
(iv) It ignores the effect of inflation on the historic cost of the assets. (Current Cost Accounting, which would counteract this limitation, is now seldom used.)

3. Techniques used in the value process

A variety of factors must be considered during the value process.

The discount rate

The Capital Asset Pricing Model (CAPM) and the weighted average cost of capital are the methods used most frequently in calculating the cost of capital.

More than 50 per cent of respondents used in the survey the weighted average cost of capital approach. This compares with a 1987 study of 177 major US companies which found that more than 87 per cent of the companies' chief financial officers used a weighted average cost of capital as the basis of their discount rate calculation (Rappaport[6]).

The cost of capital

In value-based strategic management methods, as with any discounted cash flow technique, the cost of capital has to be taken into account. The normal method is to use the weighted average cost of capital. This takes the cost of debt, preference shares and equity, weighted by the proportions in which they occur in the capital structure of the firm.

● Debt is the rate of interest paid, less the tax deduction as interest is a cost. In the equation an organisation may have debt at various rates of interest, and the figure that should be used is the weighted average of all the rates.
● Preference shares cost the rate of dividend associated with them. The gross figure should be used, as there are no tax deductions. The advantage of preference shares is that, unlike interest on debt, failure to pay the dividend cannot drive an organisation into bankruptcy.
● Equity is the hardest component to cost, as it is the shareholder's opportunity cost, that is, the return that could be obtained by investing capital optimally in other ventures with similar risks. There are several methods for calculating this, and these will be found on most books on financial management.

The following simple example illustrates the calculation of the weighted cost of capital:

Capital	Amount (£)	Cost (%)	Cost (£)
Equity	1 000 000	15	150 000
Preference shares	500 000	10	50 000
Debt	500 000	8	40 000
Total	2 000 000	12	240 000

Although it was agreed by the majority of respondents that the rate of discounting the cash flow stream should be the weighted average cost of debt and equity, it was clear that the rate may differ across business units within a group because of their relative risk exposure.

Residual and terminal values

Residual value is the price that the asset can be sold for at the end of its commercial life. *Terminal* value is the value of a business unit, project or asset at the end of a planning cycle, and approximates to the economic value from the end of the cycle to the end of the relevant unit's life.

Figure 12.2
Some valuation
methods

Equity-spread approach

The equity-spread approach to valuation focuses on the difference between the return on shareholders equity (the change in share price, plus dividends, divided by the initial share price) and the cost of equity (the shareholders' expectation for return, based on the element of risk). If the equity spread is positive, then shareholder value has been created; if negative, then it has been destroyed.

Share price theory assumes that the share price is influenced by a company's expected equity spread as well as its growth prospect. Managers will do best, then, to focus investment for growth in positive equity spread businesses. The technique's value is limited because it is based on accounting value, with likely distortions. It also ignores some very important sources of value, such as deferred taxes and terminal value at the end of the planning period, and it is also very sensitive to financial leverage.

Market value multiples

This approach seeks to find a business unit equivalent of the market/book multiple. This approach lends itself to simulating both the beginning and ending market values of a business unit on the basis of the book value of its assets.

To establish the multiple it is necessary to determine what are the measurable indicators or drivers of the market value. These variables (combinations of returns, growth, R & D expenditure, etc.) are given weighted values, with the help of specially developed models and databases to help predict share price based on book value.

The key advantage of this approach is that its accuracy can easily be tested with historical data. A test of a sample of 600 US firms found that value-creation estimates based on multiples of either assets or sales corresponded more closely to actual shareholder value creation than the accounting measures of ROI and EPS (Reimann[7]). One of the disadvantages of the method is that book values (the base to which the multiple is applied to predict the 'value') can be affected by many accounting factors which could distort the picture, so it does not necessarily prove a reliable base.

Economic value added approach

The economic value added approach is the product of the equity-spread (the difference between return on equity and the cost of capital) and the total capital employed in the business. The objective is to increase the economic earnings derived from the existing or projected capital bases. (Unfortunately, if the equity spread is negative, then the approach is 'economic value lost').

This approach is frequently used at the portfolio planning stage; and some companies only use it for making strategic decisions at the group level.

Positive-value and negative-value business unit approaches

These approaches are simply the opposite sides of the same coin. Like the economic value added approach, they are used to make portfolio decisions about business units, and in making acquisition and divestment decisions – adding to or growing those businesses for which economic returns exceed the cost of capital (positive net present values). Businesses with negative economic values will be restructured or eliminated, with capital diverted to positive-value business units.

The Q-ratio approach

The Q-ratio approach also focuses on economic value. Developed in the 1960s by James Tobin, the Nobel Prize winning economist, the approach calculates the relationship of the market value of a company's assets to the cost of replacing those assets in current money. This Q-ratio is, thus, an M/B multiple with the book value of assets in the denominator adjusted for the effects of inflation. The rationale is that investors adjust their expected returns for anticipated inflation when analysing alternative investments. Therefore, the true or 'real' value of a business should also reflect this inflation factor. (Reimann,[8])

The appropriate way to calculate residual or terminal value is a critical question, because it can form a substantial proportion of the total value of a business unit.

Terminal values are most frequently computed using the perpetuity approach. The rationale is that competitors will be attracted to any business which is able to generate returns above the cost of capital. This competition will drive the return down to the cost of capital and by the end of the planning period, the business is considered to be earning only the cost of capital on its investment. Because these cash flows do not significantly change the value of the firm (Rappaport[6]) they can be treated as though they were a continuing stream. The present value of this stream or perpetuity is the annual cash flow divided by the rate of return:

$$\text{Terminal value} = \frac{\text{Annual cash flow}}{\text{Cost of capital}}$$

Portfolio planning

The Positive/Negative Value Business Unit approach is the most favoured technique in portfolio planning. It is preferred by 70–80 per cent of respondents, with the Equity-Spread approach used 50 per cent of the time.

Most companies preferred two or more value analysis techniques. They used different approaches for different purposes and at different levels. For example, the Positive/Negative Value Business Unit approach is used in making divestment decisions at group level. The Equity-Spread approach is regarded as straightforward, and its message is easily spread to business unit managers. Some companies use the Market Value Multiples method for presentation only, finding that, although it encourages returns higher than the cost of equity, the result may not maximise shareholder value.

4. Implementation of VSM in UK companies

This survey found that VSM is used mainly at the corporate or group level, although most businesses plan to drive its application down to the level of operating units. The majority of companies use acquisition to create shareholder value, and elicit the aid of consultants at all stages of development and implementation. The 1991 MORI survey estimated that 56 per cent of top management uses economic value for specific major decisions, 33 per cent for routine planning and control, and 30 per cent for reporting to investors.

VSM begins at the top

Most value analysis takes place by a combination of resource allocation and portfolio analysis (identifying which assets or businesses to retain, sell or buy).

British Petroleum reported that it had used value analysis to divest two business units which were outside its core business. TSB has used value analysis to change the emphasis of its business after its flotation on the stock market.

Some companies have introduced a value approach which requires a particular unit to value its business at the start of the planning period, and to highlight changes during the period. Others plan to follow this lead.

Business units may also be required to use value techniques in choosing between alternative scenarios. A business unit may be required to demonstrate that it has selected the best option for implementation before funds are released. At least one company is moving towards setting targets in terms of value generation for its main activity.

Growth through acquisition to create shareholder value

The overwhelming majority (18 out of 19 or 94 per cent) of responding companies reported that their strategies include growth through acquisition to create or enhance shareholder value.

However, of those 18, only seven reported a successful acquisition record (success being defined as a company's ability to earn at least its cost of capital on the funds invested in the acquisition). Of those who reported success, one of the major reasons cited was acquiring companies in the same or related businesses or markets. Other reasons included the sound valuation of acquisition candidates and the ability to capitalise on synergies. Those companies who reported failure blamed diversification into businesses where they had little or no knowledge, experience, or expertise. All of these companies feel that value analysis, in the selection of acquisitions, is the best approach.

Help from consultants and computer models

The majority of companies who advocate the value approach use consultants and computer models in the analysis and implementation process.

The general consensus among respondents was that the complexity of data analysis has been a major obstacle to the acceptance of VSM. One solution is to bring in one of a number of consulting firms which offer specialist VSM advice. In addition, there are a number of software products which can be extremely valuable in helping with the introduction of the value approach.

There are at least three routes for establishing data support systems:

(i) Choose one of the proprietary software products offered by consultants.
(ii) Develop the value system in co-operation with one of the consulting companies.
(iii) Create company-specific software internally to support value analysis.

Building value into incentive systems

The last stage of the implementation process should be to build value into the incentive system as a means of motivation. If it is introduced too quickly or drastically it may be demotivating, especially for those who have previously been rewarded within a conventional framework.

No firms indicated the use of incentive systems which include the creation of value. However, the literature researched for the purposes of this survey suggests that the most successful VSM incentive systems are:

(i) Those which are linked to the value created in specific businesses.
(ii) Those which discourage short-term window dressing and help to ensure that managers focus on the long term.

5. Ingredients for the success of VSM

A number of factors were discovered to be essential for the successful use of the value approach.

Acceptance at director level

A prime ingredient for success is the acceptance of value theory at director level. All responding companies felt that they had the full support of the chief executive and the board. Indeed, interviews with UK companies who are proponents revealed that, in the majority of cases, the move to VSM was initiated by a new senior executive from outside the company.

There was much less acceptance and understanding at the business unit level.

Understanding of senior management teams

It was felt that senior management teams must understand the relationship that exists between their strategic announcements (not short-term performance results) and their share price (evidence of financial market response). Management teams, both staff and line, must also understand the benefits of shareholder value analysis, such as the linkages between it and product – market strategies. Value must be embedded in the culture of the organisation or it will not survive.

Is the culture right?

Having the right culture was also seen as important to the successful implementation of value at the business unit level, although there seemed to be little awareness among managers as to what that correct culture should be. It was also generally agreed that the company must evaluate the adequacy of current organisational structure and systems in integrating shareholder value analysis, and install new systems when necessary.

Value sharing: motivating managers for value creation

One of the most important goals for the value company is finding the best way of putting value theories into practice. Rewarding managers and staff for making the best long-term value decisions instead of just traditional short-term performance rewards becomes a perplexing, but not insurmountable problem. It is an issue, however, that must be properly resolved before any firm can truly consider itself a 'value' company.

In addition to traditional targets (which are basically related to accounting-derived turnover and/or profit return, growth in sales and/or margins, and some definition of targeted return on profit), many managers and employers are rewarded with stock options, gain-sharing and profit-sharing plans and the like. These last rewards all involve the issue of ownership, which is crucial to the development of a value compensation system – one that makes all workers partners in the process of adding to shareholder value. The idea is to reward managers for reaching or exceeding targeted performance measures that run parallel to the creation of value on an annual basis.

Training for VSM

Training for value is a cardinal rule for those in the United States who have successfully used the techniques. However, only four of the UK responding companies offer this type of training. The importance of educating managers about value is demonstrated by VSM consultants, who spend a significant amount of their time on educational work.

Summary

The consensus was that to be successful VSM must:

(i)   Have the support and dedication of the chief executive and board.
(ii) Be introduced into a receptive culture, with the appropriate organisational structure and systems.
(iii) Allow for an investment in training, and in incentives that encourage managers to emphasise a long-term and not just short-term view.

6. Limitations to the value approach

The practical problems involved in using the value approach are seen to be considerable. Difficulty in making accurate and relevant cash flow and discount rate projections was seen in 50 per cent of those responding as the most significant problem.

However, some of the practical limitations relate to common misunderstandings. For example, one complaint most frequently expressed was that there is too much emphasis on the 'numbers', and not enough on strategic thinking and 'value drivers', such as sales growth, profit margins, capital investment and taxation.

Another frequently encountered limitation was that VSM was considered by most operating managers to be too technical and theoretical.

The danger of creating and reinforcing a culture where managers spend most of their time analysing and planning, and not enough time 'making it happen' was also listed as a limiting factor.

7. VSM as a prevention against takeover

VSM is seen by more and more companies as a valuable weapon in the defence against unwanted takeover bids and in controlling the value gap (the difference between the market price of a firm's ordinary shares and the share value if the company were managed for the maximum share price possible at the time). If the difference between the actual and potential share price is large, it is an invitation to raiders. Managing the value gap means changing the investment community's opinion about the company's future performance. It can involve improving internal operations, adjusting the capital structure or selling some of its businesses or assets. It will most certainly mean communicating its intent to the investing community.

Hoylake's £13.4bn ($22bn) bid for BAT Industries plc in July 1989, and KKR's £15.2bn ($25bn) bid for RJR Nabisco provide two examples of takeover attempts which developed from the bidder's belief that the acquisition candidate's shares were undervalued by current investors. Concentrating on strategies designed to maximise long-term cash flows and minimise value gaps helped BAT to successfully defeat the raider. BAT's pre-Hoylake strategy was to use its cash-generating tobacco business to pay for acquisitions intended to offset the longer-term uncertainties of world tobacco sales.

The VSM process begins with a careful financial assessment of each business unit and of the level of risk inherent in alternative strategies. It strives for long-term value creation which comes from sustainable competitive advantages in the company's mix of businesses. The value analysis may, for example, help managers to determine whether to retain or discard existing activities. The simple

Figure 12.3
Value decisions

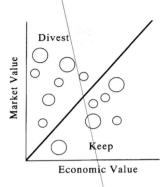

diagram in Figure 12.3 relates the market value of various business units to their economic value.

The size of the bubbles represents the proportionate investment in different businesses. The business units positioned to the left of the 45 line are worth more to a potential buyer than to the group and should be divested. If a significant proportion of business units are to the right of the line, it indicates that the group is undervalued by the market. Action must be taken to reduce the gap. Practical problems arise when the activities to the left and right are interconnected.

To increase shareholder value, managers must identify where value is being created or destroyed and be aware of the impact of different strategies. To be effective, VSM requires the extensive involvement of those managers responsible for execution, but VSM must also be part of a balanced approach that emphasises qualitative factors, including issues such as quality and customer satisfaction.

The second part of the VSM process is implementation. This involves acceptance, commitment and understanding by line managers who need to be motivated to manage for value. For the company it means different communication and training, and incentive schemes linked to longer-term cash generation, not just short-term results.

8. Case study: Lloyds Bank plc

> Lloyds Bank's primary objective is to create value for its shareholders – by increase in the dividend and appreciation in the share price. This is the driving force behind our decisions and actions. . . . We rank each business on the basis of the shareholder value they create; each activity is viewed as a creator or destroyer of value. Businesses which consume cash and destroy value are targeted for divestment. (*CEO's Report, 1989*)

Lloyds Bank was one of the success stories of the 1980s with a compound growth rate of 27 per cent (on January 1981 investment with dividends reinvested), a performance not matched by any other UK bank. During 1991 its business mix enabled Lloyds to achieve a return on assets 50 per cent higher and

Figure 12.4
Value drivers in
Lloyds' business

Value drivers in Lloyds' business

From a practitioner's point of view, Lloyds believes that identification and management of 'value drivers' should be left to the business units. Generally, though, it feels that significant number of factors drives the value to its shareholders:

- The ROE of each business unit.

- Avoiding strategic mistakes (in other words, 'getting it right the first time').

- Projecting the right image in the right market.

- Avoiding bad debts.

- Targeting customer groups prepared to pay a premium for its service.

- Quality of service to the customer: "It is cheaper to retain existing customers than to get new ones".

---

dividend growth 37 per cent higher than the peer group. Its distinct structural advantages with focus on high margin, low capital intensive domestic businesses, together with its philosophy of maximising shareholder value, have made it the core bank holding of an increasing number of investment portfolios.

The group's three basic strategies, responsible for its remarkable results, reinforce its belief in what drives value for shareholders (Figure 12.4) and its sub-targets for creating shareholder value:

(i) To achieve a net ROE greater than 18 per cent (Lloyds' cost of capital).
(ii) To increase the dividend payout ratio.
(iii) To maintain a strong balance sheet with equity grown from retained earnings.

The objectives and methodology of value strategy and management have been debated and agreed with the bank's senior management. The methodology is used for major strategic issues, and to a lesser extent for business unit strategies. Below this level the approach is simplified to the objective of achieving a sustainable after-tax return on equity, which will at least equal its cost of equity. Nevertheless, Lloyds believes that there is still plenty of scope for extending the full approach to lower levels within the organisation.

With the 1990 economic fluctuations out of the way, the benefits of the approach are clearly shown in the growth in shareholder value of Lloyds Bank compared with its peer group (which included a 35 per cent+ growth in share price during 1991). The philosophy of shareholder value, which was formulated and propagated by the current CEO Brian Pitman (appointed December 1983) places primary emphasis on creating distributable returns (free cash flow) for shareholders via profitable non-capital-intensive business.

Lloyds' strategies for creating shareholder value

Lloyds implements three basic strategies to achieve the goals stated above.

Reallocation of assets

This strategy for creating shareholder value has transformed Lloyds from a diversified international bank into a focused domestic bank. Lloyds' policy is to focus on the strengths of the market, not necessarily domestic investment versus international activities. Although it has recently disposed of some UK assets (selling its stake in Yorkshire Bank and closing its gilts and eurobond operations) and acquired others abroad (Abbey Life in Ireland and Germany), the larger proportion of its business is in the UK.

Its 62 per cent international assets in 1981 had been reduced to 28 per cent by the end of 1990. The significantly wider domestic net interest margins reflect a large component of consumer and small business lending funded from a base of cheap retail deposits. The international segment was wholesale in orientation, geared to low margin, euro-currency and large corporate lending. Now this is focused on international private banking in those countries where Lloyds is not a major player in the retail market.

Lloyds has moved away from low margin euro-currency lending and sold international offices in the USA, Canada and Portugal. It has also enhanced value to shareholders by recognising that growth, to compensate for declining (at the time) corporate loan margins, must come from other areas, such as increasing arrangement and lending fees, and enhancement of the personal customer base (thus Lloyds' acquisition of Abbey Life).

Lloyds estimates that its interest margin is almost 25 per cent higher than the peer group average because of its low percentage of international assets.

Seeking selective market leadership

Lloyds' second strategic principle concerns competitive advantage. Its stated policy, which underlies its switch from international to domestic assets, is to seek selective market leadership and to avoid those markets and products where it cannot obtain a strong position. It pulled out of gilts and eurobond operations in 1987, for example, because 'markets were overcrowded and we were marginal players'.

High margin/low capital intensive businesses

In keeping with its policy of producing high affordable dividends (distributable returns) Lloyds has sought balance sheet growth by moving away from low margin commodity lending into risk management and fee-based services. Development of its life assurance subsidiary, Black Horse Life, began with the acquisition of a 57 per cent stake in Abbey Life, projected to generate significant

269

cash flow from its existing client base. This is expected to prove extremely effective in terms of capital cost regulatory requirement (cash holdback) as requirements are minimal in relation to the costs of lending under the BIS rules. Although embedded value life profits are not technically distributable, they can be included within the group's capital and so effectively free up banking-derived earnings for distribution.

Lloyds' focus on high margin areas like personal and small business lending has resulted in a higher yield on its domestic assets and stronger net interest margin than its peers.

The results of Lloyds' adherence to its strategic principles has produced amazing results since 1986 (see Figure 12.5): its pre-tax return on assets was 185 per cent better than peers in 1990 against 33 per cent in 1986.

Return on earning assets

1986	Lloyds	Barclays	NatWest	Midland
Net interest income	3.82	3.78	3.54	3.27
Other income	1.85	1.91	1.55	2.05
Costs	-3.60	-3.82	-3.25	-3.93
Subtotal	2.08	1.87	1.84	1.39
Bad debts	-0.50	-0.64	-0.52	-0.70
Investment gains	0.00	0.06	0.01	0.10
Associates	0.05	0.11	0.09	0.05
PRE TAX	1.62	1.41	1.41	0.85

Return on earning assets

1990	Lloyds	Barclays	NatWest	Midland
Net interest income	4.29	3.07	3.34	2.74
Other income	2.84	1.97	1.88	2.45
Costs	-4.62	-3.31	-3.69	-4.00
Subtotal	2.50	1.73	1.52	1.20
Bad debts	-1.76	-1.08	-1.07	-1.17
Investment gains	0.04	0.00	-0.01	0.05
Associates	0.04	0.03	0.02	0.04
Exceptional	0.29	0.00	0.00	0.09
PRE TAX	1.11	0.67	0.47	0.02

Figure 12.5
Comparison of Lloyds with peer groups

Difficulties in implementing a value approach

The problems experienced by Lloyds in implementing VSM were primarily technical and involved retraining its own financial experts and those within the investing community to think of cash flow in terms of 'free cash' or 'affordable dividends' to shareholders rather than cash flow in the traditional sense. Lloyds' experience with the investing community was that, with a few notable exceptions, there was little awareness of, but a lot of interest in, the value techniques. Its regular meetings with analysts and fund managers has succeeded 'only up to a point' in educating and convincing the investing community of the benefits of managing for value. 'They [the investors] are convinced by the results, but not by the theory.'

Lloyds feels its value strategy can be summarised as:

(i) Ensuring profitability of ongoing businesses without going to its shareholders for more capital.
(ii) Reducing investment in those parts of the business which cannot realistically expect long-term returns which exceed the cost of equity.
(iii) Increasing investment in high return businesses.

Overall, Lloyds' objective is to maximise shareholder value, which means 'maximising the present value of (estimated) future affordable dividends'. It does not attempt to maximise ROE but instead to take on all business which at the margin will generate 18 per cent ROE. Lloyds believes that maximising ROE does not maximise shareholder value. Rather, it feels that success is better measured by the actual change in shareholder value over time.

When asked if it felt it would be a takeover target in the future, Lloyds' opinion was that it would not: 'Management is already maximising returns for shareholders.' Indeed, if the sentiments of many of the analysts surveyed are to be believed, it is a share to buy. To quote one: 'Lloyds Bank represents the best combination of dividend productivity and cheapness and should be the core long-term holding in portfolios' (UBS Phillips and Drew).

9. Case study: Dixons group plc

Dixons Group plc is an international group specialising in the retail sale of consumer electronics, photographic products, domestic appliances and related services (profiled in Figure 12.6). It trades through Dixons, Currys and Supasnaps in the UK and Silo in the USA. The Group is also engaged in property development and trading in the UK, Belgium, Germany, France, Luxembourg and Portugal through Dixons Commercial Properties International.

Dixons Group's value focus involves long-term investment to develop a mature base of operations, centred on customer satisfaction. It believes that striving for customer satisfaction will drive value across the entire business. The Group believes that the success of VSM and its benefits will depend in part on

Figure 12.6
Profile of Dixons
Group companies

Dixons. Retails consumer electronics and photographic products through high street stores.

Currys. Retails a wide range of domestic electrical products through superstores and high street stores.

SupaSnaps. Offers film processing services and photographic accessories.

Silo. Retails a wide range of consumer electronics and domestic appliances through superstores in the US.

---

developing sales staff rewards based on customer satisfaction rather than short-term sales targets. Its considerable progress with its focus on value led in part to a 75 per cent increase in its share price through 1991, a difficult time for retailers as many endured horrific recessionary setbacks.

The consumer electronics and domestic appliance sectors, although generally regarded as long-term growth markets, are cyclical. As a result, business is subject to considerable fluctuations in demand, which tend to be exacerbated by new product introductions and shifts in economic climate.

This had led to a number of problems:

(i) In the mid-1980s, when demand was strong and sales of new products such as VCRs, microwaves and computers were growing rapidly, Dixons made a number of investment decisions based on what turned out in the short term to be unsustainable levels of sales. Because the 'brown goods' (TV, audio, video, camcorders) sector is very prone to such investment 'traps', making investment decisions on the basis of high short-term profitability can lead to problems in later years as demand declines, particularly when costs are also rising rapidly.

(ii) The integration of Dixons' and Currys' logistical support and the realisation of the synergy between the two businesses were delayed because the short-term buoyancy of the market obscured the underlying problems.

(iii) Currys' competitive position was eroded because of its structure of small stores, and at the same time its cost base was high due to the location of its shops on the high street. The strategic response to the problem, the move to edge-of-town superstores, was slow to implement.

These problems were tackled in 1988 and 1989, but the solutions were poorly communicated to shareholders and analysts, and the results were not immediately apparent due to the weakness of the market and the timescale for implementation. Dixons' market share growth rate began to slow down with a simultaneous cost escalation. As a result, the share price fell sharply, and in December 1989 Kingfisher made a hostile bid for Dixons Group. Although this offer was unsuccessful, it focused Dixons' management's attention on its failure to communicate with the investment community and led to a considerably better perception of the nature of the group's business, its problems and the solutions being implemented.

The group's 1990s plan for creating shareholder value is a many-faceted strategy for building long-term customer satisfaction. Dixons Group firmly believes that value in its businesses is created when long-term customer loyalty is created. This involves not only an upmarket push for Dixons and the expansion of Currys Superstores, but also the emphasis of new concepts in systems, service, merchandising, product improvement and innovation, and staff development and compensation.

Expansion of Currys superstores

Currys, in shifting away from the high street to edge-of-town superstores, hopes to give customers a far better shopping experience: a large range of 'white goods' (washers and dryers, refrigerators, freezers, cookers, small appliances), larger more comfortable stores with a relaxed atmosphere, longer opening hours and convenient parking. This move has led to improved sales, up by 11 per cent like-for-like against a 4 per cent reduction in its high street store sales. The group expects that Currys Superstores will account for 35 per cent of retail space by April 1992, at least equal to Currys' High Street stores.

Upmarket push for Dixons

Dixons' attack on margins focuses on upgrading the mix of its merchandise to achieve higher average prices. Between 1988 and 1990 Dixons saw a 24 per cent price increase in real terms as average prices were decreasing. This meant that the volume of goods handled dropped sharply while turnover remained constant. This had a significant effect on its cost base. Retailers of white and brown goods traditionally sustain high overheads to deal with large volumes of sales (warehousing, delivery, administration, after sales service). Smaller investment in inventories has not only reduced investment in working capital, but Dixons finds itself discounting less because of obsolete and warehouse-worn merchandise.

Modernised information systems

The group is currently making considerable investment (£10m) in a sophisticated branch PC network designed to provide branches with up-to-date stock availability information as well as store profitability. It provides instant information about previously evasive issues such as discount origin, customer service history, and inventory and service parts availability. The system will eventually allow instant access to credit and repair organisations, and detailed product specification data which will give sales personnel more authority in dealing with customer enquiries.

Improved merchandising

In addition to improved merchandising of white goods in Currys' Superstores and upgraded Dixons merchandising of brown goods the group has opened new specialist departments on a trial basis, particularly at Dixons stores. More space and a wider range of computer game hardware and software is catering to the growth of the computer game market. Other specialist departments group together low-price merchandise like films and video tapes as well as general brown goods accessories on a self-service basis.

To improve its already impressive 33 per cent of the UK camcorder market 300 Currys High Street stores installed camcorder centres through the summer of 1991, with very encouraging results. In addition, Currys High Street stores have begun a trial (10 stores by end 1991) to reduce the space given to big white goods. Instead it sells them through an in-store catalogue centre, and focuses much more in store on small appliances. It is hoped that this move will improve its presence and market share in small appliances, while the large Currys Superstores in cheaper, cost efficient locations handle a larger than ever market share of the larger white goods.

Product improvement and innovation

Historically electronic goods have been made with two points in mind: ease of manufacture and number of features. 'User friendliness' has until recently not been a priority. Consumer complaints range from complex and contradictory instruction booklets to £2000 systems that are packaged without plugs. Figure 12.7 outlines some significant Dixons initiatives guaranteed to pleasure any

---

Joint customer satisfaction projects with Sony, Hitachi, Panasonic and Matsushita have been initiated to respond to calls for simpler technology.

• Circuit boards which formerly had to be soldered out now clip out, enabling repairs to be carried out in the customer's home with minimal fuss.

• Instruction booklets have large easy-to-follow diagrams with colour coding for cables and plug points, and have been rewritten to improve former badly translated Japanese and to correct contradictions.

• More care is being given to make sure that self-assembly parts are all compatible with each other.

• Design initiatives are underway for future electronic equipment which will have four or five diagnostic points built in to enable engineers to find faults quickly. 90% of engineer time is spent now in locating a fault and only 10% in fixing the fault.

• Packaging is being redesigned to make life easier for the consumer so that spending 45 minutes getting a TV out of a box may soon be a thing of the past.

Figure 12.7
Dixons initiatives to simplify consumer installation and engineer repair of electrical goods

customer who has to install his or her own TV, stereo or VCR. In addition, with the average cost of servicing a VCR at approximately £30, eliminating an estimated 30 per cent of unnecessary service callouts will mean significant financial benefits for Dixons as well as improving customer satisfaction.

The product innovation cycle has been quiet since 1983, the peak of the VCR boom. The expected launch in 1992 of CDI (interactive compact disk) as well as the DCC (digital compact cassette), a 16×9 picture format colour TV and high definition TV are all expected to boost the innovation cycle. And although the innovation in products is not expected to be really buoyant until 1994–1995, Dixons is projecting that its market share will continue to move upwards.

Staff development and compensation programmes to build shareholder value

In 1990–1991 average branch staff numbers fell by 5 per cent in Dixons and 14 per cent in Currys (which translated through to 12–14 per cent increases in sales per employee). Distribution employees were also significantly reduced (16 per cent), and branch pay increases were modest. How then does Dixons Group account for the results of a 1991 employee survey that showed a sharp drop in staff turnover and that employee perceptions of the company (and motivation to create value through retaining customer loyalty) have never been higher?

Clear career structure, trust of managers and a sharp drop in the level of customer complaints (40 per cent drop in the 18 months to September 1991) are credited for this remarkable improvement in perception. The group's plans for developing and keeping 'value' orientated staff, as outlined in Figure 12.8, are all based on its belief that staff give better care to customers when they have been with the company for some time, when they are better trained and when they are compensated for long-term sales, not just immediate sales which may not create customer loyalty.

---

1. The compensation system is based in part on commissions focused not just on sales (except for Christmas sales bonuses), but on margin improvements, add-on products, housekeeping (credit agreements, etc.) and care of stock (significant drop in lost and damaged stock in 1990-91)

2. Compensation is also linked to staff development so that those who take up offered training programmes are eligible for bonuses. Training in two key areas - product knowledge and selling skills - is carried out both in-house and through distance learning programmes, often with major input from manufacturers. Training is primarily focused on value creation, as it is directed toward solving customer problems. Training is structured with milestone targets, at which staff qualify for extra pay.

3. Staff pay is also tied to employment longevity based on Dixons Group's firm belief that loyalty for service (and presumed improved performance) must be rewarded.

Figure 12.8
Dixons Group's plan for developing and keeping 'value'-orientated staff

Substantial improvements to customer service

Dixons/Currys central service organisation, Mastercare, has improved out of all recognition. Its 'same day service' really works, and engineers even call the customer directly before a visit to check on the time of appointment. With its desire to consistently deliver the best service possible, Dixons/Currys is installing in-store repair centres for quicker turn-round times for customers. The concept, which is being introduced into 30 Currys Superstores around the country, is also expected to substantially reduce the group's costs of repair while reinforcing its fundamental philosophy of building trustworthiness.

Summary

Dixons Group's concentration on building shareholder value through customer satisfaction and loyalty has captured investors' attention, as evidenced by its significantly improved share price. The message from many analysts: It is not too late to buy!

References

1 Handler, S. *Value-based Strategic Management: A Survey of UK Companies*, Harbridge Consulting Group Ltd, London, 1991.
2 Goold, M. and Campbell, A. *Strategies and Styles*, Blackwell, Oxford, 1987.
3 Porter, M. E. 'From Competitive Advantage to Corporate Strategy', *Harvard Business Review*, May/June 1987.
4 Buzzell, R. D. and Gale, B. T. *The PIMS Principles*, Free Press, New York, 1987.
5 Prahalad, C. K. and Doz, Y. *The Multinational Mission*, Free Press, New York, 1987.
6 Rappaport, A. 'Stock Market Signals to Managers' *Harvard Business Review*, November-December 1987.
7 Reimann, B. C. 'Decision Support Software for Value-based Planning', *Planning Review*, March/April 1988.
8 Reimann, B. C. 'Managing for the Shareholders: an Overview of Value-based Strategic Management', *The Planning Forum*, Blackwell, 1987.

Further reading

Stewart, G. B. *The Quest for Value*, Harper Business, New York, 1991.

CHAPTER 13

Vision and objectives

There are many related concepts around vision: strategic intent, mission, objectives, goals and performance standards. The chapter explores them in some detail, and presents them in an integrated context.

No self-respecting organisation these days is complete without its vision statement, although writing a statement and having a sense of vision for the whole enterprise are not always the same thing. An organisation can have a clear sense of purpose, communicated to all, without a written vision statement: it is also possible to have a vision statement that is full of good words but does not derive from any clarity of purpose or direction. In fact it is very difficult to judge a vision statement from what is put on paper: whether noble words are motivating truths or empty platitudes depends more on what the organisation does than what it says.

There are semantic problems. What one person calls a vision, another may decide is a mission statement. Hamel and Prahalad[1] as we saw in Chapter 1, argued that what was needed was *strategic intent*, a term which has caught the imagination of some. They define this as an obsession with winning over a long period. The quote clarifies this:

> On the one hand strategic intent envisions a desired leadership position and establishes the criterion the organisation will use to chart its progress. Komatsu set out to 'encircle Caterpillar'. Canon sought to 'Beat Xerox', Honda strove to become a second Ford – an automotive pioneer. All are expressions of strategic intent.
>
> At the same time, strategic intent is more than simply unfettered ambition. (Many companies possess an ambitious strategic intent yet fall short of their goals). The concept also encompasses an active management process that includes: focusing the organisation's attention on the essence of winning; motivating people by communicating the value of the target; leaving room for individual and team contributions; sustaining enthusiasm by providing new operational definitions as circumstances change; and using intent consistently to guide resource allocation.

> ## How important is having a clear vision?
>
> In his paper 'Strategic Vision or Strategic Con? Rhetoric or Reality' (in Hussey, D. E. (ed.), *International Review of Strategic Management*, Vol. 4, Wiley, Chichester, 1993), Colin Coulson-Thomas refers to three surveys in which he played a major part:
>
> - In the *Managing the Flat Organisation* survey: 'Every respondent assessing it believes clear vision and mission to be important, and about three quarters of them consider it "very important".'
> - The *Quality: The Next Steps* survey concludes that: 'A clear and shared quality vision and top management commitment are essential.'
> - In the *Communicating for Change* survey, 'Clear vision and strategy' and top management commitment are jointly ranked as the most important requirements for the successful management of change.

Although useful in emphasising what the organisation is about, I do not see any significant difference between strategic intent and the way vision should be used at the level of the organisation. Vision is a term that began to become popular in the late 1970s, and was well established by the mid-1980s. What it means for me is an expression of the longer-term objectives and values of the organisation, in a way that shows what the firm is trying to achieve. The definition provided by Karlöf[2] is helpful:

> Vision, in the sense of something seen in a dream, is the term used to describe a picture of a relatively remote future in which business has developed under the best possible conditions and in accordance with the hopes and dreams of the owner or chief executive. A vision provides a benchmark for what one hopes to achieve in business, and can be a guide to the level of ambition of strategic planning . . .
>
> . . . A vision can be said to link business with corporate culture, creating a common standard of values for the individual performance of employees.

Vision is important in transformational leadership (see Chapter 3), but in that context it is a concept that may refer to any change situation, not necessarily that of the total organisation. It even applies to situations in a personal context, such as that of a married couple who want to create a garden in a new property. They are likely to achieve better results if there is an underlying vision, which they share, of how they want the garden to look after all the work is done. Vision makes sense in all change situations. However, what we are grappling with in this chapter is the application of the concept at corporate and business unit level.

The first requirement is that top management needs to have thought out what are the long-term aims of the organisation. Without this clarity of purpose and direction, any vision statement is bound to lack meaning, however fashionable it may be to have one. Normally a vision statement will also include mention of the values of the organisation. Chapter 8 looked at the two concepts for arriving at

> ## The vision guides the way forward
>
> Hans Hinterhuber and Walter Popp of the University of Innsbruck, Austria, see vision as a guiding force:
>
> > Like the North Star, therefore, a vision is not a goal, but rather an orientation point that triggers movement in a specific direction: if the vision is borne by a sense of reality and appeals to both the emotions and intelligence of a company's employees, it can be a directing force with a powerful integration effect. So every entrepreneur and every manager claiming to possess strategic management competence should be able to state his or her entrepreneurial vision, clearly and inspiringly, in just a few sentences'.
>
> (Hinterhuber H. H.and Popp, W. 'Strategic Leadership Competence', in Hussey, D. E. (ed.), *International Review of Strategic Management*, Vol. 2, 1 Wiley, Chichester, 1991)

these, stakeholder theory and constraints, and this debate will not be repeated here. However the chapter is written using the constraints concept.

The reason for a written vision statement is to aid communication of the vision across the whole organisation, and often to customers and suppliers as well. It is a first step to achieving a shared vision throughout the organisation and in shaping the culture to support the strategies. However, because it is a statement which is widely distributed, there may be elements about the strategic direction which have to be stated in a more general way than is needed for the formulation of strategy.

There is also more to getting an organisation to move in unison than a vision statement, and what is really needed is a concept of objectives which links the components of vision with ways of measuring corporate progress, and linking these with personal standards of performance.

In the descriptions that follow, the vision statement would be drawn from what are described as the primary and secondary objectives, and goals and standards of performance have a definition and control purpose. But first let us turn the clock back, and see what some of the early writers had to say about objectives.

What are Objectives?

What is meant by 'objectives', why are they required and how might they be used in management and strategic planning? As is the case with so many aspects of management, there is a problem of semantics. 'Objectives' is a word that is used with many different meanings, and, of course, has a place of its own in usage outside of the management textbooks.

Exhibit 13.1 A bottom up process to decide the mission

The debate on whether vision and mission should be determined at the top of the organisation or by a bottom-up process probably has no end. Either may be appropriate in certain circumstances. The illustration here is of the process used by the College of Business and Public Administration, the University of Louisville in the USA.

In this situation a bottom-up process was not an option. It was part of a mandatory process required by the US accrediting body for business schools. Although the majority of US universities are in the private sector, this type of external requirement which removes choice from the organisation will be very familiar to public sector organisations.

The process followed was:

Task force: volunteers from all areas of the college, but not the executive, were sought to form the task force to write the new mission statement.

Input from internal and external stakeholders: groups of people were interviewed. To stimulate strategic thinking they were asked to think about what an article in *Business Week* would say about the college if written in five years' time. Several groups were interviewed, each session taking up to 90 minutes.

Achieving buy-in by employees: Key issues were identified, such as the directions of the educational industry, the values shared by the faculty, and the type of competitive strategy that best suited the college's strengths and weaknesses. These were debated at a series of meetings with faculty, both to resolve the dilemmas and to create ownership of the mission statement.

Drafting the mission statement: drafts were prepared, and again subjected to a process discussion between stakeholders and the task force. There were several iterations of this process. Summaries of the various views went out to all members of the college, and a series of forums were held at which those who wished to express views could do so. A final version of the mission was prepared.

Vote to accept the mission: the mission statement was put to a vote across the college, and unanimously accepted.

The whole process took 6 months.

(*Source*: Magill, S. L., Johnson, S. D., Barker, R. M. and Bracker, J. S., 'The Bottom-up Mission Process in Professional Service Organisations: a Case Study', *Strategic Change*, 5, No. 2, 1996.)

It is almost true to say that there are as many definitions of 'objectives' as there are writers on strategy. It is certainly a topic that has engaged the attention of many management thinkers, and probably as much thought has been given to this as to any other single aspect of planning. Scott[3] suggests:

> Objectives here are the statements of planning purpose developed within any kind of business plan. They are established within the framework of a planning process, and they normally evolve from tentative and vague ideas to more specific declarations of purpose. Objectives, furthermore, are always present in a planning process even though they are sometimes unconsciously established.

Ansoff[4] sees objectives as: '. . . decision rules which enable management to guide and measure the firm's performance towards its purpose'. Drucker[5] maintains that a company may have a number of objectives. This viewpoint is further developed by Humble[6] into a comprehensive system of 'Management by Objectives', which is capable of application at all levels in the company. Argenti[7] takes a different view and believes that any firm has only one corporate objective:

> . . . something fundamental to the nature of a company and which distinguishes it from other types of organisation: it is therefore something permanent and unalterable. It is the reason for the very existence of the company, that for which it came into being and what it is now for. It is that which, if the company fails to achieve it, the company itself fails. It is a permanent unalterable purpose, or *raison d'être*.'

(Argenti sees the corporate objective as something distinct and separate from other types of objectives: simply as a dimension of profit.)

Many practitioners see a number of classifications of objectives, in particular into objectives and goals. For example, Ackoff[8] states:

> Desired states or outcomes are objectives. Goals are objectives that are scheduled for attainment during the period planned for.

He further divides objectives into stylistic and performance, the former being desired for their own sake and defined qualitatively, and the latter 'instrumentally', i.e. quantitatively. (However, it should be mentioned that some practitioners reverse the meanings of 'objectives' and 'goals'.) There is, too, a link between the constraints and objectives which has been discussed in some detail in Chapter 8.

Some concept of objectives is essential for the application of strategic management. The following analysis considers, first, the problem of the business undertaking and ultimately the modifications to this concept which might be applicable to non-profit-making bodies, such as government departments, hospitals, charitable, and similar organisations.

There is no doubt that Scott[3] is correct in his assertion that all organisations have objectives. They may not always be defined, and one of the first tasks of anyone undertaking strategic planning in any organisation must be to bring some clarification to the confusion – which exists in many companies – around its objectives. It is by no means infrequent for differing divisions in a company to be working to opposing objectives, or, indeed, for different people in the same division to be pulling in opposite directions. Usually this is all done in blissful ignorance, each person being certain that he or she is acting in the best interests of the company. Occasionally it is deliberate.

My own approach to objectives owes much to the combined weight of thought given to the subject by other writers. It has the further advantage of being tested and used in real, rather than theoretical, planning situations. Like most other practitioners, I see a division of the broad concept of objectives into a number of components. Those I recommend are:

1 The primary, or profit, objective of the business, set in advance of strategy
2 The secondary, and mainly narrative objectives, again set in advance of strategy
3 Goals which are time-assigned targets derived from the strategy
4 Standards of performance (often identical with goals) assigned to particular individuals.

Perhaps the most important factor is that there is a concept: each of the elements bears some relation to the others. The most vital parts of the concept are those which the company as a whole is trying to coordinate all its efforts to achieve. From these central and fundamental objectives should spring the purpose and role of every sector of the company and the personal objectives of individual people. Thus the concept is meaningful and capable of subdivision no matter how the company is organised. No change need be made to the principles whether they are applied to a one-person business, a conglomerate, or a multinational undertaking. The only modifications needed are in deciding who sets which divisional (or layer of) objectives, a point which will receive attention later.

Primary or profit objective

The primary or profit objective comes directly from a consideration of the basic duty of a chief executive, which is to manage the company in such a way that it fulfils the profit obligations to all the shareholders and at the same time provides an adequate cash flow for what may be termed 'corporate renewal'. The chief executive has full responsibility, answerable through the board to the shareholders, over the means by which these aims are achieved, and, subject only to the legitimate constraints which shareholders might apply, may choose the means to reach the targets.

We saw in the previous chapter that the creation of shareholder value should be a key aim of any chief executive. No business should be operated in such a way that profit is considered unimportant (the term 'profit' is discussed more fully later). I have heard managers speak as if a chief executive can choose between making profits or gaining turnover growth with little or no profit. The brutal fact is that, except in those increasingly rare cases where the owner and chief executive are one and the same, the chief executive does not have this choice. And even in a privately owned company lack of profits can only be tolerated for as long as the financial resources can stand it. The penalty for the chief executive who does not earn profit is elimination – either through disillusioned shareholders selling out their holdings at the first takeover offer which comes along, or because they decide to change the management, or because the company passes into bankruptcy and is closed down. Even giant companies are not immune from the effects of a disastrous cash-flow situation.

The reason for this is simple. A company that consistently fails to make profits will sooner or later cease to exist. The only factor in question is the speed at which it dies, which depends on the patience of its creditors, the size of its liquid resources, and the demands of its shareholders. We can go a step further and argue that a company that fails to make adequate profits will die either because of shareholder dissatisfaction or because the company cannot generate funds for growth and corporate renewal on which the future of every company depends. A company that does not make an appropriate level of profits, and manage its affairs so that shareholder value is gained through the share price, faces the rite of being swallowed up by another, or purchased to be broken up.

A feeling for profit must be held by all managers in the organisation if the company is to be successful. A business whose individual members have no sense of profit responsibility is a depressing sight. Successful businesses tend to develop a climate in which profit is taken into account during the planning process. Any company run by managers who argue that profit does not matter to them is very sick.

One more general point should be made about profit, and this is that the philosophy is not simply one of short-term but of long-term profit growth allowing for corporate renewal, which is something better than survival. In all decisions the company's future should be given due consideration. Most companies could increase today's profit at the expense of tomorrow's: for example, by reducing advertising, abolishing research and development, cheating the customer, or innumerable similar actions. The management task is to balance the need for current profits against the need for the company to progress in the future (of course, organisations have been set up to make a 'quick killing' and then close down, but these are unlikely to be interested in the concepts of management discussed here). That there is a need for current profits is also beyond doubt. The company that forgets this will perish, just as surely as the people who pack up eating at Easter and devote all their efforts to contemplating their next Christmas dinner. Shareholders are right never to be satisfied with *Alice Through the Looking Glass* jam – there must be some for today.

This accent on long-term considerations is not designed to lead companies into the trap of descending to platitudes. An objective such as 'we intend to maximise profit over the long term' is neither meaningful nor valid. An objective in this form is of no use to any manager. 'Maximum' profit depends on the individual manager's viewpoint. It will mean different things to different people, and there is no way of telling whether it (whatever it is) will be sufficient to satisfy shareholders. Maximised profit for some businesses might not be a profit at all, or might be such a small return that the correct action would be to wind up the company and give the shareholders back their assets. As it is unquantified, it is impossible to carry out 'gap analysis' (or any other form of mathematical exercise) to devise ways of reaching it. And as no one knows what it is, no one will know when they have got there, so the essential monitoring and controlling aspects of planning become impossible to implement. This means plans lack a cutting edge, and 'planning' degenerates to a meaningless exercise which adds only costs to the company and produces no benefit. Such a phrase becomes a shelter for the inefficient. Every manager can claim to have maximised profit; every short-term drop can be blamed on a long-term implication.

A main difference between companies which practise effective strategic management and those which have a more traditional approach to management is that the strategic companies are not satisfied with words alone. Much more meaningful is a specific quantitative statement of what profit is required. The planning company will also want to tie a time period to the profit concept. It is interested not only in what profit it requires this year; it needs to state its aims for as far ahead as it is willing to plan.

Perhaps the first step is for the company to define what it means by 'profit'. This must be established in accounting terms, and the definition should be used in all future plans. A company should never delude itself into believing it has achieved targets merely because it changes its chief accountant for one who has a different approach to the problems of reserves, depreciation, goodwill, and the like. The objective should cover two dimensions of profit – quantity and efficiency. An efficiency target (e.g. return on capital employed) is not by itself a valid objective because there may be a number of different results possible which yield the same ROI%: it is possible to foresee a situation where profit may decline even though the ROI% increases. A quantity dimension by itself is a valid target, although it is much more use to the company if linked to efficiency.

Like profit, the particular efficiency rating used should be carefully defined, and the same method of calculation used for computing results as for computing the target. This does not preclude a company from using more than one efficiency ratio provided it does not get them mixed up.

The definition of the corporate profit targets over the period selected for the plan is something which required a great deal of management thought, and there are differences of approach between a parent company and its subsidiaries, and possibly between privately owned and publicly owned companies. Perhaps the best approach is to return to the basic philosophy of a shareholder's legitimate expectations. What does a shareholder expect from a company? It may be impracticable (although not impossible as Fisons have shown - see Redwood[9]) to ask the shareholder, who may have many expectations. One thing the shareholder would particularly like is increased earnings from the investment. Put another way, this may be expressed in growth in earnings per share: this is not necessarily the same as growth in profits because the gearing effect of borrowed capital can increase earnings per share more than a proportionate increase in profits: similarly, a new share issue may reduce earnings per share although profits may rise. Earnings per share is a concept which can be quantified, and, of course, is only a generalisation until it is quantified.

Supporters of value-based strategic management, as we have seen in Chapter 12, would take a different view of how objectives should be quantified. They would use discounted cash flow techniques to measure targets, arguing that this forces decision makers to look to the future rather than the past. It also reconciles the economic approach to the evaluation of capital expenditures, which most large organisations take, to the overall strategies of the organisation.

A number of factors should be taken into consideration when a chief executive sets profit targets:

1 Trends over previous years (these provide a baseline for growth)
2 Progress by other companies of a similar size or in the same industry
3 The performance of the leading companies quoted on the Stock Exchange
4 Opportunities for more profitable investment elsewhere (for instance, shareholders tend to lose interest in a company which yields them less than an equivalent investment in a bank savings account)
5 The vision of the chief executive, and intention to give the shareholders more than they have had in the past
6 The strategic need for growth to reach a size which enables the company to at least maintain its position of influence in its trade, and to provide a cash flow to generate future growth and the replacement of assets.
7 Rates of inflation. There should be an improvement in real terms
8 Acceptable levels of risk.

The usual efficiency ratios, particularly return on capital and return on shareholders' funds, should be utilised in the study. A new chief executive who inherits a company earning a miserable 1 per cent return on capital employed will probably have a long way to go to give shareholders the type of earnings they have a right to expect: on the other hand, he or she might consider that there is a lot of scope for improvement, as things cannot get much worse.

A privately owned company might adopt a different approach, although that outlined above is valid should it wish to use it. In many such companies it is possible to find out what the shareholders want, because ownership and management may be vested in the same people or there may be strong family influences. Here it may be practicable to consult the shareholders, and there may, in the family business, be other factors. A less ambitious growth target might be preferred to prevent loss of family control (either financial or through having to open the management ranks to outsiders).

Once the profit objectives have been set for the total company it is time to think about objectives for divisions and subsidiaries. Now it is possible for a subsidiary or division to calculate its own profit objectives on the lines argued above, although I believe this task should be undertaken by the head office subject to discussion with the division or subsidiary concerned. The reason for this is that the way in which a total company profit objective is divided up is in fact a series of strategic decisions. An objective set for subsidiary A reflects the parent company's decisions that that particular activity should continue in being and that a particular growth and contribution is expected from that area of business.

Exhibit 13.2 A reminder of the terms used

Return on investment. This is profit divided by investment and expressed as a percentage. A number of different bases are available as the measure of investment. For example, depending on the purpose of the analysis, it would be possible to use:

Total assets
Total assets less current liabilities
Total assets less total liabilities (shareholders' funds)

Profit may also be taken before or after tax.

Earnings per share. The earnings attributable to ordinary shareholders (that is after deducting the earnings attributable to preference shareholders), divided by the number of ordinary shares

Price–earnings ratio. This is not mentioned in the text, but is an important ratio which has an effect on objectives. It is the market price per share divided by the earnings per share.

Discounted cash flow. A method of analysis that takes into account the time value of money. It is based on the fact that a unit of money available today is worth more than that same unit at some time in the future, because of the earnings that can be gained from it. If the money is not available until some time in the future this opportunity has to be forgone. Net streams of cash for an investment or activity are forecast into the future, and discounted back to present value, using a rate of discount which may, for example, equate to the cost of capital. This gives rise to several possible measures, the two most common of which are:

● *Net present value*: the cumulative total of the discounted incremental cash flows. If a 10%n discount rate were used, the NPV would he zero if the project equated with the standard, negative if it were below 10%, and positive if it were above it.
● *Internal rate of return*: the discount rate which would apply to reduce the NPV of a project to zero.

The proportions of the profit objective which are required from each activity area (and what is meant by this will depend on company organisation – it may be an industry grouping, a strategic business unit, a country operation, or simply something which fits in with the pattern of the subsidiaries owned by the parent) may again be divined from an amalgam of past trends, competitive activity, return on investment rates, strategic growth rates, and expectations. There should be discussion between subsidiary and head office so that objectives are agreed and accepted, but this does not alter the fact that it is a basic head office duty to set them.

It may be that, as part of a determined strategy, a particular subsidiary will run at a loss: for instance, if a new company is set up in what, for the group, is a new country. This can be reflected in the profit objectives. It is not a decision for the subsidiary alone: in fact if all subsidiaries and divisions opted to lose money, albeit for future growth, the total company would be in a sorry state. The ability of a group to accept controlled losses in certain areas depends on its ability to meet its planned profit targets by contributions from other areas. If, for properly evaluated long-term reasons, subsidiary A is to sacrifice profit for growth, subsidiaries B, C, and D must be able to make up the shortfall. Only the corporate centre can know what it can afford.

In many situations there may well be a conflict between sales growth and profit growth. This has another important aspect – cash flow. The value argument would imply looking at a business unit on the same lines as a capital investment, and subjecting the strategy to DCF analysis to ensure that there is an acceptable payback. If the subsidiary is a new venture this may well be done as a matter of course: if it is a new strategy for an old subsidiary this course may never even be thought of.

It is relevant to consider the profit targets of autonomous units under the concept of the primary objective. It is also relevant to realise that from the point of view of the total company these are not objectives at all, and in fact fit in much more closely with the definition of goals quoted earlier. From the point of view of the chief executive of the subsidiary it is a primary objective. This different viewpoint from different levels in an organisation occurs in other types of objective and will be discussed in more detail later. For the present it is enough to say that it is one of the reasons why there is confusion of thought over the topic of objectives. The fact that position does change a person's conception of an objective is part of normal life – from earth, with the naked eye, the full moon is seen as a circle: in fact it is a sphere.

Two further factors should be mentioned before the concept of secondary objectives is considered. The first is that many business groups contain subsidiaries which are not wholly owned by the group and which may have other shareholders. The duty of a chief executive is, through the board, to all the shareholders, and such a chief executive should play a much more important part in the setting of the primary objectives than the chief executive of a wholly owned subsidiary. The process may begin in the same way, but may be subject to a greater degree of thought and modification by the subsidiary chief executive. There is a duty to meet the legitimate demands of all the shareholders, and the chief executive should ensure that the objectives are in line with this.

The second factor is that, particularly in multinational business, the subsidiary chief executive may be subject to government constraints which prevent acceptance of the profit objectives. These, too, cannot be ignored, and represent an additional reason – if one is needed – for consultation between the centre and subsidiaries when objectives are set.

Secondary Objectives

Profit is an important aspect of corporate objectives, but it is not the only one. The term 'secondary' is chosen to describe the next group of objectives: not because they are less important to success but because they should really be defined after the profit objectives have been set.

Secondary objectives are descriptive and attempt to set out the key elements of the business of the future. Where the corporate appraisal seeks the present corporate identity, the secondary objectives describe the company's future identity. They paint a picture not of what is now, but what the company is determined to become in the future. They take the old question *What business am I in?* and give it a new dimension, oriented to the future rather than the present.

This type of objective, sometimes called 'the mission', should examine the nature and scope of the business, the geographical sphere of operation, and some of the key factors about the company which the chief executive feels are important. They may include a statement of the way the company intends to conduct its relations with its employees, customers, and society: there is a straightforward link with the chief executive's ethical viewpoint, already discussed in Chapter 8.

Some managers believe that secondary objectives are not really objectives at all but statements of strategy that broadly describe the means that will be used to attain the profit targets. There is some justification to this opinion, but there are three arguments that can be used against it. First, it does not really matter if the concept does venture into the realms of corporate strategy since none of the elements of corporate planning exist in isolation and all overlap to some degree. Second, this type of objective can be very useful in channelling creative thought to a desired end, and the concept can thus be justified on the grounds of expediency.

The third argument is even more compelling. Every chief executive holds a mental vision of what the company can become, regardless of the strategy chosen to reach it. There is a very real gulf between the concept the chief executive of a conglomerate might have – a willingness and ability to accept any profitable investment in any field – and that which might be held by the chief executive of a company operating in only one or two industry groups who would never, under any circumstances, consider moving too far from the fields the company understands. It may be that one day the second company would change its objectives and arrive at a broader concept of its basic purpose. As it is with a company, so it is with most individuals. As a person gains in experience and education, as family and other responsibilities increase, and as he or she gains a more realistic appreciation of strengths and weaknesses, so the concept of ultimate aims changes. There is no reason why any objective, corporate or personal, should be regarded as immutable. It need only be permanent enough to outlast the period for which strategies are prepared.

Both primary and secondary objectives should be thought of as map grid references rather than as the bull of a dartboard or shooting gallery. A map reference means that direction of travel can be changed, detours made, and the predetermined target still attained. On the other hand, a dart or bullet, once it embarks on its parabola, is committed and the action cannot be recalled or changed in any way. Objectives thought of as a map reference lead to flexibility: alternative strategies become possible and contingency planning has purpose. Objectives seen as the 'bull' would lead to inflexible plans that would shatter at the first insurmountable obstacle.

Objectives should be set with care, since the map reference should be the best one for the company. This is particularly true of the secondary objectives, as it is these which may be the most motivating and have the most impact on the total organisation. It needs no saying that the wrong map reference will lead to wrong strategies which might take the company in a direction which is contrary to its real interests.

This is one reason why the secondary objectives should be defined with thought and care, and why, like the primary objectives, they are a matter requiring the attention of the chief executive. It is also fair to say at this stage that secondary objectives may change if the chief executive changes. Although the corporate appraisal should provide the factual information on which these objectives may be based, the final result is a personal interpretation by the chief executive. Thus, as with the profit target, the chief executive's thoughts, ambitions, and belief in his or her own capability make up a large part of the company's objectives.

A statement of a company's business activity should be narrow enough to focus attention on opportunities in a meaningful way, but wide enough to enable the company to identify opportunity when it sees it. Drucker[5], gives many examples of companies whose objectives were seen in too narrow a fashion, with the consequence that they embarked upon courses of action, and passed by many opportunities which they were ideally equipped to handle. It is worth examining some examples of what this broadening of objectives has meant to certain businesses.

The UK manufacturers of various food and pharmaceutical products had many successful years when the entire reason for the existence of the company was thought of in terms of their main product: all diversification opportunities were given inadequate resources of time and money. The total accounting and management information system was geared to this one product. This position changed with the advent of a new managing director. He defined the company's business in much broader terms, laying stress on the company's area of strength – its particular segment of the food market and its strong distribution links. Within three years the company had launched a number of new products and had many others under development. In the first year the one major product contributed virtually all the home food sales: by the third year 40 per cent of turnover was coming from other products. Within the company people thought of their prospects in a different light. The major product became what it should always have been, a valuable product, not the *raison d'être*.

A company in the fruit and vegetable trade traditionally thought of themselves in terms of bananas, and geared their whole business to this concept. Admittedly they had certain well-developed skills in this product, but they had many problems and opportunities in common with other fresh-produce wholesalers. A change in outlook led to a much wider definition of the business, still within the general area of fruit and vegetables, which in turn led to expansion and diversification in several new areas.

It is easy to state that the widening of perception was in each of these examples only a statement of the obvious, and that the opportunities would have been taken up by any good management. This would be too simple an analysis. If results in terms of profits and growth are considered, each of these companies had had 'good' management, although each was facing some problems. Yet in each case it needed a change in emphasis before they could see opportunities, many of which had been available since the day the companies were incorporated. It really comes back to the problem of perception and vision. Strength of ambition is not the only factor in success, but it is very difficult to succeed without it. In a sense the secondary objectives, when combined with the profit targets, measure the strength of ambition of the company. Corporate success still requires clear judgement and good decision making, but at least a part of the recipe for success is available.

Objectives should also be defined at various levels in the organisation. Although the objectives of each subsidiary or division should be compatible with those of the total group, they need not be identical. Few subsidiaries are in the total area of business defined by the parent, and, in any case, local conditions and local perception might make it desirable to stress certain aspects not considered by the parent as important.

Goals

Goals follow naturally on the two elements of the concept of profits so far discussed. If we may regard objectives as the map reference we may consider goals as milestones and landmarks along the chosen route. They serve exactly this purpose: to enable the company to check that it is still on-course and to examine the reason why it has made any deviation.

A departure from strategy may be quite acceptable provided it is carried out with full knowledge of its effects. Alternatively, failure to achieve a goal may indicate that strategy should be changed if objectives are to be attained.

Goals can only be properly defined after strategy has been determined. They should always be expressed in quantitative terms, since they are designed as a standard of management, and it is virtually impossible to measure perform-ance against a qualitative statement of expectations. They should also be defined against time – that is, they should indicate not only what should have resulted but when it should have taken place. There is only one rule for the frequency or time intervals between goals: the usefulness of the periods selected.

In effect, a network of goals provides a form of model of the company's strategy over the whole period of the plan. The model may be as simple or as complex as the company wishes: again the criteria must be usefulness. Each goal must be purposeful and there is no value in defining targets which the company either cannot or does not intend to measure.

If goals are derived from strategy they will be compatible with each other. This is important because it is of little benefit for a company to have goals which can only be reached if other goals are sacrificed. This does not mean that a company may not apply a degree of critical targeting to all elements of its plan. For example, if inventory levels are high it may set a goal to reduce them, but this must be followed by definition of a plan to achieve that goal. In applying this element of corrective targeting the company must examine the other elements of the plan to ensure that the goals derived from these are still sensible. If, for instance, lower inventories meant poorer customer service and lower sales, these facts would have to be taken into account at the same time as the inventory goals were adjusted. The proper use of corrective targeting is, of course, during the process of developing plans and the use of goals in this way does not invalidate the contention that they are defined after strategy has been established.

The fact that goals must be capable of being measured was mentioned above. Preferred goals would be those that can be measured as a matter of routine from existing information sources, be they accounting, marketing research, or personnel records. In some cases goal setting may indicate a need for change in the management information collected or in its manner of presentation.

Goals which can only be measured by special non-routine exercises may be worthwhile if the cost of collecting the data is less than the expected benefit. A company which includes the development and change of its corporate image as an important and essential element of strategy may define this in quantitative terms (e.g. perception levels of particular aspects) and may commission a market research study to check results against these benchmarks. Similarly, an occasional analysis of internal data might be made to provide a measurement of a goal which is not measured on any routine system.

Many different types of goals may be defined, and the possibilities suggested here are by way of example rather than recommendation. Only the company itself can know what is relevant and important to it: no textbook can provide this answer. Goals might be defined for:

- Percentage market share (by product and/or country)
- A ratio, such as return on sales
- An absolute figure for sales
- A minimum figure for customer complaints
- A maximum figure for hours lost in industrial disputes
- A labour productivity ratio
- Total number of employees
- A maximum employee 'wastage' rate
- A standard cost
- A cost-reduction target
- A date by which a particular event must take place (e.g. new product launch)

Standards of performance

The fourth aspect of objectives is a derivation from goals. While a goal is a corporate, divisional, or departmental target, a standard of performance is something which is individually assigned to a named person. Sometimes the personal standard may be identical to the corporate goal: for example, a market share goal may be assigned to the product manager responsible. Sometimes the standard may be something derived from the goal: a splitting up of the corporate target into pieces for which individual people may be responsible (an example is the personal sales target given to a representative).

Performance standards may be taken from any aspect of the company's plans – the annual plan, the long-range plan, or a project plan. Frequently the standard will be a time-assigned task: Mr Smith to complete a market survey by 1 September; Mr Brown to negotiate a bank overdraft facility by 1 May; Dr Stevens to develop a new product formulation by July next year; Mr Oliver to secure the XYZ account by January next year. Such tasks may often be incorporated into networks and similar documents.

The importance of personal standards is that they provide a tool for ensuring that plans are converted into things people can do – indeed, into things people are expected to do. There is thus a direct link between the tasks of the individual person and the total corporate strategy. The function and practical use of personal standards of performance will be examined in greater detail in Chapter 20, which deals with the ways of implementing plans. In that chapter attention will also be paid to the technique of 'management by objectives' (MBO) as developed by Humble[6] and its modern cousin performance management. The system of personal standards described here is a simplified variant of MBO, although its aims are narrower than those of MBO: the differences will also be discussed later.

The overall concept as described here can be visualised as a network of targets, all interlinked in some way to the company's primary and secondary objectives. There are numerous levels, reaching right into the heart of the company. At an earlier point in this chapter the shifting of objectives from differing viewpoints was briefly mentioned. This should now be examined in greater detail since it applies to all the types of objectives described here.

The essence of this chapter has been to identify objectives as a target that is being pursued, and strategy as the means by which the organisation tries to achieve the objectives. Once a chief executive begins to examine objectives below the total company level he or she is beginning to deal with strategy: thus profit objectives set for a subsidiary are, in fact, an element of strategy. However, for the subsidiary chief executive these profit targets become a primary objective: only the way chosen to attain them can be called strategy. In general terms it is correct to say that within an organisation strategy set by one level in a business becomes the objective of the level beneath it. This can be illustrated very simply in Table 13.1.

The example is oversimplified, and in practice the company would define other objectives and elaborate its strategy in much more detail. It is very easy to

Table 13.1 Levels of objectives and strategy

Level	Objective	Strategy[a]
Total company	After-tax profit £1 m by 1975	Profits to come from: (a) Diversification £500 000 (b) Subsidiary A £230 000 (c) Subsidiary B £400 000 (d) Subsidiary C £100 000
Subsidiary A	Profit target £250 000	To concentrate effort on two departments, each marketing one product: Department O £100 000 profit Department P £150 000 profit
Department O	Profit target £100 000	Develop annual turnover of £1m (a) Existing outlets £700 000 sales (b) New outlets £150 000 sales (c) Exports £150 000 sales
Marketing managers	Develop export sales to £150 000 p.a. by xxxx	

[a] The individual sources add up to more than £1 m. to allow for overheads.

visualise the example extended to cover other types of objectives and to other levels in a company. The point is that if the manager of department O does not produce a strategy to achieve an after-tax profit of £100 000 he or she has failed, just as surely as the group chief executive who does not reach the million.

It follows that every level in the company has some delegation of freedom of decision making from the top. (When this stops, an objective ceases to be an objective and becomes a simple instruction.) This explains why it is both possible and desirable for the chief executive of subsidiary A to have his 'strategic plan' even though the strategy is subordinate to that of the group.

What has so far been discussed is the concept as applied to the normal business undertaking. The position is different when non-profit-making or publicly owned undertakings are concerned. In organisations such as a hospital or a charity the concept of the primary objective may have little value. However, I would argue that a 'cost of service' objective tied to the remainder of the overall concept is of importance. An objective of service to the community or to individual categories of people might indeed be the main *raison d'être* of the undertaking: this is no reason why a cost-efficiency rating should not be valid. Where the commercial concern tries to provide its shareholders with their profit requirements the charitable undertaking needs to give the people for whose benefit it exists the maximum service at the minimum cost. These are factors which can be defined, quantified, and used in strategic planning in a meaningful way. In my opinion an undertaking such as a large hospital requires sound commercial planning and application if the skills of doctors and nurses are to be used to the full. The criteria of decision making may be different, but certainly exist. Commercial inefficiency merely wastes the abilities of the non-commercial worker in the hospital.

Some government undertakings have a defined task which calls upon them to make profits as well as provide a service. This particularly applies to 'productive' undertakings such as – in the UK – the Post Office and agencies such as the Defence Research Agency. The British Post Office has, for example, the obligation to earn a predetermined return on assets (this, of course, is only half an objective, and would not fit the definition of the primary objective used earlier in this chapter).

The dilemma of publicly owned business undertakings should not be understressed. The prevailing world fashion is to privatise all that can be privatised, and to create market-driven agencies from as many of the rest as possible. Those that are not privatised are subject to direct control by government, and their objectives can alter with every change of political party. British Rail, for example, suffered before privatisation because of the seesaw between community service objectives and short-term profit objectives. In addition, the constraints attached to the strategic freedom of the enterprise may change. Again British Rail provided an example: one government allowed a diversification policy, the next stated that the only area of business was to be railways. It is perhaps not surprising that the managers of such activities, like the Post Office, press governments to privatise them.

Much has been said about objectives in their various shapes and forms. It would be wrong to leave the subject without some consideration of the benefits which a well-applied application of the concept will bring. The main use is the basic one: objectives enable a company to plan. The primary objective is a precursor to strategic action: how this objective is used in strategic planning – through the technique of gap analysis – will be demonstrated later.

Through their part in the strategic planning process objectives 'stretch' the organisation and help it to achieve more than may otherwise have been the case. As the plans are devised, any failure to reach objectives causes a recycling of corporate thought and calls for new ideas which will enable the looked-for results to be achieved.

In addition, the total concept of objectives, from primary objective down to the lowest personal standard set, provides a motivational tool of great potential. Objectives can be made widely known in an organisation – after all, it is only the strategy which should be confidential - and can be used to stimulate the minds of men from boardroom to factory floor. A measure of cohesion and coordination is introduced.

Although, as Scott[3] has stated, all companies must have objectives (even if they are unaware of them), it is a fact that many companies have never attempted to define them in any logical way. This means that individual managers project their own desires and interpretations on to what they think their company should be doing. Careful attention to the definition of objectives will ensure that everyone does, indeed, get on the right tracks.

Better motivation, coordination, and higher levels of achievement can be expressed as a contribution to communication, which is one of the side-aims of any process of formal planning. Perhaps, above all, objectives lead the company on its first steps along the path towards clarity of corporate thinking.

References

1 Hamel, G. and Prahalad, C. K. 'Strategic Intent', *Harvard Business Review*, May/June, 1989.
2 Karlöf, B. *Business Strategy*, Macmillan, London, 1989.
3 Scott, B. W. *Long Range Planning in American Industry*, American Management Association, 1965.
4 Ansoff, H. I. *Corporate Strategy*, McGraw-Hill, New York, 1965.
5 Drucker, P. F. *The Practice of Management*, Heinemann, London, 1955.
6 Humble, J. W. *Improving Business Results*, McGraw-Hill, New York, 1968.
7 Argenti, A. J. A. *Corporate Planning: A Practical Guide*, Allen & Unwin, London, 1968.
8 Ackoff, R. C. *A Concept of Corporate Planning*, Wiley Interscience, New York, 1970.
9 Redwood, H. 'The Fisons Shareholder Survey', *Long Range Planning*, April 1971.

CHAPTER 14

Strategy

In this, the first of several chapters about strategy formulation, the aim is to explore some basic approaches. The chapter stresses the importance of considering several options. One of the earliest tools of strategic thinking, gap analysis, is demonstrated. The majority of the chapter shows one simple way of examining different strategic options, using a matrix derived from one originally developed by Igor Ansoff. Although not the latest strategic thinking, the approach is still useful as a first stage of thinking, and may be all that is needed in very simple situations.

Some aspects of the strategic planning process have already been discussed in considerable detail. In other chapters most of the essential groundwork of the strategic plan has been worked over. At this stage in the process we may assume that the company has set its objectives, defined its social responsibility, established all the assumptions on which it will base its plan, and now fully understands its own strengths and weaknesses. All this work will, as a byproduct, have provided the company with a number of opportunities for further study.

This chapter will consider certain aspects of corporate strategy in some detail with the intention of analysing the various approaches to the formation of strategy. In later chapters attention will be focused on more detailed analysis, and eventually on the strategic plan itself.

Definitions of strategic and operating planning have already been given. Because the difference between the two activities is important, it is worth turning attention once more on these two areas. Ansoff[1] illustrates his view of the essential meaning of the terms with his well-known cow analogy. He maintains that the operating problem is concerned with getting as much performance as possible out of the company's investment in current markets – a process which he likens to 'seeking the best way to milk a cow'. Strategic problems are on a different level, and are concerned with allocating the firm's resources to activities which offer the largest potential return, which may not necessarily have anything in common with its current activities: '. . . but if our basic interest is not the cow but in the most milk we get for our investment, we must also make sure that we have the best cow money can buy.' Strategic management can opt to change the cow: operating management can only attempt to be a more efficient milker.

This does not mean that strategy does not take account of current operations. Indeed it must, for the decision to remain in them is in itself a matter of strategy. Where strategic decisions encompass all the possible paths that the company might take to reach its objectives, and where the definition of what those objectives should be, is of itself a matter of strategy; operating planning is concerned only with getting the most out of what is currently being done.

Strategy is very much a question of a choice from the alternative paths open to the company. The number of alternatives available to any company is legion, and their identification and analysis may be a complex task. Consider, for example, the relatively simple strategic problem facing a smallholder who has set himself the task of doubling his profits over a three-year period:

1 Expand by buying the farm next door.
2 Apply more investment to the land, e.g. in the form of glasshouses or irrigation sprays.
3 Change the crop to another entirely different – perhaps add a cow, goat, or rear chickens.
4 Install another process: perhaps prepackaging fruit and vegetables or turning milk into cream.
5 Attention to marketing, so that a greater realisation is obtained.
6 Become a more efficient producer.
7 Sell the business and invest the capital elsewhere.

These seven alternatives can be combined into $7 \times 6 \times 5 \times 4 \times 3 \times 2 \times 1$ possible courses of action – and the best that can be said about this is that it is a lot. And this ignores the numerous alternatives hidden in the broad listings staged (buy the 50-acre farm on one side, or the 100-acre farm on the other; grow sugar-beet or potatoes or radishes).

So far the illustration makes the point that even a relatively simple business unit has a wide field from which to choose its strategy. At the other extreme, the massive multinational, multidivisional company will have even more possibilities (and needs special ways of considering them: see Chapter 15 and 16). Yet there is also no doubt that the illustration has succeeded in making a relatively simple problem into a very complicated one.

This is because the evolution of strategy involves more than the writing down of possible alternatives. The steps omitted in the smallholder illustration were:

1 Considering the alternatives in the light of the firm's own constraints and code of ethics
2 Applying the results of the corporate appraisal so that opportunities are matched to the company
3 Considering those weaknesses established in the corporate appraisal which exclude some alternatives (e.g. lack of capital or skill)
4 Information from the environmental appraisal
5 Evaluation of the alternatives themselves: some are always potentially more profitable than others.

The strategic planning process involves the identification of alternatives, the collection of information, evaluation and selection of alternatives, and, finally,

Figure 14.1

Gap analysis

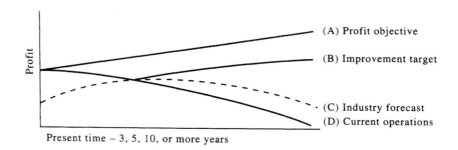

Profit

(A) Profit objective

(B) Improvement target

(C) Industry forecast
(D) Current operations

Present time – 3, 5, 10, or more years

the strategic decisions themselves. Much more will be said on these subjects: for the moment it is fair to assume that the applications of these stages during the process would have reduced the smallholder's problems to something he could manage – a choice between a few real opportunities.

Part of the disciplined thinking which must accompany the development of strategy is to assess the extent of the problem. One very useful and simple technique to assist in this is gap analysis. This sets out the targets the company is trying to achieve, what is expected from current operations, and what the 'gap' is between expectations and requirements. Filling the gap is what strategy is about. All this can more easily be demonstrated with a simple diagram (Figure 14.1).

The diagram measures absolute levels of profit on the vertical axis and periods of time on the horizontal axis (it could also be used to measure return on investment ratios or sales). Line A shows the progression of the company's primary, or profit, objective. This measures what the business intends to achieve.

Line D measures what the company expects to achieve from its current operations, assuming no basic strategic changes are made. In the early stages of planning, this line would probably be projected on data obtained during the corporate appraisal, possibly supplemented by more detailed forecasts in some areas. As the company moves further into the planning process it will be replaced by the projections from the operating plans. This should mean that the validity of this line should improve, although if the initial work has been carried out well the position of the revised line should not be too far away from the original.

The corporate appraisal should also provide the information on which lines B and C are prepared. Line B shows the effects of proposed profit improvement projects on profits and illustrates the extent to which line D can be moved towards line A – a partial closing of the 'gap'. Line B may also include profit targets to be achieved from an improvement strategy: that is, the actual means may not at this stage be known, only that the target is likely to be realistic.

One way of helping line B to be realistic is to consider line C. This is an attempt to insert the industry trend: that is, what the company would be earning if their results were based on average industry returns instead of their own individual forecast. This particular line is not always obtainable because base data are sometimes unavailable, and it is itself a forecast of trends. Nevertheless, where it can be obtained, it gives a useful perspective and aids the company in its assessment of the 'improvement gap'.

The gap between lines B and A is the 'strategic gap'. This is the area to which corporate top management must give attention, for it will only be filled if the company enters into new strategies.

In the diagram, line D shoots rapidly downwards towards oblivion. This is by no means an inevitability, and the direction and shape of this line, and the nature of the improvement and strategic gaps, will be unique to each individual company.

The gap-analysis approach may also be used at various levels in the company – subsidiaries, divisions, or departments. The only difference is that at the lower levels the strategic gap may be a 'new thinking' gap: it depends how much of the strategic task is delegated by central corporate management. In large companies it may be a great deal.

Kami[2] maintains that gap analysis can be used much more widely, and that although a simple technique it can help companies of any size. He suggests taking the analysis two stages further. First, the expected results of the various programmes devised to fill the gap should also be charted so that the impact of each can be seen. As some may fail, he advocates the identification of reserve programmes: cumulatively the results would then exceed the objectives, although the expectation is that not all would be implemented. His second suggestion is that control points be shown on the diagram (Figure 14.2), to indicate the time when the company should check that it is, in fact, on-course.

Gap analysis is thus used to help the organisation to 'stretch' itself towards its objectives. Occasionally, closing the gap may be impossible, either because of shortage of ideas or shortage of resources. Perhaps the objective for the fifth year is achievable, but only at the expense of unacceptable losses in the early years. In these circumstances, and provided the objectives have been carefully thought out, the answer may be to re-examine the company's continued role as an independent business unit. Possibly the shareholders would be better served by a merger with another company. Alternatively, the answer may be to fire the chief executive, or the planner, or both.

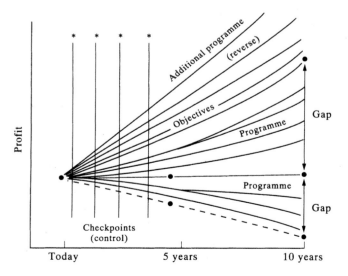

Figure 14.2
Gap analysis with control points (o). (Reproduced from Kami[2])

On the other hand, the company may find that in practice its projects considerably exceed its objectives, even after allowing for reserves. Here the company has to be very sure that all the projects are within its financial and human resources. If they are, it is in the fortunate position of being able to decide whether to change objectives and aim for a higher target, or to opt for a slower than optimum growth. The temptation to move on to a higher growth pattern is often one to be avoided, since too much growth may be as disastrous as too little.

The diagrams are designed as an aid to thought – and possibly of presentation – and it is possible, and sometimes desirable, to dispense with the drawing and analyse the figures alone. Exactly the same results can be achieved.

So far the discussion of the 'gap' has provided an indication of the strategic task. Before turning to the ways in which strategy might be further identified and analysed, it is worth considering the philosophical approaches to planning defined by Ackoff.[3]

He sees three distinct philosophies which – for want of better terms – he calls 'satisficing', 'optimising', and 'adaptivising', although in practice mixtures of the three pure forms also occur. 'Satisficing' plans aim to do well, but not as well as possible, to do enough to satisfy, but not to do more than this, although it may be possible to do better. Objectives set by 'satisficing' planners are always feasible – the 'stretching' effect of a good system of objectives is avoided. Strategies always try to avoid conflict, and rarely involve organisational change or major variations from the past. 'Satisficing' planners produce 'one-point' plans, i.e. their plans contain only one set of strategies and forecasts and make no provision for the possibility that things might go wrong: an artificial certainty is given to all planned actions. As it is assumed that the organisation is flexible enough to cope with the unexpected, there are seldom formal systems for monitoring and controlling the plans.

Ackoff[3] sums up 'satisficing':

> Not surprisingly, satisficing planning seldom produces a radical departure from the past. It usually yields conservative plans that comfortably continue most current policies, correcting only obvious deficiencies. Such planning therefore appeals to organisations that are more concerned with survival than with development and growth.

'Satisficing' planning adds little to the company's knowledge of itself or its markets. Its value to the company must be seriously questioned.

The 'optimising' planner takes a completely different view of his job. He aims always to choose the best possible course of action, and relies very heavily on operational research techniques and mathematical models. He formulates all his objectives and goals in quantified terms – and tends to ignore all those which he cannot so quantify.

> This can distort the value of his work and produce justifiable discomfort in the consuming managers who must moderate quantitative results with their own qualitative judgements on important problems that have not been taken into account.[3]

The optimiser is only as good as the models he produced. Perhaps his biggest defect is that he tends to underrate the human aspect – partly because many 'people' activities cannot be built into the model. Although control systems can be incorporated into the systems these tend to measure only what was foreseen when the model was built – the unforeseen is in danger of being ignored.

'Adaptivising' is accompanied by the belief that the main value in planning lies in the process and not the plans themselves. Again it is worth referring to the Harvard study by Vancil,[4] quoted in Chapter 2, and his suspicion that accuracy in forecasts might be the wrong objective of a planning system.

The adaptiviser believes that another main purpose of his plans is to prevent crises from arising – to adapt the organisation and systems so that difficulties are avoided, and so that management does not have to spend most of its time resolving the problems caused by past inadequacies and inefficiencies.

Perhaps the strongest point of the adaptiviser's platform is that he differentiates distinct types of risks in all future events. There are certain aspects which are virtual certainties (the point was made in the chapters dealing with the environment), for which the best solution is to ensure that adequate plans are made and actions committed so that the company may exploit these events. Many more events are a matter of varying degrees of probability: here the adaptiviser will prepare a series of contingency plans to cover every foreseeable possibility. (Examples have been given in a previous chapter).

Ackoff's analysis is useful in understanding management behaviour, and it is important to know the various approaches to strategic planning as this can often help shed a new light on the way a company plans and acts. My own bias is towards adaptivising planning although, as in so many other aspects of management, there is probably no one correct answer.

But, for most of us, there is a greater interest in the identification and selection of strategic options than in learning to classify our own approach to planning.

One simple way of looking at strategic options has appeared in many books and articles – with modifications and variations – although it can be traced back to Igor Ansoff,[5] and has been called the Ansoff matrix. The variant in Figure 14.3 derives from this source, although the terminology used is different. Despite its simplicity, the matrix is still useful, and provides a helpful starting point for thinking about strategy at a basic level. Strategic options are classified according to their positions on this matrix.

Figure 14.3
Analysis of strategic alternatives

Product \ Market	Current	New
Current	(a)	(c)
New	(b)	(d)

(a) Current products in current markets

This is improving the performance of the company's existing products in the markets in which it currently trades. Many of the data for decisions in this area will come from the corporate appraisal, and the development of plans in this box of the matrix is very much the duty of operating management. The main element of corporate strategic thinking in this area is concerned with how much, how fast, and what quantity of resources should be committed to these actions. Following Ansoff's[1] image mentioned earlier in this chapter it is concerned with getting more milk out of the cow.

Action in this area might be increasing brand share by changing any of the elements of marketing strategy – for example, sales effort, advertising, distribution channels, or the relative weightings in the marketing mix. It would also include actions which improve the profitability of current operations and thus the actions which help take the company to line B in the gap-analysis diagram.

It makes good sense for every company to fully investigate the area before moving on to the more exotic elements of corporate strategy. Although problems of the company's 'risk balance' are relevant, and although the planners must ensure that the point of diminishing returns has not been reached, it is a fact that action in the area of current products and current markets is often less risky than ventures into the unknown.

(b) New products to current markets

This is often a logical way to exploit particular marketing knowledge and capability possessed by the company. It is a path taken by business ever since the first business began, and is frequently accompanied by an economy of scale in marketing, distribution and sales operations. Examples of action under this segment of the strategic matrix are the supermarket which expands its activities into clothing and domestic hardware, the suit manufacturer which introduces shirts into its product range, the pharmaceutical company which adds a new cold remedy or the magazine which introduces mail-order selling to its readers. By definition these products should be handled by the same sales force, and purchased by the same consumers.

Again much of the initiative and most of the planning will be the task of operating management, though it is certainly a strategic planning task to ensure that adequate attention is given to opportunities in this area: it is ground that should be thoroughly worked over before the company attempts to work the lesser-known terrain in box (d).

(c) Current products in new markets

This is another area where synergy can be fairly high, as development here can often bring economies of scale in production and general management. Once again it is a method of expansion which has been used from the dawn of history.

Perhaps the most obvious example which springs to mind – since so many companies do it – is to seek out new markets in other countries. There are still companies which restrict their thinking to the domestic market.

For many companies export opportunities will either already be taken up or may simply not exist at all. This does not mean that no opportunities will be available, although they may not be so obvious. In Chapter 6, which discussed forecasting, mention was made of the concept of the product life cycle. One particular reason for introducing existing products to new markets could well be to extend the product life cycle. Such an action can be important at any point on the S-curve, but may be strategically vital as the product moves into maturity, the top point of the curve associated with low growth (or actual decline) in both sales and profits. Action taken at an earlier point of the curve may, of course, help to postpone the day of maturity.

Ovaltine in the UK, in contrast to many other countries elsewhere in the world, is a product which has traditionally been associated with bedtime drinking. Much of the advertising of the previous years – if not decades – of both Ovaltine and its competitors had created the bedtime market. In 1970 a deliberate attempt was made, through the Cool-ova campaign, to create a new market – Ovaltine, drunk in cold instead of warm milk, as an anytime beverage. A good try that did not work.

This is not an isolated example of action which might be taken to create new markets. Consider the ethical pharmaceuticals company which offers a range of its products, for 'over-the-counter' sale in pharmacies: or, alternatively, the company selling proprietary pharmaceuticals which moves into the ethical field. Plastics manufacturers have a history of creating new markets for their products, often by attacking the position of traditional materials.

(d) New products for new markets

Diversification: in effect this box of the matrix can be summed up in one word. Yet this is deceptively simple, since it is potentially the most risky and dangerous path open to any company. The pitfalls are many since the ground is usually completely unknown to the exploring company. And somewhere along the path there is often a distorting mirror which reflects a powerful and glamorous image of the manager, trapping him with dreams of empire, grandeur, and glory. Yet it can also be a rewarding path to tread. For some companies it may indeed be the only way to develop.

The way the individual firm handles the four boxes in the matrix would depend to some extent on its definition of what is a product and what is market. The definition of product which I like to use comes from McCarthy[6] and includes the intangible aspects of a product as well as its physical characteristics. The intangibles include those items which are offered by the company to induce consumers to buy – for example, aftersales service, a guarantee, or the terms of credit it offers. The tangible aspects include, besides the obvious characteristics of shape, form, and composition, less obvious elements of packaging and branding. Thus under this definition an 'own-label' version would be considered a different product from the branded item, even though all other characteristics except the label were identical.

Market definition can cause similar problems, and there can be few people who have not observed with some cynical amusement the way virtually any product can be proved to be a brand leader.

In practical terms there can be no universal definition of these words which is adequate for all companies. The right answer is for the company to apply definitions which suit its own purpose – the only rule is to be consistent.

One term which has been mentioned several times is 'synergy', the mystical force which means that the whole is greater than the sum of the two individual parts, which largely comes about because of the economies of scale which may occur in the larger unit – economies which may be in any area – management, production, physical distribution, marketing, research and development, or any other sector. In acquisition situations bitter experience has often shown that synergy is more illusory than real – but this is another story. As a generalisation, synergy might be expected to be highest in box (a) and lowest in box (d).

A further generalisation can be made about synergy in diversification. It is likely to be higher in horizontal or vertical diversification than in unrelated diversification. These terms are illustrated in Figure 14.4. Vertical diversification is integration backwards towards the raw material or forwards to the ultimate consumer. Horizontal diversification is moving towards activities on the same level in the chain, but which have common consumers or distribution channels. Unrelated diversification is moving into something which has nothing in common with the present business. Each is subject to a different pattern of risks.

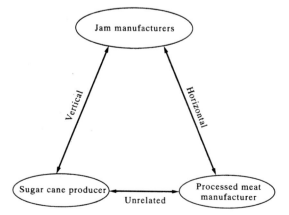

Figure 14.4
Types of
diversification

Customers	Products	Related Technology	New Technology
Existing	Existing	Wooden bedroom furniture	Metal beds
	Similar	Wooden dining room furniture	Electrically operated beds
	New	Wooden garden furniture	Electric blankets
Similar	Existing	Children's bedroom furniture	'Status' beds Built-in TV, etc.
	Similar	Fitted cupboards	Metal kitchen cabinets
	New	Wendy houses Climbing frames	Furnishing fabrics Stainless steel sinks
New	Existing	Contract sales to hotels	Bulk supply Metal school furniture
	Similar	Wooden display units	Medical inspection couches
	New	Coffins	Suspension filing systems
Firm Itself		Wooden mouldings Packing cases	Hinges Door fittings

Figure 14.5
'Synergy' chart for a company considering expansion/ diversification (in this case a manufacturer of wooden bedroom furniture). (Reproduced with permission from Hargreaves[9])

For example, although synergy might be high in vertical diversification, the fundamental risks to which the company is subject may not be changed: yet the amount of resources subject to those risks may be drastically increased.

Some writers suggest the preparation of a synergy chart as the next stage in the analysis. The example in Figure 14.5 is quoted from Hargreaves.[7] A similar approach is adopted by Ansoff.[5]

During the preparation of each of these stages of analysis, preliminary screening should take place and ideas which are obviously unattractive or impracticable discarded. This is very much a commonsense approach: the main problem being to be reasonably flexible in the rejection stage, and not to kill ideas just because they are different. The ideas which are left are intensively evaluated. One of Ansoff's[5] major contributions has been his work on this evaluation process, and the suggestion of methods of selection, which take into account both the concept of synergy and an approach to the probability of success.

Quite apart from the possible financial results of alternative strategies, it is very useful to relate the alternatives to the company's own capability profile and its available skills and resources (see Chapter 9), and the particular attributes which the corporate appraisal has revealed the most strategically desirable – for example, adjustments to the company's risk balance. The object of the exercise is to select those courses of action which most effectively fill the gap between current expectations and the primary objective, which capitalise on as many of the company's strengths as possible, remove or correct its weaknesses, which comply with its objectives and constraints, and which have the highest probability of success. The main purpose of drawing up check lists and rating opportunities against them is to ensure that no important factors are overlooked.

Screening our projects, arranging them in recommended selection order, and evaluating their prospects is an important staff planning function. The final choice of strategies is not: this is a task that management should not delegate to planners. And even in the screening process the conclusions are likely to be more valid if they are worked on by the management team rather than by the planning staff alone.

There are probably three main schools of thought over the way in which the strategic net should be cast when the company begins to fish for its alternatives. The first is that it should be solely an opportunist. Full-scale selection and screening techniques as described here are not required under these circumstances: all that the company need do is to try to keep itself in the situation where opportunities come its way. Such a company is, in fact, unlikely to practise any system of formal planning, and yet is often highly successful. This carries a lesson to the planner. Every plan should leave room for the possibility that unforeseen opportunities will arise – the possibility of the 'lucky break'. The planning system which precludes this sort of entrepreneurial activity is likely to do its company a disservice.

The second school of thought is that the net should be thrown as wide as it will stretch in an effort to draw in every single opportunity that it is humanly possible to identify. This needs a very extensive screening and evaluation process which, for many companies, may be beyond their resources. The trend of thinking through the 1980s has been to suggest that diversification leading to the conglomerate company rarely gives the best deal to shareholders. See, for example, Porter.[8]

The third school of thought is that most chief executives are only able to work in certain industry areas and have a definite concept of the type of activity they would be prepared to take their companies into. In effect the broad field is described in the company's objectives, and it would be wasting effort to try to fish for opportunities in other areas. Even so, the size of the fishing ground may still be very extensive.

As with so many other aspects of corporate planning, the 'right' answer is the one that fits the company. And as the company develops and changes so it may change its viewpoint and find another 'right' answer.

Certainly the approach selected will have an influence on the identification of opportunities. This brings us to the last topic in this chapter: before alternatives can be screened, analysed, and adopted, they must be found. The very practical question of 'How does a company identify new opportunities?' is one that causes concern to many managers. A few broad hints might help to put this problem in perspective.

At the outset it should be stressed that there is no substitute for individual creativity. Many of the best opportunities selected often arise simply because a creative person thought of them. Strategic planning can help by providing a framework through which these ideas can be channelled, as well as the use of particular techniques in the planning process (such as brainstorming meetings). The unexpected and unstructured 'good idea' is often one of the most effective. It has been said earlier that the planning process must seek to encourage individual creativity, not to destroy it.

The logical processes of analysis described in this and other chapters should also be expected to produce a good yield of opportunities. Environmental studies, the corporate appraisal, and the attempt to analyse various possible strategic moves can produce much that is worthwhile. For the analyst there may also be much that is tedious, a statement that will be endorsed by anyone that has searched industry lists for possible acquisition candidates. Frequently the clarity with which a company is, through its planning processes, able to examine its basic problems provides the new viewpoint that enables the solution to be found. Individual creativity may still be present in the finding of opportunities through analysis, but the advantage of an analytical process is that many opportunities can be uncovered even where individual creativity is low. A process of analysis, following predetermined concepts, starting wide and gradually narrowing down, can be rather like the net used by the trawlermen. Where the sea is rich the harvest of fish will be great – but if the wrong place is trawled the catch may be insignificant.

It would be wrong to conclude that all new opportunities are internally generated either by an 'ideas' person or an analyst. Most companies will also draw much from the marketplace: the more marketing-oriented the company, the more effort it will make to find out what its consumers want. In addition, some strategic alternatives may emerge from actual or anticipated moves by competitors. It is in these fields that a continuous programme of marketing research comes into its own – the continued probing of consumer requirements, and the testing of different interpretations of these should provide a flow of ideas. Some of these will lie within the strategic path determined already, although others might well take the company into new strategies.

At any point in time a company, particularly if it has invested heavily in research and development in the past, is likely to have a stream of projects ready for implementation over the next two to three years. This is today's position, and it may represent very welcome and important additions to the list of alternatives under consideration. The real problem of planning research and development is not how to make use of past ideas that have reached fruition, but how to ensure a continued flow of projects with a reasonable measure of control so that future requirements can also be met. This is a problem which will receive attention later.

The discovery of strategic alternatives is not a passive activity to be solved from behind a desk. Few planners can afford to wait for things to happen – and even fewer chief executives can afford this luxury. There is a great deal of hard work involved to be performed by the chief executive and planner or shared out among the management team. The deliberate attack on the future is by no means impossible and, indeed, is one of the aims of strategic management.

This chapter has only made a beginning, and much more remains to be discussed on the subject of strategic planning. It is a great mountain of a subject, and all we have done so far is to establish a base camp from which to begin the assault on the summit. In subsequent chapters there will be discussion of the main groups of alternatives the company might choose, an examination of techniques of portfolio analysis, particular reference to strategic planning for multinational business, and a chapter on the practical problems of writing a strategic plan. And all this before the specialist subjects of financial and human resources strategy are reached. Let us hope that the base camp is well established, for the mountain is an Everest.

References

1 Ansoff, H. I. *Planning as a Practical Management Tool*, Corporate Planning Seminar Manual, Bradford University, May 1966.
2 Kami, M. J. 'Gap Analysis – Key to Super Growth', *Long Range Planning*, June 1969.
3 Ackoff, R. C. *A Concept of Corporate Planning*, Wiley Interscience, New York, 1970.
4 Vancil, R. F. 'The Accuracy of Long Range Planning', *Harvard Business Review*, September-October 1970.
5 Ansoff, H. I. *Corporate Strategy*, McGraw-Hill New York, 1965.
6 McCarthy, E. J. *Basic Marketing: a Managerial Approach*, Unwin, London, 1964.
7 Hargreaves, D. 'Corporate Planning: a Chairman's Guide', *Long Range Planning*, March 1969.
8 Porter, M. 'From Competitive Advantage to Corporate Strategy', *Harvard Business Review*, May/June 1987.

CHAPTER 15

Strategic portfolio analysis

Complex situations require more complex methods of analysis. The intention of this chapter is to give the reader an insight into the portfolio analysis approach, and to show the relationship of the data considered to the concepts of industry analysis discussed in an earlier chapter. The value and pitfalls of the concept are described. The chapter explains how risk can be incorporated into portfolio analysis.

During the 1970s there were many major contributions to corporate planning. One of the most significant was undoubtedly strategic portfolio analysis. This technique, which can be found in many different variations, helped to satisfy the emerging need for centralised decisions on key strategic issues in multinational corporations. Portfolio analysis provided a means of comparing numerous business activities in relation to each other, establishing priorities and deciding between winners and losers.

The original work is accredited to General Electric whose concept included dividing activities into *strategic business units* with like characteristics, related to the life cycles of the products. Strategic business units may be a composite of product and geographical area. It is quite possible for a product to be in a mature stage in developed countries and in a take-off phase in less developed ones. This life-cycle difference could result in two strategic business units, instead of one on a more traditional product grouping.

The Boston Consulting Group deserve much of the credit for developing and popularising the technique. It is this organisation's 2 × 2 matrix with its evocative terminology which has captured the imagination of modern business. The broadly descriptive labels attached to each box in the matrix, cash cows, dogs, stars and question marks, have become part of the language of management and are quite frequently used by those who are ignorant of the underlying technique.

One axis of the Boston matrix measures growth and the other relative market share and the whole edifice is based on the assumption that these are the two major factors affecting profitability, which although it may sometimes be true is by no means a universal law. The Boston concept was linked to their theories of experience curves, which postulate a phenomenon that costs will fall by a regular percentage every time output doubles. Put together the two techniques postulate a strategy of competitive dominance and an emphasis on high market shares in high growth activities.

Much of this is open to question, and indeed is increasingly being questioned, and Boston Consulting have their critics as well as their adherents.[1,2] Competitive techniques to the Boston Consulting approach are numerous: most merely replace one axis with another factor empirically considered to be more relevant. On a broader front the Strategic Planning Institute runs a multicompany activity (PIMS) which attempts to isolate key variables from a study of actual data submitted by its member-subscribers. This service is well thought of by large companies where sufficient industry data exist on the PIMS files, and provides empirical evidence of links between factors such as growth, market share, promotional expenditure, research and development and the like, and can be used as a basis for portfolio analysis.

Hofer, in a diagram used in Hofer and Schendel,[3] suggests a different approach to portfolio analysis. His matrix has the stages of the life cycle on one axis (development, growth, shake-out, maturity to saturation, and decline), and competitive position on the other (strong, average and weak). This offers a useful way of seeing a number of corporate activities in a comparative way, without pretending to be a formula for strategic decisions. One of the weaknesses of the Boston Consulting approach is that it became a recipe for strategy: invest in stars so that they continue to shine, divest dogs, because they will do you no good, use the cash from cash cows to choose winners from the question marks (later christened by others *wildcats*) and to support the stars.

Barksdale and Harris[4] combined the Boston Consulting Matrix with a life-cycle approach. This had the result of questioning whether all dogs consumed resources without delivering benefit. They pointed out that there were dogs that could be turned into useful businesses, just as there were 'dodos' that had nowhere to go. Later someone else renamed the dodo 'underdogs', which is rather neat. They also identified 'war horses' as an additional variety of cash cow, where business was declining, but the activity would go on and on generating cash. Although the additional farmyard terminology helped expand the original thinking, the result is still strategy by formula: if it falls within a certain box on the matrix, do what the box says. This worries me, as it did many of the critics of portfolio analysis. Buzzell and Gale[5] published a summary of principles drawn from the PIMS database. Among their conclusions, which we will revisit in more detail in a later chapter, was:

> Many so-called 'dog' and 'question mark' businesses generate cash, while many 'cash cows' are dry.

I believe that portfolio analysis is a very useful tool, that can give insights into many strategic situations. However, I prefer to use it for two main purposes. One is to look at activities within the organisation relative to each other, so that strategic issues can be surfaced. The second is to make the analysis more future oriented by looking at the likely movements across the portfolio, and the impact of actions that the company or competitors can instigate. To do this requires an approach that generates a deep understanding of the factors which really influence business success, and which can be related to other analytical approaches. This chapter will describe just such a technique, and in the following chapter a case study will be provided to give more insight into its application and interpretation.

Only one of the techniques, as far as I am aware, attempts to develop deep understanding of the factors which really influence business success. This is the directional policy matrix (DPM) developed by Shell Chemicals[6,7] and made into a three-dimensional matrix by consultants Harbridge House.[8] The DPM is a 3 × 3 matrix measuring on one axis the factors which influence long-term profitability in the market and, on the other, those which account for longer-term competitive position. The position of a strategic business unit on each axis is determined from a weighting of numerous subfactors. What is most significant about these is that they can be related to economic theory which explains what influences power within an industry: in fact it is of value to examine this structural analysis of industry before considering the DPM in any depth.

The Harbridge House addition is in the form of a risk matrix which, with the market success axis in common with the DPM, turns it into a three-dimensional box which can easily be modelled in clear plastic; or even more easily can be handled as a narrative qualification to the analysis of each strategic business unit or recorded on two dimensions by colour codes.

That axis of the risk matrix which is not shared with the DPM measures risk from the major environmental forces. The position on this axis is scored taking both impact and probability into account, and producing a composite score from an examination of the risks to which each strategic business unit is subject. This additional dimension is very helpful when strategic decisions are being considered, and enables top management to gain a clear insight into the main strategic issues they face.

Most general economic textbooks deal with market structures, and the concepts of perfect and imperfect competition. All things being equal, we would expect a company to earn higher profits, the closer it comes to being a monopoly; conversely, profitability might be expected to decline as the company's activities came closer to meeting the conditions of perfect competition. The difference between the two conditions is the degree of power over the supply curve, in relation to demand and the degree of freedom of the firm to set prices.

The underlying theory has been worked into a practical analysis by Porter[9] (see Chapter 10). Following his line of thought it is possible to visualise an industry in the manner described in Figure 10.2, as five groups of interrelated forces operating within the framework of the external environment. The eight-sided figure represents one way of visualising the external environment, which has been dealt with in more detail in earlier chapters. These forces, although of the utmost significance to firms in the industry, are generally common to all competitors, although their impact will vary from firm to firm.

Readers will remember from Chapter 10 that the central box in the diagram deals with the competitors in the industry. Although there are a number of clear-cut factors which affect the degree and depths of competitive rivalry, this is also modified by the power of suppliers and buyers. The greater the power and influence of these two groups, the lower profitability tends to become in the industry. Both of these boxes should be analysed to the required depth relevant to the industry. Buyers, for example, would normally be divided into wholesalers, retailers and the consumer. For industrial products there may be further manufacturers. Relationships between each of these buyer groups will be significant in the overall examination of factors which affect profitability.

Not surprisingly, the industry is also affected by the availability of close substitutes. A near-monopoly position in one product may be effectively threatened by substitute products and the firm may find that this seriously affects its prospects. The question of substitutes also has to be considered in deciding on the relevant boundaries of the industry, a point which will be returned to later.

The final box deals with the possibility of completely new entrants joining the industry, and the possibility of firms leaving the industry. Ease of entry or exit is likely to affect the behaviour and profitability of firms in an industry.

Before exploring the implications of these factors for portfolio analysis, which we will deal with shortly, the analyst has to answer the question: 'What is the relevant definition of the industry?' This is often easier to ask than to answer, and has dimensions of product/market characteristics and geography. The widest possible definition of products/markets would sweep all the substitutes into the competitors' box, and result in a canvas too vast for the type of picture that needs painting. On the other hand, too narrow a focus, such as one product out of a vast industry, will distort perspective. If the portion of the artist's canvas which is examined is too small, it will not be possible to draw any conclusions about the picture. These issues were discussed in Chapter 10, but are worth repeating here.

The dilemma is illustrated in Figure 15.1, where alternative views of an industry are presented. The final decision has to be made in the light of knowledge of the industry and its markets and the purpose of the analysis. An examination of Ford might, because of its wide interests and integrated position, focus on the entire automotive industry. A manufacturer of invalid cars might gain no value from such a broad picture, and could benefit more from a study of its segment of the industry. If there is a principle, it is to start broad and to narrow down if the canvas is too big.

A related problem is one of geographical scope, illustrated in a similar way in Figure 15.2. Here the criterion is one of normal competition and the existence of

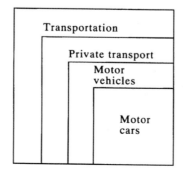

Figure 15.1
What market?

Figure 15.2
What geographical
market?

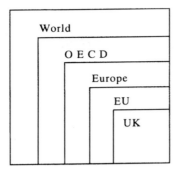

natural or artificial barriers to foreign competitors. Perspective may change over time: at one period it was possible to take a meaningful view of the UK petrochemicals industry; now a regional Western Europe view is the minimum common sense would suggest. Again the right decision is likely to be broad rather than narrow, and has to be taken in the context of the specific industry.

Neither of these problems are unique to industry analysis and they recur in strategic portfolio analysis in the definition of meaningful strategic business units and strategic business areas. A workable decision is thus essential for both types of analysis, and if both are considered together it should be possible to find common definitions.

The difficulty of reaching the right solution is one of the vulnerable areas in both approaches, since the action prompted by the analysis may well be both wrong and dangerous if the answer is wrong.

There is also the danger of treating the approaches as if they resulted in a series of natural laws which automatically dictate the only possible strategy. History proves that some companies can prosper in industries that look sick, because of particular efficiencies of operation, a carefully chosen niche in the markets, or occasionally for a reason which seems to defy analysis.

One approach which is very useful is to apply industry structure analysis at the level of the strategic business unit, using the data generated as one source of information for portfolio analysis. This has the advantage of providing valuable strategic insight of a type appropriate for each level in the company. It also means that at corporate level there is no need to request a long list of data from strategic business units which is of no value to the unit providing it, nor is there a need to embark on expensive surveys duplicating data already available elsewhere in the organisation. There may of course be a need to work independently to check data or fill gaps.

The market prospects axis of the matrix

The market prospects axis consists of three groups of factors which analyse the industry as a whole. The descriptions used vary to some degree from those in the material published by Shell,[6] and include my own experience of using the approach in a number of industries and situations. The factors are compared with points of principle from industry-structure analysis so that similarities and common ground can be seen. In this comparison the debt to both Professor Mike Porter and the Shell analysts must be fully acknowledged since the analysis is built on their original work.

Directional policy matrix weighting

1. Market growth   *4 points*

(Scored on a pre-established scale which relates to the firm or industry under consideration).

2. Market 'quality'   *4 points*

2.1.   Relative profitability of sector, and stability of profits.

2.2.   Are margins maintained in times of overcapacity?

2.3.   Is the product resistant to commodity pricing behaviour?

2.4.   Is the technology of the product freely available or protected?

2.5.   Is the market supplied by a relatively few competitors?

Industry-structure analysis

1.   Rivalry in an industry will tend to increase as growth rates slow, and competitors can no longer satisfy objectives from primary demand increases, and so begin to fight harder for brand share.

2.1.   High profitability may attract new entrants to the industry, therefore entry barriers should be carefully studied.

2.2.1.   Competition increases when fixed costs are high, incremental capital investments are large, or external factors lead to severe and often occurring excess.

2.2.2.   The degree of contention in an industry will increase when the product is perishable or expensive to store.

2.3.   The greater the differentiations between products, the easier will competition become.

2.4.   Patent and similar protection tends to restrict new entrants to the industry. It may also increase the degree of product differentiation.

2.5.   The profits of an industry tend to be adversely affected as competitors increase in number. This trend may be accentuated when competitiors are both numerous and of similar size.

314

Directional policy matrix weighting	Industry-structure analysis
2.6. Is the market dominated by a few powerful customers?	2.6. Profits tend to be adversely affected as the power of the buyer *vis-à-vis* the industry firm increases. Particular points which affect buyer power are:

- Domination by few powerful buying firms, particularly when these take a high proportion of the output of the industry;
- When the buyer offers a credible threat of backwards integration (conversely, a credible threat of forwards integration by firms in the industry may reduce the relative power of buyers);
- When the buying firms are in a low profit industry; and

2.7. Does the buyer's final product have high added value?	2.7. When the buying firm has low added value, and therefore little room to adjust margins.
2.8. In the case of a new product is the market likely to remain small enough not to attract competitors?	2.8. Refer to 2.5 and to 'Entry barriers'.
2.9. Is the product one where a change by the buyer would mean a change in machinery or formulation?	2.9. Bargaining power of buyers is reduced (and that of the industry firm increased) when the buying firm is bound by the economic costs of changing production processes, plant, methods or obtaining new clearances from regulatory bodies.
2.10. Is the product vulnerable to substitutes?	2.10. At best, substitutes put a ceiling on the prices and profits of the industry. At worst, they may capture the entire market.

3. Raw material and supplies   4 points

3.1. Are there any industry problems in obtaining supplies of components and raw materials?	3.1. –

315

Directional policy matrix weighting

3.2. What is the ratio of supplier firms to industry firms for each major component or material?

3.3. To what extent are substitute supplies and raw materials available?

3.4. Does the industry purchase a high proportion of the output of the supplying industry?

Industry-structure analysis

3.2. The bargaining power of suppliers (of important items) tends to increase at the cost of industry profits as the supplying industry becomes less 'competitive' (that is the fewer and larger the firms in the supplying industry).

3.3. This works in the same way as 2.10, but as an advantage to the industry when substitutes are available.

3.4. When this is the case, the bargaining power of the supplier is reduced, and industry opportunity for profit increased. At the same time it may encourage suppliers to try to help the growth of the industry on which they are so dependent.

But suppliers' power is enhanced when they offer a credible threat of forward integration, and reduced when the industry offers a real threat of backwards integration.

Entry/exit barriers
Entry and exit barriers receive more emphasis in the Porter analysis, since entry barriers reduce the risk of increased competition, while exit barriers force competitors to behave more aggressively since they cannot easily realise their investment.

Entry barriers include: high capital investment; specialised high cost plant; patents; product differentiation; highly efficient producers; complex distribution networks.

My own experience is that the answers to each subquestion in the directional policy matrix need to be scored and weighted (see the next chapter), and I have found empirically that the matrix has meaning when approximately half the weighting is assigned to a combination of market growth and profitability and the remainder to those other factors which are likely to affect future profitability.

The competitive capability axis

A similar comparison can be made of questions considered in the other axis of the directional policy matrix, and a further set of factors analysed in industry structure analysis. (Industry structure analysis treats these in the context of the diagram in Figure 10.1 and not as a matrix.)

Directional policy matrix

1. Market position   *weighting 4 points*

1.1. The concept is one of leadership rather than brand share.
Scoring positions are:
Leader (4) Followed by others in pricing and usually has a pre-eminent market share.
Major producer (3) When no company is a leader, but a number are well placed.
Viable producer (2) Strong viable position but below top league.
Minor producer (1) Inadequate to support position in long run.
Others (0).

2. Production capability   *weighting 4 points*

2.1. Economics of production (relative to competitors).
2.2. Available capacity.
2.3. Geographical distribution of capacity.
2.4. Security of raw materials and supplies.

3. Product research and development   *weighting 4 points*

This is a compound question dealing with the ability of the company to support its market share in the future (R&D, technical service, product development, etc.).

Industry-structure analysis

1.1. Competition increases (and industry profits tend to fall) as the number of competitiors in an industry increases, and as they become more equal in relative size and bargaining power.

It is the relative positions which are frequently as important as the absolute.
1.2. Competition becomes more volatile as companies develop different 'personalities'. A newcomer to an industry will often upset the unwritten 'rules' in the industry.

2. Competitive analysis would be made of each of these factors. Question 2.4 would also be considered in relation to the points on a credible threat of backward integration.

Again, when plotting positions on the competitive axis of the DPM, I have found it convenient to assign half of the total weighting to historical performance and the other half to those factors likely to affect future performance.

317

Portfolio analysis in practice

Figure 15.3 provides an example of the directional matrix completed for some hypothetical strategic business areas, and this may serve as an example of how all the other portfolio analysis techniques are applied.

Three of the boxes are labelled with words suggesting that divestment is the approximate action to consider, because of weakness in market growth and position. Two boxes suggest cash generators. In both cases there may be need for some maintenance investment ('Proceed with care' suggests *slightly* more generous investment policies), but for both the aim should be to harvest as much cash flow as possible.

Four boxes imply different approaches to growth strategies. 'Leader' and 'Growth' both suggest investment is worth while, but carry the implication that the growth box should aim for a balanced cash flow, while the leader box may be both cash hungry and supported. 'Double or Quit' really says choose some of these, back them to grow, and get out if they fail. It is from this box that future 'leaders' should come. The remaining box is a reminder that a little more effort might bring that leadership position.

I do not use these labels when I apply the technique, because they are statements of tendency rather than fact, at least when applied outside of the chemicals industry. It is useful to know them, but the temptation to plan by recipe should be avoided.

Now if an organisation could array all its activities on such a matrix it at least has a preliminary indication of what might be a sensible overall corporate

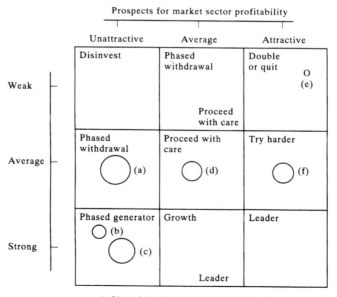

Figure 15.3
Example of DPM

1. Size of circles proportionate to turnover
2. Strategic business units indicated by letters

Exhibit 15.1 Using portfolio analysis at Vickers

Some of the early writing on portfolio analysis implied that the technique was almost strategy by formula. I have never used the method in this way. When Vickers and Rolls-Royce merged in 1980, they had around 35 business units, with activities varying from office furniture to the Rolls-Royce car, from business stationery to armoured fighting vehicles. Portfolio analysis, using the scoring method given in detail in the next chapter, was used to give a view of the prospects of each business, relative to all the other businesses, and to show how much of the corporate asset base was tied up in each. A dynamic view was taken of some businesses, showing the effect of various options that were under consideration on the position of the businesses affected. Behind each entry on the portfolio chart was a Porter-type analysis of the structure of the industry, completed by the business unit teams.

The analysis was used to give a perspective to top-level discussions about the future shape of the business, and to explore which of the businesses had to think globally if they were to continue to be successful.

A result, after two top management conferences, was that the organisation accepted that the resources were not available to support all the businesses to enable them to compete effectively, therefore the strategy had to be to determine a few core businesses, and divest the remainder of the portfolio in order to provide capital to invest in the core.

The core was initially six businesses, plus one or two others where there was some initial uncertainty. Some major investments were made in these businesses as the divestments brought results, such as the purchase of the Royal Ordnance tank factory.

One of the core businesses, making lithographic printing plates, was sold as this business became more competitive on a global scale. In 1997, press reports say that another core business making health care equipment is up for sale.

I remember saying to Sir David Plastow, then the managing director of Vickers, that portfolio analysis of this type was more helpful in signalling precisely what not to do. One dimension not covered by the portfolio analysis, but which the planning team struggled with, were the common technologies that went across the various businesses. If the portfolio analysis put down paving stones for each business, there was also a strategic need to be sure that opportunities did not fall through the cracks.

(*Sources*: personal experience D. E. Hussey; *Vickers Plc (A)*, a case study, Professor John Stopford, London Business School, 1989: press reports. Note: any details that might be considered normally to be confidential about my consulting work have appeared in the case study) strategy to each. And if each has been plotted using industry structure analysis, the positions in the matrix should be backed by carefully thought-out strategic business unit strategies. Put the risk analysis behind the matrix, in a series of categories of low risk, average and high risk, and a new dimension of thought is opened up.

A number of observations should be made. First, the position on the matrix is not an eternal truth. Over time, in line with product life-cycle theories one might expect a decline in prospects, a drift towards the left of the matrix. Similarly, one might postulate an increasing tendency for a decline in each position. The overall effect suggests that today's leaders may become tomorrow's cash generators, and ultimately candidates for divestment. Understanding and managing the drift is an important aspect of strategic management.

Second, the grids on the matrix are not finite barriers. Interpretation is very difficult when a strategic business unit falls near a boundary. A high degree of judgement in interpreting results is needed, and the techniques are certainly no black box.

Third, the importance of the point made earlier about getting the strategic business area sensibly defined becomes very apparent from a glance at the matrix. A high position in a fast-growing segment might put the SBU into the leadership box if defined in segment terms. If looked at on a larger canvas this could translate to a slow-growing market in which the company has a poor position, which might indicate divestment. Getting the approach right requires much searching thought, and is unlikely to be the same answer for each organisation.

Fourth, it is easy to see that the different types of strategic positioning of the SBUs requires managers of different capabilities, personalities and skills. The entrepreneurial manager may fit the 'double or quit' business, and be quite incapable of running a cash generator effectively. Managing an operation for planned divestment also calls for a different degree of talent. Some work has already been done on matching people to opportunity[10,11] and it is a field wide open for significant academic study.

No one should imagine that this, or any other portfolio analysis technique, can solve all strategic problems. If this simplistic view could be taken, strategy would be reduced to four or five groups of decisions and life is much more complex than this. What the matrix should do is highlight *indicative* action for further investigation, and also provide a way of seeing all parts of a complex company in relation to each other – reduced to one piece of paper for those whose managements properly understand the technique. My own experience has found it to be a useful approach to take discussions back to corporate objectives and philosophical arguments on the nature and shape of company desired and, then, into the organisational and people's problems of attaining it. Thus, strategic decisions become well rounded and give attention to all the problems involved in implementation.

Portfolio analysis will not work for everyone. Businesses where market share is unimportant for success (for example, agriculture) cannot sensibly be analysed, particularly if reasons for being in them are associated with capital appreciation and tax advantages. (Products requiring regional or local markets can usually be evaluated if the geographical scope of the market is sensibly defined.)

It may also fail in an organisation with complex production interrelationships. Give up product *x* may be wrong advice if in fact it is a byproduct and failure to dispose of this at the best price would alter the cost structure of product *y*. This is really an argument for understanding the businesses before they are plotted on the matrix, and a reinforcement for carrying out industry-structure analysis as a prerequisite step.

Risk matrix

Risk takes many forms as has been discussed in earlier chapters, and there are techniques for examining different aspects. These vary from the methods of analysing risk by discounted cash-flow methods (Hertz[12]) – DCF will be returned to in a later chapter – to a number of ways of looking at environmental risk, which we have discussed previously.[13]

Shell[14] describes another method of looking at environmental risk, primarily on a broader front. The result is again to force consideration of the issues and to gain some awareness of danger areas for which special strategies might be necessary.

The risk matrix discussed in detail here was first described in Hussey,[8] and, as mentioned earlier in this chapter, is used to give a third dimension to portfolio analysis. It could be used as a stand-alone technique but interpretation is considerably more meaningful if it is used in the way described. Although my experience has been to apply it as part of my modified directional-policy-matrix approach, it could be altered to fit any method of portfolio analysis.

There is no need to describe the axis it holds in common with the directional policy matrix. The remaining axis is a scored position based on an assessment of the specific environmental factors that appear to be of concern; the score is arrived at by considering both the probability of occurrence and the potential impact on the organisation. Figure 15.4 provides an example of the worksheet and the scoring methods.

As with all the approaches, the real issue is in deciding which of the many environmental aspects are likely to be of concern, and which for practical purposes can be ignored. (The answer will vary with the strategic business unit and area.) The methods used to arrive at this assessment vary from backroom analysis to ways of mobilising management judgement at various levels of the organisation. Both can be useful, and it is often advantageous to combine them.

I have frequently used a questionnaire approach on an individual plus small-group discussion basis to follow the backroom analysis. The questionnaire not only provides check lists which aid consideration (these are varied, because environmental issues facing, for example, a bank are not all of the same type as those of concern to an industrial company). The questionnaire carefully considers the issues in relation to the manager's view of the organisation, identifies his or her perception of the organisational response, compares with the way the organisation has responded in the past, and finishes by analysing detailed actions that should be taken. (See Chapter 7 for more detail.)

(a) Individual scoring of risk is achieved by multiplying the score for probability by the score for impact, using the following scales:

Impact		Probability		
Extremely high	6	A certainty	100%	6
	5	Very likely	84%	5
High	4	Quite possible	67%	4
	3	As likely as not	50%	3
Relatively low	2	Probably not	33%	2
	1	Highly unlikely	16%	1
None	0	Impossible	–	0

Scoring examples
Impact extremely high and Probability a certainty: 6 x 6 = 36
Impact high and Probability very likely: 4 x 5 = 20
Impact low and Probability very likely: 1 x 5 = 5

(The scores derived from the environmental assessment method of chapter 7)

(b) Example of work sheet for environmental risk (hypothetical data)

	Strategic business areas		
Environmental factor	A	B	C
Inflation above 15% p.a.	3 x 4 = 12	–	6 x 4 = 24
Labour militancy	6 x 6 = 36	6 x 5 = 30	3 x 3 = 9
Anti-pollution legislation	1 x 4 = 4	6 x 6 = 36	–
Increase in VAT	3 x 3 = 9	6 x 6 = 36	3 x 3 = 9
Nationalization of major customer	6 x 6 = 36	–	–
Social attitude–anti-profit	4 x 4 = 16	6 x 4 = 24	1 x 1 = 1
Total score	113	126	43
Average score	18.8	31.5	10.75
Interpretation	Medium–high risk	Very high risk	Medium risk

Note: (i) Probability score can vary by SBA if the geographical area is different.
  (ii) It is also possible to add scores across to see a seriousness weighting of the factor on the total company–but be careful when SBAs are in different areas, since the combined factor may then have little meaning.

Figure 15.4
Risk matrix scoring

An advantage of the risk matrix is, like the other two approaches, that it forces thought about the issues. In addition, it provides an overview of the entire organisation and one that can be related to the strategic importance of each business unit and to the importance of each to the organisation.

This last point can be covered by plotting each position on both the DPM and risk matrix by drawing circles whose size is proportional to importance. Another approach is to redraw the matrices inserting total figures for profit contributions, sales, capital employed, cash flow, etc. for the activities which fall within each box.

Figure 15.5
The risk matrix

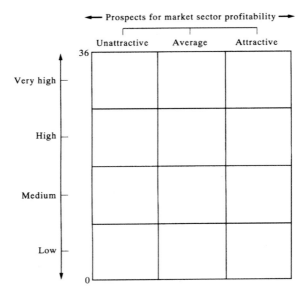

← Prospects for market sector profitability →

| Unattractive | Average | Attractive |

Figure 15.6
Combined three-
dimensional matrix,
portfolio analysis
plus risk

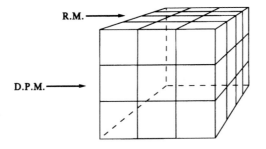

Figure 15.5 provides an example of the risk matrix. Figure 15.6 shows this as the third dimension of the DPM: the use of perspex blocks as illustrated makes it easy to provide a visual representation and has much appeal as a desktop toy, although the same visual impact can be gained at lower cost by using different colours to show different levels of risk on a single plane.

Despite their defects, the portfolio-analysis techniques have taken the practice of planning several steps forward, and have much to offer the complex organisation.

References

1 Thackray, J. 'The Corporate Strategy Problem', *Management Today*, October 1979.
2 Hamermesh, R. G., Anderson, M. J. and Harris, J. 'Strategies for Low Market Share Businesses', *Harvard Business Review*, May–June 1978, pp. 95–102.
3 Hofer, C. W. and Schendel, D. *Strategy Formulation: Analytical Concepts*, West Publishing, St Paul, MN, 1978.

4 Barksdale, H. C. and Harris, C. E. 'Portfolio Analysis and the Product Life Cycle', *Long Range Planning*, 15, No. 6, 1982.

5 Buzzell, R. D. and Gale, B. T. *The PIMS Principles*, Free Press, New York, 1987.

6 Anon. *The Directional Policy Matrix: An Aid to Corporate Planning*, 2nd edn, Shell International Chemical Co, 1979.

7 Robinson, S. J. O., Hitchens, R. E. and Wade, D. P. 'The Directional Policy Matrix – Tool For Strategic Planning', *Long Range Planning*, 11, No. 3, 1978.

8 Hussey, D. E. 'Portfolio Analysis: Practical Experiences with the Directional Policy Matrix', *Long Range Planning*, 11, No. 4, 1978.

9 Porter, M. E. *Note on the Structural Analysis of Industries*, Harvard Business School, 1975.

10 Pappas, N. 'Corporate Planning at Du Pont', *Chemicals Engineering Process*, June 1978.

11 *Business Week*. 'Wanted – a Manager for Each Strategy', 25 February 1980.

12 Hertz, D. 'Risk Analysis in Capital', *Harvard Business Review*, January/February 1964.

13 Newbauer, F. F. and Solomon, N. B. 'A Managerial Approach to Environmental Assessment', *Long Range Planning*, April 1977.

14 Shell, Societal response matrix.

Further reading

For those who would like to explore some of the other methods of portfolio analysis I recommend the following two books which are linked. The first describes eight approaches, looking at the strengths and weaknesses of each. Included are a variant of the Shell matrix and an early version of my risk matrix. The companion book is a form of tutorial for the Compass Matrix Portfolio Analysis Support System (a disk is included), and enables the user to apply all the approaches with the aid of a PC. The books are highly recommended (really you need both) for anyone wishing to explore more of the techniques).

Segev, E. *Corporate Strategy: Portfolio Models*, Thomson International/Boyd & Fraser, London, 1995.

Segev, E. *Navigating by Compass: Corporate Matrix Portfolio Analysis Support System*, Thomson International/Boyd & Fraser, London, 1995.

CHAPTER 16

Portfolio analysis in practice

Many of the criticisms of portfolio analysis are based on misunderstandings about how it should be used. The aim of this chapter is twofold, first, by practical demonstration to show how portfolio analysis can be applied and used, and second, to provide scoring rules which can be adapted for use in real situations. The chapter explores the wrong strategic indications that can arise when the market is incorrectly defined.

The purpose of this chapter is to illustrate the application and use of two particular methods of portfolio analysis. The first is derived from the directional policy matrix. The second is the risk matrix. Both were described in outline in the previous chapter. In order to achieve this purpose a fictional company, Good Investments plc, is described. This company has a wide spectrum of businesses. Although the company does not exist, the situation it faces does. The industries and dilemmas are all ones in which I have had experience, and Good Investments is a sort of disguised composite of consulting work with several clients. The data given about the industries and markets are also disguised, so do not be tempted to use it for a real analysis. The example is set in a normal period: in other words no recession is in progress. Also, because it had to be written at a certain time, industry prospects may have changed by the time you read this: if this is the case, please suspend disbelief in order to see how to score and plot businesses on the matrices, and how to use them. The material is adapted from a case study I wrote for Harbridge Consulting Group, and is used with permission.

Good Investments (GI): the background

In recent years the company has not performed well, and the institutional shareholders are demanding action. They wanted a pre-tax return on capital employed of something more than 15 per cent (which they felt was the average return in the UK), and they also wanted a profit growth target of at least 3–4 per cent per year.

GI consisted of eight major divisions with a combined turnover of about £500 million. By far the largest division was industrial fasteners (£200 million) which was currently turning in a poor performance. During the two years of the recent recession it had made small profits, and last year produced a modest increase in profit. During this period it had invested heavily in new plant 'to gain market share'.

Historically this division was very significant as it was the foundation business of the group and had in the past contributed the cash which had enabled the other business to be acquired or developed. It held about 50 per cent of its rather specialised world markets, and its current business plan was to invest several million pounds in a new-look marketing campaign, and to build a new divisional headquarters office to 'restore morale'.

The general feeling of the GI board was that fasteners had done so much for the firm in the past that it should now be supported in its time of need. Its competitors included a US group which had 40 per cent of the market, but which also operated in a number of other unrelated fastener segments not touched by GI. The remaining 10 per cent share was held by three small competitors. Everyone was aware that the fasteners market would show only very small growth in the future of not more than 1 per cent per year.

General Hydraulics was the second largest division with £100 million turnover. It had a 10 per cent market share of a large but declining world market, and was a poor third in the market to a German company (30 per cent) and a US company (25 per cent). This had always been a problem division, making profits on average only about one year in every three. It had been reorganised several times in its twelve-year history. Currently the division's management were negotiating the purchase of the hydraulics interests (about 3 per cent of market) of a diversified giant company. A purchase price of £20 million was speculated. The main benefit of the acquisition was seen as the opportunity to put more production through GI's hydraulics plant. However, the industrial relations problems and the costs of closing the other plant on acquisition had not yet been evaluated.

Pneumatics was a good cash-contributing division, with products allied to defence. At £75 million turnover, which had shown no real growth over the past few years, it managed to make 15 per cent return on capital employed and was a major cash contributor. It was estimated that it held about 60 per cent of the UK market in its specialist application, the remainder being shared between four other British firms. The market was unlikely to grow in future, but existing contracts meant that business was secure for at least another three years.

Oil Rig Services (£40 million turnover) provided an engineering support service to the offshore petroleum industry. This was an essentially local business operating out of Aberdeen and had 45 per cent of the market in that area. Previously high rates of growth of 10 per cent per year had slackened to around 2 per cent, which was the forecast rate for the foreseeable future. Expansion of market share locally was highly unlikely. If significant expansion of business was wanted the division would have to replicate its activities in other geographical locations and fight against entrenched competition.

General Engineering Contracting had a £30 million turnover. It had been very profitable but was affected badly by the recession and by technological advances which meant that to stay competitive it had to make a significant investment. It held 10 per cent of a fragmented market where all activities tended to be restricted to the UK. Its management expected to break even unless new investment was made, in which case a 3 per cent return on capital employed was forecast.

The rate of return (discounted cash flow basis) on the new investment was exceptionally high, and most board members of GI felt that the £6 million modernisation programme should be approved, despite the fact that the market showed no signs of growth. The general feeling was that past heavy investment in this division had to be protected.

GI had stumbled into machine tools almost by accident, but through the personal energies of one of the main board members had built a profitable £10 million turnover business in a growth niche in the market. The division had been yielding a 20 per cent return on capital employed. It had a respected name in the UK with a 20 per cent market share, but did not trade in other countries. Lately new Japanese competitors had come into the market. The board thought that the market share could be defended easily against the Japanese, and felt it appropriate that GI should have this stake in applied high technology.

Another high-technology business was personal computers. The product aimed at the small business. In its three years of operation in the UK market the firm had grown from zero to £25 million of highly profitable turnover. Over the next three years its sales were expected to increase eightfold, and that included allowance for a fall in market share from 75 per cent to 55 per cent. Currently 25 per cent return on capital employed was earned, but the business was cash hungry and continually had to invest to meet the increased production needs. A £50 million investment plan featured in the demands of the UK market and a foothold into the as yet undeveloped European market. Some board members believed that the division should only be allowed to reinvest what it earned itself, otherwise it would take away resources 'earned by fasteners and needed by fasteners'. There was also a feeling that the market outside the UK could wait until the British market had been dealt with.

The eighth division was GI Security which had two product areas – guarding services and security vehicle services at £10 million turnover each. The former was labour intensive and a highly fragmented market with low entry barriers. The market was static and the activity did little better than break even.

Security vehicles were profitable, and entry barriers were higher because of the investment needed for security vaults and vehicles. GI had 10 per cent of the overall market and was number four out of six competitors. However, it only operated in 20 per cent of the population areas in the UK, and in those areas success was much higher (around 50 per cent of the market). The market was growing at 3 per cent per annum, but expansion of market share was related to the investment in vaults in new geographical areas.

Analysing GI

The difficulty of the situation described above is that, through conventional means, it is not easy to see the relative merits of the components of the total company. Without this relative view, it may also be difficult to decide investment priorities. Are the schemes in hand the best use of resources? We need also to look at the question of shareholder value, and whether such a wide dispersion of activity can be good for the shareholders. In a real-life situation in which I was involved when Vickers and Rolls-Royce Motors merged, the problem was that the company had too many businesses, and not enough funds to develop them all properly: the danger was that this could have led to poor results for all of them: for a description of this work see Stopford.[1]

Portfolio analysis can help create a strategic understanding, but the information given so far for GI is inadequate for this purpose. The analyst would have to probe deeper, and Tables 16.1 and 16.2 provide the data that will enable us to plot positions on the portfolio matrix.

The scoring rules for plotting the matrix positions are set out in the Appendix to this chapter. They make a boring read, but are essential for anyone who wishes to apply the method to a real situation. Tables 16.3 and 16.4 show how the rules are applied to the facts set out in the earlier exhibits. Figure 16.1 shows the matrix with the various businesses positioned: the numbers key to the numbers on the exhibits. The sizes of the circles are designed to give an impression of the relative size of sales turnover of each business (see Table 16.5). It might have been better to use net assets as a base had this information been available. Profits are another base that could have been compared, except that I do not know the best way of treating losses on such a diagram. A further method, which is sometimes useful, is to show a pie diagram proportionate to market size, with a slice representing the company's market share. An even more ambitious approach is to show the 'served market', that is, the segment or sector in which the company operates as a pie slice of the total market, and the market share of the served market as a further slice.

In this example the impact is meant to be visual, as a reminder of the importance of each business to GI, and there is no information to go deeper than this.

The matrix offers a better way of viewing the company. At this stage I have only plotted the present situation, and have taken statements about the geographical scope of the business at face value. Later we will question some of the assumptions, and look at the impact on positioning of some of the strategies that have been suggested. Viewing all these businesses at once, in a strategic way, on one piece of paper, makes it easier to reach decisions that are in the interests of the whole.

I have avoided attaching labels to the boxes on the matrix, because I think that this can lead to a formula approach to decisions. In real life, I would never wish to plot positions on the matrix unless I had also undertaken industry analysis, as it is very easy to misinterpret the prospects for a business. The fact that a business is doing well or badly is partly to do with markets and the structure of the

Table 16.1 Acts and judgements: GI portfolio – market prospects

Market factors	Industrial Fasteners	General Hydraulics	Pneumatics	Oil Rig Services	General Engineering Contracting	Machine Tools	Personal Computers	Guarding services	Security vehicle services
1 Market growth	<1%	Declining	Static	2%	Static	3.5%	Over 100%	Static	3%
2 Industry profitability	125	5%	16%	20%	5%	16%	20%	3%	15%
3 Stability of margin	Modest reductions in margins	Significant margin erosion	Occasional price cutting	Occasional price cutting	No margin control	Occasional price cutting	Little or no change in margins	No margin control	Modest reductions in margins
4 Degree of product differentiation	Modest differentiation	Modest differentiation	Significantly differentiated	Modest differentiation	Standardised product	Significantly differentiated	Significantly differentiated	Commodity product	Modest differentiation
5 Ratio of industry to customer firms	1:100	1:50	1:10	1:10	1:75	1:75	1:100	1:100	1:50
6 Threat of backwards integration	Unlikely but possible	Quite likely	Moderate threat	Moderate threat	Quite likely	Moderate threat	None	Serious threat (in-house services)	Unlikely but possible
7 Customer added value	Average	Average	High	Very high	Average	Average	Average	Average	Very high
8 Threat from substitutes	Some threats emerging	Under threat	Some threats emerging	None in sight	Under threat (technology)	Possible but unlikely	Some threats emerging	Some threats emerging	None in sight
9 Degree of 'switching' cost protection	Low	Moderate	High	Low	None	Moderate	Very high	None	Low
10 Entry barriers	Moderate	Moderate	Fairly high	Fairly high	Moderate	Fairly high	Moderate	None	Fairly high
11 Supply difficulties	Average	Very few	Average	Very few	None	Some serious problems	Very few	Some serious problems (labour)	Very few
12 Ratio of suppliers	6:1	6:1	6:1	20:1	6:1	3:1	3:1	–	3:1
13 Threat of forward integration by supplier	Unlikely but possible	None	None	None	None	Unlikely but possible	Moderate threat	–	None
14 Degree to which supplier depends on the industry	Under 20%	20–33.3%	Under 20%	Under 20%	Under 20%	Under 20%	Under 20%	–	50–74% (vehicle)
15 Geographical area considered	World	World	UK	Local–Aberdeen	UK	UK (but should it be world?)	UK (but should it be world?)	UK	UK

Table 16.2 Acts and judgements: GI portfolio – competitive position

Competitive factors	Industrial Fasteners	General Hydraulics	Pneumatics	Oil Rig Services	General Engineering Contracting	Machine tools	Personal Computers	Guarding Services	Security vehicle services
1 Market position	Major	Minor	Leader	Major	Viable	Minor	Leader	Negligible	Negligible
2 Relative profitability	Same as industry	Consistently 10–20% lower	Consistently 10–20% better	Consistently 10–20% lower	Consistently 25% higher	25% higher	More than 20% lower	Consistently 10–20% higher	
3 Production economics	Same	Worse than average	Better than average	Better than average	Worse than average	Better than average	Better than average	Worse than average	Better than average
4 Capacity utilisation	Above 60–80%	40–50%	Above 80%	Above 80%	50–60%	60–80%	Above 80%	50–60%	Above 80%
5 Quality of plant	Better than major competitors	Worse than major competitors	Better than competitors	Worse than competitors	Worse than major competitors	Better than major competitors	Better than major competitors	–	About the same
6 Firm's supply problems	A bit better than the industry	About the same as the industry	About the same as the industry	About the same as the industry	About the same as the industry	Average	Better than major competitors	–	About the same as the industry
7 R&D services	Almost right	Has some deficiencies	Almost right	Right for the market	Right for the market	Inadequate	Has some deficiencies	–	–
8 Technical support	Better than average	As good as relevant competition	Better than average	Better than average	Worse than average	As good as competition	A leader in this field	–	–
9 Distribution	Excellent	Average	Good	Good	Average	Average	Good	Below average	Average

Table 16.3 Scores: market prospects

	Weight	(1) Industrial fasteners		(2) General Hydraulics		(3) Pneumatics		(4) Oil Rig Services		(5) General Engineering Contract		(6) Machine tools		(7) Personal computers		(8) Guarding services		(9) Security vehicle services	
		Score	Wgtd Score	Score	Wgtd Score	Score	Wgtd Score	Score	Wgtd Score	Score	Wgtd Score	Score	Wgtd Score	Score	Wgtd Score	Score	Wgtd Score	Score	Wgtd Score
A. MARKET GROWTH	5	0	=	1	(5)	0	=	0	=	0	=	2	10	4	20	0	=	1	5
B. MARKET QUALITY																			
Industry profitability	8	1	8	0	0	3	24	3	24	0	0	3	24	4	32	0	–	2	16
Stability of margin	1	2	2	1	1	3	3	3	3	0	0	3	3	4	4	0		2	2
Degree of product differentiation	1	2	2	2	2	3	3	2	2	1	1	3	3	3	3	0		2	2
Ratio of industry to customer firms	1	4	4	2	2	1	1	1	1	3	3	2	2	4	4	4	4	2	2
Threat to backwards integration	1	3	3	1	1	2	2	2	2	1	1	2	2	4	4	0	0	3	3
Customer added value	1	2	2	2	2	3	3	4	4	2	2	2	2	2	2	2	2	4	4
Threat from substitutes	1	2	2	1	1	2	2	4	4	1	1	3	3	2	2	2	2	4	4
Degree of switching cost protection	1	1	1	2	2	3	3	1	1	0	1	2	2	4	4	0	0	1	1
Entry barriers	1	2	2/26	2	2/13	3	3/44	3	3/44	2	1/10	3	3/45	2	2/57	0	0/8	3	3/37
	÷16		1.625		.813		2.75		2.75		.625		2.813		3.563		.5		2.313
	×5		8.125		4.06		13.75		13.75		3.125		14.063		17.813		2.5		11.563
C. SUPPLY POSITION																			
Supply difficulties	1	2	2	3	3	2	2	3	3	4	4	1	1	3	3	1	1	3	3
Ratio of supply to industry firms	1	2	2	2	2	2	2	3	3	2	2	1	1	1	1			1	1
Threat of forward integration by supplier	1	3	3	4	4	4	4	4	4	4	4	3	3	2	2			4	4
Degree to which supplier depends on the industry	1	4	4/11	3	3/12	4	4/12	4	4/14	4	4/14	4	4/9	4	4/10	–	1/1	1	1/9
	÷4		2.75		3		3		3.5		3.5		2.25		2.5		.25		2.25
	×2		5.5		6		6		7		7		4.5		5		2.5		4.5
TOTAL SCORE			13.625		5.06		19.75		20.75		10.125		28.563		42.81		3.0		21.063
	÷4		3.41		1.27		4.94		5.19		2.53		7.14		10.7		.75		5.27

Table 16.4 Scores: competitive portion

	Weight	(1) Industrial fasteners		(2) General Hydraulics		(3) Pneumatics		(4) Oil Rig Services		(5) General Engineering Contract		(6) Machine tools		(7) Personal computers		(8) Guarding services		(9) Security vehicle services	
		Score	Wgtd Score	Score	Wgtd Score	Score	Wgtd Score	Score	Wgtd Score	Score	Wgtd Score	Score	Wgtd Score	Score	Wgtd Score	Score	Wgtd Score	Score	Wgtd Score
A. MARKET POSITION	2	3	6	1	2	4	8	3	6	2	4	1	2	4	8	0	0	0	0
B. PRODUCTION/SUPPLY CAPABILITY																			
Relative profitability	4	2	8	1	4	3	12	1	4	1	4	4	16	4	16	0	0	3	12
Production economics	1	2	2	1	1	3	3	3	3	1	1	3	3	3	3	1	1	3	3
Capacity utilisation	1	3	3	1	1	4	4	4	4	2	2	3	3	4	4	2	2	4	4
Quality of plant (cf. competition)	1	3	3	1	1	3	3	1	1	2	2	3	3	3	3	–	–	2	2
Supply problems (cf. industry)	1	3	3	2	2	2	2	2	2	2	2	2	2	3	3	–	–	2	2
	÷8	19	2.375	9	1.375	24	3	14	1.75	11	1.375	27	3.375	29	3.625	3 (÷6)	0.5	23	2.875
C. MARKET SUPPORT SERVICES																			
R & D	1	3	3	2	2	3	3	4	4	4	4	1	1	3	3	–	–	–	–
Technical services	1	3	3	2	2	3	3	3	3	1	1	2	2	4	4	–	–	–	–
Distribution network	1	4	4	2	2	3	3	3	3	2	2	2	2	1	1	1	1	2	2
	÷3	10	3.33	6	2	9	3	10	3.33	7	2.33	5	1.67	8	2.67	1	1	2	2
TOTAL SCORE	×0.75	11.705	8.78	5.375	4.03	14	10.5	11.08	8.31	7.705	5.78	7.05	5.28	14.295	10.72	1.5	1.13	4.875	3.66

Table 16.5 Importance of GI businesses by revenue

Division	Turnover (£million)	%
Fasteners	200	40
General Hydraulics	100	20
Pneumatics	75	15
Oil Rig Services	40	8
General Engineering	30	6
Machine Tools	10	2
Personal Computers	25	5
Guarding Services	10	2
Security Vehicle Services	10	2
	500	100

industry. It may also be a result of good or bad management, and the way in which the organisation has responded to the opportunities and problems it faces.

Below I have listed the strategic actions that GI had under consideration for each business, with my provisional recommendation drawn from the analysis. They do not always agree!

Interpretation compared with board's investment strategies

1 *Fasteners*	Several million on new-look marketing campaign. Construction of new head office.
Recommendation	Operate for maximum cash, with such expenditure/investment as is necessary to maintain market share. The weighting of fasteners is important, and it should not be allowed to slip. The feeling that fasteners should be able to reinvest their own 'earnings' is wrong.
2 *Hydraulics*	Purchase of hydraulics interest of major company for £20 million.
Recommendation	Do not do this. Business should clearly be considered for divestment.
3 *Pneumatics*	No investment needed. Should be a cash generator.

Figure 16.1
GI plc – basis of
strategy. The
numbers are keyed
in Tables 16.3 and
16.4

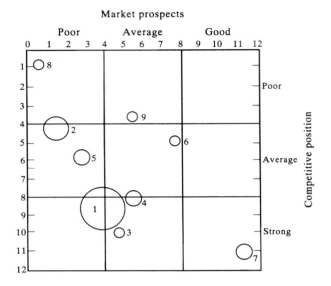

4	*Oil Rig Services*	Possible replication of other activities in other areas.
	Recommendation	May be better to run for cash. However, I would not rule out expansion subject to careful project appraisal *and* consideration against other uses of funds.
5	*General Engineering*	£6 million modernisation programme.
	Recommendations	Would the investment push it into a cash generator box? Initial indications are no. In this case divestment should be considered.
6	*Machine Tools*	Defend market share against Japanese.
	Recommendation	This business has to be looked at on a wider geographical basis, and strengths and weaknesses compared with Japanese competitors. Needs a careful market appraisal, and consideration of capital needs to give most efficient production. Investment should be balanced against risks and rewards. Indications are biased against investment.
7	*Personal Computers*	£50 million investment plan which board predisposed to reject.
	Recommendation	Depending on competitive position in key markets, this would appear to be the best opportunity for the group. Needs heavy cash support. GI should be sure they have the resources and nerve for a game that requires a speed build-up of market position across a wide front.
8	*Guarding*	Little hope, unless new concept giving unique advantage can be built up. What joint resources with vehicles?
9	*Security Vehicles*	Expansion of market share needs new facilities.
	Recommendation	On the surface, not the best use of resources.

Figure 16.2
GI using revised
assumptions

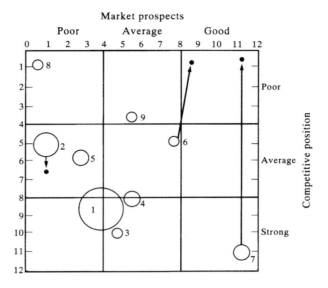

Challenging the assumptions

If this were a real situation I should like to challenge the assumptions for two of the businesses. It is extremely unlikely that personal computers and machine tools can be viewed solely in a UK context. Both are global businesses and have global competitors. Therefore, in the long term it is unlikely that either can survive by thinking only in UK terms.

A more likely positioning is indicated by the arrows on the matrix in Figure 16.2. On a world basis, machine tools might be seen as slightly more attractive in prospects, but the competitive positioning would shrink to the poor box. Similarly, viewed on a world basis the strong personal computers competitive position would become weak.

This immediately raises questions about the possible strategy. We do not have all the information to resolve them, but can suggest a hypothesis.

Machine tools

This is a long established industry with entrenched competitors. The UK position is not good. The question is whether it would even be feasible to move to become a world player from such a weak base. Acquisition might be a possibility, but the issue is to build a world position in a few products, rather than to own a diversity of products none of which have a world position. Someone would have to work very hard to persuade me that a viable world strategy is even possible.

Personal computers

Although in the 1980s the industry power was in the hands of the hardware manufacturers, such as Apple, IBM, and Compaq, by the 1990s there had been a shift. At one end the pace of technological development is dictated by a few chip manufacturers such as Intel. At the other it is Microsoft, through its domination of the operating systems and software. Any decision on this fast-moving business would need more than has been provided in this analysis, to confirm that Good Investments has the technology and marketing capability to rise above the commodity status that many assemblers of hardware have fallen into. The expected growth rate on which the portfolio analysis is based would require a great deal of careful scrutiny.

We seem to be moving from a strong position in a market where it is still possible to gain market share from technological innovation but where there is increasing danger of losing differentiation and becoming a commodity-type producer forced to compete on a low-price strategy. The first question is therefore whether it is desirable to move to become a world player from the present base. The second is whether Good Investments have the resources to compete on a global basis. If not, the options might be disposal through sale to another company or floating the business on the stock market and reducing proportion owned by Good Investments. Another option might be to form a joint venture with another firm.

Hydraulics

The final movement in Figure 16.2 is the hydraulics strategy proposed by the GI board. This shows that following this strategy would barely shift the position on the matrix, and would therefore be unlikely to improve the overall situation. In fact it would make it worse by increasing the proportion of the balance sheet held in a problem area.

Looking at risk

The analysis so far looks at only one aspect of the strategic situation. The Risk matrix enables us to add more information, and thus to gain more insight. The rules for this technique are brief, and will be described, together with an example of their application to the GI situation. In addition to scoring rules we need an assessment of the environmental factors which are important to the company. An earlier chapter dealt at length on ways of analysing and identifying the factors, so in this chapter we will assume that GI have performed this task well. Table 16.6

Table 16.6 Risk matrix score sheet: Good Investments plc

Major external threat	SBU 1 I × P = S	SBU 2 I × P = S	SBU 3 I × P = S	SBU 4 I × P = S	SBU 5 I × P = S	SBU 6 I × P = S	SBU 7 I × P = S	SBU 8 I × P = S	SBU 9 I × P = S
Emergence of focused Japanese threat	5 × 1 =	5 × 1 =	5 × 1 =		5 × 1 =	6 × 6 =	6 × 4 =		
Impact of UK trade cycle	5 × 5 =	6 × 5 =	2 × 5 =	1 × 5 =	6 × 5 =	6 × 5 =	4 × 5 =	3 × 5 =	3 × 5 =
Technological obsolescence	3 × 1 =	5 × 4 =	5 × 6 =	1 × 5 =	4 × 6 =	5 × 6 =	5 × 5 =	2 × 2 =	2 × 2 =
UK unemployment continues at high rate							3 × 5 =	3 × 5 =	
Political power of peace lobby		1 × 4 =	6 × 4 =		1 × 4 =	1 × 4 =			
Instability of major customer countries	4 × 2 =	4 × 2 =			5 × 5 =		4 × 4 =		
Decline in real oil prices				5 × 5 =	1 × 5 =				
TOTAL									
AVERAGE									
PENALTIES									
RM SCORE									

I = Impact, P = Probability, S = Score

provides the information that will be used as the basis for plotting risk. In a real situation there might be many more factors identified, but I have kept the list short for demonstration purposes.

Scoring the RM

The market prospects axis is scored according to the DPM rules. The 'degree of risk' axis requires a scoring sheet, a completed example of which is given later.

This scoring sheet lists the identified external factors and scores them for each strategic business unit, on the basis of impact and probability.

Impact and Probability are scored on the following basis:

Impact		Probability		
Extremely High	6	A Certainty	100%	6
	5	Very Likely	84%	5
High	4	Quite Possible	67%	4
	3	As Likely As Not	90%	3
Relatively Low	2	Probably Not	33%	2
	1	Highly Unlikely	16%	1
None	0	Impossible	–	0

To obtain a matrix score, the impact is multiplied by the probability score. The average score is calculated by dividing total score by the number of items with a positive score (e.g. ignoring zero or irrelevant items).

This first measure of risk ignores the problem of multiple risks. For example, businesses A and B may both score 15, but if A has in the make-up of its score a number of factors of high impact and probability, while B is only subject to two factors altogether, this would suggest that A is the more vulnerable business.

To compensate for this penalty points are added to the average score, on the following basis:

		Add
For every factor scoring	16–20	1
	21–25	2
	26–30	3
	31–36	4

The results of the scoring are built up through three stages. Table 16.7 is a repeat of Table 16.6 with the scores calculated. It is a worksheet, but provides some valuable interpretive information in its own right. A horizontal reading illuminates the factors which have most potential impact on the whole group, which are the UK trade cycle and technological obsolescence. An overall strategic response by GI, on the assumption that it decided not to change its portfolio of businesses, might be to take action to speed up new product development in order

Table 16.7 Risk matrix score sheet: Good Investments plc (as Table 16.6 with scores calculated)

Major external threat	SBU 1 I × P = S	SBU 2 I × P = S	SBU 3 I × P = S	SBU 4 I × P = S	SBU 5 I × P = S	SBU 6 I × P = S	SBU 7 I × P = S	SBU 8 I × P = S	SBU 9 I × P = S	TOTAL
Emergence of focused Japanese threat	5 × 1 = 5	5 × 1 = 5	5 × 1 = 5		5 × 1 = 5	6 × 6 = 36	6 × 4 = 24			80
Impact of UK trade cycle	5 × 5 = 25	6 × 5 = 30	2 × 5 = 10	1 × 5 = 5	6 × 5 = 30	6 × 5 = 30	4 × 5 = 20	3 × 5 = 15	3 × 5 = 15	180
Technological obsolescence	3 × 1 = 3	5 × 4 = 20	5 × 6 = 30	1 × 5 = 5	4 × 6 = 24	5 × 6 = 30	5 × 5 = 25	2 × 2 = 4	2 × 2 = 4	145
UK unemployment continues							3 × 5 = 15	3 × 5 = 15		30
Political power of peace lobby		1 × 4 = 4	6 × 4 = 24		1 × 4 = 4	1 × 4 = 4				36
Instability of major customer countries	4 × 2 = 8	4 × 2 = 8			5 × 5 = 25		4 × 4 = 16			57
Decline in real prices of oil			5 × 5 = 25	1 × 5 = 5						20
TOTAL	41	67	69	35	93	100	100	49	19	
AVERAGE	10.25	13.4	17.25	11.67	15.50	25	20	16.3	9.5	
PENALTIES	2	4	5	2	7	10	6	3	–	
RM SCORE	12.25	17.4	22.25	13.67	22.50	35	26	19.3	9.5	

I = Impact, P = Probability, S = Score

Figure 16.3
Environmental risk
matrix

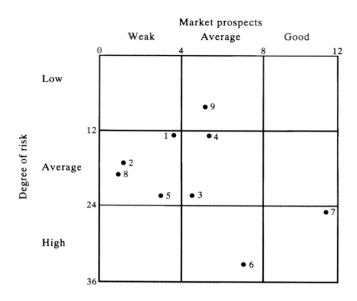

to gain extra time to benefit from products in an era of shortening life cycles. This could well be important enough to become a corporate initiative, introducing new approaches to project management, and providing more resources for new product development. The dependence on the UK economy could lead the group to consider more expansion into other parts of the world, such as South-east Asia. A later chapter will discuss global strategies in some detail, so I do not want to argue the merits or demerits of such a move here. However, it is an option that emerges from the analysis so far.

Figure 16.3 plots the scores on a matrix. The distribution of results is, of course, different from those that we saw in the portfolio analysis because one axis of the matrix has been changed. I regard this stage as an interim step, and prefer to leave interpretation to the next stage, illustrated in Figure 16.4. Here the risk matrix and the portfolio analysis are combined, and immediately a new insight is provided. Immediately we see that two businesses where we already had identified some critical strategic issues, machine tools and personal computers, numbers 6 and 9 on the chart, are also subject to high risks from environmental forces.

The next area of consideration from the information we have assembled is to see where the group is adding to shareholder value. At first sight it is difficult to see what it is that GI offers which is an addition to the value provided by each business unit. An earlier chapter discussed ideas about how value can be created, and the reader might wish to test GI against these. A key part of the GI strategy should be to increase shareholder value. I make this point because it illustrates that although we have gained considerable insight from the two analytical techniques, they cannot answer every strategic consideration.

The final decisions about GI's strategy should also take into account the strengths and weaknesses of the group and its components. We would want to

Figure 16.4
Portfolio analysis
showing risk

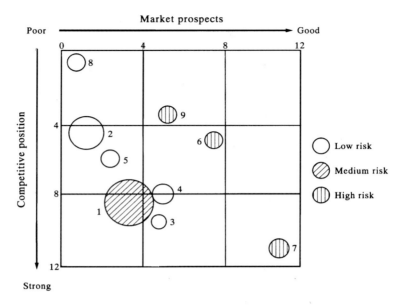

challenge some of the internal beliefs about markets and the industry, and delve much deeper into industry and competitor analysis. I should also want to see whether there are common strands of technology across the group, and identify the core competencies of the organisation. Any further analysis should also consider 'soft' aspects such as culture.

I should not, as you have guessed by now, want anyone to think that our two pieces of analysis have cracked the problem of what to do in GI. However, I hope you will agree that we have gained considerable strategic insight into the group, and that GI management did not possess this insight before the analysis was completed. We have some clear ideas about decisions which would be good or bad for the group, even if we have not uncovered all the options. Any one relevant technique of analysis will show some facets of a strategic situation. I think mistakes occur when an organisation latches on to only one technique, and bases all decisions on the outcome of this. My view is that this is a dangerous fault of many managers and analysts.

In the final event the future of GI will be determined not by the analysis but through the quality of the decisions made by management, and the creative way in which they identify responses to opportunities. Analysis helps strategic thinking: it does not replace it.

Reference

1 Stopford, J. M. *Vickers Plc (A)*, London Business School, 1989.

341

Appendix: Scoring rules and worksheets for DPM

Summary of the score weightings

Market prospects axis

Three groups of factors are considered for this axis, and are weighted to represent their importance. Weightings could vary with the type of business: the ones suggested below were worked out for manufacturing companies:

Factor Group	Weight
Market Growth	5

Here we are concerned with the underlying trend. The growth rate is assessed on historical evidence, adjusted by forecast changes, but ignoring short-term 'blips' caused by recession.

Market Quality	5

This examines the profitability of the activity. It is concerned with historical evidence, adjusted for factors which are likely to change that position.

Scoring considers the degree of product differentiation, ratio of industry to customer firms, whether margins are maintained in terms of overcapacity, threat of backwards integration, added value by the customer, technical position and entry barriers.

(Note: there are weighting differences for these subquestions which are described in the scoring rules.)

Supply Position (Total Industry)	2

This looks at supply difficulties, ratio of suppliers/industry firms, the threat of forward integration and the degree of supplier dependence on the industry.

Competitive position axis

Three groups of factors are considered in plotting this axis. Whereas the other axis asks questions about the industry/market, this axis is concerned with only answers about the firm.

Factor Group	Weight
Market Growth	2

This uses a concept of relative market position rather than an absolute share.

Note: Be prepared to modify these rules to fit the particular business.

Production-Supply Capability   1
Consider the firm's profitability relative to the industry, the production
economics of the firm, capacity utilisation, quality of productive
resources and ability to source materials and supplies. Some questions
in this subgroup are weighted more heavily than others.

Market Support Services   1
Examines the extent to which the present market position is being
supported by research/development effort, technical support, and the
distribution network.

Scoring

The scoring is organised so that the final maximum score on each axis is 12.
Another maximum figure could have been selected to avoid some of the
arithmetic in scoring, and the main reason for this choice is familiarity. Scoring
rules have been adjusted from time to time as I have used the approach in
different industries and I have found it helpful to have a constant total figure.

Note that market growth scores will be adjusted to suit the needs of each
company. The choice of midpoint for the scale is:

(a) Target rate of growth for the firm as a whole, or
(b) Average rate of growth historically achieved by the firm.

The rest of this section offers detailed scoring rules.

Directional policy matrix: scoring scales

1. Prospects for market profitability

1.1 Market growth

Assumption
3–4 per cent real growth p.a. would be a reasonable target for GI. The scale
should be amended if this objective is changed.

Rate of Growth	Points
Negative	−1
0–2%	0
2–3%	1
3–4%	2
4–7%	3
Over 7%	4

Growth should be primarily the historic pattern over recent years, tempered by any known trends for the future.

It is impossible to compare these ambitions with historic and forecast rates of GDP growth. If this suggested a growth rate of 2–3 per cent were more realistic, the scale should be amended. In practice the scale is thus set up according to the realistic objectives of the company.

1.2 Profitability record

Suggested scale:

Description	ROCE	Score
Very high	Over 20%	4
High	16–20%	3
Average	15%	2
Low	10–14%	1
Poor	0–9%	0
Loss	Negative	−1

This question attracts 21 per cent of the total weighting for this axis of the matrix.

Note: The profitability scale can be set up from statistical data on the profitability of UK industry, for example using ICC Business ratios data.

1.3 Margins maintained in times over capacity/low demand

	Score
Little or no change in margins	4
Occasional price cutting	3
Modest reductions in margin	2
Significant margin erosion	1
No margin control	0

1.4 Degree to which product seen as commodity or differentiated

	Score
Differentiated – seen as almost unique	4
Significantly differentiated from competitors	3
Modest differentiation	2
Standardised product	1
Commodity status	0

1.5 Ratio industry to customer firms

This considers the relative dependence of the industry on its customers.

Description	Ratio	Score
Numerous customers	1:100+	4
Many customers	1:75	3
Average	1:50	2
Few customers	1:10	1
Unity	1:1	0

An adjustment may be made to the rating when one buyer takes a major share of all purchases.

1.6 Threat of backwards integration

	Score
None	4
Unlikely but possible	3
Moderate threat	2
Quite likely	1
Serious threat	0

1.7 High/low customer added value

	Score
Very high	4
High	3
Average	2
Low	1
Very low	0

1.8 Threat from substitutes

	Score
None in sight	4
Possible but unlikely	3
Some threats emerging	2
Under threat	1
Already serious	0

1.9 Degree of 'switching' cost protection

	Score
Very high – ensures continuity of business	4
High	3
Moderate	2
Low	1
None	0

1.10 Entry barriers

	Score
Very high – new entrant unlikely	4
Fairly high	3
Moderate	2
Very few	1
None	0

1.11 Supply difficulties

Does the industry in the country of operation have difficulty in obtaining raw materials, components, etc?

	Score
Very serious problems	0
Some serious problems	1
Average	2
Very few	3
None	4

1.12 Ratio of suppliers to industry firms

The question applies to the key supplies by value

		Score
+30:1	Very healthy	4
20:1	Healthy	3
6:1	Average	2
3:1	Causing concern	1
1:1 or worse	Dangerous	0

1.13 Threats of forward integration by supplier

	Score
None	4
Unlikely but possible	3
Moderate threat	2
Quite likely	1
Serious threat	0

1.14 Degree to which the supplier depends on the industry

	Score	
	If suppliers large firms	If suppliers small firms
Proportions of sales		
Over 75%	0	
50–74%	1	
33–49%	2	
20–33%	3	No
Under 20%	4	score

1.15 Overall weightings for market prospects axis

Market growth	5
Market quality	5
Supply position	2

Of this	
Based on historical fact (profits and growth)	7.5–6.2%
Balance	4.5–37.5%

2. Company's competitive position

2.1 Market position

Rating	Key word	Description
4	Leader	A company which normally has price and technical leadership in the market place. The associated brand share will vary. For example, a company with 25% share (the highest) in a field with 10 other competitors each with shares varying from 1–15% will be likely to be a leader. Another company with a 30% brand share and two major strong competitors may not be.
3	Major	The position where no one company is a leader, but 2–4% companies of similar size have major shares in the market.

347

2	Viable	A company with a strong stake. Usually this will be the next position when one competitor is the leader.
1	Minor	Less than adequate to support R&D and other services in the long run.
0	Negligible	Current position negligible.

This question has 50 per cent of total weighting on this axis of the matrix.

2.2 Company's profitability relative to the industry

	Score
More than 20% higher	4
Consistently 10–20% higher	3
Same level as industry	2
Consistently 10–20% lower	1
More than 20% lower	0

2.3 Production economics

Description	Indication	Score
Excellent	Over 15% advantage	4
Better than average	5–15% advantage	3
Same	Prices roughly the same	2
Worse than average	5–15% disadvantage	1
Poor	Over 15% disadvantage	0

This question represents a judgemental effort to compare the economics of the firm with major competitors. The clue will often lie in relative prices.

2.4 Capacity utilisation

	Score
Above 80–100%	4
Above 60–80%	3
Above 50–60%	2
Above 40–50%	1
Under 40%	0

2.5 Quality of plant, etc

To some degree this is related to production economics. It is a judgemental question about the state of productive assets and methods compared with competition.

	Score
Very much better than major competitors	4
Better than major competitors	3
About the same as major competition	2
Worse than major competitors	1
Very much worse	0

2.6 Materials/components supply problems faced by firm

	Score
Considerably better than the industry	4
A bit better than the industry	3
About the same as the industry	2
A bit worse than the industry	1
Considerably worse than the industry	0

2.7 R & D services

Does the company undertake the degree of R & D necessary to sustain its position in the market?

	Score
R & D effort right for the market	4
R & D effort almost right	3
R & D effort has some deficiencies	2
R & D effort inadequate	1
R & D effort very poor	0

2.8 Technical support

Is the company able to provide the level of technical support needed to support its position?

	Score
A leader in this field	4
Better than average	3
As good as relevant competition	2
Worse than average	1
Very poor	0

2.9 Distribution network and methods

	Score
Excellent	4
Good	3
Average	2
Below average	1
Poor	0

3.0 Weightings for competitive position axis

	Score
Weightings are distributed:	
Market position	8
Production/supply capability	4
Market support	4

Approximately 63 per cent of total weightings are applied to the provable elements of market position and relative profitability.

CHAPTER 17

Strategic planning – a second look at the basic options

This chapter aims to provide another way of looking at strategic options, which is related to the nature of the action instead of the source from which it is derived. Seven major options are explored in some depth: divestment (including outsourcing), obtaining licences, giving licences, various expansion methods, research and development, acquisition and merger, and strategic alliances. The value and difficulties of the approaches are explored. Practical guidance is given to help improve the chances of success if the option is chosen.

In Chapter 14 there was a considerable discussion of the matrix (Figure 14.3) into which most strategic alternatives could be fitted. Within each sector of this matrix there are many actions that can be initiated, and these may be classified under a second list of headings on which discussion should now be turned. These are:

1 Divestment
2 Obtaining licences
3 Granting licences
4 A simple expansion approach – hiring staff
                                          partnership
                                          broking
                                          'piggy-backing' operation
                                          contract production
                                          selling own services
5 Research and development
6 Acquisition and merger
7 Alliances.

Divestment

A decision to give up a particular sphere of activity may be very difficult to make. There are often emotional or prestige reasons for wishing to continue: a dislike of admitting failure, an unpleasantly high loss to be faced in one year, problems of employee morale, and, above all, a sneaking feeling that someone else might pick up the divested area and make a success of it. For a chief executive this may be like advertising personal inadequacies. If it is a major divestment, the whole of the business world will observe it and will note the results if another chief executive does succeed where the first has failed.

The decision to divest can come in varying degrees of size. The dropping of a few minor products may cause no problems at all. In another case an entire activity area may be sold without having any noticeable effect on the day-to-day operations of the company. A decision to divest the company of a complete division or subsidiary may have a much greater impact.

Divestment may be a very important strategic decision to consider. Although my opening sentences on the subject hinted that failure could be the incentive to divestment, this is only one of the many possible causes. It is possible to divest from strength as well as from weakness.

A divestment decision might well arise from a tidying-up operation after the company has made its corporate appraisal or evaluated its portfolio. Perhaps the operation, although profitable, does not fit in with the company's perception of what it should be doing. Here it may be sensible to apply the maxim of concentration of effort by attempting to withdraw from an operation which makes demands on top management time but which has no place in long-term strategic thinking.

A related divestment decision might arise because although the company might wish to remain in a business, it may be unable to afford the capital expenditures required to make that business a successful long-term competitor. In these circumstances it is better to find a way to withdraw now, while the business is seen as successful, rather than waiting until it has lost competitive ground. It was this sort of circumstance that lay behind the reshaping of the Vickers portfolio over the three years following the merger with Rolls-Royce Motors.

Divestment may be the result of a desire to reduce risk. An assessment may suggest that the company is unwise to rely on profits from its subsidiary in an underdeveloped country because of the high probability of political unrest. It may be prudent to divest the company of all or part of its operations in that country in order to avoid a possible problem at a later date.

As we saw in the GI example in the previous chapter, the perception of risk may be related to the perception of the strategic requirements of this business, and it may be the combination of the two that brings the divestment decision to the fore.

Shareholder value has been discussed several times, and has provided a different motivation for divestment. This may take the form of reshaping the portfolio in the way already suggested, or of returning to the shareholders an equity stake in an activity hived off from the current ownership. Argos was hived off in this way from BAT Industries, and now has nothing to do with its former parent, although no doubt it still has a number of shareholders in common.

Divestment may be forced for legal reasons. In the USA, anti-trust legislation has compelled many large organisations to divest part of their businesses. This has long been an element of US business history. For example, the break-up of the great Standard Oil Company in 1911 into thirty-eight state-centred oil companies ultimately led to a number of the mammoth world players of today. There are many more recent examples, such as ITT. Monopoly legislation is not restricted to the USA, and the legislation of the EU and its component countries has made companies divest businesses that they would rather have kept, sometimes as the condition for allowing a merger to take place. In other countries, such as Malaysia, there has been legislation that has forced the sale of a major part of the shareholding to local people. This type of legislation may be the trigger that leads an organisation to withdraw from the particular country.

The final example is where the legal background to the competitive arena makes it impossible for the company to compete on level terms with its main rival. BP sold its downstream oil interests in Canada to the state-owned oil company. Not only was Petrocan in a preferred position through many government actions, but it became impossible for BP to expand to meet its challenge because of legislation which made it very difficult for a foreign-owned company to expand by acquisition in Canada.

A divestment decision from weakness might arise in order to improve the cash-flow position. The sale of a profitable activity might be the solution to a difficulty that cannot be resolved by other means. Alternatively, an activity may be divested now in order to avoid a major capital investment foreseen in the near future. In this way a potential problem is avoided, and the more favourable time (for the vendor) may be picked for the sale.

There are many divestment strategies. The simplest is to offer the business for sale, and here the skill is to do this in a way that gains the maximum price but does not cause a flight of customers or key staff. The need for what might be termed 'confidential promotion' has led to specialist acquisition broking businesses. When Vickers decided to divest the diesel division they approached it in a similar way to how they might have chosen a diesel company to acquire. In other words, which companies in the world would it best complement, in terms of development, product range, and geographical coverage. This resulted in a short list of target companies who could be approached with a carefully prepared proposition showing where the benefits were. The buyer was Perkins. The probability was that this approach brought a better price, and because it was handled by the top management of the division, may have maintained management morale and kept the key people together.

Another means of divestment is the management buy-out. This has long existed, and became particularly popular during the 1980s, often leading to businesses which prospered once they had thrown off the shackles of the head office. One well known example is the purchase of the National Freight Corporation from the British government by its management and other employees, a story which has been described by Thompson.[1]

Exhibit 17.1 Demerger

Increasingly divestment has taken the form of a demerger, with a large organisation splitting itself into discrete businesses, so that the shareholders then have shares in two quoted organisations instead on one. The reasons are usually defensive, to ward off an expected but unwanted acquirer, or in order to give more value to shareholders.

In 1993 ICI demerged into two companies, floating the pharmaceuticals and biotechnology businesses on the stock market under the name Zeneca. Bulk chemicals, paints and explosives remained under the ICI name. One advantage for shareholders is that Zeneca, because of the standing of pharmaceuticals in the stock market, would find it easier to raise capital for expansion than if it remained a part of a larger company.

Through the 1980s ICI had followed a strategy of expansion by acquisition, following clear objectives to increase the organisation's business in overseas markets, particularly the USA, and to build up its businesses in the most profitable segments of their industries. In the 1990s it began a further exercise in restructuring, selling businesses such as fertilisers, and dividing into seven core activities. It was apparent at this stage that there were two main groups of businesses, which were not synergistic with each other.

Hanson Group suddenly bought nearly 3 per cent of ICI shares in 1991. Although no intention to bid for the whole company was ever announced, ICI acted as if it had, and mounted a vigorous defence strategy. Various internal studies had shown that there were really two major strategic business groupings in the company, and this was confirmed when the company's merchant bank S. G. Warburg was invited to study the figures. The decision was made to follow the demerger option recommended by Warburgs.

In 1991, what was to become the Zeneca businesses had 32 per cent of the total turnover, but contributed 70 per cent of the trading profit. Apart for the strategic benefits to both businesses, flotation meant that shareholders would gain value as each business had its own share valuation, and full value could be obtained from the Zeneca portion of the shares. The move also made the organisation unattractive to a predator whose only aim was to release the locked-up value.

(*Source*:Kennedy, C. 'The ICI Demerger: Unlocking Shareholder Value'. In Lloyd, B. (ed.), *Creating Value Through Acquisitions, Demergers, Buy-outs, and Alliances*, Pergamon, Oxford, 1977.)

Charterhouse in the 1970s was a combined industrial, merchant banking and financial services organisation in the UK. During the late 1970s it began to reduce its investment in the industrial holdings, and to use the funds to build the merchant banking operation, including the acquisition of another major player. The divestment strategy applied to many of the strongest companies in the portfolio was to float them on the stock market, initially retaining a significant shareholding which could be disposed of later. This was a neat way of divesting, in that it gained maximum realisation without it being necessary to find and negotiate with one particular buyer. Customer confidence was unaffected: it was after all a sign that the company had grown up, and it avoided the internal upheaval of an acquisition.

It is also worth stressing that divestment does not have to be total. It is sometimes worth removing some of the problems of risk and inability to fund growth by merging a subsidiary with that of another organisation. A stake may be retained, possibly for sale later. However, there can be risks here, particularly if one partner wants to slow investment and the other to increase it. Just such a situation is described by Friedman:[2] the joint company formed in the USA from the construction equipment interests of Allis Chalmers and Fiat. Allis Chalmers wanted to reduce their stake in this business: Fiat wanted to expand. Consequently there was a clash every time Fiat called for new investment, which would in fact have increased the Allis Chalmers stake. Fiat had purchased 65 per cent of the construction equipment from Allis Chalmers. This attempt at reducing involvement in a business led to litigation and acrimony.

In all divestment decisions attention must be given to personnel, morale throughout the whole company (nothing spreads faster than a rumour that the ship is sinking), and to the public relations aspect. The divestment plan should deal specifically with these matters.

A divestment decision is based on forecasts and assumptions in much the same way as an investment decision. The main difference is the light of publicity. The outside world rarely knows when an investment opportunity is rejected or even – except in the case of large failures – where a decision to invest proves less successful than had been hoped. Divestment is a public act and calls for a higher degree of management courage. Despite this, it is an action which should be considered when a company evaluates its future strategy, for it may be the key to greater profits.

More recently there has been another form of divestment, the outsourcing of services which the organisation previously used to undertake for itself. Sometimes this has included the transfer of employees to another organisation, which has happened frequently as IT activities have been outsourced. Another route has been helping employees in the area to be outsourced to set up their own business on the strength of an outsourcing contract.

The strategic rationale for this form of divestment is cost reduction, flexibility in times of expansion and contraction, a realisation that specialist organisations can often bring a better service, and a narrowing of focus to the core competency areas. Jennings[3] argues that almost the whole value chain is open to an outsourcing decision. He gives a number of guidelines for use in the outsourcing decision, which include:

- Ensure that decisions are taken in relation to the overall strategy, and in the context of a future-oriented view of the changes that are likely to take place in the industry.
- Ensure that the service is fully defined when undertaking a cost analysis – it is easy to overlook frequent free advice that a unit may provide, which is peripheral to its main function.

The virtual organisation

The combination of outsourcing, alliances, and, sometimes, the opportunities offered by modern information technologies has led to a new form of organisation. The virtual organisation fulfils all the functions of the traditional form, but as many of them are not owned or performed in house, overheads are reduced, and suppliers are able to secure and pass on economies through specialisation. In fact the form is not as new as its name. For example, publishers have a tradition whereby they rarely employ authors, printing and book binding is outsourced, services such as copy-editing and proof reading are often performed by freelance specialists, and in some cases even sales and distribution are delegated to specialist organisations.

What is new is the greater number of organisations which have found value in treading this route, and the new opportunities that arise through the new technologies. So we have a virtual retail bank in First Direct, where telephone, hole-in-the-wall cash machines, and other computerised applications make it possible to eliminate the traditional branch offices: although, of course, there is nothing virtual about the back-office activities, where there is a very real bank.

The virtual form may reduce risks as well as reduce costs. Harbridge Consulting group Ltd established a virtual organisation to implement its strategy for Europe. Alliances were made with quality organisations in various countries, so that a service could be offered to multinational companies to run a tailored training programme in most European languages. In Germany, where there was a different strategy, a virtual office was created inside the premises of a non-competing consultancy. German-speaking London professionals were supported by contracts with quality self-employed German professionals. Had the firm not been acquired, a contact office would have been opened in Brussels in alliance with a number of firms from other European countries. What was achieved was a capability that would have taken more resources than were available to establish by traditional means, that was operational in months rather than years, and which almost eliminated risk.

Anyone considering this form should think carefully about the managerial implications, and should not underestimate the time that has to be spent with alliance partners to ensure a shared commitment to what is intended.

- Ensure that a careful costing exercise is undertaken, which means understanding which of the indirect costs charged to a unit will truly disappear if the unit is closed.
- Take great care to define the core activities, and to retain these in the organisation.
- Ensure that the outsourcing decision does not create a competitive disadvantage by leaking knowledge or technology so that it now becomes available to competitors.

Successful outsourcing decisions will often lead to forms of strategic alliance, an issue covered later in this chapter.

Obtaining licences

A decision to obtain licences may arise from a study of any of the boxes in the strategic matrix, although it is more likely to be associated with new products, whether for existing or new markets. It may be a logical decision in a situation where a licensed process can bring lower production costs for existing products or can upgrade the products so that they give a better market performance and in these situations can contribute to expansion under the two existing product boxes of the matrix.

The main drawbacks of obtaining licences are cost, continuity, security of information, legislation, and availability. A licensing agreement involves the payment of a fee, frequently on a royalty basis, over the life of the agreement. This usually means a commitment of future margins, which can cause problems if the company ever moves into a situation where these are declining.

Continuity is another problem which depends on the type of agreement, the remaining patent life (if any), and the strategies of the licensee. Unless carefully considered a licensing policy brings the risk that what has become a major product area may disappear overnight if the agreement is cancelled or lapses, there is no control by the licensee over research and development, so he or she may not know whether product improvements are being carried out or how vulnerable it is to technological developments by competitors.

Security of information may not always be a disadvantage, or at least any disadvantage may be more emotional than real. But a licensee must provide information to the licensor and, in many cases, must give access to the books of account, marketing plans, and production processes. This may be a disadvantage if the venture proceeds well, giving the licensor full information about the market which might tempt him into it on his own account with this or the next improved version of the product. In this way the licensee may, in effect, be carrying out the expensive market development work on behalf of another company. This information problem can become more acute when company ownerships change: what is quite sensible policy at the beginning may become much more of a problem if the licensor is acquired by a major competitor of the licensee.

Legislation may be a problem which has to be taken into account. For example, the payment of royalties may be prohibited by some governments. A change in legislation can be particularly difficult for both parties.

Perhaps the biggest problem of all is finding someone who wants to license a product or process. There are specialist agencies which can assist in bringing interested parties together, and it is possible to identify possibilities and make a direct approach to the company concerned. In many ways there may be similarities with identifying and negotiating with a suitable acquisition prospect. Success cannot be guaranteed, and the company must always remain wide awake to the unexpected opportunity.

The difficulties and problems should not be overstressed, for cooperation is possible even among the most aggressive of competitors (e.g. the licensing arrangements in the world's pharmaceuticals industry). There are very real benefits to a licensing agreement, and in most cases these outweigh the disadvantages. In any case many can be overcome through care in negotiating the terms of the agreement.

First a company may save time by taking a licence. It may be possible to put a new product on the market within a matter of months, where by other means it might take years. The quality of the product is known already, as may be its performance in other markets, and thus the risk of delay through product failure is considerably reduced (although a licensed product may still fail in a new market). This shortening of the time span, and the reduction of risk, can accelerate the product's ability to contribute to profits.

Licensing may further reduce risk because it provides access to a brand name which is already known if not established. This is not always the case, but it may well happen. This strategy may also give the company access to technical knowledge and skilled personnel which would otherwise be difficult or impossible to obtain. It may give a back-up service which might be beyond the resources of the company itself.

In many cases a licence will also bring the benefit of patent protection – on the one hand, enabling the company to undertake a process which would otherwise have been denied to it, and, on the other, providing it with a shield behind which it can shelter.

A licence may also reduce competition or the possible threat of competition. This may be important if the development for which a licence is sought represents a major technological advance over the company's own product. The licence, besides securing the development for the company, ensures that the licensor does not become a threat by entering the market as a competitor.

Granting licences

One way of extending existing products to new markets is to actively seek to grant licences to other companies. We have examined some of the reasons why it is worth while for a company to obtain a licence: now it is time to look at the other side of the coin to see the benefits available to the company granting the licence.

Perhaps the biggest is that it provides opportunities to profit from the product or processes without tying up working capital or carrying the risk of market development work. The licensor may also gain time – just as the licensee does, although for different reasons. To establish an effective production and distribution unit in another country may take at least a year – longer if factories have to be built and plant ordered. By granting a licence a company can often ensure that it is receiving an income from its project within a much shorter period.

A company may avoid the commitment of working capital for normal marketing and the expenditure of fixed capital. It does not have to erect overseas plants or expand domestic capacity to cope with exports. This may enable expansion beyond a company's own capital resources, and because the additional earnings are obtained for only a meagre additional working capital requirement, may dramatically improve profitability ratios.

The nature of licensing means that tariff barriers can often be jumped without subeconomic ventures being set up in high-risk countries. This may be a means of expanding or a way of avoiding all loss of profits when an export market closes its borders through protective tariffs.

Few strategies are without some disadvantages, and there are points which should be considered. A licensing agreement is often vulnerable to changes in government policy, e.g. the imposition of controls which prohibit royalty payments to external companies. There may be risks in passing on technology to outsiders who may abuse the terms of the agreement. Perhaps the greatest disadvantage need not be a disadvantage if a company does its long-range planning well: licensing agreements can make it more difficult for a company to set up its own organisation in an area which has shown significant development. It therefore behoves a company to carefully plan its strategies for a particular country or product area so that the terms and conditions are matched to its ultimate ambitions.

Simple expansion

Often in an analysis of strategic options the obvious gets forgotten. For the two boxes of the matrix dealing with existing products the best way of expanding may be the simplest way. Just do it. This is the situation when the strategy can be fulfilled from within the company's existing resources – either out of current capacity, from expanding existing factories, or from the transfer of technology to new factories and new business areas. This really is so obvious and so logical that it needs no further analysing.

In cases where technology is closely related, it may be possible for new products to be launched in this way, particularly 'me-too' products which involve no creative research and development.

Where the technological threshold of an industry is low, it is also a worthwhile possibility to take the simple approach and just start the operations required. In this case the only skills needed may be brought in through the engaging of suitable employees. Thus a decision to open a chain of hotels, or hairdressing salons, or a small factory making cement blocks, could be implemented through the recruitment of people with the requisite skills, the investment of capital in the resources needed, and, as an optional extra, the use of specialist consultants to help the venture off the ground. As the technological threshold increases, often accompanied by a rise in the financial stake needed to enter the industry, the simple method of expansion becomes more difficult and more risky. But it is rarely impossible (although it may in some industries be highly dangerous) and it is the method of growth and development which originally set many of today's mammoth companies on their paths of expansion.

There are alternative ways of tackling this method of expansion. Additional skills may be obtained, or risks reduced, by joint ventures or partnership arrangements. These may provide a safer method of, for example, expanding existing products into a new overseas market, and at the same time reduce the capital resources needed to finance the operation.

Another method may be to seek to use other companies' resources to help expansion. One example of this is contract manufacture, which may be exploited as a dynamic tool, or to protect existing market interests in a country where a new protective tariff has changed the competitive position of current supply sources.

Perhaps one of the most frequent examples of using contract production to exploit new opportunities is provided by the 'own-label' boom in the grocery trade in Europe and the USA. Supermarkets rarely own their own production sources and use the facilities of existing manufacturers to supply the required product. Expansion of the 'own-label' business would have been more risky and costly without this opportunity.

Production is not the only resource, and it is possible for a company to devise a strategy which exploits opportunities available through the marketing and distributive skills of others. Such strategies are usually medium rather than long term, and can be of great benefit to both parties. They vary from the usage of specialist brokerage firms, to what has been called 'piggy-backing'.

Management Today,[4] reports how Canada Dry used piggy-backing to break into the grocery market sector in the UK. The company was well established in the licensed trade and, rather than set up its own sales force, decided that the best way into the grocery trade would be through a company already established in that sector. It chose Wander, manufacturers of Ovaltine to 'piggy-back' it for selling, invoicing, and delivery operations.

It is possible to look at essential support service areas, and to turn these into business opportunities which provide services to outsiders as well as to those in the organisation. If spun off completely, they become an outsourcing activity, which we have already discussed. Although it is somewhat unfashionable to consider a strategy of selling such services while still keeping the activity inside the organisation, there are many examples. In both the public and private sectors of the UK there are in-house training organisations which also market their services outside, and have turned themselves into a profit centre instead of a cost centre.

In common with many other companies Tate & Lyle, the sugar group, looked very hard at their physical distribution operations. Here they found that they were able to offer a delivery service to selected clients for goods – including shoes, canned food and wine – which were compatible with their own products. This has now become a steadily expanding activity.

The 'piggy-back' example quoted above was, for Wander, a sale of part of its own service area. In this case it profited from its selling and physical distribution systems.

Modern thinking would suggest that the profitable exploitation of essential service areas is sometimes worth doing, but more often it diverts management and other resources from the core activities of the organisation, and in these circumstances outsourcing would be a better option.

Research and development

In some situations the various alternatives discussed above will provide the solution to a company's needs. Probably in many other situations they will be inadequate, and much more attention will have to be given to the remaining options, one of the most complex of which may be research and development. For many companies, research and development is an essential to survival, and at least as part of its strategy must be directed along this path. Science-based or highly technological industries may have to accept that a commitment to research and development is part of the price they pay for being in that business area. It is almost impossible to conceive of the Hoffman La Roches, the Union Carbides, the Du Ponts or the IBMs of this world without conceding the vital part that research and development plays for each of them.

Yet it would be wrong to see all research and development as one single type of problem area. For some companies a measure of basic research is an essential; for others it is a matter of applied research only; still others do little research and their emphasis is on the word 'development'.

Some definition of these terms may be helpful. Basic research may be defined as research which is carried on in the search for knowledge but without specific commercial objectives: when carried out by a firm it may seek a discovery which will benefit the firm, although the discovery may not initially be tied to any particular objectives. Applied research is, on the other hand, aimed to fulfil specific objectives. Development 'is concerned with the technical non-routine activities associated with translating scientific knowledge into marketable products' (Steiner[5]). An ethical pharmaceuticals company, for example, might have to accept a measure of basic research if it selected a strategy of developing new basic substances: on the other hand, a generic manufacturer, producing only those ethical products which have come off-patent, might only need the bare minimum of applied research. One food manufacturer might concentrate mainly on development work – for example, new products to marketing specifications based only on known technologies: another might finance a programme of basic research to produce edible protein from a petrocarbon source. The problems of planning are different for each of these research and development areas, basic research being the least predictable and reliable: probably most companies will never have to face the difficulty of trying to plan this type of research.

Research and development may be selected as the strategy for all the boxes in the matrix. It may be the path for complete diversification or the vehicle for product improvement. It may improve the margins of an existing product through the development of a new process or a change in a formula, R & D may fulfil a current and urgent need for today's operations or may be selected as the lynchpin of a future diversification strategy.

The strategic planning process should provide the framework for research and development planning, by:

1 Specifying the product or business areas to which research is to be directed
2 Setting priorities for research and development projects

3 Assigning time targets for R & D

4 Setting the cost framework in terms of both revenue and capital requirements.

Requests for research and development may emanate from operating management (for marketing, technical, or financial reasons) or may come from the studies carried out at strategic level by the top management planning group. The value of a heavy top management involvement in the setting of R & D objectives and in ensuring that these are an integral part of total company strategy has been stressed by many writers. For example, Steiner[5] states: '. . . top management involvement in choosing R & D programmes is important whether or not it considers itself technically qualified.' Quinn[6] argues: 'R & D planning and budgeting . . . must therefore be directly tied to total corporate planning.' Rance[7] stresses: 'In my experience the programme of the group R & D function must be determined through consultation at the highest possible level of executive authority in the company.'

Every R & D objective should be justified: that is, an attempt should be made to show what is required, why it is required, and the benefits the project will bring. Top management, through the planning process, must also assess the priorities for R & D work. The strategic plan should provide a clear indication of the most important areas to which R & D effort should be directed: establishing this is a part of the decision process which leads a company to select R & D rather than one of the other alternatives.

Closely tied in with priorities and the strategic decision are time targets. It is important to establish whether the work required is of the type that will respond to additional resources or whether there is a natural sequence of events that cannot be speeded in any way. If R & D is unlikely to produce results in the required period of time, the company may be forced to reject it as a method of growth or it may be compelled to develop other additional strategies to fill the gap caused by the extended time required. Unfortunately, the time required for a project and its related component cost is frequently underestimated. For example, Allen and Norris[8] found that time was underestimated by 204 per cent on average, while cost was exceeded by 46 per cent. Once a time target has been set in the plan, every available control tool should be used to ensure that the company keeps to it (see Chapter 20).

It should also be recognised that certain types of R & D projects are subject to two forms of failure. R & D may not succeed in producing the required product or process at all. Where an improvement or cost reduction exercise is involved an R & D success may be implemented immediately. A new product, however, is subject to a second type of failure: although R & D may have met all specifications, it may still die at the marketing stage. Norwood and Smith[9] report on a study of post-marketing new drug failures in the US pharmaceuticals industry over a long period. In the survey definitions, post-marketing failure rate was about 13 per cent over the period 1958–1966. However, the authors maintain that 'the pre-marketing failure rate for the pharmaceutical industry is much higher than that for all of American industry'. An assessment of the pre- and post-marketing failure rate for all American industry is provided in Figure 17.1.

Figure 17.1
Product evolution.
(From Dooley and
Ciapolla[10])

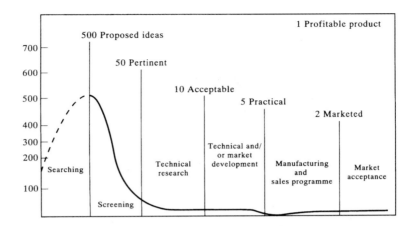

In the grocery trade, studies over a period of time (eleven years USA, fourteen years UK) by Nielson indicate that even at test-market stage the failure rate is relatively high. On average some 60 per cent of products test marketed went national in the USA, while in the UK only 46 per cent were launched. A study by Kraushar Andrews & Eassie Ltd.[11] showed that in the UK the average new product which reaches national distribution has only a 50 per cent chance of surviving four years or more. New products in this context are not necessarily new in an R & D sense, but the data give some indication of the risks involved.

Assessing the cost of a project is important for both decision and control purposes. First, the amount of resources required for a new project should be compared against the cost of alternative strategies. If it is too high and too risky, the company might well have to fill the matrix by another method. In addition to the cost of an individual project the company must consider the total long-term budget for its R & D section. It may be good policy to reject an R & D strategy because to follow it would mean spending more on total R & D than the company can justify: each project may be of reasonable cost by itself, but cumulatively the position becomes strategically unsound. (Control was referred to when time was discussed.)

Steiner[5] states that there are a number of 'rules' in practical use which are applied to the setting of R & D budgets.

> Establish the total R & D budget at some percentage of sales.
> Try to match what competitors are doing.
> Find the industry average and stick to that.
> Take a past historical average for the company and increase it by an amount equal to the internal rate of growth that is set as a company objective. If, for example, the company decides to grow at 8 per cent per year through internal product developments, then increase the budget for research and development by 8 per cent each year.
> Cost out R & D needed to meet specific product objectives and add a percentage for independent research to be determined by those doing it. Give the R & D staff what is requested if the amount is reasonable in light of the firm's financial ability. Develop in the planning process a balance among R & D and all other activities.

363

My own recommendation is that the amount of resources allocated for R & D should arise from the planning processes: that is, it should be a balance between the various activities of the company set at strategic level. In setting the balance the company should also take account of the cost of individual projects, so that these may not exceed the total allocation, and so that money is not allocated willy nilly when in fact it is more than adequate for all the projects that are required. For sustained R & D effort one of the main requirements is a measure of stability in budget allocations. This is an area where corporate planning can be of considerable assistance because, by tying in R & D effort to total corporate strategy, it helps the company to both identify and provide for its needs. If the plan throws doubt on the company's ability to finance the required measure of research, the best solution might well be to opt for a lower measure where there is more stability. No amount of planning can remove management judgement. Having set cost and time targets, only top management can decide whether to continue or to cut off once the limits are reached. Similarly, judgement is required in the selection of an R & D strategy, on its likely success, and on the cost effectiveness of such a strategy.

A further area of decision in the selection of an R & D strategy is whether to commission the work internally or externally. The availability of universities and specialist agencies should not be overlooked, and may provide a means of avoiding 'humps' in the company's internal R & D staffing needs.

The subject of R & D may be left with a final thought on the type of R & D strategy which may be selected. Pavitt[12] classifies these into 'offensive' (the intention to be first in the field with a major innovation), 'defensive' (the intention to avoid mistakes by following the leaders – never being first but reacting quickly enough to be second), and 'absorptive' (obtaining developments on licence and carrying out minimum R & D work to further develop them). The basic R & D approach selected would have a bearing on the choice of R & D instead to one of the other alternatives discussed in this chapter. Pavitt sums up the management implications of his strategy in Figure 17.2.

In this discussion of R & D strategy I have left one aspect unexplored: the technology strategy of the company. This will be discussed in a later chapter.

Acquisition and merger

A major area of strategic choice open to a company is acquisition, or its variant, merger. In many ways this strategy is too inviting, and can easily become a trap for the unwary. While the paper advantages of acquisition may be enticing, the management and human aspects – often incalculable at the early stages – may become so great that they prevent the strategy from becoming a success.

'Mergermania' can easily run riot, and the speed with which third parties frequently make intervening bids during a battle between two companies suggests that little thought or strategic planning has entered the process. The real reason for many acquisitions may be corporate or individual pride, without attention to what is good for the company or sound for its long-term future.

R & D strategy	Implications for management		
	Resource and managerial requirements	Possibilities of penetrating foreign markets	Specific problems and opportunities for European firms
Offensive	High R & D, high risk, high pay-off with success. Requires managerial flexibility and creative and perceptive science, technology and market exploration.	Relatively easy, provided that foreign demand exists.	Most difficult when US firms have strong technology/market advantages. Other advanced technologies do, however, exist and can be exploited.
Defensive	Medium R & D risk. Lower pay-off unless leader makes mistakes. Need for good knowledge of competitors, short lead times, and strong marketing capability.	Likely when lead times very short, leading firm makes mistakes, or when firm makes improvements in design or in secondary characteristics.	Best strategy when consolidating past mistakes, or when dealing with competitors with strong technology/market positions.
Absorptive	Low R & D and risk. Low pay-off, unless there exists strong advantages in man-power or material costs, or other company attributes.	Likely when market restriction clauses can be avoided, and cost advantages rapidly exploited.	More difficult as big firms prefer to invest rather than license. Possible when firm has its own technology. Medium- and small-sized firms more likely to license than big ones.

Figure 17.2
Research and development strategies. (From Pavitt[12])

Yet there may be positive and genuine benefits to an acquisition strategy: real reasons which demonstrate that this method of development can provide a sound bridge to the future, and is not necessarily a way of dissipating resources to give solid form to misty illusions of personal grandeur. It is worth studying these potential benefits, before looking at some of the practical results of merger activity, and some of the ways of ensuring that if an acquisition strategy is selected it has a good chance of being successful.

Acquisition may be used to fill every box in the expansion matrix; for example:

1 *Existing products/existing markets.* Acquiring an extra link in the chain – backwards integration to control supplies, or forwards integration to take on a further step in the distribution process.
2 *Existing products/new markets.* Buying a wholesaler in a new export market, to provide an easier means of entry.
3 *New products/existing markets.* Acquisition of a company that can be completely integrated with present operations.
4 *New products/new markets.* Complete diversification through acquisition of a company in an entirely new field.

This is something of an oversimplification of the reasons for acquisition, and needs further elaboration. In fact there may be many sound arguments in favour of acquisition.

(a) Reduction of risk

In the previous section examples were given of new product failure rates for two industries. The acquisition of a business with suitable products may provide an opportuntity for a firm to expand without carrying this risk of failure. Such a policy may be in the interests of the individual firm but will only benefit the community if the acquisition has a synergistic effect (of course, it is in the interests of the company to seek synergy).

There is also the possibility of a negative effect – for managerial and morale reasons the two companies may achieve less when put together than they would as single entities. Nevertheless, the risk to a company may still be less than one of the alternative expansion strategies, even in a situation where the cost of implementation is higher. We will look later at the research into success and failure of acquisitions.

(b) Avoidance of a profit slump

Acquisition may be a way of buying immediate profits, where one of the other alternatives would have caused a period of reduced earnings. Profits may increase in absolute terms, but still bring a reduction in return on investment, although this, too, may be avoided if synergy can be exploited. The way the acquisition is financed will also affect ROI.

(c) A means of entry into a new area

Not all new business areas are easy for an outsider to enter. The more advanced technology and high-capital industries (often the two go together) have by their very nature a measure of protection against intruders. To break in may require the injection of heavy capital resources into a business area in which the company has little experience, or the problem of somehow obtaining the necessary technical knowledge which can be difficult, costly, and with few chances of success. In these circumstances acquisition may be a very attractive strategy and may save both time and money.

(d) A means of obtaining cash

Certain types of company may have a healthy cash-flow situation, large liquid reserves, and a relatively poor history of profits. Such a situation may, for example, occur with a shipping company, where positive cash flows from depreciation on very expensive fixed assets make reinvestment of the cash a difficult strategic problem. In this sort of situation, a company with a good profit record and a need for capital to exploit its many projects may find it possible to acquire the other company on a share exchange basis – in effect buying cash for paper. Such a move may be facilitated if the stock market has valued the companies on a yield, rather than on an asset, basis. The acquiring company is left with the problem of increasing earnings so that its present shareholders are not dissatisfied – the synergy which makes this possible may be simply a use for the surplus cash.

(e) Welding together a fragmented industry

Some industries are highly fragmented. This makes it difficult for any company to gain a major share of the market by any internal strategy. The only way to build up a sizeable operating unit is through a process of acquisition and rationalisation. A move of this nature may be encouraged by government as the best means of creating a healthy industry: an example of such a situation was the UK machine-tool industry during the 1960s. It is worth pointing out that although acquisition may be the only workable strategic choice within an industry, a far better option might well be to expand into a completely different field. The danger sign to be avoided is when top management begins to see itself as the crusading saviours of the industry rather than professional managers charged with the duty of looking after shareholders' interests.

(f) Removal of competition

Example (e) above may have the effect of removing competitive products, but is not the main reason for the acquisition. On the other hand, it is possible to seek the destruction of competition through acquisition for monopolistic reasons: to gain complete control of a market in order to reduce consumer choice and increase prices. Acquisition for this reason now verges on the impossible in many developed countries because legislation exists expressly to prevent it.

(g) Opportunity for synergy

Some aspects of synergy have already been discussed, and the synergistic effect is something which should be looked for in any acquisition situation. The main reason for an acquisition may be because the company has spotted a synergistic opportunity. Cash resources have already been discussed (they are something of a special case), but opportunities may also exist in areas of research and development, production, distribution, or marketing. The only thing to add is a plea for caution: in most merger situations, what is known about a company is only the tip of the iceberg: what lies hidden under the surface may be enough to destroy the apparent opportunity.

367

(h) To obtain new ideas

A sterile company may turn to acquisition for growth because it lacks creativity and has no ideas of its own. Unless a radical change takes place such a company is likely to find that an acquisition provides it with only a short-term opportunity. The next phase of growth will also require ideas, and the company is no more likely to have these after the merger than it was before. In my experience many companies which turn to acquisition do so because they do not know what else to do. And this is not a very good reason.

(i) To obtain new people

It is sometimes said that a reason for acquisition may be to obtain particular management skills. It is difficult to think of many acquisition circumstances where such a reason is sound: the services of a firm of 'headhunters' may be cheaper and more effective. A possible exception may be when a company particularly wants a person who is running a small business and there the purchase price is small. The situation may be different in a true merger situation, where management of complementary skills and talents wish to come together for the benefit of both parties: again, this is a solution which is more likely in small- to medium-sized companies than in the larger businesses.

(j) Capital cost of growth

Acquisition may also be chosen for financial strategic reasons rather than because it is the less risky or more profitable path open to the company. A business with a poor cash flow may not have the capital to choose, for example, the R & D route, but may be able to acquire by an exchange of shares and without cash. Whether this is a good reason for acquisition depends on individual circumstances.

Chapter 2 included evidence that the benefits expected from a merger are not always achieved in practice, and referenced many studies that showed that the failure rate is likely to be around 50 per cent, and has not improved over the 30 years during which such studies have been undertaken. There is advice available on how to reduce the chances of failure. Kitching[13,14] does more than present the evidence of failure. He also shows that the failure rate is much higher in acquisitions for diversification, and makes a number of suggestions for both pre- and post-acquisition actions that will improve the chance of success. Ansoff *et al.*[15] showed that careful planning would improve the results to be gained from an acquisition.

One of the weaknesses has been that acquisitions are often looked at mainly from a financial and economic view. On paper putting two organisations together often appears to create synergy when these are the only viewpoints. In practice many other factors are as important, particularly those around corporate culture, people, and customers, and these are often ignored or given scant attention. Cartwright and Cooper[16] give what is probably the most complete guide available to the cultural and human aspects of acquisitions (much of this is relevant for alliances).

From personal experience I would add another caution. Even when an organisation appears to be a competitor of yours, it does not mean that it gains its customers in the same way. It is not uncommon for an assumption to be made that the two businesses are the same and can be crashed together, thus destroying the differentiation which might be the reason why the other company held its position in the market. It is easy to destroy, even when the intentions are the opposite. So there is a clear health warning attached to the acquisition route.

Perhaps the most important lessons to be learned from merger studies are that success calls for careful management planning, deliberate and speedy action to achieve the merger objectives, and control to study the results of the action. The planned approach to mergers tries to take out many of the elements of risks.

First, any company considering merger should clearly identify why this particular alternative strategy is being selected above all others. If an acquisition idea cannot pass this preliminary screening it should be rejected. If there is a prima facie case for acquisition, the next stage should be the identification of the acquisition objectives. This must be a deliberate and unemotional approach, and related to the general requirements of the strategy rather than a particular acquisition candidate: moving the analysis to a specific company comes later.

The acquisition objectives should serve as the framework around which the next stage of analysis can be built – the detailed acquisition profile. Again, without a particular company in mind – for this will only cloud the judgement – the planning team should prepare a pen picture of the type of company that is required in order to fulfil the strategy. The profile should specify all the factors that are considered important – and those will vary from company to company. It is rare that the ideal acquisition candidate exists in real life, but the profile provides a standard against which all candidates may be measured. For the measurement to be really useful, it follows that great care must be exercised in drawing up the profile so that all important factors are both identified and quantified. If a particular criterion is vital this must be stressed since there is no point in making an acquisition that cannot possibly fulfil its purpose. On the other hand, other points in the profile may be desirable but not essential: this, too, should be stated.

There are many ways in which an acquisition profile may be set out, and, as in so many aspects of management, there is no one golden rule. The example given here is of what might be done rather than what must be done, and refers to a hypothetical situation where the planner can be very specific about the market in which he expects his acquisition to be operating. A more general example will be provided later.

Acquisition profile: marine heating and ventilating company

1 *Size.* To cost no more than £1m at an initial return on capital employed of not less than 10 per cent.

2 *Products*. Design and manufacture of complete environmental control systems for the shipping industry.

3 *Market position*. Must have at least 10 per cent of the UK market and must have customers in more than five shipyards. Must have 25 per cent of sales in export markets, including Norway, Holland, and Japan. At least 90 per cent of sales must be in original equipment. Turnover about £1m per annum.

4 *Technical position*. Must be accepted in its industry as a leader in technical innovation. Over the past five years an average of at least 5 per cent of annual sales must have been spent on research and development.

5 *Management*. Competent management at all levels is desirable. Good top management is essential, as is technical management at all levels.

6 *Factories*. Plant and equipment must be relatively modern (90 per cent of plant must be under five years old).

Factory must be located in the north-east of England. The site must have room for expansion, and it must be physically possible to treble output within three years.

7 *Conditions*. No company will be acquired unless it is possible to obtain all voting shares.

In some circumstances a company may wish to be more general in acquisition requirements. For example, a company wishing to expand in the food business may be willing to choose a candidate from a number of subsectors of that broad industry group (the hypothetical company above was able to be much more specific than this and to say precisely which industry and which market it wished to enter). A conglomerate company may wish to define its acquisition policy in even more general terms, being willing to consider a number of candidates from a number of industries. In this sort of situation the requirements may be much more matters of financial strategy than any particular market strategy, and the intention may be to exploit investment and financial management skills, rather than to develop any particular wing of the business. Such general profiles are still an aid to the identification of acquisition candidates, and have been used by many companies. An example is given below.

The XYZ Company intends to diversify into four new business areas, and to achieve this end will acquire suitable companies in the food industry in Europe, the USA, and North Africa.

Acquisition efforts will be concentrated on companies which have a demonstrable record of product development. The companies must have strong franchises in advertised and branded consumer food products, and must hold less than 10 per cent of the domestic market.

Food industry investments will be selected from companies in any of the following areas:

Coffee and tea
Canned foods
Pet foods
Sweets and chocolates
Sauces, pickles, and condiments
Frozen foods

Restriction

Not more than two companies will be acquired in any one country, and not more than one will be in North Africa.

Size

The minimum size of any company by turnover will be £3m per annum, of which at least 75 per cent will be domestic sales.

Profitability criteria

No acquisition will be considered that does not offer the prospect of returning 10 per cent on shareholders' capital within three years and after taxes. The average return on capital employed during those three years must not be less than 8 per cent. Profits (after tax) of at least £300 000 per year must be possible.

Any acquisition in North Africa must yield 20 per cent return on capital employed, according to the above definitions.

Ownership and management

No company will be acquired unless at least 80 per cent of equity can be obtained, and 100 per cent is preferred.

The competence of management, proved by past records, and the continued availability of key people is an essential factor in any acquisition.

A great deal of thought and hard work will have been put into these first stages of the acquisition study, but this is only a beginning. The next step is to study the companies theoretically available for acquisition and to match their characteristic against the predefined acquisition profile. This statement hides what in practice may be a long and boring task: it may require an analysis of several hundred companies to arrive at two or three which are close to the profile, and even then acquisition may prove to be impossible. Much of the analysis may be at a fairly simple level, certain factors from the profile (for example, turnover range) being used to screen out the obviously unsuitable and to reduce the list to manageable proportions.

Now it may well be that no company matches very closely with the acquisition profile, and management may be called upon to decide how far they can compromise, or whether the deviations are so great that they indicate that an alternative strategy should be chosen. Each successive stage in the screening processes is likely to involve more detailed analysis work. By the time the short list is reached the company may have had to carry out original market research in order to establish some details of the companies concerned: certainly very

Figure 17.3

Stages in the
identification of
acquisition
candidates showing
sources of
information

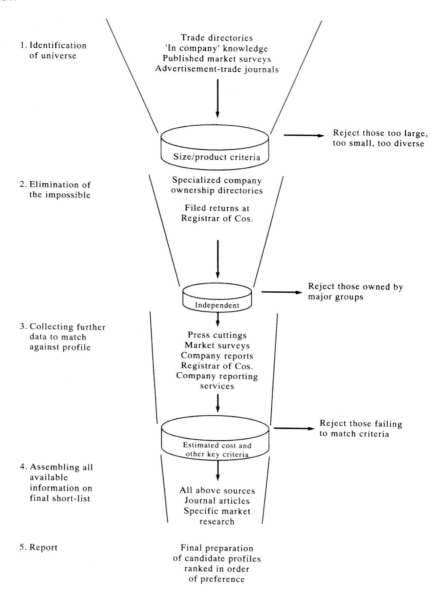

1. Identification
of universe

Trade directories
'In company' knowledge
Published market surveys
Advertisement-trade journals

Size/product criteria

Reject those too large,
too small, too diverse

2. Elimination of
the impossible

Specialized company
ownership directories

Filed returns at
Registrar of Cos.

Independent

Reject those owned by
major groups

3. Collecting further
data to match
against profile

Press cuttings
Market surveys
Company reports
Registrar of Cos.
Company reporting
services

Estimated cost and
other key criteria

Reject those failing
to match criteria

4. Assembling all
available
information on
final short-list

All above sources
Journal articles
Specific market
research

5. Report

Final preparation
of candidate profiles
ranked in order
of preference

detailed desk research will have taken place. Figure 17.3 provides an illustration
of how the acquisition research might develop, although this can only be a
generalised view, and there may be differences in particular situations.

The screening processes should result in a short list of companies which closely
match the acquisition profile. An attempt should be made to identify the probable
cost of acquiring each of these companies with the possible financial strategies
that might be adopted. An acquisition objective should then be developed for
each candidate, showing exactly what benefits the company seeks. Much of this
will be derived from the general acquisition objectives, although much may be

specific to the particular candidate. From this a provisional value of the candidate *to the company* may be established. This may be higher than the valuation of the candidate on past and expected performance because of the things the company intend to do to that company once it is acquired. The final candidates may now be ranked in order of preference, putting management in a position to decide whether to proceed with the acquisition.

Until this decision is made no indication of interest will have been given to the candidates concerned, and all work should be carried out in strict confidence. After this point the company has to approach the candidate either directly or through a third party (e.g. a merchant bank) to establish whether there is any interest in selling. There are differences between the acquisition of publicly quoted and privately owned companies: with the former an offer can be sent to shareholders even if the directors of the candidate company oppose the acquisition. In a private company, where management and financial control may be in the hands of the same people, such tactics would be unlikely to succeed. In either type of company amicable discussion is preferred, since this may give the purchaser access to much more information about the candidate, enabling him or her to define the acquisition objectives with more precision and to value the company with more confidence.

Negotiation is outside the scope of this book, as are valuation and the many legal and taxation problems which arise from acquisition activity. Before a firm offer is made, the purchaser should be very clear on what he intends to do with the company since, as has already been stated, speed of implementation is very important once an acquisition offer has been successful.

Uncertainty about what will happen may damage morale in both companies at all levels unless action is taken with speed. In addition, the expected benefits of the merger may evaporate if undue delays take place. In my opinion it is more important to move with speed, taking all necessary steps within a matter of weeks, even though this may bring the risk of a wrong decision. Change over too long a period – or rather speculation on what that change might be – can bring a psychological blight over the company. If changes are implemented quickly, people can begin to relax and accept that they are now only subject to normal business hazards rather than the abnormal ones of the acquisition situation.

The achievement of this speed of action requires careful management planning both before and after acquisition. It calls for the commitment of top management time and interest, the allocation of responsibility for merging the two companies to a specific senior manager, and the control of the implementation of the acquisition plan by a regular reporting system. Acquisition may make a great demand on managers of both companies. Problems vary from the large tasks of rationalising two factories or merging two marketing operations, to the less important but time-consuming difficulty of putting two accounting systems on to a common basis. Overall the emotional climate may be coloured by fear.

The human factors are so important in merger success that they are worth more detailed examination (see Chapter 21). The example of Penn Central Railroad's diversification efforts provides a grim warning of where a badly managed acquisition policy may lead. Penn Central's bankruptcy in June 1971 has been described as the worst collapse in the history of modern US business. (Some observers maintain that the collapse of Penn Central can itself be traced back to the formation of the company in 1968 with the merger of two railways, Pennsylvania and New York Central.) The report on the collapse by the Interstate Commerce Commission, the body which regulates all US operations, stated – among other things – that eagerness to diversify into non-railway activities led to the investment of $309m into pipeline, airline, real estate, and other activities. The total return on these massive investments was only $4–7m, and in some cases Penn Central management failed to insist on their subsidiaries paying any cash dividends.

Strategic alliances

Joint ventures have always been with us as a strategic option. Perhaps the oil industry offers the longest historical view of the use of this approach, often forced on the companies because of the costs of developing an oilfield, or the fact that control of production or markets may be divided so that limited collaboration is desirable. During the 1980s, the joint venture option became broadened to a concept of strategic alliances. A strategic alliance may involve investment by two or more companies in a specific venture. It may be broader, and involve forms of collaboration over marketing, technology, manufacture or other factors that are to the benefit of both companies. This second form of strategic alliance is appealing, but much more difficult to manage. In an acquisition or merger the partners become one. In a joint venture it is possible to set up an organisation to fulfill the required purpose, although not always without some clashes of objective between the partners. In the other form of alliance the companies may operate through their existing structures, making it difficult for either party to control what is happening.

The drive for alliances is partly fuelled by the fact that in many industries, for example the defence industries, the number of large players who may be available for acquisition is close to zero. Companies still need to find ways of competing with global competitors who may be operating on a larger scale. Alliances offer one way of doing this, or of obtaining benefits from larger market operations without the risks or requirement for high investment. The avoidance of what may be very high levels of investment may itself be the driving force. In some situations, government controls or protective rules may make alliances the only way of getting into a particular market.

The steps in selecting alliance partners are similar to those in finding acquisition candidates. However an additional essential step is to ensure that each party is aware of the objectives of the other before any agreement is signed. If the aims of the alliance partners are not compatible, the chances are that the alliance will break up quickly. A second requirement is not to underestimate the amount of management attention needed to make an alliance work. It is worth being realistic about the expected life of an alliance, since once the objectives of the partners changes, the alliance may become unworkable.

British Airways has been one of the most successful followers of the strategic alliance strategy, forming alliances with other airlines that have enabled it to be

Exhibit 17.2 Gaining benefit from strategic alliances

The intention of British Airways to form an alliance with American Airlines will bring competitive advantages to both organisations. BA has had a history of successful alliances, and has learnt from its failures. It knows that it cannot achieve its goal of industry leadership by other means.

One of the core competencies of BA is the operation of alliances, which have taken many forms. It learnt from early experiences. An alliance with United Airlines to codeshare London routes came to grief because United did not have to give up those London routes which were outside the codeshare agreement, which frustrated the arrangement when United bought Pan Am's London routes and operated them outside the alliance. BA has not made the same mistake in its other US alliances, USAir, and if it clears the regulatory authorities, AA. Despite this, the USAir agreement only lasted about three years, and BA decided to sell its shares in 1996.

Some alliances, such as that with USAir where BA bought 24.6 per cent, have involved an equity participation. This has extended into various franchise-type alliances, such as that with the French airline TAT where it initially took 49.9 per cent in 1992. All TAT international flights were operated under the BA name, and in BA livery. In 1996, BA acquired the remaining shares in this company, turning the alliance into an acquisition.

Franchise agreements with an equity stake are in force with a number of airlines, including the French Air Liberté (1996), and the German Delta Air (1992), renamed Deutsche BA. Examples of franchises without equity participation include Comair of South Africa (1996), Sun-Air of Scandinavia (1997), and some regional UK airlines.

The Qantas alliance (1993) is not a franchise, but involves joint marketing, purchasing and service agreements, the last on a reciprocal basis. BA bought 25 per cent of Qantas equity under this agreement. An alliance in India with Jet Airways is limited to marketing and frequent-flyer programmes.

What has BA gained? There are economies from the bargaining power of joint purchasing. Codesharing allows BA to offer a service to destinations it does not serve, although its planes may be used for part of the journey. Its reach is extended. Scheduling can be arranged so that franchised internal flights act as feeders for BA international flights more conveniently than for other airlines. Technology links enable, for example, an airline to be offered through another's computerised booking service. The benefits accrue to both parties, which is one of the criteria for successful long-term relationships.

(*Source*: Mockler, R. J., Dologite, D. G. and Carnevali, N. M. 'Type and Structure of Multinational Strategic Alliances: the Airline Industry'. *Strategic Change*, 6, No. 5, 1997)

the leading world operator. For a detailed case study of alliances in the airline industry, and extensive advice on the issues in multinational strategic alliances see the three linked articles: Mockler, Dologite and Carnevale[17] and Mockler.[18,19]

The 1990s in particular have seen the rise of another form of alliance, the closer linkage of suppliers and customers. These are not all partnerships of equals, but there has been a growing tendency for collaborative relationships. The thinking originally came out of the total quality movement, with the realisation that longer-term relationships were a major contributor to overall quality, and has gained momentum because of the trend to outsourcing discussed earlier. There has also been a realisation that an alliance that works together on the value chain may deliver benefits to customers that could not be achieved by organisations working alone. These types of alliance are somewhat different from those discussed above, but nevertheless require very similar management skills if they are to succeed.

Some strategic principles

The complexity of strategic decision making becomes more apparent, the deeper the exploration of the subject. Even this chapter, which appeared to be self-contained, and indeed was when I wrote the original in the first edition of this book, has thrown up a need to look more deeply into the strategy of technology (and I will link this later to some thoughts about manufacturing strategy), and the human issues in acquisition. To neglect the people issues would mean that we are looking at strategy and not strategic management. We have yet to explore any of the thinking about global strategy.

At this point in the exploration of strategy it is worth referring to one of the few extensive databases from which the cause and effect of different strategies has been studied over a long period. I refer to the PIMS database. PIMS stands for profit impact of market strategy and has been in operation since 1972. Buzzell and Gale[20] provided a useful analysis of what can be gleaned from PIMS, and at the time they wrote there were 450 corporations contributing information on a total of 3000 business units. Data are collected annually, and the length of membership varied from 2 to 10 years. Member companies came from the USA and Europe.

The top principles of strategic thinking which emerged from the analysis were:

1 The most important single factor impacting on the performance of a business unit is quality relative to competitors. They found that superior quality often brought premium prices, and in addition could lead to market growth and an expansion of market share. The word 'relative' is important, because competitors are unlikely to stay still. This strategy therefore requires constant action if the company is to stay in the lead.

Exhibit 17.3 New success factors in Japanese companies

Successful strategy is not about doing what everyone else does, nor is it always a question of doing only one thing. Akira Sawayama is the managing director of Tokyo-based consultancy Yahagi Consultants. In a presentation he made at a forum of the Japan Strategic Management Society in December 1996 (which he later wrote into an article for me) he revealed his research into the top-performing Japanese companies. He studied companies other than pharmaceuticals, with pre-tax earnings of more than 10 billion yen. One criterion was that the definition of success meant that they had to have exceeded the peak performance they had reached up to the bursting of the Japanese economic bubble. There were twenty-one such companies, whose performance was analysed over the period 1990 to 1995.

The successful companies:

- Combine operational measures with structural changes, trimming inventories, manpower, and restructuring the business portfolio;
- Know their strengths and weaknesses, and build the business on core competencies which have relevance to their customers;
- Many traditional human resource policies have been changed, moving to a meritocracy, performance-related bonus systems, and empowered managers who are held personally accountable for results in their areas. Sawayama argues that the result has 'nothing to do with the myth of Japanese consensus, but is driven by intensified competition within the organisation: accomplish or perish';
- They have powerful leadership, with clear strategic intentions, which has resulted in much more product being made outside of Japan (Aiwa, for example, now produces 86 per cent of its products outside of the country, compared with 46 per cent in 1988 – the philosophy is to make products where the currency is weakest and sell them where it is strongest). The leaders take personal responsibility for longer-term thinking, and have abandoned bottom-up strategic planning;
- Their pursuit of a competitive edge is relentless.

Successful companies have created a new strategic focus, and changed their cultures and the processes which drive the cultures.

(*Source*: Akira Sawayama, 'Back to Basics: the New Success Factors in Japanese Companies', *Strategic Change*, 6, No. 3, 1997.)

2 A second finding was that there was a link between market share and profitability. Companies with highest market shares tended to have better profitability. The authors caution against interpreting this statement as a belief that high market share at any cost is a good strategy. It is not.

3 High investment intensity acts as a drag on profits. Profitability tends to be highest where the amount of investment is lowest. This conclusion, in my opinion, should not lead anyone to the simplistic strategy of avoiding reinvestment to gain competitive advantage, a route that could eventually lead to total failure.

4 Much of the conventional wisdom about 'dogs' and 'cows' is not borne out by the evidence. This statement was discussed when we considered portfolio analysis, and is only included here for the sake of completeness.

5 Vertical integration is a profitable strategy in some situations but not in others. The analysis is somewhat complex, but basically shows that vertical integration decreases profitability in businesses with a low relative market share. Businesses with an average or high market share do best when vertical integration is high or low, but not when it is in the middle. The conclusion seems to be: avoid it if you have a low market share. If you have a stronger position only go for vertical integration if you are prepared to do it in a significant way.

6 Most of the strategic factors that boost return on investment will also boost long-term value.

These points are drawn from one chapter of the book by Buzzell and Gale. This point is made because there is a great deal of explanation and wisdom in the other eleven chapters, and these are worth reading.

As always, when considering any points about strategic principles, remember that there are no hard rules and absolutes. Conclusions such as the above are helpful, but have to be considered with all the other factors and issues that have been covered so far, and many that we have yet to cover. Getting a good strategy is not a matter of applying a formula.

References

1 Thompson, P. 'The NFC Buy-out – A New Form of Industrial Enterprise', in Taylor, B. (ed.), *Strategic Planning and the Board*, Pergamon, Oxford, 1988.

2 Friedman, A. 'Fiatallis: From Marriage to Divorce', *Financial Times*, 11 February 1985.

3 Jennings, D. 'Strategic Guidelines for Outsourcing Decisions', *Strategic Change*, **6**, No. 2 March/April, 1977.

4 Monahan, J. 'How Canada Dry Mixed its Marketing', *Management Today*, November 1970.

5 Steiner, G. A. *Top Management Planning*, Macmillan, London 1969.

6 Quinn, J. B. 'Technological Strategies for Industrial Companies', *Management Decision*, Autumn 1968.

7 Rance, H. 'Financing R & D', *Management Decision*, Autumn 1968.

8 Allen, J. M. and Norris, K. P. 'Project Estimates and Outcomes in Electricity Generation Research', *Journal of Management Studies*, October 1970.

9 Norwood, G. J. and Smith, M. C. 'Market Mortality of New Products in the Pharmaceutical Industry', *Journal of the American Pharmaceutical Association*, November 1971.

10 Dooley, J. I. and Ciapolla, J. A. 'Guides to Screening New Product Ideas', in Martin, E. (ed.), *Management for the Smaller Company*, American Management Association, 1959.

11 *New Products in the Grocery Trade*, Kraushar Andrews & Eassie Ltd, 1971.

12 Pavitt, K. 'Technological Innovation in European Industry: the Need for a World Perspective', *Long Range Planning*, December 1969.

13 Kitching, J. *Acquisitions in Europe; Causes of Corporate Successes and Failures*, Business International, 1973 (Summary published in each June 1973 issue *Business Europe*).

14 Kitching, J. 'Acquisitions in Europe', various issues of *Business Europe.* This was a summary of reference 13, and may be more easily accessible under the same title in Hussey, D. E. (ed.), *The Truth About Corporate Planning*, Pergamon, Oxford, 1983.

15 Ansoff, H. I., Avner, J., Brandenburg, R. G., Porter, F. E. and Radosevitch, R. 'Does Planning Pay? The Effect of Planning on Success of American Firms', *Long Range Planning*, December 1970.

16 Cartwright, S. and Cooper, C. L. *Managing Mergers, Acquisitions and Strategic Alliances*, 2nd edn, Butterworth-Heinemann, Oxford, 1996.

17 Mockler, R. J., Dologite, D. G., and Carnevale, N. M. 'Type and Structure of Multinational Strategic Alliances: the Airline Industry', *Strategic Change*, **6**, No. 5, 1977.

18 Mockler, R. J. 'Contingency Models for Developing Multinational Strategic Alliances: the Airline Industry', *Strategic Change*, **6**, No. 6, 1997.

19 Mockler, R. J. 'Multinational Strategic Alliances: a Manager's Perspective', *Strategic Change*, **6**, No. 7, 1997.

20 Buzzell, R. D. and Gale, B. T. *The PIMS Principles*, Free Press, New York, 1987.

Further reading

Bleeke, J. and Ernst, D. *Collaborating to Compete: Using Strategic Alliances and Acquisitions in the Global Marketplace*, 1993.

Hussey, D. E. 'Virtual Organisations: The Ultimate in Flexibility', *Journal of Professional HRM*, Issue 5, October, 1996.

Hussey, D. E. (ed), *The Innovation Challenge*, Wiley, Chichester, 1997.

Jarillo, J. C. *Strategic Networks: Creating the Borderless Organisation*, Butterworth-Heinemann, Oxford, 1993.

CHAPTER 18

Multinational and global strategy

This chapter shows the forces that are making more and more industries take a global view, both of their competitors and of the geographical arena in which they operate. The drivers for globalisation are examined, and the argument is made that globalisation is a strategic decision: it does not just happen. A method to compare whether the company is operating in accord with the pressures for globalisation is described. However, there is more to operating across country borders than taking a global view. Another aim of the chapter is to consider some of the issues in the management of multinational undertakings that affect the design of strategic management processes and the strategic decisions themselves.

Once a company begins to operate outside of its own national environment, its problems of strategic choice begin to multiply (some of these complications may also occur in a company with a number of large subsidiaries).

International business has been with us for a long, long time. It arrived at the dawn of civilisation and for centuries provided the motivation for many of the acts which shaped the path of history. If wars were not fought for personal grandeur, territorial expansion, or religion, they were usually fought for trade. By the fifteenth century the international company was well established in the shape of the banking and merchant businesses which flourished in Italy.

The international company began to get larger, and during the European colonial period was frequently entrusted with the task of government, administration, defence (and we might add aggression), as well as sordid commerce. The British East India Company, the Hudson's Bay Company, the British South Africa Company are just a few of the names which can still set the imagination reeling. Some of our modern multinational giants may be bigger, but how many can bring their private armies and navies to back up their grand strategies?

Problems of managing international business are also very old. Drucker[1] quotes the example of how the Rothschild family managed its international banking business – stationing key members of the family at the foreign courts where business was to be generated and banishing the inept members to places where there was no business.

Although many problems are old, they are still very relevant, and should be considered against the background of the different types of international business which exist today. These can be classified under four headings:

1 The company whose only international business is trading internationally
2 The company which has a high volume of export business supported by marketing companies in other countries and the occasional manufacturing subsidiary
3 The transnational company with a network of subsidiaries or associate companies in other countries, including many overseas plants
4 The multinational company that produces and markets internationally and which has a multinational management, possibly international ownership.

The transnational and multinational companies polarise into two strategic types, multidomestic and global. A multidomestic strategy is a coordinated series of country operations, possibly grouped into regions, where strategies are designed as a response to local market conditions. The global company looks at the world as one market, and in many but not necessarily all of its strategies will act on a global basis.

Strategic management for the first two types of companies presents only a few additional problems over those faced by the national business. These arise mainly from the complications of distance, language, national cultural differences, the management of additional profit centres, and the need to take account of more than one national business environment.

It is the last two categories which are the main subject matter of this chapter, and in particular the spectrum of multidomestic to global. What is it that drives a company to change from a strategy of having subsidiaries which respond individually to their own markets to an organisation which in the extreme case clones an identical response to every market? And what options lie between these extremes?

Forces of globalisation

Yip[2] argues that there are four groups of factors which are the drivers for an industry to become global: market, cost, government, and competitive.

Market

The factors here include a convergence of market requirements in different parts of the world, as life styles and tastes draw closer together. Customer organisations, who are themselves global, increasingly expect their suppliers to

> ## Exhibit 18.1 From multi domestic to global: Ford 2000
>
> In 1994 the Ford 2000 programme was announced. Ford's automotive operations had made good profits in 1994, but relative to competitors, their performance was weak. Hitherto Ford had designed, manufactured and marketed cars on a regional basis: Europe, North America, and Asia-Pacific, on the theory that a multidomestic strategy enabled the organisation to be in the best position to meet market needs.
>
> In practice, this had begun to stifle innovation, leading to worse performance than competitors on development time, the costs of new models, and standardisation of parts. The attempt to turn the Escort, designed in Europe, into a world car had failed, with each region redesigning the car. Only six of the intended 5000 parts remained in the USA in common with Europe. The radiator cap was one of the six.
>
> Ford had therefore less bargaining power with suppliers than its competitors, and suppliers had less chance of economies of scale that could be passed on to Ford.
>
> The switch to a global strategy meant that there would in future be five vehicle production vehicle centres (later reduced to four), each having global responsibility for the design, development and engineering of vehicles for a particular market segment. One centre was in Europe, the rest in the USA.
>
> Success of this strategy depends on many things, not the least of which is information and communication technology to enable local market preferences to be integrated into design and engineering in a far-distant country. Ford is now implementing a strategy that has long been followed by Honda and Toyota. However, it is much harder to change an organisation and culture than to build one from the ground floor, and success will depend as much on change management skills as it does on the ability of the vehicle design centres to produce worldwide vehicles.
>
> (*Main source*: Afuah, A., 'Is Ford 2000 the Right Strategy for Innovation: A Management Theory Perspective?', *Strategic Change*, **6**, No. 6, 1997.)

offer a global service. There are now more areas of the world which enjoy a relatively affluent life style. However, this last point should not be over stressed, as the population in the less developed world is expected to continue to increase as a percentage of total world population.

World travel creates a requirement for the same service to be available on a global basis. Visa or American Express are good examples of markets where a world-wide service is needed, and which give the companies concerned an advantage over a credit card that can only be used in the country of issue.

Demand is related to price, which in turn has connections with cost. The nature of many markets is that the market size is achieved because world requirements are compressed into a few factories, thus enabling costs to tumble through economies of scale and the experience curve effect, allowing continued price decreases in real terms. The vast increase in instant information through the explosion of information technology has meant that facts about the markets and business environment are known quickly, enabling a fast response.

Costs

In addition to the volume effect on costs that can be achieved by a global approach, such an approach may be forced by technological change and the trend to shorter product life cycles. World volumes may be needed in order to afford the required level of research and development and the capital costs of new production requirements. Because of issues like this many industries have seen a concentration that would have been unnecessary forty years ago. The number of players in the world aerospace industry has fallen as development and production costs have risen, and it is now inconceivable that anyone could contemplate entering this industry on a small scale, based only on the demand from domestic airlines.

Information technology has also helped the cost factor. Computer-aided design (CAD) and computer-aided manufacture (CAM) enable products to be designed in any country, and instantaneously be made available in any other location. This makes it easier for manufacture to be located in areas of lowest cost, and design and development in areas of high talent. It also makes it easier for engineering teams in different countries to collaborate in the design of a new product.

Government

Recent years have seen the amalgamation of separate countries into vast trading blocks, of which the best example is the European Union. In addition to creating a larger accessible market, EU regulations have removed many non-tariff barriers by setting common standards for many products. Many difficulties in reaching a standardised product, essential for true global operations, have thus fallen away. Overall barriers to trade have been steadily reduced, despite occasional setbacks as in the 1992 GATT negotiations.

There has also been a world trend to privatise industries previously in the public sector. Thus the opportunity for global expansion in telecommunications now exists, when it was impossible in the 1970s.

Competitive

Although certain local niche strategies may sometimes be successful in an industry where most players are global, increasingly it is being realised that the rules of the game are changing, and that it is next to impossible to defeat a global player through a country-by-country strategy. One reason behind the demise of the British and American motorcycle industries was that the companies concerned had been driven out of their markets before they realised that the new competitors were thinking in world terms. The reason behind the success of the global strategies is partly the lower costs that can be achieved through a mixture of high volumes and standardised products, and partly because the decision base is different. In one grocery products assignment I handled in the late 1980s, my client operated on a country-by-country basis in most European countries. The leading competitor operated on the basis that Europe was one market. Whereas my client demanded that each country made profits, the competitor took a global view and would willingly reduce profit in a particular country to combat any attempt by the other players to increase their market share. This was always possible, as my client, in common with the other competitors, took marketing decisions piecemeal at the country level, and never mounted a coordinated attack in all countries at the same time.

While many companies have evolved into global players, there is an increasing tendency for at least some organisations to be global from start up. Jolly et al.[3] studied four companies from different countries which had a global vision from start-up, and implemented that vision immediately. The companies were Logitech, a Swiss-based manufacturer of desktop aids for computers, Techno-phone, a British firm providing hand-portable telephones, Connor Peripherals, started in the USA to commercialise high performance Winchester disk drives, and Lasa, which established itself simultaneously in the USA and Europe. Lasa is also in the high-technology computer-related field. While a few years ago it might have been sufficient to watch the strategies of those companies that already had a presence in many countries, the signs are that we may see more global start-ups in the future. The pressure to go global is therefore based not only on what can be seen today but also on the way it might develop in the future.

Kenichi Ohmae[4] argues that for long-term success, global businesses have to have a sound position in all the three geographic centres of the world: the USA, Japan and Europe. Those that stay in only one or two of these areas are unlikely to succeed in the long run, because the volumes of production which will fall to those competitors that do penetrate the total triad will give an immense cost advantage. The argument is based on the fact that these areas contain some 600 million people in the largest and most sophisticated markets of the world.

Globalisation as a strategic decision

Figure 18.1 illustrates the fact that for the individual company globalisation is a strategic decision. The diagram is derived from points made by M. Cvar[5] in a 1986 study of patterns of success and failure in global competition.

The analysis suggests that there are certain characteristics in industries that become global, in that there has to be the opportunity for high levels of demand for standardised products which also give rise to economies of scale. Globalisation is not a naturally occurring state but is man-made, and the triggers are the identification of common segments in different countries that enable a product to be defined globally. In turn this enables supply sources to be consolidated, so that the competitive cost advantages can be gained.

The study also showed that the successful global companies had five factors in common. They had all developed a pre-emptive strategy, effectively becoming the agency that created the global market. All managed their companies on a global concept and measured their performance on this basis. It was also observed that all had higher than average R & D compared to their industry. All

Figure 18.1
Global competition.
(Derived from
Cvar[5])

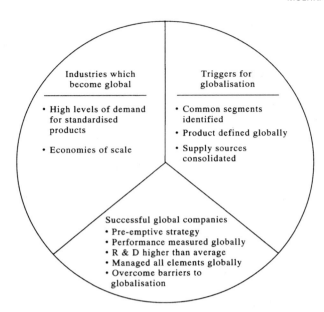

had demonstrated a measure of single-mindedness in overcoming obstacles to globalisation.

The implication of the global dimension is that for many companies strategic thinking has to stretch beyond the country dimensions that may have been traditional in the industry. Whether the company seeks to create a global business, on the lines suggested by Cvar, or whether it chooses to let a competitor initiate this process is a matter for the individual company. Once the industry goes global the opportunities for the company with only a local market view will certainly change, and may diminish.

Prahalad and Doz[6] suggest that the key factors in deciding how to operate are the need for integration on a global basis contrasted with the need for local responsiveness. If these two concerns are seen as two sides of a matrix, it follows that different businesses can be positioned on the matrix and appropriate strategy decided. However, the authors point to a factor which most strategists will have already observed, that the number of industries where global integration is the dominant factor increases every year. The pressures are created by customers and competitors, and it is dangerous to assume that an industry which has local responsiveness as the key factor today will remain like this in the future.

Figure 18.2 provides a diagram which was inspired by the Prahalad and Doz matrix. Exhibits 18.3 and 18.4 provide a set of questions to enable organisations to plot the industry situation, and the way their company is operating. In this diagram the need for a globally integrated approach is seen as one end of a spectrum, the other end of which is a need for a totally local response to the market. The vertical arm of the quadrant measures whether the company is operating in a global or multilocal way. Quadrants B and C are on the face of it potentially appropriate company responses. Quadrant D could be appropriate if

Exhibit 18.2 Going global from start up

Established companies often move to becoming a global organisation through a series of steps. Many started with the concept of a plant for each country and local marketing. Later manufacturing and marketing were coordinated on a regional basis, and some plants closed while others specialised. After this there may be a global operation, which looks on the world as one opportunity, building mechanisms to take account of the varying needs of different country markets. Research, design, and manufacturing are set up on a global basis, and in some regions there may no longer be a plant. Marketing is coordinated, and in some cases managed globally.

Research from IMD, Lausanne, found companies which depart from this evolutionary approach, and begin life with a global vision. One such example is Logitech, a Swiss-based manufacturer of peripherals for personal computers. It was founded by two Italians and a Swiss in 1982, and by 1989 had achieved sales of US$140m, and a 30 per cent share of the global mouse market. Sales were 65 per cent USA, 28 per cent Europe, and 7 per cent in the Far East.

From the outset it recognised that it was in a global business. The company was founded in Switzerland and the USA. Initially most research was undertaken in Switzerland, but very soon the major part moved to California. Initially manufacturing took place in the USA and Switzerland. In 1986 a new plant was established in Taiwan which thereafter became the main manufacturing centre.

Logitech had to solve the problems of being a new entrant competing against global players. They succeeded through a global vision from the start, a measure of focus in what they did, and the creation of a global structure from the outset. Although the difficulties they had to overcome should not be minimised, they began with an advantage of sorts: they carried no baggage of obsolete structures, culture or ways of working. They had much to do to implement the strategy, but no entrenched attitudes to overcome.

(*Source*: Jolly, V. K., Alahuhta, M. and Jeannet, J.P. 'Challenging the Incumbents: How High-Technology Start-ups Compete Globally', in Hussey, D. E. (ed.), *The Innovation Challenge*, Wiley, Chichester, 1997.)

the company has been able to identify niches in each market which are defensible. However, my experience is that the statement 'we are niche players' is often a rationalisation to explain the strategy, and often has no basis of fact behind it. It is hard to think that an answer which fell in quadrant A could be appropriate, and behaving globally in markets that cannot become global seems like a quick route for disaster.

I have not refined and tested Figure 18.2 yet in real situations, as I have with most of the other methods and models I have described in this book. So far its use has been restricted to teaching the concepts of global strategy through the

Figure 18.2
Company fit with
competitive need

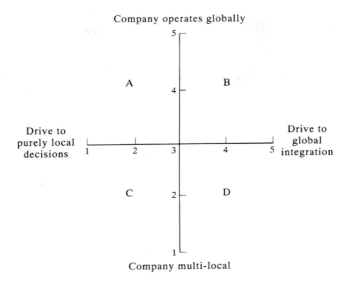

Company operates globally

A   B

Drive to
purely local   Drive to
decisions   global
integration

C   D

Company multi-local

medium of case studies. More work is required on the questions and the scoring, but I have included it here because the line of thinking it follows is valid.

The point should be made that different degrees of 'globalness' may be appropriate for different functions in the organisation. Thus design might be integrated globally, manufacture to a significant extent, while certain aspects of marketing, such as advertising might be different for each country. Once again the answer is not a formula that can be applied to give one right answer but management's strategic response to the circumstances as it sees them.

The decision-making process

Perhaps the first strategic problem a company which operates across national boundaries is called upon to solve is how far the decision-making process should be decentralised. If the intention is for all strategic decisions to be made at head office, very little more need be said. My own view is that no multinational or transnational company of any size can prosper under this approach. However, there is clearly a difference of which strategic decisions should be decentralised, depending whether the company is operating globally or multidomestically. In either case the answer lies in a *controlled* decentralisation of decision making.

Under this concept the country chief executive would have a wide degree of freedom to operate within the strategic framework established at the centre. This requires a shared understanding and commitment to the vision, clear objectives, and strong financial control to be exercised over the sources of finance and the way in which capital is used. A wide strategic freedom should not lead to abdication by the parent company. The shared vision is always important, but even more so in the global company, because many aspects of strategy have to be pulled together

387

Exhibit 18.3 Global/local responsiveness questionnaire

Please circle one number on each scale according to the position of the industry

MARKETING AND SALES

1 Market requirements diverse	1 2 3 4 5	Market requirements homogeneous
2 Few opportunities for cross-country standardisation	1 2 3 4 5	Many opportunities for cross-country standardisation
3 Numerous market segments	1 2 3 4 5	Few market segments
4 Distribution channels differ by country	1 2 3 4 5	Distribution channels the same in all countries
5 Customers all local operations	1 2 3 4 5	Customers all global operations
6 Low customer pressure for world-wide service	1 2 3 4 5	High customer pressure for world-wide service
7 Competitors all local buying	1 2 3 4 5	Competitors all global buying
8 Numerous competitors in world	1 2 3 4 5	Few competitors in world
9 High fiscal barriers to trade	1 2 3 4 5	Low fiscal barriers to trade
10 Many non-fiscal barriers	1 2 3 4 5	No non-fiscal barriers

RESEARCH AND DEVELOPMENT

11 Low rate of technology change	1 2 3 4 5	High rate of technology change
12 Low level of R & D effort	1 2 3 4 5	High level of R & D effort
13 Short development time for new products	1 2 3 4 5	Long development time for new products
14 Long product life cycle	1 2 3 4 5	Short product life cycle

OPERATIONS

15 Low scale efficiencies	1 2 3 4 5	High scale efficiencies
16 Low procurement scale economy	1 2 3 4 5	High procurement scale economy
17 Flat experience curve	1 2 3 4 5	Steep experience curve
18 High transport costs as % total costs	1 2 3 4 5	Low transport costs as % total costs

Total score _____

Average score _____

Exhibit 18.4 Questionnaire – How does your company operate?

Tick the statement which most accurately describes how your company operates

		A		B		C	
Executives' focus of vision	Local view	☐	Coordinate but define locally	☐	One view of the world	☐
Manufacturing	Each subsidiary has its own plant	☐	Plants at country level but coordinate	☐	Few plants serving the world	☐
R & D	At country level	☐	Coordinated centres	☐	Few centres, global orientation	☐
Quality concepts	Set at country level	☐	Common principles	☐	Same everywhere	☐
Culture	Each company differs	☐	Some common features in all companies	☐	Same everywhere	☐
Decisions try to maximise profit	At local level	☐	Through synergy	☐	On world view	☐
Control systems	Local	☐	Local but internationally coordinated	☐	Global	☐
New product development	Local	☐	Coordinated local	☐	Centralised globally	☐
Marketing management	Independent local	☐	Coordinated	☐	Global	☐
Area of markets	One or few countries	☐	Strong in at least one Triad region	☐	Strong in whole Triad	☐

Score 1 for each tick in column A
Score 3 for each tick in column B
Score 5 for each tick in column C

Total score _____

Average score _____

centrally to reach a world view, and these cannot be left to the country chief executives. Decisions which can be taken locally should not be taken in the centre. The worst of all worlds is when a company operates a multidomestic strategy, but determines its strategies as if it were operating a global strategy.

The reasons why the chief executive of international subsidiaries should have a large say in their own strategies are:

1 Opportunities can best be seen by the people on the spot. The larger the group and the greater its geographical dispersion, the harder it is for opportunity to be spotted from the centre. Quite apart from remoteness from and lack of understanding of the local scene – however well informed the head office management – there is also an enormous problem in organising and handling the vast volume of market and other environmental data needed to spot opportunities from many thousands of miles away.
2 Motivation is better secured in each subsidiary if the local management feel that they have a say in what is to be done. Better-quality managers can be recruited, including chief executives who think as chief executives and not as branch managers.
3 Acceptance of profit responsibility is more likely – and fairer – when local management has some freedom of manoeuvre.
4 Many subsidiaries may be joint ventures or have minority shareholders, and the rights of these partners should be observed.

The keyword is 'controlled'. Uncontrolled decentralisation will result in chaos, for any head office needs to retain certain rights.

5 The right to override a local strategy (and change the strategic framework) if this is in total group interests. For example, a cross-licensing agreement with another company might be very beneficial and profitable on a world-wide basis, but might require the sacrifice of certain products sold by a particular subsidiary. The local chief executive would never suggest this, and, indeed, would probably never be aware of the wider opportunity.
6 The right to refuse to sanction a capital expenditure (where reasons are good and valid).
7 The right to bring some international rationalisation to marketing, research, production, procurement, and physical distribution.

It follows that there will, on occasions, be a conflict of interests between parent and subsidiary. Recognition of this fact is an important part of the strategic planning process. This problem will be discussed in greater depth, but before doing this I should like to mention one way in which the effects of conflict may be mitigated.

Within limits I have argued for chief executives of subsidiaries to be given a wide degree of freedom in local strategic planning. It is possible for the talents of these managers to be used in a much broader sense to help the chief executive of the total group to identify and select the overall strategies. Considerable benefit may be gained if there is a measure of participation in the shaping of the future of the group. Such an action may be brought about through the participation of subsidiary managers in group planning exercises, in working parties, and think-tank sessions.

All this is valuable, but none of it detracts from the ultimate responsibility of the top managements of the parent company to plan the whole business in a way which satisfies the owners.

For analytical purposes five further discussions areas have been identified for close study: conflict of interest between parent and subsidiary; selecting a multinational strategy; multinationalism and Third World countries; the additional risks of multinational business; the future of multinational business.

Conflicts of interest: parent and subsidiary

One of the major problems of multinational strategic planning is the fact that there are numerous situations where a choice has to be made: a decision which will either increase parent company profits or increase those of the subsidiary. Jacoby[7] argues that such clashes need not occur provided the parent insists that each subsidiary operates under the forces of competition. This is a view which is very difficult to accept. There are often unavoidable clashes of subsidiary and parent interest, and there can be few multinational groups who would find it profitable to allow a complete state of *laissez-faire* among their own subsidiaries.

A conflict of profit interests may cause two other areas of difficulty, in addition to the basic strategic decision. The first is an internal problem, the company's own interpretation of its ethical and moral constraints (see Chapter 8). Many multinationals claim to be 'good citizens' of each country in which they operate, something which is by no means as easy as it sounds. The second difficulty is one of law. It is by no means unknown for the parent of a multinational to make a decision which would compel the board of directors of the subsidiary to commit an offence: usually a contravention of the tax or exchange control regulations through an action which effectively transfers assets or income outside of the control of that territory.

Examples of the type of decision which might well bring a conflict situation are:

1 Various subsidiaries might operate individual plants. Others might import from neighbouring countries. A group study shows that a large geographical area could be more economically served if one centralised plant were erected. For certain subsidiaries this would mean the closure of their own plants and the consequent cessation of exports. Some subsidiaries might pay more for their goods than they did before, although total group costs are lower, because some element of profit must be returned to the subsidiary in the country which operates the plant.

  Strategic decisions such as this are becoming more acute as the benefits of regional specialisation become more apparent, and as economic unions become bigger (for example, the enlarged European Union).

2 Investment proposals from a subsidiary are turned down because more profitable or less risky projects exist elsewhere. In the eyes of the subsidiary their project may be essential for profitable growth, and may comply with all the

minimum profitability criteria of the group. From their point of view there is nothing wrong with the project: from the parent's angle it is a simple question of using international resources in the best possible way.

3 A desire, because of wide margins in taxation rates or difficulties in repatriating profits, to make as much profit as possible in the parent country. There are many ways in which this aim can be achieved, and it is usually possible to find a legally acceptable formula: for example, abnormal profits may be built into raw material prices, there may be 'contributions' to research and development, royalties, management fees, and technical aid agreements. Often these are fair: sometimes they are unfair, and the payments are out of all proportion to any benefits obtained. The authorities frequently accept the arrangements because they are unaware of the amount of profit being siphoned off (in, for example, raw material prices). A danger sign is the situation where a multinational parent can 'afford' to let a subsidiary make a loss year after year. Frequently a situation like this means that the loss is only in the books of the subsidiary: a consolidation of profits in the books of the parent would reveal a profit.

4 Insistence that subsidiaries purchase products from group sources even though cheaper supplies are available in the open market.

5 Defining a trading area for a subsidiary and preventing it from seeking sales outside it: such a policy is essential for orderly international marketing, particularly with branded products which may be available in many countries. Essential though it may be, it may still reduce profit opportunity for a subsidiary.

6 Insistence on standards of quality which reflect group prestige and which are higher than those required by the subsidiary or the environment in which it operates. These standards may relate to factory buildings, office accommodation, plant, products, or commercial behaviour (e.g. insisting that all managers have written contracts of employment when such an approach is alien to the country).

As multinational companies come closer to the ideal of multinational ownership, some of these problems might fall away, since a decision on a point of conflict in favour of the parent would produce profits which accrue to investors on a wide economic front.

The strategic problems arising from such issues will, for the foreseeable future, have to be solved by chief executives operating outside of these ideal circumstances. Because the situations are more complex than simply deciding to do what gives the most *apparent* profit, there are no universal guide rules that can be applied. There are numerous considerations to be brought into the decision, many of which can only be subjective: for example, the political repercussions at home and abroad, the effect of adverse public relations on the markets of subsidiaries, and the company's internal constraints and code of ethics.

It is a fact that managers in a subsidiary are often involved in actions which, although they may not be illegal, are against the national interest of their particular country. Certainly, there is a reasonable argument that their task, like that of the management of the parent company, is to increase shareholders' value. In many circumstances this may be justification enough: often it is an oversimplification which avoids the real issues.

It is also clear that the host government of the country in which a subsidiary is based would prefer to see profits maximised locally, and would rather assets were utilised in the national interest rather than for the benefit of some other country. In Europe and North America there are fairly clear rules about what may and may not be done, and although companies sometimes find themselves in dispute with tax and exchange control authorities, there is generally an understanding of each other's viewpoint. In this environment reasonable solutions can usually be found. Both parties are also well aware of the mutual benefits of multinationalism, something which helps to balance the scales when they appear to be biased in a particular direction. Developing countries, particularly the emerging Third World countries, frequently take a different view to that of the Western world, a point which will be returned to later.

Perhaps the most difficult element of all to incorporate into the decision process is the one of management motivation. The criterion for economic decisions of this type is usually some form of accounting exercise: a quantification of expected results for each alternative. What is so often forgotten is the human motivation factor. Even when a local manager is genuinely and wholeheartedly a 'group' person it can become very depressing when because of the structure of the profit-routing decisions, the subsidiary apparently is unable to earn an adequate return on the capital employed under its control. After a year or two it is very easy to forget the local profit sacrificed to another area of the group and for the manager to be judged on the apparent results. If a situation is created where local managers become depressed and lose motivation (and therefore inspiration and creativity), the local results might well be much worse than the accounting exercise suggested. Management is a human activity: strategic decisions which forget this have a fair chance of being wrong.

Sometimes an adjustment can be made through the management accounting system, so that managers know what their real contribution to earnings is and are aware that they are given credit for it. If authority, responsibility, and accountability become mixed, a situation may be created where no one can be judged by results. This may be in the interests of a poor manager: it is never beneficial for a good manager and rarely right for the company.

These problems have been discussed at some length because they are an important consideration in the strategic planning process. They are just the type of factor which is likely to be ignored by the organisation which indulges in planning but not strategic management. Any company which does overlook them does so at its peril.

Selecting a multinational strategy

Rutenberg[8] makes the point that many companies have become international by 'creeping incrementalism' rather than deliberate strategic choice. A soundly conceived strategy should remove most of the problems of *what* to do in *which* countries. This means that somehow the company has to arrange its affairs so that it can examine opportunities throughout the world, which should include

393

relevant countries in which the company currently has no business. There should be a multinational strategy into which current and projected operations are slotted. Part of this strategy turns on the setting of objectives about which there has already been much discussion (Chapter 13): certainly profit objectives for subsidiaries can only be set realistically if they are defined within the framework of an overall strategy.

It is interesting to look at the typical development pattern of a company which becomes international without giving much thought to the process. The company is hypothetical: the situation is one I have observed in life:

> The company develops a large export trade, appointing agents and applying promotion generally on a percentage of sales basis. It has considerable variety of special packs and labels, and various methods of pricing have crept in over the years. Haphazardly, after visits by export executives, agents have in some areas been replaced by the company's own marketing subsidiaries because each report appeared logical at the time. Similarly, certain markets have been singled out for abnormal promotional expenditure: but the company has not thought of how long it will take to recover this or whether exports will be able to continue if a tariff barrier is levied. Where countries have in the past imposed protective tariffs, the company has built factories 'to protect its markets'. Each factory has come as the result of pressure, and many are inefficient and of subeconomic size.

Now contrast this situation with a similar hypothetical company, trading in the same markets and with essentially the same problems. The difference is that this company has an international strategic framework and is therefore able to make rational decisions and to bring some order to its problems:

> The company studies each of the countries in which it has (or might possibly have) business, and classifies these into three main classes which reflect profitability and development potential. Advertising and promotion support is removed from the third class of market, where the company's business is small with little chance of change. The top market grouping is of countries with good development potential, and here advertising and promotion is allocated on a mission basis subject to certain long-term considerations. The middle category has provision for some market expenditure, but only sufficient to maintain the company's position: markets in this category have little expansion potential but are profitable.
>
> An overall examination is made of the alternative merits of agents and the company's own marketing subsidiaries, and certain criteria are established. The company produces a plan to set up the type of selling operation which best suits each market, and intends to implement this over a three-year period. There is a deliberate rationalisation policy to reduce variety in packs and labels.
>
> The company also defines its position on local manufacturing plants. It now decides the circumstances under which it will open an overseas factory (size, investment, type of pack, profitability criteria). These circumstances exist in three markets, and the company decides that it is in its long-term interests to work towards establishing plants there within the next five years. Contingency plans are developed for contract manufacture or licensing for a

number of markets where a protective duty is possible but where a plant would be uneconomic.

All assessments of market development expenditure for the top grouping of countries are made in the context of the longer-term prospects of the country. Such investments are not undertaken where the risk of a protective duty being imposed is high, unless the company believes that its contingency plans are sufficient to give it a reasonable future return.

Both of these hypothetical companies are too neat to be real, but they do indicate the value of a predetermined strategy for international operations. It may seem rather too obvious that a strategy is required which conditions all actions, but it is a point which is often overlooked.

> An international company decided to concentrate most of its investment and development in Europe and the USA. In no circumstances was it prepared to invest in certain unstable countries. Nevertheless, a development plan was produced for a certain highly unstable export territory, urging a five-year period of low prices and high advertising, during which time no profit would be made. No one had considered risks of import controls, tariff barriers, or political change which could cut off exports at any time. No one had any idea what should be done if this happened apart from a determination not to open a factory. The logical decisions within the strategy were completely overlooked.

Van Dam[9] has demonstrated that it is possible – and profitable – to study countries on an international basis, so that a strategy may be developed which involves concentrating on those which appear to be reaching a stage of economic development which is 'right' for the company concerned. His work follows – and adapts for business use – that of Rostow,[10] who analyses the stages of national economic growth into: the traditional society, the pre-conditions for take-off, the take-off, the drive to maturity, and the age of high mass consumption. The classification of countries into criteria developed from Rostow's five stages can be a valuable step in the identification of the areas of value to the company, so that it can decide how each should be treated from a strategic point of view.

Unless a company has an overall outline strategy for its multinational operations it is likely to make decisions which pull it in the wrong direction.

Multinationalism and third world countries

International business is no stranger to the emerging nations. In addition to additional risks – which will be discussed later – of dealing with such nations, there are other problems which often tend to be overlooked. It is very easy for multinational business to try to continue policies which have been found workable in dealings with the Western world. Patterns of business behaviour in countries in Europe, North America, Australasia, and southern Arica may not be identical in each country, but they have a strong similarity. A policy which works in one of these areas has a high probability of working in the others.

Yet these policies may be completely unworkable in dealings with Third World countries to the extent that some companies deliberately opt to omit these countries from their sphere of operations: others, regrettably, do not know that there is a difference.

Any generalised view which purports to cover all Third World countries is bound to be wrong in some detail when applied to a particular country. Despite the weakness of generalisations, it is worth making a few, since if they act only as a warning light as multinational strategy is defined, they will have served a useful purpose. At the least they should make it clear that certain additional problems do exist.

Conflict of objectives

The impossibility of being a good citizen of every country of operation has been discussed elsewhere. This fact may become an acute strategic problem in a Third World country. A business unit in an underdeveloped country tends to be smaller than a subsidiary in a more developed area although it may be large in relation to other business in that country. The perception of the headquarters of the multinational group of its smallest subsidiaries may be vastly different from that of the host government: even more so, if the subsidiary is a member of a large, prestigious, and internationally well-known group. A mouse appears larger to a cat than to an elephant: what is insignificant to the giant is a major element of the economic diet of the small country.

Decisions which appear to be against host country interests – for example, failure to invest, failure to export, particular employment policies or dividend requirements – loom much more important in the eyes of the government of the Third World country than they would do in one of the more mature countries. This problem is made worse by the fact that the underdeveloped country may be passing through a period of nationalistic ardour, political development (or change), and may, indeed, feel that its particular needs mean that any conflicts of objectives should err on its side rather than that of the multinational company.

Local participation

Many Third World countries have legislation which compels a local equity participation in each foreign-controlled company. Other countries may not have any legal requirements, although their decision makers may consider that multinational companies should take note of local aspirations for equity participation.

When a multinational group tries to impose a concept of wholly owned subsidiaries and runs against this real feeling in the host country, resentments tend to build up. At the same time, from the multinational point of view, joint ventures and minority shareholders make administration and control more difficult. Local directors of suitable calibre may be hard to identify.

Apart from the public relations aspects, local equity participation may be a way of reducing risks, and should not therefore be rejected by multinational companies just because they have a general policy which acts as an internally erected barrier.

Employment

Restrictions on the employment of foreign nationals are not the sole prerogative of the Third World countries. Perhaps Switzerland is one of the most protective of countries in this respect, with vigorous controls and licensing arrangements for foreign workers. The USA has stringent immigration controls. The UK also restricts immigration, although this legislation was much more a question of slowing down the flood of Third World immigrants than any desire to protect nationals from competition for jobs. Naturally, business has to operate within the framework of these laws.

An underdeveloped country is likely not only to be more stringent in the application of such laws but also to be extremely suspicious when it is forced to grant permits for the employment of non-nationals, and resentful that business has not 'trained' locals to take the top management slots. These feelings can lead to unofficial blacklisting and 'problems' put in the way of the company concerned. Even where it has the support of the government, it may be a target for the opposition, the trade union movement, or the newspapers.

An example of this comes from personal discussions I once had in a Caribbean country. I was frequently told by government and quasi-government officials of the sins of a particular company – the main 'sin' being the number of labour permits it had obtained for expatriate managers. Even though each permit had been individually justified and granted, the 'sin' still led to other actions and contributed to delays in dealing with the company's applications under the price-control legislation.

Suspicion, distrust, and a different ideology

It is a fact that many Third World countries completely and absolutely distrust multinational companies: the larger the company, the more this distrust occurs. Multinational business is branded as an oppressor and exploiter, a stealer of the natural resources which make up a nation's heritage. This stigma is applied broadly and without regard to the merits of the case. For example, former President Nyerere of Tanzania has been reported as stating that his country should accept a slower rate of economic growth achieved through its own efforts rather than allow 'exploitation' by multinational companies of its natural resources, human talent, and finance. The record of the Western world at both the public and private level shows that there is much to justify this viewpoint, although it may be unfortunate for those companies whose intentions are honourable.

In addition, the concept of 'reasonable profit' is often not the same as in developed countries, and completely opposed to that of the company itself. There is often a feeling that economic activity should be undertaken by a company for social motives. Once a business is established it is expected to expand even though this action may not earn an adequate return: it has a 'duty' to employ more and more local people.

It may be argued that this view in part springs from large companies themselves, who continually oversell to host governments the benefits their subsidiaries bring to a country's economic progress (particularly at a time when they are trying to wring protective concessions out of that government). In part it is due to the unfortunate effects of successful 'blackmail' schemes through import control and protective tariffs by governments which have led to the erection of subeconomic plants by companies as a desperate measure to protect their markets. Most of all it is due to fundamental differences between the West and the Third World countries, and in views of politics, economics, and social development.

The size of the multinationals

All these feelings are inflamed by the sheer size of some of the multinational groups relative to that of the smaller countries, making government officials feel resentful in the belief that the problems of their country are never understood or debated at main board level: simply because no one at that level is ever involved in them.

It is rarely company presidents or chairmen who visit underdeveloped countries, and representatives from group headquarters, although senior managers, are not always the highest level: yet they expect to meet the key ministers and officials in the country they are visiting.

The record so far

The situation in general terms is that the rich countries are getting richer while the poor ones appear to be standing still or, in some cases, moving backwards. Natural resources of the underdeveloped world are mainly consumed by the much smaller population living in developed countries. With this record behind them, it is not surprising that Third World countries take actions which are against the interests of individual businesses.

All these factors are important because they must affect the company's approach to multinational strategy. They provide an additional reason for involving the chief executives of subsidiaries in major decisions: these managers on the spot are in a much better position to see the total problem. Emphasis is given to supporting strategic decisions with other actions. For example, any company with a large stake in the underdeveloped countries should consider a detailed public affairs strategy, to ensure that its relations with centres of influence in that country are strong enough to further its interests.

The additional risks of multinational business

Multinational operations may bring an increased opportunity for profit: they may, as some companies claim, be an agency for international understanding and a contributor to world peace. They also bring additional challenges to a company over and above the normal business risk that comes from all operations.

Some aspects of this have already been discussed in the chapters on environmental issues and, by implication at least, in earlier parts of this chapter. No discussion of international strategy can be complete without some further thoughts on this problem which must colour the overall decisions of the company. Even effective objectives cannot be set for subsidiaries unless some thought is given to the additional risks in each country: any decision to concentrate on particular areas of the world must have risk as part of its input.

The additional risks include those of fluctuations in exchange rates, which can completely alter the asset value of an overseas subsidiary (at least in the currency of the parent company), as well as changing the real value of profits earned and dividends paid. In addition, changing exchange rates can cause accounting difficulties in the books of both parent and subsidiary: a subsidiary may be in a position of meeting all its profit targets measured in local currency but failing miserably in the books of the parent.

Failure of a country to meet its international debts is another problem which strikes from time to time. This may mean that payment cannot be obtained for exports, or that foreign governments refuse to honour contractual arrangements. This is only matched for severity of effect by outright expropriation. Although there are international agreements covering expropriation and compensation these are not always observed. Even when compensation is given it may take many years before the matter is finalised and payment actually received.

On top of this there are the risks that a localisation policy will force the company to withdraw key managers and skilled personnel and to replace them with untrained and untrusted local employees. Systems of licensing may close overseas markets as may penal protective duties. Stringent price-control measures may force retirement from a market or heavy losses: often the overseas government concerned does not mind which.

The risks are not all bad ones, and there are some factors to be considered on the credit side as well. International operations may bring taxation advantages, either by facilitating the use of tax havens or by enabling the company to obtain tax holidays from some of its overseas operations. An example of the latter is the ten-year tax holiday once given by Singapore for 'pioneer' industries. (Tax is really a matter of financial planning, although it should have an impact on strategic decisions.) Tax advantages are also given by former Communist countries of central Europe.

Additional incentives are given by certain countries to encourage exports. An example is Australia, which doubles the tax allowance on certain expenses incurred in marketing exports, as well as giving other fiscal inducements. In some countries overseas debts can be insured, as through the UK ECGD scheme (subject to certain conditions).

The UK and other OECD countries also have an investment insurance scheme which covers companies for political risks as far as new capital is concerned. This makes it much easier to decide that an attractive investment in a politically unstable country really is attractive. Financial help is also given by some governments, including the USA, to aid pre-investment studies in certain overseas countries.

Overall, multinational business is attractive because it represents one of the best ways of getting maximum return from marketing, production, and research and development investment. Despite the abnormal risk of multinational business, it is often less risky to extend a developed product to another market than to commit sums to research and development in new products which carry a high normal risk of failure.

The future of multinational companies

For the most part strategic decisions are looked at in two dimensions: the viewpoints of the individual country and the individual company. These dimensions are not always in sympathy with each other, and occasionally may result in outright conflict.

There are indications that in future multinational business might also have to begin to consider yet a third dimension in its strategic planning – the world economy. The case, which is now convincingly argued by ecologists and environmentalists, is that the world be regarded as a system of finite size. Pressures on this system through population growth, urbanisation, the limitations of the world and the biosphere, the problems of industrial wastes and pollutions, and the now predictable exhaustion dates of certain natural resources (e.g. oil and natural gas) will increasingly bring the situation where the interests of an individual company although in balance with those of its host country are against the interests of the world as a whole.

The fact that a multinational company may increase its total earnings by expanding geographically does not mean that the world economy benefits to a greater extent. Sometimes a number of competing single-country businesses would serve the world better: sometimes it may be that the venture would benefit the world most if it were not done at all. Rutenberg[8] argues that in the future the multinational company will be forced to prove – to a much greater extent than hitherto – that there is a measure of synergy in multinationalism.

The conflict of the three competing dimensions can be illustrated by a simple hypothetical example. A multinational company finds that because of the high costs of air and water pollution control its home production units become more expensive to operate. An underdeveloped country sees the industry as an economic benefit and is willing to accept less stringent pollution-control measures. The factory is moved to the new country and both the company and this country feel that they are better off. But what of the world as a whole? Pollution levels are still the same: the same noxious chemicals are discharged into the air and the sea.

Although not all governments are in sympathy with the spirit of multinationalism (in fact even the US senate was recently asked to approve a bill which – if passed – would effectively have smothered all American multinational business), it is likely that the question of how far companies are to become multinational in ownership will become increasingly important. I believe that this is a strategic decision which must receive more attention from both business and governments.

It is also likely that the underdeveloped countries, which control much of the natural resources currently consumed by the developed world, will demand a fairer share of the economic activity. Some 75 per cent of the world's population live in these countries. It will be necessary for the multinational countries to redefine their multinationalism in this context. Whether we wish it or not, the economic limitations of the world, and the pressures on world peace that failure to act will bring, will mean that some transfer of activity from the developed to the underdeveloped world is likely.

One of the more significant issues to come to the fore in recent years is the international control of multinational companies (which owes something to the growth of international trade unions, many of which see the multinational company as the enemy). In 1976 the OECD published a voluntary code of conduct for multinationals, to which member governments agreed to encourage companies headquartered in their countries to adhere. This has had may effects on individual companies reacting under government pressure. The ILO has prepared its code of conduct for multinationals, and the United Nations has a code in draft form. Pressure is mounting to make such codes legally binding.

Certainly the multinational companies face more challenge and difficulty than the company which opts for single-country development. But the risks are not without reward, and, for many, multinational operations offer the most profitable of the strategic choices available. And many are multinational already, and have the problem of managing their vast complexes. The path to profit is rarely an easy one, and let no one underestimate the additional challenge that may be found on the road to a multinational strategy.

References

1 Drucker, P. F. *Managing for Results*, Heinemann, London, 1964.
2 Yip, G. *Total Global Strategy*, Prentice Hall, Englewood Cliffs, NJy, 1992.
3 Jolly, V. K., Alahuhta, M. and Jeannet, J-P. 'Challenging the Incumbents: How High Technology Start Ups compete Globally', *Journal of Strategic Change* 1992.
4 Ohmae, K. *Triad Power*, Free Press, New York, 1985.
5 Cvar, M. R. 'Case Studies in Global Competition: Patterns of Success and Failure', in Porter, M. E. (ed.), *Competition in Global Industries*, Harvard Business School, Boston, 1986.
6 Prahalad, C. K. and Doz, Y. *The Multinational Mission*, Free Press, New York, 1987.
7 Jacoby, N. H. 'The Impact of Multi-national Corporations', *Dialogue*, 4, No. 2 (abridged from an article in the *Centre Magazine*).
8 Rutenberg, D. T. 'Planning for a Multi-national Synergy', *Long Range Planning*, December 1969.

9 Van Dam, A. 'Strategic Planning for Corporate Growth in Developing Countries', *Long Range Planning*, September 1969.

10 Rostow, W. W. *The Stages of Economic Growth*, Cambridge University Press, Cambridge, 1964.

Note: Parts of this chapter were derived from a paper presented at a conference of the American – Management Association in New York in February 1972, and subsequently published: Hussey, D. E. 'Strategic Planning in International Business', *Long Range Planning*, June 1972.

CHAPTER 19

Technology and manufacturing

This chapter aims to broaden the discussion of strategy to include technology and manufacturing. First, it shows how to undertake an audit of the organisation's technology base, and this is followed by several ways of displaying which technologies are common across different activities. The chapter then shows how the strategic implications of the technology portfolio may be examined. For manufacturing, the aim is to introduce a number of strategic concepts, including the focused factory, the learning curve, the impact of modern manufacturing concepts, and the all-important concept of striving for world-class performance, which, of course, extends beyond manufacturing.

There is a relationship between the two subjects of this chapter, since the technology will affect manufacturing. However, the organisation has to get both components right, as it is possible to have a poor strategy for technology while planning manufacturing in a very effective manner. Similarly, there may be a superb approach to technology, yet the company may not get the best out of manufacturing.

Technology

While a great deal has been published about the market and economic aspects of strategy, the literature on strategies for technology is relatively sparse. Loveridge and Pitt[1] argue that awareness of the importance of technology in strategy has been greater among managers than among writers. 'So we feel confident that awareness of technological change in terms of its pervasiveness, dynamism, difficulty of managing and strategic significance is high among practitioners. In contrast, admittedly with some honourable exceptions, research-oriented writers have only recently chosen to address squarely the significance of strategic decision-making.' I wish that I could share their confidence.

Early planning literature on technology concentrated on technological forecasting, a topic discussed in an earlier chapter, and of which the book by Wills[2] is fairly typical. There may be more recent books, but most that was worth saying on this subject was written during the late 1960s and 1970s. However, forecasting and strategy formulation are not the same thing. Anyone who has tried to bring technology into the strategic planning process will know that there are immense difficulties in even describing different technologies in a way that is helpful.

The starting point that I should suggest is a technology audit of the organisation. I suppose that logically I should have included this in the chapter on the corporate appraisal, for this is where such an audit really fits. To do this would have made it harder to suggest an overall approach to technology.

Henry[3] offers a four-step approach: the audit, assessing the strategic implications of the technology portfolio, an implementation plan, and a technology monitoring programme. This is a useful way of thinking about the topic, and the first two steps are followed here, although I have added ideas from other authorities. The last two will be discussed more generally in later chapters.

Step 1: The audit

Henry[3] states: 'A technology-asset audit focuses on determining the real or perceived value that any technology node, or its individual technology links, has in the business benefit – cost chain – from raw material acquisition, to the supply of the produce or service, to the customer'. He suggests that comparisons should be made against the competitors. Several basic questions are proposed for an audit.

- What are the basic technology assumptions in the company's current business strategy?
- What are the basic technology assumptions in competitors' strategies?
- Is the customer's perception of the technological qualities of the companies important?
- What value, if any, do customers place on the technological qualities of competitors' products?
- Is corporate R & D contributing to the improvements in the company's current technology position, or are improvements starting to take longer and cost more?
- Are competing technologies becoming cost-effective? Are competitors making gains ahead of the company?
- How does the company manage information related to these questions?

There is no general right way to conduct an audit, and to demonstrate this I include a list of equally sensible questions derived from an article by Ford.[4] Some of these overlap those of Henry, but most are different:

- What are the key technologies and 'know-how' on which the business depends? This is a slightly different way of looking at Henry's first question.
- What sort of record does the company have in bringing home-grown technology to market, and what are the reasons behind this record?
- What sort of gap is there between the technological knowledge of the company and that of its key customers?
- What is the life-cycle position of each of the key technologies?
- What technologies are emerging which could affect our markets? This question harks back to the environmental assessment discussed in an earlier chapter, and is also the place where technological forecasting may be helpful.
- Where are the technological strengths and weaknesses: in product or in manufactures?
- Does the company fully exploit its technologies?
- Are there any unwanted technologies which could be sold or licensed to other companies?

To these questions I should add one inspired by Gluck and Foster,[5] which is to find out the phases of a development project where top management spends most of its time. The suggestion of this article is to look at the phases of development under the headings: study, design, development, production, marketing, and post-marketing. Top management can exercise most influence on the final outcome if it is involved most heavily in the first two phases and early stages of the third. In many companies this is the opposite of what happens and most top management effort is put on the final three phases.

However, by this time, the major technological strategic decisions have been taken, usually by someone quite low in the organisation. It reminds me a little of a presentation I once heard by a mid-level person from a city's town planning department. He declared that he alone determined the whole town planning strategy. Yes there were elected councillors, he had several managers above him, and they thought they were making the decisions. But he set all the assumptions on which the strategy was based, and no one had ever questioned them. His assumptions determined the strategies that could be followed, and eliminated many others. In technology it cannot make sense for the paths that the company will follow to be determined by people who have no responsibility for the overall vision and strategies of the firm.

We touched on another aspect of the audit in an earlier chapter, with the core competency approach of Prahalad and Hamel,[6] and I will not repeat these ideas again. However, they do have links to thinking by Abell,[7] which was not discussed earlier. Abell suggests a three-dimensional matrix which classifies activities under the headings *customer function*, *customer groups* and *alternative technologies*. Figure 19.1 shows the shell of such a matrix. It is possible for a business to serve multiple-or single-customer functions, to specialise on a narrow or broad range of customer groups, or to use one or more technologies to meet those functions and the requirements of the customer groups.

This method, which pays attention to some of the questions of Henry,[3] although technology might well be defined much more broadly under the Abell

Figure 19.1
Abell's three
dimensions for
business definition

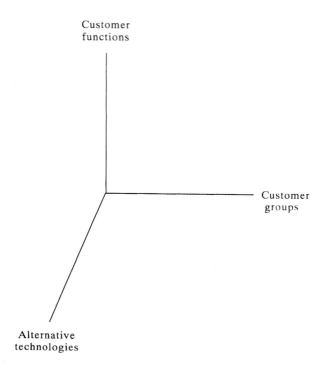

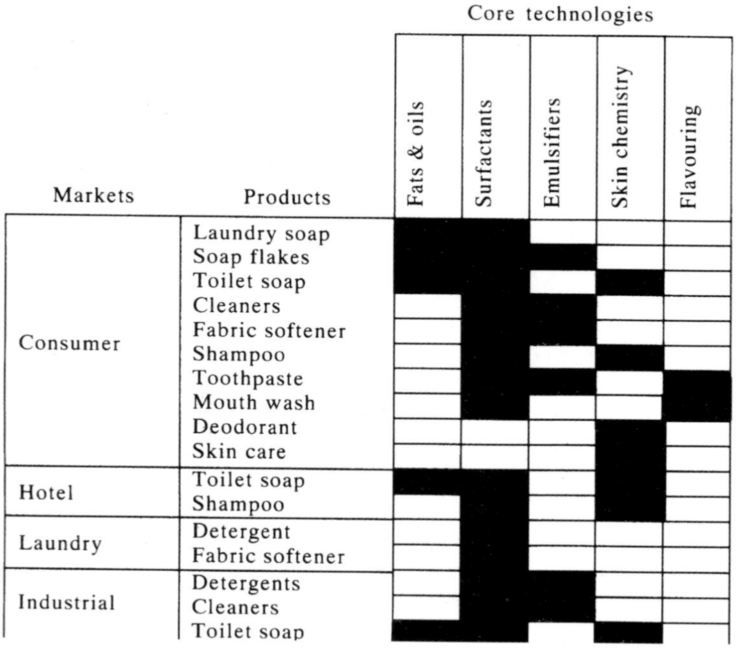

Figure 19.2
Technology analysis
– generalised
example, detergents
industry

approach, is very similar to many of the three-dimensional methods used to examine market segmentation.

Figure 19.2 illustrates a way of trying to define and examine technologies across an organisation. This particular example is derived from an assignment of mine in an unusual organisation which was a cross between consulting engineering and process engineering, although neither term is an accurate description of the activity. In essence, the business was concerned with the application of engineering principles to new applications, up to and including the installation of the proven prototype. The technical strands of a business such as this are of great importance in defining future strategy. To preserve confidentiality I have extended it to a completely different industry.

It is tempting to think that an audit of technology is only a matter for the high-technology companies, and can be ignored by all others. This is true only for as long as the technology stays static. A few examples worth mentioning of where

Exhibit 19.1 Technology – the challenger and the pioneer

In his study of Japanese companies which have been more successful since the growth bubble burst than they were before, Akira Sawayama, managing director of a leading Japanese strategic management consultancy, mentions two types of technology strategy. The challenger must possess core corporate skills which enable it to catch up and eventually overtake the leaders in the field. He gives the example of Canon, whose current core skills began in the years when the company was working out how to make a plain paper copier that did not infringe Xerox patents (there were over 600 of these). The fact that it did so is a matter of history. Mr Yamaji, former president and CEO of Canon, called it finding a different grammar to say the same thing. The message to a patent holder in a dominant market position is that patent protection can bring a sense of security which encourages technological complacency. Canon showed the dangers of this.

A pioneer is a company whose competence is based around the creation and development of new ideas, or which combines existing knowledge in a new invention. Casio Computers is such a pioneer, and began in 1957 with the invention of a relay-type calculator which sold 2 million units in its first 18 months of operation. The company produced the first digital watch in 1974 and electronic musical instruments five years later. More recently it has been the first pioneer of the digital camera. To be successful the pioneer must create the demand for its invention, and move quickly to enjoy the benefits of being first. Critical success factors therefore are more than technological skills, and include demand creation and fast movement to build a position before other firms get in.

(*Source*: The examples were from Akira Sawayama, 'Back to Basics: the New Success Factors in Japanese Companies'. *Strategic Change*, 6, No. 3., 1997. Some of the comments are my own.)

new technologies have taken over a market, and frequently led to the collapse of some or all of the traditional players are: typewriters, which have been to a great degree replaced by computers; electromechanical telephone exchanges, which are now an obsolete technology; home cine cameras and projectors, which have almost completely given way to video.

Assessing the strategic implications of the technology portfolio

Henry[3] argues: 'Step 2 of the Analysis is conducted with a view to ascertaining how best to leverage the company's technology assets to meet tomorrow's business objectives as defined by the strategic plan.' The modest techniques already illustrated provide one basis for further strategic evaluation. Neubauer[8] suggests a technology matrix, a version of which appears in Figure 19.3. This has *technology position* on one axis, moving from weak to strong. The other axis shows *relevance of the technology*, ranging from low for old technologies of little value to high for new technologies where many applications are possible. Strategic business units are plotted on the matrix, in much the same way as was described in Chapters 15 and 16.

I know of no rules for weighting and scoring the factors that enable the patterns to be plotted, and I have not had occasion to use the matrix myself. The factors suggested for each axis are:

Technology position	Relevance
Patents	Breadth of application
Licences	Speed of acceptance
Development lead times	Developmental potential
Personnel	Application in other industries
R & D budgets	Environmental acceptability

These questions would need to be applied to each technology used in the SBU, and a weighting system designed to produce a combined answer.

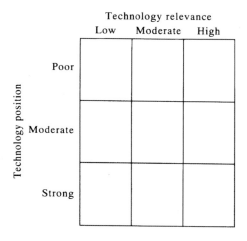

Figure 19.3
Technology matrix

The suggestion is that the final matrix would be used first to check that current investment in technology matches the need, and that priorities are shifted to reduce investment in low-relevance technologies, and increase it in business where the company needs to catch up or maintain leadership.

The suggestions I am making here can only be classed as ideas, stimulated by the technology matrix. It seems that the value of the matrix could be much enhanced if more attention was placed on the individual technologies, and particularly those which are common across several SBUs. This would aid consideration of cross-SBU technology links and help develop synergy between the businesses. It may also prevent duplication of effort, or actions which would benefit one SBU but harm another. A set of matrices could be prepared, one for each key technology, culminating in the summary matrix suggested by Neubauer.

Neubauer makes the link between the type of portfolio analysis of Chapters 15 and 16 and the technology matrix. This could be made tighter by combining the information. The simplest method might be to colour code the SBUs on the market prospects/competitive position matrix according to their position on the technology matrix. Nine codes may be a little too much to digest, but it should be possible to reduce these to a manageable four by redrawing the grid on the matrix.

Ford[4] suggests three different types of technology strategy. First there is a technology-acquisition strategy. The basic routes that can be followed are those

Table 19.1 Factors affecting technology – acquisition decisions

Acquisition methods	Company's relative standing	Urgency of acquisition	Commitment/ investment involved in acquisition	Technology life-cycle position	Categories of technology
Internal R & D	High	Lowest	Highest	Earliest	Most distinctive/ critical
Joint venture		Lower		Early	Distinctive or basic
Contracted-out R & D		Low		Early	Distinctive or basic
License in		High	Lowest	Later	Distinctive or basic
Non-acquisition[a]	Low	High	No commitment/ invest	All stages	External

[a] i.e. buying final product or part production from others.
From Ford.[4]

already outlined in Chapter 17 and need not be repeated here. Ford adds the caution that there is a need to examine the position on the life cycle of technologies or subtechnologies acquired. He provides a matrix (Table 19.1) which shows how various factors affect the decision to use internal or external sources.

There also needs to be a strategy for exploiting technology. This goes deeper than the issue of the strategic business portfolio, and includes an aggressive approach to finding other ways of gaining benefit, such as licensing others to use the technology. Again, the various ways of doing this were discussed earlier.

Finally Ford comes to the need for a strategy to manage technology, which implies making decisions on all the issues identified in the audit and portfolio analysis.

A sound technology strategy can be critical to success. Although for many industries there is often a chance to change course later to catch up, sometimes the change brought by technology is so far reaching that a company caught out of step could literally go out of business. An example of a company that had to change dramatically is STC, which until the mid-1970s was a leading manufacturer of electromechanical telephone exchanges. The change to electronics meant that many plants had to be closed and many of the core skills of the company became obsolete, with a considerable impact on human resource strategies.

Technology can give organisations a competitive advantage. Certain airlines have undoubtedly gained a lasting advantage from the electronic booking systems which they had developed, which through various means gave them a better chance of being chosen than competitors. Otis Elevators has benefited from harnessing IT to its lift service operations, giving an advantage which it is difficult for a small operator to emulate. Simon Engineering changed the North American market for mobile booms for use on construction sites by developing the much smaller, lighter, more economical and more flexible Eagle and Constructor machines which gave access to awkward and high places through an entirely different lifting concept.

More frequently, the game is about avoiding competitive disadvantage, and catching up with competitors who have got ahead. The lead time for enjoying the 'monopoly' benefits of something new are shrinking, which means that no company can afford to be complacent. Simon Engineering caught the industry by surprise, and gained a real advantage, some of which has remained with them. Within a comparatively short time their competitors were able to develop and market similar classes of machines, which reduced but did not eliminate the advantage gained.

Manufacturing

In the mid- to late 1960s the literature on technology strategy seemed to be dominated with technological forecasting, presumably on the doubtful premise that if we can produce a good forecast, somehow strategy will follow. Manufacturing strategy was being served somewhat better, with some excellent approaches to new thinking. The lead was at that time taken by faculty at Harvard, in particular Wickham Skinner, a collection of whose landmark articles, many dating from the 1960s, appeared in 1978.[9] I find it rather sad that this excellent body of work was largely ignored, and that few companies began to treat manufacturing in a strategic way until the mid-to late 1980s.

In many organisations manufacturing was the rather boring activity that followed the marketing strategy, and was treated as operational, rather than strategic. Comparatively few companies, until the 1980s, had taken strategic decisions that related marketing and manufacturing into one coherent strategy: in other words, manufacturing was treated as a sequential activity, whereas in reality there is a mutual interaction between the two. Skinner stressed the need to take a top-down view of manufacturing, rather than the traditional strategy from the bottom-up approach. Under the traditional approach the individual engineers, industrial relations experts, information technology specialists, the production planners, and other experts may all have been very efficient. Efficiency and effectiveness are not always synonymous, and it needs management input to ensure that the right thing is done.

Modern thinking raises the significance given to manufacturing, partly because of the actions of competitors and partly because new methods and technologies force manufacturing decisions to be more strategic. In addition to the Skinner idea of the focused factory, we now have to wrestle with CAD–CAM, JIT, flexible manufacturing, world-class manufacturing, and the impact of global strategies, to name only some of the modern concepts. We will look at various aspects of manufacturing strategy, although not all will apply to all organisations or to all parts of an organisation. However, if you know what to consider, you have a better chance of getting what you need.

The focused factory

Skinner[9] developed the concept of the focused factory in contrast to what is still a common practice of production units which have a broad range of objectives. His argument is that unless the factory concentrates on a narrow range of manufacturing objectives it will not achieve optimum levels of effectiveness. This implies setting up factories which have only a limited number of production technologies, meet only a few market demands, do not mix long production runs with specials, only produce products that have common quality objectives, and have a limited number of manufacturing tasks. Output is impaired when conflicting production requirements are placed on the same unit. The issue is not whether the plant and machinery is capable of producing far too many objectives but whether it is economic to keep changing. In thinking of this we have to think of the learned skills of people. For example, it is extremely difficult for a factory to mix aeronautical parts with commercial production, because it is not possible for the same operatives to keep changing the tolerances and quality to which they work to meet the lower specifications. The fact that the flame plating unit is capable of producing for both applications is not the relevant issue. A simple example is the production of spares for aftersales support on the lines that produce the original equipment. Each interrupts the other.

Skinner gives an example of two market requirements for furniture. One is for low prices and high volume, the other requires high fashion, high price, and limited editions. The manufacturing requirement for the former is for large lot sizes, mass-production machinery, and a high proportion of lower-skilled workers. Economy of scale is important, as costs will fall with volume. The latter may require fast production of new models, repeated model changes, an effective production control system to reduce lead times, and hand finishing, requiring a higher proportion of skilled workers. Mix up the two sets of production objectives in the same factory, using the same machines and work force and there is a recipe for suboptimal working.

Skinner argues that the apparent duplication of buildings and machinery caused by the separation pays back in lower costs, and better service to customers. However, where it is not feasible to have two quite separate facilities, he suggests setting up a factory within a factory: that is, establishing quite separate units within the same umbrella buildings and organisation. Hussey[10] describes how the factory within a factory concept was applied by Otis Elevators in 1984. The factory at Liverpool, England, had been laid out by machine type, following a flow-line principle whenever possible. It made architectural products for lifts (car doors, door surrounds, etc.), controllers for lift operation, and machines to drive the lift. It also produced spares for all these items. Costs were high, delivery times were long and often not kept, and an extensive computer system was used to keep track of each contract, which cost £500 000 per year to run, and could not deliver the needed information.

However, in February 1985 the managing director of Otis UK was able to give a presentation at an international conference in Singapore showing a complete turnaround in the Liverpool factory. He demonstrated how Liverpool's costs had shrunk: for example it could now produce a gearless machine 18% cheaper than Taiwan. Lead times had reduced and the proportion delivered on time had increased. This dramatic improvement was the result of considerable hard work by the Liverpool management team, implementing a major new strategy in the Liverpool factory.

The foundation of the strategy was the breaking down of the Liverpool factory into a number of workshops, physically united, each of which could be managed as a business unit. The manager of each would be responsible for all aspects of his operations. To facilitate this the central stores were broken up, each workshop operating its own, and the white collar staff associated with each operation were moved from the office block and housed in custom built offices each adjacent to its manufacturing operation.

This released 114,000 square feet of productive space which was separated from the rest of the factory by a brick wall, and sub-let to another organisation, Masons. (This also reduced the rates bill.)

The workshops were organised around the major elements that make up an elevator, plus the field workshop. The elements are Machine, Architectural Products, and Controllers.

From being a 'vendor of the last resort' the field workshop was turned into a focused activity which could be used to help salesmen gain modernisation orders; it is now frequently visited by customers, and the employees have a close association with the field activity. A fifth workshop is Consolidation and Shipping, which is the link between the other workshops and the customer. Each workshop has its own technologies.

Service spares are no longer produced at Liverpool. This activity was transferred to be close to the service warehouse in London, removing from the premises an activity which had little in common with the remaining operations.

There is no doubt that the focused workshop has produced significant financial improvements. Lower costs, shorter lead times and on time delivery have resulted in an increase of orders to Liverpool.

For the first time in memory the number of indirect staff fell below the number of direct workers. Despite lower hours per unit of production, standard hours of production began to rise as orders from Otis companies overseas started flowing back to Liverpool. The field workshop began capturing work previously given to outside vendors. (Hussey[10])

The architect of the change, John Miller, summarised the reasons for the approach:

The advantage of the focused approach was that workshops could be established from a zero base, allowing a break with past practices and the previous culture. A manufacturing resource could be created to suit the specific needs of each warehouse. Smaller focused units made it easier to use a team approach to problem solving and contributed to job flexibility. Above all, it was possible to give people something to identify with, which they could run as a business and see the results of their efforts. (Quoted in Hussey[10])

The learning curve

Learning curves were first observed in a factory producing aircraft. Every time cumulative output doubled, there was a constant fall of 20 per cent in the unit labour cost. Thus:

The   4th plane requires 80 per cent of the labour of the   2nd plane
The   8th plane requires 80 per cent of the labour of the   4th plane
The 100th plane requires 80 per cent of the labour of the 50th.

This is not the same as economy of scale, which is the fall in unit costs brought about by an increase in capacity and throughput over a given period.

Economies of scale are not cumulative in their effect. The learning curve reduction is caused by the increased skills of the labour force as more experience is gained, and has been found to apply in a variety of different industries.

A greater level of significance was given to this finding by the Boston Consulting Group, who derived the experience curve concept. 'Each time the accumulated experience of manufacturing a particular product doubles, the total unit cost in real terms (i.e. in "constant money", net of GDP inflation), can be made to decline by a characteristic percentage. The decline is normally in the region of 20–30%' (Hedley[11]). When plotted on a logarithmic scale, the experience curve appears as a straight line.

The experience curve embraces the learning curve, but the empirical findings are that it covers all the other costs of manufacture as well. The whole organisation becomes more effective through experience measured in terms of cumulative output. The implications of this are that the strategy has to exploit the maximum potential from the experience curve. If competitors manage to obtain the predicted level of benefit but your company does not, the competitive disadvantage may widen to a point of no recovery.

When demand is inelastic and there are other competitors it is difficult to make use of this concept, since it is probably not possible to increase output enough to gain dramatic decreases in cost. The situation changes when demand is sufficiently elastic, because here it is possible to gain volume from lower prices, and lower costs from the increased volume. If the equation can be pushed far enough it will mean that new competitors would find it almost impossible to obtain volumes large enough to be competitive. Similarly, the laggards among existing competitors will become increasingly uneconomic and be shaken out.

This concept has worked well in many parts of the electronics industry, where the real decline in both prices and costs is easily observable. However, it is not necessarily as simple as it sounds. For example, many small producers of personal computers are able to operate as low-cost producers because they are designers and assemblers, benefiting from the low costs of components which they buy in. The experience curve in these cases is more beneficial to manufacturers of chips, disk drives, and other components than it is to the companies that market the computers themselves.

The implications of the learning curve on strategy are clear. An experience curve concept implies relatively few plants supplying global markets, standardised products, and total coordination between marketing and manufacture. When marketing reduces the real price, manufacturing must be ready to supply the increased volume. It implies careful attention to purchasing and subcontracting. Above all, it implies the maintenance of quality, so that lower prices do not become associated with inferior goods. These are all features of the way in which Japanese electronics, automotive and motorcycle firms operate. The experience curve is a partial explanation of the forces that drive firms towards a global strategy, as discussed in a previous chapter.

The competitive impact of trying to compete against the machine like operations of the experience curve by traditional means is best illustrated by the British motorcycle industry. Just before the industry collapsed in 1974 the best British motorcycle factory produced 18 cycles per man year, compared to 350 in the best Japanese factories. Even though the British industry had consolidated, each marque still ran its own factory as if it were independent. No products were standardised, even at the components level. The British industry was beaten by a strategy that it never understood.

There are limits to the experience curve. The need for an elastic demand curve was mentioned earlier, and to this we might add a need for continued market growth. This probably explains the continued introduction of new models by the consumer electronics industry: without this growth could slacken and the experience curve go into reverse. Presumably if demand falls costs will rise, prices will rise, causing a further fall in demand.

Henry Ford had never heard of the learning curve yet he used it to good advantage with the model T Ford car. Then one day he woke up to find that nobody wanted to buy this car any more. His competitive position slumped to the bottom of the league, and the factory had to be closed for a lengthy period until a successor model could be designed and produced. This story is described at some length by Abernathy and Wayne.[12]

There is a connection between the focused factory concept and the learning curve, in that without focus it may be impossible to gain the potential benefits of the experience curve, as the experience is dissipated across other products.

Some modern manufacturing concepts

Anyone considering manufacturing strategy should include in the options some of the modern concepts of manufacture. A brief description of some of them is given here. For more details refer to Hill[13] and Hayes, Wheelwright and Clark.[14]

Flexible manufacturing system (FMS) is a way of handling small batch sizes economically, giving more flexibility of production and reducing throughput times and inventory sizes. The concept is the grouping of parts into families, with manufacture controlled by computer, using machine tools with the ability to change tools automatically. In effect small batches can be manufactured as efficiently as larger batches, which provides the opportunity to modify standard products to suit individual market needs. FMS can change strategies for global production.

Computer-aided design (CAD) is the use of computers by the designer to design products on screen, and store all the critical information electronically, including all dimensions and tolerances. A library of design elements can be retained in a design database, reducing design time for future products. Not only does CAD speed up the design process, but it makes it easier for designs to be modified and manipulated. Standardisation becomes easier because of the access to the database. It is also much easier to pass design information to others, inside and outside of the same building. Floppy disks are much more manageable than large blue prints.

Computer-aided manufacture (CAM) takes CAD a stage further by using the computer to convert drawings and designs into manufacturing instructions. Information on tools, jigs, routing instructions and the like can be incorporated into the product database. CAM can also produce the instructions needed to drive computer-controlled manufacturing processes.

Just-in-time production is a system which ensures that each item is only made at the time it is required, or in the case of purchased items, delivered to the production line when needed. The system reduces inventories throughout the process but requires careful attention to scheduling. Its adherents believe that the system prevents problems from being hidden behind inventories so that they can be dealt with. JIT offers a low-technology approach, based on demand-pulling requirements. However, it requires some stability in demand levels and considerable effort to install and make effective.

World-class manufacturing

World-class manufacturing has become an important concept since the 1980s. It requires regular benchmarking, a topic discussed in Chapter 10, although in this case the aims of the benchmarking are specifically manufacturing. Competitor performance is very important, but such benchmarking would also cover other relevant industries.

Hayes, Wheelwright and Clark[14] define world-class manufacturing: 'Basically, this means being better than almost every other company in your industry in at least one important aspect of manufacturing.' They suggest that there are four stages of manufacturing competitiveness into one of which every company can be slotted. Stage one is 'internally neutral'. The role of manufacturing is simply to make what they are told to make, and the company relies on its product designs and marketing skills for its success. Under these conditions a factory is something that you have to have, but you expect it to play second place to marketing.

Stage two they call 'externally neutral'. Here companies are concerned to meet the standards of costs, delivery and quality of their competitors. Such organisations tend to use the same suppliers as the bulk of the industry, to follow industry standards and to recruit manufacturing personnel from within the industry. The driving objective is to copy competitors to stay competitive.

Stage three is for manufacturing to be 'internally supportive' of the rest of the company. It is not just a question of making products to competitors' standards but of using manufacturing to enable the whole company to achieve more. Manufacturing does more than copy competitors: it tries to tailor manufacturing strategy to the competitive strategy of the company.

The final classification is stage four, described as 'externally supportive'. Here the company seeks to use manufacturing as a source of competitive advantage, and is not concerned with being as good as competitors but being better than them. This is true world-class manufacturing, when the organisation is perpetually seeking ways to improve. The authors suggest that such organisations are the ones sought out by suppliers when they wish to develop or test new machinery. They have higher-quality personnel at all levels than most of their competitors. They are able to react faster, meeting changes in the market far quicker than their competitors. Designs of new products are tied so tightly to the manufacturing process that competitors can only copy them if they invest in extensive retooling and major design costs. They do not recognise that they have reached an optimal state, so that effort is continually being put to improving things that others might consider to be at a state of excellence.

The philosophy that the organisation elects to follow is in itself a strategic decision, and will change how it takes every other strategic decision in manufacturing.

Strategic decisions in manufacturing

This chapter so far has covered a number of strategic manufacturing areas, both around the role of manufacturing in the company and many of the options that may become the basis of the strategy.

By implication, the discussion has touched on many different types of strategic manufacturing decisions. To make sure that nothing is lost, the final part of this chapter will summarise some of the more important areas. Skinner[9] and Hayes, Wheelwright and Clark[14] both provide guidance which largely covers the same ground. However, the latter make an interesting distinction between issues which they term 'bricks and mortar', which are to do with physical things, and those they term 'infrastructure', which are to do with people and systems.

Bricks and mortar

1 The capacity that needs to be provided, and the timing of various increments of new capacity
2 Location of capacity, including the number of locations. This issue becomes of critical importance for companies with global competition
3 Type of facilities, and the degree of focus within each
4 Production technologies, and the nature of the equipment and systems that have to be provided
5 Make-or-buy decisions for materials, systems and service
6 Health, safety and environmental issues.

Infrastructure

1 Human resource policies, covering recruitment, training, reward systems, security and skill requirements
2 Communication and management policies to support the required culture
3 Quality requirements and the approaches to be used to attain them
4 Production planning and control systems, and, equally important, the philosophy that lies behind them. Companies using JIT have to operate differently from those using more traditional methods
5 Organisation structure and design, including such issues as layers of management, empowerment, and the role of staff functions
6 Measurement and control systems
7 The processes for developing new products.

This chapter should have revealed the importance of technology and manufacturing in the strategic decision-making process. Although some aspects of these strategies are reactive to the corporate objectives and strategies, there are also times when they should be proactive, and help to reshape those objectives and strategies. This is more likely to happen when companies are operating at level four, and is very unlikely for those which are on level one.

For many managers, manufacturing and technology are closed books, and are therefore ignored whenever possible. Good strategic management should not allow this to happen, and the seeds of ultimate failure are sown whenever companies opt out of giving strategic attention to these areas.

References

1 Loveridge, R. and Pitt, M. *The Strategic Management of Technological Innovation*, Wiley, Chichester, 1990.

2 Wills, G. *Technological Forecasting*, Penguin Books, Harmondsworth, 1972.

3 Henry, J. P. 'Making the Technology-Strategy Connection', in Hussey, D. E. (ed.), *International Review of Strategic Management*, Vol. 1, Wiley, Chichester, 1990.

4 Ford, D. 'Develop Your Technology Strategy', *Long Range Planning*, 21, No. 5, October 1988.

5 Gluck, F. W. and Foster, R. N. 'Managing Technological Change: A Box of Cigars for Brad', *Harvard Business Review*, September-October 1975.

6 Prahalad, C. K. and Hamel, G. 'The Core Competence of the Corporation', *Harvard Business Review*, May-June 1990.

7 Abell, D. F. *Defining the Business: The Starting Point of Corporate Planning*, Prentice Hall, Englewood Cliffs, NJ, 1980.

8 Neubauer, F-F. *Portfolio Management*, Kluwer, Deventer, Netherlands, 1990.

9 Skinner, W. *Manufacturing in the Corporate Strategy*, Wiley, New York, 1978.

10 Hussey, D. E. *Management Training and Corporate Strategy*, Pergamon, Oxford, 1988.

11 Hedley, B. 'A Fundamental Approach to Strategy Development', *Long Range Planning*, 9, No. 6, 1976.

12 Abernathy, W. J. and Wayne, K. 'Limits of the Learning Curve', *Harvard Business Review*, 109-119, September-October 1974.

13 Hill, T. *Manufacturing Strategy*, Macmillan, London, 1985.

14 Hayes, R. H., Wheelwright, S. C. and Clark, K. B. *Dynamic Manufacturing: Creating the Learning Organisation*, Free Press, New York, 1988.

CHAPTER 20

Financial planning

This chapter has the modest aim of providing an introduction to the elements of financial strategy. Financial resources can be a limiting factor which prevents necessary expansion, and the way in which resources are obtained may make it easier or harder to obtain further resources in the future. No strategy can sensibly be decided without consideration of financial issues, and this chapter shows what is involved.

The question of financial planning has appeared on other pages of this book only to be dismissed in summary fashion with a rider stressing its importance. This is the unfortunate consequence of the need to analyse one thing at a time, and creates a measure of unreality in that in a real-life management situation many things are pursued concurrently.

Any feeling that financial strategy is something that happens after the real managers of the business have made their decisions should be rapidly dispelled. Financial plans, as documents, may appear to be the last link in the planning chain, and perhaps the final appraisal and financial strategies will be made at this point, but any major strategic decisions will have already considered financial implications: for example, an acquisition plan must be interwoven with the financial strategy since this will dictate how the plan is implemented.

Good financial management has three major aims: to keep the business solvent, to maintain sufficient liquidity for it to meet liabilities as they become due, and to ensure that in the context of these first two aims it provides the company in the most efficient way with the finance it needs for growth. A company which practises strategic management will be trying to meet these aims more effectively – a way that is future-oriented, considers more factors, is better coordinated, and which should make it possible for better financial decisions to be made. Just as strategic planning as a whole sets out to be a better way of running a business, financial planning – one of its components – sets out to be more effective in managing the finance function.

A pre-condition for good financial management, and therefore also for financial planning, is a corporate attitude of mind. Senior managers must consider cash-flow implications in all their major decisions. Every senior manager is involved in the utilisation of corporate financial resources, yet too many managers never think beyond profit (pre-tax and pre-financial charges).

Financial plans will express the company's forward plans so that they positively identify the financial needs, problems and opportunities. This is an important aspect of financial planning, but only has real value when it is overlaid by the financial strategy, which will involve the selection of the means of financing, management of surplus funds, ways of avoiding the incidence of taxation, and changes in the company's general policies. Financial strategic decisions may act as a constraint on broader, strategic thinking, drawing the investment line which the company may not overstep. It may act as a goad to stimulate further capital investment so that liquid balances are reduced, thus using money more profitably and reducing the danger of the company becoming an acquisition victim hunted for its cash.

There is a very close relationship between the financial plan and the other plans of the company, and these provide the raw material from which financial requirements can be assessed. Although most financial managers try to take a forward view of financing needs, this is very difficult where the company has no formal planning system. Strategic planning gives the opportunity for dramatically improving this view, giving greater accuracy, a more comprehensive coverage, and a method of control. Its forecasts are based on what the company intends to do rather than on trend lines constructed from past performance.

So financial planning represents (at least for the well-managed company) an improvement rather than a revolution. For the company whose financial management is weak it may well act as a revelation.

The strategic plans, discussed previously and the operating plans, which will appear later, will provide the company with an estimate of future profits under a specific and defined strategy and set of circumstances. They will also outline the capital budget needed to support and implement this strategy. Capital investment figures may sometimes be in the form of a range, rather than one definitive figure, and although this is a complication it does not cause any real problems. In reality, profit forecasts should also be seen as a range.

These plans should also provide an estimate of depreciation, an expense which, in cash-flow terms, is not a real expenditure. Specific provision should exist for calculating this in operating plans, and in plans for new activities it may be estimated directly (there is no historical depreciation in such plans, so direct calculations may be made from capital investment needs: the main complication would come from acquisitions).

In this way the financial planner is provided with some of the main parameters of cash-flow forecasts: profits, capital expenditures, capital inflows from divestments and depreciation. The way in which the planner receives them gives the figures a validity which his or her own estimates would not possess.

The strategic and operating plans also provide information on movements in sales and purchases which enable some of the other components of the cash flow to be calculated: debtor and creditor levels and inventories. Definite decisions may be made to change present ratios: for example, to reduce credit given or cut inventories. Plans, plus existing data available to the financial manager, and certain strategic decisions in the area of finance (e.g. dividends) provide the elements from which the remaining cash-flow components may be estimated.

In the initial stages the cash-flow part of the financial plan will make assumptions about the sources of funds to provide the company with the means of financing the plan. These decisions are not automatic, and are major elements of strategy in the consideration of which there are many factors to take into account. Changes in the sources of finance will affect, among other things, interest, dividends, and taxation. At this stage it is of value to quantify some of the alternatives. In many companies the amount of work involved in these calculations will justify some computer assistance.

The embryo plan should also be tested for sensitivity to various items of risk. A plan that will run the company into serious financial trouble if a few things go wrong should be viewed more critically than one which appears safe under most circumstances.

Cash-flow forecasts prepared in this way suffer from one major defect. They represent the expected position as at a certain time of the year. Most businesses have seasonal variations, and to ignore these can be very dangerous, particularly if the plan is produced in the troughs. A plan produced at the time of the peaks might lead the company to raise more capital than it requires.

The planned cash flow would, therefore, be of more value if it were accompanied by estimates of constant and variable capital needs. Constant capital may be defined as the fixed capital of the business plus that level of working capital which is needed to maintain operations in the slackest period of the year. It is 'constant' only for that year, and may change with each year of the plan. Variable capital is that extra element of working capital which may be required over and above the constant level to finance the company at other periods of the year.

Constant and variable capital levels will have a greater gap in a business with a heavy seasonal influence. A company with no seasonal influences is likely to have little or no variable capital.

Adequate financial control can only be exercised if the company works to a regularly revised short-term cash-flow forecast based on the budgetary control process. Here, more than any other area, it is necessary to constantly study and, if necessary, reschedule the actions shown in the plan. A postponement of a capital expenditure project can easily change the way in which finance is raised. Failure to control in the short term can lead to a loss of liquidity which sends it into insolvency.

Another schedule which should appear in the financial plan is a long-term capital budget (more will be said about short-term capital budgeting in Chapter 26 which deals with investment appraisal). This need not be a very complicated document, and should attempt to list each planned fixed capital expenditure over the period of the plan, phased by the expected year of expenditure (this may be different from the year in which the project is completed). Sometimes it may be desirable to give the figure within a range: sometimes, as a choice between two alternatives, only one of which will be accepted (project A £500 000 *or* project B £450 000).

This document may also be used to indicate working capital requirements from new areas of business arising from the strategic plan. Sometimes it is easier to calculate these in this way than to pick them up from ratios based on production and turnover projections. The important rules are to omit nothing and avoid double-counting.

So far this aspect of financial planning has been treated on the level of a relatively simple company. Most of the problems involved in handling the more complex (and more usual) business are matters of detail rather than of principle, and as such can easily be identified in practice. There are two practical points which deserve some additional attention.

The first is that the figures which find their way into the financial plan need not necessarily be the total of all operating plans in the company. Consolidation is not always a question of simple addition. The company that simply adds up the forecast capital requirements of hundreds of operating plans from all around the world is likely to end up with a borrowing requirement it can never achieve. The point will be made in more detail in Chapter 24 that the corporate planner must exercise an element of discrimination in selecting which figures of each operating plan go forward into the total corporate plan.

The second complication is in the area of international business. Because cash is not freely transferable from one country to another, cash flow projections are likely to be more use when calculated on a single-country basis. A shortage of cash in Australia is not compensated by a surplus in Nigeria. At the same time, the financial plan should treat capital as a corporate rather than an individual subsidiary resource. Expenditure on inferior projects should not be allowed just because that particular country has a capital surplus. Strategy should consider the funding of one country by another where this is both legal and desirable. And, of course, local financial strategies must be approved at corporate level.

International factors in financial planning make the task much more complex: it would be wrong to overstress this, however, as the complications have to be faced by financial management in any case, and arise despite – and not because of – any efforts to plan ahead.

So far attention has been concentrated on the assembly of data to give a first indication of corporate resources and needs. This is a relatively simply task, and at this stage is little more than the analysis of other people's data. Once the work is done it is possible to return to a more interesting application of skills – financial strategy itself.

It is possible that the cash-flow projections reveal a position which can safely be adopted as the financial plan. This will come about where financial implications have been fully considered at the strategic planning stage, and where plans have been based on a careful appreciation of the company's available financial resources. From the corporate planner's viewpoint this is a very pleasant state of affairs and means that there is no rethinking to do. Unfortunately it is an unlikely possibility, and the most probable outcome will be a need to reconsider sources of funds and, in some cases, their application. Projects which appeared to be highly desirable may have to be postponed or rejected on financial grounds, which in turn may open a gap between primary objective and plan, which the planner thought had been safely closed.

Three other possibilities are more likely:

1 The cash flow will reveal no difficulty in balancing sources and application of funds, but will highlight areas where financial policy is weak and requires changes, which may in turn unbalance the cash flow. For example, if the ratio of debt to equity is becoming disproportionate.
2 Despite projects which may be expected to achieve all profit objectives, the company has a surplus of liquid assets.

3 There is a shortfall of resources, which have to be made up unless planned capital expenditure is to be cut back.

Each element of the projected cash flow will have been based on either an assumption or a known financial policy, which means that it can be deliberately changed. In addition, a strategic action planned for the future may indicate a need to change policies immediately. An intention to 'go public' in three years' time may be facilitated if certain financial policies are changed next year.

Setting financial policy is one of the major tasks of financial planning, and is fundamental to the company's successful use of corporate planning. No figures in the cash-flow projections are firm, no policies which cause them are immutable.

It is possible to divide the cash-flow statements into two broad groups: elements which are internally generated and elements which have to draw on the world outside. These are, perhaps, not the most accurate descriptions, but will assist further analysis.

Internally generated elements include all working capital, fixed capital expenditure, dividends, depreciation, and taxation (although this last stretches the definition somewhat).

Working capital

There are still companies where little or no attention is given to the way in which working capital is used, although these are becoming fewer in number. Where they do exist, they are usually in the position of having a surplus of funds and reasonable profits. In companies such as this there is often 'flabby' management with no top management interest in debtors or inventory levels. The need to borrow money, particularly at a time of credit squeeze or high interest rates, often forces such a business to turn its attentions inwards and economise in its use of working capital. Such an outlook may also come about with a change in management.

A reduction in working capital through greater efficiency has three main effects: an improvement in liquidity, a saving in (or earnings of) interest, and an improvement in return on investment ratios. Savings may be made by adjusting the length of credit period given to customers and taken from suppliers (by agreement), or by reducing inventories.

No financial manager should act alone on these points, since they are also matters which concern operational management. In some circumstances precipitate action can cause more problems than it solves. Solutions may be complex and require the assistance of skilled services: as in the design of an inventory control system, a change in the order-handling procedure which gets invoices out quicker, or a detailed study to cut down inventories by reducing the number of distribution depots, or standardising products so that raw material and finished stock levels may be set low.

Good management will demand that measures such as these become part of day-to-day considerations. Operating managers should be encouraged to think about working capital when planning any new decisions. In a less well-managed company opportunities for improvement should have been uncovered through the corporate appraisal.

The chances of a normally well-managed company releasing large flows of capital by changing policies which affect the use of working capital are not high, but the possibility should not be overlooked.

Fixed capital expenditure

Investment requirements for fixed capital can only be defined in broad terms in any long-range financial plan, but, nevertheless, these estimates may be accurate enough as a basis for financial strategy.

If it appears that finance is going to be a problem it may be necessary to reconsider these expenditures and take one of the following actions:

1 Ration the available capital according to profitability, risk levels and strategic needs
2 Identify expenditures which can be postponed for a defined period without unduly upsetting overall strategy
3 Concentrate on investments with the earliest payback
4 Re-examine alternatives.

Item (4) requires some explanation. One possibility is to consider ways of implementing the project which involves less capital expenditure, or which phase the same expenditure over a longer time period. Shortage of capital may mean that new projects should be based on renting property, rather than buying; hiring assets rather than purchasing them; or even buying on hire purchase. It may suggest changing a project from one of expansion to acquisition, giving a better opportunity to purchase for paper rather than cash.

What all this indicates is a critical examination of the projects and their effects on profits, and is probably best carried out as a joint exercise between financial management and the strategic planner.

Dividends

One of the ways in which capital may be generated internally is to distribute less of the profits to shareholders. In a family business, where ownership and management are the same, it is much easier to decide on policies which restrict or reduce the distribution of profits to the owners. In this case, there is full knowledge of the reasons for the decision and an acceptance that a sacrifice now will bring greater benefits later. In small business such methods of financing are frequently adopted.

In a large business with many shareholders, and particularly in the case of a quoted company, there are likely to be valid reasons against financing by a reduction in dividends (except possibly where earnings have fallen). Such an action would alter the yield of the shares and cause a fall in share price on the stock exchange. Existing shareholders would lose capital as well as income. This in turn could make the company more vulnerable for takeover.

A policy of holding dividends to existing levels, despite increases in earnings, is unlikely to be so upsetting, at least in the shorter term. (A continuation of the policy over a longer term could result in a situation where market price was less than break-up value, and this too might attract the eye of the hunter in the acquisition jungle.)

Dividends are by no means the only factors which cause fluctuations in share prices. They are – subject to adequate profit performance – one of the areas over which the company has some control. It may be that other elements of the financial strategy require the maintenance of a strong share price: if it is planned to enter the acquisition field it would be more costly if any paper exchange were made on the basis of a low share price. The better deal is likely to come when the shares are strong.

In international operations there may be taxation or exchange control advantages in ensuring that subsidiaries pay a reasonable dividend, even if this causes them difficulties in financing capital expenditures. A bird in the hand from a potentially unstable country is probably worth two in the bush that may be locked in by exchange control measures, or that carry a risk of being lost through expropriation.

Depreciation

Depreciation rates may, within limits, be set by the company itself. There are variations between companies and although auditors generally protect investors against a change of depreciation rates in a way that is designed only to manipulate profits, it is possible for companies to alter their policies from time to time.

Overprovision, once a sign of cautious financial management, is now generally considered much less desirable, in that its effect on profits and real asset values may make the company an attractive acquisition possibility.

The importance of depreciation in cash flow will vary from company to company, but it is often – as, for example, in a shipping company – one of the largest generators of cash the company has.

Taxation

Taxation cannot be evaded, although it is frequently possible to plan the affairs of the company in such a way that the burden of tax is reduced. On an individual project basis (see Chapter 26) taxation is an important item in the appraisal process, and will influence discounted cash-flow calculations. Investment allowances against tax will be usually assumed in project analysis to be available in the year in which they are due: that is, the assumption is that other areas of the company will be earning profits so that the allowance can be set against these. One of the aims of financial strategy must be to ensure, as far as possible, that this assumption is true. The financial benefits of ensuring this can themselves lead to a particular corporate strategy: for example, a company with low profits and high allowances seeking to acquire a company with high profits that will mop up the allowances. If tax allowances cannot be taken, it may be preferable to avoid capital expenditure and lease instead.

In a multinational group it may be possible within the constraints of the law, to choose policies which attract a lower incidence of tax. In all such groups there is some freedom of decision over where profits are made (see Chapter 18).

Under the second group of strategic decision areas there is a consideration of ways in which the company may raise finance. In broad terms these are all matters of relationships with bodies or people outside the company itself, although within the limits of availability the decision to tap these sources is one taken by the company. Strategic consideration will include the basic categories of financial requirements, equity sources, and borrowing.

Categories of finance

There are a number of ways of categorising sources of finance, and these are useful for setting the scene even though they may only influence – and not dictate – the eventual financial strategy of the undertaking.

One classification is into short, medium, and long term. A traditional, and largely outdated, view is that the type of borrowing should fit the type of need: short-term borrowing should never be used to finance the purchase of fixed assets. Certainly there is a point to be watched in defining the financial mix, since excessive reliance on short-term funds for long-term needs can put the company in a vulnerable position. The problem is one of balance, rather than doctrine, and will be returned to when gearing is discussed.

Another classification is risk, fixed assets, and working finance. Risk capital is finance which belongs to the owners of the company (either from retentions or share issues) and which the company is prepared to stand the risk of losing. Both fixed asset and working capital may, of course, be financed from risk capital. Although companies need not necessarily use separate sources for each, it is worth considering that the greater the risk attached to a venture, the more desirable it is that it is financed from equity sources. A heavy investment of loan funds in an R & D project which is unsuccessful could have a much more serious effect on the company than a similar loss of risk capital.

Equity sources

One of the first platforms of financial strategy must be to define the extent of gearing which is acceptable to the company. Initially this will be only to set the parameters of future decisions and will lay down the maximum debt:equity ratio which will be considered acceptable.

The company's basic objectives must be considered here. Many firms now define their profit objective in terms of growth in earnings per share. Additional equity finance in many circumstances would, despite the increasing profits, cause a reduction in average earnings per share, thus preventing the company from achieving its objective. This would tend to drive business with this type of objective to loan funds rather than equity. Similarly a value-based strategy approach would lead to a different mix of strategic–financial decisions.

Objectives are only one aspect of the decision. Financial strategy must also consider a number of factors varying from the state of the money market to control, to cost of finance, as well as the ever-present need to maintain liquidity and solvency. Some of these points should be examined in more detail.

A public company, with a widespread of ownership of its shares, is unlikely to face any direct problems from loss of control when floating an additional issue. Indirectly, the possible weakening of share price on the stock exchange could lead to changes. The company that has all shares concentrated into a few holdings, and which is forced to go outside its existing shareholders for the new issue, is likely to find the control problem of more importance.

Additional equity participation carries the advantage that its servicing costs are related to overall profits. If there is no profit, a dividend need not be paid (or indeed, a dividend can be withheld even when there is a profit). Interest on a loan has to be paid regardless of profits. Equity may, in some circumstances, cost more than a loan. It means giving away a share of the profits of current operations, even though the new operation for which the additional equity is required may be making a lower marginal contribution (although this may be avoided if preference shares are issued). While borrowing provides the opportunity of increasing the return on shareholder's funds, additional equity is likely to reduce that ratio, although total profits may increase.

The decision may also be affected by the current and forecast state of the money market. From the market's viewpoint there are times when it prefers equity to loan investment (or the opposite). A share issue which is unsuccessful, even if taken up by underwriters, may reflect very badly on the company's public image. In times of credit squeeze, when the pressure is to reduce loan finance, equity may be the only available source: but this is not a justification for raising long-term equity to meet short-term problems, unless the plan shows that the additional equity would in any case have to be raised in the near future.

427

Equity becomes of particular importance in acquisition strategy, for an exchange of paper is often a means of avoiding a cash outlay. Such moves are popular with vendors because they may solve certain personal taxation problems. In many circumstances the acquiring company may obtain liquid funds for the exchange of paper. Control may become a much more urgent problem in these circumstances since large blocks of shares in the 'victim' may translate to even larger blocks in the 'hunter'. A combination of cash and paper may avoid this.

Sources of equity are the stock exchange, intercompany deals in an acquisition, or, of course, the traditional personal sources. Additionally, an injection of equity may sometimes be obtained from merchant bankers or other finance houses. In an international business, advantage may be taken of local sources of equity to finance the development of subsidiaries, although the disadvantage of such an action is usually the complication of having minority shareholders.

Many different types of equity are possible, and a company may protect its existing shareholders by issuing preference shares or shares which have voting right restrictions. These may, on the other hand, prove unattractive to the market.

Borrowings

Some of the issues associated with loan finance have been covered in the discussion on equity. One of the major issues to consider is the burden of interest which heavy borrowing will incur. In theory no money will be borrowed unless it earns more for the company than it costs. There are some problems here. First, the calculations must be made on expectations – which may be wrong, either through error or a change in the basic circumstances. Companies do not always make the profits they forecast. This is really a question of acceptable risks, which must be taken into account when the plan is prepared.

Second, to maintain a positive cash flow, the *retained* profits on the projects for which finance is required must be greater than the interest.

Third, a project may be a good investment, but may not break even for several years. During this early period the interest burden – along with other unrecovered costs – must be paid from elsewhere. This is another indication of the need to have an overall financial plan since the total picture may alter conclusions which would be drawn from a study of individual projects.

Cost is as important in considering borrowed finance as it is with equity. With borrowed funds there may be the added complication of having to choose between fixed and fluctuating rates, which requires an assessment of future interest levels before any sensible decision can be made.

Probably the most widely used source of short-term finance is the bank overdraft, which can often be the simplest and cheapest method of obtaining working capital. In times of credit squeeze this source may not be so readily available, and levels of overdraft previously negotiated may be reduced. One of the advantages of overdrafts is that levels can usually be negotiated in advance, but only taken up as required. Additional sources of finance are factoring debtors and discounting bills of exchange. The former may be an expensive and unpalatable solution. The latter is nowadays more likely to arise in companies with export business.

It is possible to obtain long-term loans from banks and finance houses of various types. In some countries there are government-backed development corporations designed to provide this type of credit. The stock market may be tapped through the issue of debentures, although success is likely to be dependent on both the standing of the company and the state of the money market. It must be remembered that debentures carry a fixed interest rate, which may present the company with a long-term disadvantage if an issue is floated at a time when interest is abnormally high. (This, of course, is a comment which applies to all fixed-interest loans.)

Long-term finance needs may also be obtained from mortgaging existing property or taking out a mortgage to buy a new property. In these cases the funds are likely to come from houses which specialise in this type of operation. A variation of using property to raise finance is sale and leaseback. This is venture capital and not a loan. Although it brings in an immediate capital sum it may be expensive (although not necessarily when looked at over the long term if in a situation of rising rents) and suffers from the further disadvantage that it reduces flexibility. Once sold in this fashion, the property is no longer available as specific or general security for other loans – and in a normal situation of rising property prices may remove from the company an asset which increases steadily in value.

Medium-term credit can be obtained from most of the sources mentioned and in addition from leasing and hire purchase.

Taxation implications must be considered in making the decision, since the effect of tax may change the real cost to the company.

The final financial strategy selected should be fully integrated and include provision for contingencies – both for failures by the company to achieve plans and failures of the proposed source of finance to be available at the expected cost. Although the company should be trying to set a long-term strategy, it must be aware that finance is an area where there may be sudden and dramatic environmental changes which can affect the comparative cost of various sources and their availability.

A good financial plan is more than projection of the application and sources of funds statement. In addition, there are few companies whose strategic decisions in the area of finance are as simple as the factors so far discussed might suggest.

One overriding strategic consideration is that the company should try to select its sources in a way that leaves it the utmost flexibility. This means, all other things being equal, that unsecured loans are preferable to secured loans, or that equity might be better than a loan which puts a charge over all the company's assets.

This flexibility question also has implications in the next point. It pays to be right in the assessment of funds needed. Often it is simpler to raise one large sum than two smaller ones, and the costs of so doing are likely to be less. If the loan requires the mortgaging of property, it may be less easy to raise a second mortgage than to obtain the whole sum on a first mortgage – a smaller loan can take away as much flexibility as a large one. On the other hand, the raising of too much finance, of either equity or loan is expensive and strategically dangerous.

Financial strategy in multinational operations has added complications quite apart from the legal ones. Some international companies try to arrange finance so that subsidiaries remit as much money back to the centre as is possible, and the subsidiaries themselves operate on the largest local loans they can raise. This is not solely financial in its implications, and may impinge on operations: for instance, the 'loading' of raw material prices to get money back to the centre may make the subsidiary avoid certain operations which appear to be unprofitable in its own eyes, while the burden of interest payments may further decrease the company's apparent earnings.

Certainly any multinational strategy must give consideration to national and international sources of funds, and one element which should be defined in the plan is the constraints which should be observed by subsidiary companies. The backing of the parent is often sufficient to enable the local subsidiary to obtain larger loans more easily than it would if it relied solely on its own assets.

Equity stays with the company. Loans have to be paid back (although in practice certain types of loan finance may continue almost indefinitely). Provision must be made in the plan for any refunding operations which might be necessary over the period of the plan. In some cases the intention may be to pay back the loan: in others it may be to renegotiate for a further period.

A further aspect of the plan should cover financial public relations, which may be a helpful tool in giving the company credibility, and ensuring that it is known to the financial world and the investing public. Credibility will often hold up share prices when there is an off-trend drop in profits because the explanation given is accepted. It may help the company in driving off an attack from a would-be acquirer or getting the terms of its own acquisition bids accepted.

No one should believe that financial public relations will have more than passing value unless the company is basically sound. A massive edifice cannot be erected in safety on crumbling foundations, and although a PR 'front' may prop things up for a short while, it will not last for long unless backed by facts and results. Although financial public relations may be a specialist area it cannot be separated from the general public relations activities of the company. It is not possible to present two different pictures of the company without both losing credibility.

Financial plans may have to deal with surplus liquid funds as well as shortages. Strategic changes and implications of too much cash have already been discussed. If surpluses do exist, it is up to financial management to make the best use of them, and this is a requirement whether the funds available are moderate or excessive. A well-prepared plan will aid this task in two ways. The projections of capital needs will reveal the changing amount of excess funds available and, therefore, the length of time for which financial management can afford to offer when investing, and sensitivity analysis will help the assessment of the risks in tying up cash in this way. Environmental assessments will enable investments to be made against the background of an appreciation of the money market, changing interest rates, and general economic conditions.

The financial strategy of an organisation may be highly creative and innovative, and this is frequently an essential.

British Petroleum financed its Alaskan oil field, and secured a major strategic position in the USA by a brilliant move. At a time when it was financially stretched it acquired a minority holding in Sohio in exchange for Alaskan oil and other US activities. Sohio were to take over the financing of Alaskan production and had the strength to do this. As Alaskan oil began to flow BP would gain additional equity participation in Sohio in which it would eventually be the majority shareholder. As it was initially an investment, not a subsidiary, BP could not present consolidated accounts which meant that none of the Alaska financing affected its balance sheet.

Much of the company's future success will depend on the skill with which it prepares its financial strategies. It is an area which it cannot afford to neglect, and where failure can render useless all the effort expended by others in the organisation.

CHAPTER 21

Strategic planning for human resources

The other key resource is people. This chapter shows why a strategic approach to human resource management is important, both as a means of ensuring that resources match strategic needs and also as one of the ways to help ensure that strategies are implemented. The chapter shows how these aims can be achieved, and provides a number of check lists and questionnaires to help facilitate the assessment of the degree to which the organisation takes a strategic approach to HRM.

Business is a human activity (despite the fact that many actions take place in the name of business which the cynic might claim would suggest inhumanity). Although labour requirements change, clerical workers may be replaced by computers and factory workers by automation, middle managers may disappear as their organisations de-layer, there still remains a basic fact: no company can operate without people.

The two fundamental resources of any business, of whatever size and whatever nature, are people and money. And of these two, the people resource is the most complex. Money is money whether it comes from loan or equity sources: it does not need to be distinguished from any other money; one five-pound note has the same value as another. People, on the other hand, are all different. They have different physical characteristics, different temperaments, different educational levels, different personal values, different skills, and different abilities. A company, at any one time, has a requirement not for people in general but for specific people who are able to fulfil the function for which they are needed. When it requires managers, it cannot satisfy its need by recruiting labourers: nor can a surplus of managers make up for a shortage of skilled production workers.

In addition, the resource of people is always needed in a particular place. The financial needs of a plant in Glasgow can be met from a bank account in London. The people who work in that plant can be in no other place but Glasgow. Because people are not pawns on a chess board, and have relationships and responsibilities, desires and preferences, and a life outside business, they are a relatively immobile resource.

When money is in surplus there is always a way in which it can be utilised. When the people resource of the company is in surplus it becomes a drain on profits – an unnecessary expense. Because they are human beings, there are good reasons why they should not be treated casually – indeed the social climate and legal constraints of the day may prevent this.

The people resource cannot easily be turned on and off like a tap, yet the effectiveness of the company depends on getting the balance of human resources right. This means that if a company is to be sure that it can achieve the strategies it has set itself, it must give full consideration to the human factor, and must give a priority to planning the personnel aspects of the business. This means bringing people considerations into the strategic selection and implementation process, and ensuring that a strategic orientation is given to the planning and management of the human resource function.

In Chapter 3 we looked at the relationship between strategy, structure, systems and culture, and this thinking is important when we consider a strategic approach to human resource planning. The human issues in strategy will be looked at in more depth later in the book. In this chapter the concentration will be on strategic planning for human resources, a topic which although it began to emerge in the 1960s is barely recognised, and not understood by the majority of managers and human resource specialists.

The first attention to human resource planning began in the 1960s with books on manpower planning, although most of these dealt to some degree with organisational planning. Of these McBeath,[1] Lynch[2] and Bramham[3] are a good sample. I still find these books helpful, although the philosophy behind most of them is more reactive to corporate strategy than proactive.

In the 1980s attention began to be given to the value of linking management development to corporate strategy, both to ensure that management development was more cost effective for the company by incorporating more bottom-line discipline into it, and because the power of training initiatives as a way of implementing strategy was not generally recognised. Useful references here are Bolt,[5,8] Hussey[4,6] and Nilsson.[7] To the best of my knowledge these cover the two early articles, and the only three books so far published on this topic. An increasing number of articles are now appearing in planning and human resource journals.

My own work moved from strategy, through some manpower planning, to management development strategy, and on to a total strategic approach to human resource management. So far the literature on a total approach is scanty, although the idea of such an approach has crept into seminar titles. I know of some works that are being written, but at this point the only reference I can give is Salaman.[9] It will be very different when the time comes to write the next edition of this book. I expect it to become a much more important topic in both theory and practice.

A framework for strategic HR management

The strategic elements of human resource management are the areas which should alter to reflect changes in the organisation's strategy, and which should

433

also have a proactive relationship with the development of that strategy. They are all areas where the investigator should expect to find differences compared with similar activities in other organisations. These are not necessarily differences of basic concepts, but of the interpretation of those concepts so that they fit the unique needs of the company.

The strategic elements of human resources are only a portion of the work that goes on within the HR function. Behind the strategic activities stand a host of administrative and support services. The direction of these is, of course, shaped by corporate policy and strategy, but many more would be directly transferable from one organisation to another. For example, the policy towards recruitment may be strategic: the actual processes of recruitment may be very similar between organisations. Record keeping is an administrative task of all HR departments, not very different between organisations: what information goes on the records may be changed by the organisation's specific approach to competencies, manpower planning and management development.

Figure 21.1 sets out the framework in diagrammatic form. The heart of the model holds the vision, values, objectives and strategies of the organisation. These should drive the strategies and policies of the activities in the middle ring. As mentioned, there is a two-way influence, in that the activities in this ring can affect the corporate strategy. For example, the manpower planning activity may show that the strategic assumptions behind a new strategy are fallible, in that the people needed to implement a new strategy may be unobtainable.

The inner-ring activities are management development, manpower planning, succession planning, climate and culture, competency assessment, and a group of policies towards recruitment, remuneration, and industrial relations. The activities in this group may vary in their degree of strategic importance from time to time.

The outer ring shows the support activities mentioned above. These will only be dealt with in the context of the inner ring activities in this chapter.

In planning HR activities a starting point should be the corporate strategic elements at the heart of Figure 21.1. There are a number of steps to go through which are illustrated in Figure 21.2. Most of this diagram is self-explanatory, but two steps are worth stressing.

1 The figure suggests that if the HR department is not given access to the strategic information, the whole planning process should be abandoned. It also suggests that if no plan exists, and it is not possible to clarify the strategy officially, assumptions should be made. The different view taken is to do with how the HR department is perceived. If in good esteem, it is worth making assumptions to fill gaps. If not esteemed highly enough to share the plan, then assumptions would be a waste of time because someone else has the true picture, and assumptions from a source that lacks credibility would have no meaning. The implication of what I am saying here is that no worthwhile strategic plan for HR can be prepared if the function is shut out from other strategic discussions: in addition, no organisation that excludes HR can expect to produce sound strategies that are capable of being implemented.

2 There is a box in Figure 21.2 which questions the depth of the analysis. This is a point born from experience and supported by Harbridge Consulting Group

Figure 21.1
Human resource
management and
corporate strategy

Figure 21.2
Relating HR actions
to corporate plans

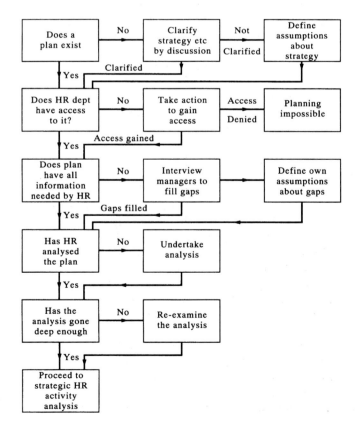

research.[10] It is possible to treat a de-layering and downsizing decision at two levels. The first is the obvious one, of redundancy actions, early retirement, and communication. The second is more subtle, like how do we make the organisation work now that we have de-layered? This involves new management processes such as empowerment and performance management, and the training that enables both the empowered and the empowerers to understand how to make the new concept work. The research showed that very few companies were thinking at the second level. It is not surprising that the sort of motivation problems identified in Scase and Goffee[11] should be found when no action is taken to make the new organisation function.

Figure 21.3 shows how to begin to see the corporate plan in HR terms. The example is illustrative only, and the examples are deliberately kept at a simple level to show the method. Behind each tick should be a list of explanations: for example, what is it that management development will have to do to support the de-layering strategy?

It is worth mentioning that few strategic plans are written with HR in mind, and that very often HR thinking will not appear in those plans. There is always a need for intelligent interpretation, and it may often be necessary to take the interview route suggested in Figure 21.2 to fill some of the gaps. An alternative to one to one interviews is to organise a meeting where senior managers are

Figure 21.3
Using matrix displays (illustrative only)

Strategic sources		HR areas impacted						
Type	Description	Mangmt dev.	Succession planning	Manpower planning	Competencies	Climate/ culture	Others (specify ➝ reward	
Vision	Customer responsive	✓			✓	✓		
	Global	✓			✓			
Strategies	European expansion	✓	✓	✓	✓	✓		
	New R&D unit			✓				
	Delayering	✓	✓	✓	✓	✓	✓	
	Strategic alliance	✓				✓		
Values	People centred	✓	✓	✓		✓		
	Performance management	✓			✓	✓	✓	
	Integrity				✓		✓	
Objectives	25% PA Revenue growth	✓	✓	✓	✓	✓	✓	
	Double market share	✓	✓	✓	✓	✓	✓	

persuaded to think through the HR implications of the plans. The point is that if this type of thinking is new to the company it may be rather more ragged than the figures suggest. This is how experts earn their keep!

Relating to the external environment

The Human Resources strategy, like other business strategies, is impacted by what is going on in the outside world. It is important that HR looks at these events and trends, as in most organisations no one else will be doing this from an HR viewpoint.

Earlier chapters suggested ways of thinking about and assessing the environment, and these will apply equally to the HR strategy. As with strategic changes, it is possible to think deeply about these issues or be superficial in looking at the HR impact. For example, the changes in demography in many countries of the world are well documented. It is possible to look at these only in terms of recruitment and retention, and overlook more subtle impacts such as increased diversity in the cultural and ethnic backgrounds of the workforce in certain age groups, making it important that the organisation plans to handle this diversity in the most constructive way. At one extreme there may be a need for training in cultural diversity. At the other there may be a need to modify the work place and work place procedures to make people from minority groups feel more welcome. Laura Tovey[10] in her research found that most organisations in the UK were only planning to deal with the obvious things, and had not considered the less obvious but potentially more important issues.

Another example is that changes in technology may bring a long-term shift in the nature of jobs in a company and in the people who are competent to fill them. Amin Rajan[12] showed in his research how the financial businesses, such as insurance, were changing to require more knowledge workers where previously the overwhelming requirement had been for clerical people.

Figure 21.4 sets out a matrix for considering environmental issues from an HR perspective. This is a special adaptation of the method given in Figure 7.2 and although the subheadings given are illustrative, and would need to be expanded to fit the specific situation, they give a good idea of the sort of trends and issues that should be considered in an HR plan.

It is also important to consider the level of environmental turbulence and its impact from an HR view point. This concept, described in detail in Ansoff[13] and Ansoff and McDonnell,[14] was summarised in an earlier chapter.

Each level of turbulence calls for different managerial characteristics, because the business has to be managed in a different way. Ansoff and McDonnell provide profiles for management skills, management climate, and management competence required for each level of turbulence.

The implications for HR management are mainly as we move from the present to the future. If the position on the scale of turbulence is changing, it may be that the nature of management in that organisation must also change. This can change succession plans, may have a training implication, and will alter other aspects such as performance management and recruitment policy.

Figure 21.4
Assessing the
impact of
environmental
issues on HR
activities

Broad headings	Example checklist	The important changes	Impact	Probability	Importance	How does it impact HR?
Demographic	Age structure of population					
	Migration levels					
	Size of population					
	Diversity of population					
Economic	Inflation reflation/recession					
	Wage and salary levels					
	Taxation					
Legal	Employment law					
	H & S legal					
	EEC rules					
	Information disclosure					
Technological	IT					
	Production methods					
	Product life cycles					
Infrastructure	Educational system					
Industry/market	Competitor employment practice					
	Industry norms					
Ecology	Environment movement					
	Pressure groups					
	'Green' attitudes					
	Smoking attitudes					
Social	Work attitudes					
	Cultural differences					
	Educational values					
Political	Likely pressures					
	Government changes					

A strategic approach to management development and training

Now it is possible to explore the circles on the inner ring of Figure 21.1. All will be approached in a strategic way. It is worth mentioning that this is not the way in which most organisations currently think about HR issues, although research by Harbridge Consulting Group (Kate Ascher[15] and Laura Tovey[10]) shows that an increasing number of organisations have adopted this view.

The concept for management development is shown in Figure 21.5. The argument is that the philosophy for management development should put emphasis on corporate needs, in addition to the traditional view which looks at individual needs in the context of what the organisation is willing to spend.

In order to make this effective, those drawing up the management development plans and programmes must have an intimate knowledge of the corporate strategy, and the ability to get behind the strategy to the management development actions needed to support it. This may require the actions to survey senior managers as mentioned in the first part of this chapter, additional analysis by human resource specialists who have an appreciation of the firm's strategy as

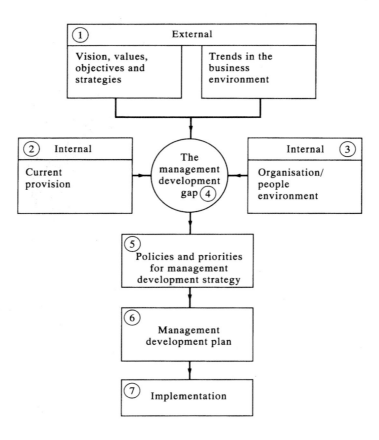

Figure 21.5
Strategic framework for management development

well as a knowledge of their own craft and a large supply of common sense. Management development and training people who expect to be able to find a company book with all the answers will be disappointed. It is they who have to be proactive and write the book!

My experience suggests that once a company begins to adopt this model, it will find that it also has to change how it assesses individual needs. One possibility is the use of company-relevant competencies, which can be used as a basis for assessing needs. These have value in many methods of assessment, including assessment centres. Some brief thoughts on a strategic approach to competencies will be given later. The assessment of individuals remains an important element of the mix, but a strategic view may well lead to different ways of making that assessment.

Matrices should be developed to help relate individual needs to corporate needs. Figure 21.3 provides a starting point, and the following hypothetical example shows how the corporate need for training in specific skills and knowledge might be derived from the data in this figure. Only the items listed under strategy are considered for the purposes of the example, although in reality all of the strategic sources would be covered. I make no claim that the example covers all that the organisation might require from its managers, nor that the answers would be the same for other companies following a similar strategy.

Strategy	Corporate management development need
European expansion	Market planning
	Country cultural differences
	Working of the EU
	Managing change
	Visionary leadership
	Project appraisal
Delayering	Empowerment
	Career management
	Situational leadership
	Interpersonal communication
	Performance management
Strategic alliance	Successful alliance management
	Understanding cultural differences

Such matrices would need to be developed for various levels of management, and possibly for different areas of the organisation, and in some cases for specific jobs. It should also be clear that these matrices are a starting point. Each item needs to be looked at in more detail to specify exactly what the need is, and what subtopics would also have to be covered.

Another box on the diagram is the audit of current management development provision. All the researches already quoted, and other studies with which I have been involved, suggest that cost–benefit analysis is not a regular feature of management development management, and that there is a tendency to hold on to training programmes, and the resources which deliver them, even when there is a high level of dissatisfaction with the providers.

Figure 21.6
Audit of current
training provision

For each initiative	
1. Aims	**2. Results/current plan**
• Objectives	• Number of events
	planned 1992
• Corporate goal, KSF or	actual 1991
strategy supported	actual 1990
• Other rationale for	• Number of
initiative	participants 1992
	1991
• Target population	1990
• How target population	• Participants as %
identified?	of target groups 1992
	1991
• How are people selected	1990
to attend	
	• When did the initiative
	start
	• How is it resourced?
	• Breakdown of costs
	• What are the course
	ratings
	• How are the benefits
	measured
	• How has the initiative
	contributed to the
	objectives?

A framework for auditing all current management development activities, of which the majority will be training programmes, is offered in Figure 21.6. Many organisations find it surprisingly difficult to answer these simple questions, which suggests that the management of the function has been less than professional. (A longer checklist, covering the policy issues, appears in Figure 21.8.)

From the gap that emerges out of the audit, it becomes possible to define new policies and priorities for management development. This leads to another box on Figure 21.5, the development of a management development plan. The final box is a reminder that plans have to be implemented, and to support this some guidance will be given on selecting external resources to help implement the training elements of this plan.

The integration of these various types of information in the approach shown in Figure 21.6 allows management development to be viewed in a business-oriented manner. Most organisations that work in this way change the priorities they had been following, and alter many of their approaches to development and training. It also allows more initiatives which can be tied directly to bottom line results,

Figure 21.7

Some policy issues

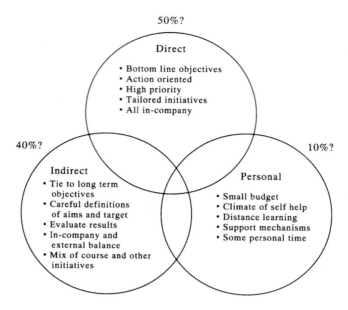

50%?

40%?

10%?

Direct
- Bottom line objectives
- Action oriented
- High priority
- Tailored initiatives
- All in-company

Indirect
- Tie to long term objectives
- Careful definitions of aims and target
- Evaluate results
- In-company and external balance
- Mix of course and other initiatives

Personal
- Small budget
- Climate of self help
- Distance learning
- Support mechanisms
- Some personal time

Increase areas of overlap to achieve
multiple policy objectives

thereby making it easier to demonstrate the value of training to the organisation.

Figure 21.7 suggests three groups of training needs that might be defined from such a study. Without trying to be dogmatic, because the decisions will vary by company, I have indicated on the diagram possible proportions of corporate effort that should be devoted to each group. Initially I should like to discuss each circle on the diagram as if it were a watertight entity, but later will try to show how initiatives that fall in the overlap areas of the circle may enhance the value of the initiatives, by killing two or more birds with one stone.

By direct priorities I mean initiatives that contribute directly to corporate aims and objectives, such as training events designed to implement a strategy or structural change, formulate strategy, deal with an issue from the business environment, implement a policy change, change culture to enable a strategy to succeed, or provide solutions to a specific problem or issue. By their nature these needs are likely to be met by initiatives that are action oriented, have bottom line objectives, and have a high degree of urgency. In turn this affects the solutions, which may well be courses that cascade through several levels of an organisation, are entirely run in company and have a high degree of tailoring. Only if they have these characteristics can these initiatives deal with the type of issue that is identified as a direct need.

Indirect priorities may be equally important for the company, and many of the initiatives will be more long term in both their objectives, and the time over which personnel are involved in an initiative. However not all will be lengthy initiatives. Under this heading I include induction training, career development programmes, and actions to improve personal performance. I believe that the policy here should be to tie to long-term objectives where appropriate, to be very clear about the aims of and target population for the initiative. Here there may be a balance between in-company and external initiatives, and a mix of training and development actions. Many in-company courses under this category would benefit from being tailored, but the depth of tailoring may often be less than for a course dealing with a corporate issue. The decision hangs on the learning objectives of the various components of a course or programme.

The final category are needs which are identified by individuals in discussion with their managers, but which are personal in that they do not have a high corporate priority. If people are motivated to develop themselves, there is likely to be value to the organisation in giving encouragement. What I believe is appropriate here is not company courses but the creation of a climate of self-help and the provision of support. Under this heading I should consider giving financial support for distance learning, for example, and perhaps establishing a resource centre where self-study can take place. In return for this support I would expect individuals to give some personal time to the course of study.

Clarity emerges from such an analysis, but the benefits to the firm may be increased if deliberate attention is given to the overlap areas. For example, indirect needs can be tied closer to direct needs through the use of competencies as the standard against which the developmental and remedial needs of individuals are evaluated. Competency assessment will be the next circle to be considered from Figure 21.1.

A second way of adding value to 'indirect' initiatives is to build in some of the direct issues into the longer-term development programmes, through teaching materials and project work.

Another example is to use a workshop initiative to help business units to develop sound strategies, which with modification can be used later for an indirect development need, to train less senior managers in business planning.

Creative thinking can help an organisation obtain much more from management development than the three-circle diagram may initially suggest, but the value of the planned approach cannot be overstressed.

This approach does not mean that organisations should never do any training that can only be looked at as an act of faith. It is a question of balance. Just as it is poor management for the total management development strategy to be built from the bottom up, so it would be equally poor if it were to be totally built from the top down.

There should be a switch from a purely cost-based decision on available options to one of cost–benefit analysis. It is common practice for training managers, for example, to take an out-of-pocket expenses view of training initiatives. The cost of participants' time in attending training initiatives is rarely considered, and almost nobody adds in the real economic factor, the opportunity cost of this time. As a result many current decisions on training matters are aimed at reducing the cost of the initiative rather than increasing the benefits. This has led to many decisions which are wrong for the companies concerned.

A different slant to assessing individual needs

It may be of interest to record that Tovey[10] found that all of her sample of large UK companies used a performance-appraisal method to establish needs, and for 40 per cent it was the only method. Only 10 per cent used competency assessment, and assessment centres, where used, were on a selective basis (which is sensible). Other methods such as surveys and assessments by training managers were used by the 60 per cent that did not rely solely on assessment centres.

The annual appraisal interview is a notoriously poor way of assessing development needs, as it depends on two levels of perception, the subordinate and boss, both of which could be erroneous. Greater use of the competency approach can ensure that the right questions are asked, but does not remove the bias.

I have found that bottom-up assessment is particularly good at identifying needs that may have otherwise remained hidden, but I have only used this method for looking at management and interpersonal skills. On a confidential basis questionnaires are completed by the subject manager and by at least three subordinates and/or peers. These are aggregated and the individual reports are not revealed to the subject. What is of value is the 'photograph' of management behaviour, which is often different from the self-perception. This method can be used in a general way, although there are also approaches which are related to researched topics, such as the management of innovation, leadership, and organisation climate.

Surveys can be a valuable periodic tool, and can be focused on the competencies that are important to the firm. We have found it useful to obtain ratings on perceived abilities and the perceived importance the person places on them. This is particularly useful in a change situation, when management sees the need for new skills and this view of relevance is not shared by those below them.

The use of assessment centres is well known. What might be less well known is the way in which they can be designed to mirror the strategic requirements of the organisation, both in ensuring the selection of the right people for a particular situation and in identifying the strategically oriented training needs. Most experts in assessment centres come from the industrial psychology route and they give more emphasis to the individual than to the firm. Put a business orientation to assessment centre design and a very powerful tool is created. *HR Reporter*[16] shows how Pratt and Whitney used an assessment centre approach to help restore their competitive position. Their response to being pushed out of the number-one position in aero engines by GE was to break down a 21 000-person operation into fifty two smaller business units. Managers had to be selected and trained to operate as small business managers, a move considered necessary to respond to the changed business situation.

Conclusions

The strategic view postulated here enables management development to add more value to the corporation without necessarily spending more. At the same time it provides a permanent mechanism for aiding the implementation of strategies, an issue which will be discussed in more detail in a later chapter.

Figure 21.8 provides a longer check list of questions for an audit of management development using the principles of the model in Figure 21.5.

A strategic approach to competency assessment

The idea of defining management standards and competencies is not new, but in the UK received a new emphasis after the publication of the report into management development by Constable and McCormick.[17] This led to the formation of an organisation called the Management Charter Initiative (MCI), one of whose activities was to research and publish generic management competencies for various levels of management. So far competencies have been published for supervisory, first-line and middle management (MCI[18-20]). These competencies are intended to 'provide a basis against which managers may be assessed, their performance improved and their skills more effectively utilised'. Properly used, competencies have value in management development, manpower and succession planning, recruitment, and performance management.

MCI use the following headings to define competencies:

1 *Units of Competence*: the broad descriptions of what is expected from a competent person at each level
2 *Elements of Competence*: a breakdown of the units
3 *Performance Criteria*: which specify the outcomes which have to be achieved for competent performance
4 *Range Statements*: which describe the range of instances and circumstances in which the element is applied
5 *Evidence Specifications*: what evidence is required to show that competence is achieved.

The MCI competencies are well loved by the British government, which likes the idea of standards that can be universally applied, and by many academic organisations, which use them as the basis for developing new educational programmes, in the belief that relevance to industry is thus assured.

While the concept of competencies has undoubted value, the generic approach has serious faults. Figure 21.9 shows in an approximate way how levels of management are affected by the strategic decisions of the firm. While the job of a supervisor may be almost entirely the same, regardless of the vision, values and strategies, it is hard to argue that senior management jobs are equally identical. In the diagram, the black area shows where generic competencies are likely to be of value: the white area where they have doubtful validity. Exact positions of the boundaries will vary by company, so the argument is not that the generic approach is never appropriate, but that how and where it is appropriate will vary considerably between organisations.

Figure 21.8

Checklist of
questions for an
audit of
management
development

1. What is management development contributing to the achievement of corporate objectives?

2. Do you know whether it is helping you to gain competitive advantage?

3. How do you know?

4. What explicit connections are there between training initiatives and corporate strategy?

5. When was the management development plan last fully reviewed against the strategic needs of the company?

6. Is there a mechanism for top management involvement in such a review, for example by a regular steering group, or by periodic detailed consideration by the chief executive?

7. How are management development plans determined?

8. Do management development initiatives cascade from top to bottom of the organisation, or is all effort concentrated on one or two levels?

9. When training initiatives are designed to help implement strategies, do you start at the top of the organisation and work down?

10. How are budgets for management development activity determined?

11. Are budgets related to the corporate need, based on a clear management development and training plan, which is broken down into defined and costed projects?

12. What is your total expenditure on management development?

13. Are all elements of expense of management development under the same budgetary responsibility: or is it possible for one part of the organisation to save expense by causing increased costs to another part? (For example, by the training manager choosing a cheaper hotel in the country because this looks better against his budget, but in doing so causing much higher travel costs which fall under other budgets.)

14. Are the opportunity costs of the people attending training programmes identified and considered when planning such courses?

15. Does the control system force actions to minimise the expense of training without any consideration of whether this minimises the return on the opportunity cost?

16. How large is your training budget compared to competitors? In your home country? In other countries?

17. How does your management development effort compare with best practice in the world at large? (e.g. bench-marking yourself against the leaders)

18. When you require a global training initiative to develop a common approach across all subsidiaries, do you run the programme in the language of the company, or do you deliver a programme which keeps the integrity of the original, but makes adjustments for country cultural difference, and offers the programme in the various mother tongues of participants?

19. Do you have a clear policy difference for the different categories of need identified in Figure 21.7?

20. How are people selected to attend a programme: in relation to the corporate need, or on a 'volunteer' basis?

Figure 21.8
Continued

21. How is management development organised in your organisation?

22. Does the structure enable corporate priorities to be identified and addressed?

23. How are differences of perception, about what is of corporate importance, between different areas identified and resolved?

24. How are management development activities coordinated between corporate, divisional head offices, country offices and other organisational units of the organisation?

25. What actions are taken to ensure that management training results in changed behaviour in the job situation?

26. How do you evaluate the effectiveness of a management development initiative?

27. Do you do anything more than give a reactions questionnaire at the end of a course?

28. There are 500-600 providers of training services in the UK alone. Do you understand the differences between the various types of competitor, so that you can relate their particular competencies to your need, or have you stereotyped providers so that you automatically use business schools for senior management initiatives without evaluating whether there are other high quality providers who may be more appropriate for the task?

29. Do you insist that when an outside provider is quoting you for a tailored course that the proposal shows the effort that will be spent researching the course in the company, and developing the right amount of company relevant teaching materials? Are your tailored courses really tailored, in the sense of being unique to your organisation and its needs?

30. How long have you used all your present training suppliers?

31. Is there a mechanism so that you can judge their performance?

Figure 21.9
Generalised diagram: impact of strategy on competencies at various management levels

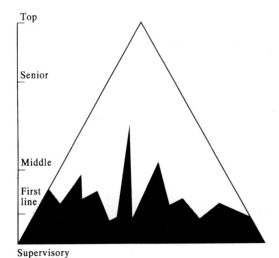

A second disadvantage of the MCI approach is that it does not set out to cover all competencies. It aims to cover the generic rather than the functional skill elements of management jobs. Even if all the generic descriptions were right for a particular organisation, the competencies would still not cover all the things that needed to be done to enable the organisation to achieve strategic success.

One example will suffice to question the value of the generic approach. Two multinational grocery product companies face up to their markets in very different ways. One operates a global strategy, where country differences are subordinate to the overall strategy. The other works on a multicountry basis, with every country operation being an ROI centre, and having a high degree of strategic freedom. The management and business skill competencies for most senior-level jobs would be quite different between the companies. A successful country managing director in the global company has to operate in a different way from his competitor in the multicountry company. A successful career in one company does not guarantee success in the other.

Figure 21.10 shows a more strategic approach to competency assessment. Like the strategic management development approach, to which it is related, it

A strategic approach to competency assessment

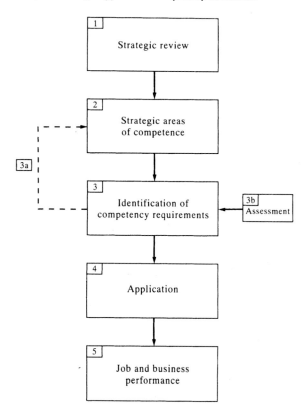

Figure 21.10
A strategic
approach to
competency
assessment.
(Copyright
Harbridge
Consulting Group
Ltd: used with
permission)

begins with a strategic review (step 1). This is fundamentally the process described earlier in this chapter. In step 2 the competencies the company requires at each level, in order to implement the strategy successfully are defined. These are blended in step 3 with the assessment of required competencies at the level of the key jobs. There is a recycling loop at this point to ensure that the individual competency assessments are properly related to the corporate needs. The most likely issue is that a change of strategy could bring a requirement for new strategic areas of competence which are not seen by those who should be affected, because either they are unaware of the strategy or of its implications for them. The approach, with case histories illustrating different aspects of its implementation, has been fully documented by Tovey.[21]

To make sense of competencies derived by the above method requires a way of grouping competencies once they have been identified. Figure 21.11 shows a method we have used which is related to our research into leadership. The core of the model is flexibility, because it is believed that this is a prerequisite for success in modern competitive conditions. The inner ring consists of the individual skills and attributes each manager should have in order to perform effectively in the particular company situation. The outer ring shows the elements each manager should possess to be an effective leader in the particular company. Other ways of grouping could be used.

Figure 21.12 gives an example of the competencies that might be derived for a specific company under one of the subheadings of the model in Figure 21.11. Although some elements might appear in a similar exercise undertaken for a different organisation, what we find is that there are differences in priorities,

Figure 21.11
Strategic competency profile. (Copyright Harbridge Consulting Group Ltd: used with permission)

Figure 21.12
Example of
competencies
related to one
element of Figure
21.11

Visionary

Conceives longer term direction for the business in the context of
opportunities, competitive factors and profit requirements: causes a
desired future state to be defined that is realistic, motivating and
meaningful to others: shares this with conviction so that people know
where they are going and what they have to do to get there.

Strategic thinking

Able to combine analytical method and mental flexibility to produce creative
and realistic responses to changing business situations

• Insightful analysis
• Solution oriented questions
• Non linear mind set

Industry and market knowledge

Understands the key external factors and trends which help to shape the direction of
the company and underpin the formulation of its vision and mission

• Being customer focused
• Knowing the competitors
• Understanding the external environment

Knowing the company

Understands the key internal factors and issues which enable the best operating
decisions to be made for the company, its customers, and the business units and the
individuals who work in them

• Strengths and weaknesses/distinctive competencies

Core values

Behaves in a way which reflects the values and beliefs of the company and is
consistent with its vision and mission

• Being credible
• Showing conviction
• Display integrity
• Constancy of purpose

---

detail, and nuances of meaning because of the different business activities and
strategies. The example company operates in only one country: additional
elements would have to be introduced if it were to have a multinational
strategy. Similarly it is a single-industry company. Additional competencies
would be needed at the top if the company operated more broadly, perhaps
competencies in portfolio management. The reference to customer focus is not
because the consultants considered this to be a good thing but because it was
a key plank in the company's strategy. Similarly, there is no reference to
competence in value-based strategy concepts, which there would be in another
company which was dedicated to this concept.

Climate and culture

There are three dimensions to the audit of corporate culture:

1 What is the current culture?
2 What is the desired culture to achieve corporate success?
3 What should be done to change or reinforce culture?

In everyday terms organisational climate can be paraphrased as 'how it feels to work around here'. It is closely related to culture, and some authorities see little difference between the two. It is important because an organisation's climate has a direct impact on what that organisation can achieve. This is increasingly recognised, and some of the major repositioning moves of large companies have been accompanied by a deliberate attempt to change the culture. Examples include the 1980s drives by Jan Carlsen of Scandinavian Airlines and Jack Welch of General Electric. Publicly announced actions in the UK include those by British Telecom and British Petroleum. It is not easy to change the culture of an organisation unless there is a crisis situation which is widely accepted, as there are always many factors within the organisation that reinforce the historic situation. What is widely observable is that there are now many top management groups in companies who have assessed what culture they believe is necessary if their companies are to be successful over the next decade, and have issued edicts which say things such as:

> Our culture will be open and honest, giving appropriate recognition to and respecting the rights of the individual. The company puts the customer first, and makes decisions as low down the organisation as it can. It is dedicated to creating an environment which encourages entrepreneurial attitudes and individual creativity.

The reality is often different!

Inside the company there is an attitude that the business would be fine if only the customers would stop complaining, no one knows what decisions are being taken at the top, there is no delegation, the people are risk averse, and everyone will always try to pass decisions upwards. This example is not an exaggeration.

Figure 21.13 shows the dimensions of climate used by my firm. A critical determinant is the management practices of superior managers. The research on which this model was based[22] showed that certain practices dramatically affect climate, that these can be measured objectively by taking a reading from the people who report to the manager, and that any desired changes to climate can best be achieved by persuading managers to modify their work practices in critical areas.

The clusters of practices that have been found to be critical are:

- Structure – clarity of roles and responsibilities
- Standards – pressure to improve performances coupled with pride in doing a good job
- Responsibility – the feeling of being in charge of one's own job
- Recognition – the feeling of being rewarded for a job well done

451

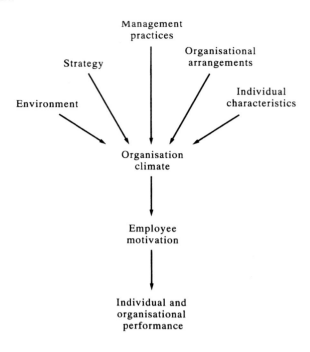

Figure 21.13
A model of organisation climate and performance – the determinants. (Copyright Harbridge House Inc.: used with permission)

- Support – the feeling of trust and mutual support
- Commitment – a sense of pride in belonging to the organisation.

The advantage of using an objective method to audit climate is that it is easier to see what is compatible or incompatible with corporate strategy, discussion internally on what should change is focused and has more credibility, it is possible to remeasure at some future time to monitor the effect of changes, and it is possible to compare the cultures in different parts of the company.

Because virtually all ways of looking at climate or culture are proprietary or protected by copyright, it is not possible to provide a check list for any detailed approach to measuring climate. Readers may care to refer to Handy,[23] where an alternative approach to assessing the culture of organisations is provided. This includes a questionnaire attributed to Harrison.

A strategic approach to succession planning

Succession planning may be considered as one aspect of manpower planning, and is only looked at separately because of its strong links with management development. It is also possible for an organisation to gain considerable benefit from succession planning without necessarily undertaking any other manpower planning activity.

As with all other HR activities, succession planning can be either a dynamic and powerful tool which supports the corporate strategic effort, or it can be a bureaucratic exercise which results in neat succession charts which do not contribute in any way.

Since our approach is strategic, succession planning should begin with a consideration of the impact of the strategies and changes in the external environment on the structure of the organisation. This by now will be a familiar approach, and much of this consideration will have already been given if the analyst has followed the order of this chapter. It is self-evident that any change, or projected future change, in key jobs will affect the skills and qualities looked for in any potential successor to the present incumbent. In addition, the nature and pace of change resulting from the strategy may bring a need for more, or different, managerial positions.

Succession planning also requires a means for identifying people with the potential to move upwards in the organisation. There are dangers if the only means of making this identification is the assessment of superior managers. These include:

1 Different perceptions across divisions: a person judged in one area not to have succession potential may in fact be better than another from a different area, judged by his or her manager to be a strong candidate.
2 There may be a tendency to judge that people have potential, but that they will not be ready for, say, two years. However, when the exercise is repeated the following year the same people are still seen as being two years away from being ready.
3 The perception of the superior manager of another person's suitability to succeed may be based on what the job is now rather than how it will be by the time that person succeeds.
4 Judgements may also be biased because the candidate is compared against the manager's belief in his or her own capabilities. An interesting sidelight is thrown on this by Akira Ichikawa.[24] He observes that all Japanese business leaders are short people, despite the overall growth in the height of the Japanese population. However, leaders are always selected by their predecessors, and the culture means that a successor will not be appointed if he is in any way seen as superior to the present incumbent. Someone who is taller, unless he has family ties, has little hope of appointment. Western culture is somewhat different, but not so different that selection is always unaffected by using oneself as the ruler against which potential successors are measured.

A more balanced view of potential may be obtained if assessment centres are used in addition to assessment by superior manager, and if there is a review mechanism so that all potential successors are considered by a high-level management group on a regular basis.

A strategic approach to manpower planning

Figure 21.14 offers one way to approach the task of preparing a manpower plan. It suggests certain steps which have to be followed in order to end up with a meaningful and comprehensive plan. And as will now be familiar to

Figure 21.14
Strategic framework
for manpower
planning

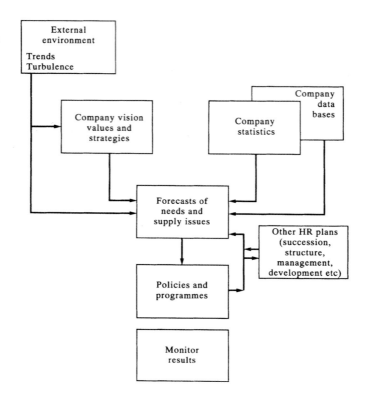

the point of becoming boring, the critical starting points are the environmental trends and the vision, values and strategies of the company. The strategy issue has been thoroughly debated, and there is no need to add anything at this point. The environmental box is worth a brief mention as there are some things to consider which have not so far been dealt with at any length.

If the full audit of the environment has been undertaken carefully most of the trends which affect manpower planning will have been picked up. Obvious trends include demographic changes, not only to population size and the age structure of that population but also to ethnic mix at different age levels. For some businesses, the analysis may have to be undertaken at a local level for certain types of labour. Although overall there may be a surplus of a certain type of low-grade labour in a country, this may be an academic fact to a company which operates in an area where there is a shortage.

The external study should also cover education and skills. Thus it may be important to understand the changes in the expected output of graduates in certain disciplines, or the speed at which the supply of a profession (for example, actuaries) can be adjusted to meet expansion in national demand.

It is almost impossible to make effective use of the information covered in the environment and strategy boxes, unless there is a strong base of company statistics. If, for example, you do not know how many people there are at a particular level or function there is not much that can be done with an assessment that implies that the company will need this particular skill to support its expansion plan. Without knowledge of the rate of labour turnover, and the reasons for people leaving, it is impossible to begin to estimate the number of people that the company should plan to recruit.

Figure 21.15 lists some of the statistics that the organisation should be collecting. Although in most cases the most recent information is the most important, time series can be very useful to allow the study of trends, and to examine the impact of new policies. In addition, there will be needs from time to time for additional information. Behind the regular series of statistics there should be a comprehensive database, which allows the identification of individuals with particular attributes, and the collection of specific statistics. In addition to basic employment records, the database might contain details of training given, particular skills (such as language capability), psychological profiles (e.g. tolerance of ambiguity, career aspirations, and particular experi-

---

1. Total number of employees by:

   Grades
   Business areas
   Locations
   Meaningful jobs/skills
   Sex
   Basis of employment (e.g. permanent, part time, etc.)

2. Age and length of service structure by grades, business areas, locations, meaningful jobs/skills and sex.

3. Labour turnover rates, by grades, etc: by age and by service length.

4. Productivity data by grades, business areas, location, meaningful jobs/skills and sex.

5. Potential of employees in critical jobs (see succession planning), and statistics on promotion

6. Accidents and other occupational health data, by activity, location, age etc.

7. Time lost through sickness, by grades, business areas, etc.

8. Industrial relations disputes, by grades, etc.

9. Trade union membership statistics, by union.

10. Recruiting activity and success rates, by grade, etc: number of unfilled vacancies by grade, etc.

11. Overtime statistics, by grade etc.

12. Contract and agency employees, who are substituting for full time employees.

13. Number and type of transfers across business units and across functions: across countries.

14. Number of employees by grade etc who are on secondment or temporary transfer outside of the planning unit.

Figure 21.15
List of some of the internal statistics needed for manpower planning

ence (such as service in a particular country), salary grade and level, and salary history). Competencies could be used as one of the parameters for the database.

Because all organisations are different, the planner should construct his or her own list of statistics needed. It is not untypical to find even large organisations which have trouble tracking basic statistics, such as the total number of employees each month, and sometimes two conflicting figures are passed to top management: one from the accountants, based on payroll, and the other from the personnel area. While it is possible for there to be legitimate differences in these figures (such as someone being on the payroll in the month following departure because overtime or bonus payments have to be paid), a good place to start an audit of manpower planning is the availability, timeliness and accuracy of the HR statistics.

The interpretative part of the manpower planning process is in the box where forecasts of needs, and the supply issues in meeting them, have to be drawn together. If good information is available, the main problem here is uncertainty. Even forecasts for one year ahead can be inaccurate in a turbulent environment. Those for longer periods may justify considerable sensitivity analysis, so that the impact of changes can be properly understood.

The policies and programmes which result from the forecasts may cover any or all areas of HR management. For some issues the solution may lie in training: for others it may be recruitment or remuneration. And sometimes the right solution is not an HR issue but a change in the management process of the organisation as a whole.

Other policies

There is only one box left to consider from Figure 21.1, and this is not looked at in detail because what is strategic will vary from time to time. For example, remuneration may for much of the time be a purely administrative function. However, it may achieve strategic importance if the remuneration policy is hindering achievement of a corporate objective, such as a bonus scheme which emphasises individual effort, whereas the required climate of the company is to emphasise team working. Here the bonus system may be driving people to behave in the wrong way.

One way to determine areas which need attention for strategic reasons is to rate what each activity does to aid the achievement of the corporate objectives. A matrix such as Table 21.1 may be helpful.

This analysis will probably need to be undertaken at various levels in the organisation. Any activities which prove to be strategically critical should then be examined using the principles used for each of the other components of the model.

Table 21.1

Activity	Hinders 1	2	Scale neutral 3	4	Helps 5
Recruitment					
Remuneration					
Benefits					
Welfare					
Industrial relations					
Employee relations					
Communication					
Pensions					
Records					

Intercultural issues

One area which should receive strategic consideration is cultural differences between countries and the way these can affect operations. The overall trend is for the management world to become smaller, and for more organisations to mix nationals of various countries in management teams. The assumptions behind this are often that cultural differences will iron themselves out. In the days when a minority of expatriate managers spent long periods of time in other countries this may have been a reasonable assumption. The assumption is not true of most modern business situations, and particularly untrue when organisations are trying to become pan-European or truly global. Of course, cultural differences extend not only to colleague managers but also to customers, suppliers, politicians, and public servants.

Every country has stereotypes of people from other countries, and these get in the way of understanding. A stereotype is a nationally shared view of people from one country, race or religion by people of different countries, race or religions. One of the earliest psychology books I read carries an amusing chapter on stereotypes. A short example appears below:

> The English consider themselves sportsmanlike, reserved, tradition loving, conventional, and intelligent; astonishingly enough, Americans agree, adding however that the English are also sophisticated, courteous, honest, industrious, extremely nationalistic, and, I hardly dare put this down, humourless![25]

Now ask someone from France and someone from Spain what they think!

Stereotypes get in the way of understanding. An objective understanding of the differences aids communication and enables managers to achieve better results. For example, appraisal systems and reward systems which work well in British and US cultures can be a total disaster in other countries. This does not mean that the objectives of those schemes cannot be achieved, but that a different vehicle would be more effective. Cultural understanding is not about trying to be like the other person, but being aware of the interaction of your culture and that person's so that you act differently, and interpret differently.

Fortunately we can get behind the stereotypes to at least some of the real differences. The leading authority is Hofstede,[26] whose Institute for Research on Intercultural Management (IRIC) continues to explore and validate intercultural differences. An alternative approach has been developed by Trompenaars.[27]

The Institute for Training in Intercultural Management (ITIM), headquartered in Holland, has links with IRIC. The five dimensions which they use to measure cultural differences between countries have been applied to almost the whole world, with the result that it is possible to study the interaction of any national culture on almost every other culture. The dimensions, taken from ITIM literature (direct quotes in inverted commas) are:

- Power distance: 'extent to which the less powerful members of society accept that power is distributed unequally.'
- Individualism: an individualism/collectivism scale. Are the predominant attitudes to look after the interests of oneself and one's immediate family, or to look after the interests of the group to which one belongs?
- Masculinity: Are the dominant values achievement and success (masculine), or caring for others and quality of life (feminine)?
- Uncertainty Avoidance: 'The extent to which people feel threatened by uncertainty and ambiguity and try to avoid these situations.'
- Confucian Dynamism: 'The extent to which a society exhibits a pragmatic future-oriented perspective rather than a conventional historic or near term view.'

The strategy may change the required skills and capabilities of the organisation's managers

Earlier I gave the example of how a global strategy would affect the competencies required from senior managers, compared to a multidomestic strategy. Same industry, similar products, same market, but different competencies are needed because the management situation is different. However, this example was only the tip of the iceberg, and all the elements of Figure 21.1 may be impacted by strategic changes. In this discussion I am excluding the obvious acquisition of new skills the company does not possess when the strategy takes the company into new technologies or new markets. It is the less obvious that is worth stressing.

In particular I should like to draw attention to two strands of thinking. The first concerns the portfolio techniques which were discussed in Chapters 15 and 16. Pappas,[28] writing about Du Pont, argued that different management skills were required for businesses in different positions on the matrix. An unsigned article in *Business Week*[29] continued this line of thinking. The argument is that it takes different skills and approaches to manage a cash-generating business than it does one selected for expansion. Similarly, managing a poor business, which may well be disposed of, is a different matter again. It is possible for a manager to have the flexibility to adjust to the situation, but it is dangerous to assume without careful checking that a successful entrepreneurial type could be equally successful in managing a business for maximum cash.

We can take this idea of situational management a stage further. In Chapter 3 the environmental turbulence concept of Ansoff was discussed. Ansoff and McDonnell[14] deal at considerable length with the position of the organisation on the scale of turbulence, and the implication this has for management competencies, organisational climate and structure. There are considerable variations in the ideal profiles they provide of managers under each of the turbulence headings: mentality, external versus internal orientation, time orientation, model of success, risk propensity, power of general management, leadership style, problem solving, knowledge, and leadership skills.

This is not really surprising when one thinks about it, and it is easy to see how an effective manager at level 1, where the environment is repetitive and there is more administration than entrepreneurship in the job, could be an utter failure if in a level 5 company where the environment is surpriseful and discontinuous. It helps explain many of the problems of managers in the UK's National Health Service, who for decades have operated at around level 1 and now find themselves at the stroke of the government's pen coping with a level 4 situation. The move to a competitive market type way of operating takes away all the previous stability. It may well be better in the end, but in the short term almost every manager is out of step in terms of accumulated experience, success formulae, and skills to cope with the new. As outsiders looking in, we can see great needs for culture change, management training, different ways of appraising people, new recruitment policies: in fact something different has to happen in each box on Figure 21.1.

What is equally important, and much more difficult to spot, is for each organisation to think of where it is now on the scale, and where it is likely to be in the near future. The analysis will not bring the same result for every business in a diversified company, but is likely to throw up many factors that are important for strategic HR planning.

Results of a comprehensive HR strategy

The benefit that comes out of a strategic review of HR activity is, of course, directly related to how well HR is already contributing to the strategic aims of the firm. The experience and research I have been associated with suggests that the organisations which take a strategic view of all aspects of HR management are still in the minority, at least in the UK. If this is correct, most organisations that make a serious attempt to follow the ideas set out in this chapter should obtain considerable benefits.

If every organisation followed the advice of this chapter, there would be a much greater commitment of top management to the critical HR issues, and it would be easier for HR managers to demonstrate the value of their work. Much less would be an act of faith. This seems to be a move towards more business-oriented and professional HR management than exists in many organisations.

This has been a long chapter, but it by no means exhausts the people issues that must be considered in strategic management. We will meet a few more of them in later chapters.

References

1 McBeath, G. *Organisation and Manpower Planning*, 2nd edn, Business Books, London, 1969.
2 Lynch, J. L. *Making Manpower Effective*, Pan, London, 1968.
3 Bramham, J. *Practical Manpower Planning*, Institute of Personnel Management, London, 1978.
4 Hussey, D. E. 'Implementing Corporate Strategy: Using Management Education and Training', *Long Range Planning*, **18**, No. 5, 1985.
5 Bolt, J. F. 'Tailor Executive Development to Strategy', *Harvard Business Review*, November/December 1985.
6 Hussey, D. E. *Management Training and Corporate Strategy*, Pergamon, Oxford, 1988.
7 Nilsson, W. P. *Achieving Strategic Goals Through Executive Development*, Addison-Wesley, Reading MA, 1987.
8 Bolt, J. F. *Executive Development*, Harper Business, New York, 1989.
9 Salaman, G. *Human Resource Strategies*, Sage, London, 1992.
10 Tovey, L. *Management Training and Development in Large UK Business Organisations*, Harbridge Consulting Group Ltd, London, 1991.
11 Scase, R. and Goffee, R. *Reluctant Managers: Their Work and Lifestyles*, Unwin Hyman, London, 1989.
12 Rajan, A. *Capital People*, Industrial Society, London, 1990.
13 Ansoff, H. I. 'Strategic Management in a Historical Perspective', in Hussey, D. E. (ed.), *International Review of Strategic Management*, Vol. 1, No. 1, Wiley, Chichester, 1991.
14 Ansoff, H. I. and McDonnell, E. *Implanting Strategic Management*, 2nd edn, Prentice Hall, Hemel Hempstead, 1990.
15 Ascher, K. *Management Training in Large UK Business Organisations*, Harbridge House, London, 1983.
16 *HR Reporter* 'Training Small Business Managers for a Big Business Atmosphere', *HR Reporter*, **3**, March, Los Angeles, 1988.
17 Constable, J. and McCormick, R. *The Making of British Managers*, British Institute of Management, London, 1987.
18 Management Charter Initiative. *Occupational Standards for Managers, Management I and Assessment Guidance*, London, 1991.
19 Management Charter Initiative. *Occupational Standards for Managers, Management II and Assessment Guidance*, London, 1991.

20 Management Charter Initiative. *Management Standards, Supervisory Management Standards*, London, 1992.

21 Tovey, L. *Competency Assessment: A Strategic Approach*, Harbridge Consulting Group Ltd, London, 1992.

22 Litwin, G. H. and Stringer, R. H. *Motivation and Organisational Climate*, Division of Research, Harvard Business School, Boston, 1968.

23 Handy, C. B. *Understanding Organisations*, 2nd edn, Penguin, London, 1981.

24 Ichikawa, A. 'Leadership as a Form of Culture', in Hussey, D. E. (ed.), *International Review of Strategic Management*, Vol. 5, Wiley, Chichester, 1993.

25 Eysenk, H. J. *Uses and Abuses of Psychology*, Penguin, Harmondsworth, 1953.

26 Hofstede, G. *Cultures and Organisation*, McGraw-Hill, Maidenhead, 1991.

27 Trompenaars, F. *Riding the Waves of Culture*, Economist Books, London, 1993.

28 Pappas, N. 'Corporate Planning at Du Pont', *Chemical Engineering Progress*, June 1978.

29 Anon. 'Wanted: A Manager to Fit Each Strategy', *Business Week*, 25 February 1980.

Further reading

Bate, P. *Strategies for Culture Change*, Butterworth-Heinemann, Oxford, 1994.

Hall, W. *Managing Cultures: Making Strategic Relationships Work*, Wiley, Chichester, 1995.

Hussey, D. E. *Business Driven Human Resource Management*, Wiley, Chichester, 1996.

Mockler, R. J. and Dologite, D. G. *Multinational Cross-Cultural Management*, Quorum, Westport, CT, 1997.

Tyson, S. (ed.) *Strategic Prospects for HRM*, Institute of Personnel and Development, London, 1995.

CHAPTER 22

Preparing the strategic plan

Although many argue that strategic thinking is more important than writing a formal plan, there are many occasions when a written plan is useful. It may be demanded by the owners of the organisation, or may be a useful tool to help gain financial support, or retain it in hard times. This has the limited objective of showing how a strategic plan for a relatively simple organisation might be written.

Several preceding chapters have been devoted to aspects of corporate strategy and the choice between options. In an earlier chapter it was postulated that action was the end product of planning, and that plans were the intermediate product which enabled action to result. So somehow the chief executive or strategic planner, having guided the company through its decisions, has to write all this into a document that can be used as the basis for action.

For many, the preparation of strategic plans will present few difficulties. There are others who find the task of translating concepts into plans a daunting one. This chapter is designed to provide a measure of practical advice about writing a strategic plan, and is supported by a hypothetical example of what such a document might look like.

Once again it should be stressed that the principles discussed here are matters of judgement rather than dogma. There are few approaches that are definitely right or definitely wrong: the best solution is one that works in the circumstances of the company. Nevertheless, a suggested solution is often valuable as a starting point, even though the reader might then choose to approach the task in another way.

A good place to start is with the types of strategic plans that might be prepared. Some planners suggest that the strategic plan should show the broad outline strategy. Each major element should then be treated in greater detail in separate plans dealing with acquisition, diversification, divestment, and research and development.

My own approach has always been slightly different. I believe in the use of project plans for the detailed examination of a particular element of strategy. Thus there might be a project plan to launch a new product, acquire a particular company, or build a new factory. Each of these project plans is a detailed investigation, supported by full financial analysis, and designed to confirm that the conclusions drawn in the strategic plan are still valid. A project plan is always prepared on an 'as required' basis and becomes self-extinguishing. It is not the same as a separate long-range plan dealing with one particular aspect of strategy.

I also believe in separating the research and development plan, because once the strategic decisions have been made the administration of the R & D department is no more a matter of strategy than the operations of a marketing department. The definition of what to research and how much to spend on it is very much strategy: the interpretation of these decisions into something that can be implemented is very much an operational task.

I also like to distinguish two other types of top-level plan which form part of the total strategic viewpoint of the company – finance and human resources.

So my approach to writing a strategic plan would be to include all the detail of the acquisition, diversification, and divestment plans, but the major strategic decisions only in the areas of research and development, finance, and HRM. Relevant elements of strategy will, as they begin to harden, be investigated in-depth depth as projects.

There is another point about the subdivision of strategic plans which springs out of statements made earlier in this book. In Chapter 13 it was maintained that strategy and objectives change places in the eyes of different levels in the organisation. The profit objective given a subsidiary is strategy for the parent, an objective for the subsidiary. In Chapter 18 it was argued that the chief executives of subsidiaries could be given a high degree of freedom of strategic decision making, subject to the overall strategic framework set by the parent. The nature of that freedom will vary depending on whether the company is following a global or multicountry strategy.

It follows from this that part of the strategic task is delegated – again it is stressed that the portion delegated is within a detailed framework – and that certain detailed elements of strategy will not therefore appear in the group strategic plan. Instead these will be worked up in the strategic plans of subsidiaries. In a large multinational company it is possible to see a network of subsidiary strategic plans, each of which makes a contribution to converting the group outline framework into a defined course of action. To me this appears to be a meaningful subdivision of work.

One rather naive question which is sometimes asked is how long a strategic plan should be. The answer is that all plans should adhere to the principle of good business reports: they should be succinct, and therefore as short as possible, but should also contain all the necessary facts. A strategic plan need not include a blow-by-blow account of the boardroom debates which centered round each strategic decision. It need not necessarily list every course of action considered and rejected, although it is sometimes useful to include decision trees which summarise the main actions and chance events. Any alternatives reserved as contingency plans should be mentioned. The plan should be cross-referenced to the studies and reports which led to the conclusions.

A number of factors influence the length of a plan (quite apart from the style of the person writing it). A complex company, with geographically diverse units operating in several industries, is likely to have a longer document than a company of similar size which is based on one industry in one country. The larger the company, the longer its plan is likely to be, although this is by no means an invariable rule. The ambitious company will have more actions planned than the stagnating company of similar size. A company with major problems and planning many corrective actions may have a more complicated – and therefore longer – plan than an organisation with few problems. Companies which hug all their decisions to the centre will end up with a fatter document than those which delegate. What goes into corporate strategic plans of a complex multinational may be based very firmly on portfolio analysis: either businesses or core competences or both. Important top-management issues are different from those faced by the simpler companies which are illustrated in the example at the end of this chapter.

All this is common sense, and reinforces what we know to be true. The value of a plan is measured by the quality of its content, not its weight, dimensions, or number of pages. The fact that one planner's plans appear different from those described by other companies in articles and at seminars is not significant.

Plans should be presented in a way which makes them easy to read and handle. Nothing is worse than the business document (of any kind) which physically falls to pieces whenever it is used. Plans are meant to be used. It is also a mistake to present them too well. A typeset document, with multicolour diagrams and bound in leather, may look, smell, and feel impressive: it will also carry a false idea of permanence and authority. Plans are working documents, and those using them should feel free to write on margins, tear out pages, and scribble comments across the text.

Charts and diagrams also help understanding, and can link into visual aids used in presenting and discussing the plan. Decision trees have already been suggested, and may be augmented by graphs and histograms. Portfolio and risk matrices are of immeasurable value for complex organisations. The key principle is to keep to what is useful and not to chart facts which have little impact on the decisions involved. The idea is not to produce a child's guide, with a picture on every page, but a usable business document.

There can be no firm rules about what items should make up the content of a strategic plan, although I should recommend that the following at least be considered.

Introduction

It is always worth allocating some space to describing the scope of the plan and its relationship with other plans. Because it is as a photograph of a situation, seen at a particular moment of time, every plan has limitations, and it is important that these should be understood by all who read and use the document.

Assumptions

Those assumptions which are important for a proper understanding of the plan should be detailed. Specific opportunities, or problems which spring from these, will appear later in the document, and some form of cross-referencing is useful. General effects of the assumptions will occur throughout the plan and will not need this treatment. In Chapter 5 it was argued that many assumptions defined and used on the way to the final plan are not essential to its interpretation and should not appear in it.

Primary objective

A statement of the profit objectives of the company, expressed in the way that is most useful for the company. As these objectives will have been accepted by top management at an early stage in planning, there is no need to give all the reasoning which led to the particular choice of figures.

It is sometimes convenient to show in this section how the total objective has been allocated to divisions of the company, and what is the target left to be filled by completely new strategies.

Secondary objectives and constraints

The statements of purpose and other similar objectives should be clearly stated, as should the self-imposed constraints under which the company intends to operate. Only factors which are really meaningful to the plan should be included: again, the supporting reasoning should be omitted, as it should already be top management policy.

Strengths, weaknesses: the current situation

In any military plan an appraisal of the current situation is of considerable importance. The same is true of the strategic plan, which should show the main strengths and weaknesses of the company as defined in the corporate appraisal and subsequent work.

This should not be a repetitive listing of factors which have lost their value, and 'weaknesses' which have already been corrected should be excluded. The list is designed as an integral part of the plan, not a means of flattering top management by showing how much they have achieved.

The section becomes of much greater value if it is indexed to subsequent parts of the plan which make use of the information, and if the weaknesses are divided into two parts: those which are corrected by the plan and those with which the company has to live for some time to come.

Some companies like to include a narrative appraisal of the current position, emphasising problems and the events which have led to a need for action. Statements of this nature are of considerable value if somebody intends to use them: they are worth little if their only use is as padding to make the report look better.

The key to the decision to include anything in a plan is the value it has in defining, explaining, and recording the intended actions, or in their subsequent monitoring or controlling.

Statement of expected results

Somewhere in the plan there must be an interpretation of its meaning in terms of money, and a comparison of results with the targets and objectives set. It is often convenient to have this at this point, so that it summarises actions before the reader becomes involved in the details of strategies. If the 'gap' between target and expected results is *not* closed, this is something which top management should be aware of from the beginning, as it will condition their interpretation of the plan.

The expected results should show key figures using the company's standard accounting definitions, but under main summary headings only. The figure should illustrate profits, cash flow, and the main efficiency ratios. It is always helpful to back up this summary with several previous years' history (often a chart of key figures showing the projected position and a long period of history is a key to better understanding).

It is good discipline to include a section here, comparing previous plans with actual results and the new plan. Although I always recommend completion of a strategic plan on a rolling basis, with the opportunity to update and revise annually, this does not mean that changes should be made without thought. Any changes must be made responsibly and the fact that a record is kept helps this to happen.

Risk and sensitivity

Logically, risk and sensitivity analysis should appear at the end of the plan, since it is difficult to think coherently about the risks attached to a strategy until the strategy itself is understood. On the other hand, the statement of results lacks meaning until those reading the plan have some feel for the profitability of success or failure, and the expected impact of either of these events on the results. Although risk should have been taken into account during the strategic selection process, whatever strategies are finally selected will still carry some risks, and these must be understood by all concerned.

Really, the positioning of this section of the plan is a matter of judgement, and is not the most difficult problem the planner will have to face.

Strategies

The word 'strategies' covers innumerable ways in which the meat of the plan – what the company intends to do – may be presented. Some possible ways of analysis are:

1 By present operations, and then the appropriate choice of main headings from Chapters 14 and 17
2 By strategic business unit, showing, for each, strategies in relation to new and present operations

3 By strategic business areas of operation, perhaps further subdivided under one of the two systems shown above

4 By order of importance to the company: often the most dramatic presentation, but confusing when operations are complex.

5 By core competencies.

One of the problems in writing any plan is that narrative has to be written as a sequence of words, and in most companies even the tightest of prose will run into a number of pages. This makes it hard to see the total picture. A diagrammatic representation of the decision path – perhaps in the form of a decision tree or portfolio matrix – may mean that pages of narrative can be summarised in one diagram, giving an overview which is otherwise difficult to obtain.

'Strategy' should not only include the main actions in the fields of marketing, production, acquisition, and divestment. It should show organisational changes which result from these strategies, manpower policies, financial policies, and, where relevant, ancillary policies such as public relations. Each of these subjects may be taken up in more detail elsewhere, but where the action is an important condition to the success of the company it should have a place in the strategic plan.

Contingency strategies

Details should be given of those strategic courses of action reserved for contingency purposes. One point that is often overlooked in the preparation of strategic plans is that the information available at the time the plan is made will vary in quality between strategies, and between one plan and the next. It is therefore not possible for the company to write down each of its strategies with the same degree of exactitude. Some strategic paths will be crude lines on the company's map of its future; others will be painted in finite detail and every bump in the road identified and understood.

To attempt to delay the plan until all strategies can be identified with equal confidence would mean, in many companies, that no plan was ever produced. The problem is that any plan is but a static photograph of a dynamic scene.

The knowledge should not tempt the company into letting its strategy plan become vague and meaningless. Vision is required, but not wistful dreams. Some evaluation should have been done, however crude, on every option that appears. It is, in my opinion, also valid to indicate areas in the plan where the company has not yet made up its mind: thus one part of the company's strategy may be to take one of two indicated paths, both of which are subject to further evaluation.

The plan may reveal an intention by the company to enter a particular industry by acquisition. Although the exact cost of this action may not be known, it is possible for the company to have ascertained that acquisition candidates are potentially available within certain limits of capital costs and returns, and that – provided this proves to be true – acquisition is a better choice of action than any other option. Thus the plan can carry the matter much further forward, although there are still some uncertainties.

The company may also, through its strategic plan, have decided to move its factory, sell the old buildings, and update its production equipment. Costs and benefits may initially be known only within broad parameters.

Other actions may have progressed much further – as these two examples will have done by the time subsequent strategic plans are prepared – and the company may have in its possession its final appraisal of its course of action.

It is pleasant to visualise a situation where plans are all neat and tidy, where things can be clearly labelled and pigeonholed, and where the strategic plan can, accordingly, be used as a handbook for a sequence of actions the effect of which is known to the last penny. But we live in a real world, not a fairyland, and it is only occasionally that a company will find that its strategic plan fits so neatly into place that there is nothing to do over the next five to ten years but sit back and watch it all happen. The real world is untidy: so most strategic plans will contain some loose areas with ragged edges. And the world also has a habit of changing!

When a plan is written (and provided it appears that the actions selected are adequate to enable the company to meet its targets) this mixture of levels of detail could result in statements of this kind:

- The company will select three of the five courses of action identified in this plan, and will initiate one of them in each of the next three years.
- The company will enter the furniture industry in Australia in year two of the plan and will invest up to £1m in this project, with the intention of breaking even in year one, and with expectations of achieving an internal rate of DCF return of 15 per cent assessed over a fifteen-year period. Five alternative ways of achieving this result have been identified, and a selection of the most beneficial course of action will be made during year one.

In the next planning cycle the company will have completed more of its studies and be in a position to be more specific about some things. In each case the company has committed itself to a strategic course of action although it still has flexibility. It is because there are so many uncertainties that the company needs a portfolio of options: contingency plans that can be brought in at short notice to replace actions which subsequent events show are no longer valid.

No strategic action should be implemented without a final detailed examination. This is the function of the project plans discussed earlier.

In order to help bridge the gap between theory and practice an example is given of a hypothetical strategic plan. Because it is a hypothetical situation, it includes simplifications which enable the plan to be shorter than might be the case in a real situation. This is to avoid boring the reader and although slightly unreal does serve to stress what was stated earlier: that plans of any type should be as short as possible. It is also a plan for a relatively simple company where the concept of strategic business units is not really suitable.

The object of the example is to demonstrate how the document known as the strategic plan might be written. It is not intended to be a study of the actual strategies chosen: for present purposes it is not relevant whether the chief executive of the hypothetical company has chosen wisely or badly.

The example is a strategic plan for a hypothetical company – Thru-Draught Heatvent Co. Ltd – engaged in heating and ventilating contracting. At present all profits emanate from this activity. Last year's after-tax profit was £250 000 arising from a turnover of £20m. Total capital employed is £10m, giving a return on investment of 2.5 per cent. The company's activities are closely linked with the building trade, and are therefore subject to cyclical fluctuations. In the last five years the lowest after-tax profit was £50 000. Last year's figure is the peak for this period (although higher profits have been achieved in the past), but the current year's estimate is also £250 000.

All the equity is owned, in equal proportions, by four members of one family. More capital is available from family sources if prospects can be improved and if the risk of profit fluctuations can be reduced. Alternatively, the family is willing to consider 'going public' and raising equity funds for future development through the stock market. In any case, the company currently has no loan finance.

The managing director is forty-five and had held his appointment for about eighteen months. He was brought in from outside, and entered the business on the retirement from executive roles of two of the shareholders. The remaining shareholders hold the positions of production director and financial director respectively.

At the time the new managing director joined the company it was facing a number of problems. He believes that it was his efforts which led to last year's profit improvement. He caused work to begin on a corporate plan shortly after he joined the company, and after much thought, analysis, and internal discussion has now reached a point when he has a detailed five-year plan ready for presentation to the board.

This is the document that is set out on the following pages. May I plead with the purists to take the plan at face value, and not to view it as an exercise in accounting? Anyone who follows the accounting too closely is bound to find anomalies, as the figures were prepared only to give body to the example, and have no particular significance of their own.

Strategic plan: years 1–5: Thru-Draught Heatvent Co. Ltd

1. Introduction

1.1 This document presents the aims and intentions of the company, and the main strategic path that it should follow. It is an ambitious plan, but one that is achievable and realistic. It also will bring a considerable improvement over results achieved during the previous five years.

1.2 The plan does not purport to solve all the problems of the company, and has identified many areas where further investigatory work must be carried out before firm conclusions can be reached. This work is in hand, or projected in the plan.

1.3 Support is given to these board strategies by separate and detailed plans covering the area of finance, manpower and current operations.

2. Assumptions

2.1 The general level of prices will increase by 8 per cent per year in the first two years of the plan, and thereafter at 6 per cent per year. Steel is expected to increase in price at 8 per cent per year throughout the plan.

2.2 The company will continue its present pattern of good industrial relations and will not itself be subject to any strikes or disruptive labour disputes.

2.3 The government will continue to implement its announced five-year programmes for the rebuilding of obsolete hospitals and the establishment of health centres.

3. Primary objectives

3.1 The intention is to treble after tax profits by the fifth year of the plan.

	Last year	Current est.	Year 5
After tax profit (£000)	250	250	750
Return on capital employed (%)	2.5	2.5	5

(Note: the minimum acceptable average return on investment for new projects is 12%.)

4. Secondary objectives and constraints

4.1 The company is in the business of environmental control wherever and whenever it is required. It is engaged in the operations of designing, manufacturing, and installing such systems.

4.2 For the next five-year period the geographical area on which the company will concentrate is Europe.

4.3 The company intends to be a 'good citizen' of each country in which it operates, although it will always give preference to shareholders' interests whenever this is legally possible.

4.4 The company will always endeavour to treat its employees fairly and to give employees the opportunity of sharing in the growth of the company.

4.5 Obligations to customers are treated very seriously, and the company prides itself on its high standards of workmanship and quality. It is a matter of fundamental belief for the company that honesty and integrity of performance are more important to it than quick profits, and that in all areas of the company quality specifications must be observed and inferior work rejected.

5. Strengths and weaknesses

	Strengths	*Implications*
5.1	A reputation for quality and technical excellence.	See paragraphs 8.1 to 8.4.
5.2	A special leadership position (55 per cent of domestic market) in specialist heating and ventilation systems for computer rooms, laboratories, and other buildings housing sensitive equipment requiring a high degree of dust and temperature control (currently 15 per cent of sales) split in the ratio 2 domestic to 1 export.	See paragraphs 8.1 to 8.4, 8.8.
5.3	An established position in European export markets (10 per cent of sales).	
5.4	Strong technical management.	See paragraphs 8.1 to 8.4.

	Weaknesses	
5.5	85 per cent of sales related to general building activity, and consequently subject to fluctuations in volume and profits.	See section 8.
5.6	40 per cent of profit emanates from the 15 per cent turnover in the specialist control area.	See section 8.
5.7	One in every five general contracts is undertaken at breakeven, in order to secure the business.	See paragraphs 8.5 and 8.7.
5.8	All business in France (50 per cent of export sales) has been undertaken at a loss due to overestimation of the competitors' prices.	See paragraph 8.4.
5.9	The company, with its two UK plants, has double its required capacity without allowing for overtime working.	See paragraphs 8.5 and 8.14.
5.10	Marketing management is generally poor.	See paragraph 8.10.
5.11	Management information is rudimentary. Lack of data is a contributory reason for several bad decisions taken in the company.	See paragraph 8.12.

5.12 The company has reached a point when it must make many changes. Its profitability from current operations must be improved, and new activities must be started, both to bring profitable growth and to reduce the effect of profit fluctuations.

5.13 If the company does nothing new and merely continues to operate as at present its turnover will increase to £25m by the last year of the plan. Profit, at its best estimate, will have declined to £200,000 – or much less if the general building industry does not develop at the rate expected. This gives a 'gap' of £550,000 between the profit objective and the current forecast, as well as indicating a worsening position and a declining return on investment.

5.14 The company has also to think beyond the five-year period, and must commit research and development resources to produce a new generation of environmental control equipment to meet the needs of the future.

5.15 Many decisions have to be taken, and a new pattern of risks accepted. The company is fortunate in being in a position from which it can make the necessary changes to assure its future.

6. Statement of expected results

	Profits (£000)					
	Current year	Year 1	Year 2	Year 3	Year 4	Year 5
Computer and speciality	207	250	350	400	450	500
General building	310	400	420	420	430	430
Licensing	–	50	150	200	250	250
Domestic air conditioning	–	(50)	(50)	50	200	250
Profit contribution	517	650	870	1070	1330	1430
Administration expenses	(100)	(130)	(150)	(160)	(170)	(180)
Profit before tax	417	520	720	910	1160	1250
Tax	167	200	280	365	465	500
Profit after tax	250	320	440	545	695	750

		Current year	Year 5
Capital employed	(£m.)	10	14
ROI	(%)	2.5	5.4

(Detailed cash-flow statements are not shown here – although essential in any plan – but an example will be found in Figure 31.2.)

Note: The simplifying assumption is made that sales and contract completions are the same.

7. Risk and sensitivity

(Detailed sensitivity analyses should appear here. Because they are somewhat tedious to read, unless they are for your own organisation. I have not included an example.)

8. Strategies

Licensing

8.1 The company has its main strengths in its reputation for quality, its technical skills, and its leadership position in the specialist ventilating field. One of the main areas of expansion will be the further exploitation of these strengths. There are opportunities in Europe and the specialist ventilating market is expanding at 10 per cent per year.

8.2 To fully exploit this opportunity and attempt to obtain a higher share of the market by the traditional methods would involve major capital expenditures (£500,000), would run at a loss for two or three years, and would have a high degree of risk.

8.3 The alternative of licensing has therefore been chosen, and negotiations are in an advanced stage with the XYZ Company of Paris to license this company to produce for the French market. This will involve the conversion of our current business in France to the new arrangement, but as these sales have been at a loss this in itself is a means of profit improvement.

8.4 In return for technical assistance, specifications, the use of brand names and marketing advice, and all rights in France, we will receive a royalty of $7\frac{1}{2}$ per cent of turnover – which will yield an immediate profit of £50,000 in the first year of the plan, rising to £250,000 by year 5.

Operational improvement

8.5 All current production activities will be rationalised into one factory. This will bring a reduced unit cost and thereby improve the profitability of all contracts.

8.6 The personnel implications of this move are still under study, but are unlikely to be severe because of the new use that will be made of the factory which will be released in this way (see paragraph 8.14).

8.7 A deliberate short-term reduction of general building business will be sought and no break-even contracts will be entered into. The effect of this policy on turnover is forecast as:

	Current year	Year 1	Year 2	Year 3	Year 4	Year 5
General building – domestic (£m)	16	14	13	13.5	14	14

An immediate profit improvement of £90,000 will result from the combination of this policy and the plans outlined in paragraph 8.5.

8.8 Domestic market concentration will be on the area of greatest strength – the specialist market. Sales forecasts are:

	Current year	Year 1	Year 2	Year 3	Year 4	Year 5
Computer and specialist – domestic (£m)	2.0	2.25	2.5	3.0	3.5	3.5

8.9 These forecasts will be achieved through an improved marketing approach (the subject of a separate report), and the results of a continued R & D effort. Profits from this area of our business (net of a continuing £100,000 per year expenditure on R & D) will rise from just over £200,000 this year to £500,000 by year 5.

Organisation and management

8.10 The marketing department is being strengthened and reorganised under a product management concept. Full supporting services will also be provided. The detailed organisation is the subject of a consultant's report.

8.11 Increased emphasis will be placed on management development to support the company's intention to expand (see consultant's report). A nucleus of young graduates will be built up, trained in the company, and thus be available for the major diversification discussed below.

8.12 An information technology strategy will be developed next year, and the first stages of this will be implemented immediately. Training will be provided to managers and secretaries to enable an electronic environment to be operative by the end of next year.

Diversification

8.13 Anticipated improvement in the efficiency of current operations as outlined above will enable the company to give adequate attention to a major diversification into the home air-conditioner market.

8.14 Initial products will be based on the technology of an American firm from whom a licence has been obtained, the agreement including technical assistance. Production will be carried out in the factory released from normal production (paragraph 8.5). (Feasibility and market reports are reaching their final stages.)

8.15 The immediate impact of this strategy will be a reduction of profits in years 1 and 2. Thereafter the project will be profitable and by year 5 will be contributing £250,000. There will be no sales in year 1, the loss in that year being due to initial expenses. Turnover will develop to:

	£000		
Year 2	Year 3	Year 4	Year 5
200	500	750	800

8.16 The project is subject to different risks from those of our present business and should therefore have a stabilising effect on profits.

Finance

8.17 Full financial implications are developed in the Financial Plan. All requirements can be met if dividends are held to current levels and if short-term needs are met by bank overdraft (£200,000 ceiling) in years 1 and 2.

8.18 By year 3 the success of these strategies will have been proved. At this point the shareholders may consider 'going public'. It is because there is doubt over this intention that earnings per share objectives have not been set.

9. Contingency plans

(This section has not been completed since it has a relationship with risk and sensitivity and is unnecessary for demonstration purposes.)

A note on the example

The example was written for the first edition of this book, and although I have updated it a little, I have allowed inflation to make it an example for a much smaller company than was the original intention. Lack of information, which they recognise, means that they have not undertaken careful industry and competitor analysis. Most of us as observers might have many reservations about the particular strategies in favour. However, it offers a practical example of what a plan might look like.

In doing this it takes us very neatly to the next chapter. When you are asked to evaluate a strategic plan, such as the one in the example, how do you set about it? In the final event, success is not a question of neat plans but of sound strategies, properly implemented. In the next chapter there is some guidance on how to think critically about a plan.

CHAPTER 23

Evaluating a business plan

Many managers are given strategic plans to comment on during their careers. The aims of this chapter are to show what to look for if you are placed in this position, to aid the process of critical evaluation. A secondary aim is to provide guidelines which can be used to evaluate any plan that you may be called upon to write.

It is not easy to review a plan that someone else has written, although many of us are required to do just that. If you prepare a plan yourself, you know the background situation, the analytical approaches applied, the gaps in the information used to formulate strategy, and you have a good grasp of all the elements of the strategy. The position may be very different when you are asked to evaluate a plan that someone else has prepared. This may happen in situations where the context is known, such as commenting on the strategic plan for your own company or of one of its divisions. It may also happen when the context is not known, such as when evaluating the plan of another SBU, or foreign subsidiary, or of another organisation in a friendly merger or joint venture situation. Professional organisations, such as banks and accountancy firms, often also frequently face situations when they have to judge plans of other organisations for various purposes. The same need often occurs with management consultants. The problem which this chapter tries to solve is how to begin.

There are at least two aspects which need consideration. The first is the quality of strategic thinking that goes into the plan: the second is the quality of the planning document – the plan – as a communication medium and an aid to implementation. Both are important, and the simple matrix in Figure 23.1 can be used as a way of exploring their significance.

Adapted from Hussey, D. E. 'Evaluating a Business Plan', *Journal of Strategic Change*, March/April 1992, used with permission. (It also appeared in *Strategic Management Review*, Japan **17**, No. 2, 1993.)

Figure 23.1

Relationship of
quality of plan to
quality of strategy

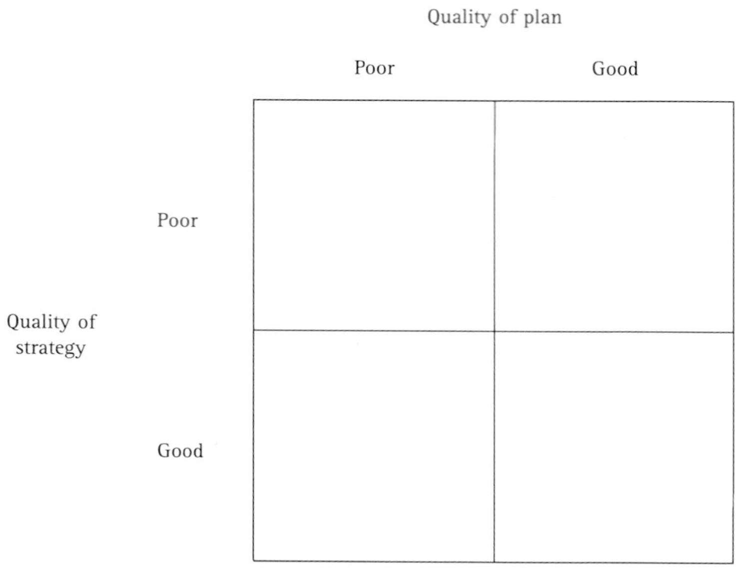

Quality of plan

	Poor	Good
Poor		
Good		

Quality of
strategy

It is worth spending a little time thinking about this matrix. The preferred situation is when the strategy is sound, and the plan that describes this is clear and concise, yet comprehensive. There can be few attempts at planning that do not strive for this condition. It gives the organisation the best chance of both deciding and implementing the right things.

When the quality of the strategy is good but the plan is poor there is a real danger that it will not be communicated adequately. An SBU, for example, may find that the level of corporate support it expects is not forthcoming because of misunderstandings over the strategy. At any level there may be a failure to implement if there is no clarity about what has to be done.

Perhaps the most dangerous situation is when the plan is good, and therefore convincing, but the underlying strategy is poor. This can result in the wrong things being done with considerable zeal. The quality of the document may be such that the right questions are never asked about the appropriateness of the strategy. The document looks so good and reads so well that everyone believes the strategy is sound.

The poor/poor box, which is occupied more commonly than is desirable, leads to a situation where little of the planning effort brings any benefit to the organisation. The reasons for this planning failure may be varied. It could be that the rapidity of change in the business environment is too great for traditional approaches to strategic planning to have any impact. It may be that the style of top management makes planning impossible. It may be a lack of competence in those concerned in the planning process.

In this chapter attention will be given to both aspects, but before we start I should like to draw attention to a widely observed tendency which I am sure many readers have themselves noticed about plans.

The 'laws' of planning

Years ago I defined two laws of planning, which all written plans seemed to follow. They are as noticeable in project plans supporting requests for capital expenditure as they are in strategic plans.

1 *In any written plan, everything comes right in the third year.* This does not mean that it will come right, only that the plan says it will. The third year is close enough to appear to have meaning but far enough away to escape retribution. The underlying psychology is that three years is long enough for things to work out.
2 *The third year never comes.* My second law of planning is that the bounty of the third year is never delivered. Somehow the cornucopia expected three years ago when the plan was made is as empty in the third year as it was in the first two.

Of course, things can come to pass as the plan suggests. However, knowing that so many plans show two lean years followed by a time of plenty makes me want to probe very deeply into any plans which follow this pattern. This usually means exploring the information on which the plan was based, as well as studying the strategy itself.

Does it have a purpose?

Both of those aspects of the plan which were identified earlier should have a purpose. The most important is the strategic aspect. What objectives are the strategies trying to achieve, and is the expected outcome consistent with the aim? This does not mean that the strategy is sound or the plan good, but it indicates whether the writer believes it to be appropriate. If there are no stated objectives, and the expected results are not stated, the plan will be in a vacuum.

The purpose of the written document should also be understood. Clearly it is to describe the strategy that will achieve the objectives. Behind this is another layer of subtlety: for whom is the plan being written? The written document may well take a different form depending on its target readership, and this will affect any critical evaluation of that plan. For example, a business plan written mainly to record the strategy and communicate it within an organisation that is well aware of the background situation may need to contain much less information about the market and company situation than a plan, covering the same strategy, written to gain the support of a remote parent company. In the latter case the decision makers may have a preferred format for plan presentation, but may lack understanding of the local situation. Part of the rationale for the document may be to persuade and convince upwards, whereas in the first case the purpose was to communicate downwards. A business plan written partly with an intention of gaining support from bankers or major external investors may require a different format again. Before evaluating the quality of a plan, it is worth finding out what it is to be used for.

Testing a strategy

Strategies may be good or bad, and even a good strategy may fail through poor implementation, or a poor one succeed because of the skill and flair of individual managers. It is useful to test strategies for basic flaws, and the following points are designed to help this process.

Is the strategy identified and clearly stated?

It is impossible to assess a strategy until the strategy is known, a point which is self-evident. Yet surprisingly a very high proportion of the written plans I have seen fail this test. I have ploughed through pages of material on many occasions, and found a history lesson on the company, but have had no idea of the strategy the organisation was following. When this happens there is no plan.

Has it considered competitors and the industry structure?

Competitive positioning is a critical element of strategy. In addition, the strategy should be developed with an awareness of competitors, and the moves which they are likely to make. The competitive structure of the industry will also affect the possible strategies that might be successful, which implies that the strategy should be considered in the context of the industry structure. If the strategy is to break the rules, by changing the power structure of the industry, the method should be clear from the plan. Many of the plans I have examined assume that the desired changes will happen without there being any reason why they should. Wishful thinking is not the same as a strategy!

Does it match the realities of the market?

All strategies face the test of market realism. New products will only have a chance of succeeding if they meet a requirement of the buyers. Old products will not suddenly increase their sales unless there is a reason. One of the hardest things is to persuade an organisation that has been expanding rapidly on the back of one major consumer durable that there is a saturation point and that product life-cycle theories do in fact apply. Equally hard has been to convince companies to strike a note of realism when taking a successful product into a 'new' country. People will not necessarily flock to buy that product just because the corporate plan says they should.

Is the geographical scope appropriate?

In some industries the need for global integration is more important than the need for local responsiveness. The 'globality' of the industry must be examined, and strategy tested against this. What appears to be sound on a one-country basis may not be sound when the global nature of the industry is understood. And this is not a static analysis, in that global pressures affect more industries each year. In the UK I have often found that managers do not take a world view of their businesses. When I helped in implementing the merger of Vickers and Rolls–Royce Motors in 1980, one of the major achievements was bringing about an understanding of the global nature of many of the markets. This led to strategies that were quite different from those previously formulated under the assumption of local businesses (see Stopford[1] for a description of this process).

Is it consistent with environmental forces?

The assumptions on which the strategy is based should be stated. No strategy exists in a vacuum, and there are many environmental trends and forces that have an impact on strategy. One test is to examine the extent to which the strategy considers the outside forces.

Are the levels of risk acceptable?

A strategy may look very elegant, but it may also be a disaster if it is a 'bet the company' move. In testing a strategy it is important to think of the economic risks the company can afford. It may also be valuable to consider whether the chief executive responsible for the strategy is willing to accept the personal risks involved. If not the strategy may be good, but is unlikely to be implemented.

Does it enhance shareholder value?

Some might argue that this test should be number one. I have put it in its present position only because it is not possible to assess the impact on shareholder value until the underlying soundness of the thinking can be gauged. Increasingly companies are using value-based planning approaches to measure contributions to shareholder value, effectively expressing the outcome of the plans in discounted cash-flow terms. There is more to shareholder value than this. A simple example is whether synergy is gained between business units, or whether they are so competitive that they duplicate resources and miss opportunities for joint working, or shared resources. Another example is the role of a head office and whether it adds value through how it operates, or merely adds to costs.

481

Does it match corporate competence and resources?

In other words can it be done? A common fault is for plans to be too ambitious, to ignore existing factors, or to expect things to happen faster than the organisation can implement them. A related question is: does the plan identify and build on core competencies?

Is the company structure appropriate?

Structure and strategy have to be compatible. Even sound strategies can fail if the structure is designed to fulfil a different strategy to the one chosen.

Does it match the company culture?

This is a difficult question to answer, but is important. If the strategy calls on the company to act in a manner totally alien to its culture, the strategy has a high chance of failing unless the culture is changed. Scandinavian Airlines offers a good example. In the early 1980s it introduced a strategy one plank of which was customer responsiveness. The culture at the time was bureaucratic, with all decisions referred upwards. To be responsive meant driving many decisions much lower in the organisation, and to make this happen meant that the company had also a plan for a major change in company culture.

Does it have an appropriate time horizon?

The plan should be developed to cover the time period necessary to fulfil it. A strategy that ended with a major investment, with no outcomes shown for that investment would clearly be deficient. The plan should not be positioned on the salami system, with just a few slices of investment shown, disguising the fact that the real shape is a tubular sausage and not a flat circle! There may sometimes be a need to develop the strategy for a longer period than the company's planning process requires. In fact one of the problems of business units of a larger corporate entity is that often the corporate planning horizon is too long or too short for their situation.

Does the plan have internal consistency?

The final test question asks whether the plan is logical and hangs together. It may sound a trivial point to those who plan well themselves, and it is not usually the obvious that goes wrong, such as marketing planning to expand volumes without manufacturing being able to produce them. In my experience the two most common problems are quantification and people. The quantified results of a plan should be related to the strategies in the plan, but sometimes they are put together using ratios and growth factors which do not take account of the costs and rewards of the actual action planned. The second coordination area which seems to defy logic is the changes that have to be made to structure, culture, and human resources. This section of the plan often appears to be put together without any consideration of the strategies.

The missing question

The discerning may feel that this list of points to look out for misses the most important, which is whether the strategy appears sound. This is, of course, the most critical issue, and one of the most difficult to reduce to a few sentences. Experience in strategic thinking and knowledge of those principles that have been defined are the two most important elements. Yet experience also shows that because most of the principles are statements of tendency, rather than rigid rules, a strategy that defies the accumulated wisdom of the experts is not necessarily bad.

There is also an element of fashion in strategic thinking, which may be another way of saying that strategies have to fit the age in which they are made. In the 1970s portfolio arguments of having cash cows to fund stars, and wildcats that may become future stars would have figured in the judgements of strategy, whereas today adding shareholder value is seen as of more significance.

However, there are some principles, dealt with in greater detail elsewhere in this book, that are worth repeating, even though they cannot be used slavishly.

1 Porter[2] has codified many principles around the relative positions of the various players in different industry structures. An appropriate strategy for an industry where there is a dominant leader may be totally wrong for a fragmented industry with no entry barriers. There may even be differences between fragmented industries like the guard and patrol sector of the security industry which has little opportunity for differentiation, and few niches, and an industry like management consulting which has many opportunities for differentiation, and numerous niches. An awareness of the industry principles is an essential starting point for evaluating any strategy.
2 Buzzell and Gale[3] drew a number of lessons from some fifteen years' experience of operating the PIMS database, which collects cause-and-effect data from its members to allow the derivation of strategic factors. Among other things, these principles show the importance of market share, the importance of quality, and the impact of vertical integration. The danger is if anyone tries to interpret these findings blindly. Yes, higher market share is associated with higher profitability, but as the authors point out, using this to justify a strategy to move from the bottom of the share league to the top may be the road to a totally uneconomic course of action.
3 James[4] offers some interesting thoughts on mega strategies, and draws comparisons between business and military principles. The insights here are of particular value when the strategy involves expansion into another country or market, or when considering defence against an incursion by an invader who is trying to do the same thing to you.

483

4 Remember that all the evidence is that more acquisitions fail than succeed. Kitching[5-7] provides many principles derived from research in Europe and the USA, and shows the types of merger that have the highest chance of success. Porter[8] showed that the success chances of mergers and acquisitions had hardly changed since Kitching's work. The practical implication of all this is that I look very hard at any strategy which depends on acquisition, and want to see the actions that are planned to increase the chances of success. In many strategic plans acquisition is a form of cop-out, and a statement of intent to acquire replaces real thought about the situation.

All this advice is important. But in evaluating strategy we can borrow the words of the great economist Alfred Marshall.[9] 'It is doubtless true that much of this work has less need of elaborate scientific methods, than of a shrewd mother-wit, of a sound sense of proportion, and of a large experience of life.' He goes on to add a qualification: 'Natural instinct will select rapidly, and combine justly, considerations which are relevant to the issue in hand; but it will select chiefly from those which are familiar; it will seldom lead a man far below the surface, or far beyond the limits of his personal experience.' Although it applied to economics, the words are equally relevant to another branch of economic activity, the formulation of strategy.

Testing a plan for quality

Plans are written for different purposes, and the particular purpose should be considered when the plan is evaluated. There is a wide spectrum of styles and formats that could be applied, and the suggestions below accept that there is no one right way to write up the plan.

Concise but clear

A plan should be as brief as possible, but must communicate the strategy: a verbose plan may be less clear than a concise one, particularly if it is also poorly structured. Sometimes it is useful to impart information that is relevant to the plan: a good plan would probably separate the information (for example, market evolution) from the strategy section, but would demonstrate that the information has been used through the way the strategy is presented. Experience shows that lengthy narrative information sections that appear in plans often have nothing to do with the decision process in the plan. What is there should be integrated.

Use of diagrams

One of the best ways of relating strategy to complex data is through diagrammatic displays. For example, an industry 'map' may show the key data about the competitive structure of the industry on one piece of paper. A portfolio diagram allows the strategic situation of various business units to be compared, again on one piece of paper. Matrix displays of any type may add clarity, compress information, and relate the strategy to the information.

Structure of the plan

The plan must have a structure, and that structure should aid understanding. Without being dogmatic about order of presentation or content, there should be as a minimum sections on the strategic situation, internal strengths and weaknesses, vision and objectives, the chosen strategies, expected results and the action plan. It does not mean that a plan is bad if it lacks these, but it raises a line of questioning.

Too many actions

Corporate strategic plans are fairly broad. Plans at lower levels exchange breadth for depth. In both, a common error is to be over-optimistic about the number of new initiatives that can be implemented in a given period. All strategic actions planned must be considered against the resources of the unit, other claims on time, and should include realistic assessments of the elapsed time an action will take. A plan should not become a do-it-yourself hangman's kit.

Implementation

The final test is around implementation. Even a sound strategy can fail if attention is not given to implementation. The plan should address this, by establishing goals (milestones) to measure progress, breaking down the strategy into main action plans, and dealing with the issues which arise from this.

Issues may include involvement of those who will be required to implement, training in new skills needed to implement, communication and appropriate control mechanisms.

Summary

All the points in this chapter can be compressed into a few sentences. The evaluator needs to:

- Understand the strategy
- Be convinced of its soundness in relation to industry structure, competitors, the market and the environment
- Be convinced that it fits the competence and resources of the organisation
- Establish that it can be implemented
- Know the purpose for which the plan is written.

References

1 Stopford, J. M. *Vickers Plc A*, London Business School, 1989.

2 Porter, M. E. *Competitive Strategy*, Free Press, New York, 1980.

3 Buzzell, R. D. and Gale, B. T. *The PIMS Principles: Linking Strategy to Performance*, Free Press, New York, 1987.

4 James, B. G. *Business Wargames*, Penguin Books, London, 1985 (originally published in 1984 by Abacus Books).

5 Kitching, J. 'Why do Mergers Miscarry?' *Harvard Business Review*, Cambridge MA, November/December 1967.

6 Kitching, J. *Acquisitions in Europe: Causes of Corporate Success and Failure*, Business International, Geneva, 1973.

7 Kitching, J. 'Winning and Losing with European Acquisitions', *Harvard Business Review*, Cambridge MA, March/April 1974.

8 Porter, M. E. 'From Competitive Advantage to Corporate Strategy', *Harvard Business Review*, Cambridge MA, May/June 1987.

9 Marshall, A. *Principles of Economics*, 8th edn, Macmillan, London, 1956.

CHAPTER 24

Operating plans

This chapter is about preparing plans at lower levels of the organisation, which include critical areas such as marketing. Through some worked examples, the aim is to provide guidance on these aspects of planning.

Much has been made of the strategic decision process and the type of plans which are prepared for use at the company's highest levels. There is need for widespread participation of managers in the selection of strategy, and preceding chapters have suggested some ways of achieving this.

It is easy to argue that the strategic plan is the most important document the company possesses. From the use that top management makes of it this undoubtedly has some truth: yet it is rather like the argument that the roof garden of the millionaire's penthouse flat is more important than the foundations of lower storeys of the building. Seen in this light, the argument no longer seems so emphatically strong.

One of the foundations of a sound corporate planning process is a strong system of operational planning: that is, plans for the company's existing areas of business activity. Continuation of an area of activity is in itself a strategic decision (it must be if it is accepted that divestment is a possible alternative of strategy), and top management, with the help of the operating managers concerned, will have tried to define the place of each operational area within the overall strategic framework.

Subject only to the constraints and targets set from the top, the initial task of planning for an existing area of business activity should be completely delegated to the line managers responsible for that area. In other words, having decided the broad parameters, the chief executive should expect the line managers themselves to demonstrate what they should do with the area of business entrusted to them and how they intend to go about providing their share of the action which will attain the corporate objectives. In practice, certain additional elements of strategy may be delegated to managers, such as new products which bear a close relationship with the existing business.

One point which occasionally causes confusion is that many operational managers have dual roles. On one side they are charged with the duty of planning for their own business areas, in doing which they have a subordinate role to the total business strategy. On the other side they may, as members of the top management team, carry an important responsibility in the strategic planning process itself. This dual role – which is encountered in other aspects of management by every executive director – should not prevent the concepts of strategic and operational planning being separated.

This chapter concentrates on long-range operating plans. The questions of short-term plans, and other ways of converting long-range plans to deeds, are discussed in some detail in the future chapters. Because operating plans are a wide subject, most of the examples given here will relate to marketing and production. At the outset it should be stressed that other areas of the company may also be brought into this aspect of planning process: for example, some of the key areas which should receive attention with longer-term aspects in mind may be office accommodation, computer facilities, or a management information system. The simplification is not meant to confuse the complexities which exist in any real situation.

Most people who write about strategic planning, or who are themselves successful practitioners, agree that planning processes must have maximum involvement from managers. Planners should not attempt to do planning on behalf of operating managers and should not construe this as being any part of their duty. They have to make planning happen: they should not themselves make the plans.

There are few managers who would be content to allow others to plan their actions for them. Planning is an integral part of every manager's task, and a manager is no longer managing if this element of his function is removed from his or her control.

One decision about the system of planning designed for the company must be which managers should be called upon to prepare a long-range plan, and how far down the line involvement in long-range planning should go. Planning responsibilities must follow organisational lines: it would be a bad system that allowed a manager to bypass a superior and submit a plan directly to the chief executive. As a general rule, the higher the managers are in the organisational pyramid, the more they should be involved in the longer-term aspects of planning. Lower levels of management can contribute to idea sessions, and in a much fuller way in short-term planning.

As a guide I would suggest that in any major unit of the company the prime responsibility to prepare a long-range plan must fall on the person in charge. However, he or she should call upon all senior managers with a major responsibility for a part of that unit to contribute a long-range plan for their particular areas and to participate in discussion over the total plan of the unit. The planner – in large companies there may be separate divisional planners for each unit – should assist by helping the manager in charge to split up the planning task.

How these principles work may be seen from the simple example of a marketing manager who has as direct reports a general sales manager, four senior product managers, and a few service areas. Responsibility for preparing the marketing plan must belong to the marketing manager, yet it is good sense for senior managers to be invited to participate in setting the general policy of his department, and therefore to write long-range plans for their own activities. The general sales manager may call for thought contributions – but probably not complete plans – from the regional managers. The senior product managers should certainly be expected to prepare their plans in conjunction with their assistants.

Unfortunately, strategic management cannot make a dramatic change to the capability of the individual manager. It can help a good manager to become more effective: but even a major increase in the effectiveness of a poor manager is unlikely to change him or her to a good manager. If a manager avoids decisions, the fact that problems are now defined in greater depth will not cause decisions to be made. The really poor manager may seize on planning as a way of avoiding action: it can be used as an excuse; a means of finding all the reasons for not doing things.

The good manager will find benefits. It will lead to better decisions, and provide a clearer knowledge of his or her part in the total company effort. A tool will have been gained which helps to motivate and control subordinates. Such a manager may need help from the planner in learning how to improve planning and use plans more effectively. Unlike the mediocre manager, he or she will benefit from this help.

The reason for stressing this is that there are still some chief executives who believe that planning will solve their management problems and will miraculously turn the dullards into intellectual giants, the sluggards into power packs of energy, and the timid into dashing front-runners. Planning may force the chief executive to solve these management problems because it may isolate the weak and mediocre to an extent that they can no longer be ignored. This may force the chief executive to undertake unpleasant tasks to modify the management team, although planning will only be the means of exposure and not the reason for the action.

Any company that begins planning must expect its managers to accept a planning discipline, although this may be only a mild one. Timetables must be observed, certain key data must be included in plans, their subordinates must be involved, assumptions must be taken into account, the planning process they use must be compatible with the total corporate approach. Many companies write up the essential elements of the system into a handbook or manual.

One of the problems in defining a system of operational planning is that it is very easy to produce a good argument which proves it is impossible. Long-range sales forecasts will be an important element of both the analysis of alternatives and the final plan. It is possible to 'prove' that such forecasts must take into account the forward cost structure of the company and be related to general economic trends in the market. Cost accountants will demonstrate that forward costs can only be estimated if production output can be defined in relation to capacities and changing methods of production. And, of course, production will argue that they would welcome the opportunity to produce these data – if only someone would give them a sales forecast.

The procedures must break this circle and thus enable planning to take place. This means that essential time-lags must be allowed for in the system, so that where possible a department only begins its plans when it receives the input of key data from another department. Someone has to set assumptions so that work may proceed: for example, on the cost of goods – so that sales forecasts may be made, and price, promotion, and other strategies linked with them. Information has to be passed from one department to another, and departments whose efforts affect each other must have provision for general discussion, and coordination. Opportunity must be given for the final draft of plans to be reviewed to take account of changes caused by the intentions of other departments.

Production cannot, for example, complete their plan until marketing have provided data on sales – quantities, packaging, and product specifications. In turn the production plan may modify that of marketing – to meet the required level of sales may be costly, involve major capital expenditure, or occasionally be completely impossible. Unless the system provides for coordination and the exchange of information, plans are unlikely to be very realistic. Although the planner should assist in this coordinative task, the responsibility must be shared by the operating managers themselves – and even more by any general manager who has a responsibility for both an area of production and of marketing.

The best service a planner can perform is to design the procedures and time-tables so that coordination is a matter of course and cannot be avoided, rather than regarding it as a job to be done afterwards.

It was earlier reported that other areas of the company (e.g. IT) might be required to complete operating plans. At the least an expense forecast will be required so that total profit figures may be arrived at. This takes the planner to another decision: How far should service department expenses be allocated to operating divisions? In planning terms, allocation is usually not necessary, and better long-term plans can be made if items such as office accommodation are viewed in total. However, the annual budget probably does allocate. The planner needs to decide how far incompatibilities of budget and long-range plans are acceptable, and whether any compromise is desirable in either or both.

Operating planning can be improved if each planning cycle is formally started, rather than leaving managers to their own devices. This removes any excuses for forgetfulness or failure to complete plans, and at the same time provides an opportunity for providing managers with any planning information they need to have. One good way to begin the process is to issue a letter, setting out the detailed timetable for the cycle, including the dates of any coordination and review meetings required, finalisation dates for plans, the names of people who should receive advance information (and when), and an official routing for the completed plans.

At the same time all managers will need to be informed of any assumptions on which plans must be based (a good planning system will have already provided an opportunity for discussion on these). Examination may be requested of specific alternative courses of action: either alternative strategies or the same strategy under different assumptions.

The letter should also provide clear guidance on the strategic policy for each division or subsidiary, which must be taken into account during the preparation of the plan. This can be issued in the form of a set of guidelines to each divisional manager, incorporating the objectives set for the division, stressing areas of weakness which must be corrected, clarifying the availability (or otherwise) of capital for the division, and generally relating the plan to the overall strategy in which it fits.

A good rule is for this letter to be issued and signed by the chief executive, as this can avoid suspicion that the planner is dictating policy, which is not a planner's function. Sometimes it may be simple to separate the guidelines from the timetables in which case the planner will not cause problems by signing the routine instructions.

If they are planning effectively, every responsible divisional head will reissue the start-up letter, with their own guidelines added, to each of the managers who is to contribute to the plan. This is an important step because it can avoid subordinate managers wasting their time on ideas and strategies which will ultimately be rejected. Assistance may be given by the planner in preparing these guidelines, but, again, it is important that they be issued by the person responsible and not by the planner.

The system of operational planning should cover the position of committees. Some companies set up 'planning committees'. These may be useful as forums of coordination, discussion, and review, but are dangerous if they are set up to replace the individual planning responsibilities of managers or the planner. Where adequate provision already exists in the company for discussion, special regular committees may be superfluous – although *ad hoc* working parties put together for a particular task are likely to be of considerable value.

Managers who have never before produced written plans frequently find their first plan of great difficulty. The planner can help by ensuring that the planning manual gives clear guidance, by designing the system with the problems of operating management very much in mind, and by being available to give help during the planning cycle.

There are a number of principles which can be applied to any form of plan, and managers should be made aware of these:

1 A plan should be concise yet long enough to give a clear understanding of what is intended. Verbosity should be discouraged. Despite the frequent claims by line management that they are short of time, many operating plans are overlong. This is a difficult dilemma for the planner. To request that the plan be rewritten is likely to cause bad feeling, and will certainly mean that even more time is spent on writing plans. A more gentle approach often results in the same mistake being made the following year. Each planner has to find an individual solution to this problem.

2 Every well-prepared plan has a purpose. There must be a reason for the plan. It must set out to do something. Failure to understand the purpose frequently leads to the diversion of management thought into unprofitable byways.

3 There is always more than one possible course of action. Good planning will identify all practicable alternatives – the decision tree technique is useful here.

4 The course of action chosen must be properly defined and the reason for the choice understood. Not only must the plan have a purpose, but it must show how that purpose will be attained.

5 Results expected from the course of action must be specified so that management can follow the logical outcome of accepting the plan and also measure progress against the plan.

6 If the plan is to result in deeds it must allocate responsibilities in a clear way. There must be no doubt over who is to do what task.

What items of information are included in the long-range operating plans will depend on the requirements of the company and its individual components. It will also vary depending on whether the units are businesses with a high degree of strategic freedom or departments. A dogmatic approach, with piles of forms from corporate headquarters and giving no discretion to individual managers, is likely to be damaging. The object of the planning system is to persuade managers to consider the future and to face up to the challenge of change – it is not to constrain their thoughts along innumerable little boxes on innumerable sheets of paper.

Yet some formalisation of content is necessary. To ask managers to prepare plans without giving them any guidance is merely to increase their problems. Similarly, all financial data must follow some rules or it will not be possible to monitor the plan through the accounting system or even to judge whether results improve or decline. The company's normal accounting definitions should be used although global headings should replace unnecessary (from the planning sense) detail.

Most companies will need to include some forms – or prescribe a format for financial data, which is really the same thing. The golden rule is to keep the forms simple, and few in number, and not – as some companies do – to try to extend the annual budget into the future.

Guidance should also be given on the sort of thing which is likely to be relevant in a plan. Although I believe that every plan should have two parts, a narrative 'programme' and a 'budget', I believe that the keyword should be 'guidance'. Managers should be given freedom to write the narrative parts of the plan in their own style and fashion, and to include the essential information in the way that suits them best. At the same time the guidance should be comprehensive enough to cater for the managers who are so new to writing plans that they will follow all the suggestions in the manual as if they were edicts, given force by severe punishments for those who ignore them.

Again, the planner, working with the managers, has to decide individually what the balance is and which approach best suits his company.

All this advice is rather general. It is useful now to look at operating plans for marketing and production to suggest (with examples) how these might be completed. The guidance given here assumes that these are departments within a business unit which is also preparing a strategic plan.

Marketing plans

Before they can make marketing plans with confidence, all marketing managers will wish to survey the background of information available to them on their products and performance in the market place. At a later stage in the proceedings they will be reviewing their strategies with the chief executive or the board. They, too, will need to have access to facts about the market, although they will not necessarily need to use them other than for reference.

Marketing planning is greatly assisted if the provision of this information is made an integral part of the planning system. It is usually better to treat the background data as an appendix to the plan, bound as a separate document, rather than trying to fit both plan and information between one set of covers.

Marketing is vitally concerned with change in the needs, desires, attitudes, and opinions of its consumers, the way in which product reaches the consumers, and what competitors are doing in the marketplace. This is something of a simplification of the marketing task, but it is in these areas that many forecasts and assessments have to be made if marketing plans are to be more than wild hopes coupled to blind guesses.

Information on the market usually is available from many sources: published economic and demographic statistics, published market studies, specially commissioned market surveys, consumer panels, retail audits, and sales records. Many more sources are available to the dynamic marketing research department.

The coordination of data, of varying sources and degrees of accuracy, into a comprehensive handbook is a valuable first step in marketing planning. The discipline ensures an understanding of the available information, and identifies gaps in the data, where assumptions must be made or additional marketing research commissioned. It is a step that can be justified for every major market (or product), although it may not be worth while giving such extensive treatment to minor product areas.

This is an area where I should recommend the company to prepare set formats, so that data for each product area always appear in the same order. Products of a completely different type – e.g. industrial and consumer – may need separate formats. Figure 24.1, reproduced from Hussey,[1] provides a check list of the information headings which might be used to develop the format.

Much of the handbook will consist of firm data abstracted from reliable sources, the compilation of which may be a relatively junior task. The handbook should be future oriented – after all, it is for use in planning rather than the control of past results – and for this reason will include certain forecasts and predictions. These, together with assumptions set to cover gaps in the data, are a more senior responsibility. At the least they must be fully accepted by the marketing manager as a reasonable basis for the plans: responsibility for the actions planned from these forecasts remains with the marketing manager.

Carefully prepared handbooks of this nature, updated at regular and frequent intervals, are invaluable for future planning. They help the marketing manager to appraise current strategies against the hard facts and expected developments of the markets. Critical examination of what is currently done is always a good starting point for doing something new. (If the strategy is still valid, there will be no need to change it.) The handbook forces the separation of hunches, informed opinion, and facts: it ensures that where facts are available the manager is aware of them, and that he or she does not guess where there is already knowledge.

From this solid base, the marketing manager is able to venture into the less than solid future.

The general outline of a marketing plan might well include the following points:

1 Marketing targets and objectives
2 A sales forecast for each year of the plan (supported by back history) for each main product, or product grouping, and in both value and quantities
3 The marketing strategy for the period of the plan, *in broad outline*

493

Figure 24.1

Broad indications of some possible data headings for the market background appendix

```
1. GENERAL DATA
   (a) Population              age and sex
                              region
                              households
                              social class
                              urban/rural
                              working/non-working
   (b) National income        per capita
                              per household
                              regional differences

2. PRODUCT PROFILE (by relevant headings as in 1A)
   (a) Demography             present users
                              heavy users
                              non-users
                              competitive product users
   (b) Product image
   (c) Analysis of uses of products
   (d) Time or day of usage analysis
   (e) Frequency of usage
   (f) Frequency of purchase
   (g) Price/volume relationships
   (h) Brand shares

3. DISTRIBUTION (by relevant headings as in 1A)
   (a) Source of purchase     all users
                              heavy users
                              competitive product users
   (b) Brand shares by source of purchase
   (c) Retailer attitudes     to product
                              to company
                              to competitors
   (d) Wholesale attitudes    to product
                              to company
                              to competitors
   (e) Profitability of product retailer
                              compared with all products
                              compared with competitors
   (f) Degree of customer service
                              given for product
                              given by competitors
   (g) Retailer attitudes to  trade packing
                              consumer packing

4. MARKET SIZE (by relevant headings as in 1A)
   (a) Definition of market
   (b) Size of total market   by value
                              by quantity
   (c) Market forecasts       by value
                              by quantity
   (d) Market size per pack size
   (e) Details of substitute products
   (f) Quantity and value of market by various channels of distribution

5. PRICE
   (a) Analysis of consumer prices
   (b) Analysis of trade prices

6. PROMOTION
   (a) Advertising            by media
                              by competitor
   (b) Merchandising activity
   (c) Special offer etc. activity
   (d) Response of retailers to promotions

7. MARKET SEGMENTATION

8. HISTORICAL DATA

9. PRODUCT COST DATA       by standard costs
                           by fixed and variable costs
```

All these headings are indicative only. A full listing can only be made after a study of the firm's particular problems. Such a list can be prepared by any competent marketing manager. There is no significance in the order in which headings appear.

4 Details of price movements planned for each product over the period of the plan (really an element of strategy, but of particular importance if the company is to cope with inflation)
5 Clear definition of goals so that strategies may be monitored (e.g. future market shares)
6 Anticipation of problems and methods designed to deal with them.

The whole marketing programme must be conceived against the background of the market and competitive forces in that market.

One of the most difficult tasks for managers is setting strategy in outline: that is, concentrating on the longer-term elements. Plans frequently contain a great amount of information on the next special offer, this year's market research programme, and very little about the future of the product in the long-term marketing portfolio, the long-term product image that is required, or the improvements needed to enhance its performance. Getting the balance right takes a fair amount of practice: lack of it results in plans which are confused and lengthy.

It is easier to write about marketing strategy if the plan is prepared within a conceptual framework, which means breaking down the total strategy into various elements. A number of classification schemes exist and are widely used by marketing managers, and the planner need not be dogmatic in insisting that plans follow his or her preferred classifications. Planners will find it useful to have a preference so that they can make a constructive recommendation to managers who do not have an acceptable approach of their own. A very useful format is the 'four P's' approach suggested by McCarthy[2] which divides total marketing strategy into price, product, place, and promotion.

The company must decide at an early stage how it will treat inflation in its long-range plans (see also the previous chapters on the external environment). In a situation of inflation, price strategy is particularly difficult to plan. Some companies solve the problem by ignoring cost and price rises and making the sweeping assumption that any additional costs will be recovered from the marketplace. This may make it easier to put plans together, as it simplifies many of the issues. But it is not planning. Avoidance of an issue does not make it disappear: one of the reasons for planning is to help the company cope with future problems, and to pretend that one of the most complex problems of all does not exist is not a solution. In some countries it is not possible to increase prices without government permission. In any circumstances complete recovery of cost increases may take some substantial planning and thought.

In common with any operating plan there should be a section dealing with future organisation structures and people. It is important that line managers give considerable thought to these aspects of their forward plan, even though there will be an overall corporate plan dealing with human resource issues. The reasons why I believe this to be important were given in Chapter 21: that all mangers have a responsibility towards people which they should never be allowed to abdicate. Additionally, any change in marketing requirements and sales efforts may bring a need to change the numbers, types, or relationships of the people required to fulfil the plan. In turn this affects costs and profits. Many plans fail because it is assumed that the present organisation can cope with the future intentions, and the 'people problem' is often not recognised until valuable time has been lost. The programme must be supported by the budget section of the plan. Exactly how this is set out, and which information headings are important, must be a matter for the individual company. Accounting definitions will vary between companies, so any general suggestions made must be subject to alteration to suit the particular company.

Nevertheless, a way of setting out the data is suggested in Figures 24.2 and 24.3. If required an additional line can be inserted in Figure 24.3 to show quantities by product.

The approach suggested is capable of easy modification to provide separate information for home and export sales although a company should really be thinking of individual markets, rather than an amorphous lump called 'export'. 'Product' may be interpreted as a group of products, or widened to deal with specific pack sizes. Sales costs are shown as allocated to products, although many companies may prefer not to do this. Depreciation is shown as a notation, as it has a place in the financial plan.

The essence of the suggested forms is simplicity. Long-range budgets should be supported by a schedule of intended capital expenditures, although these are more likely to occur in a production plan (although they may be heavy in a marketing department which is responsible for physical distribution).

Figure 24.2
Summary of results

	Department		Five-year plan 19 –19			£000
	Last year 19	Current year 19 Estimated	Five year plan			
			19	19	19	19	19
Total sales (after discounts)						
Cost of goods sold						
Gross margin						
Gross margin (% of sales)						
Direct marketing costs						
Direct marketing contribution						
Direct marketing contribution (% of sales)						
Indirect marketing costs						
Total contribution to company profit						
Notational only – depreciation						

Figure 24.3
Product details

Department...............

Five-year plan 19 – 19   £000

	Product............							Product............					
	Last year 19	Current year (Est) 19	19	19	19	19		Last year 19	Current year (Est) 19	19	19	19	19
Sales (after discounts)													
Cost of goods sold													
Gross margin													
% of sales													
Advertising & Promotion													
Product mkg. research													
Direct selling exps:													
Sales force													
Commissions													
Other													
Physical distribution													
Other direct marketing costs													
Total direct marketing contribution													
Direct marketing contribution													
% of sales													

Example of a format for a long-range marketing plan

The example shows (simplified) extracts from the marketing plan of a hypothetical company. It begins after the definition of objectives and assumptions and shows the general marketing strategy of the company, and the specific strategy for one of its products. All the 'facts' were invented for the example, and the reader may assume that the budgets would quantify adequately the revenue and expenditures.

1. General marketing strategy

1.1. Introduction

The plan is a continuation of the strategies laid down over the past two years, leading to a reduction in the company's profit-dependence on garden ornaments, and on sales through the specialist garden shop. Garden ornaments currently produce 75 per cent of profits (95 per cent two years ago) and this will be reduced to 50 per cent by year 5. Garden tools and accessories will be the company's major target over the next five years.

1.2. Garden care market

The tools and accessories sector of the market is still increasing at the rate of 30 per cent per year and currently is worth £30m at retail prices. Ornaments have been declining by 10 per cent per year and the market is worth £10m. The tools and accessories sector is forecast at £45m by year 5. Some recovery in the ornament market will enable it to reach £12m over the same period.

There are seven main elements to the company's plan for this market:

1 *Brand policy.* All garden accessories and ornaments will in future be marketed under the brand name 'garcare'. Research shows that this brand has a significant image among consumers, suggesting quality and skilful design, which extends beyond the accessories on which it has hitherto been applied. It is a platform of the long-range plan that this strategy be continued for all *relevant* new product introductions.

2 *Changing the image of garden ornaments.* The intention is to move the products away from the 'small suburban' image of garden ornaments, through:
   (a) Market segmentation (see 3 below)
   (b) Branding of all products and building up an image to support each product (see below and product strategies)
   (c) Use of public relations to stress the value of the products to all garden lovers
   (d) Product promotion to move selected items from the garden to the home.

3 *Market segmentation.* New variants of products will be introduced to segment the market and will be supported by specific promotion through media which reaches the target buyer. The accessory market will be segmented into the 'garden fanatic', the 'garden lover', and the 'keep it tidy' buyers, which research has shown to be meaningful segments.

4 *Promotion.* Emphasis on advertising and promotional expenditures will be on the accessory market (60 per cent), group promotion featuring the 'garcare' brand for a range of products (25 per cent), and ornaments (15 per cent). (Total promotional expenditure is given in the budget.)

5 *Sales force.* A new sales force of forty people will be formed over years 1–2 and the system of agency distribution progressively abandoned. (The distribution targets for individual products are given in the product sheets.) The main target outlet will be the 'garden centre' where the company currently has no business. (See personnel section for details of organisation and manpower.)

6 *Supermarkets.* The private label participation in this business is worth £1m split equally between the two market areas, of which the company currently has 90 per cent (ornaments) 1 per cent (tools and accessories). An effort will be made to increase the tools and accessory business to 20 per cent of the market by year 2 (see detailed programme).

7 *Mail order.* A mail order division will be opened in year 2 (see detailed programme and targets).

1.3. Competition

There are two main competitors in each field ....
(details omitted to simplify the example)

2. Individual product strategy – garden gnomes

2.1. Promotion

(a) Ninety per cent of advertising expenditure will be designed to change the 'small garden in suburbia' image of gnomes to the broader 'A gnome makes a home', stressing the aesthetic delights of gnomes in both garden and house.

(b) This will be effected through both television and press advertising (exact allocations will be made in the annual plan) over the whole period of the plan.

(c) In addition, the new branded pack will be used promotionally and carry a theme message.

(d) There will be a medium-term (two years) public relations campaign with a budget of £5000 per year to stress the novel features of garden gnomes. (Detailed plan to be prepared by Mr Brown.)

(e) Supporting expenditure by direct mail shots will promote the special gnome for special people theme (e.g. the 'Zurich' gnome for persons interested in finance). This will be aimed at the Christmas trade to reduce the winter seasonal drop in sales.

499

2.2. Distribution

(a) No other branded gnomes are currently on the market. The company aims to increase its overall share (retail audit: value of sales) of the garden gnome market to:

	Goals				
	Years				
Current	1	2	3	4	5
25%	25%	40%	40%	45%	45%

Monitoring responsibility – Mr Green.

(b) Brand share performance will be increased in the following areas of weakness, through tactical adjustments to local distribution, pricing and in-store promotional activities.

	Goals (retail audit – value)					
	Current	Year				
		1	2	3	4	5
Southern	10%	15%	20%	25%	30%	35%
Midlands	15%	20%	25%	30%	35%	40%
York	10%	15%	20%	25%	30%	35%

Monitoring responsibility – Mr. Green.

(c) Certain minimum penetration levels will be attained in the major outlets through own sales force activity and tactical adjustments to merchandising allowances and tailor-made promotions.

	Goals (retail audit – value)					
	Current	Year				
		1	2	3	4	5
Garden shops	75%	75%	75%	75%	75%	75%
Garden centres	–	35%	70%	75%	80%	90%
Departmental stores	5%	10%	15%	20%	20%	20%
Supermarkets	1%	25%	30%	40%	45%	50%

Monitoring responsibility – Mr. Green.

2.3. Product

(a) The range of normal garden gnomes will be rationalised from twenty-five varieties to not more than twelve, within a two-year period.

Action – Miss Smith.

(b) Up to six special 'indoor' gnomes will be available in any one year for the Christmas trade.

Action – Miss Smith.

(c) All products will be packed in branded boxes with transparent display panels, twenty-four to an outer. This change to be effective during year 1.

Action – Miss Smith.

2.4. Price

(a) General retail price policy is to demonstrate the superior quality of the product through a price structure which commands a 2p premium over competitive products. This policy will be maintained.

(b) A new price structure will be designed to provide an incentive for quantity purchase and to meet requirements of supermarkets. This will be introduced in year 1.

Action – Mr Green.

(c) Production cost increase can be held for years 1 and 2 (through the effect on unit costs of the expected increase in volume), and will rise by about 5 per cent in year 3. New technology will be available by year 4 and should hold costs steady. Price policy will be to maintain prices for two years (unless competitors increase their prices in which case strategy will be reviewed), increase by 10 per cent in year 3 and thereafter hold steady. Regular review of price policy is essential.

Action – Mr Green.

2.5. Key results

	Current	Year				
		1	2	3	4	5
Sales (£000)	1000	1400	1675	1750	2000	2250
Advertising and promotion (£000)	75	140	168	175	140	158
Advertising and promotion as % sales	7.5	10	10	10	7	7
Direct marketing contribution (£000)	100	140	250	260	300	335
Direct marketing contribution as % sales	10	15	15	15	15	15

501

Production plans

Marketing plans show what products are to be sold, changes of form and pack required for marketing purposes, and the profitability of the products. It was mentioned earlier that, during the planning process, there must be coordination with production.

The purpose of the production long-range plan is to show how the marketing requirements can be made available and at what cost. It should examine the capacities of the various areas of the factory, the ways in which these may be changed in the short term (e.g. overtime) and in the long term (new equipment). If the company has more than one production unit it may require a plan for the optimum sourcing of product. It should take account of technological developments, alternative methods of production, and ways of improving profitability (see also Chapter 19).

One area of difficulty in production planning is the objective the unit is to work to. If the accounting system allows the 'sale' of product to the marketing department it may be possible to set a 'profit' objective. For many companies production will be treated as a cost centre, and the only objectives which can be set are in terms of efficiency – either based on physical units (as with wastage factors) or a maximum standard cost which has to be beaten.

The main reason for the plan must be the profitable running of the production unit and the anticipation – and therefore avoidance – of problems. Terms used in the plan should be internally defined. Capacity calculations may require particular care: in any case it is not enough to examine theoretical annual capacity against forecast requirements, unless some consideration is also given to the pattern of requirements during the year. A product with seasonal peaks may have an average monthly surplus of capacity and yet be unable to meet marketing requirements for six months of the year.

In many instances production planning will require the examination of many options: capital investment or additional labour; overtime or new plant; higher inventories or more capacity to cope with seasonal peaks.

As with all operating plans, the production plan should pay attention to problems of organisation and people, although (as has been stated in the discussion on the marketing plan) the intention should not be to replace an overall personnel plan for the company. The chances are that the production area is the company's biggest employer of labour, it may have the most acute problems in industrial relations or wage negotiations, and it would be unrealistic to request a plan which ignored these factors.

The budget requirements of the production plan should be kept to the simplest terms. Individual product costs of production will appear in the marketing plans, so in most companies it would be superfluous to state them again in the production plan. So the production plan should show summary figures: total expenditures on each of the major raw materials, other direct costs in total for each of the major departments, and production overheads. Again depreciation should be itemised separately to assist cash-flow calculations, a point which applies to any operating plan.

Equally important is the long-range capital budget. In most cases this will deal with broad estimates, but should be designed to give a clear indication of expenditure needed to support the production plan. Each major project should be itemised.

An example is provided of how the narrative section of the long-range plan of one department in a production unit might be set out. General issues of personnel and organisation, and capital and revenue budgets are not included in the example, and would appear as part of the total plan for the unit. The example is meant to provoke thought, and is not intended to be the last word on writing an operating plan: as in almost any other aspect of corporate planning there are many 'right' ways of doing the same thing.

Example of a format for a long-range production plan

Extract from the plan of a hypothetical pharmaceutical company

General packaging department

Objective

To package the 'SIX' and 'OPQ' ranges of pharmaceutical products to the defined standards to ensure compliance with government and health regulations and the quality requirements of marketing.

Production requirements (000 packs)

	Year				
	1	2	3	4	5
Hard packs	80	75	60	60	60
Strip packs	260	280	300	450	325
Auto-line packs	1000	1200	1500	1800	2000
Liquid packs (small)	500	520	550	600	700
Liquid packs (large)	200	200	220	240	250
Total packs	2040	2275	2630	3150	3335

Capacity

All calculations are based on 2000 hours production per year (250 days by 8 hours).

	Packs per year
Automatic tablet counting line	3 million
Syrup packaging (100–150 ml)	2 million
(1–21)	75 million

	Tablets per year
Strip packaging	12.5 million

Programme

(1) Manual packaging. Rationalisation of packs and products (in conjunction with marketing) is expected to steadily reduce the need for manual packaging operations. The need will remain for certain large packs containing 5000 tablets or more tablets as these cannot easily be processed by available automatic or semi-automatic methods.

Action – Rationalisation studies to be completed year 1: implemented years 2–3: Mr Young. Working party to study ways of mechanisation or work simplification.

Report end year 1: Mr Briggs.

(2) Strip packs. The capacity of this section is estimated at equivalent to 12.5 million tablets per year. Tablet numbers to be processed are:

This year	Year (million tablets)				
	1	2	3	4	5
5.0	12.0	13.0	13.4	14.0	15.0

This suggests that capacity will be exceeded in year 2. It is not planned to order new capacity until year 3 for installation in year 4 (estimated capital cost £5000) because:

(a) This will give time for sales forecasts to be evaluated against results in view of the large increase of sales expected from as yet untried products.

(b) Requirements up to and including year 4 can be met through overtime working, although this becomes less economic in year 4 than purchasing a new machine.

(c) A new machine would double present capacity.

Action – Check production requirements during year 1 – Mr Young. Evaluation of machine required year 3 – Mr Young.

(3) Automatic tablet packaging line. This line packages the standard range of small tablets into plastic tubes of various sizes. All tablets are currently counted semi-automatically, using King TB-4 electronic counters. Filled tubes are automatically capped, labelled and placed manually in outers. Capacity is adequate for the period of the plan, with sufficient flexibility to meet seasonal factors or unexpected increases in requirements.

Action – Working party to investigate ways of fully automating all aspects of the operating: to report in year 1 – Mr Briggs.

(4) Syrup packaging unit. Seasonal factors are such that syrup packaging capacity will be utilised 50 per cent during the winter months and 25 per cent during the summer. A constraint of higher utilisation is caused in the syrup manufacturing unit which has a lower capacity than the packaging plant. No new plant is required during the life of the plan.

(5) General opportunities. Surplus capacity in various sections of the packaging unit provides an opportunity for increasing revenue by taking in outside contract packaging. This possibility will be investigated (Miss Jones) during year 1, with a view to implementation towards the end of the year. (As this is an unproved opportunity, no account has been taken of it in the budget.)

General

These plans are not produced solely for the benefit of the operating manager. They are an important part of total company planning and must be integrated into the total system. This means that something must happen to them once the operating manager has completed them.

It is worth remembering that operating plans are a form of communication between managers and the chief executive. The planner must not become a blockage. The help and advice given to managers as they complete their plans, the way the planner tried to ensure that they have evaluated the logical implications of each course of action; have studied alternatives; and have taken account of the company assumptions – all these must be carried out in a way which does not destroy the plans as a communication channel.

Good planners will enjoy the confidence of line managers – although this is something which may take time to win – and will be able to help and guide them informally during the planning preparation. The borderline between help and interference is a very fine one which the planner must be careful not to cross.

Plans should be routed to the chief executive through the planner. The planner's task at this stage is to relate the plans to the outline strategy and corporate policies, to check them for completeness, and to coordinate them with the plans of other operating divisions. At this stage the planner may informally or formally go back to the manager on aspects of the plan.

Eventually they should be passed through to the chief executive with a note (copied to the line managers concerned) of the main issues for decision – results, areas of risk, main problems, strategic issues, and the like.

There should always be a review of plans by the chief executive and, possibly, other members of the top management team. Reviews may be held of all plans in one major meeting attended by all concerned. Alternatively, and I prefer this, they may be small meetings consisting of the chief executive, planner, the operating manager, and whatever team he or she wishes to bring with him. Sometimes a private meeting between chief executive and manager may be better, in which case the planner should not expect to attend as a right.

In large companies the strategic planner may have a number of divisional operating plans, all broadly accepted, to integrate into total company strategy. Some companies simply add up the profits and capital needs of all divisions and call that the plan. In my view consolidation is not as simple as that, and may require adjustment to the figures carried through for strategic planning. An example of this is with estimates of capital requirements: in operating plans these are frequently high for two years (where managers have firm projects in mind) and tail off to nothing for the rest of the plan. The planner may need to adjust these estimates.

Review may lead to modification. Once a plan has been agreed and accepted it becomes an instruction from top management to the operating manager to begin to implement, which should lead to the preparation of the tactical plans discussed in Chapter 24.

It is not a blanket authorisation to commit vast sums of capital expenditure, although it is an agreement that, provided the detailed appraisal of the expenditure indicates acceptable results, the capital will be made available. Chaos is often caused in companies where plans are accepted but no thought is given by top management to capital needs. If there is no intent to provide the necessary capital, the lubricant which makes the plan work, the plan itself must be changed.

Techniques may be used to aid the task of operational planning. Some have already been described in earlier chapters, and a number will be discussed later. Success in this type of planning is not a matter of techniques, but of the method of approach and motivation. If this goes wrong, much of the company's planning effort will be wasted. If it succeeds the company will reap many rewards.

References

1 Hussey, D. E. *Introducing Corporate Planning: Guide to Strategic Management*, 4th edn, Pergamon, Oxford, 1991.
2 McCarthy, E. J. *Basic Marketing: A managerial Approach*, Irwin, Homewood, IL, 1964.

Further reading

Kotler, P. *Marketing Management: Analysis, Planning, Implementation, and Control*, 8th edn, Prentice Hall, Englewood Cliffs, NJ, 1994 (or a later edition).
Piercy, N. *Market-led Strategic Change*, Butterworth-Heinemann, Oxford, 1992.
Wilson, A. *Marketing Audit Checklists*, McGraw-Hill, Maidenhead, 1993.

Part 4

Implementation and the Management of Change

CHAPTER 25

Project planning and appraisal

This is the first of three chapters which deal specifically with the implementation aspects of strategic management. The aim is to show how project plans may be used as a means of confirming the strategic decision, and providing a means of breaking down the strategy into actions which can be monitored. A second aim is to show the linkage which should exist between project planning, strategic management, and financial control mechanisms such as capital budgeting.

The need for project plans, as one of the ways in which a company moves its long-range plans into today's actions, was mentioned in Chapter 3. The company's strategic plans may be regarded as a snapshot of the entire company and its intentions taken at a particular moment of time. Project plans are an enlargement of one specific piece of that snapshot, which is studied with microscopic attention.

Although there should be a close link between the strategic plans and project plans – indeed, so close that they should all be regarded as part of the same system – projects may be investigated at any time of the year and are not tied to the planning cycle. Similarly, the length of time chosen for the evaluation of the project need not be related to that chosen for the strategic plans.

Ideally there should never be a need to investigate a project unless this has appeared in the long-range plans. If this policy could be maintained it would ensure that the place of the project within total corporate strategy had been established according to all the best rules. Unfortunately, real-life situations rarely occur with this degree of nicety: managers are human and will sometimes omit things from their plans; strategic planning is, in any case, a continuous process, and new opportunities may be uncovered between plans; environmental changes may cause new projects to arise.

It is because of this that no company can afford to issue a blanket edict that only capital expenditure mentioned in the plans will be authorised. To do this would mean that sometimes the company would have to act against its own interests and refuse investments for doctrinaire reasons rather than from good business sense. However, it is a good idea if top management makes known its displeasure when 'surprise' projects are dropped on its table for no good reason. The degree of acceptable 'surprise' depends in some measure on the company's position on the scale of environmental turbulence (see Ansoff and McDonnell[1]).

What is needed is a subsystem in the corporate planning process which deals with projects. The components of this subsystem are: a method of short-term capital budgeting; a routine which ensures that each step in the project planning process is undertaken at the right time; rules for the appraisal of capital expenditures; and a method of control.

There is nothing particularly novel about any of these elements, and the approach outlined is followed by many companies who practise no other element of formal planning in their organisation. It is possible to develop a very efficient way of dealing with projects, which contributes much to the effective use of corporate resources, without having any form of strategic plan. The danger here is that although each project is dealt with carefully on an individual basis, it is not necessarily the action that is best for the company.

It is not possible to operate a complete process of corporate planning without treating projects effectively. This is why this important aspect of planning appears in this book, even though the methods described are not the sole prerogative of corporate planners. The fact that planners often find themselves in situations where no effective project planning system exists is justification for its inclusion.

Capital budgeting procedure

Long-term capital budgeting has been discussed in Chapter 20 as a component of the financial planning process. Short-term capital budgeting is much more of a control process, and aims to provide procedures for authorisation of different types of capital expenditure to budget for expenditures over, for example, a twelve-month period, to provide for management review of capital requirements and to control expenditures against budget.

Although minor capital expenditure does not require overelaborate methods of evaluation, it does need to be justified and controlled. In a large company minor expenditures can accumulate to a significant total sum, and one which the company has to provide from its financial resources. It is very easy for any company to become undisciplined and to waste its resources.

For minor expenditures it should be sufficient for a simple system of authorities to be introduced, using a form which requests explanation but not financial evaluation. This ensures that expenditures can only take place on the approval of the responsible manager who, in any case, is held accountable for keeping within a capital budget. Thus a departmental manager may be allowed to authorise expenditure up to £10,000, and a divisional manager up to £25,000, with anything above this coming out of the 'minor' category and requiring different treatment.

There may be exceptions to this rule. For example, the company may insist that these authorities apply only to items which appear in the capital budget, and that approval for anything excluded must in any case come from the board. Or an embargo may be placed on specific types of expenditure (such as new furniture), which means that power to authorise money spent on these items is restricted to certain higher levels of managers.

The system may also be used to cover revenue expenditures although exceptions will usually have to be made for certain departments: for example, advertising expenditures by a marketing department because of the size and nature of its transactions.

Operation of any system of authorisation of minor expenditures (and it should not be forgotten that for many items the difference between a revenue and a capital expenditure is a matter determined internally by the company's accountants) will be assisted if the company has standing policies. Much unnecessary expenditure can be avoided if there are firm policies laid down to cover the type of word processors which may be purchased, what functions may have microcomputers, what variety of furniture may be chosen, and so on. Often the reason for capital expenditures on small items is a 'want' rather than a 'need', and is a desire to enhance status on the part of individuals. Such expenditures rarely contribute to corporate profits, and frequently lead to a chain reaction from other people who in turn wish to make similar expenditures.

A second category of capital expenditure, which requires slightly different treatment, is the replacement of fixed assets. Certain replacements are a routine expense for which a simplified system of authorisation may be introduced, even if the amounts are outside the 'minor' expenditure limits. An example of this is the replacement of sales personnel's cars. Provided the replacement is within the policy laid down, there is little point in making the authorisation system too complex. Replacements of all types should be estimated in both the long-term plans (in global figures) and in the short-term capital budget (in detail).

Not all asset replacement situations are as simple as this. Major plant also wears out and from time to time has to be renewed. Such renewals should not be automatic, and should be fully studied well in advance of their need. Provision should be made in the appropriate plans for the financial commitment, so that the need to make capital available for this purpose is not overlooked. The time to replace plant and machinery does not always coincide with the book depreciation, so it is important that the plans reflect management thoughts rather than financial extrapolations.

Technological development and other forces may cause obsolescence long before assets are fully depreciated. From a planning point of view the most important element in a replacement decision is time. If it is left too late, a crash programme may have to be introduced to replace the item so that production is not impaired. If considered in time, it becomes possible to examine options, some of which may be far-reaching and also involve expenditure on additional plant. The authorisation system should ensure that these studies are carried out and the need for them identified well in advance.

Profit-improvement capital expenditure is the third important area to be encountered. (Sometimes a replacement expenditure may also be profit improvement.) A general feature of this type of expenditure is usually a high return and quick payback, coupled with the difficulty of identifying individual projects on more than a short-term basis. The authorisation system should provide for speedy investigation and approval of these projects, but should not overlook the fact that the implementation of some may be accompanied by changes in the personnel area. Some companies with continuous profit-improvement systems have a quick-routing system for capital expenditure requests of an improvement nature. Except where personnel problems are involved, the strategic positioning of the unit under review or the amount of capital is very large, there is rarely a good reason for delaying the introduction of a profit-improvement measure.

In some circumstances it may make sense to increase the authorisation limits of certain managers for improvement projects. This should reduce delays. Capital budgeting should provide a lump sum for investment projects (as noted earlier, it is often impossible to forecast individual projects).

The largest amounts of capital expenditure are, in most companies, for investment and corporate development. (There may be exceptions: for example, ship replacement may for a shipping company be the main use of its capital.) The capital is required to do something new to secure growth for the company. Each development project should arise from the decisions taken in the strategic plan, and the implications of the outline project on corporate strategy should already be known. (The possible treatment of projects omitted from these plans has already been discussed.)

Major development and investment projects are the ones which require the closest and most detailed evaluation before capital is committed, and this should include network or other systems for ensuring implementation. In other words, although the decision to proceed will be largely financial, the strategic decision having already been made, the evaluation must also cover all non-financial aspects.

In most companies major authorisations of this type must be made either by the board or by a special subcommittee set up by the board. These may be exceptions where authority is delegated, within specified limits, to the board of a subsidiary.

One of the main problems in setting a system of capital budgeting is to make sensible delegations of authority to approve capital expenditure. The balance must be found that gives operating managers and chief executives of subsidiaries enough flexibility to act, and yet does not remove all control for those ultimately responsible for the well-being of the company.

It is also important that the authorisation system does not create too much 'red tape' and too many bureaucratic delays. The longer the chain of approval, the greater the delays will become, and it is not unusual for subsidiaries of multinational companies to wait several months before answers come back from the centre. Frequently the job of evaluation is done twice, which is wasteful – once by the subsidiary and once at head office. In a competitive situation no company can afford to have systems which impede its progress.

The British subsidiary of a multinational group gave advance warning in its plans that it would have to make a major investment in a replacement boiler house. The opportunity was taken to study the possibility of relocating the plant, and after proposals were rejected by the head office (on strategic grounds) a project was prepared to request capital for the new boiler house. Six months went by before there was a word from the head office, and over a further six months the head office insisted on re-examining all the engineering alternatives. Eventually the insurance company – as had been predicted – threatened immediate withdrawal of coverage. The whole organisation went into a panic, approval was given to replace the boiler house, and the only obvious result from the delay was that the time-lag had caused costs to rise by 40 per cent, relations with the insurance company were impaired, and many hours of engineers' time were lost.

Capital budgeting systems should regularly report actual expenditure against the budget. This requirement does not replace the need to control individual projects, a point which will be discussed in some detail later.

Project–evaluation routine

The planning system should include a routine which ensures that all projects go through a number of defined stages, and that the right people are brought into the project at the right time – for investigation, coordination, approval, and implementation. Unless this is clearly defined, the company may well find that important stages are overlooked, and that decisions are made before the project has been evaluated. Such a system also improves interdepartmental communication and helps to prevent managers from keeping projects to themselves and deliberately denying access by people from other departments who should play a part in their evaluation.

As mentioned earlier, the project planning system cuts across the strategic planning system of which it is a part. The relationship can perhaps be visualised as a series of horizontal and vertical bars. The horizontal bars are successive strategic and operating plans which are joined together by the various vertical bars of project planning. Some vertical bars may overlay several horizontal bars – occasionally they may be so short that they barely embrace one horizontal. This relationship is illustrated in Figure 25.1.

There will be variations in the project planning system to suit different types of projects. The development and introduction of a new product is likely to follow a longer path than a project to install a new piece of equipment. The internal organisation of decision taking within the company will also affect the way in which the system is organised.

Even with these qualifications, it is still useful to consider an outline of what a project planning system might look like. The example (Figure 25.2) is of a procedure for the development of a new product, and was designed for a company in the food industry.

This example simplifies some of the problems; particular projects may need to add further stages. A decision to launch a new product may mean that the

Figure 25.1
Relations of project
plans to long-range
plans

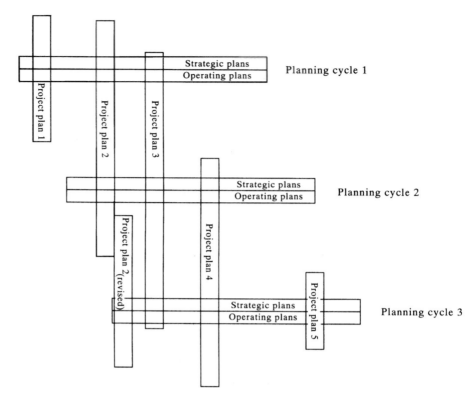

company has to extend its premises, which in turn means a detailed study of the physical and financial alternatives. The amount of work within each of the stages will vary from project to project, and may be complicated by failures at certain points which bring a need to go back to the beginning again. The system does not indicate control mechanisms. It becomes apparent from a study of this simplified system that it requires a coordinator. Someone must be responsible for ensuring that each step is completed, that everyone knows the part he or she is to play, and the completion date.

Different types of project require different coordinators. In this particular example it could probably be adequately filled by the product manager responsible for the project. For other projects there may be other sensible choices: the best coordinator is one who has a personal interest in seeing that the project is completed to its targets of finance, physical performance, and time.

Complex projects require the assistance of coordinating and controlling techniques. Networks are particularly valuable, the more so when it is remembered that each of the substages may include a number of tasks which themselves have to be carefully planned and coordinated.

Figure 25.2

Stages in project planning: a new product

1. Identification of idea
   Ideas may come from many sources, including:
   (a) Inspiration
   (b) Marketing research
   (c) Brainstorming and similar "ideas" sessions
   (d) Competitive action

2. Initial prospects study
   Desk research to establish prospects for the idea, leading to definition of a preliminary product marketing concept and postulation of an ideal launch date.

   Action:
   Marketing

3. Preliminary product marketing concept
   Defining the outline concept, *possible* level of sales (within perhaps a wide range), request for research and development work.

   Action:
   Marketing

4. Definition of research and development objective
   A statement of the meaning of the product marketing concept in R & D terms, assessment of product flexibility, estimated time needed to complete task, estimated cost of research, any problems arising from priorities.

   (Note: see also Chapter 17)

   Action:
   R & D

5. Decision to proceed

   Action:
   Top management

6. Refined product marketing concept
   At a point where R & D work, and such complementary marketing research work as is possible and desirable, shows sign of success the PMC should be refined. This stage will include provisional financial data – costings, range of margins at various possible selling prices, process and investment data.

   Action:
   Marketing assisted by appropriate departments

7. Decision to proceed
   If stage 6 shows a probability of acceptable results the project may proceed without reference to top management. If failure is detected at this stage, the project should be referred to top management for a decision whether to abandon or continue.

   Action:
   Marketing or top management as appropriate

8. Feasibility study
   The project now moves into a stage when a full feasibility study is possible. The completion of this study requires the initiation and completion of work in a number of areas, such as:
   (a) Marketing research, such as concept testing
   (b) Process development
   (c) Further R & D work
   (d) Technical feasibility investment needs
   (e) Packaging development
   (f) Revised costing
   If these steps do not indicate any revision of thinking (e.g. complete rejection of the concept at the marketing research stage), it becomes possible to move to the next step.

   Action:
   Marketing
   R & D
   R & D
   Process engineering
   R & D
   Accounts

9. Marketing plan (Project) and project evaluation
   (a) Preparation of outline marketing plan, broad sales, and marketing cost estimates.
   (b) Detailed test market (or alternative) plans.
   (c) Examination of project in relation to corporate strategies.
   (d) Detailed financial appraisal, including sensitivity analysis.

   Action:
   Marketing
   Marketing
   Planning
   Planning and/or Accounts

10. Decision to proceed
    The immediate decision to be made is whether to proceed to test market. However, this will only be made if the expectations for the project still appear to be good. In practice investment decisions may have to be made at this stage, although ideally they would be deferred until stage 12.

    Action:
    Top management

11. Completion of test market: Re-evaluation
    Stage 9 should be repeated using the results of the test market and updating all forecasts.

    Action:
    As appropriate

12. Decision
    Final decision to launch or reject.

    Action:
    Top management

Rules for the appraisal of capital expenditure

Certain of the stages in the system demonstrated above showed the need for appraisal of the project. Some projects may be so simple that complex appraisal techniques are unnecessary: for example, a project to reorganise the flow of paperwork in a company.

Wherever a project involves a significant expenditure of capital, the company should insist that a careful financial appraisal is made. To ensure that results are comparable between areas of the company over time (and to build in a means of monitoring and controlling) the investigation and appraisal should follow defined rules.

Many companies find it useful to set out these rules, including a description of the techniques of evaluation to be used, in a handbook or manual. Techniques of appraisal can be applied manually, but computer assistance is virtually essential if any complicated sensitivity analysis is to be undertaken.

The original landmark book on techniques and methods of appraisal was Merritt and Sykes.[2] Since then the techniques have become almost commonplace, and are described in most books on financial management, managerial economics, and some on operational research. The techniques now come built into spreadsheet programs, and even in some calculators.

Project evaluation is essentially the study of and selection between alternatives. The strategic planning process should have settled the main lines of action and development, and will itself have been a choice between broad alternatives. A project narrows each of these strategic choices to a particular choice of action. Within each project there may be many different ways of achieving the project objectives, each with different profit and cash-flow implications. This can be illustrated by taking as an example a project to market a new product by a company whose factory is operating to capacity. The options which should be examined might include:

1 Withdrawal of existing products of lower profitability to make capacity for the new product
2 Constructing a new factory for the new product
3 Extension of existing factory premises
4 (possibly) Building a new factory on a new site to house both the new and the old activity
5 Having the new product manufactured by someone else.

Within the chosen alternative there is another selection of choices. How big a factory extension? What type of plant and why? Rent or buy premises, plant, and equipment? Which firm of contract manufacturers? The list is apparently endless.

Although many options may be eliminated fairly quickly and without too much difficulty, the company should aim to identify and evaluate as many as appear to be practicable solutions. It is not always the 'obvious' option which provides the best answer to the problem. In any case, for financial reasons, the company may prefer to choose a solution which is not the best: it has already been demonstrated (Chapter 20) that sometimes a project with a quick payback is more expedient than one with higher profits but a slower payback. Companies sometimes have to take the course of action they can afford rather than the one they would prefer.

Mathematical analysis techniques, although essential in the evaluation, are not the only factors which should be considered. The strategic requirements of the company (particularly a need to shift into a different area of risk), the public relations effect of the company's action, or the personnel and morale problems caused by the action, are among the qualitative factors which should be given considerable weighting in the decision process. The answer does not lie only in the numbers but in a combination of numbers and business judgement. In any event, no quantitative analyses of an expected future development can be read as if they were audited statements of past performance.

Each analysis is based on assumptions (which should be defined) and forecasts (which should be explained). Sensitivity analysis will assist in the interpretation of the figures.

The best thing a company can do to ensure that its quantitative appraisal techniques have meaning is to see that they are based on a careful and objective study of the project. Any technique is only as good as the data that go into it, and it is fair to claim that a crude profitability measure (such as percentage Return on Investment) based on well-founded data is of more value than the most sophisticated discount cash flow (DCF) analysis of data which has been thrown together without thought.

Objectivity is easier to achieve in theory than in practice. The responsible line managers must play a part in the appraisal and evaluation of their projects if only to ensure that they have a commitment to their implementation, and so that they can accept the standards defined in the project plan as something for which they are held accountable.

Many managers understandably find it difficult to be objective about their own projects. They are likely to see as obstacles anything that slows down or prevents their projects obtaining the required capital appropriation, and in their eyes no other project in the company could possibly be as important. Already prejudiced about the view of their project, many are not averse to taking a deliberately optimistic view of sales and profits – or to suggest unjustified changes to their forecasts should the first DCF analysis look unfavourable. Pushing through the new project in this way means that they are not wasting their effort which they personally have put into the scheme, and cannot be accused of doing nothing.

Once top management starts to exercise control through the project plan the trouble starts. This is hitting below the belt (after all, every thinking person knows that managers will try to make pessimistic forecasts which they can exceed, if they are to be judged against them). Excuses follow, reasons why the project forecasts just have to be different – the time factor, new developments, someone else's figures were wrong: who has not heard the answers before?

The best way of improving objectivity and avoiding this sort of unprofitable conflict is for all appraisals to be a matter of teamwork between operating management and staff expert. Each has to convince the other of the validity of any conclusions which may be drawn, and the final report is binding on both.

From the outset, the control use of the document must be known, and specific data built into the project to facilitate this. Both sides must understand the methods of analysis: the staff expert because he has to make and interpret the calculations; the line manager because he is bound by the results. A manager's understanding may be at a different level to that of the expert. He or she need not be able to make the calculations, but must understand the principles of the technique used and the meaning of the answers.

This team work and understanding should be backed by an insistence that the financial calculations be supported by written project plans and, where desirable, networks or other ways of ensuring implementation. It must be very clear what action has to be put into effect to achieve the results shown in the project plan. Insistence on this type of plan will often improve the accuracy of the figures on which the analysis is based.

Before discussing the content of project plans, it is worth spending a little time thinking about the team which makes the appraisal. The reasons for a line and staff partnership have already been made clear. The combination helps to ensure objectivity, without moving into an 'ivory tower' situation, where all judgements are made by a remote planning staff. On the management side, input may come from a number of different areas and departments. The staff experts would in most companies come from a special project-appraisal unit. Strong arguments can be made for attaching this to corporate planning, but these are matched by reasons of equal validity which suggest that the accounting side is the right home. The real answer is that it does not matter, the important thing being the calibre of the people employed in the unit, who should be experienced in the methods of appraisal and used to the real problems of working in close association with busy line managers.

Most companies will from time to time have projects which, when implemented, will not be the responsibility of any present operating department. In these cases the company should use the best talents it has available to form the appraisal team, which may mean drawing on a line manager even though he or she may have no ultimate responsibility for the project.

In many ways an outline format for a project plan will resemble an outline for a long-range plan. Information will be required under headings which have many similarities with those in the long-range plan, as it has been argued that project plans are only enlargements of part of the 'photograph' which is the strategic plan, and it would therefore be surprising if there were not similarities.

The company has to decide on the time span over which forecasts will be made and the project evaluated. Although it is possible to make useful analyses of data over a five-year period, it may often be desirable to extend this to at least ten years (the longer the period, the less the impact on DCF calculations of the theoretical treatment of the residual value of fixed assets: in a five-year calculation the need to credit these as a cash inflow in the last year has a much greater distorting effect and can lead to the wrong conclusions). Each company may choose its time span to suit itself, but should try to apply it to all projects to facilitate comparison between different projects.

Only a generalised view can be given of the narrative contents of a project plan since there are obvious differences between projects. An investigation of a project to relocate a factory must result in a report which bears little resemblance to a new product launch. The suggested outline refers to a marketing project with some production investment, and is not meant to be the answer to every project problem which might arise.

Assumptions

Those assumptions specific to the project should be carefully defined. This requirement includes assumptions on which sales forecasts are based.

Objectives

The purpose and aim of each project should be defined before the investigation begins, and preferably should form part of the terms of reference of the project-appraisal team. A well-thought-out statement of purpose can assist the board in understanding the significance of the project when it comes up to them for decision.

The project objective should be cross-referenced to an action listed in the long-range plan. If it is additional to the long-range plan this fact should be clearly stated, with an explanation of the reasons for its omission from this plan.

Marketing

A glance back at the new product system will show some of the steps that have to be taken to arrive at a satisfactory marketing plan. It is rarely adequate for the sales forecasts used in appraisal of the project to be conjured out of the air (although it is unfortunately true that many companies throw their forecasts together in this way, as if the ballpoint pen which writes them were a magic wand). Many projects may require extensive marketing research. The information background, as well as the marketing strategy and tactics, should appear in the project-appraisal report. Exactly what marketing research is carried out, and how much money is invested in investigations, is a matter which each company has to decide on its merits.

A detailed marketing plan will provide cost estimates for advertising and promotion, sales force, and similar items. It will also provide sales forecasts.

For practical reasons it is often useful to have only a summary marketing plan in the main report, all the detail being placed in appendices. Those finally authorising the capital expenditure are unlikely to need to read the detailed plans: they must be satisfied that they exist.

Production

The project should include a full technical assessment of the process of manufacture, the plant recommended, and the specifications of the raw materials required. This analysis leads to forecasts of capital expenditure and of costs of production. Although few would claim that forecasting capital expenditures is easy (especially when considering the need to estimate expenditure in each year of the project), it is child's play when compared to the problem of forecasting production costs. The difficulties of making accurate assessments for new products to be produced on new plant by a new process cannot be overstated: neither can the need to put every effort into making forecasts which are reasonably accurate. To make any sensible cost assessments the project team must have an intimate knowledge of the project and the experience necessary to interpret a manufacturer's rating for a new piece of equipment into what throughout will actually be obtained in practical operation. (It goes without saying that a cost assessment is easier to make when for the expansion of an existing product, of which the company has practical experience.)

Costs in projects should be looked at from a number of ways. A DCF calculation calls for assessment of the *additional* revenues and costs brought by the project, and, of course, ignores depreciation as this is a positive cash flow. (The cash leaves the organisation when the asset is purchased: annual depreciation is an attempt to match those previously incurred costs with the period in which they will produce income.) A more traditional calculation should also be made, so that the company can examine its pricing policies in relation to the full costs (and the market), and so that a study may be made of the effect on variable costs of different levels of production.

Projects may also involve additional problems, such as where to locate the new plant, or which of several plants in various countries to expand. Often the optimum solution of these problems requires extensive operations research help.

Again the detailed technical appraisal should form a subplan with only a summary in the main report.

Personnel

Once again the importance of that other major resource, people, comes into the limelight. Any project will fail if adequate supplies of manpower are unobtainable, and this aspect must be given close attention.

There may also be ways in which the project affects current employees, and these, too, should be studied, the problems identified, and solutions found. A project to close an old plant has an obvious and direct effect on the people working in it. An expansion of a factory may also alter the rhythm of the lives of present employees. There may be promotion opportunities, training needs, and disputes because it is believed that the working conditions in the new unit are better than those in the old, and additional pressures on employee facilities, such as canteens. All these problems are possible: it is equally possible that none will trouble the company. Certainly some considerable time and thought should be devoted to examining the possibilities in the project planning stage.

Risk analysis

It is good management for a company to examine the various risks to which its new project is subject and, through a sensitivity analysis, to assess the possible financial effects of the various risks. Some will spring from the assumptions made about the factors influencing the project (e.g. competitors' reactions to the new product). Others should examine risks connected with political events, fiscal changes, raw material cost changes, technological development, and like factors.

The aim is to understand the project, to be awake to particular dangers, and – if the effect of these is outside the company's limits of acceptable risk – for the board to know this. Risk analysis can lead to the abandonment or modification of apparently profitable projects.

Financial appraisal

All the subsections of the project plan should be designed to yield quantified data which can be analysed to show the full financial effects of the action planned. This means taking account of fixed and working capital as well as profits, and implies the discipline of trying to foresee all the capital expenditures over the period studied. This is so that the shape of the whole project is known, and that top management is not asked to approve investments on a piecemeal basis. There is a great difference between authorising an expenditure of £5m, which completes the project, and allowing a similar investment which is followed by annual calls for more capital in order to 'protect' the original investment. Simple examples are:

1 The project to expand a factory this year, which can only work efficiently if accompanied by an increase in warehousing space next year
2 A major overseas expansion which will not be workable unless head office also expands
3 An acquisition project which requires further capital expenditures to modernise it to 'protect the investment'.

The board may, of course, approve only the first phase of the investment and require the rest to be re-evaluated at a later date.

Another choice to be made is whether all calculations should be taken at constant prices or allow for inflation. It is certainly true that in certain types of project, inflation – the effect of which is subject to forecasting errors – can tend to increase the apparent rates of return. On the other hand, the real world is subject to inflation, and for this reason I should argue – as I have over the total corporate plan – that the figures should try to be as close to reality as possible. In other words they should allow for the effect on costs and income of expected price changes. Again, a strong secondary reason is that monitoring and control, already difficult, become almost impossible if the figures are not at current prices. There is, however, considerable value in converting figures back to a real rate of return after assessing all inflation effects.

Inside the company, standards should be set below which projects would normally be considered unacceptable and automatically rejected. (Exception may be made for specific strategic reasons.) This rate does not have to be the same for all areas of the company: it may be 12 per cent DCF rate for division A and 15 per cent for division B, with further differences for operations in specific countries. Rates may be adjusted in relation to the position of the division in a portfolio analysis matrix (see Chapter 15). Acceptance of a standard does not imply automatic authorisations of anything that exceeds it: it is merely the entrance qualification.

Some companies have schemes which alter the rates of return predicted in a project through a reliability index. This is based on a comparison of the accuracy of performance against forecasts over the past few years. Those managers with a high rating are assumed to be able to continue thus into the future, and their projects are judged likely to be close to the figures calculated in the appraisal. Those whose record has been poor have their calculated returns reduced, which may mean that their projects are rejected.

Although I stated earlier that projects should be assessed on a marginal basis, judgement should not be based on these results alone. The reason for this is that a loss-making operation may still be loss making, even after the addition of a capital expenditure with a very high rate of return. If the project is examined in isolation it may appear to be highly desirable. When looked at on a consolidated basis the conclusion could well be that it is throwing good money after bad. The actual techniques of project appraisal are beyond the scope of this chapter.

Financing

Each report should include recommendations on the financing of the project. For small projects there may be little to say, as they may present no problem. Larger projects may be quite different, and may, as intimated earlier, require the investigation of several options. Certainly at the final decision stage the board must know that the projects it authorised are capable of being implemented.

Monitoring and controlling

Implementation is a keyword in planning. Top management must have a method of monitoring and controlling projects so that it can ensure that the actions are carried out, and that the results are acceptable. No one can control the future, and there are occasions when forecasts just cannot be achieved. If this happens, top management should be aware of it, and the fact that they are aware is often enough to ensure that corrective or compensating actions are implemented, which bring the results closer to the planned position. The idea should be for management to be aware of deviations either before or while they are occurring: knowledge after the event may be of educational value and help the company to avoid such mistakes in future, but it can do nothing to improve the situation.

The capital budgeting system discussed earlier is useful for overall control but insufficient for the management of individual projects. On an individual project basis the company needs to control capital expenditure, financial results, and the physical application of the resources. Top management has to be able to know that a sum authorised for the purchase of a particular piece of equipment has in fact been used for this purpose.

Capital expenditure and the way in which it is used can be controlled through networks and schedules, and a regular system of reporting. For both it is probably advisable to report at least once a month, to compare actuals with the plan, and to project the total position forward so that the new expectation may be compared with the plan. This implies the discipline of breaking down expenditure into the same periods and into very detailed stages. It is no use, for example, waiting for a building to be completed before finding out whether it has cost more than planned: construction must be broken down into timed stages, such as site preparation, foundations, and each subsequent stage completion. In this way a major deviation at an early stage will be known early in the proceedings – as will a failure to meet the timetable. (Delays in time may affect an actual DCF result as much as overexpenditure of capital.) Someone must be held responsible for coordinating and controlling the project and reporting to the board (on an exception basis).

The usage and expenditure of capital are relatively easy to measure (although there should be no illusions that they are simple to control), and it also becomes apparent at a very early stage if there are any major delays in implementation. The new factory which is late being built, or the new product which lags behind its planned introduction date, are factors that become obvious very quickly.

Much more difficult is to measure the overall results against the project appraisal. Every analysis will show how the capital expenditure is to generate profits, and most analyses rightly look on the marginal contribution made by the project. Sometimes the project might be for a completely new division which will be a separate accounting unit: more usually it is to do something which is fully integrated in the activity of an existing accounting unit. Sales of a new product may be easy to identify: the real effect on output and costs of improving one part of the plant may be very hard to isolate, particularly when other factors, unconnected with the expenditure, are also changing.

The basic problems are that it is unlikely that the accounting system would normally make it possible for the company to examine the results of all projects, and that in any case the figures recorded are likely to be on a total rather than a marginal basis. The implication of this is that companies should give thought to how they are going to monitor projects at the time they approve them.

If the company makes it an essential part of its system that its project appraisal unit examines progress against plan and reports on major variances at a certain period after implementation – say the first full year's trading after the initial expenditure has been completed – an incentive is provided to ensure that results are recorded in a way that facilitates comparison with the project.

It would be a mistake to insist that only those results which can be ascertained through the accounting system should be measured. In many circumstances it is useful to go one stage back and measure against non-financial standards. If a machine is supposed to produce a certain number of units per year, this can be measured. If new plant is expected to reduce the number of people employed in a unit by 10 per cent, it becomes possible to see whether, in fact, the number of people is so reduced.

By careful thought at the outset it is possible to express most projects in terms which can be measured later. How long into the future the company continues to monitor performance against individual projects is another matter. For most projects one report is sufficient: beyond that the project should become part of the normal planning and control processes and integrated into the long-range plans and budgets.

References

1 Ansoff, A. and McDonnell, E. *Implanting Strategic Management*, 2nd edn, Prentice Hall, Hemel Hempstead, 1990.
2 Merritt, A. J. and Sykes, A. *The Finance and Analysis of Capital Projects*, Longmans, London, 1963.

CHAPTER 26

From plans to actions

The aim of this chapter is to show that strategic decisions result from a mix of analytical and behavioural drivers (the best results come form a blend of both). In this chapter the analytical and systematic side is explored and the reader will understand the systems and processes which should be established to make it easier to implement a strategy and to measure progress. The chapter is supported by recent research findings on why strategic plans so often are not converted to action.

Action must be the end product of planning, for without action planning is a pointless and empty activity. All the benefits – of mental stimulation, careful analysis, the integration of more facts into decision making, and of the involvement and greater participation of managers in defining the future of the company – become ghostly shadows that lack substance and vanish in the harsh light of reality. No company anywhere in the world has ever added a single penny to its profits from making plans: the rewards are only realised when plans are implemented.

Figure 26.1 looks at the planning process in a different way from the models used so far. What it shows is that there are two aspects to strategic management: analytical and behavioural. So far we have looked deeply into the analytical, although with occasional forays into the behavioural. However, it is clear that when we begin to think about turning plans into action, we have to give attention to both.

Although there has been considerable research into the success and failure of planning systems, much less attention has been given to the implementation of strategy. Bomona[1] suggests that when a company finds that its strategy has not produced the right outcome, it is as likely to assume that the strategy is wrong as it is to recognise that the problem may have been a failure to implement. This often leads to a change in a perfectly appropriate strategy, which is hardly the way to effective strategic management. When considering the implementation of strategy, we should remember that we are really looking at an aspect of something that may be much broader: the implementation of strategic change.

Observers (e.g. Ringbakk[2]) have noted that many managements fail to use their corporate plans. It is surprising that the planning systems that many companies have installed frequently end with a long-range plan, and rely on the annual

Figure 26.1
Two dimensions of
strategic decisions

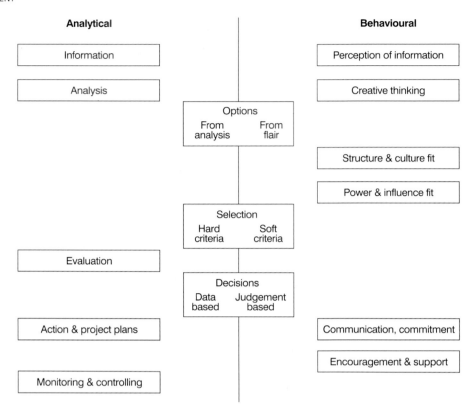

budget, informal measures, and luck to convert those plans into firm actions which really happen.

Alexander[3,4] researched the problems which American companies found when implementing strategy, and later extended this to public agencies. The ranking of the factors in each study is shown in Table 26.1. However, the important fact is not only the problems themselves but the fact that more of them related to issues of culture, structure and human behaviour than to analysis and formal system.

Kaplan[5] found that many organisations have a '... fundamental disconnect between the development and formulation of their strategy and the implementation of that strategy into useful action'. Four major barriers to effective implementation were identified:

● Vision that could not be actioned, because it was not translated into operational terms
● Strategy is not linked to departmental and individual goals (incentives are tied to annual financial performance instead of to long-range strategy: only 21 per cent of executive management and 6 per cent of middle management have objectives that are tied to the strategy)
● Resource allocation is based on short-term budgets and not the strategy (only

Table 26.1 Strategy implementation

Problems		
Problem	Order of importance	Nature
	Pvte firms	Public Orgs	Hard/soft
Implementation took longer than expected	1	1	H or S
Major unexpected problems arose during implementation	2	3	H
Inadequate coordination of implementation activities	3	6	S
Other activities distracted attention	4	4	H
Inadequate capabilities of employees	5	–	S
Inadequate training at lower levels	6	–	S
Uncontrollable external factors	7	2	H
Inadequate leadership and direction at departmental level	8	9	S
Implementation tasks not fully defined	9	–	H
Inadequate information systems to monitor	10	–	H
Employee resistance-incongruent goals	–	5	S
Lack of teamwork by key people	–	9	S
Overall goals not understood by employees	–	7	S

just over a third of organisations have a direct link between the strategy and the budgeting process)

● Control is directed at short-term performance and rarely evaluates progress on long-term objectives.

In this chapter the concentration will be on the systems and procedure issues necessary to implement plans. The more complex, softer issues will held over to the next chapter.

Only when plans have been turned into deeds can a company claim that its planning makes sense. Actions bring results – which may or may not be as forecast – and results give management the ability to exercise a control function and to interpose additional actions, or cancel others if its intentions are being frustrated.

A planning system without a formal method of creating actions is likely to lead to poor-quality planning. If managers cannot be held to account for failing to fulfil their plans, the plans themselves will have less validity, and will become as a knife that has lost its cutting edge, instruments that lack a point. And the chances are that the planning system itself will fail, and all the time and money invested in it will be wasted.

Moving from plans to actions and controlling against results is not an easy task in any company, and may become extremely complex in large or diversified organisations. It is also an area which may meet unusually strong opposition from managers because life for them would be easier if the implementation was left to them on a purely informal basis. It is not possible to conceal dust under the carpet if someone looks under the carpet every day.

The wise planner will incorporate a number of steps into the planning system. These will be intelligent steps, which allow for the consideration of deviations from the plan which should be made in the best interests of the company. No manager should be expected to slavishly follow a plan to the letter, when events or further analysis shows that the action is no longer appropriate. The plan should be the slave of the manager: horrific results may occur when the opposite is true.

Some of the particular steps recommended are 'planning'. Others are very much 'control'. Conceptually it is possible to distinguish between the two (e.g. the views of Anthony[6]). In this instance, as the object is to show how a total approach may be used to bring about the implementation of plans, an overall view is taken of a complete system.

The steps may be divided into seven essential and one optional, which may be used as an alternative to one of the essential steps. They are:

Essential
1 Conversion of long-range plans into short-range tactical plans
2 Assignment of tasks to individuals (standards of performance)
3 Budgetary control
4 Monitoring performance against plan
5 Monitoring assumptions
6 Updating and reconsideration of plans as required
7 Yearly report on planning activity

Optional
Management by objectives.

Tactical plans

No complex organisation can easily implement the usual type of long-range plan because there are many key actions which are not defined in detail and that are not broken down into tasks that can be assigned to a particular person. The long-range plan of the company, covering periods of perhaps up to fifteen years (though more usually five), needs to have elements lifted out of it and examined in depth. Perhaps the only sound way of doing this is to prepare tactical plans which will be further developed into tasks for individuals and linked with the company's budgetary control processes.

There are two main types of tactical plans, each of which fulfils a specific need: short-term operating plans and project plans.

The short-term operating plan is an expansion of part of the long-range plan. The period of time it covers may be chosen on an arbitrary basis, although there is a strong argument for choosing a year: basically 'year 1' of the long-range plan, together with such actions as have to be committed in 'year 1', in order to bring about the results required in subsequent years. A year is a reasonable period of time to handle in detail, and has the added advantage that it can be closely linked with the annual budget. Thus the annual operating plan and the budget become two sides of the same coin, and together provide documentation that is capable of tight management control.

Project plans, on the other hand, have a time span that is dictated by the implementation time of the project itself. It may be shorter than a year (as in certain profit-improvement plans) or may extend considerably beyond this (as in the construction of a new building). For detailed evaluation purposes the financial implications of a project plan may be studied for much further ahead than the long-range plan itself: for control and implementation the emphasis is on the short period. The plans cover what their title suggests – projects – which may be of any nature whatsoever: installation of a computer, construction of a building, marketing of a new product, development of a new technology. Networks are of particular value in controlling and implementing project plans. These particular tactical plans were discussed in detail in the previous chapter.

The annual operating plans are organised around functional areas (whereas the project plans may – and usually will – involve many different functions). Each operating plan will also embrace, perhaps only by cross-referencing, the projects in which the functional area has an interest.

Annual operating plans should always be seen in context of the longer period. They are not isolated documents and should be fully integrated into the process which leads to the production of the company's longer-range plans. Among the most important constraints on the preparation of the annual operating plans is that they must translate to the immediate future the strategies of the longer term: they should never be used as a means of introducing additional strategies unless the long-range plan is also modified at the same time.

There should be no surprises in the annual plan: there may, nevertheless, be a considerable amount of detailed work. Greatest effectiveness is reached when the annual operating plan is seen as the raw material of the budget: in this way the budget becomes closely integrated with the long-range plan, reflects the intentions of that plan. More will be said on this later in this chapter.

For corporate control purposes, annual operating plans should be prepared for each area where there is a long-range operating plan. What these areas are is something which comes from the shape and size of the company itself, but which may in the simplest terms be considered as the main functional areas of the company. In most companies this will be an oversimplification, but it requires little imagination to consider the various possibilities – and in any case some of these have been discussed in previous chapters.

Long-range operating plans are best prepared with a wide degree of management participation. The annual operating plans offer an opportunity of gaining even more participation through the involvement of numerous levels of management. The part of a regional sales manager may be used as an example to illustrate the different approaches. A manager at this level is unlikely to play any part in writing a long-range plan, although he or she may contribute to the plan of the division through group discussion. Little benefit may be obtained from demanding a five- or ten-year plan from a manager in this position in the organisation chart. On the other hand, it may be of considerable value to ask such a manager to define a planned course of action for the forthcoming year, even though the plan may consist of only one or two pages.

In an article[7] I described how Fyffes Group Ltd had extended their annual operating plans to cover their fifty branch managers. The existence of a plan of action for each branch (a branch had responsibilities for banana ripening, local purchasing, physical distribution, sales, certain marketing decisions, and cash collection) proved to be a sound way of translating the divisional long-range operating plan into an effective tool of management.

Lower-level plans need never be seen beyond divisional management, and are certainly not the type of document which should go through to corporate headquarters and the chief executive. The corporate planner will have little direct interest in them except to ensure that they are prepared, or if giving specific help to a divisional manager to improve planning right down the line.

Plans at this level must be prepared within the context of very detailed policy guidelines and targets issued by the divisional manager, and drawn from divisional plans. In this way it is possible to be sure that the plans will be compatible with the agreed long-range plan for the division. In effect this is delegating part of the planning tasks to subordinates in much the same way as he or she has received part of the chief executive's task. What the divisional manager receives from the more junior managers is a detailed programme for the performance of certain elements of the overall plan: these submissions have a parallel with his or her own submissions to the chief executive which are within the framework of the strategic plan. As in the day-to-day function of management, there are many more constraints at the lower levels, and the lower the level, the more constraints are imposed.

Annual operating plans of this type give the divisional manager a tool for controlling development and progress, assist in motivating managers, and help to spread the formal approach to planning throughout the organisation. This may stimulate new ideas, and certainly will ensure that junior managers become fully aware of corporate policy, as it affects the division, because this has to be defined before they can plan their contribution. Tasks and actions which are identified and accepted by junior managers have more chance of being fulfilled. Managers at the lower levels are individualists, just as much as their seniors, and the more they exercise their own individualistic creativity, the more satisfied they are likely to be.

The annual operating plans which are used at the corporate level are those of the units or areas which contributed to the long-range plan. There should be an annual plan for each long-range operating plan. Top management should take a careful interest in these documents because they show how the strategies detailed in the long-range plan are to be carried out.

It makes sense for the annual plans to cover the same general headings used in the long-range plan but treating the subject in a different way. The object is not to repeat what has already been said but to change the broad statements of policy and intent into an itemised programme for action.

The long-range marketing plan would discuss the place of a particular product in the marketing plan, its positioning in the market, the general image of the product, and the way it is to change. The annual plan, within this broad strategy, gets down to detail and should become a blueprint for the year's activity, capable of implementation even if the managers concerned leave the company for any reason. Advertising will be looked at in terms of detailed campaigns, media schedules, and supporting promotional activity.

The quality of annual operating plans can be improved by careful attention to procedure. A comprehensive timetable should be issued by the planner, so that all understand the part they have to play and the date by which their contributions must be received. (The timetable should be related to that for the annual budget in view of the close association of this with the operating plan.) It is frequently wise for the instruction to begin preparing the annual operating plan to go out under the signature of the chief executive, who may add any additional policy guidelines and planning assumptions which should be taken into account. For the most part, these should come from the long-range plans.

Each operating plan should be scrutinised by the planner, to check that it is compatible with the long-range plan. It should be reviewed by top management at the same time as the budget.

Assignment of tasks to individuals

One of the most important components of any annual operating plan is the list of goals and personal standards of performance (see Chapter 13). These give the company the ability to measure performance against the plan.

The financial effects of the annual plan will be reflected in the budget and controlled through the time-proven processes of budgetary control. This by itself will not ensure that the company is working to its plan, since budgets can be made to come right for the wrong reasons, and many essential actions cannot be measured through the budget.

Quantified goals and the assignment of tasks to particular people provide the company with a means of controlling all the aspects of the plan: a point which will be discussed in more detail later.

One of the tasks of the planner in the scrutiny of the annual operating plan should be to ensure that managers have converted all generalised statements of strategy into specific action steps. It is also necessary to ensure that actions which must be committed next year in order to make possible the plan for future years are also correctly identified and listed.

In a practical situation it is very easy for key actions essential to the long-range plan to be 'lost', and for the company not to discover this until too late. The administrative task involved in preventing this is complex – but not difficult – and must be rated as an important part of the corporate planning process.

All personal standards of performance should be grouped by organisational responsibilities so that control can be exercised through normal management reporting lines. It also follows that the person who is expected to perform the task must be properly informed about it: an obvious requirement but one that is often overlooked.

Budgetary control

The process of budgeting and budgetary control will be familiar to every reader of this book and needs no description. What is less well known is the relationship of the budget with the long-range planning procedures of the company. Mention has already been made in this chapter of this link, and it is now time to explore it in greater detail.

It is true to say that many managers confuse planning and budgeting. There are also many who consider that ruling a few more columns and extending a budget for five years ahead turns it into a plan. Yet although planning and budgeting are different, and are carried out for separate purposes, they have a close relationship.

I like to think of the annual budget as the quantification in financial terms of the annual operating plan, which itself derives – as we have seen – from the long-range plans. In this way the budget defines the expected effects of a planned course of action, tied in with longer-term strategies, and expected to achieve certain profit targets.

The long-range plan provides a standard for judgement of the budget: for strategic actions through the annual operating plan and, equally important, the profit targets which the budget should achieve. In the long-range plan the company identified the results that each major unit should achieve.

A budget that has no relationship with any long-term plan tends to be a shallow document. The actions allowed for may, or may not, be in the long-term interests of the company. Similarly, it is more difficult to be sure that the results of the budget are what the company ought to be aiming at.

The annual budget goes into much more detail than the long-range plan – it has to, as it is a control document and must provide control information for many responsibility centres split down to all meaningful items of expense and income. Postage may be a very important item in the budget but of no interest as an isolated expenditure in the long-range plan. Because of this difference of detail, and also because there is a time lag between the completion of the long-range plan and the commencement of the budget, there are likely to be some differences in the figures. I believe this is inevitable.

However, the availability of the narrative description of the budget (annual operating plan) and the predetermined profit targets give top management sound criteria against which the budget can be compared. Areas of shortfall can be identified, and it is possible for annual operating plans and budgets to be referred back if they are inadequate. As divisional managers have already committed themselves in a general way to the long-term strategies and profit objectives, it is not unfair to expect them to sort out any differences.

At this point the annual operating plan and budget should be read together. Any significant change in budget should cause a re-examination of the annual plan, which in turn may put a question mark against a particular long-term strategy. Eventually budget, annual operating plans, and long-range plans should be reconciled.

The budget is, of course, broken down into time periods. Monitoring results against budget, considering the effects of these on the chances of hitting targets, and identifying action areas to bring a straying company back on course are well-known aspects of a budgetary control procedure. At any reporting period during the year the company should have a latest estimate of expected results.

The budget, from the beginning of the new year, becomes a way in which information on the results of long-term strategies begins to come back to top management. It provides an early warning system to allow management to begin to re-examine the validity of its strategies. Some discretion is needed in relating short-term results to long-term strategies, and deviations either way do not necessarily mean that the plan is wrong. On the other hand, it is often possible to see the validity of a new strategy at a very early stage.

There may be three main reasons for a deviation between budget and results – wrong implementation, wrong assumption, or an erroneous expectation of results (i.e. a wrong forecast). None of these necessarily mean that the plan is wrong: for example, a deviation from the expected sales because of abnormal weather conditions will rarely be a reason for altering all strategies. The combination of planning and budgeting makes it easier to identify which of the three causes of deviation actually applies (they may occur in combination), thus making it easier for management to decide what needs to be done.

Monitoring performance

The goals and standards of performance (including tasks which have to be completed) set during the process of preparing the annual operating plan are there for a purpose. Because they are defined and assigned they can be monitored. The planner should consider a way of doing this when he or she designs the company's planning procedure.

Before studying ways in which this might be done it is worth thinking about the reasons for monitoring. Certainly it is not to ensure that all planned actions are carried out regardless of their present validity. Earlier in this chapter it was stated that the plan should be the slave of the manager, and not the other way round. In the first century BC Pubilius Syrius stated: 'It is a bad plan that admits to no modification.' The words are just as true today.

The fact that it may be desirable to change a planned course of action is not a licence for neglect. Managers are expected to fulfil all plans which are still appropriate and to substitute modified plans where plans are inappropriate. The important element is deliberate decision and evaluation and understanding of the implications of the change: it is not action by default. It is not an offence to change, but it is an offence for managers not to know that they have changed.

There are some actions which should be referred back to the chief executive before a final decision is taken. No company can have a situation where a major strategic action is changed because an individual manager prefers something different. But most of the tasks and performance standards measure aspects of the plans which lie within the competence and responsibility of the manager implementing them.

Monitoring these standards should give top management an opportunity to see the effect on the overall plan of failure and changes. A situation where actions rarely proceed according to plan may indicate lack of planning ability or fast-changing circumstances which are difficult to forecast. Lack of attention to plans in the first place is something that can be improved in time – provided the lesson is learned. Fast-changing circumstances may suggest that more attention should be given to contingency plans or that an attempt should be made to improve forecasting ability.

However good the company is at planning, events will change from time to time. The wise planner will accept this, and will devote efforts to ensuring that implementation changes are made responsibly and with intelligence. The planner will also identify the key goals and standards of performance. Many can be altered without any major effect on the company's overall strategic plan, particularly where an alternative action is substituted. A few are fundamental, and the planner must be aware of these.

The planner has a number of factors to consider when designing a monitoring procedure:

1 How far is it possible to use organs for review and discussion which already exist in the company (e.g., committees)?
2 How far can the process of monitoring be delegated to line management?
3 Whether reporting should be on a total or exception basis
4 The frequency of the monitoring procedure
5 Whether the feedback procedure should be formal or informal, written, or verbal
6 How far the management information system has to be changed so that it regularly provides data needed to measure progress.

One simple procedure is to list all the objectives – used here in the sense of personal standards of performance – classified by organisational units and completion dates. A series of preplanned review meetings is established and the lists of objectives arranged so that all are reviewed on the meeting following the due date of completion. The lists become the basic agenda for the meeting, while additional columns on these lists can be filled in to provide the minutes.

Figure 26.2 provides an example of the format. If the objective has been achieved no further time need be spent on it (if the financial results turn out other than as forecast they will be picked up through the budgetary control system).

		Agenda				Minutes			
						If not achieved, complete this section			
Date due	Person responsible	Description of objective	Source of objective	If achieved tick		Actual results attained	Reason for failure	Implications of failure	Action taken

Figure 26.2
Example of a review
sheet for personal
standards of
performance

Where it has not been achieved it becomes necessary for the responsible manager to account for his actions, state why he has failed, and assess the implications of failure. The review meeting may assist in examining the implications and helping the manager to define what should now be done.

Any actions which are rescheduled are entered on to the appropriate agenda sheet for control at a future meeting. Careful organisation of the meetings can mean that they can be graded by seniority, so that each manager is effectively reporting upwards through the review meeting. It is also possible to add other key objectives which might be set during the course of the year, and to monitor these at the same time.

Heads of subsidiaries or major divisions report to the corporate management on an exception basis. They control their areas of responsibility through the system, and are in turn accountable to a higher level for achieving what their tactical plans and budget have promised.

This procedure works very well. In companies which already have a committee system it has the advantage of considerably reducing the length of the meeting, simplifying the minutes, and focusing attention on the important issues. It is a flexible system that can easily be fitted into any organisational need. It provides an opportunity for all managers who are affected by a failure in implementation to be aware of this. The system works mainly on an exception basis. Above all, it is simple to administer, requires little paperwork, yet ensures that nothing is neglected or allowed to go by default. Responsibility is firmly pinned to a particular individual from start to finish.

An alternative procedure is for the planner to abstract the list of items on a regular basis and for a letter to be sent to the relevant operating managers asking them to report on progress and explain the failures. Items which are known to have been implemented may be excluded. In addition to the regular reporting, a check should be kept on items of major significance on an *ad hoc* basis. If this system is used it is often valuable for the letters to be signed by the chief executive, thus stressing that it is top management which is most concerned with the plan's progress and making managers realise that it is the boss – and not the planner – who is going to be upset by a failure.

This procedure is more cumbersome than the first, and makes it harder to introduce exception reporting. It also raises the possibility that managers may feel that the planner is playing an unfortunate disciplinary role: something which they might resent. Certainly the planner cannot disguise the part played in the control procedure. Much ill feeling can be avoided if the planner sets out to be helpful to managers, reminding them of actions which he or she knows have been overlooked so that they have an opportunity to perform or explain the failure before they receive the letter from the top.

In any organisation there may be managers who consistently fail to implement. It is up to the chief executive to deal with them – not the planner. Failure to enforce some of the discipline will endanger all the company's planning effort. If no one appears to really care about implementation, the whole process of monitoring becomes an empty administrative exercise, and the plans themselves are debased.

The monitoring of capital expenditure appraisals, another important aspect of the control system, was discussed in the previous chapter.

Monitoring assumptions

The fact that all plans are based on assumptions, and the importance of these in trying to bring the company to terms with its environment, are things which have been stressed several times in this book. One important aspect of the control of plans is to continue to study and assess environmental trends so that the company may know whether its assumptions are still correct. If there are fundamental changes they may suggest that the plan should be reconsidered or altered. A computer model of the company can be of considerable help in examining the effect of these changes.

A company which is planning well will have contingency plans ready to implement in the event of a failure of key assumptions. Any company, including those who have neglected the preparation of contingency plans, should ensure that it becomes aware of major changes.

The organisation of a system to monitor assumptions need be little more than an extension of the company's continuous assessment of the environment. This may be carried out in a central planning department by the company's economic section or through its market research unit. The exact assignment of duties must depend on the company itself: the principle of this aspect of control is the same for every company.

Updating and reconsideration of plans as required

Most companies are likely to prepare their long-range plans on a rolling basis with the opportunity to review annually. There are companies which expect a five-year plan to last them five years without amendment, but they are in the minority and certainly will not be following the advice of this book.

The need for flexible planning has also been stressed frequently, as has the fact that plans may have to be changed from time to time. Even the annual revision of strategies is an arbitrarily chosen period of time, and the events which bring the need for a change in plan cannot be guaranteed to occur at these chosen intervals. Something major is just as likely to happen on the day of publication.

When a fundamental change occurs it may be necessary to update a part or all of the plan outside of the normal planning cycle – a task made easier where the company has contingency plans and/or a computer-based corporate model. Recognition of the need to amend the long-range plan is not an indication of failure by the planner: indeed, it is possible to claim it is a success. The ability to identify something that is going wrong before it happens and the flexibility to react speedily to external influences are factors which all chief executives should seek in their approach to planning. There can be no doubt that a certain amount of replanning may be essential between planning cycles, nor is there likely to be much difficulty (assuming an effective control system) in identifying the circumstances when this is advisable.

Some planners recommend a regular updating of the financial results of the long-range plan rather than the *ad hoc* response to circumstances outlined above. A regular revision of all expected results for the whole of the period of the long-range plan is made as a matter of routine at quarterly or six-month intervals, under the theory that such a revision forces managers to correct for the multitude of developments which might otherwise have been ignored until the start of the next planning cycle, and at the same time forces the managers to see their plans as a dynamic document which they have to use. The concept is that such measures will provide top management with a clear idea of what the company is to achieve over the five-year period (or whatever time span is used in the company's plan) rather like the 'latest forecast' column which may be compared with the annual budget under a normal control system.

The great danger is that such a system can easily become empty, mechanistic, and bureaucratic. Usually nobody takes any notice of the data generated (often this is the fate it deserves), and there is a great danger that the company will slip into a system of extended budgeting rather than real planning. It is also very difficult for participants to be fully objective, and the expected results of the next few years tend to be unduly influenced by yesterday's sale, last week's strike, or the indigestion which started after lunch. The theoretical benefit of constant updating is that the manager, through being kept aware of his or her long-range plan, will make all decisions against the longer-term strategy. The practical result is, at best, usually a meaningless chore and, at worst, can be dangerous for the company. Where the complete processes of preparing a long-range plan demand several days thinking time from a manager, much evaluation, and spirited discussion, the partial regular revision is likely to be a ten-minute exercise.

Yearly report on planning activity

The combination of the measures outlined so far will provide a motive force to drive the company to implement its plans. There is yet another step which should be taken as a means of measuring progress and as a tool to assist in the overall improvement of the company's planning ability. This is an annual progress report by the planner to the chief executive (to which specific managers may be invited to contribute) which should include:

1 A comparison of progress of the company against the long-range plans, including a note of revisions to plan which may have been made from time to time
2 An analysis of the progress of the past year, its successes and failures and the reasons for variances
3 The implications of the past year on future plans
4 Ways in which the planning procedures may be improved.

Naturally the first item suggested above will have little value in the first year, but will build up into a useful dossier of planned results and performance. Much can be learned from this about the company's planning and forecasting ability.

The second section is not intended to be a repetition of the final report of results against budget, as there is little sense in duplicating work that has already been done. The planning report should analyse performance against all key goals and concentrate on the reasons for deviations: failure by managers to fulfil key tasks, overambitious targets, pessimistic forecasting, and lack of attention to assumptions. There may be some minor overlaps with the budget reports but basically the planner is seeking to draw planning lessons for the company so that it is possible to help managers to improve their planning and so that it is easier to move to the next stage of assessing the implications of the past year on future plans. Needless to say, the report is easier to write when things have gone well than when the company has had a bad year.

One of the most difficult problems is to assess how far a short-term reversal justifies a revision of strategy. Because so much depends on current profits – including the survival of the top management team – a shortfall creates an emotionally charged atmosphere with the danger that managers will deduce a trend from what has happened, haphazardly change long-term plans, and proceed to short-term cost-reduction methods which are not always in the company's interests. It may not be an easy situation, but it is always one which an objective analysis by the planner can help the company to act sensibly.

Logically there is no reason why any company should not encounter bad years from time to time. Acceptance of the logic does not, unfortunately, make the problem much easier when it actually occurs.

The planner should be just as objective in the assessments when the company has had a good year. Often this is accompanied by a wave of optimism which has as little foundation, in fact, as the pessimism which surrounds a bad year.

At any time the planner should be thinking of ways of improving the planning procedures, through changes to the system, the introduction of refinements, or the use of new techniques. The planner's annual report should, against the background of the company's ability to plan, suggest actions that should be taken to do the job better. Planning is a dynamic process, and the company can easily outgrow its methods if it is not careful.

The planner's report should, although submitted to the chief executive, be designed for use by the company. It should be made available for all senior managers, and opportunity should be created for discussion on its assessments and recommendations.

It has to be accepted that a report of this nature may sometimes be critical of certain managers or divisions. While adverse criticism is rarely enjoyed by those singled out for mention, it is sometimes essential for progress. In this case the planner should take the manager concerned into his or her confidence before submitting the report, discuss the matter fully, and provide the opportunity for the manager to make any comments. Relations between managers and planner are likely to be better when everything is open than if there is a suspicion that any points made about them are done behind their backs. In any case, the planner in this report should concentrate on the results and should make no comments about abilities or skills.

The combination of all seven of the stages discussed in this chapter can make a very important contribution to the company's ability to implement and use its plans, to be more aware of what is happening to it, and to generally improve its planning expertise. My own experience suggests that together the stages make a powerful tool which is adequate for most companies: a tool which has sufficient flexibility to allow for modification to suit the needs of individual companies.

There is another approach which can replace some of the methods suggested here, and which is used effectively by many organisations: management by objectives.

Management by objectives (MBO)

Much has been written on MBO – one of the most useful books is that of Humble[8] – and the brief résumé given here cannot do full justice to the subject. However, it can identify the main elements of MBO to show how these can fit into a total corporate planning process.

MBO really starts where the process of defining corporate and divisional objectives finishes (see Chapter 13). There have been instances of MBO being successfully introduced into companies which do not have any defined objectives or formal approach to planning, but this is not the recommendation of most of those who developed the system.

One of the first steps is what Humble[8] calls a key results analysis. This is an assessment worked out between each manager and his or her superior, identifying the key results which the manager must achieve to be successful in the job. From these are quantified standards of performance, a method of measuring results and identification of problems which have to be overcome.

Perhaps the biggest difference between this and the systems already described in this book is that MBO deals with all aspects of a manager's job, and can be used right down the organisation to managers whose direct influence on the implementation of the plan may be hard to see. The method described earlier in this chapter is designed to deal only with actions which arise out of the corporate plans, and is therefore applied only to managers whose link with those plans can be clearly identified. MBO is intended to be much more comprehensive than the other method: and being more comprehensive means that it takes much more effort to apply. Most practitioners recommend the appointment of MBO advisers to install and maintain the process.

Figure 26.3 provides an example of one key task for each of three functions. Exponents of MBO normally expect to identify about eight tasks, or key result areas, for each manager.

The manager is invited to set out in the key results analysis his or her own ideas for improving personal effectiveness and that of the company. These improvement plans are, in conjunction with the key tasks and control requirements, discussed between the manager and his or her superior, and firm improvement plans drawn up from them.

Control information goes to both the manager and his superior at frequent intervals, and is discussed between them. The idea is that such discussion will identify individual strengths and weaknesses, and areas where further training should be given. Figure 26.4 shows the link between MBO and the personal development of individual managers.

The complete process of MBO is shown in Figure 26.5 which illustrates the relationship of individual performance with that of the unit in which the manager works.

The strength of MBO is that it is a participatory process in which the manager and his or her superior are both fully involved. Because it is a process which demands joint participation it can fail if senior managers do not fully contribute to it. It also leads to a much greater understanding by each manager of what his superior expects from him, what the important elements of his job really are, and how far he needs to change in order to be able to perform them in a satisfactory manner. The key idea is obtaining more enthusiasm and better motivation in a controlled atmosphere which descends directly from the corporate objectives and plans.

Its weakness is that it is not something to be entered into lightly, and demands a great deal of senior management attention. A simpler method of controlling plans may be made fully effective in a much faster time: but this is all it will do. It will not, like MBO, embrace all managers, nor will it be connected with training and other aspects of personal planning.

Figure 26.3
Key results analysis. (Reproduced by courtesy of Urwick Orr & Partners Ltd.) This analysis includes a summary of the *Main Purpose of Job; Position in Organisation; Scope of Job; Personal Activities;* and *Limits of Authority.* The heart of the analysis is the *Key Tasks* section

Key task	Performance standard		Control data	Suggestions for improvement
E.g. of a key task for a Production Manager Use of resources. To ensure that the most effective use is made of available resources	Labour: When average waiting time never exceeds 0.5% in any month. When ratio of direct to indirect labour does not exceed 4.0. When labour turnover, including staff, does not exceed 15% p.a. When pay performance is 95%.		Returns from wages office. Quarterly check on personnel records. Quarterly check on personnel records. Returns from wages office	
	Machines: Average machine utilisation never falls below 75%. No machine is utilised for less than 85% of its time.		No control information available at present. No control information available at present.	This information must be produced.
	Floor space: When not less than 90% of available factory floor area is utilised for production.		Annual check on floor area by works engineer.	
	Stocks: When the money utilised in providing stocks never exceeds the specified figure.		Monthly accounts.	These figures are based only on past experience; suggest a project be carried out to determine optimum figures
E.g. of a key task for an Area Sales Manager To establish with each customer the stock levels he should hold so that delivery times can be kept economic with minimum risk of stock-out.	Following delivery times are acceptable to customers and met: 		90% Orders within	97% Orders within
Cat. A	7 days	14 days
Cat. B	4 days	7 days
Sp. Accts.	7 days	14 days			(1) Outstanding orders analysis (2) Customer complaints	If we are to meet even these generous delivery times reliably, either depot stocks of some items will have to be increased or lead times from the factory reduced. I suggest an OR investigation of optimum stock levels.
E.g. of a key task for a Research Manager To recognise competitors' technological strategy and to advise M.D. when objectives should be modified.	Company's marketing and operating programmes never require "crash" changes due to failure to recognise competitors' technological strategy.		No record needed. Any such occurrence will be recognised by all.	Our methods of collecting news of competitors' technological strategy need improving. (See improvement plan for first half of 1966.)

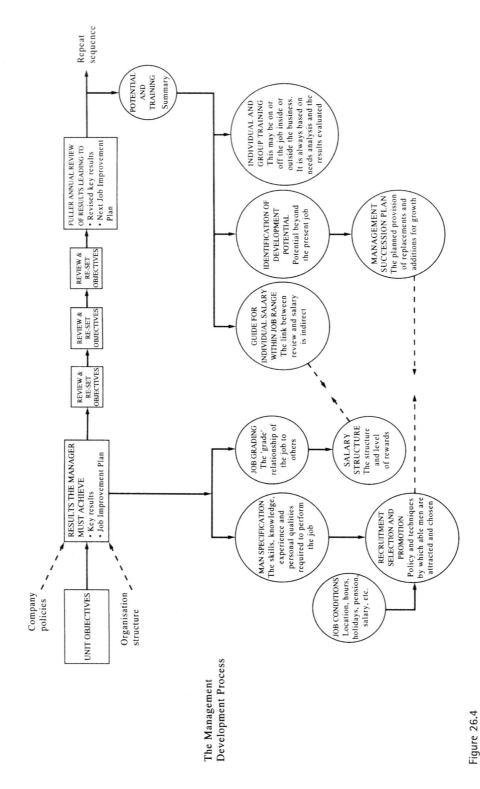

The Management
Development Process

Figure 26.4
Improving management performance. (Reproduced by courtesy of Urwick Orr & Partners Ltd)

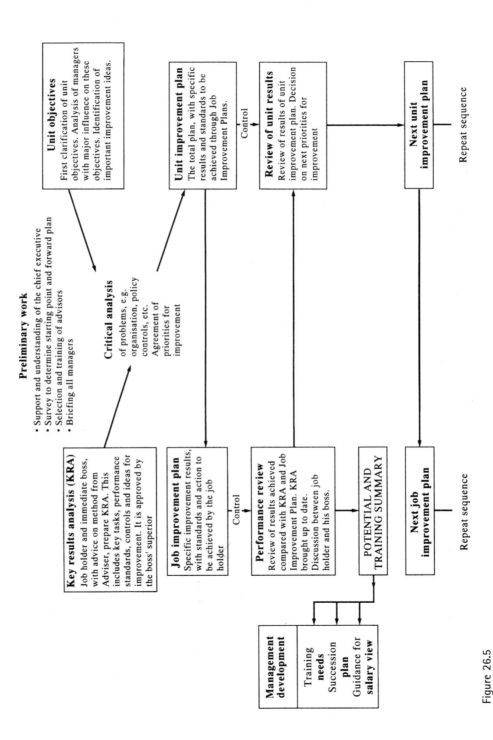

Preliminary work
- Support and understanding of the chief executive
- Survey to determine starting point and forward plan
- Selection and training of advisors
- Briefing all managers

Unit objectives
First clarification of unit objectives. Analysis of managers with major influence on these objectives. Identification of important improvement ideas.

Critical analysis
of problems, e.g. organisation, policy controls, etc. Agreement of priorities for improvement

Key results analysis (KRA)
Job holder and immediate boss, with advice on method from Adviser, prepare KRA. This includes key tasks, performance standards, controls and ideas for improvement. It is approved by the boss' superior

Unit improvement plan
The total plan, with specific results and standards to be achieved through Job Improvement Plans.

Job improvement plan
Specific improvement results, with standards and action to be achieved by the job holder

Control

Performance review
Review of results achieved compared with KRA and Job Improvement Plan. KRA brought up to date. Discussion between job holder and his boss.

Review of unit results
Review of results of unit improvement plan. Decision on next priorities for improvement

Control

POTENTIAL AND TRAINING SUMMARY

Management development
Training needs
Succession plan
Guidance for salary view

Next job improvement plan

Repeat sequence

Next unit improvement plan

Repeat sequence

Figure 26.5
Typical launching sequence for MBO. (Reproduced by courtesy of Urwick Orr & Partners Ltd)

The company has to decide for itself which of the methods of control it will apply. The company which puts in no control mechanism will find it very difficult to bridge that wide gulf between planning and action.

MBO has many behavioural aspects, and many consider that it has been overtaken by more recent concepts of empowerment.

References

1 Bomona, T. V. 'Making Your Marketing Strategy Work', *Harvard Business Review*, March/April 1984.
2 Ringbakk, K. A. 'Why Planning Fails', *European Business*, Spring 1971.
3 Alexander, L. D. 'Successfully Implementing Strategic Decisions', *Long Range Planning*, Vol. 18, No. 3, 1985.
4 Alexander, L. D. 'Strategy Implementation: Nature of the Problem', in Hussey, D. E. (ed.), *International Review of Strategic Management*, Vol. 2, No. 1, Wiley, Chichester, 1991.
5 Kaplan, R. *Building a Management System to Implement Your Strategy: Strategic Management Survey: Summary of Findings and Conclusions*, Renaissance Solutions, London, 1995.
6 Anthony, R. N. *Planning and Control Systems: A Framework for Analysis*, Harvard University Press, Cambridge, MA, 1965.
7 Hussey, D. E. 'Corporate Planning at Fyffes Group', *Long Range Planning*, September 1969.
8 Humble, J. W. *Improving Business Results*, McGraw-Hill, New York, 1967.

CHAPTER 27

Management of change

This chapter targets the behavioural issues in implementation, and aims to provide an introduction to change management and one view of change leadership. It gives practical guidance on applying the approach to change management discussed. It is not an objective of the chapter to provide a summary of every viable approach to change management and leadership.

In the previous chapter we looked at some of the behavioural issues in implementing plans, but concentrated mainly on the systems rather than the people. Change is going on all the time, and not always as the result of a predetermined strategy, which is why I have given a somewhat broader title to this chapter. However, the subject matter is critical to the successful implementation of strategic decisions.

Figure 27.1 shows a typical change sequence. Something triggers off a need for change. It may be the result of a considered strategy, or of a reaction to something that happens outside of the business. Whatever it is, change is unlikely to happen until someone has recognised the trigger event. Since we live in the real world, it is worth stressing that the trigger event is often not a major change in circumstances but the arrival of a new chief executive whose perception is different from that of his or her predecessors. We saw this in the Lloyds Bank example in Chapter 12, where the trigger was not a new strategy but realisation that looking at issues in a different way would lead to innumerable new strategies. We saw it in Chapter 10, where one of the danger points in competitor analysis is when there is a change of top management. Empirically we see it in examples of major transformational change, such as British Petroleum, GE, and British Telecom. In each of these companies, change is associated with a particular chief executive, who recognised triggers that others might have missed.

A trigger event can take place, but will only cause change if the need is seen. Thus many organisations miss the signals. Ansoff might well argue that companies which are managing in a style inappropriate to their level of environmental turbulence would probably miss the signals, or react in an inappropriate way (see Ansoff and McDonnell[1]).

Chapter 3 discussed the idea of leadership and vision, and as we will see these are important ingredients in the management of change. In Figure 27.1 the

Figure 27.1
Typical change
sequence

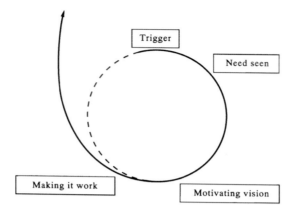

reminder is that unless the perceived need is translated into a new vision of what has to be done, change is unlikely to occur. The really hard work starts in the next box on the diagram, making it work. The future course of the company depends on how well each stage of this model is carried out. In the diagram, the thick line symbolises success and movement to a new and appropriate future. The dotted line implies that although much energy is expended, nothing much happens, and the company ends up in the same place from which it started. Not shown, but also possible is the end state being considerably worse than the present, either because the wrong strategy is implemented, or the right strategy is not implemented.

Different circumstances of change

Before proceeding further, we should consider a variety of different change circumstances. My thinking here owes a considerable debt to Stace and Dunphy,[2] who pointed out that there are both different types of change, and different change strategies that can be successful.

Figure 27.2 uses some of their ideas. It draws attention to two fundamentally different types of change: incremental which moves in a series of small steps, some of which may be hardly noticeable, and transformational where the change may be vast and fundamental. This is related to the situation in the company, the degree of support for the change from the key players. Stace and Dunphy provide a spectrum of styles:

- Collaborative
- Consultative
- Directive
- Coercive.

Box A shows incremental change where there is a high degree of support from the key people. The change may be known, as in a marketing plan which involves

Figure 27.2
Types of change
and the degree of
support for change.
Based on the ideas
of Stace and
Dunphy[2]

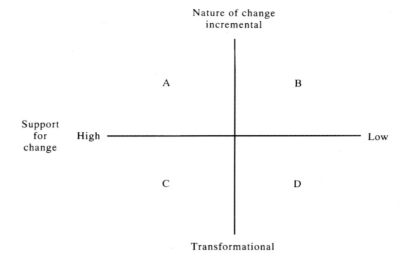

the launch of a new related product, or it may be unknown in the sense that the aims are clear, but empowered teams or individuals are determining the actions that are to be implemented, as in a continuous improvement process. Under the circumstances of box A, the most appropriate style is likely to be collaborative or consultative. This does not mean that leadership is unnecessary (see Chapter 3), but that there is likely to be minimal resistance to, and possibly even enthusiasm for, change. Because the gap between where the organisation is now and the next step is not too vast, there may be little fear of the effects of change. Continuous improvement and total quality management processes are an excellent example of collaborative incremental change in action. Teams are empowered, but coordinated, and ideally are drawn from across the organisation to avoid a 'functional chimney' view. The philosophy under which the teams work is shared, and there is continuous measurement of progress. Under this concept the amount of change attained may be very great, although each action is one step on a journey without end. The continuous improvement concept will only work when there is support through the organisation, widespread involvement at all levels, and adequate training of everyone who is touched by the process. It also requires much top management time.

In box B there is an incremental change without the support of the key people. The assessment here is whether support can be gained in a reasonable time, in which case a consultative approach could be appropriate, or whether to use directive means which may involve making people take certain actions. A mix of both is possible. Directive methods do not necessarily imply that commitment by those involved is not achievable. Although attitudes to a large degree affect behaviour, and logic suggests that the right thing to do to build commitment is to change attitudes first, the evidence is that in many situations a change of behaviour can bring about a change in attitudes. In fact there are situations when behaviour is not in line with an attitude: for example a number of smokers may now hold an attitude that smoking is not a good thing, but they may still smoke.

Box C moves to transformational change. Stace and Dunphy use the term charismatic change to describe this box. Support may be there because of the charisma of the person leading the change, and a willingness by all to accept that the vision painted of the new future is the right one, because of faith in the qualities of the leader, or it may be because the logic of the situation is apparent: the company faces insolvency unless urgent action is taken. Collaborative or consultative styles would be appropriate here, provided there is enough time to apply them. The greater the shared perception of urgency, the more likely are people to be willing to follow a directive style without this causing any negative effects.

Transformational change which implies hard actions, like restructuring an entire business, closing down loss-making divisions, or expanding into a new geographical area is usually easier for people to relate to, even if they are numbered among the losers, than accompanying changes in culture. It is hard to see how culture can be related to the new vision, without some flexing of styles between directive and consultative. Scandinavian Airlines went through a major change of strategy and culture during the 1980s, moving from a system driven to an empowered, customer responsive organisation. Much of the change was achieved through communication and consultative methods. At times the style was much more directive, as for example when key managers were asked to leave and replaced by others with empathy for the change.

Box D represents the toughest situation of all. The change may be massive, but is not supported by many people.

Figure 27.3 pulls together two models which were described in Chapter 3. It is a reminder that whatever change is envisaged will always take place within an existing organisational context. This does not mean that the activity in the inner model will have to take the outer model as immutable. In reality, the need may be to change something in the outer ring. Thus culture change in order to achieve a strategic aim has been very much a part of management thinking through the 1990s.

The labels in Figure 27.3 were defined in Chapter 3, so all that is needed now is to offer a few prompts to aid thinking at each step in the inner model. The points made below can be found in expanded form in Hussey.[3]

Envisioning
Points to consider in formulating a vision
Remember that vision in this context does not necessarily mean the vision for the whole organisation. Here, it is the picture of what the change will bring, and the benefits of it. It may be a total reshaping of an organisation, or it may be the management of an innovation, a new structure within one department, a re-laying out of the plant in a factory, or any other form of change which affects other people.

1 Is the vision credible?
2 Is it challenging?
3 Does it have internal integrity?
4 Is it clear?

Figure 27.3
Change leadership
and the
organization
(derived from
figures published in
Hussey, D.E.
*Business Driven
Human Resource
Management,* Wiley,
Chichester, 1996)

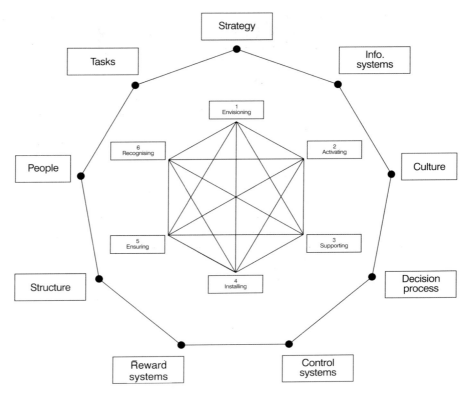

5 How does the vision relate to the past, present, and future?
6 Do you, as the leader of the change, believe in the vision?

Barriers to overcome
Even when the vision looks sound, there may be barriers which prevent it from being an effective driver for change:

1 Does the vision meet most of the above criteria?
2 Do day-to-day actions reinforce the vision?
3 Does every aspect of your own behaviour reinforce the vision?
4 Have the implications of the vision been thought through?
5 Can the vision be converted to strategies and actions?

Activating
Ways of activating the organisation
1 Demonstrate your own belief in the vision and feeling of excitement about it all the time.
2 Extend personal contact as far as possible through the organisation, to communicate your own sense of excitement, and to explain the vision.
3 Workshops of key people may be a valuable way of building commitment, and allowing them to participate in the process.

4 Ensure that there are opportunities for two-way communication.
5 Supplement the personal messages with other media, such as the company newspaper, videos for internal use, personal letters to employees, e-mail, and voicemail.
6 Use the everyday meetings to emphasise the message.
7 Consider how external public relations might aid the communication process inside the organisation, and with the influencers outside, such as customers.
8 Seek out and use examples of success that reinforce the vision.
9 Select the members of the team that will work with you with considerable care, and do not be afraid to take tough decisions to sideline or remove people who you fear might obstruct the change (but do this in a dignified and humane way).
10 Audit the nature and content of internal training, to ensure that the key changes are reflected in the courses, and that appropriate skills are provided where appropriate for those who are affected by the changes.

Barriers to overcome
1 Resistance to the change, in individuals, departments, or the entire organisation
2 Lack of change management skill in the leader
3 Unwillingness to take tough decisions about individual people whose behaviour is frustrating the change.

Supporting
Ways of giving support to people
1 Express confidence in subordinates and peers involved in the change.
2 Provide coaching to help them overcome difficulties.
3 Ensure that key people are properly empowered to play their part in the change process.
4 Be empathetic to their situations, and take account of them during the change process, but without deviating from the main thrust of the change.
5 Use praise and thanks as a positive way to enhance motivation.

Barriers to overcome
1 Lack of time to manage the change effectively
2 Lack of consistency in the behaviour in change management compared to day to day management.

Installing
Points to consider to Consider
1 Develop a plan for the change.
2 Ensure that this is carefully related to the organisational context (the outside model in Figure 27.3).
3 Consider contingencies: what might the effect be if things do not turn out as expected, and what should be done about it?
4 Ensure that ambition does not outstrip capability.

5 Do not underestimate the time that is needed to implement a major change.

6 Make sure that the plan for the change covers descriptions of the actions being taken, and provides a large enough budget to achieve the task.

7 Make it clear what actions are to be undertaken, and who is to take them.

8 Set time limits and short-term goals, to enable monitoring systems to be set up.

9 Think through the interface between the change project budget, and the normal process of budgetary control.

10 Responsibility for the success of the various elements of the change project must be clearly delegated.

11 Ensure that there is adequate project management, particularly with extensive or complex projects.

12 Use appropriate techniques such as Gantt charts and network analysis.

Pitfalls to avoid

1 Failure to think through all the consequences of the change, so that unexpected issues keep arising

2 Underestimating the time and resources that complex change requires

3 Planning only the first step of a change and assuming that the rest will follow (for example, assuming that an acquisition plan is implemented when ownership is transferred, but before the objectives of the acquisition have been secured).

Ensuring

Factors to consider

1 Are all the controls and incentives driving the organisation in the same direction?

2 Are you satisfied that there is congruence between the personal aims of the key people in the change process and the organisational goals?

3 How far can self-control be used as a driving force in this change?

4 Try to exercise the controls in a way that increases the degree to which the vision of and strategies for the change are shared by all the players.

5 As far as possible use the control process for the change as a learning opportunity, and as a way of overcoming new challenges that emerge as the change is managed.

6 There are two facets which require regular, timely flows of information: did we do the things we said we would at the right time; did the outcome of those actions achieve our expectations?

7 Ensure that the right information flows are set up to monitor all the critical elements of the change.

8 Ensure that the control system does more than pass information along: be willing to replan the change activity when things are not working out as expected.

9 Bring all the control information for the whole process together regularly, so that the person with overall responsibility for managing the change is not taken by surprise.

10 Pay particular attention to those tasks which will delay the whole project if they are not performed to time.

11 Do not assume that the normal control processes of the organisation will be adequate to monitor the change, and be willing to supplement them.

12 Accept that things will go wrong, and that quick response is therefore vital.

13 Understand that some expense may have to be incurred to monitor and control the project.

Recognition
Factors to consider

1 Ensure that you give constant recognition for the part others play as the change process moves forward.

2 Use all opportunities to reinforce the behaviour you want from others, by making them feel that what they are doing is important, and has been noticed.

3 Keep any negative comments you might have about a person for private one to one meeting, but take opportunities to acknowledge achievements in public.

4 Make sure that your superiors are aware of outstanding performance by others, and that your team knows that you are not taking all the credit for efforts they have shared.

5 Do not indulge in empty praise, and insincere comments.

6 Have regular reviews of personal performance of people who are reporting to you during the change process, so that you both have the opportunity to develop relationships and avoid surprises.

There are, of course, strong arguments for managing change in a way that gains the support of the people in the organisation. However, it is not the only model, and again I am grateful to Stace and Dunphy[2] for drawing attention to the coercive approach, where change is steamrollered through by the top person and anyone who does not go along with it is, in a manner of speaking, squashed flat. One example is the way Rupert Murdoch changed the way his newspapers were produced, in the teeth of ferocious opposition by the print unions. The change was imposed, and everything that needed to be done to drive the change through was done. It did not matter if at the end there was a complete change of employees, as the ultimate vision of a cost-effective production process was all that mattered. The power of the unions over the manning levels and methods of production was broken for ever, and few would argue that the industry as a whole is not better for it. But there is no doubt that the methods used were totally coercive. Lewis[4] provides a detailed research study of coercive transformation in an Australian college, where change was achieved through 'short sharp bursts of activity, that is by discontinuous change'. The model mirrored the freeze–unfreeze–freeze approach of Lewin[5] and although attempts were made to supplement the coercive change strategy with other methods, these failed because of luck of trust. All the new objectives were achieved and sustained over a lengthy period, and the change was achieved quickly at each unfreezing stage.

The downside was a long-term situation of demoralised staff, with a gulf of trust and understanding between academic staff and management.

A steam roller approach fits the personal style of some managers, and is therefore something that they may feel comfortable with. However if we are trying to make a rational choice of the appropriate method to achieve change, we should exclude this factor (a preference does not necessarily mean that the approach is appropriate) and consider when transformational change might best be achieved by draconian means. I suggest the following circumstances for consideration:

1 When the change has to be completed at maximum speed and there is no realistic alternative
2 When consensus is impossible under any circumstances, which was probably the case in the Murdoch newspaper example
3 When the price that has to be paid in employee motivation, resignations, loss of trust, and complete lack of shared vision and commitment is seen as less important than a fast result, or of little importance at all.

Some examples of transformational change

Most major transformational change will follow a mix of styles, and in some way following the thinking if not the letter of the leadership model. It is about creating, defining and building commitment to a new vision, and supporting this with the management effort that enables it to work. The two examples that will be mentioned are of British Telecom and British Petroleum, and in both cases the information has been drawn from published sources.

British Telecom

The vision of British Telecom is to become the most successful worldwide telecommunications group. The trigger for changes was a mix of external pressures and internal constraints which by 1990 had reached a point where the chief executive felt that action had to be taken. External pressures included the pace of technological change, with a 30 per cent per annum fall in the costs of telecommunications as new technologies became available. The complexity of the telecommunications industry had increased, to the point when it was difficult to see the joins with other industries, such as computers. The degree of turbulence in the environment had increased dramatically. Internally there was a mismatch of the organisation and its old public utility culture with the vision and the external world. Managers' perceptions were not always appropriate, and the culture was introspective and controlling, rather than outward-looking and proactive.

The desired change included a need to alter the culture of the organisation. Before the change strategy was implemented the culture was prescriptive, with individuals being expected to conform to requirements. The desired change was to a culture that enabled individuals to excel, with the company providing the support that made this possible. At the same time there was a need to reduce the number of jobs and, partly to reduce costs and partly to enable the organisation to be more customer responsive, this included a new structure which would remove nine layers of management.

On 26 March 1990 the chairman addressed the top 300 managers. They were told that the organisation would change over the next 12 months, and that all 36 000 managers would take on new jobs. They were informed that there would be fewer jobs, and that the new organisation would be in place by 1 April 1991. One purpose of the change arose from a TQM initiative which had begun in 1985, which was to gain more customer focus by using culture change that included values that addressed the customer. A team was set up to implement the changes.

After 4 months organisational design had become an industry in its own right. Many of those involved in this new 'industry' were demonstrating the behaviours that the new design was intended to remove, such as the withholding of information, arbitrary decision making and a growth in bureaucracy. This led to a measure of cynicism in the organisation. A survey was made which showed that actions were at odds with the vision, help was needed if managers were to behave differently, the whole process had made people more inward-looking, and individuals were seeking sustained and continuous leadership from the board.

One result of this survey was the introduction of a two-and-a-half day leadership programme. By 1 April 1991, 600 managers had been through the programme, with a heavy involvement of the chairman. The balance of managers had seen a video presentation, with a board member present to answer questions. By March 1992 there was a widespread recognition that the business was more turbulent, that most senior managers had been operating operationally rather than strategically, and a level of awareness had been developed among many people to enable them to participate in translating the group strategy to action.

Much of this change process was highly visible, because of the high profile of the company. The need for communication and effort to build shared values is clear from what happened, as is the need to train people to enable them to play the right part in the changed situation. Also clear is the length of time needed to change values in a long-established organisation.

British Petroleum

It is not possible to have a higher profile in a change process than to invite a journalist to sit in and write about the board meetings where the change strategy is decided. This is what BP did, with decisions being taken over several meetings in the presence of a *Financial Times* journalist.

BPs change strategy was the result of a very detailed analysis involving many people. In July 1989, the chairman designate, Robert Horton, commissioned 'Project 1990', a major internal study which had the aim of showing how to reduce complexity in the organisation, to redesign the head office organisation, and to reposition the company in approach and style for the 1990s. The project team consulted widely inside and outside of BP, undertaking over 500 interviews and processing some 4000 questionnaires.

The implementation of the culture change began in 1990, when Horton was appointed chairman. Its objective was to achieve the BP vision through the people, within a simple, supportive organisation. The process followed a number of principles:

1 The need for change was analysed in a way that took information from many people, as described above.
2 Considerable effort was given to inspiring enthusiasm for change, involving communication of various types, and including explanations of the need for change.
3 The emphasis was on building an organisation for the future, and the structure chosen was unusual enough to be exciting.
4 Top management drove the change process, and provided adequate resources for implementation.
5 There was widespread involvement of everyone in the change process, including a major educational initiative.
6 Processes were developed to support the change, including the identification of the competencies needed for employees working under the new culture.
7 There was continuous review of the change process.

Of course things did not always go smoothly, and a major problem was an increase in environmental turbulence at the time the change process started. The UK moved into recession in 1990, and the oil industry worldwide found oil prices declining. This meant that certain strategies for disposing of non-core businesses became more urgent, and more costs had to be taken out of the company. This meant that in addition to the planned changes leading to a smaller head office and more putting out of work to third parties, there were other factors which meant that many people had to leave the company. Change was thus implemented against a background of budgetary pressure, terminations and early retirements. Part-way through the process the chief executive left the company. However, the strength of the change process was that culture has changed in the direction desired, despite all the additional complications and individual uncertainties.

Change and people

One popular myth is that people resist change. Like all myths, there are some elements of truth in the statement, but we could also argue that many people welcome change. The fact is that our daily lives take place in an environment where change of one sort or another is a normal state. What may make people react adversely to change is:

1 Lack of understanding of the need for change
2 Belief that the change proposed is not appropriate
3 Failure to appreciate the urgency behind a planned change
4 Concern that the change will have an adverse personal impact
5 Failure to appreciate the many small actions needed to implement a major change.

The leadership model discussed earlier deals with how to overcome some of these problems. There is an additional concept which may help to explain why people sometimes appear to resist change, even though they may agree with its objectives. This is the concept of the psychological contract, the unwritten part of the relationship between employer and employee. It embraces the expectations of both parties, and because it is internal to the parties, and could never be made totally explicit (partly because some components only become critical when they are threatened), it may be difficult to deal with. Let me give an example.

A managing director of a subsidiary may have reported direct to the main board, and may have felt that the relationship with the board is a critical part of the job, giving prestige, a feeling that there is an influence on main board strategies, and regular contact with the top people. The structure changes, and the managing director now reports to a regional office, which also determines many aspects of broad strategy. The job title, salary, and subordinate relationships have not changed, but what has been lost is something that the incumbent felt was an important part of the job. The psychological contract has changed, and this change may be enough to make the managing director resist the change. Resistance may take many forms. It may be passive, in that there is apparent acceptance, but the excitement has gone out of the job, levels of effort reduced, and there may be a few telephone calls to executive search consultants. It may be very aggressive, with active opposition of the new order, and even sabotage. Resistance may take the form of working to rules, and no longer doing more than is demanded by the new procedures.

The important point in considering change management is that psychological contracts exist at all levels. One argument for consultation during a change process is that it provides the opportunity for the expectations to be clear, and for issues to surface before they become problems. Later in this chapter there will be some discussion of empowerment, but it is worth remembering that the introduction of a process of empowerment is likely to break the psychological contacts of both empowerers and 'empowerees', and may be reinforced by uncertainty of both about how they should work under the new concept. Such changes are more likely to be successful if accompanied by counselling and training, as well as the changing of company processes and systems that do not reinforce the concept. Just issuing a policy statement that the organisation follows the principles of empowerment is unlikely to bring about any effective change.

Figure 27.4 draws heavily on some ideas by Alexander,[6] one of the few people who has undertaken research into the implementation of strategic plans. It suggests that there may be two factors which work either together or against each

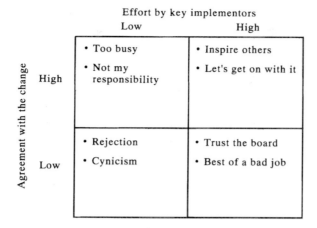

Figure 27.4
Typical responses to strategic change. Inspired by Alexander[6]

other to contribute to successful implementation: agreement with the change and the degree of effort put in by key implementors. It is possible to have low effort combined with an agreement with the change. This may be because the implementers are preoccupied with normal work, and do not give the time to the change, it may be because they do not understand the role that has to be played by them, or think that it is someone else's job. It may also be that the psychological contract gets in the way. Alexander calls this tokenism, and it is important for those trying to cause change to develop approaches to overcome it.

The second low effort box is when there is little or no acceptance of the change, either because the need is not seen, or because the strategy is believed to be wrong. This can cause outright rejection, cynicism ('We've heard that one before', 'Open communication with that lot upstairs!' or 'I'll believe that if it happens'). Good communication, with clear explanation of the need to change may change this situation, although there will always be a problem if the rejection is justified, and the change is inappropriate!

The ideal box is where both dimensions are high, and the key implementors take on the task of inspiring others and driving the change forward. The final box may lead to successful change, but can indicate a problem. 'I don't agree with it, but I expect the board is right' as a response may help the change forward, but is unlikely to lead to many creative inputs from the implementors. Making the best of a bad job conceals disagreements that would be better in the open.

All the boxes in this diagram reinforce the value of the leadership model in Figure 27.3.

Getting managers to plan the implementation of strategy

We saw in the previous chapter that there are many things which may prevent a strategy from being implemented, and in particular we were able to look at the top problems identified in Alexander's research.[6] One of the practical issues which I find is that many managers have little experience of planning the implementation of strategies, particularly strategies that are transformational. It is at this stage when we have to move from the broad statements of intent, to the detail of what particular people must do. We touched on this in the last chapter in a system sense. However, just planning the actions that people have to undertake is not the whole story. It may not be enough to agree that a particular action has to happen, and we may also have to ensure that the people who have to carry out the action have the skills and knowledge to do it well.

Figure 27.5 is an example of a method I have found useful in strategy workshops to get managers discussing and identifying the mix of hard and soft issues that should be considered. It takes a number of negative statements from Alexander's research, and turns them into positive things that have to be done.

Figure 27.5

Factors to consider in implementation

	Factor	Rank up to 10 factors in order of concern to you (10 = highest 1 = lowest)*	Rate your chosen factors on difficulty to overcome (1 = easy 5 = very hard)
1.	Defining key implementation task and activities in enough detail		
2.	Foreseeing all the issues and problems that should be tackled		
3.	Preventing day to day operations from distracting implementation		
4.	Ensuring that major changes in the business environment do not block implementation		
5.	Ensuring understanding by your managers of the strategy		
6.	Creating a shared vision at all levels of management		
7.	Ensuring that managers possess the knowledge and capabilities needed to implement		
8.	Ensuring that other employees have the skills and capabilities to implement		
9.	Dealing with the situation when the new strategy is not compatible with manager's personal goals		
10.	Ensuring that there are enough resources to implement		
11.	Setting an achievable time scale		
12.	Setting a system so that implementation may be monitored and controlled		
13.	Ensuring that senior managers have the time to implement		
14.	Communicating the implementation plan to the right people		
15.	Overcoming employee resistance to implementation		
16.	Dealing with the fear that change can provoke		

Please add any other factors that you think should be in your top 10.
* Score the most important factor 10. The second most important 9, etc.

Sixteen items appear on the list. It would be possible to add more, and this may be desirable if there are particular situations in the company that should be considered. All managers in the workshop are asked to rank 10 of the 16 items. The scoring method is designed to make it easy for all the questionnaires to be aggregated, so that a top 10 for the whole group can emerge. After ranking, they are asked to assess the degree of difficulty they see in dealing with each issue. When producing a total difficulty score for all people on the workshop, it is worth remembering that the appropriate average is of the people who have ranked the factor, not of the number who have completed the questionnaire.

The value of the approach is that it helps managers to consider the hard and soft issues in the context of what they have to do. This means that there is a norm (the total picture drawn from all questionnaires) with which individuals can compare their answers, which provides a rich ground for discussion. Unless all the managers are from the same function and business unit and are facing the same change, there should be differences between the answers. The facilitator also has a secret weapon. If no one appreciates the importance of what are clearly critical factors, it is always possible to force a discussion by comparing their answers with the overall results of Alexander's research. The differences between the research results and this questionnaire are in timing. The questionnaire tries to anticipate what must be considered, so that ways of doing this can be constructed. The research looked back at what went wrong in implementing strategies.

Management training and strategic change

In Chapter 21 the case was argued for a more strategic view of management training and management development. The value of using training as a key part of a change process cannot be over stressed, although to be successful may involve throwing out some preconceived ideas about the design and delivery of training courses.

In Chapter 21 the types of situation where training could contribute to strategic change were listed briefly. In a little more detail they are as follows.

Strategy formulation

The right programmes can be used to challenge the assumptions to which current plans are based, or to examine strategic options.

Strategy implementation

An appropriate initiative can be used to enable an understanding of the strategy to be gained in the broad terms, and in its impact on an individual and his or her job. Commitment can be built as people discover the reason for the strategy, and decide for themselves that it makes sense. Implications of the strategy can be explored and converted into personal action plans. Appropriate training can be given to correct deficiencies in the skills or knowledge of those who are involved in implementing the change.

Policy implementation

A change in policy, such as a decision to put more effort behind competitor analysis, can often be effectively implemented with the aid of training programmes, which can build commitment to the policy and ensure that people are both able and willing to implement it.

Corporate culture

Training may be a major tool in creating a culture or changing a culture. In turn this will help ensure that strategies and culture are compatible.

Environmental change

Significant changes in the business environment may provide threats or opportunities. Appropriate training initiatives can help the organisation identify and deal with major changes.

Solving problems

Training programmes may also be designed to solve particular problems, such as how to increase market share, or improve profitability. The mechanism is similar to the other categories shown, and among other things is based on shared understanding, involvement, and the enhancement of skills needed to deal with the situation. A glance back at the factors in Figure 27.5 will reveal that many would be partly solved had the power of management training been used to help implement.

A training initiative does not have to be positioned as training. It may be logged as work, since it may deal totally with real issues, and the educational element may be hidden. An example is the questionnaire discussed above. A good facilitator could bring out the importance of the issues and their consequences in the context of developing an action plan for implementing a strategy.

As can be seen from the example a training initiative can be used to develop knowledge and skills the lack of which would frustrate implementation, it can be part of the communication process, and it can provide a collaborative approach, either in the formulation of strategy itself, or more frequently in defining the detailed implementation issues. It can build commitment to the change.

I argued that some preconceived ideas may have to be discarded. The first is that we are not talking about a routine programme. The initiative has to be specifically designed, and totally tailored to meet the needs of the company. If issues are included, the materials for the programme must be developed to include those issues. Such a programme cannot be lifted off the shelf, and must be specially designed for the company, which means that it may be more expensive than a routine training initiative. Few internal training staff have the experience and capability to design initiatives of this type, which by their nature stretch across many functional skills, and require a different approach to a standard training course. Even in companies that normally staff all training events from internal sources, there is a need for the services of external, uninvolved, senior consultants to make the concept work. In many companies, the training function lacks the credibility to perform the task, even if it possesses the skills.

It is indicative that in both of the transformational case histories given earlier, training was used as a means of facilitating change. Many of the problems that do occur would be removed if more organisations chose this route, and supported it with an adequate budget.

Empowerment

The final topic of this chapter is to turn attention to modern concepts of empowerment. In doing this I have drawn on an unpublished paper by Phil Lowe,[7] of Harbridge Consulting Group, who has helped me to appreciate the difference between the modern concept of empowerment, and the long established issue of delegation. It is something more than old wisdom dressed in new clothes.

Of course, it is possible to argue that empowerment as a concept has been around a long time, even though it may not have found its full place in management. The earliest writing I have found on this, also incidentally about what is probably the first recorded management consulting assignment, is found in the Bible, Exodus, Chapter 18, verses 13 to 27.

Moses' father-in-law watched him judging and counselling the people in the ways of God, and noted that the process lasted from morning to evening, exhausted Moses and tied up most of the people. I pick up the story at verse 17.

> 17. And Moses' father in law said unto him, The thing thou doest is not good.
> 18. Thou wilt surely wear away, both thou, and this people that is with thee: for this thing is too heavy for thee: thou art not able to perform it thyself alone.
> 19. Hearken now unto my voice, I will give thee counsel, and God shall be with thee. Be thou for the people to Godward, that thou mayest bring the causes unto God.

20. And thou shalt teach them ordinances and laws, and thou shalt shew them the way wherein they must walk, and the work that they must do.

21. Moreover thou shalt provide out of all the people able men, such as fear God, men of truth, hating covetousness; and place such over them, to be rulers of thousands and rulers of hundreds, rulers of fifties and rulers of tens:

22. And let them judge the people at all seasons: and it shall be that every great matter they shall bring unto thee, but every small matter they shall judge: so shall it be easier for thyself, and they shall bear the burden with thee.

23. If thou shalt do this thing, and God command thee so, then thou shalt be able to endure, and all this people shall also go to their place in peace.

24. So Moses hearkened to the voice of his father in law, and did all that he had said.

25. And Moses chose able men out of all Israel, and made them heads over the people, rulers of thousands, rulers of hundreds, rulers of fifties and rulers of tens.

26. And they judged the people at all seasons: the hard cases they brought unto Moses, but every small matter they judged themselves.

27. And Moses let his father in law depart: and he went his way into his own land.

History does not record the size of the consultancy fee, but in this extract we see aspects of training, competencies, structure, definitions of responsibilities, limits of authority, and delegation. Had the advice been given now, no doubt there would have been some de-layering! In true consultant's style, Jethro the father in law also painted the benefits to Moses of following the advice. Unusually he seems to have stayed around to see it implemented.

Empowerment is defined by Lowe[7] as: 'A process by which individual employees are given the autonomy, motivation and skills necessary to perform their jobs in a way which provides them with a sense of ownership and fulfilment while achieving shared organisational goals.'

An empowered organisation is more responsive, in that people closest to the source of problems are able to deal with them, it gives flexibility in managing change, and is essential if organisations are to function once layers are torn out of the structure. Reaching a state of empowerment is difficult, because it challenges many things that the managed and managers had taken for granted. Managers, for example need to see their roles as facilitators, coaches and sponsors, where historically many have been organisers of others, and supervisors. To make this change, and those managed may find it as difficult as do those who manage them, requires the alignment of company systems and processes to the new concept, considerable training, and counselling over a period to ensure that managers actually apply the new concept.

An empowered organisation should provide individuals with:

1 A sense of purpose and a commitment to company goals
2 Recognition of individual achievements, and continuous feed back on performance
3 Training where it is needed
4 Autonomy to perform their jobs in a way that suits them, providing it is consistent with organisational goals and values.

It means that all employees are able to see the results of their work, accept responsibility for their own performance, feel that they have an identity in the organisation, are able to have a say in things which affect their work, and share a commitment to continuous improvement.

TQM is a driver towards empowerment, as is much of the modern thinking on manufacturing. The pressure for improved customer responsiveness is another driver, for adequate responsiveness can only occur when those close to the customer are empowered to make most of the decisions about issues that affect the customer.

Summary

What perhaps separates strategic management from strategic planning is perhaps this emphasis on the totality of strategic change. Planning strategy is not easy, but the difficulties are as nothing compared to managing a process of strategic change. If strategies are not implemented they are a waste of time, and as we have seen implementation calls for a variety of different skills, not all of which may be possessed by the average manager. Today's manager cannot rely on miracles, as Moses is reputed to have done, and few have father in laws who can give such sensible advice. There we have to find other ways of coping, and I would put leadership and the management of change very high in the list of competencies which managers at all levels should possess.

References

1 Ansoff, H. I. and McDonnell, E. *Implanting Strategic Management*, 2nd edn, Prentice Hall, Hemel Hempstead, 1990.
2 Stace, D. A. and Dunphy, D. C. 'Translating Business Strategies into Action: Managing Strategic Change', *Journal of Strategic Change*, Vol. 1, No. 4, July/August, 1992.
3 Hussey, D. E. *How to Manage Organisational Change*, Kogan Page, London, 1995.
4 Lewis, D. 'Power-based Organisational Change in an Australian Tertiary College', *Journal of Strategic Change* Vol. 2.6, December 1993.
5 Lewin, K. *Field Theory in Social Science*, Harper and Row, New York, 1951.
6 Alexander, L. D. 'Strategic Implementation: Nature of the Problem', in Hussey, D. E. (ed.), *International Review of Strategic Management*, Wiley, Chichester, 1991.
7 Lowe, P. 'The Background to Empowerment', Harbridge Consulting Group, London (unpublished working paper, 1993).

Further reading

Bate, P. *Strategies for Cultural Change*. Butterworth-Heinemann, Oxford, 1994.
Carnall, C. A. (ed.) *Strategic Change*, Butterworth-Heinemann, Oxford, 1997.
Hussey, D. E. (ed.) *The Implementation Challenge*, Wiley, Chichester, 1996.
Sadler, P. (ed.) *Strategic Change: Building a High Performance Organisation*, Pergamon, Oxford, 1995.
Tichy, N. M. and Dervanna, M. A. *The Transformational Leader*, Wiley, New York, 1990.

Part 5

Introducing Strategic Management to an Organisation

CHAPTER 28

Introducing strategic management

Not every authority on strategic management believes that there should be a formal process of strategic management. The aim of this chapter is to show how to introduce a successful process into an organisation.

Throughout this book the aim has been to present strategic management at both a conceptual and a practical level. In order to make sense the practical implications have been restricted to the particular aspect of planning which was under discussion. It is now time to leave the discussion of individual components and to look again at the complete process. The next chapters are very much a continuation of the first three, which also examined corporate planning from a holistic viewpoint.

This and the following chapters deal solely with practicalities. In this chapter are presented some thoughts on the problem of introducing strategic management into an organisation. Some problems will still remain, and these will be discussed in the next chapter, which draws heavily on the published surveys of planning in practice.

I think it is true to say that many attempts at introducing strategic management have been doomed to fail from the outset simply because too little forethought was given to what was really involved. A technique such as marketing research, a new forecasting method, or discounted cash flow can be applied to a company at will in as large or small a dose as desired. We saw in Chapter 1 that strategic management is not a technique but a complete way of running a business. The application of strategic management is not like taking a patent elixir in casual doses, but is a strict regimen that transforms the patient and which can do harm if administered haphazardly.

Strategic management in any company should begin with a decision. The only person who can take this decision is the chief executive, who must reach the conclusion that this is the way in which he or she wishes to manage the company. Ideally at this stage the top management team should share this enthusiasm. The chief executive's enthusiasm must also infect others with the same feeling. The decision to implement planning should not be taken lightly.

The first problem the chief executive will encounter following the decision is how to implement it. If the company is of any significant size, the probability is that it will need some full-time professional help in the person of a corporate planner. Smaller companies may need this assistance but may not be able to afford the services of a full-time person: for them there is another solution – the use of part-time specialists. At the start-up stage it is possible for a chief executive to use a firm of management consultants, although this solution is usually only economic in the short term, and a more permanent arrangement is needed once the problems of introduction have been overcome.

The best solution of all, if it is workable, is for the chief executive to be the planner. This will only work where he or she is fully conversant with all aspects of the strategic planning process and if it has been possible to delegate enough of the other work to allow adequate time for planning matters. Unfortunately, the nature of top management being as it is, these circumstances rarely apply. In many ways this is a pity because maximum enthusiasm would be generated in a situation where the chief executive was so obviously deeply involved in the process.

Part-time professional planners are a solution which has been rarely applied. For many small companies the specialist need is probably for only three to four days' attendance a month, and could be achieved by the appointment of a suitable non-executive director to the board (or, more exactly, a part-time executive director). From the point of view of the specialist planner the ability to work for a number of non-competing companies makes this an interesting and economic proposition. The company gains expertise from someone with a continuous involvement in the business: this, too, can be an economic concept. There are one or two firms of consultants who specialise in this type of service. I believe that it is a concept which will become increasingly important in the future.

Much of the impact of strategic management throughout the world still depends on the professional corporate planner. Few effective planning processes have been installed without the skilled services offered by this type of manager.

The chief executive who decides a corporate planner is needed is faced with another choice. Should someone be recruited from inside the organisation or brought in from outside? Each possibility has advantages. The person from inside may know the business well and already command the respect of senior managers. On the disadvantage side he or she may know nothing about strategic management. This disadvantage may be removed if there is sufficient time to learn about the subject before being turned loose on the company. Too often, planners appointed in this way are expected to do the impossible – to become experts overnight. A person appointed from within should always be a manager 'who cannot be spared': anyone who can be easily spared is unlikely to hold the good opinions of colleagues. It is unfortunate, too, that planning positions filled in this way are often pitched too low: the temptation to do this is much stronger where the chief executive can virtually force anyone from the company into the new job.

An outside skilled planner should bring particular benefits through expertise. He or she will be unfamiliar with the specific company (although not necessarily the industry), but this problem can be overstressed. A good corporate planner can learn the key areas of the company very quickly and should have a consultant type skill for adapting to new situations. Above all, the person should be expected to know what to do in the new job.

It is very easy for those inside a company to overstress the time it takes to learn the business. A line manager who has spent an entire business life learning the craft from the shopfloor upwards is likely to believe that no one can understand the dynamics of the business without following a similar career pattern. This is just not true, and confuses two different types of knowledge. A production manager in the iron and steel industry needs to have an encyclopedic knowledge of how to make iron and steel. The corporate planner does not have to be able to make the product: but has to understand what makes the business tick.

The chief executive must, however he or she decides to recruit the planner, set the position at the right level of seniority. The person chosen should be able to walk on equal terms with the senior management of that company, and should be a member of the board or management executive committee – or whatever the senior organ of management is in that company. This immediately answers the question of how much a planner should be paid. Salary (and status) should be within the band applicable to the most senior managers in that company. The planner need not be the highest paid nor need be regarded as the most senior of the group, but must be within that group.

The reasons for this are sensible and straightforward. The planner and the chief executive, to be a successful combination, have to develop a level of rapport that is much greater than that of other managers. In many ways the planner is only an extension of the chief executive: it is only possible to function in this way if there is mutual support and confidence. Without it, the planning function will wither and die, like a plant whose roots have been severed. If the gulf of seniority and standing is too wide, the required relationship will never develop. No good planner is a 'yes' man (or woman) and no good chief executive will want anything but a self-confident individual in this particular function. Criticism of an idea or decision of the chief executive is often a delicate task: it may well become impossible if the planner is positioned as a keen, middle-management type rather than a high-level executive.

Similarly, relations with other managers are conditioned by seniority. Few managers like to meet opposition to, and criticism of, their ideas and decisions: yet in a planning situation this need may arise from time to time. Such moves by a management peer are tolerable. If the planner is not seen as an equal, many of the actions he or she must take to do the job properly will do nothing more than erect a barrier of resentment which will effectively close the way to a process of strategic management. The chief executive, too, can be put in an impossible position when forced to arbitrate between two managers of highly disproportionate seniority. Arbitration between equals is carried out in a much less emotionally charged atmosphere and, because of the dynamics of the situation, the need for such intervention to settle disagreements is something that rarely arises.

Managers are human. In any circumstances there may be some hostile feelings to the idea of an additional person who will hold the confidence of the chief executive. If the planner is too junior this can well change to bitter jealousy, coupled with the fear that the planner is a 'whispering Rasputin' who is really only out to get their jobs. If already an equal, many of the fears will not occur: the planner has a job as good as theirs already, and has no incentive to work against their interests.

From the foregoing it is clear that much of the success of strategic management in an enterprise will depend on the personality and ability of the person selected to be the corporate planner. If this person's behaviour and attributes antagonise managers continuously it will not be possible to succeed at the job whatever the person's paper qualifications and however distinguished the record. Planners also need to be respected by those in the company for their skills as a planner and as a manager. Corporate planners have been called 'specialists in general management'. It is very easy to move from broad statements of this nature to long lists of the disciplines and personal traits which should characterise the good corporate planner. Unfortunately such an approach would do nothing more than resemble the lists of the personal attributes of leaders, and the qualities of leadership, which were produced by the early industrial psychologists. One is left with the impression of a saint-like creature, barely human, the identification of whom would defy the efforts of the most skilled and efficient of management 'headhunters'. There is no single person who exists who fulfils the requirements of the 'ideal' planner. But there are many people who are excellent corporate planners.

Before any real consideration can be given to the selection of a planner, it is necessary to give some thought to the real nature of the job. There are at least two levels of planning in any organisation: strategic (the duty of the chief executive and the top management team) and operational (the duty of line managers). The corporate planning function has to be able to operate at both levels, which really means that there are two closely integrated but very different planning requirements. At all times it is worth remembering the maxim that the real planners in any company are the managers. The job of the planner is to help make planning happen; to coordinate all planning efforts; to help the company more clearly see the issues that affect its future and the alternative paths it may take to systemise planning procedures in the company, including control methods; to analyse and evaluate various issues; to draw the plans together. It is no part of the planner's job to replace any manager's duty to perform the planning elements of management.

In a previous publication[1] I outlined a generalised job description for a corporate planner. This is reproduced in Figure 28.1, and although there will be variations between companies I believe that it still includes the main functions of the job and the requirements of the person.

The organisation of the planning function is another matter that requires careful thought and consideration. There may be a great temptation to establish a large centralised planning department in order to ensure the mix of disciplines which go to make up the 'ideal' (and non-existent) planner. This may be

Title: Corporate Planner
Reports to: Chief Executive
Purpose: To assist top management to plan the future of the company in an orderly and
               systematic way.

Principal Responsibilities

1. Introducing a system of formal long- and short-range planning covering all areas of the organisation.

2. Assisting management in the definition of objectives and goals.

3. Identifying long-term internal and external factors and their potential effect on the company.

4. Assisting the Chief Executive in the development of strategies to achieve corporate objectives.

5. Analysing and making recommendations on alternative courses of action, including capital investment, acquisitions, divestment, and expansion.

6. Ensuring that the future implications of all decisions are taken into consideration.

7. Appraising corporate strengths and weaknesses.

8. Advising all management levels on planning matters.

9. Writing strategic plans to reflect the decisions of the Chief Executive: co-ordinating the plans of line managers.

10. Monitoring plans and the assumptions on which they are based so that the Chief Executive can control progress.

11. Maintaining a manual to describe the planning system and to specify the part each person has to play in that system.

12. Initiating special studies and research appertaining to the future of the company. (Where available, working through appropriate departments within the organisation.)

13. Training management in planning principles and methods.

14. Applying appropriate techniques to the solution of problems.

Qualifications:
     Should be qualified to degree standard in an appropriate discipline, but should not be a narrow specialist. A wide range of disciplines are suitable, e.g. economics, business administration, market research, mathematics, statistics, marketing.

Experience:
     Should have experience of corporate planning principles and methods, and ability in some management techniques (ability in *all* techniques is virtually impossible). Appropriate techniques and concepts include:

DCF	Decision theory	Strategic portfolio analysis
Risk analysis	Marketing research	Organisational development
Network analysis	Forecasting	Competitor Analysis
Decision trees	Change leadership	Core Competencies

Should also be thoroughly experienced in management theory and philosophy. Must be able to express his thoughts fluently both verbally and in writing.
Must have integrity in his approach and must not be afraid to make recommendations that may be unpopular.
Must be able to communicate with all levels in the organisation.

Age:
     Not younger than 30.
     An example of an actual specification is shown in Figure 28.2

Figure 28.1
Job description of a corporate planner

HEAD OF CORPORATE PLANNING

Province:

The introduction, development, and maintenance of a system of corporate planning in the group which is sufficiently comprehensive and all-embracing to be capable of achieving the full potential benefits of such a system.

Responsibilities:

1. To be responsible to the group managing director and to work within the authority laid down by him.
2. To keep abreast of developments in the external environment (political/economic, social, technological, competitive) and to make periodic written reviews on it, exercising judgement with regard to possible future trends and developments.
3. To ensure that due emphasis is placed on the need for change within the group to reflect developments in the external environment, particularly on the technological and competitive fronts; to accept the entrepreneurial role of being alert to new opportunities for the group in the widest sense; to assist in the evaluation of such opportunities as are considered by the managing director to be worthy of study.
4. To initiate and actively progress corporate planning procedures throughout the group.
5. To provide an advisory service to subsidiary companies and group functional management to aid them in executing their own planning responsibilities. (Such assistance will not of course relieve them of these responsibilities.)
6. To assist in the creation of a climate positively favourable to planning by a continuing informal educational campaign and through participation in formal training courses and contribution to house journals.
7. To co-ordinate the group's planning activity, monitoring its progress in relation to an approved time-table.
8. To integrate plans prepared by subsidiary companies and group functional management in such a way that a corporate plan is produced which is realistic and which properly reflects group aims.
9. To carry out other assignments of a co-ordinating nature in order to progress matters which may have been held up because of pressure of work elsewhere – as approved by the group managing director.
10. To recruit and maintain a multi-discipline staff (at present limited to three people) who will be able to make their main contribution through their specialisation but will also assist in the general aims of the function.
11. To maintain discipline and morale within the function; to appraise the performance of staff and recommend salary increases as appropriate; to assist in the development of staff and make recommendations to group personnel with regard to their promotion.
12. To keep abreast of developments in corporate planning and in business management generally through reading, contact with other companies and attendance/participation in outside courses.

Approved   *Group M.D.*
Agreed   *Head of C.P.*

Figure 28.2
Example of an actual job specification from a British industrial company

reinforced by a common belief that the worth of a manager is measured by the number of direct reports: thus empire building is seen as a way of increasing the status of the manager.

Whatever the temptation, a large planning department is something to be avoided. As a general principle it may be said that the employment of every additional person in the planning department is a relative degree of failure, something to be undertaken only when it is so essential that no other answer is possible. This is a good principle for all chief executives or planning managers to keep at the back of their minds but there are further guidelines which might be suggested.

Decentralisation of planning

In the larger companies, particularly those with major operating subsidiaries, multinational operations, or particularly complex or diverse activities, it may be impossible for one person to fulfil the total planning role. This problem is unlikely to be solved by building up massive central planning staff who attempt to do everything. A much better approach is to put divisional planning managers in the major divisions or subsidiaries of the company, reporting to the chief executive of that division, or subsidiary, with a functional relationship to the central planning manager. For such divisional appointments, the same basic principles apply on the selection and seniority of the person concerned. It is particularly important that the divisional planner be associated with the divisional management.

Avoidance of duplication

There is a great temptation to set up duplicate services in a planning department. Special studies, the analysis of projects, the quantification of plans, and the application of OR techniques to planning problems are all activities which make a heavy demand on specialist services. Certainly many projects can be completed more quickly if the planner has a dedicated team of accountants, market researchers, and similar people.

Yet this can be a great danger. Studies might be completed at a faster rate, but they are more likely to be accepted if they have been carried out in participation with others. Accountants who deal in plans are likely to find themselves at loggerheads with their colleagues in budgeting departments. A more practical solution is to approach the process of planning with the firm intention of involving as many of the company's employees in the system as is humanly possible. This means that existing services should be expected to contribute to planning activity, and the need for rival teams of specialists is avoided. Just as managers are the company's real planners, so their specialists are the support staff of planning.

The effect of this principle will be to keep down the size of the planning department.

Confirm that planning is the right umbrella for new services

Existing functions in the company will not always have the specialists that corporate planning requires, and in many cases there will be a need to employ support staff. The fact that a corporate planner has identified the need is not of itself a good reason why the specialists must of necessity report to that function. Each situation should be examined on its merits.

Use working parties where possible

Often implementation of corporate strategy brings a requirement for additional staff in the planning department. A decision to acquire another company may bring an immense burden of essential work. This may carry a need to increase the number of central planning staff. Again, there is an alternative which is frequently better: to set up special working parties of people drawn from other areas of the company.

A maxim to consider at all times is that the larger the planning staff, the harder it will be to obtain the full involvement and participation of managers. For this reason a less obvious way of getting things done is frequently to be preferred if it brings the opportunity of drawing the company as a whole much more into the process. Strategic management should be something which is part of the company concerned: it is not something clever which stands aloof and separate from the main stream of company life.

It is worth mentioning one solution to the function of planner which has been used in some companies: no planning staff are permanent and the position of planner is held for a temporary period by each senior line manager in turn.

So far in this chapter it has been taken as datum that the planner should report to the chief executive. In practice, other solutions are employed, and planning is frequently 'delegated' to the top financial manager, who then has the planner responsible to him. Although in planning many solutions may be found to work, my personal belief is that the planner should be regarded as an extension of the chief executive and can therefore report to no other person.

Many attempts at introducing strategic management fail because of the approach taken in the initial stages. One of the difficulties of writing about the things that need to be done at this time is that the importance of the various steps will vary between companies. Similarly, the length of time a particular step takes will also vary, which may mean that compromises have to be made if the work is to follow any form of time-table. Sometimes it is more convenient to change the order in which certain steps are taken. The whole point is to come to the problem with an open mind. This does not mean that the planner should not have any idea of how to proceed, for if the problem is approached without expertise it is likely to lead to a mess.

Figure 28.3 shows in network form an approach to the problem of introducing planning into an organisation. Though subject to all the factors mentioned above, it provides a generalised framework which is capable of amendment to suit the particular set of circumstances.

Exhibit 28.1 Implementing a process for the development of a strategic plan

In 1990 the UK operations of Zürich Insurance decided to implement a new participative process of strategic planning. The outline process was designed internally, and launched at a management conference, and it was at this point that the magnitude of the task was realised. Harbridge Consulting Group was asked to provide consultancy help to support the process.

Some help was given to improve the design of the process, but the main task was to achieve a measure of participation in the organisation, to tap into the knowledge people had, and to provide some analytical approaches which would give new insight into the current situation of the organisation, and challenge current thinking.

The client set up a number of planning teams, one for each business unit, and an additional team which looked at central services. Each team included the senior people from the unit, plus a cross-section from branch and support services. In addition, some head office task forces were set up to help secure the information needed by the teams. About sixty people had an active, but focused, role in the process.

A timetable was established for each team, with a series of meetings scheduled, which would eventually enable each team to produce a draft plan for the unit.

The first meeting of each team was a workshop, designed by the consultants, which provided an overall model for the development of the strategic plan, to build capability in strategic thinking, and to enable the teams to understand and apply some methods of analysis which it was thought were appropriate for the task: various methods of looking at strengths and weaknesses, industry analysis, and competitor analysis. Preliminary collections of information were assembled for the teams to use in beginning the analysis, and the analytical methods themselves were presented in workbooks which described how to use the methods, and blank analysis sheets for completion by the teams.

Enormous enthusiasm was generated by the workshops. The output from each was an initial analysis of the business unit situation, some tentative strategies to be worked out in detail, and shopping lists of missing information. Subsequent meetings of the teams enabled each unit to prepare a strategic plan of what it wanted to achieve and how, for discussion on a total top management basis.

The consultants were involved in giving hands-on help at this and many subsequent stages of the process, working in a partnership role with the client.

(*Source*: A case study in strategic planning, by D. E. Hussey, originally a client-approved briefing paper, later published in Hussey, D. E. and Lowe, P. (eds), *Key Issues in Management Training*, Kogan Page, London, 1990.)

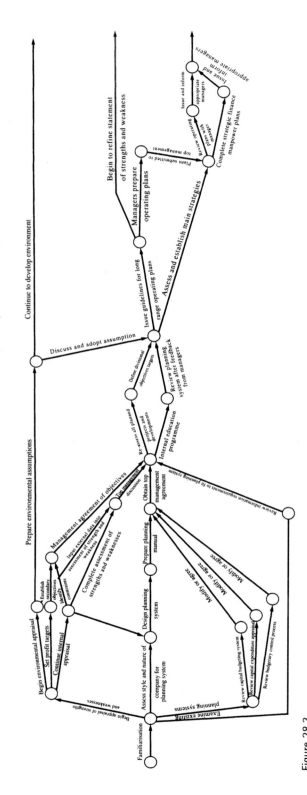

Figure 28.3
Network of main events on introduction of corporate long-range planning

(i) Familiarisation

This period is required whether a planner is recruited from inside or outside the company. In the first situation it is the time needed for the 'insider' to gain knowledge of corporate planning, and may last several months. In the case of the 'outsider' it is a shorter period, of perhaps two weeks, to get to know the broad scope of the company, the key people involved, and the geography of the company and its buildings. First, the planner should establish the culture of the company and its organisational style, so that planning solutions fit. There is a need to ensure that the planner and the chief executive hold similar views of the objectives of the planning initiative. Failure to do this can lead to an impossible situation later as philosophies clash.

It is during this period that the chief executive should begin to exercise a very important function – controlling the introduction. The planner should be required to produce some form of implementation plan – perhaps in the form of a network as in this example – which should be presented and discussed at a board meeting or whatever other organ is the company's main committee of policy and control. In this way the chief executive becomes familiar with what the planner is doing, and demonstrates a personal involvement to the senior managers.

Regular progress reports and, where necessary, the updating and amending of the implementation plan should be a part of the system of control which the chief executive uses. This may seem very elementary, but it is a fact that many planners have taken an overlong time to get corporate planning off the ground, because there was neither pressure nor interest from the top.

After the familiarisation period is over, the planner begins four tasks which may be carried out concurrently, yet which have a close relationship with each other.

(ii) Begin appraisal of strengths and weaknesses

This really is a natural development of the familiarisation period. As shown on the network, it is very much an initial period collecting available data, and planning the approach to the corporate appraisal, and rapidly reaches a stage where the task subdivides into three.

(iii) Environmental appraisal

Appraising the external environment of the company is a task which begins in parallel with the internal appraisal. Relevant data is input into the overall assessment of strengths and weaknesses at an early stage. At a later point in time planning assumptions are defined as the basis for plans. The main task of monitoring and assessing the external environment is continuous and outlives the network itself.

(iv) Set profit targets

After the first stages of the corporate appraisal (assessment of strengths and weaknesses) have begun, including the study of past results and trends, it becomes possible to establish the profit targets or primary objectives. This is desirable even at this early stage because it helps to provide the company with a framework for the other on-going tasks. Although not shown on the network, it is implied that these first objectives may be revised at a later stage (provision is made for them to be agreed by management).

(v) Establish secondary objectives

The identification of the company's statement of purpose is a logical evolution from the profit objectives, although I believe that these cannot be defined until the company has nearly completed its assessment of strengths and weaknesses.

(vi) Continuation of internal appraisal

The continuation of the assessment of strengths and weaknesses moves simultaneously with the start of the environmental appraisal, and leads naturally to the completion of this assessment, with the full integration of all relevant external data, and a detailed top management discussion. (It is, of course, possible for management to discuss objectives at the same meeting.) The word discussion implies, in this concept, acceptance, rejection, amendment, and – most important – action, for as has already been seen the appraisal is a key stage in the development of any plan.

(vii) Identify constraints

During the appraisal of strengths and weaknesses the planner should reach a point when it is possible to help top management identify any self-imposed constraints which they wish to apply to the running of their business. This definition forms part of the total package of objectives which has already been discussed.

(viii) Examine management information available

One of the initial tasks of introduction is to examine the management information available and to take a close look at the management information system. Management information is necessary as an input to the corporate appraisal, although the emphasis here is the selection and usage of relevant data. The examination shown on the network is much more concerned with the suitability of current information for long-range planning needs.

It follows that the system may either be adequate, or may require revision. In the latter event consideration should be given to amending the system so that it provides a better fit with the total approach to planning. The network suggests that this be done at a relatively early stage: however, in a practical situation it must be accepted that the complete reshaping of a management information system could take much longer than the network suggests, although the objectives of the system could be specified at this early stage.

(ix) Examine existing planning systems

There can be no company in the world that has no current systems which fulfil at least a part of its planning requirements. It is always good practice to make maximum use of whatever currently exists, and to make as few changes as possible. In some cases it may be that some systems are inadequate or non-existent: for example, there are still companies which do not have any formal methods of appraising capital expenditure projects. The end product must be a compatibility of these particular systems with the total approach to planning which is finally adopted.

The network shows three such systems – capital budgeting, capital expenditure, and budgetary control – but there may be others which should also be examined. Other possibilities are standing policies, personnel administration, and manpower planning procedures.

(x) Assess style and nature of company for planning system

The planner has to be familiar with the company, the philosophies of management in that company, its current organisation and reporting relationships, and various other factors which help to see the company in terms of a planning system. Much of this assessment can be developed from work that has to be carried out for the corporate appraisal. It is a time for reconsidering views formed during the familiarisation phase.

(xi) Establish if major strategic or organisational changes are needed

This is an essential spin-off task from the corporate appraisal, and must be completed before the planning system is designed. The line on the network envelops what may in some companies be a very complex series of investigations and decisions.

Problems in this area are critical to the future success of planning, and may act as a bottleneck which prevents further development. The situation will vary from company to company, and many planners may find that there are no problems to face.

In many organisations the decision to begin strategic management arises from a change in top management or a realisation that the company faces severe difficulties. It may be that an outline strategy has to be prepared by top management before a process of strategic management is extended to the total company. This strategy may call for profit improvement measures, the reorganisation of operating units, and even the closure or divestment of certain operations. Planning will lose credibility if these major changes are made later in the introductory process. A manager who is told to start devising plans for a business area one day and is made redundant the next is unlikely to have a feeling of confidence in the planning process: neither will his or her old colleagues who remain with the business.

Other situations may arise where although there are no drastic strategic upheavals, organisational relationships are poorly defined or inadequate for planning purposes. There are still companies which move towards strategic management from a point where one of the basic things they lack is an organisation chart. No adequate total planning system can be designed unless it is related to a clear management structure. Again this particular situation may prevent further development until it is resolved.

(xii) Design planning system

Once the above problems have been removed, the planner can design the system of planning which the company will use. Implicit in this statement is the need to work very closely with key managers so that the system fits the business, ties in with its existing timetables (year end, budgetary meetings, and seasonal factors), and is something that converts the textbook concepts into a process unique to the particular company.

(xiii) Prepare planning manual

It is logical that the complete system should be written up into a planning manual and subsequently accepted by top management as a description of the process that company will use. The manual may be one of the agents for training the whole company in corporate planning. However, the design of the manual and the way it is used internally must be compatible with the style of the company.

(xiv) Reassess all planned projects and developments

Introducing a process of planning into a company would be much easier if the company would close down for six months. This, of course, is an impossibility, and one of the challenges the planner faces is how to organise planning in a dynamic situation. In a way it is like a stunt man who has to jump onto a moving vehicle. At first this main task is to keep his footing and gain a position in that vehicle: at this point he can do nothing to change its momentum. Later, he is able to alter the speed of the vehicle or to make it change direction.

In all companies there are projects which are underway, and which it would be inadvisable to postpone during the first stages of introduction, although any major projects which were incompatible with the company's outline strategy would have come to light when this was examined.

The company has now reached a point on the network when objectives are set, strengths and weaknesses defined, and major anomalies corrected. A reassessment of on-going development projects is in order at this stage, with the possibility of postponing those which do not, in the light of all the new information, appear right for the company.

(xv) Define divisional objectives and targets

One of the hardest tasks is splitting up the total company objectives between divisions. This is an important prerequisite of any form of divisional planning, and is linked to all the investigatory work which the company has already carried out.

(xvi) Internal education programme

In many companies managers have to be helped to plan more effectively, and this is a key task for the planner. The system of planning has to be explained to managers throughout the organisation, and the right frame of mind created in all those who will participate. This line on the network summarises a number of actions and these will be discussed in some detail later in this chapter.

It is reasonable to expect that detailed discussions of the system throughout the organisation might suggest areas of improvement which should be incorporated. If it is seen as a participative system, the opinions and recommendations of managers should be welcomed.

(xvii) Issue guidelines for long-range operating plans

The company has now reached a point in time when it is ready to prepare its first long-range plans. The actions divide into strategic and operational planning, the link between the two being the guidelines, which incorporate objectives, environmental assumptions, strategic constraints or intents (often provisional at this stage), and the detailed planning time-table.

(xviii) Managers prepare operating plans

Long-range operational plans are prepared by managers, submitted to top management, discussed and debated, and themselves provide part of the input of the strategic planning process. At the same time the information generated leads to refinements of the statements of strengths and weaknesses, a process which outlives the network and continues into the next planning cycle.

(xix) Assess and establish main strategies

The main strategic choices, on which some work has already been carried out, are made, and re-examined in the light of the operating plans. The strategic plan and its associate financial and personnel (manpower) plans are drawn up. Simultaneously operational plans are reviewed in depth with line management.

(xx) Issue plans

All plans are issued to the appropriate managers and become instructions to begin implementation.

The network is of necessity compressed, and could be enlarged for a particular situation. The time span covered will vary with the complexity and nature of the company, and has been found by many investigators to take up to three years to complete in full, although some divisions of the company may be involved earlier than this. My own experience suggests that the company need not wait this long, and can be in possession of its first valid set of plans within twelve to fifteen months of start-up. This target is much more likely to succeed if the whole approach is tightly planned and controlled, as in the example, and if the company from the top down gives planning a reasonable degree of priority. The fact that much of the work causes an involvement of managers from an early stage is one factor which assists a reasonably speedy movement to a complete process of planning.

In the review the importance of an educational programme was stressed. For practical purposes the word 'educational' is emotively bad and any planners who announce that they are employed to 'educate' their fellow managers are doomed to failure. Perhaps a much better approach is to stress the need for managers throughout the company to fully understand both the principles of planning and the process being applied in their company.

This may be a great stumbling block in the way of the innocent corporate planner. Many of the concepts of strategic management are alien to what many managers have done in the past. In any company there are variations in the age, ability, function, and educational attainments of managers, and they can by no means be regarded as a homogenous group. Many managers will regard the task of management as an exciting science, and will keep up to date with the latest developments (including strategic management): others will lack the time or inclination to ever read a book or journal on a management subject. Many would go so far as to argue against the view that management can be studied, believing it is something that is inborn and instinctive (and they will not be reading this book).

Much of the task of changing the outlook of the management falls on the chief executive. It is impossible to avoid this. By personal example the chief executive must demonstrate the value of strategic management: by actions and attitudes the chief executive must motivate managers to the extent that they are willing to attempt to play their full part in the planning process. The chief executive who opts not to employ a corporate planner must bear all the burden of this personally.

584

Where there is a planner the burden is eased, for the corporate planner should do much to ensure that fellow managers become familiar with the essence of corporate planning. This requires a high quality of leadership by the planner who has no power to *make* managers follow the paths indicated, but may help them perceive the paths and wish to follow them of their own volition.

Like the chief executive, the planner has to prove the point by personal example in day-to-day conduct. Insincerity quickly becomes apparent, and managers will soon have the measure of someone who does not practise what is preached.

The planner must be able to communicate with the managers, must talk in terms they can understand, and must be knowledgeable enough about their functions to be able to appreciate their problems and what they are saying. Communication is one of the most difficult areas of management. It is important that the planner never speaks over the heads of managers – which means never sheltering behind the jargon of the techniques or position as an 'expert'. Similarly, the planner must never be condescending and speak down to managers.

The methods which a planner should consider using to fulfil the task of showing the path include:

Personal discussion

One of the most effective methods of moulding opinion is still discussion on a personal basis, talking over with managers points of planning detail in relation to their own problems and getting to know them as individuals. This begins during the familiarisation period, and gains in intensity as the planner becomes more deeply involved in the company's business and help managers in the preparation of their own plans.

Planning manual

A manual, which clearly defines the system of planning and shows how each part of the system fits into the whole is a very important tool. The reasons for this are that a concise record of the process, besides protecting the company's investment in planning, is important if managers are to understand their own part in it. The manual may be a vehicle for general planning concepts, and may form the basis of subsequent methods of planning development. A well-constructed manual will also save managers their most precious commodity – time. It will remove from them the task of thinking out the problems of setting out a plan and leave them free to face the more important task of considering decisions.

Internal planning conferences and courses

I am a great believer in the value of holding internal conferences and courses to explain to managers what is involved in corporate planning, to describe the overall process being used in the company, to highlight the reasons for introducing planning in that company, and to demonstrate to each manager that he has a part to play. A course gives opportunity to improve planning skills at the individual level.

Conferences and courses may be held at various levels in the organisation, and senior management should be dealt with separately although, apart from this, it is often a good idea to deliberately mix up seniority, departments, and functions. The content may be varied to suit the audience, as may the length of the conference.

One useful conference format is to use an outside speaker to talk on the concept and general principles, and to follow this with a presentation from the planner on these principles as applied to the company. Where possible the chief executive, or an appropriate deputy, should participate by providing a brief speech of encouragement and policy. It is vital that the chief executive plays a major part in the conference for senior managers.

Each conference should provide for adequate discussion time, and should be designed to encourage and stimulate discussion. To achieve this means limiting the numbers attending to between 20 and 30, and if necessary repeating the performance several times in order to accommodate everybody.

Conferences are often improved if they are designed by professionals. This is even more true of courses where amateurism can impede learning. The ideal course would have between 15 and 20 people attending, and would be based on participative learning methods. Case-study approaches and real planning projects can be very valuable for teaching business strategy, analysis, the use of techniques, the problems of change, and the nature of planning systems (to list but a few examples). Provided they are professionally prepared, it is often valuable to write cases based on company experience to demonstrate the relevance of the concepts.

Attendance at outside seminars

Every planner has biases which are built into the approach to strategic management. There are usually other ideas and concepts which because of this bias are not presented to managers. Yet a virile planning system requires the development of the company's approach to planning by the managers themselves. If they are herded along one path alone, they may never have the opportunity of extracting benefit from some of the opposing planning ideas. Realisation that planning is a live subject, and that real contributions can be made to methodology by managers at all levels is important both for planners and the company in general. The planner should not be positioned as the high priest who alone holds the key to the revelations of the gods.

This problem can be solved by asking selected managers to attend external seminars on strategic management. Those on offer are usually useful in exposing participants to new ideas, but should not be seen as a substitute for education.

All these approaches are of limited use unless backed by the total involvement of the company in strategic management. Training and development of any kind is best when of a continuous nature closely related with day-to-day activities and duties. Thus the best training in planning comes from using this method of management consistently, with the chief executive and planner both acting as guides to smooth the way.

Reference

1 Hussey, D. E. *Introducing Corporate Planning*, Pergamon, Oxford, 4th edn, 1991.

CHAPTER 29

Why planning sometimes fails

There has been much research on what can go wrong in a formal planning system. The aim of this chapter is to provide a guide to the pitfalls, and ways of avoiding them, drawing on research and the personal experiences of the author.

Several times in this book it has been stressed that planning can fail because of the way it is introduced or managed in a particular company. The previous chapter set out to give positive advice on the way the introduction of planning might be handled. This chapter attempts to look at the problem from a different way – to diagnose failure areas and warn against them.

Much of the material of this chapter comes from personal experiences, backed by numerous discussions with individual planners who were facing some of the difficulties that will be mentioned. It is reinforced by the writings of others, particularly those who have carried out original surveys. One leading work on this is still that of Warren,[1] which cannot be too highly recommended, but the research of George Steiner[2] has added much at a practical level. Steiner's list of pitfalls in planning is invaluable.

It should be noted that this topic was a subject for research in the 1960s and 1970s. More recent research, much of which has been quoted elsewhere, is concerned with strategy formulation and implementation. Because the research on which this chapter draws is from an earlier period it uses terms of the time to describe planning. I have not updated these to modern times. The conclusions are still valid.

Behaviour of the chief executive

It has always been stressed that planning will fail if the chief executive does not believe in it, or does not understand it, and accordingly shows a lack of interest in the process. It is sad that chief executives still introduce planning for the wrong reason. Irving[3] discovered two companies out of his sample of twenty-seven who admitted introducing corporate planning because it was 'fashionable'. Ringbakk[4] found in a survey in America that 40 per cent of respondents had difficulty in getting top management support for corporate planning.

Irving[3] also found that planners did not experience internal political difficulties where there was strong leadership and participation by the chief executive. As corporate planning is a complete way of running a business it is not something about which a chief executive can be neutral. Those who are not for it are against it: they cannot sit on a fence and still remain chief executive.

Unfortunately, belief and understanding are not necessarily both present at the same time. If a chief executive is to truly benefit from corporate planning, he must understand the processes which are involved. He or she must be as expert in corporate planning – although not necessarily in all the detailed technique – as his planner.

Pennington[5] makes the point that the type of involvement required from a chief executive is selective. He must come in at key points, and not allow himself to be swamped with so much detail that he neglects other aspects of his work. On the other hand, underinvolvement 'robs planning of its impact on operations'.

Success in applying planning as a process of management can usually be ascribed to a relatively simple fact. Managers throughout the company realise, from the words and actions of the chief executive, that this is the way he or she intends to run his business, and that anyone who does not like it can vote with his feet.

Actions and words must fit together. There is no instrument as sensitive as a company in the detection of insincerity. Success will not come simply through top management utterances. The chief executive who cannot be seen to be taking the medicine he prescribes for others will soon find himself with a planning failure on his hands. Ringbakk[6] observes: 'In many companies lip service has been paid to planning. Although management at the top has in words recognised the importance and desirability of formal planning, the necessary action and involvement have not resulted.'

Acceptance by management

Carson[7] quotes Ken Lander, then a senior partner with consultants Urwick Orr & Partners Ltd, as saying: 'It takes about two years for line managers to kill a planner through passive resistance.'

Ringbakk[4] found that in more than half of the businesses in his survey the major problem was getting operating managers to accept planning as part of their job. In a much earlier assessment Wrapp[8] stated that the most serious obstacle to planning '. . . is the subtle, but occasionally open, opposition of some executives which appears in the early stages of development'.

Warren's[1] survey supports these views, and maintains that managers too often '. . . dilute the efforts of those who seek to remove the obstacles to effective long-range planning'. He suggests that the introduction of planning is always accompanied by a 'wait and see' attitude by line managers, and their eventual support depends on the *real* backing that is given by the chief executive.

There are many reasons for opposition by line managers, including preoccupation with day-to-day tasks, systems of payment which are related to current results, and the high turnover in managers, which means that they are not around long enough to live out their long-range plans. A new person, close to the top, as a planner must be, threatens existing power structures, and may also be seen as a barrier to future progress by the managers themselves.

My view is that there need be no situation of armed hostility between planner and managers, and the steps outlined in the preceding chapter will do much to ensure that relations begin and remain on the right track. Nevertheless, the motivation of managers to use a process of corporate planning is very much a task that falls on the shoulders of the chief executive, and which depends for its success on his behaviour.

Planning will certainly fail if it does not gain a wide level of support throughout the company.

Allowing some managers to opt out

A process of corporate planning must be total. No one manager or division can be allowed to opt out of the planning system. This applies to the deed as well as the word, for commitment must be complete and must not be just a question of paying lip-service to the idea.

This does not mean that the introduction of planning may not be phased. It is quite logical, in a large company, to begin planning in one or two areas and gradually extend over the whole company. But no manager must be allowed the right of deciding that planning is not for him once his area has been brought into the planning process.

Failure by the chief executive to enforce this rule will be like glazing a cracked china cup. Sooner or later the fault will come to the surface and ruin all the work that has been done since.

Confusion about corporate planning and its meaning

Warren[1] makes the point that corporate planning is often confused with one of its elements. Some managers think they are enthusiastic supporters of planning, but really do not understand what it is about. It is common for managers to confuse it with forecasting, budgeting or computer models. Ringbakk[6] states:

> Much planning today consists of extending budgeting. In the average firm this has meant planning starting with today and going five years into the

future. The concern has largely been with the financial and quantitative results with which one is concerned in one year budgeting. However the underlying causal factors which determine the financial rules often have not been adequately covered. More fundamental qualitative thinking is required. What appears to be needed most urgently is strategic planning.

Lack of understanding often leads the entire company to expect miracles. Problems do not disappear just because the company has a corporate planner, and although immediate benefits may result (from, for example, the corporate appraisal), most must by definition be of a longer-term nature. von Allmen[9] stresses this point:

> Again, many companies decide that some formal corporate planning will give them a 'shot in the arm', when a little reflection would indicate that the start up investment of time and energy will result in just the opposite. More sinister, the launching of a major effort into corporate planning is often the signal of a panic reaction to impending serious problems which are already in so advanced a stage that only some outside miracle could successfully intervene.

Time and again it is stressed by writers on planning that it must be seen as part of the total process of management. Time and again companies ignore this advice, and try to establish planning as an operation which is additional and isolated from the total management system.

Any of these misunderstandings can – and usually do – lead to the complete failure of corporate planning, however well intentioned the original motives might be.

The planner and current activities

Some companies who employ planners give them terms of reference which effectively prevent them from taking any interest in day-to-day activities. They can do what they like – so long as they do not 'rock the boat' or upset the line managers.

No good planner will think for a fellow manager nor will he tell him how to run his business. But any plans made, and any systems devised, must be firmly rooted in the present activities of the company. Control of plans can only be carried out if the elements of the plans come down to things people are actually going to do.

It is impossible for any planning system to work if it is isolated from line managers. Plans made in a vacuum are likely to remain plans – and never be converted to actions.

The corporate planner has a rightful place in the top management committee of the company. Failure to give him or her this place is another step on the road to the ruin of corporate planning in that company.

The planner must accept the limitations of his role

Much has been said about the role of the planner and what the function should be in an organisation. It is important for the planner to understand – and accept – that, despite its importance, it is a role which has definite limitations.

The planner does not magically become the company's chief decision maker or the arbiter of its alternative policies. It is not a planner's function to foist personal pet strategies on the company or to see the role as one to be set above fellow managers. Any touch of arrogance, any impression that the planner is an overlord, will bring the planning efforts crashing down.

The planner who believes that the whole future of the company lies under his or her sole charge is doomed to failure.

All senior staff functions are difficult, and the planning function is the most difficult of all. The temptations to the planner to overstep the boundaries are very real.

von Allmen[9] mentions the 'high frustration tolerance level' which planners must have, as the '. . . commonest experience of the planner is high risk of failure with ultimate partial success'.

The avoidance of ivory tower planning

If the planner understands and accepts this role, there is little risk of introducing an 'ivory tower' type of planning. Too often, companies expect planning departments to produce plans: too often planners see their jobs in these terms.

Perrin[10] states bluntly: 'No ivory tower theorist – however brilliant – will ever be successful.' Ringbakk[1] argues from his survey that active management participation is essential at corporate and divisional levels: 'It can be argued, that this is the most fundamental condition which must be met since staff planners alone cannot do the planning.' In a different forum[6] he gives the fact that 'management at different levels in the organisation has not properly engaged in or contributed to the planning activities' as a main reason for the failure of planning in some companies.

A planning system which does not involve operating management will collapse and fail. It may appear deceptively quicker for a planner to write operating plans, and – out of a desire to avoid paperwork – line managers may initially urge that this be done. Later, line management disengages itself, claiming that the plans have nothing to do with it and are a staff matter: so no one implements them, no one has any accountability for them. A good planning system will involve every manager to an extent which will vary with function and seniority. It is not something which is reserved solely for divisional heads and chief executives. Not all managers will write long-range plans – but most should be allowed to contribute to the process.

Plans are not used

Perhaps the saddest problem area of all is that of the management which fails to operate by its plans. This may occur either because of the faults of management itself or because the planner neglects to build in any form of monitoring and control activity into the planning system.

What so often happens is that the company produces a set of impressive documents which involves a hectic period of corporate activity. The plans disappear into a series of filing cabinets, and are then lost for twelve months until the process starts again. Nothing is able to lose the confidence and enthusiasm of managers more quickly than the feeling that they are competing in an annual game of bluff and the writing of fairy stories, where the prize for all is a cloak of invisibility to ensure that no one actually does anything with the plans.

Smalter[11] states: 'The success of corporate planning is not measured by the production of impressive looking books titled "five-year plan – company confidential". Any aspiring plan will not happen merely because it is neatly documented. It is still very necessary to *make it happen*.'

The neglect of a follow-up and control system as part of the planning procedure can lead directly to its downfall. Planners can design the control procedures but only management can ensure that they are implemented. Unfortunately, many planners design no control mechanisms, and even when they do exist many managements fail to use them effectively.

The changing of a plan is not the same as neglecting a plan. Every manager has, from time to time, to deviate from a planned course of action. A consciously decided deviation made against the background of a firm is vastly different from a complete failure to use the plan at all.

Failure by top management to use the plan is something which is another manifestation of the first failure area discussed in this chapter, and is a reflection of a lack of understanding by the chief executive of what planning really is.

The planner is of too low a calibre

The planner contributes to the success or failure of the company's planning effort, and many statements have already been made about this difficult role, and the type of person who should fill it. Success in any job depends on the abilities of the person who holds it, and there are many functions in any form of organisation which bring success, mediocrity, or failure by the way in which the person holding the function fulfils the duties. The functions where personal failure can cause a companywide effect are comparatively few in number. One of these is certainly the corporate planner.

An inferior person can, despite the best of intentions, frustrate the planning efforts of the company, and in some cases will make it difficult or impossible for an effective process of planning ever to be applied in the company (this is quite apart from poor strategic decisions which may be made). Irving[3] maintains:

> Because of the unusual nature of the planner's role, and the rare combination of qualities required for its performance, the personal attributes of the planner are one of the most important determinants of the development of planning in any organisation. People with the required personal qualities are difficult to find and therefore expensive and either of these factors can result in lower calibre appointments.

The importance of the planner is stressed in Warren's[1] work and that of many other serious writers on the subject.

Despite all this excellent advice, many companies still rush down the road to planning failure by appointing the wrong person. Advertisements still appear which show that the recruiting companies see the planner as a low-level coordinator. Other companies see the position as a convenient resting place for a loyal senior executive, close to retirement, who has to be sidetracked.

Any chief executive who appoints the wrong calibre person (except in the occasional circumstance where there is a misassessment) is revealing a lack of knowledge of what planning is about. Frequently the key advisers in the company will recommend a lower calibre appointment than should be made in order to preserve their own vested interests. In general, managers like to take action which keeps the number of their equals as low as possible.

I would advance as a hypothesis for a future research programme that planning fails in a company as much from too low a calibre person being appointed as planning manager, as for any other cause. It is sad to see chief executives who are prepared to endanger all the investment of time and money the company is to make in planning for the sake of a quick or cheap appointment.

Planning through a committee

Committees and other forums for group meetings may often be used to great advantage in a company's planning processes. Elsewhere examples have been given of their use in setting assumptions and monitoring plans, to mention but two valid and worthwhile functions they can perform.

What I personally believe is impossible, and a contributory factor to planning failure, is the use of committees to replace a corporate planner. Any group with the special title 'planning committee' tends to be a danger sign (I believe that committees which are used should not be special to planning but should be part of the total management process in that company). Where the committee is the only organ the company has of creating and coordinating planning, the risk of failure rises to a very high level indeed.

By all means create forums for the involvement and participation of managers in planning, and develop these as a key element of the company's approach to corporate planning. But these should always be a tool of the planning system, not the method by which planning is introduced.

In any case, it is generally a good rule to have as few committees as possible.

Confusion of strategic and operational planning

The problem of confusing techniques of planning with planning itself has been discussed, as has the need to involve managers at all levels. Companies which manage to get these points in focus often miss another, and are blind to the differences between the two major but related types of planning. This leads to difficulties in deciding who should be involved in what, in defining the planning system, in writing the plans, and in organising the flow of planning information.

Strategic planning is, as we have seen, very different from operational planning. It is sometimes useful, but not always desirable, to involve 'grassroots' managers in the writing of the strategic plan (though often valuable to devise ways that enable ideas to come from all levels of management into strategic thinking).

'Involvement' in terms of strategic planning means the full participation of the top management team in the production of the strategic plan. This one might term as essential involvement for long-term planning success. Optionally, lower-level managers may also participate either because they have skills and knowledge on which the company should draw, or because the motivational value of such involvement is very high. This optional involvement may be selective both as to the choice of managers who are invited to participate and the extent to which they are involved. It is not always desirable for a company's total strategic plan to be known too widely in the company – particularly where there is a major acquisition strategy – although it may be valuable for selected aspects to be published.

For operational plans 'involvement' is different. Here I believe the principle should be that the head of each operational area must be responsible for his own plan, and should certainly enable all of his senior managers and as many of his more junior managers as the circumstances indicate, to play a part in the planning process.

Failure to understand the essential difference between the two types of planning leads to confusion. It prevents planning from becoming a properly integrated part of the company's overall management system. It also leads to the production of inadequate plans which do not cover the needs of the organisation and become rapidly unusable.

595

Insufficient care given to the format of plans

There are two great temptations to avoid in the preparation of plans and in the design of the planning system. One is to produce a mountain of paper in long-winded documents which are designed on the basis of what somebody thinks a plan should look like rather than what the organisation really needs. The second is to place too much emphasis on forms, so that the process of planning is viewed much in the same way as the annual completion of an income tax return.

Every organisation is unique, and must decide for itself what essential data its plans must include. In addition the requirements of detail will vary through the different levels of the organisation. A divisional manager will, for example, need more control data and information in his operating plans than he should send to corporate headquarters. Some form of 'pyramiding' is essential, together with the insistence that executives are only required to read those parts of plans which are valid and useful to them.

It is very easy for a planning system to become nothing but an empty, and vast, generator of scrap paper. Overelaboration should be avoided at all costs, and simplicity should be the design keynote.

An overelaboration of forms brings a different state of mind. A planning system which is nearly all forms is usually nothing more than an extended budgeting operation. Some forms may be required, but again they should be simple in concept and few in number. A plan should be written to do a job – not to demonstrate the cleverness of the person who prepared it.

The problem of oversophistication in planning systems

The planning system should not be too sophisticated for the company it is serving. A company which lacks elementary basic management tools, such as market research, management information systems, or adequate budgetary control, is not ready for a planning process that is too complex.

Many planners try to use advanced planning techniques immediately (such as complex computer models of the company) and design systems which depend on these. They force the company into something it is not yet ready to handle.

Similarly, there is a temptation to make planning as complex as possible in an attempt to produce a perfect plan. Frequently it is better practice to simplify, to hold the more complex areas back until the company gains in experience of planning. It is better to produce a less than perfect plan than to delay the preparation of plans for some years until the company can cope with the sophistications of the system or to force the company along paths it cannot understand.

This list of problem areas, when read in relation to the rest of this book, has a parallel with the type of instruction book which frequently comes with cars, washing machines, or other complex domestic appliances. Each part of the car is described in some detail, and the buyer is shown what it is, what it does, and what he should do. Nevertheless, at the end of the booklet there is a checklist of faults. If the engine does not start check (a) the ignition is switched on, (b) there is petrol in the car, (c) the plug leads are connected – and so it goes on.

Often the checklist enables the driver to take swift corrective action. It prevents him from calling a mechanic when all that is wrong is that he has not turned on the ignition.

Exhibit 29.1 Testing an existing planning process

These questions should be asked to gauge the effectiveness of a planning process. If the response is frequently a 'no' the chances are that the process is failing and needs to take account of some of the principles discussed in this chapter and elsewhere

- Is top management committed to the concept of corporate planning through deed as well as word?
- Are strategic actions, particularly the major ones, based on the plan?
- Are plans seriously reviewed and discussed up the hierarchy?
- Does management as a whole become widely involved in the planning process?
- Is management involvement wider than the narrow line of functional responsibility of the individual manager?
- Is there a top-down strategic input to plans (e.g. are the plans anything more than a consolidation of individual submissions)?
- Are external environmental issues studied seriously and integrated into the plan?
- Is management performance measured at least partly on the basis of the corporate plan?
- Does the planning process link up with budgetary control, performance standards, personnel appraisal schemes and management development programmes?
- Would the main competitors be grateful to receive a copy of the corporate plan? (Many are so useless that even competitors can gain nothing from them).
- Is it those managers who are good planners who get promoted?
- Are corporate plans normally completed on time?
- Is there a monitoring and control mechanism attached to the planning process?
- Is the management style compatible with a management process which requires participation?
- Is the Director of Planning a high calibre person?
- Does the Planning Department have a good co-operative working relationship with finance and accounts?

(© Harbridge Consulting Group Ltd, 1991: used with permission)

This list of failure areas is presented with something of the same purpose in mind. It is needed because we live in a real world where opinions are often in twilight shades of grey rather than the jet black and brilliant white of the textbooks.

In the first problem area mention was made of the need for a chief executive to understand planning. Unfortunately this is not a simple yes/no area. There are, in addition, degrees of understanding. Thus a chief executive may have a strong feeling for what the topic is all about but still have areas where his understanding is deficient.

Alternatively, he may have been in disagreement with a statement made or argument advanced in a previous chapter of this book. His disagreement may be partial, qualified, or absolute.

The checklist provides an opportunity for a reconsideration to be made of the importance of the issue. Often what goes wrong with the introduction of planning is just one of these very simple areas discussed in this chapter – as simple as turning the ignition key, and as stultifying on all progression if the action is omitted. If it prevents him from calling in an expert to correct it, the list will have had as much value as the handbook which avoids finding a mechanic for such simple problems.

Although few people would throw away a car that will not start, it is unfortunately true that many companies will discard their investment in corporate planning when this fails to fire. And it is doubly unfortunate when the cause of failure is preventable and often as trivial as the neglected ignition key.

References

1 Warren, K. E. *Long Range Planning: The Executive Viewpoint*, Prentice Hall, London, 1966.
2 Steiner, G. *Pitfalls in Comprehensive Long Range Planning*, Planning Executives Institute, 1972.
3 Irving, P. *Corporate planning in practice: a study of the development of planning in major United Kingdom companies*, MSc dissertation, University of Bradford, 1970.
4 Ringbakk, K. A. 'Organised Planning in Major US Companies', *Long Range Planning*, December 1969.
5 Pennington, M. W. 'Why Has Planning Failed?' *Long Range Planning*, March 1972.
6 Ringbakk, K. A. 'Why Planning Fails', *European Business*, Spring 1971.
7 Carson, I. 'The Big Leap in Corporate Planning', *International Management*, April 1972.
8 Wrapp, H. E. 'Organisation for Long Range Planning', *Harvard Business Review*, January-February 1957.
9 von Allmen, E. 'Setting up Corporate Planning', *Long Range Planning*, September 1969.
10 Perrin, H. F. R. 'Long Range Planning: the Concept and the Need', *Long Range Planning*, September 1968.
11 Smalter, D. J. 'Anatomy of a Long Range Plan', *Long Range Planning*, March 1969.

CHAPTER 30

Strategic management to strategic change?

The aim of this chapter is to provide some personal views on the way strategic management might develop, and to add a few thoughts about strategic success.

Strategic management has made great strides since it emerged as a topic under its old name of long-range planning. We now have better techniques of strategic analysis, and new concepts of strategy formulation, and we understand more about the behavioural aspects of managing strategically. It is perhaps of interest to try to speculate where the subject might be heading.

In trying to forecast its future I should like to steal from some of my editorials from the early issues of the *Journal of Strategic Change*, and from material that Igor Ansoff wrote to mark the launch of this journal in early 1992.

I have always been an admirer of elephants, and once lived in a country where they roam wild. There is something that I find appealing about these majestic animals, and I have in the past used them to illustrate some of the issues around strategic change.

Despite this, I was unprepared for the brief report which appeared in the *Daily Telegraph* of 22 May 1992. 'Rider trapped for 2 days on mad elephant'. Naturally I read on. The story was about an Indian elephant rider who, it said, was trapped on the back of an elephant while it ran amok for 200 miles before it could be tranquilised and he could be rescued. It was in a state of sexual frenzy, known as a must (what else could it be called!). However, the mahout did not suffer from hunger, as he grabbed fruit that had been tied to trees for him along the elephant's route. This implies some careful planning and forecasting, in order to predict the route correctly, and needed a high degree of accuracy. An inch too far to the left or right, and the poor mahout would have gone hungry, with food just out of reach. I do not know if the story was a left-over from 1 April although from the tone of the article I think the *Telegraph* were keeping their options open.

From observation over many years, I believe that many organisations follow a strategic path in a somewhat similar fashion to this elephant, stimulated by something, and charging off down a path without thinking about the implications.

Quick response, of which the hanging down of food for the mahout is a simile, saves some of the problems from becoming disasters. Somehow we do not seem to learn as much as we should from past experience. To my knowledge there has been at least one major study of the failure rate in acquisitions at roughly ten yearly intervals. The conclusions in the 1970s, 1980s and more recently 1993 had one thing in common. The failure rate was around 50 per cent. Either something continually goes wrong in the pre-merger strategy, or we are still struggling to learn how to implement the strategies which are so perfect on paper.

The headlong rush of the maddened elephant reminded me of a cartoon sequence I devised some years ago for a lecture about the difficulty of making change happen in organisations. The first picture showed a number of bowler-hatted, pinstriped city gents trying to make a reluctant elephant move, pushing and prodding with their umbrellas: it dealt with the difficulty of getting any willingness to change at all. The second slide showed the same characters trying to restrain an elephant that was charging off in the wrong direction. I now know that it was suffering from a must! This was to illustrate the difficulty of ensuring that the right change was implemented. There were other cartoons in the sequence, which ended with a suggestion that the wrong strategy could result in the organisation becoming a white elephant.

My previous company, Harbridge Consulting Group, has had encounters with elephants, both of the varieties illustrated in the cartoons and the real thing. A few years ago, two of my colleagues were running a course in Zambia. The hotel, in a game park, consisted of a series of low buildings with verandahs which were used for breakout groups. Into the hotel compound strolled a bull elephant with one broken tusk. Whether the students by that time had learnt much about strategic change was doubtful, although they demonstrated that they needed no coaching in how to beat a fast tactical withdrawal in the face of changed prospects. The elephant was not undergoing a must, and among our corporate souvenirs is a photograph of the animal attentively studying the flip chart. We have had no reports that he has applied the learning he gained within his own community!

The elephant theme has been used by others, including the mind-blowing image of teaching elephants to dance, although this probably owes more to Rudyard Kipling than to Rosabeth Moss Kantor.

My belief is that the next decade of advances in strategic management will be much more about managing strategic change than formulating strategy. Indeed one could see the term 'strategic change' becoming the new byword for the next phase of strategic management.

Strategic emphasis has, over time, been moving to a greater focus on implementation. I think the future will bring a greater merging of formulation skills with those of organisational behaviour and change management. Put another way, successful change comes about through a blend of the hard and soft disciplines, the analytical and the behavioural. Neglect of one in favour of the other is likely to lead to actions which do not yield the desired results.

Trends in management rarely appear from nowhere, and the emphasis I see on strategic change is a logical step in the evolution of strategic management. Nevertheless, it does challenge the traditional boundaries between functions, and requires a closer binding of many functions which have traditionally been regarded as independent. This does not mean that planners have to report to organisational development people, or that human resources in some way comes under planning. It does mean that traditional views of roles have to change, and that each should be seen as a non-watertight element of an overall task that has to be conceived as an entity.

Igor Ansoff can fairly be described as the father of strategic management, first exposing the concept of strategic planning and later leading the thinking that developed this to the concept of strategic management. In a letter to me about the new journal, he observed: 'The role of the corporate planner . . . is already obsolete, both in theory and practice, and the journal could contribute to the concept of the strategic change manager ... who combines four disciplinary perspectives: analytic, psychological, sociological and political.'

While the title of corporate planner – or the many other variations on this theme – may live on, the role in successful organisations is much as Igor describes it. Similarly, organisational development can no longer be a staff activity whose efforts are unrelated to the corporate objectives and strategy, while those organisations which give little thought to organisational behaviour must find mechanisms to bring these skills into the change process. The same argument can be made for many of the activities of the human resource function, such as management development. Overall there is a need for leadership and management of a high order, activities which cannot be separated from strategic decision making or organisational development. The real issue for all players is how to manage strategic change in an era of increasing turbulence. While there are many structural solutions, the most important step is the realisation of the mutual interdependence of all these players, if successful change is to take place.

The turbulence in the business environment is a driver of change, and leads to what might be called a situational approach to strategic management. In particular I refer to the recent thinking by Igor Ansoff which appears elsewhere in this book. However, the events which change the business prospects also change the expectations and attitudes of the people we employ. The future of strategic management, which I see as strategic change, will also be a future which takes far more account of the economic value of human resources. I foresee far more emphasis on approaches and techniques to address this issue than has been the case in the past, and I would hope for a kit bag of tools which matches the range of choice now available for dealing with other aspects of strategy.

I should like to leave the last new thought with Igor Ansoff[1]:

> . . . important as they are, unidisciplinary perspectives of a multidisciplinary problem do not automatically add up to a solution of the total problem. This fact is amply supported by the voluminous literature in cybernetics, general systems theory and sociology.
>
> The second reason is that I cannot think of any really important problem in today's society and its organisations whose solution is not vitally dependent on intimate contemporaneous interplay of the whole range of 'hard' and 'soft' sciences.

(The extract refers to the role he sees for the journal, and the omissions do not distort his intentions.)

If I try to summarise this chapter, it is to say that strategic management will move to a new dimension of strategic change management in intent if not in name. More emphasis will be placed on methods that provide a better strategic insight into human resource management; leadership and management of a much higher order will be required; and a more situational approach to strategic management will become the norm, in order to relate to the degree of environmental turbulence faced by the particular organisation.

But let me finish with a caution. New ideas are important, and take strategic management forward. However, we should never allow an author's enthusiasm to destroy our own judgement. A sign of true professionalism in the development of management theory and practice is that a body of knowledge is built up over time. The new may be very different from the old, and be designed to deal with situations that did not exist in the past, but we should distrust the hype that surrounds so many of the new concepts. There seems to be a need to persuade the world that all that is needed is the new idea, and everything previous is of little account. Well, as we saw in Chapter 1, not all new concepts are as original as their authors believe, and even the language they use to promote them is the same as has been used to 'sell' many previous ideas.

Management should not be about following fashions. It should be about choosing the ideas, concepts and techniques that are appropriate for particular situations. In order to make an informed choice, managers need to know the concepts they are rejecting, as well as the one they have chosen.

It is obvious that no concept can have the same degree of success for every organisation. For example, proponents of core competencies as the 'right' way have claimed that it can enable an organisation to transform an industry. Controlling your own destiny, and pulling the rug from under the feet of competitors, may appeal to the emotions. But think about it. The competitors read the same books, and it is clearly impossible for every competitor to transform the industry. If the game is to win, someone must lose. Core competencies have something to offer as a concept, but so do many of the other concepts and techniques. Nothing should be taken in isolation from the rest of the body of knowledge, and the wise will use several approaches to help them on the way to taking strategic decisions.

Reference

1 Ansoff, H. I. 'Welcome to the Journal of Strategic Change', *Journal of Strategic Change*, 1, No. 1, January/February 1992.

Part 6

Case Studies

CHAPTER 31

SWK Zimbabwe Ltd

Dermot Knight, now CEO of SWK Central Africa, had spent much of the last two years in extensive planning activity designed to help the SWK activities in the region to position themselves to take advantage of the opportunities that were opening. One result of this work had been the division of African businesses, present and potential, of Scott Wilson Kirkpatrick into two regions. SWK South Africa covered South Africa, and countries closely related to it. SWK Central Africa was responsible for the whole of the rest of Africa from headquarters in Harare. Included in that responsibility was the biggest company in the region, SWK Zimbabwe and its related companies.

In January 1996, Dermot and his management team were faced with the task of developing a business plan for the Zimbabwe operations, in the context of the new regional structure. Code-named Operation Bridge, the aim was to revitalise the Zimbabwe business. But first the marketing strategy had to be determined.

Background to Zimbabwe Environment

Zimbabwe is a developing country whose economic growth is not keeping pace with the expansion of the population. In Zimbabwe at this time the currency had been losing value in relation to many foreign currencies, some of the protective shields for local industry had been removed, allowing more products to enter from other countries (particularly South Africa), and the amount of money the government could make available for public sector projects was much less than the infrastructure needed, and had reduced in recent years. The government's need for funds meant that some of the taxation policies, such as a tariff on raw materials for industry and on plant and machinery, restricted the development of the private sector.

This case study has been prepared by David Hussey for teaching purposes only. Some facts have been disguised for commercial reasons. The generous help of Dermot Knight, CEO, SWK Africa, is gratefully acknowledged. © 1996 D. E. Hussey. Written for NUTAC TRAINING, Harare.

It is also worth mentioning that the country had operated in the past as an economy of shortages, caused by the civil war and its aftermath, during which time most industries had demonstrated innovative 'can do' philosophies, finding ways to produce most of the products that could not be imported. This had resulted in a seller's market, where availability was more important than price or quality, and little marketing effort was needed to sustain sales. This situation had now changed, competitive products were available from outside the country, and there were few gaps on retailer's shelves. Suddenly marketing had become important, and competition more acute, and manufacturing companies had to think in terms of a market share, rather than planning expansion of facilities to scoop the whole market. At the time of the case study the whole situation in most markets had become more competitive, and many organisations in all sectors had to face up to significant external forces, as they moved from selling what they had available to meeting the real requirements of customers.

Background to SWK Africa

Part of the international Scott Wilson Kirkpatrick group, SWK Africa is an engineering, development and management services network. The firm offers a comprehensive range of integrated services which embrace all facets of development including: development policy and trends analysis; civil, structural and water engineering; development and economic planning, urban and regional planning, urban design, project packaging and programming, project and development management, environmental studies, social studies and transportation services. The firm offered a wide range of professional services at all stages of a project from initial planning and feasibility studies, site investigation and design through to implementation and operation. The firm has had experience in Zimbabwe over some 40 years.

Membership of the international group brought certain benefits to SWK Central Africa. There was access to over 2000 people in fifty countries, which meant that local expertise could always be extended from elsewhere in the group: a disadvantage was that fluctuations in exchange rates and the low value of the Zimbabwe dollar against major currencies could make such help expensive and of unpredictable cost. Another benefit was that the international headquarters had access to international aid sources. The head office was sometimes awarded contacts for work in various parts of Africa by international aid agencies. It was sometimes convenient for some of the work to be formally subcontracted to the Zimbabwe organisation. For example, a recent contract had been placed with the international head office by the UK's Overseas Development Agency for the rehabilitation of feeder roads in one province in Mocambique: SWK Central Africa had been awarded a part of this contract and Zimbabwe Operations was assisting. Such opportunities may well not be available to a purely local firm without international connections. The information in the Appendix at the end of this case study shows some of the assignments of SWK Africa, including a number undertaken by the Zimbabwe operations.

Some facts about the Zimbabwe business

The firm in Zimbabwe, excluding a laboratory which is not part of this case study, has a total staff of eighty-six made up of:

Technical partners and staff   65
Other staff   21

Although additional professional skills can be obtained from other SWK companies, particularly the UK, the areas where SWK Zimbabwe has local expertise are:

Airport planning
Project management and development management
Civil engineering   Highways and pavements
    Township services
Railway planning
Geotechnical services
Mechanical and electrical engineering
Structural engineering
Environmental planning.

SWK Zimbabwe had local arrangements for environmental planning skills, land surveyors, quantity surveyors and architects, although it did not itself employ these skills. Zimbabwe experience was particularly strong in private sector industrial projects, all sectors of project management, airports and highways. One idea under consideration was to establish a separate business for project management services, in partnership with an organisation with an established position in this area, in order to further differentiate and exploit the opportunities for this type of service.

Table 31.1 Revenue of SWK in Zim$ million

Financial year	$ million
1989–90	4.4
1990–91	5.7
1991–2	9.8
1992–3	11.7
1993–4	13.5
1994–5	16.7
1995–6 (estimated)	18.9

The trend in revenue is shown in Table 31.1. The growth over the period has been roughly the same as the rate of inflation. The 1990s had been a turning point following a boom period for SWK through the 1980s, caused by a loss of skills to the country as a number of people emigrated, an expansion of development in the country, and exchange control restrictions which reduced the ability to hire experts from outside the country. During the 1980s SWK had as much work as it could handle without increasing productivity, and little management time had been given to thinking about what might happen when the boom ended.

SWK had 250 active projects which were being undertaken for 120 clients. Project fee sizes varied from a low of Zim$20 000 to a high of Zim$15 000 000. Smaller projects were usually completed within a year, often within a few weeks: larger projects rarely took more than two years to complete. Projects could cause cash-flow problems unless adequate payment stages were agreed, and one of Dermot's problems was how to develop product concepts which improved cash flow.

Image of SWK Zimbabwe

The firm was well known to its clients, and had a reputation for quality service and professional integrity. Dermot wondered how far this might be different from the way other high-quality competitors were regarded. He had some concern that SWK lacked a public profile, and that although it had good contacts, its narrow client base made it more difficult to be sure that it was on the bid list for all major projects that lay within its sphere of interest. The firm was undoubtedly stronger in the private than the public sector, and did not have many strong relationships with the influencers and decision makers in the public sector bodies. In order to expand, the organisation might have to seek and find more competitive bid situations, and it was relatively inexperienced in these (the reason is explained later). The firm was not seen as the leader in any particular discipline, although it was the major player in the industrial sector.

Most work gained was either repeat business for an existing client or a referral by an existing client. Sometimes boards at sites where work was undertaken carried the firm's name. (Ove Arup had become very well known because its name appeared prominently in this way on many commercial city centre sites.) Recently SWK had introduced a periodic newsletter to strengthen relationships with clients, and ensure that clients had a better knowledge of the breadth of services offered (for example, one problem was that a large client might use the firm for only one type of project, and fail to realise that SWK had expertise in other areas where it was not asked to bid). The frequency of this publication was four issues per year. Advertising was banned by the profession.

Over a long period there had also been an annual Christmas lunch for clients and potential clients, usually attended by about 100 people.

Market details

There are around thirty firms of consulting engineers bidding for business. Although it is not difficult for any professionally qualified person to become a competitor, lack of size limits the opportunities to bid for work. The consulting engineers are listed in order of size in Table 31.2. Ove Arup is the biggest, and has clear leadership in the commercial sector of the market. SWK was the leader in private sector industry, although only third in overall size. Others had leadership

Table 31.2 The competitors: human resources 1994

Firm	Ptrs		Assoc	Other tech	Total tech	Non-tech	Int. links
	Res	NR					
Ove Arup	4	2	9	91	106	23	y
B Colqhoun & P	5		5	74	84	19	y
SWK & Ptners (+ MSW)	3	4	1	57	65	21	y
Stewart Scott NCL	5	1	5	46	57	23	y
Nicholas O'Dwyer & Partners	3	2	3	44	52	11	y
Burrow Binnie	4	3		20	27	5	y
Knight Piesold (Zim)	1	6		20	27	7	y
CPP	4			21	25	35	y
CNM	2			17	19	5	n
Muir Assoc	2		4	12	18	6	y
Young Bamu Jennings	3		1	13	17	5	n
Atkinson Dickie	2		5	9	16	4	n
Bicon	2	1		12	15	9	n
Sir Alexander Gibb & Partners	4			9	13	5	y
Stewart Scott Kennedy	3			9	12	1	n
Steffan Robertson & Kirst	1	5		5	11		y
Cresswell Assoc.	2			8	10	2	n
AG Georgiadis Cslt Eng.	1			7	8	3	n
Marcussen & Cocksedge	2	1		5	8	2	n
Merz & Mclellan (Zim)	1	5			6		y
Peter Williams & Partners	2			4	6	2	n
Halcrow Zim Partnership	1			4	5	3	n
John Goddard Cslt Eng.	1			3	4	2	n
Brad Rutherford & Ass.	1			1	2	2	y
JN Jordan & Assoc.	1				1		n
Lyle Engineers	1				1	1	n
Prof. W. R. Mackechnie	1				1		n
Totals	62	30	33	491	616	196	

in particular skill areas: for example, Stewart Scott was the recognised leader in water projects.

Competition was not restricted to firms of consulting engineers, nor to firms that are resident in Zimbabwe. A few years previously SWK had won a bid for some work at Harare Airport in competition with, among others, a specialist firm owned by the operator of Paris airports. Many of the world's airport operators now had a consultancy wing, and their offerings included the management and operation of airports as well as design and development.

In Zimbabwe, some services which might have been thought to be the preserve of consulting engineers, such as feasibility studies and project management, were also offered by quantity surveyors, management consultants and the large accounting firms. Dermot believed that the merging of traditional professional service industries would continue, as this was part of a larger world trend.

Buyer's risk varies with the assignment, but is perceived as high on any large project where poor advice or performance can cause delays or affect the economics of operation. Traditionally consulting engineers worked in a way that meant that they took no project risks, and that price competition was in theory eliminated as the whole industry used the same fee rates. The two ways of quoting were a percentage of the project value or industry standard day-based fee rates where fees were charged on time actually spent. The latter method was used in situations where the project value could not be calculated.

Buyers did not like either method, arguing that the percentage of project basis meant that it was not in the industry's interest to seek the most cost-effective solutions, as this would reduce the overall fee, while the ability to charge for all time spent on a project transferred any cost of inefficiency to the buyer. It also made it harder for a buyer to budget for a project, and uncertainty could make it more difficult to arrange finance. The Association of Consulting Engineers argued that the removal of price competition meant that clients were better placed to judge the quality of competing proposals, and were attempting to gain statutory backing for the scale rates.

SWK had tried to remove some of the buyers' uncertainty for time-based charges by quoting a project as a series of steps against an overall budget estimate, so that the client was able to review progress through the project, and to modify or curtail the assignment should it appear to be costing more than was expected. This still meant that buyers were left with the financial consequences of any time needed for the assignment. Dermot had to find some way of meeting buyer needs for value on all assignments, and to remove some of the uncertainty buyers faced: he wondered whether this might be done by combining traditional consulting engineers services with other services to offer unique concepts which gave more added value to the client.

Some buyers favoured partnering arrangements, where a team of architects, surveyors, consulting engineers, surveyors, the contractor, and the developer was assembled at the beginning of the project, and worked as a team to give value to the client. This eliminated much traditional hostility between the various parties in a development, as it put them all in the same boat at the beginning, and did not allow any one party to pass off all the risks to another. The partnering concept was dependent on the willingness of all parties to work in this way, and success required the building of strong relationships.

Some buyers were more interested in price, and believed that this was best achieved by playing the field. Others saw value in some form of preferred relationship, and this was very prevalent in the industrial sector. There were also buyers who would prefer to pay a somewhat higher price for a fixed-price relationship, in order to remove the risk of unexpected bills.

Turnkey contracts were another approach sometimes used, where one organisation would take total responsibility for the whole project, awarding all subcontracts and making any essential purchases.

Using SWK ratios of revenue to technical staff (including partners) Dermot calculated that total industry revenue in 1994 was around Zim$168.5 million, and that SWK held about 10 per cent of this. However, the margin of error in these figures was high, and he put it at plus or minus 20 per cent.

The market as a whole grew in real terms during the decade of the 1980s because of the expansion of public sector business. Through the 1990s there has been no growth in real terms, and there may well have been a decline as public sector business fell away.

SWK had commissioned an economic forecast for 1996. This suggested that a good 1995/6 rainy season could stimulate the construction activity, particularly in the commercial sector where there was a pent-up demand for office space. In any event, the tourist industry was expected to continue to grow. Prospects for manufacturing as a whole were seen as gloomy in 1996, although a good rainy season would stimulate those sectors which processed agricultural products.

Longer-term public sector prospects had to be good, because of the need for many infrastructure projects if industry were to be able to develop. However, short- to medium-term economic difficulties meant that these necessary projects would not take place in the immediate future.

Inflation was expected to rise, to peak at around 25 per cent in early 1996, and the Zimbabwe dollar was forecast to continue to depreciate against major world currencies during the same period.

Public and private sectors

One way of looking at the market was in the broad sectors of public and private. Public sector buyers were the main government departments, and the municipalities. Firms were invited to bid individually, or sometimes through advertisements, and were given the terms of reference on which to bid. Frequently invitations were given to a restricted short list of five or six bidders, and there were rarely more than ten. Tenders were on a sealed-bid basis, and decisions were most likely to be highly influenced by price considerations. Terms of payment for public sector projects tended to be worse than for those in the private sector, and payment was more likely to be delayed.

Historically the industry had gained 75 per cent of its revenue from the public sector, although SWK had never had more that 25 per cent from this sector, and currently had only 5 per cent. The recent trend was for more firms to give attention to the private sector, as economic management issues had reduced the available public sector finances. Competition was likely to increase in this sector.

Although some private sector work was put out to public tender in a similar way to that of the public sector, much more was dealt with through preferred relationships with one to three firms. There was a tendency for a company to stay with the same supplier(s) over a long period, possibly partly fuelled by the standardisation of fee rates across the industry and a belief that better value could not be obtained from another source. This gave Dermot a particular problem. Although SWK's client base was a strength, how could market share be increased when many non-clients had similar relationships with competitors? Any inability to increase market share would condemn SWK to following market trends, whether they were up or down, and limit prospects for growth. There were several hundred buyers in the private sector, although SWK was not known to all of these.

A bid could be complex to prepare, and there was a cost for every bid, mainly in the time spent on it. A typical average cost of preparing a bid was around Zim$100 000. A small environmental bid would not cost as much, and would lie in the range of Zim$20 000 to $30,000.

Some issues

Dermot was aware that not all work undertaken was of equal profitability, and that the percentage of project method of quoting bore no relationship to the professional time that had to be spent on it. Historically, consulting engineers had not given enough attention to planning and budgeting time requirements for each project, or to monitoring and controlling the fee-earning and non-fee-earning activities of employees. As well as not relating to costs, the traditional approaches did little to reflect the value to clients of different services.

A study of the revenue per employee of international firms on a global basis showed that the Big SIX accountants averaged US$123 000 per employee, whereas the average for ten international firms of consulting engineers was only about half of this figure.

SWK Zimbabwe had to find a way of increasing revenue, and this meant increasing market share by a point or two, taking advantage of any growth in the market, and improving the profitability of projects undertaken.

Dermot struggled with the possibilities. Should SWK expand its client base, in which case what effort needed to be made to increase awareness and give the client a reason why SWK was a better choice than the firms they currently used? Could more be done to manage professional resources, so that all projects were more profitable and labour needs were more predictable? Was it possible to combine the traditional skills of the consulting engineer to other requirements of the client which were important to the economic success of the project, so that the total offering was both different and gave more added value to the client? Were there options such as alliances with other professional firms like lawyers, accountants, and management consultants which would be better than assembling all the skills from within SWK? Were there other ways of securing the future by developing stronger relationships with clients? Was it possible to price services in relation to the value to clients, and demonstrate that the value really existed? What should the firm's segmentation strategy be? Could a market be created for a service product which did not currently exist?

This plan had to employ more innovative thinking than had been necessary in the past, and had to give SWK prospects for long-term success.

Appendix: Extracts from the SWK brochure

Introduction

SWK Africa is an Engineering, Development and Management Services Network. Part of the international Scott Wilson Kirkpatrick group, it operates offices throughout Africa. The firm offers a comprehensive range of integrated services which embrace all facets of development including: development policy and trends analysis; civil, structural and water engineering; development and economic planning, urban and regional planning, urban design, project packaging and programming, project and development management, environmental studies, social studies and transportation services. A comprehensive range of professional services is offered at all stages of a project from initial planning and feasibility studies, site investigation and design through to implementation and operation.

Over the past 40 years we have developed an extensive understanding of local conditions. Our network of locally trained staff, supported by expertise from our international network of offices, enables us to produce the most appropriate solutions and project designs. This provides an efficient integration between Africa and the international SWK group, which employs over 2,000 people in 50 countries. SWK Africa provides access to this expertise and experience for clients who include the private sector, public sector, community organisations and major funding agencies.

SWK Africa is committed to meeting the needs of its clients through the use of appropriate technology, computer applications, local expertise and international experience. The company is dedicated to remaining fully abreast of the latest technological developments in design and innovation and their application for the benefit of the communities within which it operates.

Expertise

- *Airports* Master planning, runways, taxiways, pavement evaluation, terminal buildings, maintenance and cargo facilities, infrastructure, military airbases.
- *Environmental* Impact assessment, audit and monitoring studies, pollution control, solid waste disposal, landfill.

613

- *Geotechnics*   Engineering geology, soil and rock mechanics, foundation and pavement design, soils and materials testing, deep excavations, retaining walls.
- *Information systems*   Systems analysis, remote sensing, applications and software development, geographic information systems.
- *Human resource development*   Labour based management, technical assistance and operational support, project related training.
- *Maritime and coastal*   Master planning, ports, harbours and marinas, navigation and dredging, coastal engineering.
- *Roads, bridges, tunnels*   Motorways, trunk roads and gravel roads, feeder roads in urban and rural areas. Interchanges, bridge design and inspection, tunnels, car parks.
- *Railways*   Light rail and heavy rail, travel demand, route alignment, rail freight handling and terminals.
- *Social impact assessment and management*   Social impact assessment as part of integrated environmental procedures, social surveys, public involvement, management of mitigation strategies.
- *Structures*   Multi-storey buildings, steel and concrete structures, commercial and industrial buildings, recreational, health and educational facilities. Maritime structures, bridges, effluent treatment structures.
- *Transportation planning*   National and regional transport studies, public transport operations, traffic management, inter-urban and bypass studies, traffic advice and planning enquiries.
- *Urban and Regional planning*   Regional, metropolitan, urban and community planning, structure, framework and policy, township design and establishment, informal settlement upgrading.
- *Urban development*   Institutional studies, services reticulation design and planning, design and project management of mass housing.
- *Water and wastewater*   Water resources, treatment and supply, drainage, sewage treatment, hydrogeology, flood defences, river engineering and irrigation.

Services

- *Development planning*   Regional, local and site plans including economic, social, demographic and spatial planning from concept plans to statutory approval.
- *Planning studies*   Financial and economic appraisal, traffic forecasts, functional and operational analysis, modelling, social and environmental impact assessments.
- *Site surveys*   Hydrographic, topographic and geotechnical investigation and mapping.
- *Project implementation*   Design, tender and contract documents, contractor prequalification, tender evaluation, site supervision and commissioning.
- *Project management*   Integrated systems/process approach to project planning, implementation and delivery including budget control and programming, co-ordination, operation, procurement and training, management of change and the development process.

- *Maintenance and refurbishment* Asset valuation, inspections, damage investigations, repair and refurbishment, maintenance management.
- *Quality management* Project evaluation, technical audit, design checks, codes and standards certification.
- *Dispute resolution* Expert witness, arbitration and conciliation.
- *Training* Training requirement analysis, programme design, courses and material, personnel policy and systems, job profile.
- *Environmental impact assessment* Collection of baseline biophysical and social data, assessment of project impact, suggestion of mitigation measures.

Relevant experience

- *Transportation* Road, rail, air and sea. Experience ranges from roads in Cameroun, Tanzania, Madagascar and Mozambique to rail in Zimbabwe and from airports at Entebbe, Lilongwe, and Kasane to port development in Dar es Salaam, and Tanga.
- *Commercial and industrial development* Factories, process plants, hotels and offices. References include multistorey offices in Nairobi, new abattoir in Bulawayo and government offices in Abuja, breweries in Durban.
- *Public service* Water supply, sewerage, sewage treatment, power stations, government offices, police and fire station facilities. Clients include many national government authorities, in South Africa, Zimbabwe, Malawi and Botswana; private utilities companies and funding agencies.
- *Urban development* Structure and master plans, development of utilities, public buildings and housing projects including work in Botswana, Swaziland, Nigeria and South Africa.
- *Rural development* Agricultural development, rural roads, water resources and supplies. Projects include work in Gambia, Sudan, Somalia, Zambia, Kenya and Zaire.
- *Urban and regional planning* Structure, master plans and framework plans for areas in Zimbabwe and South Africa including Kwekwe, Umkomaas, Umlazi, Inanda, Estcourt, Verulam and Westville. Tourism and economic development planning, integrated development plan for Richards Bay/ Empangeni area.
- *Social impact assessment* - Assessment and management of projects in South Africa and Lesotho.

Contact Offices

Harare, Zimbabwe
PO Box 3143
SWK House
80 Mutare Road
Harare
Tel: 2634 487107
Fax: 2634 487101
E Mail: swkzim@harare.iafrica.com

Bulawayo, Zimbabwe
PO Box 2272
2nd Floor Price Waterhouse House
55 Jason Moyo St
Bulawayo
Tel: 2639 67778/69856
Fax: 2639 76864

Offices in Africa

Botswana: Gaborone
Ghana: Accra
Lesotho: Maseru
Malawi: Lilongwe
Mozambique: Maputo
South Africa: Durban
South Africa: Johannesburg
Tanzania: Dar es Salaam
Uganda: Kampala
Zimbabwe: Bulawayo
Zimbabwe: Harare

Offices Worldwide

Australia
Bahrain
China
Germany
Greece
Hong Kong
India
Malaysia
Nepal
Saudi Arabia
Sri Lanka
Turkey
United Arab Emirates
United Kingdom
United States of America
Vietnam

CHAPTER 32

Colgate-Palmolive Oral Care Division in the Italian Market

Colgate is a truly global company serving 5.7 billion people around the world with consumer products that help make their lives healthier, cleaner, and more pleasant. Colgate serves global consumers with products in five major categories: Oral Care, Personal Care, Household Surface Care, Fabric Care, and Pet Nutrition.

Its business focus was only in the USA until the early 1900s when the company began an aggressive expansion programme that led to the establishment of Colgate operations throughout the world. Today, Colgate-Palmolive is an $8.4 billion company, marketing its products in 206 countries and territories. To meet the needs of this vast market, Colgate sets and attains high standards for its products. Quality is the hallmark of everything it does. So, too, is consumer value. The company continually works to understand consumers' changing needs, and then meet those needs with innovative products that are affordable to the greatest number of people.

The Oral Care division is concerned with three different kinds of products, Toothpaste, Toothbrushes, and Mouth Rinses. Oral Care is the most profitable category with 26 per cent of Colgate total sales in 1994. Specifically, it accounted for $1972.9 million in 1994 worldwide sales.

In Italy, Colgate shares the market with several large competitors such as Unilever, Procter & Gamble, SmithKline Beecham, and Gillette. The future in this country appears complex as well as interesting. In early 1997, Colgate's management faced the problem of how to increase its market share in Italy. In developing a strategy for its Italian business unit, in the light of the intense competitive market. Colgate's planners were concerned with answering several questions. How will manufacturers be able to extend their own market shares in a market such as the Italian one which is highly saturated? How can they most effectively communicate the product's characteristics to the consumer? Should they consider other distribution channels?

This case study was written by Professor R. J. Mockler of St John's University, New York and A. Faccini. © R. J. Mockler 1997

In answering these questions, the planners felt it was necessary to first carefully study the Italian market, especially the strengths and weaknesses of competitors in specific opportunity areas. Within that competitive market framework they then studied the company's comparative position as a first step in developing an overall strategic business unit strategy.

The Italian market

Prior to the case, the Italian oral care market had been growing mainly due to consumers' increasing awareness of the importance of oral hygiene. The market included three different kinds of products: toothpaste, toothbrushes, and mouth rinses. Italy is not in line with the main European countries in terms of sales, thus, there appear to be very strong growth opportunities.

An important factor in this business is advertising which has allowed consumers to be aware of the existence of different formulations, demonstrating how important oral hygiene is. The concept of prevention, extendable to toothbrushes and mouth rinses, enabled the beginning of a diversification process and of a specialised supply. Consequently, new items appeared on the shelves of distributors.

Between 1980 and 1993, sales of toothpaste, toothbrushes, and mouth rinses had high growth rates and this trend is expected to continue.

Products

Toothpaste

Until ten to thirteen years ago toothpaste was generally considered as a 'soap' to clean teeth. At the same time there were so many different brands that the consumer became confused very easily. In fact, the discriminative factor was still price. In the mid-1980s, Italians began to become aware of the importance of using toothpaste formulated to prevent cavities. Therefore, innovation led to new products on the market. Pastes with grumes represented the first alternative followed by a totally innovative toothpaste made of gel. These were the main innovations, and since then toothpaste became a highly standardised product differing only in colour or packaging.

In 1993, in the mass-market channel, the toothpaste segment grew by 4.7 per cent in value and by 6.5 per cent in volume. This is not as good a performance as it appears when compared to 1990 and 1991 when sales in value increased by 16.3 per cent and sales in volume by 14.6 per cent. This trend shows that demand developed in terms of both quality and quantity. In fact, the mass market channel is the place where most people purchase toothpaste and the chemist is not as important as it was in the past. People purchase specific products in a chemist, while toothpaste can be found elsewhere and more cheaply.

Toothbrushes

The toothbrush has always been purchased as a support to toothpaste, and only in recent years has it started to be considered as a fundamental instrument for prevention of cavities. Nevertheless, the substitution level is still very low: a toothbrush lasts, on average, 8 months, whereas dentists suggest changing it every 3 or 4 months. Through an efficient and sensitive advertising campaign, sales in this segment could at least double.

Toothbrushes normally sold are the result of a compromise between aesthetics and the functional characteristics that the instrument must have. To this end, leading companies, through their R&D departments, have tried to develop the best shape in terms of efficiency and practicality. Variations in brushes are mainly in the handle and the upper pan. The bristle length, its hardness and layout are varied based on different demands and requests. Generally, toothbrush quality depends on how it is produced and on the raw materials utilised in its production. Natural bristles were very popular for some time in the past, and then were substituted with synthetic bristles that offer a high degree of versatility and are cheaper than their natural counterparts. In Italy sales in 1993 were 55 million units for a total amount of Lit 120 billion, 80 billion of which were generated from the mass-market distribution channel and the remainder from chemists.

Mouth rinses

These products represent a recent innovation in the oral care industry. In Italy a mouth rinse was made for the first time in 1990. Its qualities may be therapeutic or cosmetic. The therapeutic mouth rinse is generally suggested by dentists in cases of gingival problems and is particularly recommended to those people who usually suffer from these. The cosmetic mouth rinse, on the other hand, can be used daily to have a fresh breath, and no specific recommendations are made.

Following the Anglo-Saxon countries' example where mouth rinse growth reached incredible levels, the product was shifted from the specialised channel to the mass-market one, where it attained remarkable sales success. A mouth rinse is addressed to younger consumers, who are more sensitive to innovation. As the youngest segment of the oral care market it had the most potential. In 1993, 2,382,000 litres were sold in Italy for a total amount of Lit 36.2 billion. The mouth rinse market was in a growth stage, therefore, it was expected to grow in the near future.

Customers

The Italian consumer was willing to spend growing percentages of his or her budget for personal care to increase or maintain physical and aesthetic wellbeing. The average net income of Italian people was high enough to allow them to invest part of their budget in purchases of oral hygiene products. Thus, the market was very large.

Dividing the Italian people by age groups allowed industry experts to identify people, particularly in the age range of from 13 to 40, as the most important market. Despite the demographic reduction, it is a target market characterised by an increasing consumption propensity, since younger people tended to pay attention to their looks. Specifically, the several groups were divided by product as follows:

Toothpaste

- Under 14. This age group included children who tended not to be interested in cleaning their teeth. For this reason they showed low interest in the toothpaste.
- 14–17. This age group included adolescents who understood the importance of practising correct oral hygiene. Nevertheless, they still were not particularly attracted by this product, showed a medium interest, and preferred to spend their money in different ways.
- 18–34. This age group was absolutely aware of the magnitude of a good oral care. In fact, they were willing to spend more money if they appreciated a product's quality. For this reason, they showed a very high interest in using toothpaste.
- 35–40. This is an age group in which few people were attracted by a particular toothpaste, and were driven by price in making their purchases.
- Over 40. This age group included people who do not use this product correctly. They show a low interest for this item and they usually buy the cheapest brands.

Toothbrushes

- Under 14. The real purchasers of this product within this age group were the children's parents. Thus, this was a group in which the interest for this product was very low.
- 14–17. Adolescents were a very heterogeneous group in which some, looking for the best, bought toothbrushes themselves; others accepted what their parents used without considering the product features. Generally, this age group showed a medium interest in this product.
- 18–34. Almost all of this age group were aware of the importance of practising correct oral hygiene. In fact, they were usually well informed about the toothbrush characteristics and bought the product that met their needs at that moment. They paid close attention in their purchases, showing a very high interest in this product.
- 35–40. This age group included people oriented differently towards this product. A few components were highly interested in toothbrush features paying attention when they bought it. Others considered the price as the only important factor to worry about. Generally this age group showed a medium interest in purchasing this product.
- Over 40. Most of the people belonging to this age group were no longer interested in purchasing a toothbrush with particular features. They brushed their teeth because they were accustomed to doing it. In general, they showed low interest towards this product.

Mouth rinses

- Under 14. Like the toothbrush, mouth rinse was usually bought by the children's parents, but in this case children sometimes pushed their parents into buying it because they were attracted by its colour, its taste, or simply by the nice little bottle. This age group generally showed a medium interest for this product.
- 14–17. This was an age group particularly attracted by this product because it was considered totally new. For this reason they used it, and showed a quiet high interest.
- 18–34. This age group was interested not only in the novelty that this product represented in the Italian market, but also in its characteristics. Therefore, they showed a very high interest towards mouth rinse.
- 35–40. Very few people within this age group were interested in mouth rinse characteristics, and they bought it when they had gum problems or when the dentist suggested that they use it. Their interest for this product was low.
- Over 40. Most of the people within this group were not interested at all in this product, even considering it as totally useless. Hence, they showed a very low interest for mouth rinses.

Since the 1960s, the consumption of oral care items has been increasing but Italy was not yet at the level at which the English or Americans used these products, mainly with reference to the frequent substitution of the toothbrushes. As for the demand by the diverse age groups, the one that paid the most attention to oral care was the 18–34 group as shown above. Women generally showed more care for the teeth, perhaps due to their consideration of this practice as an aesthetic operation. Moreover, immediately after lunch, most women were at home or were able to carry a toothbrush and paste with them.

Promotion

Promotion was particularly important in the mass-market of the oral care industry. In Italy in 1993, companies in the oral care industry invested Lit 110.4 billion to promote their product lines and Lit 70 billion between January and September 1994, confirming a downward trend started two years earlier. Compared to 1992, investments in promotion decreased by about 5 per cent. This situation showed a reduced interest of the companies towards the promotion tool, since the promotion expenses reached about 18 per cent of total sales. So high investments were due to the presence of particularly aggressive competitors with the financial resources to support their actions.

Investing in promotion within this industry was both necessary and extremely binding. In a crowded market like this, convincing the consumer to buy one product instead of another, becoming a part of his or her purchasing habits, was not very easy. In 1993, the most widely used advertising tool was television. In fact, producers spent Lit 87.7 billion in both public and private networks, representing 78 per cent of the total annual budget. The remaining 22 per cent was invested in promotion through newspapers (15 per cent), magazines (6 per cent), radio (2 per cent), and specialised magazines (1 per cent). Analysing the promotion investments by brand, it came out that a few large manufacturers increased sales because of TV advertising. In 1993, Unilever was the major investor with Lit 30 billion. In the second position there was Procter & Gamble with Lit 24 billion, and finally Colgate with about Lit 16 billion.

Bill-postings were totally absent due to the big advertising power of television. However, producers found television to be the ideal tool because it reached millions of people.

In addition to the traditional ways of advertising, other promotion tools were used in the Italian oral care industry, such as sales promotion and personal selling. Sales promotion based on 'three for the price of two' was particularly effective in the oral care market. Also promotions based on a kit including several products like one toothpaste, one toothbrush, and one mouth rinse, were very effective and attracted many consumers. Obviously, initiatives like these could not last for long. Their objective was not only to determine a lasting sales increase but also to withdraw as many consumers as possible from the competitors.

Personal selling was a kind of promotion mainly used for chemists and independent stores. Sales people were assigned to a certain number of chemists or stores within a specific territory and periodically they called on them. Since their salary was mainly based on commissions, sales people were free to make discounts, within a fixed range, based on quantities ordered.

Distribution

The distribution channel was a very important marketing mix choice. Several factors were considered to select the right channel such as the product characteristics, consumer behaviour, competitors' behaviour, and government regulations. Oral care producers, generally, used two main channels: the mass market (GDO) and the pharmaceutical.

The manufacturer that decided to market an oral care product line through the pharmaceutical channel understood the consumer who would have been able to purchase the same product in a large chain store. Since in a chemist the consumer could get personal treatment by specialised personnel, it played a fundamental role in the consumer's final choice. In fact, for this added value the consumer was willing to pay more for the same product. Consequently, the producer pursued higher advantages from the distribution through a specialised channel, despite the higher costs. In the long run, in terms of revenues, it was a profitable choice, because the price per unit in the chemist was higher than that of the chains.

On the other hand, the big chains were chosen when the purpose was to increase the company's presence in the mass market, aiming for an extremely high number of units sold. In the mass market, companies dealt with important distributors who were able to sell the product at a national level. As for the chemists, on the contrary, every single sales point had to be directly contacted.

Table 32.1

Company	Brand	Shelf space (%)
Colgate-Palmolive	Colgate	16.0
Unilever	Mentadent	15.3
Procter & Gamble	AZ	2.3
Gillette	Oral B	7.0
SmithKline & Beecham	Aquafresh	5.5
Ciccarelli	Pasta del Capitano	5.0
Smithkline &Beecham	Macleans	3.9
Unilever	Durban's	3.9
Henkel-Cosmetics	Antica Erboristeria	3.0
Stafford-Miller	Sensodyne	1.9
Unilever	Benefit	1.8
Manetti & Roberts	Chlorodont	1.6
Colgate-Palmolive	Defend	1.4
Unilever	Denti in Crescita	1.3
Henkel-Cosmetics	Thera-Med	1.1
Others	–	18.2

Source: GDO 1994

To be present in a big chain was very important for a company, but even more important was how the product was positioned on the shelves. Since brand loyalty was very low within the oral care industry, a good position on the shelf can be a determinant in consumer purchasing behaviour. Table 32.1 provides an overview' of several brands' positions, on average, on the shelves of the main Italian chains.

Independent stores represented a very small share of total market sales, and in the near future sales were expected to be constant. The reason was that their prices were higher than those of the big chains and many brands were not present in independent stores. Thus, consumers preferred to buy products either at a chemist or from a big chain. Independent stores still survived in small towns where big chains did not have sales points, and in mountain villages.

In terms of total sales it was obvious how much more important the mass market was if compared to the specialised retail and independent stores. In a few years the mass-market sales increased from 44.7 per cent in 1989, to 92 per cent in 1994 while the chemists' channel had only 7 per cent, and independent stores 1 per cent.

Multinational companies found it difficult to enter the Italian oral care market. In fact, after the usual market research to monitor the environment, market regulation, consumer behaviour, and so on, they met cultural obstacles. In Italy, unlike the USA and the main European countries, big chains, small stores, chemists etc. are not open 24 hours a day but have different opening hours depending on the season, except for the big chains, that usually open from 9.00 a.m. to 7.00 p.m..

This situation limited a lot each company's sales that, moreover, had to face very high personnel costs. These were the main reasons that could be considered as a kind of entry barrier. Nevertheless, the Italian oral care market still remains highly profitable and leading companies fight to gain market share.

Competition

The oral care market was characterised by the presence of very large multinationals, such as Procter & Gamble, Unilever, Colgate-Palmolive, SmithKline Beecham, and Gillette. The market was also characterised by a low brand loyalty that consequently led to a continual engagement of the companies with the consumer. It was a competition that involved all marketing choices, they fought over prices, product characteristics, distribution choices, even communication. Investments in advertising were high, and the market segmentation never ended.

Procter & Gamble

Procter & Gamble was born in 1956. It manufactures and markets detergents and soaps, and distributes and sells pharmaceutical products, cosmetics, perfumes, hygienic products. and food products. It invests $800 million in R&D every year, and 6000 researchers are engaged all over the world. In 1986 the company acquired the 'AZ' brand from Pierrel, and in a few years it has been able to implement this product line and launch three new products: AZ Tartar Control (paste), AZ Verde (paste), AZ Tartar Control (gel). P&G decided to market this product line on the mass market with two new products of the same line in a 'Double Package'. This strategic choice was made to meet the needs of consumers who asked for more than one package, and the double package allowed a savings of 20 per cent compared to the single one.

P & G's strategy was based on a constant evolution and differentiation of the product to create the most complete product line existing in the market. Odontological research was the starting point of each strategy. The many different products were developed as a consequence of direct cooperation between the R&D department and the dentists.

Unilever

Unilever was formed in 1930. It operates in seventy-five countries and has over 300,000 employees in more than 500 subsidiaries. Net sales in 1992 were Lit 53,000 billion: 60 per cent of sales came from Europe, 20 per cent from North

America. and 20 per cent from other continents. In Italy Unilever had 7,700 employees and net sales of Lit 4,000 billion in 1992.

In the oral care market the company was present through its important division Elida Gibbs, which offered all the typical oral care products – toothpaste, toothbrushes, and mouth rinses. In the toothbrush segment Unilever was the absolute leader with 37 per cent market share in volume; 21 per cent market share in the mouth rinse segment, and 28.8 per cent market share in the toothpaste segment. Its brands included Mentadent, Durban's, Benefit and Pepsodent. Its leadership stemmed from precise strategic planning based on the combination of different brands positioned at different levels on the market, therefore, not in competition with each other.

Colgate-Palmolive

Founded in 1806, Colgate-Palmolive has been recognised as the global leader in oral care for well over one hundred years. These achievements are possible because Colgate consistently demonstrates superiority in meeting professional and consumer needs for oral care products. More than 40 per cent of toothpaste and 25 per cent of toothbrushes sold around the world carry the Colgate name. Throughout Colgate's oral care history, the constant goal has been to improve oral health through superior technology and ongoing patient education programmes.

Colgate provides leadership in establishing and maintaining worldwide oral health education programmes. Colgate literally taught many of the world's people how to brush and care for their teeth. Each year, 24 million children in forty-three countries take part in Colgate programmes. In the USA, the 'Bright Smiles, Bright Futures' educational programmes and materials are designed to help dental professionals, and elementary school teachers bring good oral health to the next generation of American children. Today, Colgate continues to deliver products and services that improve the oral health and overall quality of life for consumers everywhere. Colgate achieves continued innovation by linking the health of consumers with the latest research findings and technological advances in dental science. Colgate has long recognised the value of maintaining a firm partnership with the worldwide professional dental community, as well as the wisdom of a substantial investment in professional education, clinical research, and technology.

In 1993 Colgate Oral Pharmaceuticals Inc., a subsidiary of the Colgate-Palmolive Company, was created in Canton, Massachusetts. This subsidiary was formed to emphasise the company's commitment to developing innovative therapies specifically for the dental professional. Investing in advanced technology, listening to the profession, and encouraging innovation are key elements of Colgate Oral Pharmaceuticals' leadership in professional oral health products.

Company mission

Since the early 1900s, when the company began its expansion throughout the world, the mission statement of Colgate was one word – *quality*. Other objectives for the Italian market included establishing Colgate as a major competitor for contractual manufacturing work, such as government contracts to supply the Italian Army, Air Force, and Navy. Colgate applied its strategic ideal of quality to everything it did. It always made heavy investments in research and development in order to find the right product to meet consumer needs.

Products

Products manufactured by Colgate-Palmolive in the Italian oral care sector consist of two main lines:

- Products addressed to the big distribution and independent stores
- Products addressed to the specialised channels.

Each product line is composed of several sub-lines. Table 32.2 lists the many different products made by Colgate-Palmolive in the oral care segment:

Table 32.2

Toothpaste	Mouth Rinses	Toothbrushes
Colgate	Plax	Colgate
Defend	Periogard	Zig Zag
Periogard	Chlorodex	Total
Fluorigard		
ABC		
Gel Kam		
Platinum		

Colgate-Palmolive, as a product strategy, tends to lengthen the life cycle of each product line in order to attract consumers with different needs and tastes, and to give an image of completeness of the product line. At the same time it adds several variations to some single products, increasing the number of products for every brand. Toothbrushes are offered in different shapes and colours, mouth rinses in the half-litre size only. The segmentation operated by Colgate-Palmolive in the toothpaste market depends on the attitude/interest the consumer has towards oral hygiene practices. This is a factor depending on the education level, the age, and the social and economic level.

Customers

In the oral care market, brand loyalty was very low; seldom did consumers buy the same product and the tendency was towards a diversification of the purchase. In this situation, advertising, especially on television, becomes a central point, absolutely important for the consumer who is also influenced by the packaging. A survey in 1993 about oral care products shows the consumer is attracted by:

- the packaging (36 per cent)
- the price (26 per cent)
- their recognition of the product (21 per cent).

From this survey the importance of the packaging was underscored. In fact, over the last few years it has been experiencing an evolution mainly concerned with the material utilised. It has shifted from a metallic tube to a soft plastic one which is lighter and more manageable. More recently, the dispenser was the most important innovation and consumers found it attractive, which increased demand as soon as it was marketed. It is not easy to delineate the classic Colgate consumer's profile due to the low brand loyalty existing in this field. Nevertheless, the 18–34 age group remained Colgate's main target market since this was the group most interested in purchasing oral care products.

Towards the future

In 1997 the future for Colgate-Palmolive looked just as promising as the recent past had been successful. For the oral care segment, characterised by a continual launch of new items, keys to success were distributed in two functional areas: in the R&D department product innovation was the determinant, while in the marketing area a good relationship with the distribution channel was important. In addition, the qualitative standards and the price were important but not fundamental.

Some executives argued that to keep pace with new trends, the introduction of new items with additional characteristics rather than the usual products always carrying the same features became critical to success. These innovative products, in the toothpaste segment especially, could present a dramatic increase in the preventive action against cavities, or they could be natural products. Other managers argued that the innovative engagement had to focus on the packaging, through new shapes, new materials, and graphic variants. Others said that a standardised package could be considered a true innovation by the consumers. Some other executives argued that a good choice would be to create more products carrying new brand names to be sold in the mass-market channel, trying to copy Unilever's strategy.

Because of this new continually changing scenario, brands of leading companies were expected to be present in a growing number of niche markets. As for the toothpaste segment, Colgate, in order to respond to this market trend, marketed different brands, each one covering a diverse area: Colgate and Defend in the mass-market channel, and specialised items such as Periogard, Fluorigard, Gel Kam, ABC, and Platinum in the pharmaceutical channels.

In Italy Colgate has been known since the Second World War, therefore it was considered a traditional brand. Competitors' products were younger and it was easier for them to build the image required by the market in that moment. In fact, the toothpaste market in the mass-market channel is extremely crowded,

Table 32.3 Decision chart

Kind of decision	Alternative 1	Alternative 2	Alternative 3
Toothpaste Innovation	New formula with a more effective preventive	New formula with natural ingredients	New formula with a more effective preventive
Packaging	New and different packages for high and low-priced items	One standardised package for each differently priced items	New and different packages for high priced and low-priced items
Brand name	Different brand names for items positioned at different price levels	One brand name for all items	Different brand names for items positioned at different price levels
Toothbrush Innovation	New colours and shapes	One standardised shape	New shapes and colours
Bristles	Natural fibres	Synthetic fibres	Synthetic fibres
Mouth rinse Kind of product	Therapeutic	Cosmetic	Both therapeutic and cosmetic
Size	Different sizes	Half a litre only	Different sizes
Distribution channel	Big chains and independents for low/medium-price products and chemists for high price (specialised products)	Big chains and independents for low/medium price products and chemists for high price (specialised products)	Big chains and independents for low/medium-price products and chemists for high price (specialised products)
Promotion Advertising	Concentrate investments on TV advertising	Advertising on TV, radio, magazines, newspapers	Advertising on TV, radio, magazines, newspapers and bill postings
Sales promotion	No investment in sales promotion	Investment in 3 × 2 sales promotion	No investment in sales promotion

Table 32.4 Market shares

	Share	Brand shares
Toothpaste		
Unilever	28.7%	Mentadent 19%
		Durbans 2.9%
		Pepsodent3.7%
		Benefit 2.7%
Colgate-Palmolive	22.3%	Colgate 19.6%
		Defend 2.7%
Procter & Gamble	18.4%	Az Verde 7.8%
		Az Tartar Control 6.4%,
		Protezione
		Gengive 3.6%
SmithKline Beecham	9.7%	Aquafresh 5.8%,
		Macleans 3.5%,
		Iodosan 0.4%
Farm. Ciccarelli	8.7%	Pasta del Capitano
Henkel Cosmetics	4.5%	Antica Erboristeria 3.5%,
		Thera-Med 1%
Gillette	1.9%	Oral B
Manetti & Roberts	1.7%	Chlorodont
Stafford-Miller	0.9%	Sensodyne
Sodalco	0.4%	Fresh & Clean
BYK Gulden	0.1%	Emoform
Toothbrushes		
Unilever	36.9%	Mentadent 21.3%
		Gibbs 15.6%
Gillette	14.4%	Oral B
Colgate	8.7%	
Procter & Gamble	8%	Az
Piave	8%	
Squibb	5%	
Others	19%	
Mouth rinses		
Colgate	52%	Plax, Actibrush
Unilever	21%	Mentadent
Johnson & Johnson	9%	Reach
Gillette	8%	Oral B Fluorinse
Sodalco	4%	
Ciccarelli	4%	
Others	2%	

consequently new opportunities to increase the business come from other segments such as toothbrushes and mouth rinses.

For the toothbrush market, some managers said that sales within this segment could double, and this could occur through a sensitive advertising campaign aimed at making the consumer aware of the importance of a necessary toothbrush change every 3–4 months, as dentists suggest. Other executives thought the right strategy to pursue would be the aesthetic route through new shapes or even new materials. Some managers argued that, like toothpaste, a standardised shape for the toothbrush to become 'the classic Colgate shape' could represent a good alternative. These alternatives include a different economic expectation for this segment, and each proposal has to be thoroughly evaluated by the top management.

For the mouth rinse segment, some executives argued that Colgate should produce therapeutic rinses only or just cosmetic rinses. Others said the company had to manufacture both. Some other managers thought the right way would be to offer different sizes as opposed to the current one size.

In short, management is considering ways in which Colgate can differentiate itself from its competitors and improve its strategic position in the long run (see Table 32.3).

CHAPTER 33

Ratner/Signet Group plc: 1984–97

'People ask me, how can you sell this product for such a low price? I say it is because it is total crap. We even sell a pair of earrings for under £1, which is cheaper than a prawn sandwich from Marks & Spencer, but I have to say the earrings probably won't last as long.' This statement was made by Gerald Ratner, the managing director of the world's largest retail jewellery chain, in April 1991. It was not the first time he had made these and similar jokes, and they had been reported regularly in the financial press, which was not the normal reading of his mass-market customers. On this occasion he thought the meeting at the Institute of Directors was private, but his remarks were heard by a reporter from one of the tabloids, and became headline news, also reaching the television and radio news broadcasts. Suddenly it was his group's customers that read or heard the comments, and the joke was no longer funny.

The Ratner strategy

The family firm was begun by Gerald Ratner's father, Leslie, who started with one shop in 1949, the year in which his son Gerald was born. It went public in 1965, and six years later Gerald joined as a shop assistant at the age of 21. In 1984 he took over the managing directorship. At that time it had 130 stores in a fragmented retail market, trading under the Ratner name. His initial vision was to expand the retail market for jewllery, and to gain a 50 per cent share within a few years . There are reasonable, but not conclusive, estimates of the size of the retail market in the UK. By 1988 it was probably around £2.5bn (including VAT), or £2.1bn with VAT stripped out. Ratners' share was estimated at around 23 per cent. He expected the market to double over the next five years, and for the Ratner share to reach the desired 50 per cent. In fact it reached around 30 per cent by 1991.

This case study was written by D. E. Hussey, for teaching purposes only, in September 1997. © 1997 David Hussey & Associates

By this time his vision had expanded to embrace the USA, where the aim was to obtain a 10 per cent share of the US market over a 5–10 year period. This would have made Ratner the largest chain in the US market, and required a build-up to about 1500 shops.

The Ratner Company grew rapidly, by a mix of acquisition and internal development, and pre-tax profits climbed to a peak of £101m before tax in financial year 1991, compared to a loss of £400 000 in 1983. Sales reached over £1bn in 1991. A note of caution is needed here. The company year-end was 31 March until 1987, when it was changed to the end of January. This means that 1991 results were mainly of trading in 1990, and as the norm for the business is that 80 per cent of profit is made in the run-up to Christmas, it is important not to confuse the company year with the calendar year. Christmas 1991 appears in the Ratner figures under 1992. The stock market valuation of the company was around £827m in calendar year 1990, compared to £1m in 1984.

The opportunity Ratner saw when he took over the family Ratner chain was to position jewellery for the mass market. He summarised this as giving people 'jewellery they could afford, rather than quality they could not', giving an element of replaceable fashion purchases to this segment of the market. It is probably not exaggerating to suggest that his actions created this segment, and did much to expand the market. The 1988 annual report stated 'We believe that a significant part of the 20% growth in the market in the last 12 months is attributable to our expansion.' It has been estimated that in the UK as a whole the average price for a jewellery item was £200 in 1982: this had fallen to £25 by 1992. Ratner jewellery was not aimed at the investment market (Ratner is once reported to have quipped 'Diamonds are a bad investment, particularly ours'). Ratner's vision of his segment was to offer jewellery that lower-paid working women could afford to buy for themselves, and throw away when they were tired of it. The actions taken to support this basic strategy for the Ratner stores included:

- Build-up of buyer power, both to achieve lower costs and also to persuade manufacturers to design costs out of a product. One Ratner innovation was hollow gold jewellery, which enabled the cost to be shaved.
- Insisting that suppliers accepted Ratner contract turns, which meant that any unsold stock could be returned. This moved the risk of overstocking to the supplier, and around 20 per cent of purchases were returned to the suppliers. This policy antagonised suppliers. It was claimed by one supplier, Slade Holdings, that return of stock after Christmas 1990 was a major cause of its collapse in February 1991.
- Selection and purchase of merchandise was handled centrally. Systems were set up so that stock was automatically called off from the warehouses, and in most places delivered before business began the next day.
- All shops were laid out in the same way, and, subject to physical limitations, all window displays were identical. These were determined centrally.
- All prices were set from the centre, and discounting decisions were made centrally.
- The market offering included money-back guarantees, price matching, interest-free credit, and both in-store and external credit cards (1988 annual report).
- Attention to the fashion element of the products sold.

- Media promotion, handled centrally.
- A computerised order-picking system at each of the two warehouses (Birmingham and Colindale). Ratner claimed that a 150-item order which used to take 3 hours to assemble could now be put together in 5 minutes. The order pickers were put on an incentive bonus scheme.

The original Ratner stores were positioned as low cost, low quality (quality in the relative sense of a Rolls-Royce compared to a Lada, not in the normal TQM meaning). Shop windows had a bazaar feel, with much glitter and little empty space between items, an impression which was reinforced by periodic discounting. But the formula, supported by an increase in the number of Ratner shops, brought results. Gerald Ratner claimed in October 1988 that the average Ratner shop made £57 000 p.a. profit, compared to the average for Zales of £26 000.

The UK acquisitions

Ratner made his first acquisition of Terry's in December 1984. These were brought under the Ratner systems, but continued to carry the Terry's name. In May 1986 he reached agreement to buy H. Samuel, which included Watches of Switzerland. He recognised that Samuel operated in a more up-market segment, which could be described as middle price, middle quality. Watches of Switzerland was a more exclusive chain, offering high quality and expensive items. The acquisition added 370 stores to the network.

In a press interview describing the strategy for the acquisition, Ratner mentioned that at the time of the purchase, Samuel shops had an average turnover per square foot of £32, compared to Ratner shops of £66. He felt that the Ratner systems would enable a rapid improvement to be made, as well as increasing the purchasing strength of the whole group. By January 1988, Samuel turnover figures had been increased to £62 per square foot, but Ratner shops had also improved to £95. In a press interview, after the merger he stated that every Samuel shop now carried the same merchandise, put in the window in the same position, and offered at the same price. New lower-priced merchandise had been introduced. However, higher-priced items were still sold, including diamond rings of up to £1600 each, which, because of the purchasing power, were better quality than similar-priced rings offered by competitors. In the 1988 annual report, which covered the first full year of trading of Samuel under the new ownership, Ratner was able to claim:

> ... progress has continued with outstanding results, and the new merchandise and marketing techniques have contributed to significant growth. The trading formula which we have developed successfully in the Ratners chain is now fully operational in the H. Samuel group. The number of shops in the H. Samuel chain increased from 357 to 364 during 1987/8. In the current year, we plan to open a further 50 shops and to refurbish 72 shops. Like for like sales growth in the year under review was over 38 per cent and sales in the current year are buoyant.

633

Watches of Switzerland were largely outside of the Ratner system, but were provided with finance to enable shops to be refurbished and a limited number of new stores to be opened.

By the start of the calendar year 1987 Ratner was ready for a bigger challenge, and bid for Combined English Stores, a group which included retail chains of chemists, fashion clothing, sweets, jewellers Zales/Collingwood and Salisbury (luggage, costume jewellery, handbags, and fancy goods). It also owned Eurocamp, a leisure facilities operation. In fact Ratner was outbid by the Next organisation, and afterwards he stated that if he had been successful, he would have kept only the jewellery and Salisbury chains. In August 1987 he bought Ernest Jones. This chain sat somewhere above H. Samuel on both price levels and quality. In the 1988 annual report Ratner commented on the intention to 'Position Ernest Jones at a level in the market slightly above H. Samuel, where it will become the diamond ring specialist of the group.' Ernest Jones, too, was being given the Ratner system treatment. A key advantage seen was Ratners' ability to buy more effectively for all the chains. Within a few years the overlap of merchandise in all the chains was around 50 per cent.

In November 1988 Ratner bought the Zales/Collingwood and Salisbury chains from Next. These were the companies he had originally hoped to gain from the Combined English Stores bid of the previous year. £150.75m was paid for these businesses, of which £80m was attributable to Salisbury. The purchase of Salisbury was a departure from the previous strategy of building up the jewellery chain. Ratner argued that Salisbury had little direct competition, the shops were of a high standard, so improving the merchandise, and putting in Ratner systems would enable the chain to be very profitable. Zales were at about the same price level as Ernest Jones, but as it was in the second quartile of perceived quality would be subjected to the same formula that had been applied to the other UK acquisitions. The purchase was financed by a rights issue of £80m, preference shares issues to Next for £25m, and £30m from internal resources. The balance of nearly £16m was debt obligations assumed with the purchase. The previous year the two chains had earned £9.5m in operating profits, and Ratner expected them to contribute £5m for the remaining months of his financial year.

In 1990 Gerald Ratner seriously considered making a bid for Dixon's, the chain selling consumer electronic goods and cameras.

The US acquisitions

The US retail jewellery business is even more fragmented than the UK. In 1990 it was estimated that there were 61 000 outlets, but only 3000 of these were owned by public companies. In the 1988 report, which covered most of the 1987 calendar year, Ratner estimated the US retail market to be worth around $18bn per annum. The first US acquisition was completed in August 1987, when Sterling Inc. was bought for £126m. This, the fourth largest retail jewellery chain in the USA, operated 117 stores, mainly in the mid-West, but with some presence in the mid-Atlantic and West Coast regions. In the 1988 report, the choice of

Sterling was justified, as it was '.... the most efficient and best managed of the US speciality retail store chains'.

A month later the privately owned Westhall group was acquired for £29.4 m. 'Westhall met the strict acquisition criteria for our US expansion plans, particularly in its successful merchandising, prominent positions in shopping malls and well respected trading names. As well as wider geographic coverage, the acquisition is providing us with economies of scale and operating efficiencies resulting from the integration of Westhall into Sterling' (Annual report, 1988). In addition, effective credit systems and controls were to be introduced into Westhall, to enable it to increase its volume of credit sales. The acquisition added seventy-one stores to the portfolio, in the Eastern and mid-Western regions.

At this point the Ratner Group had less than 1 per cent of the US market, and saw considerable opportunity for expansion. The US stores were geared to the popular-priced end of the market, and were located mainly in shopping malls. Each store offered a variety of styles and prices, with an emphasis on quality diamond and gemstone products. The average store sale in the period covered by the 1988 report was US$200 and 55 per cent of sales were made on credit. Sterling claimed the lowest bad debt ratio (1.7 per cent) in the jewellery retail business.

Further acquisitions took place in 1988 and 1989 (calendar years), when Osterman, Ringmaker/ Allens and Westfields were added. All were merged into Sterling, and a new headquarters was built for the US operations in Akron, Ohio.

In October 1990 £426m was spent on the acquisition of the Kays group. A comparison of Sterling and Kays from the published accounts of the preceding year is given in Table 33.1.

The poor bad debts record of Kays was, of course, known. There was an unpleasant surprise in the Kay inventory, which was of a poorer quality than expected. In effect, Ratner was buying staff and premises, and the acquisition moved the US operations to a total of 1000 stores in forty-three states, and a 5 per cent share of the market. The 1991 report showed that the group now received 36 per cent of sales and 41 per cent of profit from the USA. It was expected that the Sterling systems would improve sales in Kays, and there would be significant

Table 33.1

	Sterling 03/02/90	Kays 31/12/89
Sales ($m)	402	427
Sales per store ($000)	1122	850
Operating income per store ($000)	137	46
Operating margin (%)	15.6	5.4
Bad debts written off (%)	2.5	7.5
Number of stores	456	494

cost savings, including the closure of the Kay head office. The Kays purchase was financed partly by exchanging each ordinary share of Kays common stock for one convertible preference share of US$0.01, partly from a rights issue, and partly through existing and new bank facilities (Annual Report 1991).

From the pinnacle of success

The peak year of the Ratner Group was 1990, when the profit attributable to shareholders reached £79m, which was roughly three times larger than the turnover had been in 1983. Although sales rose in 1991, profits were lower at £69m. Nearly £7m of the difference between the two years was extraordinary costs, the profits on ordinary activities being much closer. The 1991 annual report stated:

> During 1990, trading in both the UK and USA has been carried out against a deteriorating economic background, with the full impact of the recession and uncertainty arising from events in the Middle East hitting consumer confidence in the all-important Christmas trading period. In these adverse trading conditions, the resilience of our businesses has been shown by the market share gains we have achieved.

Elsewhere there was reference to 'a most difficult year for retailers'.

The report claimed that in the UK market share had increased from 30 per cent to 33 per cent.

> In the 1990s the UK jewellery market is not expected to grow as rapidly as in the 1980s. It is no longer an underdeveloped market. Nevertheless, there is significant room to enhance our market share. The emphasis of our strategy will be more focused to ensure that we improve our operational efficiency whilst continuing to utilise our buying power to maintain our competitive position in the market place.

In the USA the group now claimed 5 per cent of the US market, although this had declined by 3.6 per cent during the 1990 calendar year, and £14m of the profit contribution came from the newly acquired Kays. The future strategy for the USA was '...to complete our geographic coverage by selective expansion over the next few years, funded from the significant cash flows generated by the UK and US businesses.'

The first three months of the 1991 calendar year (the report was dated 22 April) had continued to be difficult, with the increase in VAT having a significant effect on UK margins.

> With the reduction in interest rates, the indications are that consumer confidence will recover and I am hopeful that trading conditions should be significantly better for our all important Christmas trading period. I am confident that we have established a sound operational structure for the continued profitable growth of the group.

Things began to go wrong for the group after the jokes at the Institute of Directors. In Christmas of that year the volume of sales was only achieved through massive discounting, of up to 25 per cent, in the run-up to Christmas. Although discounting had always been part of Gerald Ratner's method, with shop windows plastered with money-off announcements, there was another reason. Many of the suppliers had rebelled, and had only agreed to supply the group on a firm sales basis. Unsold stock could no longer be returned. The result was that although sales were slightly up on 1991, the 1992 financial year showed a loss attributable to shareholders of £125 950. A major US competitor, Zales, went into Chapter 11 bankruptcy in November 1991, bringing the threat of increased discounting in the US market.

By January, 1992, press articles were appearing with titles like 'How Ratner's dream became a nightmare'. From a 1990 peak stock market valuation of £827m, the value had fallen to a little over £6m, as the extent of the losses became known. A few months earlier. Ratner had been telephoned by Sir David Alliance, chairman of Coats Viyella, and a family friend, advising Ratner that investors had lost faith in him, although they still respected his operational skills. The sensible thing to do was to stand down as chairman, while remaining managing director. Alliance recommended Jim McAdam, as chairman. McAdam at that time was 61, and had just retired as deputy chairman of Coats. His whole career had been in the textile industry, part of it overseas. The appointment of McAdam gave confidence to the City, and was one of the factors that gained the continued support of the banks, who at that time were owed £217m.

On 25 November 1992 Gerald Ratner resigned. There had been some disagreement with McAdam over discounting during the pre-Christmas period. Ratner wanted to discount to stimulate trade. McAdam was determined to raise margins, and would allow no discounting until the New Year.

McAdam's recovery strategy

McAdam's initial strategy was built around the need to reduce costs, increase margins, and secure the support of the banks so that there was adequate finance to enable the business to continue. In August 1992, in an interview with *Marketing Week*, he described his recovery plans for the jewellery chains, with a greater emphasis on service and segmentation of the three main chains. Ratners were to stay in the low-price segment, but Samuel and Jones were to be refocused. Samuel in particular was to move further up market from 'look-alike Ratners', and would no longer have product overlap or use the same promotional material as the Ratner chain. 'We will focus H. Samuel on the middle ground of the mass market,' James McAdam is reported as saying. Ernest Jones would continue to compete in the upper segment of the mass market, offering more sophisticated services such as stone setting. The marketing budget was to be reduced. All UK jewellery activities were put under a single management board.

In the 1993 annual report he described 1992 as a year of consolidation and achievement. In the UK, in addition to focusing each chain, he put particular emphasis on margin improvement and the reduction of 'the over-reliance on discounting'. At this time the US 'policies were found to be robust, marketing strategies were redefined, and changes were initiated to improve operational efficiency'. Watches of Switzerland was sold in June 1992 for around £23m.

Cost-reduction actions taken during the year in the UK included a shift from full- to part-time pay for many employees, a wage freeze, and the closure of the Collingdale warehouse. Fifty-seven jewellery stores were closed, and 182 identified for closure over the following three years. More emphasis was placed on staff training. Operating costs were reduced by £32m and stock levels fell by £53m.

In the USA operating costs were cut by £19m, through the closure of unprofitable stores, and savings in marketing costs and bad debt charges. Inventory levels were cut by £31m (some sales were lost in the final quarter because of inventory shortages). Discretionary discounting at branch level was reduced. The support of the banks had been obtained, and a new facilities agreement negotiated to follow on the expiry of the old agreement in June 1993. The company name was changed to Signet in 1993, but the original Ratners chain continued to trade under the old name.

These actions were not enough to restore the organisation to health, although the 1993 annual report showed a considerable reduction in the loss. The market was still suffering the results of the recession, and the group had to service a high level of debt. By the end of the 1994 financial year, McAdam was able to report that both the UK and US jewellery operations were again trading at a profit, although the Salisbury chain was underperforming, and the overall results were still in loss. One key action taken to preserve cash was not to pay the dividends owed to preference shareholders, which amounted to £30m each year.

The next stage

The Salisbury chain was a problem, and had made losses consistently. In the 1991 report Gerald Ratner had referred to improvements being made to distribution and a plan to close fifty unprofitable stores. 'We are remerchandising Salisburys, concentrating on its core product strengths of handbags, luggage and gifts, whilst introducing more flair and originality.' Losses continued. In 1994 a decision was made to dispose of the chain, and in the 1994 report a provision of £87.056m was made to cover the anticipated loss on such a sale, mainly the writing off of goodwill.

In May 1994 McAdam was still convinced that the jewellery activities could trade their way out of difficulties. Although attempts had been made to test a new retailing concept for Ratner shops, using the Equa brand, performance of the low-price chain was still poor. The whole chain was closed down during the 1994 calendar year, so that by the year end all UK efforts were concentrated on H. Samuel and Ernest Jones.

In August a buyer was found for the Salisbury chain. Stephen Hinchliffe purchased Salisbury for the sum of £3.18m, paying £2.75m in cash, and taking over £430,000 of debt. However, he did not buy a warehouse operation at Crawley, and Signet had to provide £1.5m for the closure of this operation. In the period of the 1995 financial year up to the sale, Salisbury had revenues of £24,649m, and an operating loss of £4.736m. The loss on disposal was £87,070, with a further loss on disposal of fixed assets of £1.5m. As the majority of the loss had been provided for in the previous period, the impact on financial year 1995 was only £6.262m.

After the sale McAdam said 'We can now focus all our efforts on our core jewellery business and just get on with it'. Hinchliffe, the buyer, said 'We can return to profits a lot faster than people imagine. There is nothing wrong with the fabric of the business.' He intended to expand, improve the quality of merchandise, and cut the number of distribution centres to bring an immediate seven-figure saving. Some commentators argued that Signet had neglected the business.

In September 1994 Signet announced a plan to refurbish up to 150 stores, spending £40m on this over a three-year period. There was a fall-off in the US market during the year, and at year end the operating profit from this source was down by about 25 per cent.

Dissident shareholders

Although Signet moved into the black in the 1995 financial year, it was not out of trouble. Many of the preference shares had been bought up by an organisation called Active Value, which specialised in buying up low-priced shares in organisations that were in trouble, and pressing for action that increased the value of its holdings. This organisation owned 25 per cent of the US-owned preference shares, and pressed for a capital reconstruction during the whole of 1994. Preference shareholders had around 29 per cent of the total voting rights on any such resolution. In 1994 Active Value argued that management was putting off a problem that had to be faced, and that it was not possible for the company to trade out of its difficulties.

In February 1995 McAdam reviewed the actions he had taken over the past three years as part of his response to the plans being put forward by the dissident shareholders who were now grouped around Active Value. Although he had taken over an organisation with more than 30 per cent of the jewellery market, not all the business was profitable. The Ratner shops were discredited, and although Jones and Samuel had good reputations there was little differentiation between the chains, with much overlap of products. Nine hundred UK stores had been closed. In some places there were two Ratner stores near each other, which had cannibalised sales. The strategy was now to concentrate on Jones and Samuel in the UK, and these had been re-established with separate identities. Margins were now higher in the UK. In the USA McAdam intended to rebuild Sterling. A two-year banking agreement to secure facilities for £400m had been agreed, and was due for renewal in the summer of 1995.

The dissident shareholders were pressing for the sale of either the UK or the US businesses to reduce debt, and to restructure the capital of the company in their interests. McAdam saw this as an action which was not in the interests of all the shareholders.

An extraordinary general meeting was requisitioned by the dissidents for 5 May 1995. Their plan had come down to the break-up of the company, as, they claimed, buyers were already interested in buying the various parts of it for around £700 m in total. Ordinary shareholders would receive 20p per share (or more if the sale realised more than £800m), and after the repayment of debts, the preference shareholders would gain about £290m (around two thirds of what they were owed in capital and arrears of dividends). Although any remaining original preference shareholders would lose money, those like Active Value, who had bought shares at a price below face value, would make a profit.

The motion was defeated, McAdam arguing that a fire sale would mean that the business was sold for less than its value, and that the scheme was not in the interests of all the shareholders. Rumblings from the dissidents continued through the year, and through an organisation called Parcon, Active Value began to buy ordinary shares to increase its voting power, eventually achieving nearly 20 per cent of this class of share. There were threats to call another extraordinary meeting to oust the board and force consideration of another reconstruction plan.

The 1996 financial year results showed an improvement, but not on a scale that would solve the company's debt situation. In January 1996 Signet announced that the board was reviewing the possible sale of the UK businesses. Formal bids were invited, and initially seven were received, including one from Gerald Ratner. Eventually only one bidder was in the running at a price of just under £280m. The deal eventually foundered in September over leases. When a lease is assigned, the original leaseholder remains liable should the assignee default. Recently this contingent liability had become a reality for Sears when Fascia collapsed after buying one of their chains, and all the obligations of the leases had to be picked up by Sears. This proved to be an insoluble problem for Signet.

Meanwhile the market was picking up, and the modernisation of H. Samuel was resulting in an increasing market share. The results for the year showed a considerable improvement in results, with after tax profits almost doubling.

The board called an extraordinary general meeting on 26 June 1997, as well as meetings for each class of shares, to consider a capital reconstruction. It approved the conversion of preference shares to ordinary shares, and preference shareholders agreed to forgo their rights to arrears of dividend. As a result of this, the preference shareholders would own 82.5 per cent of the ordinary shares. Active Value and its supporters own about 35 per cent of the shares as a result of the deal.

McAdam said 'We will listen if any one comes to us with a pot of gold, but we are not putting either our UK or US businesses up for sale.'

Historical summary

(£000, except per share data)	1983	1984	1985	1986	1987[c]	1988	1989	1990
Sales	25 900	27 600	32 300	44 800	158 000	360 200	635 160	898 102
Exceptional items								–698
Profit/(loss) on ordinary activities pre-tax	–400	1 100	2 100	4 300	22 500	50 400	86 010	120 790
Tax on profit on ordinary activities							–31 824	–41 730
Profit/(loss) attributable to shareholders							54 186	79 060
Fully diluted earnings per 10p share[a]	–1.4p	2.4p	4.1p	8.4p	15.2p	21.1p	25.6p	26.9p
Ordinary dividend payable							14 862	20 098
Ordinary dividend per share							7.5p	9.5p
Capital expenditure							52 143	63 281
Depreciation							16 536	23 060
Net assets							184 635	297 900

	1991[b]	1992	1993	1994	1995	1996[d]	1997
Sales	1 113 922	1 128 634	928 625	987 960	924 079	894 682	901 952
Exceptional items	–12 100	–97 965	–18 047	–87 056	–14	0	0
Profit/(loss) on ordinary activities pre tax	101 957	–122 328	–40 079	–85 437	8 143	25 016	45 066
Tax on profit on ordinary activities	–33 040	–3 622	14 523	1 020	–5 792	–7 499	–11 211
Profit/(loss) attributable to shareholders5	68 917	–125 950	–25 556	–84 417	2 351	17 517	33 855
Fully diluted earnings per 10p share[a]	21.3p	–50.5p	–19.2p	–38.3p	–9.0p	–8.4p	2.5p
Ordinary dividend payable	29 177	7 033	0	0	0	0	0
Ordinary dividend per share	10.0p	2.4p					
Capital expenditure	71 984	32 215	13 092	21 739	24 417	16 923	15 202
Depreciation	28 932	39 319	37 299	39 478	28 339	26 815	24 619
Net assets	397 648	302 553	256 560	248 890	248 892	271 327	300 745

[a] As adjusted for the rights issue in 1990
[b] Re-stated to reflect the adoption of Financial Reporting Standard 3
[c] Year end changed from 31 March to January
[d] 53 weeks

Ratner/Signet selected final accounts

Consolidated profit and loss account: £000

	52 weeks ended 1/2 1992	52 weeks ended 30/1 1993	52 weeks ended 1/2 1996	52 weeks ended 3/2 1997
SALES	1 128 634	928 625	894 682	901 952
Continuing operations	1 106 970	923 796		
Discontinued operations	21 664	4 829		
Cost of Sales	−1 127 733	−888 070	−784 343	−781 119
Gross profit	901	40 555	110 339	120 833
Administrative expenses	−68 032	−42 661	−46 400	−44 328
OPERATING PROFIT/LOSS	−67 131	−2 106	63 939	76 505
Continuing operations	−67 540	−1 177		
Discontinued operations	−409	−929		
(Losses) on disposal of fixed assets:				
continuing operations	−28 040	−9 764		
Profit: disposal of discontinued operations		4 161		
Profit/loss before interest & tax	−95 171	−7 709	63 909	76 505
Interest payable, net	−27 157	−32 370	−38 923	−31 439
Profit/(loss) on ordinary activities pre tax	−122 328	−40 079	25 016	45 066
Tax on profit/loss	−3 622	14 523	−7 499	−11 211
Profit/loss attributable to shareholders	−125 950	−25 556	17 517	33 855
Dividends	−22 702			
Additional finance costs: non equity shares			−42 075	−26 398
Retained Profit/loss	−148 652	−25 556	−24 558	7 457

Consolidated balance sheet: £000

	01-Feb 1992	30-Jan 1993	03-Feb 1996	03-Feb 1997
FIXED ASSETS				
Tangible assets	235 887	205 249	149 660	128 938
Investments			2 472	
	235 887	205 249	152 132	128 938
CURRENT ASSETS	822 666	723 140	722 236	711 657
Stocks	425 725	359 268	339 995	326 953
Debtors	122 298	152 607	228 498	220 771
Short term investments	18 111	5 348	900	900
Cash at bank and in hand	256 532	205 917	152 843	163 033
CREDITORS (within 1 year)	−723 525	−632 595	−181 104	−409 032
NET CURRENT ASSETS	99 141	90,545	541 132	302 625
TOTAL ASSETS LESS CURRENT LIABILITIES	335 028	295 794	693 264	431 563
CREDITORS (more than 1 year)	−5 878	−6 031	−394 872	−123 748
PROVISIONS FOR LIABILITIES & CHARGES				
Deferred taxation			−2 409	
Other provisions	−26 597	−33 203	−25 016	−7 070
TOTAL NET ASSETS	302 553	256 560	271 327	300 745
CAPITAL & RESERVES				
Called-up share capital	66 287	66 287	66 287	66 281
Share premium account	175 123	175 123	175 128	175 129
Revaluation reserve	3 660	2 239	1 084	1 784
Special reserve	43 118	43 118	61 241	80 433
Profit & Loss Account	14 365	−30 207	−32 408	−22 882
SHAREHOLDERS' FUNDS	302 553	256 560	217 327	300 745

Consolidated cash flow statement £000

	52 weeks ended 1/2 1992	52 weeks ended 30/1 1993	52 weeks ended 1/2 1996	52 weeks ended 3/2 1997
NET CASH INFLOW FROM OPERATIONS	61 093	103 428	97 539	109 397
RETURNS ON INVESTMENTS & SERVICING OF FINANCE				
Interest received	13 962	14 909	8 415	6 505
Interest paid	−35 580	−59 594	−47 914	−34 642
Dividends paid	−48 333			
NET CASH OUTFLOW FROM RETURNS ON INVESTMENTS & SERVICING OF FINANCE	−69 951	−44 685	−39 499	−28 137
TAX RECOVERED/PAID	−26 377	23 507	−1 322	−1 754
INVESTING ACTIVITIES				
Purchase of tangible fixed assets	−32 215	−11 984	−16 923	−15 202
Disposal of subsidiary undertakings (net)		23 231		
Proceeds on sale of fixed assets	7 732	13 303	−801	5 262
Payments from disposal of ESOT shares				−13 883
NET CASH FLOW: INVEST ACTIVITIES	−24 483	24 550	−17 724	−23 823
NET CASH IN/OUTFLOW PRE FINANCING	−59 718	106 800	38 994	55 683
INCREASE/DECREASE IN BANK DEPOSITS			4 433	12 882
FINANCING				
Issue of share capital	60 008			
Expenses in connection with share issue	−3 328			
New bank loans	35 196		−15 309	−5 175
Issue of loan notes	43 576		−5 296	−28 983
Repayment of 4% conver. Bonds 2002		−43 960		
Repayment of subordinated notes	−19 892	−4 319		
Reduction/increase in external financing of credit receivables	8 480	−98 828		
Other long term creditors	−6 594			
NET CASH IN/OUTFLOW FROM FINANCING	117 446	−147 107	−20 605	−34 158
INCREASE/DECREASE IN CASH & CASH EQUIVALENTS	57 728	−40 307	22 822	8 643

Average number of employees

	1992	1993	1996	1997
Management	333	319	323	331
Administration	1 084	754	1 196	1 090
Distribution & sales staff	18 935	15 437	10 476	9 797
TOTAL	20 352	16 510	11 995	11 218
Aggregate payroll costs £000	228 110	200 826	179 065	171 961

Segment Information: £000

	1992	1993	1996	1997
UK, Channel Islands & Eire				
Sales	629 038	472 220	336 783	343 495
Profit/loss before interest & tax	-92 734	-27 952	18 057	22 725
USA				
Sales	499 596	456 405	557 899	558 457
Profit/loss before interest & tax	-2 437	20 243	45 882	53 780

Share capital; fully paid: £000

	1992	1993	1996	1997
Ordinary shares of 10p each	29 305	29 305	29 306	29 306
Preference shares, various	36 982	36 982	36 976	36 975
Total	66 287	66 287	66 282	66 281

Creditors: Amounts falling due within one year: £000

	1992	1993	1996	1997
Bank borrowings				
overdrafts	50 140	34 872	39 905	30 130
loans	311 733	375 252	22 356	206 995
4% convertible bonds 2002	44 000	40		
Loan notes	70 241	79 355	3 969	42 405
Trade creditors	91 890	42 436	36 497	35 416
Corporation tax	20 085	7 743	9 767	19 982
Social Security & PAYE	4 733	3 054	3 828	4 042
Other taxes	22 681	19 636	15 217	15 868
Other creditors	33 075	9 303	7 386	10 144
Accruals & deferred income	74 947	60 904	42 179	44 050
Total	723 525	632 595	181 104	409 032

Creditors: amounts falling due after one year: £000

	1992	1993	1996	1997
Bank loans falling due between 2–5 years			344 820	119 675
Loan notes			45 756	
Subordinated notes issued by subsidiary	3 631	4 371	4 248	4 064
Other creditors	2 247	1 660	48	9
Total	5 878	6 031	394 872	123 748

Retail Prices Index   *13 Jan 1987 = 100*

Year	All Items	All exc mortgage interest & indirect taxes
1987	101.9	101.9
1988	106.9	106.6
1989	115.2	113.1
1990	126.1	121.4
1991	133.5	129.5
1992	138.5	135.1
1993	140.7	139.0
1994	144.1	141.3
1995	149.1	144.5

Source: Office of National Statistics

Retail trade: volume index

Year	Index	Other specialised non-food stores
1987	91.5	85.8
1988	97.3	94.1
1989	99.3	98.5
1990	100.0	100.0
1991	98.7	94.8
1992	99.4	91.6
1993	102.4	94.3
1994	106.2	97.6

Source: Office of National Statistics

Ratner market shares

Calendar year	UK (%)	US (%)
1985	2.6	
1986	12.1	
1987	23	<1
1988	27	2
1989	30	
1990	33	5
1991		
1992		
1993		
1994	20	5[a]
1995	20	5[a]
1996		4.5[a]

[a]Speciality jewellery market: share of total market about 40% of these figures

Figure 33.1
Jewellery retail sales
1983–92 (£m)

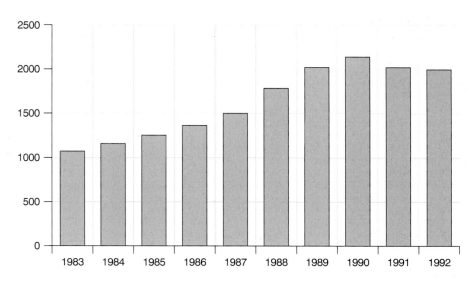

Ratner/Signet shops: number at financial year end – UK

	H Samuel	Ratner	Terry	Ern Jones	Watches of Switzerland	Zales	Jewellers UK Total	Salisbury
1984		130					130	
1985			26					
1986								
1987	337	143		58	20			
1988	367	199	85	58	20		727	
1989			merged					
1990								
1991	437	248		200	24	merged Jones	781	220
1992							1500	
1993	434	120		174	SOLD		1030	186
1994	433			170			603	
1995	428			167			600	
1996	428			166			594	

Ratner/Signet shops: number at financial year end – USA

	Total
1987	
1988	218
1989	
1990	456
1991	
1992	
1993	928
1994	871
1995	839
1996	778 (of which 440 trade under the Kays name)

Ratner acquisitions

Date	Company	Loc.	Store No.	Cost (£m)	Method
Dec-84	Terry's	UK	26	4.25	shares/loan
Jul-86	H Samuel	UK	370	149.00	shares/cash
Aug-87	Ernest Jones	UK	60	25.00	shares/cash: cash element financed by rights issue
Aug-87	Sterling	US	117	126.00	cash: financed by rights issue
Sep-87	Westhall	US	71	29.40	convert bonds
May-88	Osterman	US	56	36.00	shares
May-88	Time	Jersey	21	5.30	cash
Nov-88	Zales/Salisbury*	UK	442	150.75	£110m cash, £25m pref shares, £15.75 debt
Aug-89	Ringmaker/Allens	US	87	12.00	cash
Oct-89	Westfields	US	87	39.50	cash
Oct-90	Kays	US	426	236.00	£114.9 preference shares exchanged for Kay common stock: Balance was debt taken over, financed by bank loans & rights issue

* Includes 73 Collingwood

Ratner disposals

Date	Activity	Loc.	Store No.	Price (£m)	Details
Jun-92	Watches of Switz	UK	25	23.50	Asprey
Aug-94	Salisbury	UK		3.18	Stephen Hinchliffe: £2.75m cash plus £430m debt taken over, but Signet to carry £1.5m for Crawley warehouse closure

CHAPTER 34
AGIP Petroli entering the Indian market

In early 1997 India, like China, was a rapidly growing market that many multinational companies had entered or were planning to enter. India's oil market was, in 1995, 1 million metric tonnes (MT) (60 per cent automotive, 40 per cent industrial) and was expected to grow in volume in the industrial sector and in monetary value in the automotive. The share of higher-quality products was expected to increase and therefore provide an opportunity for premium brands for companies like AGIP.

The main alternative entry strategies available to AGIP were:

● Export products to be sold through local distributors
● Establish a wholly owned company
● Set up a joint venture with an Indian partner.

In addition, should a strategic alliance be selected, AGIP management realised that careful attention would need to be paid to how the alliance was structured and managed.

A new entrant can mainly use the retailers and workshops channel, which accounts for about 270 000 MT; other channels are almost a monopoly of public sector companies. As the country is huge and the market highly fragmented. distribution becomes the key factor.

In early 1997 the management of AGIP Petroli was preparing for a meeting to discuss plans to increase its business. After having expanded worldwide in the past decades, the company was considering how to take advantage of emerging market opportunities in India. Among the issues the top management had to carefully consider were how AGIP Petroli should enter India as a foreign company, and how best to take advantage of the resources and capabilities available in the host country.

This case study was written by Professor R. J. Mockler, St John's University, and A. Cornetti and Scordino, New York, for teaching purposes. (© R. J. Mockler, 1997

Company overview

AGIP Petroli, a subsidiary company of ENI (Ente Nazionale Idrocarburi), is a leading supplier, refiner and distributor of petroleum products in Italy. The company is not only a major competitor in the Italian market; it also plays a substantial role in the international oil market through subsidiaries, branches. joint ventures, and representative offices throughout the world.

History

AGIP (Azienda Generale Italiana dei Petroli) was founded by the Italian government in 1926 with the objective of 'pursuing all activities relating to the industrial and commercial aspects of petroleum products'. The company grew rapidly and was soon engaged not only in oil exploration and refining but also product distribution.

The 1929 depression brought progress to a halt. During the period of autarchy in the 1930s AGIP again started to expand and consolidate. In 1945 the government decided to liquidate the company. However, the strong results which rapidly began to emerge from oil and gas exploration induced the government instead to reorganise and recommence operations in all sectors. In 1953, the government established the Italian National Hydrocarbons Corporation – ENl – with AGIP as the core company.

A period of growth followed for the company in a wide variety of fields: motor-vehicles, agriculture, industry, shipping, aviation, domestic heating and even tourism – with the AGIP Motel chain. Meanwhile the company was reinforcing and upgrading its distribution, building service stations offering a wide range of facilities for driver and vehicle alike.

The change in conditions in the energy and petroleum markets which occurred in the mid-1970s induced the government to give ENI's Energy Division a broader and a more systematic structure so as to enable it to tackle the various phases of the petroleum cycle in a more flexible manner.

AGIP Petroli was established in 1977 and became sector-head of the ENI group in 1981. Between 1978 and 1983 AGIP Petroli's operations were strongly conditioned not only by market uncertainties but also by the fact that as a state-owned company its definite mission was 'to guarantee the country's energy supplies.' Moreover, it was asked to play a social political role by replacing the various firms that were encountering hard times. Hence, instead of pursuing a policy of expansion in the commercial and production sectors, AGIP Petroli had to adopt a strategy of defence and reconversion.

After some delays, the long process of reconstruction finally got under way. Industrial and commercial operations were rationalised and changes were made in strategies, organisation and the entrepreneurial approach. Recovery of economic efficiency was a lengthy struggle, involving a major effort to upgrade technological and organisational aspects of the company, while developing the capacity to operate effectively in very complex, high-tech sectors. More generally, all this called for the abandonment of the behavioral pattern of a state company and the adoption of a model based on market efficiency, flexibility and profitability.

AGIP Petroli in the international markets

AGIP began its international efforts in the 1950s. Its CEO's policy of negotiating direct agreements with producer countries to ensure crude oil supplies led to the decision to allow the company to operate worldwide in the exploration, refining and distribution sectors. It also led to the establishment of subsidiaries and joint ventures all over the world.

In 1997, AGIP Petroli operated in the downstream petroleum sector in Italy and abroad, ensuring close integration of the crude-oil supply, refining and product-marketing system. Supply of crude oil involved complex negotiations with numerous international business interests, long-term purchasing contracts and spot deals. Supplies originate from fifteen countries, mainly in North Africa and the Middle East. The company had seven refineries processing over 40 million tons per year of crude and feedstock. Its industrial system outside Italy was based on collaboration agreements in Germany and a number of African countries.

The organisation focused especially on research which is handled by Euron, a subsidiary concerned with studies and experimentation covering all phases of the petroleum cycle. Thanks to the constant revamping of its industrial system, AGIP Petroli retains a prime position worldwide as regards refining capacity, advanced technology, prime product yields and environmental safeguards which enable the company to market high-quality products all over the world.

Products

AGIP Petroli is one of the few companies in the world operating in all segments of the lubricants cycle, including production and marketing of base oils and finished lubricants for the most varied uses, as well as the recovery and rerefining of used oils. It is also engaged in the design and manufacture of products for rallying and racing on land and sea, as well as the production of LPG and its distribution using cylinders, road tankers and piped mains systems. In addition, AGIP Petroli is one of the first five companies worldwide manufacturing special products such as additives for fuels, lubricants and solvents.

AGIP brand lubricants, created in the San Donato Milanese research laboratories, join the excellence of raw materials with continual experimentation and constant cooperation with car manufacturers to provide the guarantees of reliability and safety that drivers all over the world have come to appreciate. In

1969, AGIP Petroli was the first European company to introduce a motor oil with a synthetic base, Sint 2000. Since then it has continued its research, providing the market with products increasingly aimed at special requirements like Sint Turbo Diesel for diesel engines and Sint Catalyst for catalytic cars.

In early 1997 the goal of the management was to introduce its high-quality products in the huge and fast-growing Indian market. The evaluation of the different alternatives leading to the final decision were expected to affect the international future of the entire company.

An introduction to India

It is often said, with some justification, that India is not a country but a continent. Almost 900 million people live within the borders of the world's second most populous nation. Although still predominantly a traditional agricultural economy, India was developing rapidly as one of the world's largest industrial powers. The government was pushing through a programme of modernisation and economic liberalisation which aimed to transform India into one of the leading industrial economies by early next century.

Although potentially an economic giant, almost two-thirds of the population worked on the land and literacy rates were low: it was estimated by the World Bank that perhaps a third of the world's 'absolute poor' lived in India.[1] Nevertheless, it was the marriage of an enormous potential market and the new opportunities for investment which had attracted foreign companies to India in increasing numbers, particularly in the last two years.

Geographical and cultural considerations

Despite its great size and diversity, India had achieved a notable level of political stability; the governing Congress Party was unique in having a national focus, in comparison to the more regional bias of rival parties. The strong lead which central government had been able to provide had given much impetus to the recent process of economic reform. Nevertheless, any company hoping to develop a role in the Indian market first had to realise that the country was made up of very distinct regions and that individual states or groups of states might be large enough or sufficiently homogenous character to be treated as separate 'national' markets in themselves.

India was divided into twenty-five states and seven other Union Territories. State governments had a high degree of autonomy in handling certain activities, including, most notably, local industrial policy. Although English was the most commonly spoken language of the government and business classes there was no 'national' language. The country was divided into a great number of local languages and, in many cases, the state boundaries were drawn on linguistic lines. The cultural heritage was rich. Hinduism, Buddhism, Jainism and Sikhism originated in the North, supplemented much later by Christianity and Islam.

Distances between major centres were often considerable and land communications were either slow (by rail) or very poor (by road). Bombay (the main economic centre) and New Delhi (the capital) are 1400 km apart: an express train covered the distance in 17 hours, and by road the journey could have taken as long. India's physical size was made more daunting by infrastructure deficiencies, which continue to place major constraints on economic growth. Although major investment programmes were underway to improve the transport and telecommunications networks, their lack of development was a major constraint on companies operating on a nationwide strategy.

The move to a liberalised economy

For over forty years after Independence in 1947, the Indian government, guided by the socialist principles of Jawaharial Nehru, pursued an economic policy characterised by central planning and protectionism and an increasing drive towards self-sufficiency. This policy reached its apogee in the 1970s when, for example, the foreign oil companies, which had been dominant, were forced by increasingly restrictive regulations to leave India. A major portion of industry became state-owned and was subjected to strict licensing, labour and pricing regulations. Free enterprise was not encouraged.

By the mid 1980s it became clear that a controlled economy could not produce the desired results and liberalisation measures were first introduced, with the aim of freeing Indian companies from excessive regulations and controls and making the protected industry more competitive. However, by the time of Rajiv Gandhi's assassination in May 1991, India stood on the brink of a major economic and political crisis.

Rajiv Gandhi was succeeded by prime minister, P. V. Narashima Rao, who immediately set about giving the liberalisation process its strongest impetus by the New Economic Policies in July 1991. This set in motion a series of further and continuing reforms of major significance to Indian and foreign companies alike. The main components of the new market conditions are summarised below:

Trade policy
- Almost all import restrictions have been removed.
- Import licensing has largely been abolished.
- Ceiling rates of import duties were brought down significantly in the 1993 budget from levels which once approached 300 per cent on some goods to an average of 35 per cent. Import rates for priority sectors like petroleum refining have been reduced still further.

Foreign investment policy
- Direct foreign investment has been actively encouraged to allow technology transfer and multinational linkage.
- Restrictions on foreign firms entering the industrial sector have been greatly reduced.

653

- Automatic approval for investments of up to 51 per cent in high-priority industries; specific approval for 100 per cent foreign-owned ventures is possible.
- Restrictions on expansion and diversification of companies with majority foreign ownership have been greatly reduced; investors are now allowed to use their own brand names, buy property, open their own branches and accept deposits.
- Liberal tax and non-tax concessions are available for new investment.
- For approved investments, capital earnings can be freely repatriated subject to normal taxation and exchange control procedures.
- Elimination of manufacturing programmes requiring a progressive increase of indigenous content in joint ventures.

Industrial policy
- Only six industries still reserved solely for the public sector.
- A private sector is evolving rapidly with participation in all other industries permitted; private competition has been particularly encouraged in banking, internal airlines and telecommunications.
- Major relaxation in the rules allowing branches of foreign trading and manufacturing companies to operate in India.
- Substantial deregulation and simplification of procedures for setting up and operating in business. For example, industrial licensing has been virtually abolished, clearance from the Monopolies Commission has been dispensed with and changes have been made to company laws to allow mergers and acquisitions.
- Business taxes have been substantially reformed.

Foreign exchange policy
- Devaluation of the rupee has allowed for its partial conversion in foreign markets; the exchange rate has been stabilised and a unified exchange rate system has been in place since February 1993.
- Amendments to the Foreign Exchange Regulation Act mean that the importers can pay for goods with foreign exchange bought at the market rate without the permission of the Reserve Bank of India.
- Indian foreign exchange reserves rose from $1 bn to over $20 bn between 1991 and 1994.

The remaining obstacles

India's progress towards full economic reform had been likened to the slow yet stately progress of an elephant in comparison with the frenetic pace of the other Asian economies, most notably China. Although the implications of reform in India were dramatic, the process they had set in motion was likely to take a number of years before the most far-reaching effects were seen.

Widespread reform of the state sector had been avoided, largely to mitigate the catastrophic effects of unemployment in a labour-intensive economy. India had no welfare system, but strong trade unions and a number of long-standing labour laws stated that, for example, workers could not be sacked except for serious disciplinary offenses, so loss-making factories could not be closed; anyone leaving a particular job voluntarily had to be replaced; and any employee working for a particular company for ninety days was entitled to a pension for life. Instead, the government sought to improve the competitiveness of the state-owned companies by allowing private operators to set up alongside them.

Enormous investment was required in the infrastructure, particularly transport and telecommunications, if the benefits of the reform process were to be widely distributed. The traditional and hidebound Indian bureaucracy continued to act as a brake on policy directives from above. Thus, while broader issues concerning setting up and managing business had been tackled, more immediate 'local issues', for example those concerning premises and setting up telephones, could still take several months to complete.

Although there was a large, skilled and cheap labour force available, levels of literacy were still very low by Western standards; foreign companies were often convinced of an 'ethical' need to improve labour conditions with their partner companies in India, particularly in traditional industries, a policy that could lead to increased investment costs. Cultural differences and the protection afforded by the labour laws had created working habits which differed markedly from the traditional Western work ethic. Foreign companies needed to understand the Indian 'way' when examining working practices. Although India had maintained a high degree of political stability over the last four decades, occasional outbursts of tension had proved temporary setbacks to the reform process and disputes between religious factions still formed a threatening backdrop.

Lubricant supply and demand in india

The oil industry

The oil industry was mainly divided into *upstream* and *downstream*. *Upstream* includes the processes from exploring areas to finding curds, drilling up (the excavation itself), pumping up the crude, and the logistics and the trading of the crude. *Downstream* includes all the processes related to the refining of the crude and the commercialisation of the oil derivatives. Among these products, lubricants played an important role. The base oils were the raw material of the lubricant and there were diverse types of bases, classified according to their viscosity and other chemical and physical parameters.

A lubricant is a mix of a base oil with additives. According to the percentage of oil base (against a synthetic base which was obtained from non oil substances) it could be classified as mineral (100 per cent base of oil origin), semi-synthetic and synthetic (more than 70 per cent of synthetic base). In any case, the three types of lubricant had additives to enhance the lubricant properties.

There was another industry which produced lubricants – the petrochemical industry, whose product was synthetic. Lubricants had mainly two uses: automotive (lubricants used in vehicles, e.g. the lubricant used in the charter of

655

the engine) and industrial (used in industry, e.g. the lubricant used in the axis of a pump). The AGIP project focused on automotive lubricants.

Base oils and additives supply

In India, base oils were manufactured in three main refineries (IOC, Hindustan, and Madras). Local production, in spite of extension plans by PSUs and private sector companies, was falling behind demand. In fact almost one third of lubricants were manufactured with imported base oils (see Table 34.1).

Table 34.1   Demand and supply scenario (000) tonnes

Product	1990/91	1991/92	1992/94	1999/2000
Lubricants demand	892	932	862	1376
Base oil production	552	390	533	827
Imports lubes and base	340	542	329	549

Source: BTS

Margins in this market were quite high, in fact prices covered transportation costs from the Mediterranean. Companies like Gulf Oil were currently buying base oils from the Mediterranean and reselling them in India.

The two main additives suppliers in India were Lubrizol India LTD and Indian Additives.

Lubrizol was the absolute market leader covering about 80 per cent of the demand. The local base oils provided poor quality, therefore increasing volumes of additives was required to manufacture high-quality lubricants. The whole market of additives was estimated around 65 000 MT in 1994.

Lubricant manufacturers

In India about twenty-seven major blending plants and several small plants run by minor private blenders operated. IOC accounted for almost half of the national blending capacity, whereas the other PSUs (HPC, BPC, IBP) altogether covered about 30 per cent. Castrol was the biggest private sector blender with four plants and 10 per cent of the capacity.

As seen in Table 34.2, there was excess capacity to cover the consumption of new entrants in the next few years. In fact, each oil company started its operations blending on third parties' plants as fees were cheap and quality reliable. As soon as the critical mass was reached, foreign oil companies started building their own plants, releasing further blending capacity.

Table 34.2 Current and planned lubricant blending capacity

Company	Tonnes (1994)	Planned additional capacity by 1997–8 (tonnes)
IOC	395 000	340 000
Hindustan Petroleum	162 000	105 000
Bharat Petroleum	90 000	75 000
IBP	35 000	50 000
Castrol	86 000	
Tide Water	13 300	
Pennzoil	9 000	
Gulf		75 000
Elf	15 000	
Others	30 000	40 000
Total	835 300	685 000
Total capacity		1 520 000

Source: BMS – Total Research, Business opportunities in the market for automotive lubricants in India

The automotive sector

Automotive lubricant use in the Indian market made up 60 per cent of the lubricant use. Lubricants were used in vehicles such as jeeps, commercial vehicles, passenger cars, tractors, buses, and two- and three-wheelers. While only one Indian in 300 used a car, one in fifty owned a scooter, moped, motorbike or two- or three-wheeler (Table 34.3). Of this group, two- and three-wheelers accounted for over 70 per cent of vehicles used in India. Cars and jeeps accounted for ten per cent of the total vehicle population.

The number of vehicles in use in India had been rapidly increasing. Since 1981, the vehicle population had effectively doubled every five years. One explanation for the expansion in vehicle use was an increase in ownership of two-wheeler vehicles. Car ownership, despite tax concessions initiated in 1993, was still unaffordable to the vast majority of Indians. Thus, given their relatively low cost, two-wheelers promised to capture the disposable income of the growing middle class. The continued growth of the two-wheel vehicle was expected to contribute to the demand for lubricants in India.

Medium to heavy commercial vehicle growth was estimated to continue at a lesser rate, while the demand for lighter vehicles widely used to carry a majority of consumer goods in urban and suburban areas was likely to double. The small number of tractors and agricultural vehicles was expected to double by the year

Table 34.3 Vehicle ownership by main regions expressed as no. of inhabitants per vehicle in use

Region	2/3 wheeler	Cars/jeeps	CVs	Tractors	All vehicles
North West	30	245	294	111	20
North	59	300	719	526	42
North East	148	291	279	2479	63
Center	59	625	747	703	45
West	34	177	408	767	25
East	146	355	486	1915	40
South West	48	199	422	1470	34
South East	54	324	472	2716	41
All India	57	279	482	683	39

Source: Ministry Of Surface Transport (MOST)

2001. Even though the economy was booming, a car or commercial vehicle was still too costly for Indian consumers. Indian vehicle owners tended to keep their vehicles running for as long as possible, hence there were many older model vehicles that consumed lubricants at a much quicker pace than their newer counterparts.

Overall market size

In 1994 the estimated size of the market for automotive lubricants in India was 590 000 tons. This represented a 22 per cent growth in consumption since 1990. The market was worth Rs 29 300 million ($968 m) in 1994. This represented a growth in value of 35 per cent since 1990.

Table 34.4 Automotive lubricants market by value, 1990–94

Year	Rs million	$ million at 1994 exchange	% change
1990	21 820	716	
1991	23 000	754	5.4
1992	24 670	812	7.3
1993	26 740	877	8.4
1994	29 500	968	10.3
% change 1990–94			35.2

Source: Vehicle manufacturers / BMS – Total Research

The market size by geographic region

The largest markets for lubricants were the west (principally Bombay) and north (principally New Delhi) which collectively accounted for almost half the total market. In general, the lubricant market was largest in regions which had the best-developed parcs. Although the west was not the largest region in terms of population (the north, east and south-east were larger), it did have the largest vehicle parc, largely reflecting Bombay's status as the commercial hub of India. Car ownership in the north, east and south-east was approximately half the level in the west, while ownership of two-wheeler and commercial vehicles was also among the highest in India in the west.

A high concentration of commercial vehicles which consume ten times the amount of lubricant per year compared with cars could also inflate the volume of smaller regions. The north-west, for example, had a relatively large commercial vehicle parc and was thus a more important market than its size would have suggested. Despite containing India's second largest city (approximately a fifth of the population in total), the east was a relatively poorly developed market. Vehicle ownership lagged well behind the west and north and the region had been stagnating economically. The south-west, and particularly Bangalore, was experiencing a rapid economic growth and car ownership was second only to the west. The south-east was developing less rapidly. Vehicle ownership was similar to the east and centre, although the two stroke market was growing more rapidly. Central India, broadly defined as Madhya Pradesh, but in effect taking up large parts of eastern Maharashtra and Andhra Pradesh, was the least developed market; largely rural, car and commercial vehicle ownership was the lowest in India. Although the smallest region studied, the north-east had a relatively large commercial vehicle parc (since rail transport was less well developed). However, the region was remote, fragmented and blighted by political instability.[2]

The market by product type

The market was broken down by engine oil, two-stroke and other automotive lubricant products. Monograde engines once dominated the Indian market, but the picture had changed considerably in the last two to three years. Multigrade oils were now the most common engine oil, accounting for 70 per cent of the engine oil market. Synthetics and semi-synthetics were very recent introductions and had very limited application for vehicles currently in use.[3]

Given the relative size and growth of the two-wheeler market in India, two-stroke products had a share of the market considerably in excess of that found in Western markets. Two-stroke oil was viewed as a simple 'commodity' product by most vehicle owners, with low cost and simplicity of use taking precedence over quality. Consumption per vehicle was, therefore, relatively high. Other lubricants accounted for 17 per cent of total lubricant consumption. The largest segment consisted of gear oils, transmission fluids and brake fluid. Consumption of these products per vehicle in Indian conditions was relatively high: most vehicles had manual gear boxes. The market for automotive grease accounted for 27,000 tonnes; again, consumption per vehicle was high, but was gradually falling with the introduction of long-life greases.[4]

Table 34.5 Market size by product type, 1994

Product	Volume (000 tonnes)	Volume share (%)
Engine oils	415	70.2
Monograde	125	21.2
Basic SC/CC multi	224	37.9
Standard SF/CD multi	65.5	11.1
High-perf. SG/SH/CE/CF multi	0.5	neg
Synthetics/semi-synthetics	neg	neg
Two-stroke oil	72	12.2
Commodity & TA/TB	62	8.5
TC and above	8	2.7
Semi synthetic/synthetic	2	1.0
Other Lubricants	102	17.0
Gear oil/transmission fluid	59	10.0
Brake fluid	16	2.7
Grease	27	4.3
Total	589	100

Source: Vehicle manufacturers / BMS – Total Research

The lubricant automotive supply

Lubricant oil was composed of base oil and additives. In the late 1970s the government forced the multinational corporations out of India through tax policies aimed at protecting the state-owned companies: Indian Oil Corporation. Hindustan Petroleum, Bharat Petroleum, and Indo-Burma Petroleum. These producers were known as PSUs. Local production of base oils, for lubricants had been falling behind demand. The country imported 6 300 000 tons of petroleum products to meet the gap between supply and demand.[5] Almost all base stock for lubricants was manufactured from imported crude oil, and one third of lubricants was manufactured with imported base oils. Due to these supply factors, there was an upward trend in the wholesale price of crude oil and petroleum products. Currently, multinational corporations were collaborating in joint ventures with PSUs.

Import tariffs on base oils and finished products had fallen by forty-three per cent. Base oil imports were expected to increase as domestic production fell further behind increasing demand. In 1992 and 1993 petroleum oil and lubricants accounted for 28 per cent of India's total imports, making it the largest single imported commodity. After reaching a peak of 34 million tons in 1990, production had fallen while demand had been rising by 6–8 per cent per annum. Given the relatively poor quality of base oils manufactured in India, significant volumes of additives were required to manufacture high-quality lubricants.

Eighty per cent of additives was produced domestically and the remainder of the supply necessary for lubricants was imported. Recent reductions in import duties promised to create an augmentative effect on additive imports.[6]

Sales channels

Apart from industrial oils, which were sold directly by oil companies or their distributors to customers, the main sales channels were the following:

1 *Fuel stations* – There were about 16 000 fuel stations in India and all of them were operated by the public sector companies. Officially only lubricants from the fuel supplier or their joint venture partners (Caltex, Mobil, Shell and Exxon) were sold through these channels, although, unofficially other brands like Castrol were likely to be found in these shops.

2 *Retail outlets* – The retailers' channel was known in India as Bazaar, which was basically spares and accessory shops and oil shops. In the whole country there were about 50 000–100 000 spares shops and about 5000–10 000 oil shops. Both types of shops were generally very small and stocked very small quantities.

3 *Workshops* – This channel consisted of about 6000 authorized workshops and about 50 000–70 000 independent service outlets. Most of these outlets serviced two- and three-wheelers. Vehicle owners went to authorised workshops mainly during the warranty period and then the loyalty decreased dramatically. However, this segment would have enjoyed some benefits: since more sophisticated and expensive vehicles were being introduced, the quality-concerned population was increasing.

4 *Fleets* – There had been a huge growth in goods and passenger transport by road as a consequence of the economic boom, although investments were still needed in the infrastructure and in new vehicles. Most of the fleets operated with less than five vehicles and none of them was expected to have their own workshop. Almost 60 per cent[7] of the lubricants sold through this channel were bought by state passenger fleets which privilege PSUs.

5 *Direct sales* – These were the sales achieved directly by oil companies or major wholesalers to large customers of which about 50 per cent[8] was the oil consumption of the Indian railways, supplied almost exclusively by IOC.

Future supply and demand in India

Market growth

The market accounted for about 1 million MT in 1995, of which about 600 000 MT were in the automotive sector only. The government forecast about 1 300 000 MT consumption by the year 2000. Such an increase in volume was mainly due

Table 34.6 Estimated market growth by product, 1994–99

Product	1994	1995	1996	1997	1998	1999	% change 1994/99
Engine oils	415	428	423	141	404	391	(6)
Monograde	125	110	100	95	89	84	(33)
Basic SC/CC multi	224	245	241.5	226	207	177	(21)
Standard SF/CD multi	65.5	72	79	87	96	106	62
High-Perf. SG/SH/CE/CF multi	0.5	1	2	4	8	16	3100
Synthetics/semi-synthetics	neg	neg	0.5	2	4	8	(1500)
Two-stroke oil	72	72	72	71	69	67	(7)
Commodity & TA/TB	62	56	51	46	41	36	(42)
TC and above	8	12	14	16	18	20	150
Semi-synthetic/synthetic	2	4	7	9	10	11	450
Other lubricants	102	105	103	101	98	95	(7)
Total	589	605	598	586	571	553	(6)

Source: BTS

to industrial oils whereas the automotive lubricants were expected to increase in terms of value only.

In the year 2000 the total size of the market for automotive lubricants in India will be an estimated 600 000 tons. Lubricant consumption per vehicle will reduce as new makes with modern specifications are introduced, drain periods increase and the vehicle parc becomes younger. The net result is that although the Indian vehicle parc is expected to increase by at least 40 per cent by 2000, the total volume of lubricants consumed will be 6 per cent less than at present. Market value will, however, continue to grow as the market for higher-quality/higher-value lubricants increases, although the growth rate will slow by 2000 as market volume begins to decline.

The share of the market held by engine oil was forecast to remain steady at approximately 70 per cent although overall consumption of all main lubricant types was going to decline by 6–7 per cent (Table 34.6).

In the engine oil market, consumption of monograde began to fall again after a recovery during 1994, but there was expected to be a 'hard core' of purchasers to ensure the residual importance of these products. Basic SC multigrades were anticipated to increase in consumption between 1994 and 1995, picking up former monograde users, but then decline in importance gradually, as these grades were in turn replaced by SF quality products. SG/SH quality mineral oils and synthetic/semi-synthetics should rapidly increase their consumption over the next five years, but would not account for more than 6–10 per cent of the market by 1999. SC multigrades were still to be the predominant product but SF quality grades have secured almost 30 per cent of the engine oil market.

The two-stroke sector was likely also to change significantly by 1999. Higher-quality packaged oils which had less than 15 per cent of the current market were estimated to increase to such an extent that consumption would be almost equal to commodity products by the turn of the century.

The largest decline in consumption was estimated to be in regions where the vehicle parc was already high and/or where new vehicle sales would have been greatest – the west, north-west, north and south-west. Although the vehicle parc was expected to increase rapidly, these regions represented the best opportunity for higher-quality, long-drain lubricants. In the east and south-east, vehicle ownership was lower than in more developed regions and usage of higher-quality lubricants was at a lower level. An above-average increase in the number of vehicles, coupled with a less significant fall in lubricant consumption per vehicle, suggested that overall lubricant consumption in these regions would have fallen less dramatically. The north-east and centre were likely to continue to be relatively undynamic markets; the vehicle parc was not expected to increase as rapidly as elsewhere and per vehicle consumption was not going to be greatly reduced.

Authorised service and repair outlets were the only purchaser channels likely to actually increase consumption of lubricants for the following five years: this would have been a reflection of developments in the vehicle market with many new manufacturers entering the market. Owners of new vehicles were much more likely to use authorised outlets rather than independent mechanics and, with more new vehicles on the road, the independent mechanics might lose some of their traditional, cut-price business.

Petrol stations and retail outlets were not expected to suffer a more than average decline in consumption. Petrol stations were going to continue to be the primary source of lubricants, particularly if higher-quality joint-venture brands proved successful, although some of their oil change activities were going to be lost to authorised outlets. Retail outlets were expected to continue to be an important source for mechanics and truck owners. Although the number of fleets with workshops was expected to rise slightly and the commercial vehicle parc itself was going to increase, per vehicle consumption was likely to fall by up to 50 per cent and the sector itself to shrink in volume, while increasing in value.

The changing competitive scene

The PSU suppliers (state sector composed of four main companies: Indian Oil Corporation, Hindustan Petroleum, Bharat Petroleum and Indo-Burmah Petroleum) had been losing market share but still retained the largest share of the market, with sales of 413 000 tonnes during 1994 (approximately 70 per cent of the market). IOC (Indian Oil Corporation) was the largest single supplier; the Servo brand, accounting for 4 in every 10 litres of lubricants, sold more than the other PSU brands put together (Table 34.7).

Castrol, in particular, had benefited from the declining share of the market held by the PSUs and was estimated to be the third-largest supplier, selling 72 000 tonnes during 1994. Castrol had thus moved ahead of Bharat, the third-largest

Table 34.7   Estimated market shares by volume, 1994

Company	Volume (000 tonnes)	Volume (% share)
IOC	242	41.0
Hindustan	97	16.4
Castrol	72	12.2
Bharat	56	9.5
Tide Water	25	4.2
Gulf	22	3.7
IBP	18	3.0
Pennzoil	10	1.7
Elf	10	1.7
Others[a]	37	6.2
Total	589	100
Approximate non-Indian share		16/17

[a]Includes smaller manufactures (often recycled products) and 'bogus' products largely sold through spares and accessory shops
Sources: Indian Petroleum & Natural Gas Statistics

PSU supplier. Castrol sold almost three times as much volume as its nearest sector rival, TideWater, who had enjoyed a recent revival in sales. Gulf, Pennzoil and Elf were the only other foreign suppliers to have made significant inroads to date. In total, foreign brands accounted for 16–17 per cent of lubricant sales. The remaining 6 per cent of the market (35 000 tonnes) was shared between a large number of smaller local manufactures (mainly rerefining used oils) and 'bogus' products, whose share of the market was increasing.

Table 34.8   Market shares by main sector, 1994

	PSU suppliers	%	Foreign non PSU	%	Total volume
Fuel Station[a]	204.6	98	4.0	2	208.6
Retail	52.5	37	91.0	63	143.5
Service/Repair	63.0	48	67.0	52	130.0
Fleets	36.0	88	5.0	12	41.0
Railways	30.0	100	0.0	0	30
Other channels	27.9	76	9.0	24	36.9
Total	414	70	176	30	590

[a]Includes joint-venture petrol stations selling foreign brands
Source: BTS

The figures show that the PSU suppliers and foreign private sector suppliers effectively operated in parallel markets. The PSU suppliers dominated sales through fuel to fleets and to the railways. and through rural LPG dealers to the agricultural sector. Foreign brands were sold unofficially through fuel stations to a small extent and some fleets had recently switched from sourcing from the PSUs. Foreign and private sector suppliers were predominant in the retail sector and also sold marginally more than the PSU suppliers in the third-party service and channel, particularly to authorised outlets.

Protected market shares

It was not possible to estimate market shares over the following five years with any accuracy. The market had suddenly become very competitive, but most of the new entrants had not yet established a solid platform.

There was no consensus in the industry itself about the number of suppliers the market could successfully sustain. Although there was a widely held opinion that, as the market 'shook down' and prices, in particular, became more stable, a number of the current suppliers were going to leave the marketplace. [9]The main trends to note were as follows:

The PSUs had been losing market share for the last three years (industry sources indicate by as much as 14 per cent per annum). This trend was certain to continue: conservative estimates, for example, felt Servo's share of the market was going to dip below 30 per cent over the following two or three years.[10] The introduction of joint-venture brands was certain to cannibalise sales of higher-quality PSU brands which might have otherwise had benefited from the growing share of the market regained by PSU brands. Thus, while it was reported that Mobil was going to start by offering equivalent Servo and Mobil brands in the higher-quality sector of the market, Bharat Shell was expected, instead, to phase out the Bharat brand name altogether over a period of time. In the past, the PSU brands sought to stave off the competitive threat of Castrol and Gulf in the fleet sector by providing storage facilities for established bulk clients and linking fuel and lubricant sales, thus helping them to keep down their inventories. This had proved a major advantage in retaining market share in this sector, but depended, to a large degree on the PSU brands holding on to their price advantage.

Castrol had been the main beneficiary of the PSUs decline in market share and should have continued to increase market share in the following five years. However, Castrol was facing an unprecedented competitive situation. The PSUs had all adopted, through joint ventures, international brands which competed with Castrol in the 'quality' market. The sudden influx of new entrants also challenged Castrol's supremacy in the 'quality' market and immediately targeted the channels upon which Castrol had based their success (retail outlets and mechanics).[11]

TideWater had shown a marked recovery in recent years and had the advantage of a well-known brand name (Veedol) and an extensive network. The technical collaboration with Mitsubishi had given TideWater an opportunity to target the tiny but growing high-quality sector of the market and the company stated their intention of doubling market share in the following few years.[12]

The new entrants that had been most successful to date – Gulf, Elf and Pennzoil – were not yet selling in sufficient quantities to guarantee a long-standing position in the market, but at least they had the advantage of establishing themselves ahead of a flood of more recent entrants. At that time, Gulf looked the most likely to succeed, having a well-recognised brand name (from its former relationship with Petrosil) while the tie-up with Ashok Leyland might prove advantageous. It was far too early to comment on the likely prospects for other new entrants, but, given the planned capacity of the new blending plant, it would have seemed that 15 000 tonnes was the critical mass required to gain a reasonable foothold in the market.[13]

The smaller Indian private sector suppliers were likely to keep a toehold on the market and some might even increase their share by specialising in supplying basic quality grades. Despite the entry of foreign competitors, there was optimism among the Indian private sector suppliers. The current import prices of base oil and finished lubricants continued to make local blending and/or filling an attractive proposition (as was going to be the selling of 'bogus' products).

The PSUs were finding that, as their prices increased, their low-end products were less competitive and they were, in any case, seeking to build up their 'quality' profile. The high-volume/low-margin sales might, therefore, be left to others for as long as rerefined products retained their price advantage. Nevertheless, as the demand for higher-quality products gradually increased, many smaller suppliers were going to be driven out of the market.

It is important to note that some of the larger private sector Indian companies were optimistic. Motorol (formerly Rinki), for example, was looking at markets outside India and planning lubricant plants in Mauritius, Indonesia and South Africa, having already transferred technical know-how to a manufacturer in eastern Malaysia.

The decision to enter the market

In order to decide whether and, eventually, how to enter the Indian market, AGIP's management focused its attention on all the possible opportunities and threats for a new entrant. On the one hand, there were some factors which the company could use to its advantage. The market was rapidly growing: industrial oils were increasing in terms of volume and automotive oils in terms of value. The private sector was gaining market share in contrast to the public sector. Moreover, more sophisticated models and further vehicle manufacturers were expected to enter the market, thus the demand for higher-quality lubricants was expected to grow and premium brands were going to enjoy an advantage. Among sales channels the Bazaar market was increasing its share. In this context, retailers and mechanics played a very important role in the purchase decision process: however, they knew very little about lubricants. Providing training was considered to be an advantage.

On the other hand, management was aware of the fact that a new entrant had to face several difficult problems. Industrial supply was largely provided by PSUs, best-selling oils were still low-price (and low-margin) and OEM (original equipment manufacturer) approvals were necessary to qualify a new brand. The competition was intense: there were about sixty market players of which about twenty were multinational companies. From the distribution point of view, the fuel stations channel was closed to a new entrant and the best distributors had already been taken. Moreover, the Bazaar market was highly fragmented so that the average lube consumption per outlet was low.

Entry strategies

Having all this in mind, AGIP's management planning team considered alternatives in several areas. There are several ways to enter a new market for a company. AGIP, took into consideration only the more consistent strategies:

1 *Export products to be sold through distributors*. As India is such a large country, it takes at least a distributor for each state (twenty-five plus seven Union Territories). For AGIP Petroli, it could be difficult to handle such a large number of distributors from Europe.
2 *Establish a wholly owned company*. For AGIP Petroli it is risky and costly to build a distribution network nationwide from scratch as the best have already been taken by the competitors (mostly Castrol and ELF). Besides, the country is huge and the market is highly fragmented. Therefore it requires extensive knowledge of each factor, including bureaucracy and politics, which is quite difficult to achieve from the beginning as a new entrant.
3 *Set up a joint venture with an Indian partner*. This alternative could be pursued entering the market through a 50 per cent joint venture between AGIP and an Indian partner. AGIP took into consideration the following supply policies:
   - Importing finished products: though the import tax has been reduced to 30 per cent (down from 80 per cent), all competitors produce locally, thus they can enjoy a cost advantage.
   - Local production: production can be performed in a joint venture's own blending plant or on third-parties' plants. Third-parties' blenders are cheap, reliable and have enough blending capacity. Furthermore, before the critical mass is reached, production at variable costs is very low risk. However, as volumes increase it becomes more difficult to keep quality and production control on third parties' blenders. On the other hand, the construction of a local blending plant requires higher initial investment and the risk associated with it.

The Indian partner

Once it has been decided to enter the Indian market through a joint venture, the key factor to success is to find a partner with a distribution network already in place in the automotive market. This partner should be selected within engineering companies, small Indian oil companies or vehicle producers.

One partner under consideration is Escort Ltd. Escort was a conglomerate with interests in the areas of agriculture, transportation, construction, and tele-communications with a turnover of US$688 m and 22 000 employees in 1994. The group is structured in several joint ventures which also manufacture and sell the following items of major interest for AGIP:

- Motor cycles – 90 000 Rajdoot and 120 000 Yamaha RX-100 in a 50 per cent joint venture with Yamaha (market share 33 per cent)
- Mopeds – 24 000 units of the new model Toro (market share 8 per cent)
- Tractors – 20 000 Escort tractors and 18 000 in a joint venture with Ford (market share 25 per cent).
- Pistons and piston-rings – These products are sold both directly to engine manufacturers (market share 60 per cent) and to the spare-parts market (market share 40 per cent).

Escort's sales organisation is very capillary and dealers/distributors are at a very high level compared to the country standard, with a good hold on the market. Besides, the link between dealers and Escort is very strong, and Escort can rely on a long relationship and count on their support for improvements and restyling of the outlets. These dealers are very well located and look for Western or Japanese standards. Escort also has a strong link with original OEMs whose approvals are required to qualify a new brand. A market-oriented corporate culture, training facilities, and a highly professional management are other features that contributed to choosing Escort as a possible partner.

On the other hand, Escort has no know-how of lubricants and no current involvement in the production of cars. In addition, there might be possible overlaps among the sales organisations of the group companies. AGIP Petroli therefore has to carefully evaluate all these factors before deciding whether and how to enter the Indian lubricant market.

Joint venture structure

The company would be a 50 per cent joint venture between AGIP and an Indian partner. AGIP would bring the technical know-how and the brand to the deal which was still unknown in India, whereas the Indian partner would provide the distribution network which was the key factor for the success of the venture and of the entire operation.

As India is such a huge country, four regional offices are foremost to retain the distributors and promote sales:

North – New Delhi
East   – Calcutta
West   – Bombay
South   – Bangalore

The organisational structure required for the short and medium term appears in Figure 34.1.

Figure 34.1
Organisational
structure

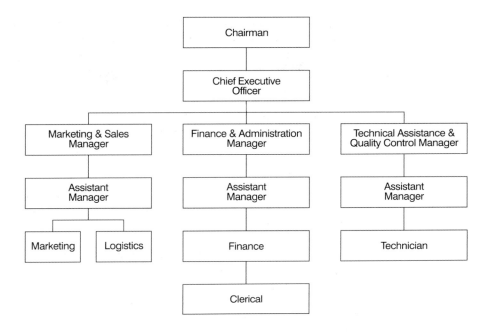

Table 34.9   Decision chart

Kind of decision	Alternative 1	Alternative 2	Alternative 3
Method of entry	Export products	Establish a wholly owned company	Joint venture with an Indian partner
Production	Italy	India	India
Distribution	Through local distributors	Build a distribution network	Partner's distribution network
Regions	North and west	North and west	All India

References

1 Economist Intelligence Unit Country Report, 4th Quarter, 1995.
2 BMS-Total Research, *Business opportunities in the market for lubricants in India*, Vol. 1, pp. 80–81, 1995.
3 *Ibid* pp.. 83–84.
4 *Ibid* p.85.
5 CNR, ENEA, ENEL, ENI, *Rapporto sull Energia*, Il Mulino, Bologna, 1995.
6 Dames & Moore International, *Analisi Comparativa del Business Lubrificanti*, January, pp. 152–155, 1995.

7 BMS-Total Research, *Business opportunities in the Market of Automotive Lubricants in India.*

8 *Ibid.*

9 Icconocol, *Proposal for joint venture with AGIP Petroli*, 1995.

10 Escorts, Lubricant project, 1995.

11 Biria Technical Services Lube refinery project in India, pp. 40–41, 1995.

12 *Ibid.* p.42.

13 *Ibid.* p.43.

CHAPTER 35

Xerox: transforming the corporation

Over the last thirty years Xerox Corporation has moved from being a dominant player in its markets in the 1970s to being threatened with extinction in the 1980s, and then back again to being the world's foremost document creation and reproduction company in the 1990s. The strategies which have underpinned the survival and success of the company are described in two case studies.

'Xerox: envisioning a corporate transformation' traces the story from the 1970s to 1992. In a reaction to a quite overt threat from Japan, Xerox was transformed from an inward-looking company, dominant in its markets, protected by its patented xerographic technology, to one of the West's most managerial innovative corporations. During this period Xerox employees invented benchmarking, pioneered employee involvement techniques previously unused, at least outside Japan, and adopted Total Quality Management so successfully that the company was the first ever to win the triple crown of quality (the Deming prize in Japan in 1980; the Baldridge award in the USA in 1989; the European Foundation for Quality award in Europe in 1992). During the latter part of the 1980s the company focused externally, and its definition of quality reflected this, i.e. 'Quality is defined as satisfying or exceeding customer requirements'.

At the end of the 1980s Xerox began to thoroughly investigate its internal processes, particularly in terms of their effectiveness and efficiency in satisfying the corporate objective of being the world's top-ranked document company in relation to customer satisfaction. Xerox realigned its thinking to recognise the importance of business processes and the deficiencies of its segmented, functionally disjointed way of doing business. The company thus became a pioneer of business process management techniques, with significant improvement in financial results and in its customer satisfaction ratings.

This introduction is by Dr Frederick Hewitt, Pro-vice-chancellor, Aston University, who was a director of Rank Xerox throughout the 1980s and a Vice-president of Xerox from 1988 to late 1993. The first part of the case study is by Fred Hewitt (Aston Business School, Birmingham) and Greg Bounds (College of Business, University of Tennessee). It was originally published in *Strategic Change* 4.1, 1995 © John Wiley & Sons, 1995. The second part is by Fred Hewitt, © F. Hewitt, 1997.

In 'Creating the holistic process-oriented learning organisation', the story is brought up to date to 1997. The company's efforts are now focused on the creation of an environment in which empowerment, innovation and flexibility are the norm, reflecting the fact that change is seen as a never-ending influence in business. Today Xerox is an extremely profitable and highly respected company, in marked contrast to the state of most western companies targeted by Far Eastern competition. For this reason alone the Xerox story is worth careful analysis.

Xerox: envisioning a corporate transformation (Greg Bounds and Fred Hewitt)

Xerox is a global company engaged in a total corporate transformation. This case study provides a case history of that transformation. It shows:

- The dramatic results achieved
- The actions taken to achieve those results
- How the change in management approach was managed
- How all employees were mobilised to bring about changes
- The tools involved, including quality, benchmarking and process improvement
- Restructuring for continuous change.

Xerox's global success

Bernard Fournier, managing director of Rank Xerox Ltd, received the first 'European Quality Award' from King Juan Carlos of Spain in Madrid on 20 October 1992. For Xerox and its affiliates this was the latest accolade in a series stretching over more than a decade. Twelve years earlier, Fuji Xerox had won Japan's premier quality award – the Deming Prize. In 1989 Xerox won the Malcolm Baldridge National Quality Award in the USA. Winning the Baldridge Award was particularly remarkable since Xerox had entered all 50 200 employees at the ninety-three US locations of its Business Products and Systems Group into the competition. Other comparably sized companies tended to enter only one division or focused their quality initiatives on one location.

In the period between the Deming Prize and the European Quality Award, Xerox affiliates also won national quality awards in Australia, Canada, France (twice), Mexico, the Netherlands and the UK. The geographical diversity of this decade-long success story is a clear indication that Total Quality Management has become internalised within Xerox to a level which is evident in few other Western companies. An all-pervasive obsession with quality is generally associated only with Japanese companies, such as Toyota, and is rarely evidenced in the West.

It is probably significant that Fuji Xerox, in Japan, was the first Xerox success on the road to global recognition; and it is also significant that much of Xerox's competition which emerged in the 1970s is Japanese. In the early 1970s, MITI identified office products in general and copiers in particular, alongside cars, motorcycles, cameras and televisions, as business areas in which low-cost, high-quality products could and should dominate the market. Faced by such fierce competition, Xerox had no choice but to match or beat its Japanese rivals in terms of quality. In any event, Xerox's response has been dramatic.

The headline of the leading article in the *New York Times* Business Day Section on 3 September 1992, read: 'Japan is tough but Xerox prevails.' In this article, an NEC Corporation spokesperson in Japan, referring to the Xerox 5100 duplicator which is manufactured in the USA but has captured 90 per cent of the high-speed duplicator market in Japan, is quoted as saying: 'The machines are better than anything we can get in Japan. We are not concerned it is an American product. We wanted the best and most efficient machine.' Perhaps this, more than any formal award presentation, indicates how well Xerox has responded to the quality challenge.

So what is it that this corporation has done? What are the characteristics of its approach to Total Quality Management? What is its vision for the future? How have Xerox leaders attempted to transform the company? Answers to these questions can be found in the following description of three general phases of the ongoing transformation at Xerox.

Phase 1: Immediate quality improvement

From its beginning, in the early 1980s, Xerox's quality focus was external and business oriented, relating employees and internal work processes to external customers' requirements. The stimulus came from outside the company in the form of competition. The reaction was also to look outside the company and, thus, Xerox pioneered competitive benchmarking. In 1983 David Kearns, the then CEO of Xerox, gathered his top twenty-five managers together at Xerox's Leesburg Virginia Training Center to review benchmarking data which showed Xerox to be way off the competitive mark in measures of quality, cost and delivery. The benchmarking process motivated Xerox leaders to make immediate quality improvement a top corporate priority, starting with the creation of a quality policy.

The Xerox quality policy

Before leaving Leesburg, these twenty-five leaders defined the Xerox quality policy which has worldwide applicability and is still in effect today. It states:

> Xerox is a Quality Company. Quality is the basic business principle for Xerox. Quality means providing our external and internal customers with innovative products and services that fully satisfy their requirements. Quality improvement is the job of every Xerox employee.

Among the most interesting aspects of this policy is the definition statement. The definition of quality as 'meeting the customer requirements' seems less remarkable today than it really was in 1983. At that time quality was still defined in most companies in terms of negatives and inanimate objects (e.g. defects per hundred machines assembled). Xerox's outward-looking, positive view of quality as meeting customer requirements was quite different.

Another interesting feature of the quality policy is the accountabilities statement. By making the bold statement that within a quality company, quality improvement is the job of every employee, the mystique and remoteness of 'the quality department' or 'the quality officer' was put aside. Xerox began what was, in effect, a cultural revolution within the company. Xerox had already pioneered employee involvement programmes, and these were now married to the total quality initiative.

Massive doses of training

Building upon these earlier successful experiences, Xerox's 'Leadership Through Quality' initiative was purposely implemented through a management-led training cascade approach (Figure 3.5.1). Starting with David Kearns and his

Figure 35.1
Training cascade

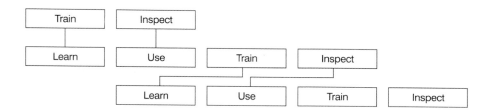

direct reports, each layer of management was trained in quality practices, sent back to their jobs, inspected for conformance to leadership through quality practices and only then certified as proficient practitioners of total quality management. Only after certification were these managers allowed to act as trainers for their own family groups. Total involvement was required, lip service and authorising others to train one's staff was not acceptable. The managers themselves trained their own staff. When the last trickle of the cascade was complete, Xerox had provided all its employees with at least 28 hours of training in problem solving and quality improvement techniques (at an estimated cost of more than 4 million labour hours and $125 m).

The cascade training technique provided employees with a common language and approach to continuous improvement. Every employee was educated and skilled in the problem-solving process and quality improvement process shown in Figures 35.2 and 35.3. This education and multi-level shared experience provided the foundation for all Xerox's subsequent efforts to transform its corporate culture.

Figure 35.2
Problem-solving
process

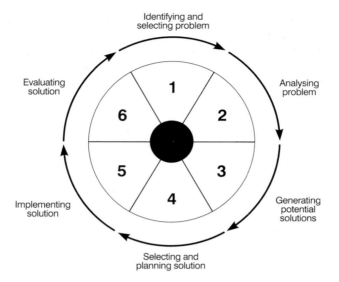

Identifying and
selecting problem

Evaluating
solution

Analysing
problem

Implementing
solution

Generating
potential
solutions

Selecting and
planning solution

Figure 35.3
The quality-
improvement
process

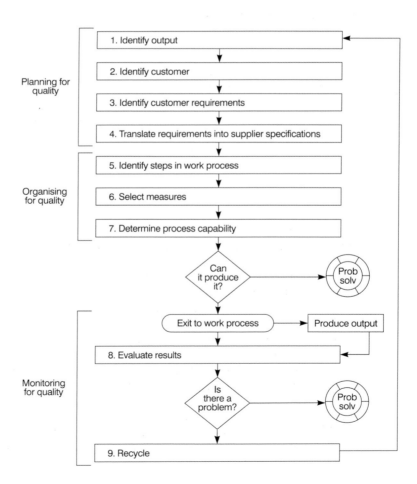

Planning for
quality

1. Identify output

2. Identify customer

3. Identify customer requirements

4. Translate requirements into supplier specifications

Organising
for quality

5. Identify steps in work process

6. Select measures

7. Determine process capability

Can
it produce
it?

Prob
solv

Exit to work process → Produce output

8. Evaluate results

Monitoring
for quality

Is
there a
problem?

Prob
solv

9. Recycle

Team Xerox

'Leadership through quality' was not the only major cultural change taking place within Xerox in the 1980s. The company had designated itself as 'The Document Company'. It had pledged to help its customers to reach breakthrough levels of productivity within their work practices through dramatically more effective ways of harnessing 'the power of the document', and to do this required careful team work.

Armed with the new quality tools, techniques and a process, salaried and hourly workers were grouped into teams vested with authority over daily work decisions and asked to make continuous improvements in their work activities. Some 75 per cent of employees participated in one or more of the 7000 quality improvement teams. These teams reduced Xerox costs by millions of dollars and made the phrase 'Team Xerox' more than an empty slogan. They reduced scrap, tightened production schedules, and devised other efficiency and quality-enhancing measures in all functions. As a natural next stage, Xerox extended the concept of 'Team Xerox' beyond its own organisational boundaries to incorporate suppliers and customers into the teams. Xerox gave suppliers training and support in such areas as statistical process control and ensured that suppliers' production control processes were 'process qualified'. Within 3 years, this approach reduced by 73 per cent the number of defective parts reaching the Xerox production line.

The role of benchmarking

Xerox has been involved in benchmarking since the late 1970s. In fact, modern benchmarking can be said to have begun with a 1979 Xerox trip to Japan to study manufacturing performance and practice. It is no surprise, therefore, that the Xerox teams seeking continuous improvement used benchmarking, combined with extensive customer preference surveys to direct their performance improvement activities. The company *assessed* its results in over 200 areas of product, service and business performance identified as key determinants of customer satisfaction. Targets were set at performance levels achieved by world leaders, regardless of industry, and in achieving these benchmark targets 'Team Xerox' also achieved the company's Phase 1 goal of immediate quality improvement. It also identified residual shortcomings and thereby defined the requirements for further improvement.

Cross-functional ineffectiveness a Phase 1 deficiency

Although they had established a good foundation for continuous improvement in most functions, Xerox managers realised that in these early efforts they had failed to achieve the degree of cross-functional team work that would be required to maintain world-class status against ever-increasing competition. Traditional organisation structures hindered cross-functional cooperation and, therefore, impeded the consistent adoption of the cultural changes required for sustained

676

competitiveness. Xerox's hybrid structure was defined by geography, function and product type. Its products were sold and serviced through geographically delineated organisations – Rank Xerox (Europe); Americas' Operation (Canada and Latin America); Fuji Xerox (Asia/Pacific); and US Operations (USA). Xerox was also functionally divided between marketing, on the one hand, and product development and manufacturing on the other.

Overall, this structure was complex, confusing, fragmented and costly, and it reduced Xerox's responsiveness to customer needs. One particular negative result of this functional fragmentation was that the learn–use–train cascade of leadership through quality had filtered down the organisation in a reductionist manner. Having been trained by their immediate supervisors, employees tended to use the training to address only their own narrowly focused functional or departmental concerns. The quality process was rarely applied across functions. Although part of the process was to identify internal 'customer/supplier' relationships, this rarely led to joint customer–supplier improvement initiatives, since bonus schemes, resource-allocation processes and information were all still functionally aligned. The exception, however, appeared to be related to a particular type of problem analysis. Where managers had defined work in terms of processes, they were not only more likely to undertake successful improvement initiatives, but these were much more likely to be cross-functional. On the basis of these observations, the next steps in the corporate transformation process became clear. Phase 2 should build upon Total Quality Management, but with a particular focus on process improvement, emphasising cross-functional processes as an area of particular opportunity.

Phase 2: Re-engineering business processes

Reorienting training

In Phase 2 Xerox modified in some respects its approach to training. Tools and techniques were now related to their applicability to specific work processes and market-driven goals. Employees were trained in multifunctional groups and skills were taught on an 'as-needed' basis just in time for application to identified process improvement initiatives. The team approach was modified, it was not abandoned. The challenge was to work cross-functionally as a team. The aim was to take a total multifunctional business process and to demonstrate how to optimally use information technology and best practices to streamline and improve the whole process. Xerox focused on what it called 'high-impact' teams, cross-functional teams responsible for defined basic business processes which have outputs that significantly impact business results. (These process teams are high in strategic importance and not necessarily high in the hierarchy.) Ed Leroux, then Director of Training and Education, illustrated the cross-functional nature of these high-impact teams:

> For example, previously we defined distribution as simply the transfer of the product from the assembly line to the warehouse. But now we recognise that the distribution process touches everything from the point of supplier

deliveries, through where the product gets produced, to the trunk of the service representative making repairs at the customer's site. Now distribution has a much more cross-functional, process orientation. And the process teams are composed of cross-functional representatives from throughout the distribution process, like manufacturing, warehousing, and customer services.

Planned learning experiences

Xerox began to provide these high-impact teams with 'planned learning experiences', rather than just training and educational courses. Under this approach the level of knowledge and skill of the specific team is taken into account, and the learning experience adjusted to their needs. Tools and techniques were provided as needed, just in time to be applied to a process. The team was required to produce a 'readiness check list', identifying the knowledge and skill level of the team members in respect of relevant tools and techniques, and also describing the documented business processes to be addressed.

Documented processes

A documented process in this context is defined in terms of activities, outputs and purposes. To understand the purpose of the process, team members must understand the relationship of the process to the company's customer-driven goals and objectives. For workers and managers within the process, this understanding provides answers to questions like: What is the organisation trying to accomplish? What does this process contribute? What is my role in that contribution? To ensure the process activities contribute effectively to corporate goals and objectives, team members must also understand the root causes of variation in process outputs. In order to understand the root causes of these variations, usually through the application of statistical process control techniques, the team members must first map activity sequences, decision points, inputs and outputs, usually in the form of flowcharts and time lines.

Carefully constructed documentation thus provides the basis for the identification of potential process improvements and also defines the boundary conditions for potential empowerment of the employees within the process. Within this approach empowerment is not the 'manager getting out of the worker's way'. Having properly framed the improvement initiative in terms of documented processes, empowerment need no longer be seen as the manager delegating authority to the point of having nothing to do. Instead, the manager continually refocuses the team's contribution in terms of the company's objectives, and specifically communicates the scope of employee authority in relation to activities and output. The manager provides workers with a business process context for their team initiatives, and then coaches and supports process re-engineering. Coaches are assigned to assist the process team not only with readiness but also with continuous learning and applications. Xerox recruits coaches who already have full-time jobs, typically line managers and not just staff professionals. Although the coaches are trained and certified, they are usually already well grounded in improvement techniques.

Comprehensive, multilevel applications

Under the revised approach Xerox employees set out to improve business processes throughout the organisation along multiple fronts. Broad cross-functional processes which are strategically important and greatly impact business success commanded the attention of senior executives, and those of more limited scope were managed by managers with more restricted responsibility. Individuals at every level of the organisation were empowered to improve their work processes and activities. Some of the more detailed improvement work may be integrated with the work of higher-level process teams, while other improvement work is self-directed and not integrated with higher-level activities. In fact, Xerox recognises a need to continuously improve existing processes, at all levels, while also working on new processes which might make the old ones obsolete. It might seem to be a waste of time to have workers and supervisors labouring to improve their work processes only to have them subsequently eliminated through re-engineering. However, Xerox does not regard any improvement as waste. Xerox prefers to have all employees engaged in improvement all the time, even at the most atomic (or *grass roots*) levels of the organisation, partly because managers cannot always anticipate which activities will be kept and which eliminated and partly because experience shows that employees who have participated in successful small change initiatives are more likely to be open to radical change than those who have no change experience at all.

Directions of process improvement: error reduction, cycle time reduction and customer-satisfaction improvements

To guide these improvements throughout the organisation, Xerox has set forth three fundamental directions for change: error reduction; cycle time reduction; and customer-satisfaction improvement. These directions for change ensure that, although improvement efforts are sometimes fragmented and dispersed, they will always be good for the company and its customers.

Like Motorola's Six Sigma campaign, Xerox promotes $10 \times$ error reduction, so that whatever the rate of errors happens to be, it should be improved tenfold. Error reduction is stressed more at the atomic levels of the organisation, particularly in areas of direct contact with customers.

Cycle time reduction can be sought at all levels of the organisation, but is particularly important at a macro-process level, where cycle time reduction through process re-engineering may totally eliminate activities at more atomic levels.

Error reduction and cycle time improvement should in themselves improve customer satisfaction. Xerox leaders, nevertheless, felt it important as part of the Phase 2 initiative to explicitly articulate that the purpose of improvements to the company's processes remains, above all else, to provide increased satisfaction to its customers. There should be no doubt that business process re-engineering is compatible with and indeed built upon the company's original Xerox quality policy. It may be a way of cutting costs, but it is not a way of cutting value to customers.

Figure 35.4
Functions versus
processes

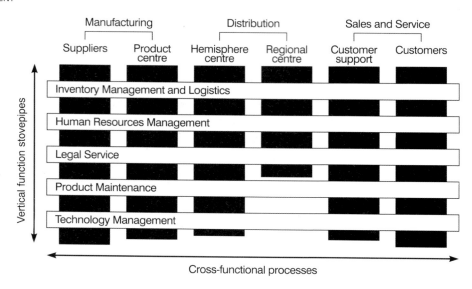

Xerox business architecture

Although the relationship between business process re-engineering and leadership through quality was at first tenuous, the two initiatives soon became intertwined and synergistic. It became evident that the key to empowerment and performance improvement was a radical simplification of business processes. Specifically, taking a cross-functional view of ways of doing business in support of satisfying customer requirements could lead to breakthrough levels of performance improvement. It was recognised that this approach could yield a quantum simultaneous improvement in quality, customer satisfaction and business results.

One example of this process-focused approach can be seen in Xerox's supply chain integration efforts. The matrix in Figure 35.4 represents a depiction developed by Xerox executives of the key business processes or cross-functional flows that serve customers. Prominent among these was the process by which Xerox manages its trading assets and ensures that customers' orders are fulfilled in a way which always meets their requirements, without the company incurring competitive disadvantage in terms of logistics cost or inventory-carrying cost. In fact, three business processes received priority attention, namely customer engagement, product design and engineering (soon renamed as time to market) and inventory management and logistics. By studying the last named in detail, it is possible to illustrate Xerox's overall approach at this stage to total quality-driven process re-engineering.

Inventory management and logistics

Each of the key business processes is assigned a process owner (or sponsor), a clearly defined set of missions and objectives, and resource in the form of a high-

Table 35.1 Business process sponsorship

Responsibilities	Execution/Implementation Approach
Provide strategic direction to business process area owners and process improvement projects	Establish business process area goals, desired state and critical success factors
Initiate BAA and process improvement projects to achieve goals and desired state	Determine projects required, commit resources and assign responsibility for process improvement projects
Provide quality assurance to ensure that process improvement projects meet strategic and business architecture requirements	Acts as primary customer for process improvement projects outputs Conduct periodic inspections of process improvement projects
Demonstrate role model commitment and support for business process management	Represent business process area (direction, resources, cross-functional and cross-organisational issues, etc.) in senior team management process
Manage cross-process and cross-organisational/functional boundaries/seams to ensure process integration and effectiveness	Resolve and/or escalate cross-organisational, cross-process issues

impact team responsible for accomplishing the mission. The responsibilities of a process sponsor are listed in Table 35.1. The position of process sponsor is not usually full-time, but a collateral activity of a manager who also holds a full-time corporate or line position. For example, Dr Fred Hewitt became the sponsor of inventory management and logistics (IM&L), the process essentially responsible for 'getting the right things, to the right place, at the right time'. At the time of his appointment, he was Director of Distribution and Technical Services for Rank Xerox in Europe, and a pioneer in developing multinational systems for optimizing inventory levels among European operating units.

The IM&L team's mission was to (1) develop IM&L strategies and processes, (2) ensure their implementation through procedures and systems across Xerox worldwide and (3) share with the operating units the responsibility for achieving ongoing improvements in customer satisfaction, logistics costs and asset utilisation.

The multinational inventory optimisation council (MIOC)

As the IM&L process sponsor, Hewitt was primarily responsible for orchestrating the involvement of other key managers and executives through their participation in IM&L process councils and subgroups. The multinational inventory optimisation council (MIOC) was the top-level council of the IM&L business process. The MIOC executive team was composed of handpicked senior managers who not only displayed the right sort of mind set but also were significant stakeholders in the change efforts that would follow. These senior level directors and vice-presidents from all different parts of the Xerox Corporation (from engineering, manufacturing, sales, service, from Europe, North America, Latin America and the Far East) were charged to look for cross-functional, cross-unit opportunities for radical process improvement.

The integrated supply chain process principles and vision

The MIOC executive team developed the following integrated supply chain process principles:

- Customer satisfaction is key
  - 100 per cent customer satisfaction at the lowest cost and levels of inventory is the objective of the IM&L process.
  - Customers will be provided with an integrated approach to all IM&L activities.
- Demand-driven supply chain
  - Customer orders will drive actions in all echelons of the supply chain.
  - Manufacturing flexibility is essential.
  - Build/customise to order, deliver to customer in 1 week are key targets.
- Time to customer is a competitive advantage
  - Removing time from the physical supply chain requires Xerox to remove time from the information pipeline.
  - Information pipeline effectiveness is critical for quickly empowered responses.
- Common product language
  - Customer requirements must be easily and unambiguously translated into items to be delivered, the components necessary to build these items and the raw materials necessary to assemble the components.
- Complexity managed through high-performance work systems
  - Complexity in the product array will be transparent to our customers and managed by our employees through high-performance work systems.
- Recycling is a key feature of the supply chain
  - To both fully utilise all assets and meet environmental concerns, Xerox will recover and recycle whenever possible.

Overall the vision was seen as creating *An integrated supply chain which never fails to meet customer requirements.*

Meeting only three times a year, MIOC addressed issues ranging from the mundane to the esoteric, directly or through a number of subcouncils. MIOC essentially served as an advisory council to then president Paul Allaire and the top five senior executive vice-presidents, to give feedback on the changes needed to realise the vision of a world-class inventory management and logistics process.

Central logistics and asset management

The MIOC executive council significantly enhanced Xerox's vision of what an ideal logistics and asset management business process should look like, but a further initiative was deemed necessary if the vision was to become reality. In the autumn of 1988 Fred Hewitt was appointed vice president of a new group, central logistics and asset management (CLAM) to provide full-time coordination of the implementation of the changes required in each business to realise the IM&L process vision. Over the next 3 years he built an organisation of change agents who worked as full-time business architects to re-engineer and transform Xerox's supply chain processes worldwide. Inventory management and logistics is a core process in itself, but CLAM as early change agents also facilitated work in other areas, particularly those that were highly integrated with the IM&L agenda. The vehicle for this coordination was a business process board composed of process sponsors from all areas actively involved in change initiatives.

As with all process re-engineering initiatives at Xerox, the CLAM team was responsible not only for solutions definition but also for working with line organisations to ensure that the improved processes became institutionalised within those organisations. Such institutionalisation clearly requires creative behavioural modification, as well as technical implementation, as can be seen from one of the first IM&L process innovations introduced across Xerox, the revised production planning process.

Revised production planning process (P3)

Xerox developed P3 prototypes with new product showcases before applying it broadly throughout the corporation. P3 moved the manufacturing and ware-housing planning away from a negotiated quarterly forecasting process. In the past, manufacturing and marketing organisations had established manufacturing production schedules with fixed lead times, based upon a demand forecast suggested by the marketing groups. The gamesmanship that ensued usually resulted in suboptimal results for the objectives of the integrated supply chain, with either surplus inventory or poor service levels being the outcome.

With P3, however, warehouses are nothing more than a central staging area which holds only replenishment stock. Inventory levels and associated production schedules are determined on a factual basis, not on forecasts or opinions. Instead of shipping out to a forecast, manufacturing ships products in reaction to a defined event, which may be an end-customer order or the generation of an internal replenishment order. Production planning becomes nothing more than replenishment control, with minimum/maximum inventory levels determined statistically and empirically based on factors such as time in the pipeline, likely need of safety stock, supplier lead times and forecasting error.

Institutionalisation of these changes in the supply chain has required the establishment of a significantly different mentality throughout all functions of Xerox. P3 teams make data-driven production decisions on the production floor, and are empowered to shut down production and send workers home or off to training, without vice-presidential signatures. P3 teams communicate with warehousing managers and work within the empirically determined limits for inventory levels. For some product types, warehouse inventory is now non-existent. Through the removal of barriers across the supply chain, Xerox has been able to significantly improve the quality of its delivery process. Customer satisfaction levels concerning Xerox's ability to 'deliver as promised' have reached an all-time high, despite the fact that business results have also dramatically improved in terms of reduced supply-chain costs and reduced inventories. Empowered employees, using simplified, fact-driven business processes, are well on their way to effecting the Xerox vision of *a supply-chain process which never fails to meet customer requirements.*

P3 and other process re-engineering initiatives orchestrated by CLAM within the IM&L process illustrate the progress which Xerox made in Phase 2 of its change agenda implementation strategy. To the functionally oriented gradual continuous improvement process of Phase 1 had been added a cross-functional process-oriented set of change initiatives capable of achieving step-function breakthroughs in productivity. Both approaches shared a common total quality-based commitment to customer satisfaction. Each approach complements the other. But even so, the question remains as to whether they represent a sufficiently radical approach to ensure ongoing success in the ever-changing and increasingly more competitive world of the 1990s and beyond. Senior Xerox managers chartered to look forward to 'Xerox 2000' apparently think not.

Phase 3: Restructuring for continuous change

To take Xerox to a new level of effectiveness and make sure that its structure reinforces the strategy and the culture that its leaders have been trying to develop, Xerox has recently (1992) structured its organisation. Chairman and CEO Paul Allaire described the purpose in the introduction of the communiqué used to announce the restructuring in February 1992:

> I have said on a number of occasions that we will need to change Xerox more in the next five years than we have in the past ten. The shape of that change is becoming clearer to us as the result of the work that we've been doing since 1989 when I announced our '*change* agenda'. In 1990, the senior management of the company participated in a set of activities called the Xerox 2000 strategic planning process. As that strategic work was reaching its conclusions, I initiated the second effort, using the quality process, to understand how we could run the company more effectively to achieve the Xerox 2000 vision.
>
> As a result of our work over the past 15 months on the nature and shape of this new Xerox, we have decided to move forward. During 1992, we will be implementing a major change of the governance, structure, process, and leadership of our company. Since this change is a direct outgrowth of the Xerox 2000 strategic work, we should think about this as a second phase of Xerox 2000, where we will be 'putting it together'. We will be working together to create an enterprise that builds on the improvements we've achieved in the past five years to ensure growth and competitive success in the 1990s.

The changes required are significant. But there are things that absolutely will not change! First are the Xerox corporate values. They are the bedrock of Xerox. They go back to Joe Wilson – they are what make Xerox special. The second is quality as our basic principle. Leadership Through Quality enabled us to survive in the 1980s. We've used the quality process to design these changes and will now use it to implement them.

Xerox's new structure

When Xerox restructured in 1992, it established a number of global business divisions (Figure 35.5). According to Xerox, a business division is a set of activities, people and assets that approximate a complete 'end-to-end' business capable of managing its own income statement and balance sheet. Each division has effective control over the complete value-added chain, including business planning, product planning, development, manufacturing, distribution, marketing, sales, and customer service and support, although some of these activities may be subcontracted to agents. Each division has a clear set of product and service offerings, a set of primary markets towards which those offerings are targeted and an identifiable set of competitors. Xerox in fact created the following nine business divisions:

- Personal document products
- Office document systems
- Office document products
- X-soft
- Advanced office document services
- Document production systems
- Printing systems

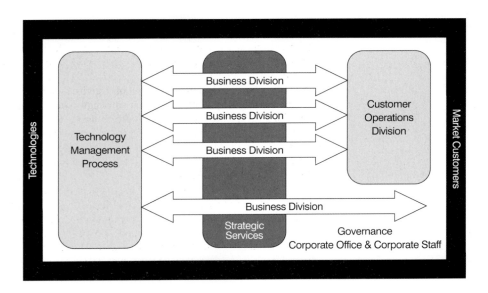

Figure 35.5
Xerox 2000
structure

- Xerox engineering systems
- Xerox business services

Within the new structure there are also two functionally specialised entities that serve all business divisions, the technology management process council and the customer operations divisions. These entities help to make sure that Xerox forms an effective linkage between the most advanced technologies available and the customer needs in the marketplace across all business areas. The technology management process council has responsibility for research and development of technology that sustains the core technological competencies for the corporation. Customer operations divisions are assigned to specific geographies. Their function is to maintain and improve the customer interface on behalf of the business divisions and make sure that Xerox, as a whole company, is easy to do business with. The customer operations divisions are responsible for support of all activities which relate to the customer, including service, administration, integration of major customer relationships, sales support, and providing local administration of the business division sales force.

The two other elements of the new structure are the strategic services and governance (corporate office and corporate staff). The strategic services exist to support the business divisions, particularly in the areas of manufacturing, logistics, supplies (materials) and strategic relationships. These services ensure that Xerox does not throw away the strategic advantages that stem from the size and scope of the Xerox corporation as a whole, even as it breaks into small, more autonomous and more responsive units. CLAM is now a part of the 'integrated supply chain' group within strategic services. Governance consists of a redesigned corporate office and a refocused corporate staff who face the challenge of 'putting it all together' on a strategic level.

Envisioning the future

Leadership and communications are recognised as two of the keys required for transforming an organisation's culture towards the emerging paradigm. Structural change is not a panacea. It must accompany technological change, business process change, strategic change and, perhaps most important of all, cultural change. Xerox has, over the years, been led by a number of unashamedly visionary individuals. In a personal message to the students, in the textbook entitled *Beyond Total Quality Management* (1994), current Chairman and CEO Paul Allaire describes the vision that he believes will lead Xerox into the future:

> We've embarked on a bold new journey. We are putting in place the *hardware* (the new organisation) and the *software* (new ways of managing and working) to enable us to seize the opportunities identified by the Xerox 2000 work. But more needs to be done. All of the work we have done in the past few years has set the stage for realising a vision for a new Xerox.
>
> What is the Xerox that I envision? I see an enterprise that has very special and unique qualities – an organisation that is looked to when people want to

figure out what will be effective management in the next century much as they do today when they want to understand total quality management. I see a company that values and celebrates the diversity of its employee body and creates an environment where each individual feels motivated to apply his or her creative energies to the work at hand. I also see a company made up of teams and communities of people who have the capacity to manage their own piece of the business, who have the freedom to use their own judgement and creativity, and who share in the risks and the rewards. Finally, I see a company that is a learning organisation – a company in which learning is pervasive and second-nature, a company in which learning becomes the norm, not the exception. The company I envision will enable and depend on continuous learning throughout the organisation – a company in which failures are seen as opportunities, where successes are studied with an eye to improvement, where new ideas are nurtured and implemented, where learning is defined as doing things differently. We're off to a very good start! We are already one of the most diverse work groups in the world. Our work on quality has given us a leg up on empowering our work force and working together effectively as teams. Our presidential reviews and training infra-structure are important ingredients of a learning organisation. We are on track to achieve the new Xerox – and it is the right track. So, much of the 'it' is already in place or being put into place. The critical ingredient now is 'putting it together'. To me, that means management. I have become more and more convinced that managing the 'it' – putting it together – is the last big frontier of competitive advantage and the most powerful lever to productivity growth.

To the outside observer the Xerox quality policy, leadership through quality, team Xerox, Xerox business architecture, business process re-engineering, and most recently, restructuring for Xerox 2000 may appear to form a logical continuum. Certainly each successive initiative has been based upon the successes and the failures of prior experiences. In reality, however, the logical nature of the progression is at least in part a matter of post-rationalisation on the basis of hindsight. The Xerox story is, in fact, all the more impressive because the participants in that story agree that the only true continuum was a refusal to ever accept the status quo. Envisioning and enacting a corporate transformation require the acceptance that the race has no end – the change agenda will never be completed. Change is the permanent state in which corporations now exist, and unless they transform themselves not into a new 'steady state' but rather into a 'state of continuous change' they must ultimately fail to meet their objectives. Perhaps this is the challenge for those wishing to envision and enact the ultimate corporate transformation.

Reference

Allaire, P. In Bounds, G., York, L., Adams, M. and Ranney, G. (eds.) *Beyond Total Quality Management*, pp. 775–777, McGraw-Hill, New York, 1994.

Creating the holistic process-oriented learning organisation: xerox 1992–1997 (Fred Hewitt)

Putting it together

At the 4 February 1992 meeting of Xerox's top fifty or so managers from around the world Paul Allaire, by then chairman as well as Chief Executive Officer of Xerox, majored on two themes – the need to accelerate the change process; and the need to take a holistic approach to managing Xerox. On the question of the speed and nature of the change Allaire was typically straightforward:

> We will change our organisation structure, we will change job assignments, we will change the way we empower and reward people. Perhaps most importantly, we will be changing how we think about our business and how we behave as we lead our business day to day... We will need to change Xerox more in the next five years than we have in the past ten.

Those present were left in no doubt that the corporation was entering yet another stage in its ongoing and relentless search for success, an effort which Allaire's predecessor David Kearns had dubbed 'The race with no end.' For those present who had seen the corporation invent benchmarking, absorb the concepts of TQM and Customer Focus, and become a pioneer of Business Process Management, a further acceleration of the change process was neither unexpected nor threatening.

Perhaps the most intriguing part of the Allaire speech and the subsequent workshops, however, was the emphasis on holism – both as regards the approach to the change process itself and also as a fundamental element of the future-management process of the corporation. Indeed, the theme of the meeting was 'Xerox 2000: Putting It Together.' Whilst making it clear that organisational realignment was part of the change required, Allaire dwelled much more than ever before on the 'soft' aspects of the 'New Xerox':

> A key catalyst in this change in the way we run the business is a change in the basic architecture of our organisation... .but [this] is not sufficient to achieve the changes that we need. If we change the structure but still try to run the company in the way we have in the past we will fail, so the structural change must be accompanied by changes in management process, in our management style, in our systems, in our processes, in our rewards approach, and in our bahavior [sic]. We might think of these elements as the software which must be changed along with the hardware of the structure.

In his concluding remarks Allaire returned to this theme:

> In the long run, the benefit of our new approach will come from how we work together... .Putting it together implies a whole new way of working together. It requires a new approach to leading and managing. It demands a new type of organisational [sic] culture for Xerox. Ultimately, it is the actions of each of us, individually, that will create this new environment.

The magnitude, urgency and all-pervasive nature of the required changes was spelled out for all to see. What was perhaps less clear was how such a transformation would be accomplished – what was the vehicle that would carry the impetus forward?

XMM – The Xerox Management Model

The first half of 1992, during which the 'Putting It Together' meeting took place, was also the period during which Xerox's European affiliate, Rank Xerox, was finalising its successful submission to the European Foundation for Quality Management (EFQM). The format of the submission is strictly prescribed. Applicants are required to use the EFQM's nine elements of management, as illustrated with weightings in the model (Figure 35.6), and to provide substantive information on the application of best practice within the applicant organisation, using the nine elements as chapter headings in the submission.

Figure 35.6
The EFQM model

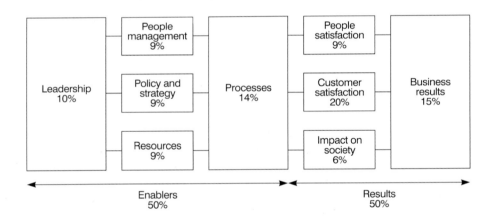

As already noted, the Rank Xerox application was successful, making Xerox the first company to attain the triple crown of Quality – with Deming in Japan, Baldridge in the USA and EFQM in Europe. Along the way the Xerox team, led by Brendan Rogers and Rafael Florez, came to appreciate the power of the EFQM model as a tool for self analysis. They also understood intuitively that used as an ongoing tool for identifying process improvements the model was compatible with Allaire's desire to introduce a customer-focused, process-oriented and holistic management approach into the company. Whereas many companies would have seen the attainment of the EFQM award as an objective, Xerox once again saw the assessment process as a way of refining its ongoing management and business processes. Following on from benchmarking, Leadership Through Quality and the Xerox Business Architecture initiatives, and retaining the best elements of all of them, Xerox developed its own model, the Xerox Management Model (XMM) (Figure 35.7).

689

Figure 35.7
The Xerox
Management Model

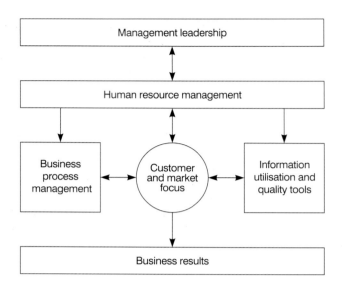

Despite the fact that the Xerox model has six elements rather than nine, the similarities between the two models are obvious. It is the differences, however, which give particular insight into Xerox's unique approach to the development of a holistic process-oriented organisation. First, in the XMM the 'Customer and market focus' element of the model becomes the engine driving the model. It links directly with all but one of the other model elements. Second, the EFQM's 'Processes' become, in XMM, 'Business Process Management' and are associated more closely with 'Business Results'. Third, the very title of Xerox *Management* Model, as opposed to Quality Management Model, is meant to indicate the total pervasiveness of the model and its incorporation of both Allaire's software and hardware elements. In the supporting literature provided to Xerox employees as part of the extensive XMM deployment process stress is laid upon the fact that although the Xerox 2000 XMM has its roots deeply embedded in the earlier programmes it is, in contrast to them, a toolbox for all Xerox employees containing everything needed to run the company. Dick Leo, a Xerox vice-president heavily involved in the deployment, stresses that XMM is 'a holistic management model because it addresses every aspect of Xerox work: planning, creating, leading, managing, changing, organizing [sic], communicating, learning, and rewarding.'

XMM deployment

The deployment of XMM began with the creation of the simple block diagram as a means of bringing together the Xerox 2000 concepts. Behind the six boxes, however, lie more than sixty process improvement tools, interlinked to provide a self-assessment tool kit which is both process-oriented and customer-focused.

During the self-assessment exercise Xerox organisational entities are led through a series of steps which analyse their performance in thirty-five business practices linked to seven specific, quantified business results. Desired process states are defined and feedback loops ensure that weaknesses are identified, both in the 'software' and the 'hardware' of the entity; process-improvement activities are generated and resources for improvement projects are put in place. Involved employees claim that during the deployment process over the last four years two- to ten-fold performance improvements in process performance have become commonplace. After self-assessment, entities have their analyses and results validated by Xerox employees from another part of the corporation. This includes a final agreed rating against model practices on a seven-point scale and an agreed level of 'Certification'. This in turn leads to an agreed set of improvement initiatives, again encompassing both 'soft' and 'hard' activities. Furthermore, since the process measures improvement in terms of both productivity and customer value, investments of both time and capital are targeted towards the longer-term objective of market leadership as well as the short-term imperative of cost effectiveness.

In effect, what Xerox is attempting to accomplish with the deployment of XMM, based upon its long-established benchmarking, TQM, Customer Focus, Business Process Management experience, is the creation of a working environment in which all processes are continuously scrutinised for their relevance to the customer and for their inherent process efficiency. Given the heavy emphasis on Allaire's 'software' and the explicit recognition of the role of individuals within the process, it may also be described as a brave attempt to establish the learning organisation, which focuses externally on the customer and internally on a holistic set of business processes operating at benchmark levels of efficiency.

On the basis of a compendium of measures Xerox continues to prosper in the late 1990s. The share price, which was $29 in 1990, reached $150 in 1996 before a three-for-one split, and has subsequently risen from the $50 split price to over $80, an eightfold increase in less than seven years. During the same period Customer Satisfaction and Retention rates have improved significantly, a plethora of new products has been introduced, and Xerox has gained market share in all continents, including a significant improvement in Japan, the home of its only significant copier competitors after its main Western rivals IBM and Kodak have both pulled out of the market.

Clearly, to claim that Xerox's commercial success is directly attributable to its deployment of a succession of change initiatives is overly simplistic. On the other hand, the fact remains that it is now fifteen years since the Japanese Ministry for International Trade and Industry (MITI) formally targeted the office equipment market for exploitation and the president of Canon famously declared his company's goal as to 'Kill Xerox'; and yet Xerox has not only survived, it has prospered in an extremely difficult market. At the very least it is valid to speculate that the willingness of Xerox's leadership and other employees to accept the need for change has been a critical if not necessarily sufficient factor in the story of the last fifteen years. The extent to which Xerox has now created the holistic, process-oriented learning organisation which it would like to be will presumably be evident in another fifteen years' time.

Index of names and organisations

Index of subjects

Tutor Support Material is available online...

A selection of tutor resource material for
Strategic Management is available
via the Internet.

*For more information, contact the Management Division at
Butterworth-Heinemann on (01865) 314496,
or e- mail sally.north@repp.co.uk*